Business Modelling : Multidisciplinary Approaches

OPERATIONS RESEARCH/COMPUTER SCIENCE INTERFACES SERIES

Series Editors

Professor Ramesh Sharda
Oklahoma State University

Prof. Dr. Stefan Voß
Technische Universität Braunschweig

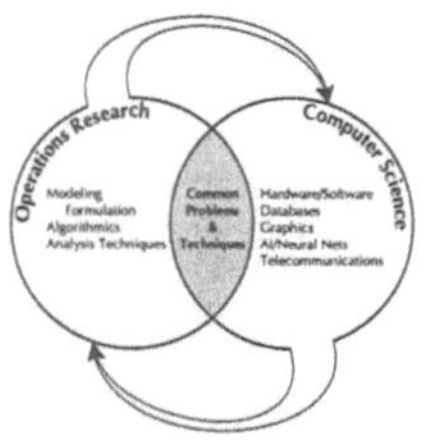

Other published titles in the series:

Greenberg, Harvey J. / *A Computer-Assisted Analysis System for Mathematical Programming Models and Solutions: A User's Guide for ANALYZE*

Greenberg, Harvey J. / *Modeling by Object-Driven Linear Elemental Relations: A Users Guide for MODLER*

Brown, Donald/Scherer, William T. / *Intelligent Scheduling Systems*

Nash, Stephen G./Sofer, Ariela / *The Impact of Emerging Technologies on Computer Science & Operations Research*

Barth, Peter / *Logic-Based 0-1 Constraint Programming*

Jones, Christopher V. / *Visualization and Optimization*

Barr, Richard S./ Helgason, Richard V./ Kennington, Jeffery L. / *Interfaces in Computer Science & Operations Research: Advances in Metaheuristics, Optimization, and Stochastic Modeling Technologies*

Ellacott, Stephen W./ Mason, John C./ Anderson, Iain J. / *Mathematics of Neural Networks: Models, Algorithms & Applications*

Woodruff, David L. / *Advances in Computational & Stochastic Optimization, Logic Programming, and Heuristic Search*

Klein, Robert / *Scheduling of Resource-Constrained Projects*

Bierwirth, Christian / *Adaptive Search and the Management of Logistics Systems*

Laguna, Manuel / González-Velarde, José Luis / *Computing Tools for Modeling, Optimization and Simulation*

Stilman, Boris / *Linguistic Geometry: From Search to Construction*

Sakawa, Masatoshi / *Genetic Algorithms and Fuzzy Multiobjective Optimization*

Ribeiro, Celso C./ Hansen, Pierre / *Essays and Surveys in Metaheuristics*

BUSINESS MODELLING

Multidisciplinary Approaches

Economics, Operational and Information Systems Perspectives

(In Honor of Andrew B. Whinston)

Editors

Clyde Holsapple
University of Kentucky

Varghese Jacob
University of Texas at Dallas

H. Raghav Rao
SUNY Buffalo

Associate Editors

Abhijit Chaudhury
Bryant College, Rhode Island

Manish Agrawal
University of South Florida

Springer Science+Business Media, LLC

Library of Congress Cataloging-in-Publication Data

A C.I.P. Catalogue record for this book is available from
the Library of Congress.
ISBN 978-1-4613-5291-4 ISBN 978-1-4615-0893-9 (eBook)
DOI 10.1007/978-1-4615-0893-9

Originally published by Kluwer Academic Publishers in 2002
Softcover reprint of the hardcover 1st edition 2002

Printed on acid-free paper.

Contents

CONTRIBUTORS

W.W. Cooper is currently the Foster Parker Professor of Finance and Management at the Red McCombs School of Business in the University of Texas at Austin. He was previously the first Dean of the School of Urban and Public Affairs and University Professor of Management Science and Public Policy at Carnegie Mellon University. Prior to that he was one of the founding faculty for Carnegie's Graduate School of Industrial Administration. He also occupied the chair of Arthur Lowes Dickinson Professor of Accounting at Harvard University's Graduate School of Business. Author or coauthor of more than 470 scientific professional articles and 22 books he holds honorary D.Sc. degrees from Ohio State and Carnegie-Mellon Universities and the degree Doctorado Honoris Causa from the University of Alicante in Spain.

William Hamlen is an Associate Professor of Finance and Managerial Economics in the School of Management at the State University of New York at Buffalo. His research is in applied economics and finance. He has published on a wide range of topics. His articles have been published in journals including: *The American Economic Review*, *The Bell (Rand) Journal*, *The Review of Economics and Statistics*, *The Journal of Economic Dynamics and Control*, *Economic Inquiry*, *Southern Economic Journal*, *Accounting Review* and the *Journal of Econometrics*. Two of his current research interests are in the areas of "superstardom in the music industry" and " the role of human capital in asset management".

Vicente Salas-Fumas (Ph.D. Purdue 1976) is professor of Business Economics at the University of Zaragoza (Spain). He has been professor in the Autonomous University of Barcelona and Visiting Scholar in Stanford. His research interests are in economics of organization. He has recently published in *Journal of Banking and Finance, International Journal of Reseach in Marketing, Journal of Ecomics and Management Strategy, International Journal of Industrial Organization*. In 1992, he received the Award "Rey Jaime I" for his contributions to the research on Spanish firms. From 1994 to 1998 he was appointed member of the Board of the Spanish Central Bank.

Francisco Ruiz-Aliseda is a graduate student in the MEcS program at Northwestern University. He graduated from the University of Zaragoza in 1998.

Ming Fan is an assistant professor in the Mendoza College of Business, University of Notre Dame. He received his Ph.D. from the Graduate School of Business at the University of Texas at Austin. His areas of research include telecommunications, decentralized mechanism design for organizations, and technologies for financial markets.

Xiaorui Hu is an assistant professor at the Department of Decision Sciences and MIS, Saint Louis University. She received her Ph.D. from the University of Texas at Austin. Her research interests include electronic commerce, financial risk management, and experimental economics.

Han Zhang is an assistant professor at DuPree College of Business, Georgia Institute of Technology. He received his Ph.D. in Management Information Systems from the University of Texas at Austin. His research focuses on the design of trusted third parties for facilitating electronic markets.

R. Preston McAfee is the author of over sixty articles published in scholarly economics journals and is co-author of Incentives in Government Procurement, a book that investigates and promotes the privatization of government-supplied goods and services. He is a co-editor of the *American Economic Review*, the most prominent economics journal. He is a Fellow of the Econometric Society.McAfee is a recognized expert in industrial organization. He has advised clients, including the Department of Justice and Lockheed-Martin, on matters concerning mergers, collusion, price-fixing, electricity pricing, procurement, bidding, and sales of government property. In 1994, he advised the Federal Communications Commission on the design of auctions for the spectrum for personal communications services, one of the three designers of what has become known as the simultaneous ascending auction. Professor McAfee is a professor of economics at the University of Texas at Austin and the University of Chicago. He was the FTC's expert on the Exxon-Mobil merger, and the BP-Arco merger

Edna T. Loehman is Associate Professor of Agricultural Economics at Purdue University. She formerly was on the faculty at University of Florida. Her Ph.D degree in economics was received at Purdue University, with Dr. Andrew Whinston as thesis advisor. Her interests include environmental and resource economics. Recently, she has been developing and experimentally testing algorithms to address group decision-making for local public goods. She has edited several books on the subject of institutional design for alleviating environmental problems including water.

Rabih Karaky is a doctoral candidate and research assistant in Agricultural Economics at Purdue University. He is currently a short term development consultant at the World Bank. His areas of interest are resource and development economics. His thesis concerns climate variability implications for agricultural policy in Morocco. He holds a Masters degree in Agricultural Economics from Purdue University and Bachelor and Master's degrees in Agricultural Engineering and Animal Sciences respectively from the American University in Beirut, Lebanon. He has served as a Credit Officer for the United Nations Integrated Rural Development Programme and as a Monitoring and Evaluation officer for the Irrigation Rehabilitation Sector Project, both in Lebanon

Gary J. Koehler is the John B. Higdon Eminent Scholar and Professor of Decision and Information Sciences in the Warrington School of Business at the University of Florida. He received his Ph. D. in Management Science from Purdue University in 1974 working under Professors Andrew B. Whinston and Gordon P. Wright. He has held various academic positions at Purdue, Northwestern University and the University of Florida. From 1994-1995 he was Professor and MIS Area Head at the Krannert Graduate School of Management at Purdue University. From 1979-1987 he held various top management positions at Micro Data Base Systems, Inc., which was a collaboration between Andrew B. Whinston and Koehler, amongst others. He has published in *Decision Support Systems, Operations Research, Management Science, ORSA Journal on Computing, Evolutionary Computations, SIAM Journal on Control* and Optimization, Annals of Operations Research, European Journal of Operational Research, Decision Sciences, Annals of Mathematics and Artificial Intelligence, Computers and Operations Research, Complex Systems, Neural Networks, IEEE Transactions on Engineering Management, Managerial and Decision Economics, Naval Research Logistics Quarterly, Discrete Applied Mathematics, Journal of Finance and others. His current research interests are in e-commerce related areas

Aimo Hinkkanen is Professor in the Department of Mathematics at the University of Illinois at Urbana-Champaign. Previously, he had been on the mathematics faculty at the University of Texas at Austin. His main research interests are complex analysis, geometry, and dynamic systems modeling. He is currently working on a supercomputer project supported by National Center for Supercomputing Applications to visualize certain limit and approximation phenomena in complex dynamics, including animation. Professor Hinkkanen's extensive work has appeared in the leading mathematics research journals. More biographical information and selected publications may be found at http://www.math.uiuc.edu/~aimo/.

Karl Reiner Lang is an Assistant Professor in Information Systems at the Hong Kong University of Science & Technology HKUST). He received his MBA from the Free University of Berlin, Germany (1988), and holds a Ph.D. in Management Science from The University of Texas at Austin, USA (1993). Before joining HKUST in 1995, he had been on the faculty of the Business School at the Free University of Berlin. Dr. Lang's has been teaching courses on Information Technology and Electronic Commerce at the undergraduate, postgraduate, and executive education level. His research interests include management of digital businesses, decision technologies, knowledge-based products and services, and issues related to the newly arising informational society. Dr. Lang's recent publications have appeared in leading research journals such as Annals of Operations Research, Computational Economics, Journal of Organizational Computing and Electronic Commerce, and Decision Support Systems. He has professional experience in Germany, the USA, and Hong Kong.

Roger Alan Pick is an Associate Professor of Management Information Systems at the Henry W. Bloch School of Business and Public Administration, University of Missouri - Kansas City. He has also taught at Purdue University, the University of Wisconsin - Madison, the University of Cincinnati, and Louisiana Tech University. His research interests include decision support systems, model management, economics of computers, and knowledge management. His research in these topics have appeared in *Communications of the ACM, Decision Support Systems, Journal of MIS, Management Science*, and numerous other outlets. He earned his doctorate from Purdue University in 1984 under the supervision of Andrew B. Whinston.

George P. Schell is Associate Professor of Information Systems at the Cameron School of Business, University of North Carolina at Wilmington. He has also taught at the University of Tulsa. Dr. Schell received his Ph.D. from Purdue University in 1983 under the supervision of Andrew B. Whinston and Robert H. Bonczek. His research interests include valuation of information systems, web-based teaching resources, and decision support systems. Dr. Schell has published articles in *Information & Management, Electronic Journal of Information System Evaluation, Interfaces, Computer Personnel*, and others

Abhijit Chaudhury is an Associate Professor at Bryant College, Rhode Island. He has over ten years of industrial experience working with European Multinationals in the field of engineering and business process automation. His research is in the area of management of the information systems function. He has published in the Communications of the ACM, several transactions and publications of IEEE, Information Systems Research, European Journal of O.R., International Journal of Production Research and Journal of Management Information Systems. He has co-authored a book on e-business infrastructure technologies, which is being published byMcGraw-Hill.

Riyaz Sikora is an Assistant Professor of Information Technology at the College of Commerce and Business Administration at the University of Illinois at Urbana-Champaign. Dr. Sikora has published refereed scholarly papers in journals such as *Management Science, Information Systems Research, INFORMS Journal of Computing, IEEE Transactions on Engineering Management, IEEE Transactions on Systems, Man, and Cybernetics*, and *IEEE Expert*. He is on the editorial board of the *International Journal of Computational Intelligence and Organizations* and the *Journal of Database Management*. He chairs the SIG on Enterprise Integration in the INFORMS' College of AI and is a co-chair of the SIG on Agent-based Information Systems sponsored by the Association on Information Systems.

Michael J. Shaw is Hoeft Endowed Chair in IT Management and director of the Center for Information Technology and eBusiness Management of the College of Commerce and Business Administration, University of Illinois, Urbana-Champaign. Shaw is on the editorial boards of eight academic journals and he has published a large number of refereed scholarly papers in journals such as *Management Science, Information Systems Research, INFORMS Journal on Computing, Communications of the ACM, IEEE*

Internet Computing, IIE Transactions, and Decision Support Systems. He is an editor of the Handbook on Electronic Commerce recently published by Springer-Verlag

Alok Gupta is an Associate Professor of Information Systems at Carlson School of Management, University of Minnesota; from 1996 to 2001 he was an Assistant Professor at Dept. of OPIM, University of Connecticut. He received his Ph.D. in Management Science and Information Systems from The University of Texas at Austin. His research has been published in various information systems, economics, and computer science journals such as *ISR, CACM, JMIS, Journal of Economic Dynamics and Control, Computational Economics, Decision Support Systems, IEEE Internet Computing, International Journal of Flexible Manufacturing Systems, Information Technology Management, and Journal of Organizational Computing and Electronic Commerce.* In addition, his articles have been published in several leading books in the area of economics of electronic commerce. His research on dynamic pricing mechanisms on the Internet is supported by ***NSF CAREER Award***. From 1999-2001, he served as co-director of Treibick Electronic Commerce Initiative (TECI), an endowed research initiative at dept. of OPIM, University of Connecticut. He is also an affiliate of Center for Research in Electronic Commerce (CREC) at University of Texas at Austin. He serves on the editorial boards of DSS and Brazilian Electronic Journal of Economics. He can be reached via email at: alokgupta@acm.org

Boris Jukic, Assistant Professor, School of Management, George Mason University, received his B.S. in computer science from the University of Zagreb and a MBA from Grand Valley State University. In 1998, he received his Ph.D. in Management Science and Information Systems from The University of Texas at Austin. His research interests include estimation of user demand characteristics and efficient infrastructure investment strategies for the Internet, as well as management of network resources. His research has been published in various information systems, economics, and computer science journals such as *Journal of Computational Economics, Information Systems and IEEE Internet Computing.* He can be reached via email at: bjukic@som.gmu.edu.

Prabhudev Konana is an Associate Professor of Management Information Systems, and Assistant Director for Center for Research in Electronic Commerce (CREC) at the McCombs School of Business, the University of Texas at Austin. He received Ph.D. in MIS from the

University of Arizona, Tucson. His research interests are in the design of electronic brokerages, assessment of e-business value, determinants of adoption of internet-based procurement, and study of beliefs and attitudes of online investors. His research received the best-paper runner-up award at the International Conference on Information Systems (ICIS), 1996. His research is supported by ***NSF CAREER Award***, ***Dell***, and ***IBM***. His research on e-business value assessment is highly cited in popular media including ***CNNFn***, ***Fortune/eCompany Now magazine***, and ***Business2.0***. Dr. Konana's work has appeared in major refereed journals, such as Sloan Management Review, Communications of the ACM, INFORMS Journal on Computing, Information Systems Research, Operations Research Letters, and Information Systems. He can be reached via email at: pkonana@mail.utexas.edu

Zhangxi Lin is currently an assistant professor of information system in the College of Business Administration at Texas Tech University. He obtained a M.Eng. degree in computer science from Tsinghua University in 1982, a M.S degree in economics in 1996 and a Ph.D. degree in information systems in 1999 from the University of Texas at Austin. His research interests include network traffic management and congestion-based pricing, economic modeling of online auctions, economic experimental system design and experimental testing, and the Internet and its application in China. He is a guest professor/researcher for four universities in China.

Peng Si Ow is currently a consultant on the deployment of innovations from R&D into operations. She began her work at IBM where she was involved in developing and deploying state of the art production planning and control systems into the field. Her work later extended from manufacturing systems to the deployment of corporate intranets and more recently to medical imaging systems. She has a Ph.D. in Systems Sciences from Carnegie Mellon University.

Dale Stahl is currently the Malcolm Forsman Centennial Professor of Economics in the Department of Economics at the University of Texas, Austin. He obtained B.S. and M.S. degrees in electrical engineering from M.I.T. in 1969 and a Ph.D. from the University of California at Berkeley in 1981. His early research was in general equilibrium theory and price adjustment mechanisms, followed by research in strategic pricing and advertising. After many years of contributions to game theory, he began investigations and experimental testing of theories of bounded rationality and learning. He has also become involved in economic analyses of the Internet infrastructure with emphasis on congestion-based pricing. His publications include a book on electronic commerce, and 60 articles in top journals.

Sulin Ba is assistant professor of information systems and the co-Director of the Electronic Economy Research Program (ebizlab) at the Marshall School of Business at the University of Southern California. She focuses on the study of intermediaries – social, economic institutions building on information technologies that facilitate electronic market transactions between buyers and sellers – from both the theoretical as well as the technological perspectives. Her current projects involve the design of trusted third parties to help small business overcome the online barriers such as security and product quality uncertainty. Her work on the institutional setup to help small business survive and grow in the digital economy has been used as the basis for testimony before the Congressional House Committee on Small Business. She has published in *Management Science, Information Systems Research, MIS Quarterly, Decision Support Systems*, and other academic journals.

Jan Stallaert is assistant professor of Information Systems at Marshall School of Business at the University of Southern California. His research focuses on the interplay between Economics, Information Systems and Organizational Theory. His past research has focused on developing new types of Decision Support Systems and their organizational impact. More recently, he has directed his attention to the new opportunities created by Electronic Commerce. He has designed and developed a patented method for trading assets in bundles, a method that has a wide variety of applications, from Financial Portfolio Theory, Financial Derivatives Trading to Creating Internal Markets for Knowledge and Supply Chain Coordination. Dr. Stallaert has published in journals such as *Management Science, Information Systems Research, Discrete Applied Mathematics, Interfaces, IEEE Computer, International Journal of Electronic Commerce, Communications of the ACM*. His research has been funded by the Office of Naval Research and numerous grants from Intel. He has consulted and implemented Decision Support Systems for various Fortune 500 companies. Prior to joining the faculty at the Marshall School, Dr. Stallaert was an Assistant Professor at the University of Texas at Austin.

Prudence T. Zacarias Kapauan is a Distinguished Member of Technical Staff at Lucent Technologies in Naperville, IL. She holds B.S. and M.S. degrees in Mathematics from the University of the Philippines in Quezon City, an M.S. in Computer Science and a Ph.D. in Management Information

Systems, both from Purdue University in West Lafayette, IN. Dr. Kapauan's current responsibilities include architecture and reliability for a 3G wireless platform. Other interests include computer telephony, service creation environments and specification languages. She is a senior member of the IEEE and an elected member of both the Phi Kappa Phi and the Beta Gamma Sigma Business Honor Society. *Correspondence*: Lucent Technologies, 2000 N. Naperville Rd., 6K-204, P. O. Box 3033, Naperville, IL 60566-7033,USA. Tel: +1.630.713.5353. E-mail: ptzk@lucent.com.

Eugenia Fernandez is an Assistant Professor of Computer Technology in the Purdue School of Engineering and Technology at Indiana University-Purdue University Indianapolis. She holds a B.S. in Mechanical Engineering from Worcester Polytechnic Institute in Worcester, MA, a M.S.E. in Computer, Information and Control Engineering from the University of Michigan in Ann Arbor, MI and a Ph.D. in Management Information Systems from Purdue University in West Lafayette, IN. Her main interests are in database, XML, and computer pedagogy with particular emphasis on learning assessment and web-based tutorials. *Correspondence*: Computer Technology Department, Indiana University-Purdue University Indianapolis, 723 W. Michigan Street. (SL 220), Indianapolis, IN, 462002-5132, USA. Tel: +1.317.274.6794. E-mail: efernand@iupui.edu

Anitesh Barua is Professor of Information Systems, Spurgeon Bell Centennial Fellow, Bureau of Business Research Fellow, Distinguished Teaching Professor and Associate Director of the Center for Research in Electronic Commerce at the McCombs School of Business, the University of Texas at Austin. He received his Ph.D from Carnegie Mellon University in 1991. Dr. Barua's recent research on the Internet Economy (sponsored by Cisco Systems) and e-business value assessment (sponsored by Dell Computer) have been featured in every significant media outlet around the world. Contact: barua@mail.utexas.edu

Ramnath K. Chellappa is an Assistant Professor of Information Systems in the Department of Information and Operations Management, Marshall School of Business, University of Southern California. He is also the co-director of the Electronic Economy Research Lab at the Marshall School (ebizlab) and is also affiliated with the Center for Research in Electronic Commerce at the University of Texas at Austin. He received his Phd from the University of Texas in 1991 under the supervision of professors Andrew Whinston and Anitesh Barua. Contact: ram@marshall.usc.edu

Melody Y. Kiang is Associate Professor of Computer Information Systems at California State University, Long Beach. She received her M.S. in MIS from the University of Wisconsin, Madison, and Ph.D. in MSIS from the University of Texas at Austin. Prior to join CSULB, she was Associate Professor at Arizona State University. Her research interests include the development and applications of artificial intelligence techniques to a variety of management problems and in electronic commerce research. Her research has appeared in *Information Systems Research (ISR), Management Science, Decision Support Systems (DSS), Journal of Management Information Systems, IEEE Transactions on SMC, EJOR, Journal of the Operational Research Society,* and other professional journals. She is an Associate Editor of *DSS.*

Robert Chi is Professor of Information Systems at California State University, Long Beach. He obtained his Ph.D. from University of Texas at Austin and his MS from University of Wisconsin at Madison. Dr. Chi has published many articles in major information systems journals such as *Decision Support Systems, Journal of Management Information Systems, and Journal of the Operational Research Society.* He is the Chief Editor of *Journal of Electronic Commerce Research* and the Advisor of Electronic Commerce Society at CSULB.

Kar Yan Tam is currently Professor of Information & Systems Management and Asssociate Dean of the Business School at HKUST. Before joining HKUST, he was a faculty member at the University of Texas (Austin). He has also held a Research Scientist position at EDS where he worked in the area of software engineering methodologies and tools. His research interests include information technology applications and electronic commerce. He has published extensively on these topics in major management science and information system journals. Prof. Tam has been project manager for numerous consultancy projects with local and multinational companies. He is currently Director of the Center for E-Commerce at HKUST.

Beomsoo Kim is an assistant professor of Information and Decision Sciences in the College of Business Administration, the University of Illinois at Chicago. He has a Ph.D. in Information Systems from the University of Texas at Austin. His research interests focus on the effectiveness of the digital economy, and on business models for electronic commerce and business.

Byungtae Lee is an associate professor of Information and Decision Sciences in the College of Business Administration, the University of Illinois at Chicago. He received his Ph.D. in Information Systems from the University of Texas at Austin. His research interests include IT productivity measurement, strategic IT investments, electronic commerce, electronic auction markets, IT applications for the health industry, and the economicsof information systems.

Seung Kyoon Shin is a doctoral candidate in management science and systems in the School of Management at the State Univeristy of New York at Buffalo. He was a database design consultant for years before joining academia. His research interests include strategic database design for data warehousing and data mining, electronic commerce, knowledge management, information system success, and cultural study related to IS.

R. Ramesh is Professor of Management Science & Systems, School of Management, University at Buffalo. His primary areas of research are Database Systems, Enterprise Frameworks, Learning/Training Systems Development and Collaborative Teams Modelling.

H. Raghav Rao is a Professor of MIS at SUNY Buffalo. He graduated from Purdue University in 1987 where his dissertation co-chairs were James Moore (Economics) and Andy Whinston (MIS). His current research interests are in e-commerce and outsourcing and are funded by NSF. He has published in journals such as ISR, MISQ, DSS, IEEE Transactions in SMC etc. He is a co-editor-in-chief of Information Systems Frontiers: A Journal of Research and Innovation (http://www.som.buffalo.edu/isinterface/isfrontiers). He spends his spare time mediating disputes between his 8-year-old daughter and 12-year-old son.

Kyeong Seok Han is an associate professor of management information systems at Soongsil University. He was a visiting scholar and a part-time lecturer at The Wharton School of the University of Pennsylvania. He holds a Ph.D. in management information systems from Purdue University. His research interests include electronic commerce, entrepreneurial high-tech ventures, and e-business. He has published articles in 'Accounting, Management, and Information Technology', International Journal of Electronic Commerce, The Journal of MIS Research, and Korea Database Journal.

James H. Gerlach is professor of information systems at the University of Colorado at Denver. His research interests include software engineering and management of information systems technology. Gerlach holds a MS in computer science and a PhD in management, both from Purdue University. He is a member of the IEEE and the ACM. His work appears in such notable journals as *Management Information Systems Quarterly, IEEE Computer, IEEE Software, Decision Support Systems,* and *The Accounting Review.* His article, "Determining the Cost of IT Services" will appear in the *Communicatons of the ACM.*

Amitava Dutta holds the LeRoy Eakin Endowed Chair in Electronic Commerce and is Professor of MIS in the School of Management at George Mason University. His research interests include business performance models for electronic commerce, telecommunications policy, systems thinking and decision support systems. Dutta's research has appeared in journals such as *IJEC, JMIS, CACM, IIE Transactions, Management Science, EJOR, Operations Research, and IEEE Transactions on Communications*. He serves on the editorial boards of several information technology journals, and is a member of IEEE, ACM and INFORMS. Dutta has consulted and conducted executive courses for several government and private sector organizations in a variety of Information Technology Management areas. He received the University-wide teaching excellence award at GMU in 2001. Dutta holds a B.Tech from the Indian Institute of Technology, MS from University of California Santa Barbara, and PhD from the Krannert School at Purdue University.

Rahul Roy is Associate Professor of Management Information Systems at the Indian Institute of Management Calcutta, India. Dr. Roy's research interests include systems dynamics, software project management and growth dynamics of high technology firms. His research has appeared in journals such as CACM and EJOR. He serves on the editorial board of Systems Dynamics: An International Journal of Policy Modeling. He has consulted for a variety of public sector organizations in the state of West Bengal. Prior to joining IIM Calcutta, he was an engineer with one of the leading industrial organizations in India. Dr. Roy received his B.Tech, M. Tech and Ph.D. from the Indian Institute of Technology and is an active member of the Systems Dynamics Society of India.

Varghese S. Jacob is Associate Dean and Professor of Management Science and Information Systems in the School of Management at the University of Texas at Dallas (UTD). Prior to joining UTD at The Ohio

State University. He obtained his Ph.D. degree in Management, majoring in Management Information Systems, from Purdue University. His research interests are in the areas of Artificial Intelligence, Data Quality, Decision Support Systems, and Electronic Commerce. His publications include articles in *Management Science, Information Systems Research, Decision Support Systems, IEEE Transactions on Systems, Man, and Cybernetics, European Journal of Operational Research, Psychometrika, Group Decision and Negotiation* and *International Journal of Man-Machine Studies*. He is the Co-Editor of the journal *Information Technology and Management* and serves as an Associate Editor for *Decision Support Systems*. He also serves on the editorial board of *Information Systems Frontiers: A Journal of Research and Innovation*.

Clyde Holsapple has held the University of Kentucky's Rosenthal Endowed Chair in Management Information Systems since its inception in 1988. His recent teaching activities include courses dealing with decision support systems, intelligent systems, and electronic commerce. He has supervised 20 doctoral dissertations. In 1993, he was recognized as Computer Educator of the Year by the International Association for Computer Information Systems. In 1995, he was awarded the University of Kentucky's Chancellor's Award for Outstanding Teaching. Professor Holsapple's publication credits include a dozen books and over 125 articles in journals and books. He has served as inaugural Area Editor for both Decision Support Systems and ORSA Journal on Computing, Editor for the Journal of Organizational Computing and Electronic Commerce, and Associate Editor for Management Science. He is a Research Fellow of the International Center for Electronic Commerce based in Seoul and an Affiliate Member of the Center for Electronic Commerce Research at the University of Texas.

Hsiangchu Lai is professor of Information Management at National Sun Yat-sen University of Taiwan. Lai received her Ph.D. in management information systems from Purdue University. Her articles have been published in IEEE Computer, Group Decision and Negotiation, International Journal of Electronic Commerce, Decision Support Systems, etc. Her research interests include electronic commerce, negotiation support systems, and knowledge management.

Yen-Ching OuYang received her M.Sc. in Information Technology from Napier University of Edinburgh in 1993. She is currently a Lecturer of Information Management at the Fortune Institute of Technology.

Ting-Peng Liang is professor of information systems at the Department of Information Management and Director of the Electronic Commerce Research Center at National Sun Yat-sen University in Kaohsiung, Taiwan. He has published a number of articles in journals such as Management Science, MIS Quarterly, Decision Support Systems, among others. His primary research interests include electronic commerce, knowledge management, and decision support systems.

Manish Agrawal is at the University of South Florida where he is an Assistant Professor in the Department of Information Systems and Decision Sciences. His doctoral work was done at SUNY Buffalo. His research interests include Electronic Commerce, Information Systems Outsourcing and Intermediaries. His research has been published in several conference proceedings including the Americas Conference on Information Systems (best paper award) as well as the Encyclopedia of Electrical and Electronics Engineering. Two of his papers on Mobile Terminals in Police Work and Information Systems Piracy have been conditionally accepted in the Journal of Organizational Computing and Electronic Commerce.

David E. Pingry is currently Professor of Management Information Systems and Economics at the University of Arizona and formerly served as Head of the Department of Management Information Systems and as Acting Head of the Department of Economics at the University of Arizona. He began his career on the faculty of VPI and has held visiting positions at Purdue and at Texas A&M. David received his Ph.D. in Economics from Purdue University, studying under Andy Whinston. He has a lengthy list of publicatons in production theory, water quality, and management of information, much influenced by or co-authored with Andy Whinston.

James R. Marsden is currently Shenkman Family Chair in e-Business, Head of the Department of Operations and Information Technology, and Executive Director of the Connecticut Information Technology Institute at the University of Connecticut. Formerly, he served as Philip Morris Professor of MIS, Founding Chair of the Department of Decision Science and Information Systems, and Professor of Economics at the University of Kentucky. He has held visiting positions at Purdue University, the University of Arizona, and the University of York (England). Shortly after receiving his Ph.D. in Economics from Purdue, Jim began working with David Pingry and Andy Whinston in a lengthy and productive collaboration. His list of publications in production theory, environmental management, management of information, and controlled laboratory experimentation owes much to his interactions with Dave and with Andy Whinston.

Foreword

Andrew Whinston

A beginning

W.W. Cooper

Foster Parker Professor of Finance and Management (Emeritus)

The Red McCombs School of Business

University of Texas at Austin

Austin, Texas 78712-1174

cooperw@mail.utexas.edu

This book constitutes a festschrift in honour of Andrew Whinston on his 65th birthday. It appropriately exemplifies multi-disciplinary approaches to business modelling. The emphasis is on the development of new approaches to newly emerging problems and opportunities in business by some of Dr. Whinston's former students and colleagues. These types of research efforts provide badly needed guidance for both business practice and public policy formation.

How did this come into being in the prominence displayed by these authors? One way to provide illumination is to turn to Andy's own beginnings as a doctoral student at Carnegie Institute of Technology (now Carnegie Mellon University). Having served as chairman of his thesis committee, I thought I might provide some of this illumination by describing events that led to Andy's doctoral thesis. This is important because this thesis "Price Coordination in Decentralized Systems" (Pittsburgh, Pa: Carnegie Institute of Technology, 1962) quickly became a classic (much cited reference) in its field. It also guided a good deal of his subsequent work.

Andy had come to us as a student steeped in economics from the University of Michigan and then found himself responding to the wider variety of research oriented activities that were being put together in novel ways at the then new GSIA (Graduate School of Industrial Administration) at Carnegie. At the time we were in the process of trying to formulate new approaches to management education.[1] To implement these approaches we had recruited a rather unusual (at the time) research oriented faculty drawn largely from the social science disciplines. A good deal of these activities were oriented toward new approaches to management and the use of new research tools built, inter alia, around possible uses of the electronic computers that were coming to the fore at that time. The Dean (G.L. Bach) had also recruited a smaller cadre of more traditional "business oriented" faculty who were familiar with contemporary business practices and experienced in the contemporary traditions of management education. One very distinguished member of that cadre singled out Andy at a faculty meeting and argued that the school should not be producing students like him. According to this faculty member he would give the school a bad name because Andy was (and was likely to remain) too "far out."

Andy had been a student in one of my courses where I became impressed with his lively intelligence and his far ranging interests. I therefore requested that he be assigned to me for the summer term as an assistant so that I could have a chance to interest him in more practical managerial problems. For this purpose I asked Andy to go through all of the recent issues of the *Harvard Business Review* and brief me, once a week, on their contents.

A recurrent topic in these articles was the problem of price coordination of decentralized systems. In each of his reports Andy commented critically on the display of a lack of knowledge of the economic theory which he believed the authors of these articles could use to resolve the problems that they were addressing. In reply I pointed out to Andy that there might be aspects of these problems that had not really been dealt with in a satisfactory manner in the economics literature of that time. I suggested therefore that he try to concentrate on identifying the underlying problems rather than the proposed solutions, and thereby perhaps open new paths for research.

It so happened that I was a consultant to the Controller's Office of the Ford Motor Company which I knew was grappling at that time with problems involved in designing satisfactory systems of decentralized pricing

[1] These efforts and their results have been documented in detail in numerous monographs and papers published by the Graduate Management Admission Council. See, for instance, *The Beginnings of Graduate Management Education in the United States*, GMAC Occasional Paper by Steven Schlossman, Robert Gleeson, Michael Sedlak and David Allen (Santa Monica, Ca: Graduate Management Admission Council, 1994).

to guide the activities of the company's far flung operations. I therefore arranged for Andy to spend a week visiting with staff concerned with these problems.

This proved to be the turning point I had been looking for. Andy quickly discovered the pervasive nature of the "externality problems" that Ford confronted in dealing with these designs. Not only had economics failed to deal with these externality problems in an adequate manner but many of these problems had also been "swept under the rug" by assuming that incentives to internalize such externalities would eliminate their presence (in the long run).

This provided the needed start for a thesis by Andy. The rest is history and Andy has gone on to other accomplishments so I won't deal further with this topic other than to say that the thesis Andy wrote not only dealt with this problem of practice but also treated it in ways that stimulated new kinds of research that were needed in economics as well as management. Thus Andy showed how a concrete problem in management could be analysed in a manner that had an impact on far removed fields of theoretical research.

In conclusion I only note that Andy's own wide ranging interests have carried him into fields (like those described in the present book) that did not even exist in Andy's student days. He has continued to be at the forefront of research in these newly developing fields. Reflecting back on the attempt to oust Andy from GSIA I am led to remark that it has always been true that the job of our business schools has been to prepare students for the future. Preparation for dealing only with problems of the past and contemporary practices are by themselves not enough. This book in honour of Andy on his 65th birthday provides ample testimony of what this means and what can be accomplished by a person possessing his talents, abilities and motivations.

Acknowledgements

The Editors would like to thank Gary Folven of Kluwer for encouraging us in this endeavor, Ramesh Sharda and Stephan Voss for their enthusiasm regarding this project. Eugene Colucci, SUNY Buffalo helped us in the design of the website for uploading all files. We would like to extend our appreciation to all the referees who scrambled to get their referee reports in time. Thanks of course go to our respective Deans and Department Chairs for all their support. Finally our grateful thanks to our respective families without whose understanding, this may have taken longer than it did. Last but not least, thanks to you, Veronica and Andy, our guru, for leading us to where we are today.

PART 1

BUSINESS MODELLING FUNDAMENTALS

Introduction

Business Modelling: MultiDisciplinary Approaches

Essays in Honor of Andrew B. Whinston

Clyde Holsapple: Varghese Jacob: H. Raghav Rao: Abhijit Chaudhury: Manish Agrawal

Univ of Kentucky: Univ of Texas at Dallas: State University of New York at Buffalo: Bryant College: University of South Florida

Key words: Business modelling, Electronic business, festschrift, analysis, simulation, e-commerce, decision making

1. INTRODUCTION

Business modelling is a vast arena of research and practice, which has taken on considerable importance over the past few decades. The ability to utilize advanced computing technology to model, analyse and simulate various aspects of ever-changing businesses has made a significant impact on the way businesses are designed and run these days. This book is a *festschrift* to Professor Andrew B. Whinston (currently Hugh Roy Cullen Centennial Chair in Business Administration at the University of Texas, Austin and formerly a faculty member at Purdue University, University of Virginia and Yale University), a pioneer in business modelling, who has inspired many multi-disciplinary approaches to problem solving in the business environment.

How is modelling related to business and more specifically to the current day e-business and e-commerce enterprises? The world of e-business represents a paradigm shift in the way business architects and decision makers appraise business processes and evaluate enterprise alternatives. This has become particularly true especially as e-business initiatives grow, and businesses increasingly move key processes beyond the boundary of the corporation to a global audience consisting of customers, suppliers, partners, collaborators and competitors.

The movement toward global e-business has resulted from a rapidly changing environment where a number of critical issues need to be resolved. Issues such as uncertainties and incomplete information in the business processes, increases in the intricacies of processes, increases in information loss in tandem with information overload, increasing availability of information from and for a select few end-users to a global set of consumers (albeit oftentimes with increasing loss of accuracy), and the necessity for businesses to react quickly and reliably to fleeting windows of opportunity all call for improved and more formal approaches to business modelling. This has indeed, been happening in varying degrees throughout industry.

In such a rapidly changing environment, how may such issues be resolved to make decision making more effective? Perhaps a comprehensive set of business and system services that could enforce business rules and filter value from key business processes would help in addressing the complexities that enterprises face in the new economy. However, for effective enterprise decision making, it is important to have clear, concise business models that allow the extraction of critical value from business processes and specify the rules to be globally enforced. Particularly in e-business specifications, the need to be unambiguous, accurate, and complete becomes even greater, because there may be no human mediator or agent to rely on in complex or unforeseen situations.

This *festschrift*, arranged in three parts, brings scholarly perspectives from various disciplines to bear on some of the critical aspects of business modeling. The first part (CHAPTERS 1-8) focuses on business modeling fundamentals and starts with a series of economics and operations research perspectives. The second part (CHAPTERS 9-19) concentrates on modeling in electronic businesses and focuses on Management Information Systems and Decision Support Systems. The third part (CHAPTERS 20-22) centers on multidisciplinary business modeling progress, in particular on the seminal work of Professor Andrew B. Whinston. The following sections summarize the three parts that make up the book.

BUSINESS MODELLING FUNDAMENTALS

The collection starts off with some gleanings from 'The Theory Of Second Best'. William A. Hamlen Jr. writes about the theory of the second best, a major topic of interest and concern in the field of economics beginning in the late 1950s and extending all the way to the present. A combination of discovery and insights by Negishi (1960) and Davis and Whinston (1965) redeemed the virtues of the laissez faire principle. In this paper the author clarifies the original and most important controversy surrounding the theory of the second best.

The second chapter deals with 'Transfer Pricing'. Here, Vicente Salas-Fumas and Francisco Ruiz-Aliseda show that, in oligopolistic markets where firms face strategic interactions, profit maximizing firms have incentives to deviate from the price equal to marginal cost rule and that the sign of the deviation depends upon the structural conditions of the market, such as homogeneous versus differentiated products and price versus quantity competition.

The third article, 'Trading Mechanism Design for Swap Markets' by Ming Fan, Xiaorui Hu and Han Zhang, proposes an electronic market for swap exchanges. The authors designed a trading mechanism that allows multiple swaps, futures and forwards to be traded on the same market and guarantees that traders will get either the combination of assets or nothing.

In the fourth article, 'Production Capacity for Durable Goods', R. Preston McAfee provides a theory of manufacturing capacity choice for a durable good. The remarkable conclusion is that efficient production may entail ten to fifty years before full market saturation is reached. The time to market saturation is increased as the good becomes less durable, and the size of the crash when saturation is reached falls as the durability decreases. The monopoly seller is efficient provided it does not ever undercut itself, a feature of some equilibria of the "no gap" case, where demand intersects marginal costs.

The fifth chapter, by Edna T. Loehman and Rabih Karaky, is concerned with 'Cost-Sharing For Pollution Abatement'. It presents a method of ameliorating externality problems when polluters and sufferers would like to take a cooperative approach, sharing costs of abatement and jointly deciding expenditure for abatement and environmental goals. The method for solving this joint problem uses decentralized messages among the involved participants concerning willingness to pay and proposals about environmental quality. The iterative process starts from exogenously specified cost shares that are then adjusted through personalized prices (which can be taxes or subsidies). The process arrives at equilibrium through price adjustment rules. The equilibrium of the process satisfies social efficiency by design. A simulated example shows that the method can solve a complex problem in relatively few iterations.

In the sixth article, 'A Study on Coefficient Reduction of Binary Knapsack Inequalities', Gary J. Koehler focuses on the work by Bradley,

Hammer and Wolsey (1975) who characterized the minimal representation of binary knapsack problems. A linear programming formulation for this problem often gave integral solutions leading the authors to state "We know of no satisfactory explanation of why the large fraction of linear programming optimal solutions are integer for this problem." This paper provides a study of this phenomenon and shows that these problems are close in structure to problems having a dual that is an integral, dynamic Leontief Substitution System.

'Qualitative Reasoning' is the seventh article. Here, Aimo Hinkkanen and Karl R. Lang present a general theory of qualitative reasoning (QR) systems which includes, as special cases, reasoning methods that use representations of qualitative differential equations and qualitative difference equations. The paper emphasizes the significance of discrete, dynamic models and optimization models in the management and economics fields, both of which have received relatively little attention in current QR research.

Modelling is a knowledge-intensive activity and modelling systems are essentially systems that manage knowledge: representing knowledge about real-world phenonmena (e.g., business situations) and processing that knowledge to derive new knowledge in the guise of expectations, implications, assessments and solutions. The last chapter in the first part of the book presents an 'Architecture for Knowledge Management Featuring Metaknowledge'. In it, Roger Alan Pick and George P. Schell describe an architecture for a general knowledge management system, and give examples to illustrate how metaknowledge could assist in a knowledge management system.

2. MODELLING IN ELECTRONIC BUSINESS

The second part of the book begins with a treatise on 'Multi Agent Enterprise Modeling'. Riyaz Sikora and Michael J. Shaw present a multi-agent framework as a paradigm for achieving enterprise integration. The coordination mechanisms needed for ensuring orderly operations and concerted decision making among the components (i.e., agents) of an enterprise are emphasized.

The second chapter in this part, 'Designing IT-Supported Market Mechanisms for Organizational Coordination', is authored by Sulin Ba and Jan Stallaert. They discuss issues that differentiate IT-supported internal markets from IT-supported commerce between different companies. Drawing on recent research by Dr. Whinston and his colleagues on market mechanisms, this chapter illustrates how such systems might be designed.

The third chapter deals with 'Congestion Based Pricing and Management of Distributed Computational Resources'. Alok Gupta, Boris Jukic and Prabhudev Konana address fundamental objections to externality based pricing, i.e., the problem of acquiring customers' private information regarding their demand characteristics. The coverage ranges from demonstration of computational feasibility of such prices based on transient system information to the issue of incentives of network infrastructure owners in the presence of multiple co-existing pricing paradigms.

'Pricing Virtual Private Networks - An Economic, Engineering and Experimental Approach' is the fourth chapter on modeling in electronic business. In it, Zhangxi Lin, Peng Si Ow and Dale O. Stahl present a network traffic-pricing model for a virtual private network (VPN) deployed on packet-switching networks. A transaction-level pricing architecture based on proxy server technology is proposed for the implementation. Analytical expressions of pricing formulas for first-in-first-out and round-robin bandwidth are derived. Both agent-based simulations and human subject based direct experiments have been conducted using real-time test data. The experimental outcomes furnish strong evidence that the pricing mechanism can effectively improve a VPN's transmission efficiency as measured by the service welfare rate.

In the fifth chapter, 'Knowledge Representation: A Classification with Applications in Telecommunications and the Web', Prudence T. Zacarias Kapauan and Eugenia Fernandez review knowledge representation schemes found in the AI literature. They identify commonalities in perspectives and underlying philosophies of the various representation schemes. A close examination of the different schemes reveals that they can be classified under one or more of four major knowledge representation philosophies: objects, networks, frames, and logic. Newer knowledge representation applications of these philosophies, specifically XML, UML and ontologies, are discussed and examples of their use in telecommunications and Web applications are given.

The sixth article concerns 'Quasi-naturally Occurring Experiments With Electronic Markets and Digital Products'. Here, Anitesh Barua and Ramnath K. Chellappa make the case that in the absence of well-developed and tested theories in the area of digital products and markets, quasi-naturally occurring experiments will be critical to testing underlying design assumptions and rationales of electronic markets.

Next, Melody Kiang, Robert T. Chi and Kar Yan Tam write about 'Finding the Right Products and Devising Marketing Strategies for E-Tailing'. They examine the use of the Internet as a virtual storefront where products are offered directly to customers. The authors' contention is that both product characteristics and consumer purchase behaviors play major roles in the success of marketing on the Internet.

In the eighth article, 'To Surf Or To Ride: An Analysis of Channel Competition Between Electronic and Retail Stores', Beomsoo Kim and Byungtae Lee study the competition between two shopping channels: electronic stores and retail stores. They focus on the profitability and expansion strategies of these channels as a function of consumer characteristics and store cost structure. A consumer's choice of a store is determined by price differences, perceived risk in online buying, network comfort level, and retail discomfort level (logical distance between a consumer and a retail store). The authors make an interesting observation that the number of retail stores has no effect on the optimal pricing strategies of either the electronic store or the retail store.

The ninth article is 'Organizational And Economic Mechanisms For Buyer-Supplier Contracts' by Seung Kyoon Shin, R. Ramesh and H. Raghav Rao. It presents an overview of the nature of contracts in a buyer-supplier business environment and identifies factors that affect contract relationships. Concepts from transaction cost theory and agency theory as well as the resource-based view are applied to develop an outline for mechanisms that can govern buyer-supplier contracts. Such contracts lie at the core of electronic commerce.

In the tenth article, 'The Intelligent Internal Accounting Control Model' is studied 'Under E-Business Environment' conditions. Kyeong Seok Han and James H. Gerlach review the history of the development of TICOM (The Internal Control Model), a computer-assisted method for designing and evaluating accounting internal control systems. The latest proposed model, TICOM-V, is based on a logical specification of an auditing domain problem in the e-Business environment and utilizes artificial intelligence and logic programming language concepts. This helps produce a system that offers greater audit ability and maintainability in the e-Business environment than previously possible.

The last article in this part of the book takes a global perspective. In 'Internet Diffusion In Developing Countries: A Socio-Technical Model', Amitava Dutta and Rahul Roy report on initial efforts to develop a model that takes a systems view to analyze how social and technical forces are likely to interact and drive Internet diffusion in developing countries. These countries, in particular, need to understand the complex mechanics of this diffusion process in order to realize their potential for growth in the new world of digital- based trade and business. The systems dynamics methodology is used to develop the model allowing for simulation of various growth scenarios and policy alternatives.

3. MULTIDISCIPLINARY BUSINESS MODELLING PROGRESS

The final part of the book looks at both the multidisciplinary nature of business modelling and Professor Andrew Whinston's significant global contributions to it throughout his career. In each research initiative that Professor Whinston undertakes there is certain to be something original, interesting and enlightening.

In the chapter on 'Advances In Business Problem Solving: Bridging Business And Computing Disciplines', Clyde W. Holsapple presents a framework for understanding the multidisciplinary nature of the business computing field. Using this framework, the chapter examines the still unfolding legacy of Professor Whinston's work, which provides an outstanding role model and inspiration for both seasoned colleagues and beginning students throughout the business computing field.

'The Intellectual Contribution Of Professor Andrew B. Whinston To The Field Of Information Systems In The Past Two Decades', by Hsiangchu Lai, Yen-Ching OuYang and Ting-Peng Liang, explores Professor Andrew B. Whinston's intellectual contribution to research in information systems over the past two decades. A citation analysis is performed using the Science Citation Index and Social Science Citation Index since 1980.

The book concludes with 'IT Reference Disciplines - Andy Whinston, A Case Study' by James R. Marsden and David E. Pingry. This work results from the support, collegiality, and synergies so characteristic of the Center for the Study of Unique Non-Convex Technologies, a circa 1970s unofficial but very productive K-school (name deleted to protect the innocent) research center.

4. CONCLUSION

Most of the authors of the articles in this book have had the good fortune to be associated with Professor Whinston over several years. We have had the benefit of his wisdom, his indomitable spirit and his ability to envision the future. To us, he has been the ultimate guru; an inspiring beacon of light for researchers, students and practitioners travelling within and across various disciplines. To him and to Mrs. Whinston, who has also played the role of advisor and friend to all of us, a heartfelt thank you!

Chapter 1

Gleanings into the Second Best Debate

William A. Hamlen Jr.
Department of Finance and Managerial Economics, School of Management State University of New York at Buffalo, Buffalo, N.Y. 14260

Abstract: The theory of the second best was a major topic of interest and concern in the field of economics beginning in the late 1950s and extending all the way to the present. Stimulated by observations made by Paul Samuelson in his Foundations of Economic Analysis (1947) and formalized by Lipsey and Lancaster (1956), the theory represented a formidable challenge to the accepted model of free enterprise and perfect competition. It concluded that if even just one sector of the economy did not act in the way described by the perfectly competitive model, and thus the first best solution was not being attained, then it was possible that the "second best" solution would require that no sector act in the manner prescribed in the perfectly competitive environment. In addition, due to the complexity of the second best requirements, it would be very unlikely that even the second best solution, or "third best," etc., solutions could be attained in real world applications. However, a combination of discovery and insights by Negishi (1960) and Davis and Whinston (1965) redeemed the virtues of the laissez faire principle. In this paper the author attempts to clarify the original and most important controversy surrounding the theory of the second best

Key words: second best, welfare economics, Pareto optimality, general equilibrium.

1. INTRODUCTION

The Academy ran on the honor system. Every student was assumed to be honest in all aspects of his or her life, but particularly with regard to academic honesty. This policy made life extremely efficient for all concerned. When Professor Jones gave a three-hour exam, he would hand the exams out in class, tell the students to take a seat and to work quietly by themselves. This relaxed test-taking atmosphere clearly helped students to perform better. Meanwhile Professor Jones would sit and work on his own research. This research eventually brought added value to his own career, to the Academy, and to the degrees of the students who graduated from the Academy. However, a situation arose which brought into question the honesty of one student, Jack, during exams. Professor Jones believed that he had caught Jack with "roving eyes." Even speaking to Jack and warning him of the possible consequences seemed to have no effect on Jack's behavior. There was, of course, a well defined solution for cheating. That was to expel from the program any student found guilty. Such a stiff penalty would quickly eliminate the problem and return the Academy to its normal optimal system. However, Jack came from a rich and prestigious family of lawyers and the evidence of Jack's dishonesty was considered insufficient to expel Jack and thereby risk a potential lawsuit. In fact, it was decided that the question of Jack's possible dishonesty could not even be made public. Another solution was to just allow Jack to go on as he was. Yet this did not seem good for the long run reputation of the honor system and for the reputations of its graduates. Another solution was to eliminate any presumption of an honor system. This implied that in order to prevent Jack from getting answers from someone next to him, all of the students and professors would have to change their behavior, and, in essence, be less efficient. Then someone made a brilliant observation and suggestion. Since Jack was the only student under suspicion, but couldn't be accused of dishonesty, one only needed to develop a seating chart for the class and place Jack in the first row, first seat. Next to Jack, in the only seat he would be able to observe, would be placed the worst student in the class. Thus, Jack, if he chose to look upon his neighbour's answers, would probably not help himself. At the same time no other student, nor Professor Jones need deviate from their efficient ways.

The story described above is an illustration of a "second best" solution. The "first best" solution was obtained when all students acted, and were assumed to act, with complete honesty. When Jack was thought to be cheating it was deemed a very inferior solution to just allowing Jack to go on cheating under the existing environment. The first best solution could have been retained if Jack could have been penalized. Then the normal optimal behavior of Professor Jones and the other students would have been unaffected. However, since this penalty could not be enacted and Jack's potential cheating behavior could not be eliminated, it at first appeared that the "second best" solution required altering the optimal behavior of Professor Jones and all of the students. Fortunately, it was realized that the true second best solution could be attained with a "piecemeal" approach to dealing with Jack and one other student. While this is only one simplistic story, it hopefully brings out the generality and scope of the second best concept. Despite the fact that the "General Theory of the Second Best" was originally discussed in technical and sophisticated mathematical economic terms, all those entering into or following the discussions and debates understood that there was also an underlying philosophical issue that had far reaching implications.

In the 1950s and 60s the field of economics was in one of its peak periods of prestige, at least among the scholarly minded. The introduction of mathematical economics by individuals like Paul Samuelson (1947), Kenneth Arrow (1951) and Gerard Debreu (1959) had elevated economics from something of a pseudo-science to a full fledged analytical science. The influences of John Maynard Keynes (1936) on world economics and politics were still worthy of front page news. Among economics graduate students the names of prestigious contemporary economic professors were discussed in a manner that is reminiscent of the general public's discussion of today's athletes and popular singers. The theory of the "second best" was one of those topics that engendered names and reputations which were considered at the time to be part of the new elite class of mathematical economists. These included names like R.G. Lipsey and Kelvin Lancaster (1956), Maurice. McManus (1958), Takashi Negishi(1960) and Otto Davis and Andrew Whinston (1965). Most of their early articles on the second best were published in the Review of Economic Studies. It was the privilege of this writer to attend Purdue University, largely based on a recommendation by Professor Maurice McManus while attaining an M.A. degree from the University of Hawaii, and to obtain a Ph.D. at Purdue under Professor Andrew Whinston. It is my association with both professors that motivates me to review the historical debate on the theory of the second best. In the following section I offer a succinct review of the theory of the second best and describe the most significant debate arising from the topic. Like others before me I will attempt to simplify what appears, to the uninitiated examining the original papers, to be a very tedious and somewhat difficult set of technical arguments surrounding the debate that took place in the literature.

2. SAMUELSON'S CONJECTURE

The debate on the second best is better appreciated if it is placed in the larger context of the theory of perfect competition and its relationship to social welfare. Perhaps the appropriate starting place is to offer a quote from Paul Samuelson's famous Foundations of Economic Analysis, first printed in 1947.

"Beginning as it did in the writings of philosophers, theologians, pamphleteers, special pleaders, and reformers, economics has always been concerned with problems of public policy and welfare. And at least from the time of the physiocrats and Adam Smith there policy and the time of the physiocrats and Adam Smith there policy and welfare. And at least from the time of the physiocrats and Adam Smith there never has been absent from the main body of economic literature the feeling that in some sense perfect competition represented an optimal situation."(p. 203, 1967).

Perfect competition, in its usual formulation, resulted in a Pareto optimal outcome, i.e., no individual could be made better off without reducing the welfare of another individual. In Chapter VIII of his Foundations Samuelson outlined the numerous efficiency conditions known to be necessary behavioural conditions for a perfectly competitive market, e.g., price equals marginal cost in an economy of price-taking firms. He recognized that all of these necessary conditions might be generalized as the solution to some grand constrained optimization problem that had yet to be fully determined. As such it might take the following form (p. 222, 1967):

$$\text{Maximize } F(x_1,...,x_n) \tag{1}$$

subject to:

$$f(x_1,...,x_n)=0 \tag{2}$$

Although Samuelson was specifically interested in the perfectly competitive economic system, Equations (1) and (2) could be the general problem used to represent any economic system.

In equations (1) and (2) the n-variables are choice variables by consumers and producers. In addition a Lagrangean multiplier λ is associated with constraint (2). The following n first-order conditions for this problem are defined as the necessary conditions for the "first best" solution to the above problem.

$$F_i + \lambda f_i = 0 \quad (i=1,...,n) \tag{3}$$

Again, while the first-order conditions given by (3) were assumed by Samuelson to describe natural behavioural actions of the participants in a perfectly competitive economy, they might also represent the behavioural actions of some other type of economy.

The motivation for the second best theory emanated from Samuelson himself. In describing the necessary conditions for optimality in a perfectly competitive economy, he made the following conjecture (p.252, 1967):

"First, what is the best procedure if for some reason a number of the optimum conditions are not realized? What shall we do about the remaining ones which are in our power? Shall we argue that "two wrongs do not make a right" and attempt to satisfy those we can? Or is it possible that failure of a number of conditions necessitates modifying the rest? Clearly the latter alternative is the correct one."

3. LIPSEY-LANCASTER AND THE FORMAL THEORY

Lipsey and Lancaster (L-L) (1956) sought to rigorously analyze this statement and construct a general framework for what they called the "second best" problem. They began with the original problem proposed by Samuelson, consisting of objective function (1) above and the general constraint (2). The necessary conditions for the "first best" solution are given by (3) above. In order to set up the second best problem, they followed the usual solution technique of first eliminating the Lagrangean variable λ from (3). This is accomplished by dividing each of the n-1 conditions by the remaining n'th condition, or:

$$F_i/F_n = f_i/f_n \quad (i=1,\dots,n-1) \tag{4}$$

where the solution to the problem should not be affected by the particular choice of the n'th variable. L-L then introduced a problem in the first-order solution by requiring that one of these n-1 first-order conditions be unfulfilled. Seemingly without loss of generality, they chose the first sector as the one which fails to meet its first-order condition. Thus:

$$F_1/F_n = k[f_1/f_n] \quad \text{where } k \neq 1 \tag{5}$$

They then appended constraint (5), along with the new Lagrangean multiplier μ, to the original problem consisting of (1) and (2). The revised first-order conditions for a second best optimal solution become:

$$F_i - \lambda f_i - \mu\{[F_n F_{1i} - F_1 F_{ni}]/F_n^2 - k[f_n f_{1i} - f_1 f_{ni}]/f_n^2\} = 0 \tag{6}$$
$$(i=1,\ldots,n),\ k \neq 1.$$

In general, the necessary conditions for the second best solution given by equation (6) imply that all sectors of the economy should deviate from their first best solution. This is despite the fact that only the first sector initially and incurably violates its necessary condition for the first best solution. Of course, despite any discussion to follow in the subsequent debate, this was the remarkable conclusion alluded to by Samuelson. The implication was that if even one sector of an economy, and specifically within the context of a free enterprise market economy, failed to act in the manner described by the known first-order conditions, then all sectors could potentially be encouraged to deviate from the behavior associated with the first best solution. Taken to its logical conclusion this result has two negative implications: First, it would justify government intervention into every aspect of the economy and imply that fully regulated economies could provide a higher level of welfare to its citizens than the free enterprise system described by Adam Smith. Second, even if government's intervention is justified in correcting one sector's deviate behavior the general second best solution would require an overwhelming amount of information on all sectors.

4. MCMANUS AND THE N'TH SECTOR

Maurice McManus (1958-59) provided the first attack on the L-L theory of the second-best. He was quick to point out that the L-L generalization of the problem is not as general as they suggested. In particular the arbitrary use of the n'th sector to eliminate the Lagrangean variable λ is not as neutral as assumed by L-L. McManus correctly noted that different second best solutions would result if different sectors were used instead of the n'th sector. This is true both mathematically and also if one attempts to actually apply the L-L rules to a particular problem in economic policy. The specific form of the violated constraint is very important to the outcome of the second best problem. Two problems with the L-L generalization are fairly obvious. First, from the new constraint given by equation (5) it is not possible to determine whether it is the first sector, the n'th sector, or both sectors that are failing to satisfy the first-order conditions. Second, the second best conditions given by equation (6) require use of the cross partial derivatives between each sector and the n'th sector, thus demonstrating that the n'th sector is acting as more than a simple numeraire. McManus' conclusion was that, in the general formation of the social optimization problem given by equations (1) and (2), the second best solution inherently involves more than a single sector. It requires that one sector consistently violate the first-order condition for the first best solution and that other sectors consistently maintain their first-order conditions, unless interference comes from a central authority.

The question arises: How might L-L have formulated the problem such that no extra n'th sector is involved in the violated constraint, at least in its mathematical formulation? An alternative solution was eventually presented by Henderson and Quandt (1980, p. 316) to illustrate that no n'th sector need be involved. Assume that sector one maintains the following condition which violates its first best solution:

$$F_1 + kf_1 = 0, \quad k \neq 1$$

(7)

Appending (7), with Lagrangean variable μ, to the original problem (1) and (2) and deriving the new first-order conditions for this second best solution we have:

$$\partial F/\partial x_i + \lambda \partial G/\partial x_i + \mu[\partial^2 F_1/\partial x_1 \partial x_i + k\partial^2 G/\partial x_1 \partial x_i] = 0, \quad i = 1,\ldots,n$$

(8)

Here, the additional terms found in the second best solution of equation (8), but not in the first best equation of equation (3), do not involve an arbitrary n'th sector. While McManus' criticism was valid with respect to the original L-L formulation, i.e., their original formulation was perfectly general, L-L (1958-1959) maintained that their basic conclusion was still valid and dependent on the inclusion of an n'th sector, i.e., if one sector violates the optimal first best conditions then the second best solution, in the general case, requires that many other sectors, and possibly all other sectors, be forced to violate their first-order conditions associated with the first best solution.

5. NEGISHI'S MODEL OF PERFECT COMPETITION

As noted above Samuelson had hypothesized that the Pareto optimal conditions associated with a perfectly competitive economy might result from the optimization of some general problem described by Equations (1) and (2). Nevertheless, the specific form or properties of the objective function given by these equations were yet to be determined when Samuelson published the Foundations in 1947. However, in 1951 Arrow published his famous "Impossibility Theorem" which made it clear that whatever the true underlying objective function a perfectly competitive economy attempted to maximize, there were limitations on the positive attributes of the function. At the time, Arrow's theorem was sometimes misunderstood and interpreted as implying that economies had no possible objective function. In fact, it only implied that whatever objective function was the one pursued by a particular economy, it could not satisfy all of Arrow's attributes. Since every economy inherently seeks to solve some constrained optimization problem similar to equations (1) and (2), even though it does not explicitly recognize that it is doing so, no economy satisfies all of the positive attributes described by Arrow. But what is the constrained optimization problem being optimized by a textbook type of purely competitive economy?

In 1960 T. Negishi published a model that finally revealed the exact form of this optimization problem. Negishi found that the perfectly competitive economy seeks to:

$$\text{Maximize} \sum_{i=1}^{n} \alpha_i U_i(x_i) \tag{9}$$

subject to:

$$\sum_{i=1}^{n} \bar{x}_{ij} + \sum_{k=1}^{r} y_{kj} - \sum_{i=1}^{n} x_{ij} \geq 0,\ j = 1,\ldots,m \tag{10}$$

$$F_k(y_k) \geq 0,\ k = 1,\ldots,r \tag{11}$$

where: U_i = the utility function for individual i.
x_i = the m–vector of goods demanded by individual i.
F_k = the production function of the k'th firm.
y_k = the m–vector of inputs and outputs in F_k.
x_{ik} = the consumption of good j by individual j.
$\overline{x}_{ij}$ = the initial endowment of good j by individual i.
y_{kj} = the quantity of good j provided by firm k.
α_i = the reciprocal of the marginal utility of income of individual i.

Thus we see that the perfectly competitive model requires an objective function and set of constraints that is more specific than the general formulation proposed by Samuelson using equations (1) and (2). It was also interesting to note that the competitive economy placed a weight on every household's utility. This weight is the reciprocal of the marginal utility of income. Thus in the hypothetical case where every one had the same utility function the rich would tend to have a lower marginal utility of income than the poor and thus the relative weight the economy placed on each rich household would be greater than on each poor household.

5.1 Davis and Whinston and the Piecemeal Approach

Negishi's model has been used in numerous applied and theoretical contexts. However Davis and Whinston were the first to demonstrate the value of Negishi's model in seeking a solution to the problem of the second best. Re-examining the general second best solution given by either equation (6) or equation (8), we note that if enough cross-derivatives are equal to zero the added conditions of the second best solution disappear and the second best behavioral conditions are the same as the first best. In this case sectors not involved in the original violation of their first best behavior can be encouraged to continue to maintain these "first best" actions. Mathematically this can be described by stating that the cross-derivatives would be zero if the functions are "weakly separable." A function given by equation (1) is weakly separable if:

$$F(x_1,...,x_n) = F(h^{12}(x_1,x_2),h^{34}(x_3,x_4),...,h^{(n-1)n}(x_{n-1},x_n)] \qquad (12)$$

Where it should be noted that a function is defined as "strongly separable" (and thus also weakly separable) if:

$$F(x_1,...,x_n)=F(h^{12}(x_1,x_2)+h^{34}(x_3,x_4),+...+,h^{(n-1)n}(x_{n-1},x_n)] \quad (13)$$

Davis and Whinston recognized that the objective function of Negishi's model, given by equation (9), is "strongly" separable and thus weakly separable in the choice variables available between individuals. Individual i might not set the marginal utility of good j equal to the price of good j, weighted by his or her marginal utility of income, as the first best solution requires, but this should have no effect on the optimal behavior on any other consumer. In other words as long as consumers tend to make choices which, except for price effects, are independent of the choices made by other consumers the second best behavioral solution will be equivalent to the first best and no government intervention is necessary.

Next, the supply and demand conditions given by equation (10) in Negishi's model are all linear and thus the second derivatives will be zero, i.e., weakly separable. Therefore they will not have any impact on creating an additional term of equation (8), either for the individual or firm having the deviate behavior, or for any others maintaining their first best behavioral rules and the second best rules will be the same as the first best rules. This finding lies at the heart of the free enterprise system. Markets governed by the laws of supply and demand and free moving prices tend to eliminate the need for additional regulation.

It is the production functions ("production transformations"), given by the equations (11) in Negishi's model, which create the most potential problems of not being weakly separable. They are by nature not weakly separable in inputs and outputs, e.g., the familiar Cobb-Douglas production function. Each firm has within its optimal choice its own outputs and the optimal choice of inputs that are usually another firm's outputs. Thus if government intervention would be necessary to obtain a second best solution, when the first best cannot be attained, it would most likely be in the production sector. But is it also likely that in having one deviate production sector would require intervention into all other production sectors? Fortunately, most firms produce only "some" outputs and use only "some" inputs from other firms. Therefore intervention to obtain a second best solution would, for all intents and purposes, be limited to a few firms or industries. It should also be kept in mind that the problem does not arise if another firm k's output is embodied within inputs used to produce output of firm k' but are not explicitly used themselves. For example, firm 1 might use some of firm 2's output as its only input and firm 2 might use some of firm

3's output as its only input, but this does not imply that firm 1 considers output from firm 3 as a choice variable. Thus firm 1's production function is weakly separable from firm 3's output and firm 2's production function is weakly separable from firm 1's output.

The realization that most of the functions in Negishi's model were at least weakly separable in all but a few choice variables led Davis and Whinston to proclaim the merits of a "piecemeal approach" to the second best problem. In essence, regulatory action to control a few deviates can be useful but limited and there is, in general, no need to extend the controls to every other sector of the economy. For example, inability to remove all or even most of the monopolistic practices by firms in the American economy justifies a second best solution of allowing labor to also act as imperfect competitors by forming unions. However, there is no need to encourage other more competitive industries to also act as imperfect competitors.

6. EPILOGUE

Davis and Whinston's piecemeal conjecture was in direct opposition to the views of others, particularly the early writers, Bohm(1967) and McManus(1967). The latter writers viewed the second best solutions as something to be actually sought and applied to all industries through use of a general equilibrium model. These views emanated at a time in which the debilities of large scale government control had yet to be fully appreciated. Davis and Whinston believed that the amount of information needed to implement a complete general equilibrium solution was prohibitive. Therefore unless the piecemeal approach was the appropriate and preferred option the entire second best exercise was meaningless. The piecemeal approach to the second best is clear example of practical problem solving in economic policy. It rests on the belief that the infinite number of "minor policy implications" will not outweigh the few "major policy implications" and for the most part the minor implications can be neglected. It does not imply that general equilibrium analysis is useless. Such analysis does provide valuable insights to economists as they attempt to maintain a perspective of both the forests and the trees associated with various economic policies. Nevertheless, if one is to accomplish anything in the way of practical recommendations in economic policy it will almost always be through some "piecemeal approach" to the problem.

The economics of the second best did not slip quietly into the night as do many economic topics. The problem of "the existence of a second best" was analyzed by Sontheimer (1971). The use of decentralization methods to achieve the second best solution was considered by Allingham and Archibald

(1975). Sherman and Visscher (1978) extended the second best concept to situation where the demand is stochastic. Numerous articles re-examined McManus' criticism of the problem of the n'th sector discussed above and improved on the generalized second best solution, e.g., Morrison (1968), McFadden (1969), Santoni and Church (1972), Dusansky and Walsh (1976), Hansen (1999), and Hatta (1977). Other articles accepted the piecemeal approach recommended by Davis and Whinston and applied it to specific sectors such as international trade and tariffs, e.g., Negishi (1969), Bertrand and Vanek (1971), and Rodriguez (1976), public good pricing, e.g., Hamlen (1977) and Sandler (1978), health care, e.g., Gaynor, et. al, (2000), and general antitrust problems, e.g., Hettich (1975), and Hansen (1999).

Being at the right place at the right time, and having the right tools can mean the difference between a career of distinction and one of general mediocrity. Those who were there when the second best was initiated by Samuelson's observation on welfare economics and Pareto optimality, i.e., Lipsey-Lancaster, McManus, Negishi, and Davis-Whinston, solidly established their positions in the history of economic thought.

REFERENCES

Allingham, M.G., and G.C., Archibald (1975) "Second Best and Decentralization," *Journal of Economic Theory*, 10, pp. 157-173.

Arrow, K. (1951). *Social Choice and Individual Values*, John Wiley & Sons, Inc., New York.

Bertrand, T.J., and J. Vanek (1971). "The Theory of Tariffs, Taxes, and Subsidies: Some Aspects of the Second Best," *American Economic Review*, 61, pp. 925-931.

Bohm, P, (1967). "On the Theory of the Second Best," *Review of Economic Studies*, 34 (3), pp. 301-314.

Davis, O.A., and A.B. Whinston (1967)."Piecemeal Policy of the Second Best," *Review of Economic Studies*, 34 (3), pp. 323-331.

Davis, Otto.A., and A.B. Whinston (1965). "Welfare Economics and the Theory of the Second Best," *Review of Economic Studies*, 32, (1), pp. 1-14.

Debreu, G., (1959). *Theory of Value*, John Wiley & Sons, New York.

Dusansky, R., and J. Walsh (1967). "Separability, Welfare Economics, and the Theory of the Second Best," *Review of Economic Studies*, 43, (1), pp. 49-51.

Gaynor, M. D., Haas-Wilson, D., and W. Vogt (2000). "Are Invisible Hands Good Hands? Moral Hazard, Competition, and the Second-Best in Health Care Markets," *Journal of Political Economy*, 108 (5), pp. 992-1004.

Hansen, C., T. (1999). "Second-Best Antitrust in General Equilibrium: A Special Case," *Economic Letters*, 63, pp. 193-199.

Hamlen, W. A. (1977). "The Quasi-Optimal Price of Undepletable Externalities," *The Bell Journal of Economics*, 8 (1), pp. 324-334.

Hatta, T. (1977). "A Theory of Piecemeal Policy Recommendations," *Review of Economic*

Studies, 44 (1)1, pp. 1-21.

Henderson, J.M., and R.E. Quandt (1980). *Microeconomic Theory*, McGraw-Hill, New York.

Hettich, Walter, (1975). "Second-Best Aspects of Horizontal Equity Questions: A Comment," *Public Finance*, 30 (3), pp. 468 - 472.

Keynes, J. M. (1936). *The General Theory of Employment, Interest and Money*, Macmillan, New York.

Lipsey, R.G. and K. Lancaster (1956-57). "The General Theory of Second Best," *Review of Economic Studies*, 24 (1), pp. 11-32.

Lipsey, R.G. and K. Lancaster (1958-59). "McManus on Second Best," *Review of Economic Studies*, 26, pp.209-224.

McFadden, D. (1969). "A Simple Remark on the Second Best Pareto Optimality of Market Equilibria," *Journal of Economic Theory*, 1, pp. 26-38.

McManus, M. (1967). "Private and Social Costs in the Theory of the Second Best," *Review of Economic Studies*, 34, pp. 317-321.

McManus, M., (1958-59). Comments on the General Theory of Second Best," *Review of Economic Studies*, 26, pp., 209-224.

Morrison, C.C. (1968). "Generalizations on the Methodology of Second Best," *Western Economic Journal*, 6, pp.112-120.

Negishi, T. (1969). "The Customs Union and the Theory of the Second Best," *International Economic Review*, 1, pp. 391-398.

Negishi, T. (1960). "Welfare Economics and Existence of An Equilibrium for a Competitive Economy," *Metroeconomica* 11, pp. 92-97.

Rodriguez, C. A. (1976). "On the Second Best Optimality of Tariffs in the Presence of Incentive Schedules," *Canadian Journal of Economics*, 9 (2), pp. 301-308.

Samuelson, P. A. (1967 edition). *Foundations of Economic Analysis*, Atheneum, New York.

Sandler, T. (1978). "Public Goods and the Theory of Second Best," *Public Finance*, 33 (3), pp. 331-343.

Santoni, G., and A. Church (1972). "A Comment on the General Theorem of the Second Best," *Review of Economic Studies*, 39 (4), pp. 527-530.

Sherman, R. and M. Visscher (1978). "Second Best Pricing with Stochastic Demand," *American Economic Review*, 68, pp. 41-53.

Sontheimer, Kevin, C. (1971). "An Existence Theorem for the Second Best," *Journal of Economic Theory*, 3, pp. 1-22.

Chapter 2

Transfer Pricing

From price guidelines to strategic interaction

Vicente Salas-Fumas : Francisco Ruiz-Aliseda
Department of business economics, University of Zaragoza, Zaragoza, 50005, Spain : Graduate student, Department of managerial economics and decision sciences, Northwestern University, Evanston, IL, 60208

Abstract: The most well-established rule for transfer pricing is that the transfer price should be equal to marginal costs, in order to maximize total profits. This paper shows that, in oligopolistic markets where firms face strategic interactions, profit maximizing firms have incentives to deviate from the price equal to marginal cost rule and that the sign of the deviation depends upon the structural conditions of the market, such as homogeneous or differentiated products and price or quantity competition.
Key words: Transfer prices; Strategic Competition; Organizational Structure; Responsibility Centers; Unobservability

1. PREFACE

In August of 1973, the senior author of this article entered the doctoral program in Management Science of the Krannert School of Management. The expectations were to see if it could be possible that the teachings of Management had the same analytical rigor that he had detected in Economics during his Bachelor's Degree studies in Spain. The first clear signal that it could be so came about in a Management Accounting class, in the Masters program, when the professor referenced the work of Andrew Whinston, "Price Guidelines in

Decentralized Organizations," in order to justify that transfer prices could serve to co-ordinate the decisions of administrative units inside the firms in a simmilar way as market prices coordinate the decisions of buyers and sellers in the market. When I read the work in question, I realized that it responded perfectly with what I was seeking: the analysis of the internal operations of a company from the logic of economic analysis.

I have always considered "Price Guidelines in Decentralized Organizations " to be one of the precursor works of what subsequently has been consolidated into a branch of Economics with its own personality, Organizational Economics. In the sixties, the organizational problem was mainly a problem of ensuring coordination towards the organization's objective of maximum profit, of the decentralized decisions of divisions and departments. Subsequently, the problem of incentives is added when there are conflicts of interest, asymmetry of information, and opportunism. Unfairly, I believe, the main stream of Organizational Economics has forgotten that fruitful literature from the sixties and the beginning of the seventies.

The work that follows this preamble places emphasis on another facet of transfer prices: their possible use as a competitive variable in oligopolistic markets, whereby transfer prices go beyond their pure accounting scope, and they acquire a central position in the organizational design of companies.

Andrew Whinston was a member of Krannert's academic staff during the graduate student years that I am now recalling. After reading his "Price Guidelines in Decentralized Organizations," I asked him to supervise my education during the doctoral studies. Andy not only accepted this supervision, but he also directed my doctoral thesis.

My intellectual debt to Andy is high, as well as my gratitude to him for having honored me with his and his family's friendship throughout all of these years.

2. INTRODUCTION

The most recent literature on transfer pricing has focused mainly on the informational problems that affect the firm`s general management (Holmstrom and Tirole, 1991: 201). For example, upper management is unaware of the marginal costs that, conversely, are well known by the managers of the responsibility centers. A large majority of the academic studies on the determination of transfer prices has been centered, then, on how to design the mechanisms that lead to revealing the relevant information for decentralized decision making (e.g., [Harris *et al.*, 1982: 604-620] and [Ronen and McKinney, 1970: 99-112][1/]). Subsequent expanded studies have introduced additional elements of interest, such as the uncertainty of the production costs (Ronen and Balachandran, 1988: 300-314) and the demand (Kanodia, 1979: 74-98) or various assumptions about the possibilities of *ex ante* communication. Thus, for example, Ronen and Balachandran (1988: 300-314) show that when communication is not possible, mechanisms exist for finding out the marginal cost starting from the delegated decisions (i.e., the volume of output).

The literature that analyzes the problem of setting transfer prices under asymmetric/private information conditions is very extensive. Nevertheless, it is primarily centered around the cases where the final product market is either monopolistic or perfectly competitive and for the most part has neglected the role which imperfect competition, found in oligopolistic product markets, play in the setting of optimal trnsfer prices. In other words, the determination of transfer prices has been studied mainly as a decision that is separated from strategic considerations.

The main purpose of this work is to model the problem of choosing the transfer prices by taking into account the strategic inter-dependencies between companies caused by an oligopolistic market structure. In agreement with Alles and Datar (1998: 451-461) and, more recently, Zhao (2000: 414-426)[2/], this approach reveals that the generaly accepted rule of seting the transfer price equal to the marginal cost of the exchanged resources, may be inadequate for profit maximization when firms compete in oligopolistic markets. In this respect, Alles and Datar show that, in an oligopolistic market with differentiated products, the recognition of the strategic interactions leads companies to rationally choose a "cost-plus" type of transfer price, that is, a price greater than the marginal cost.

Our work starts from the results of Alles and Datar, but it introduces important novelties that contribute to provide a more general and comprehensive scope to the choice of the transfer price, inluding its relationship with the decision about the organizational structure of the competing firms.

First , Alles and Datar do not analyze the question of strategically setting the transfer prices when the product is homogenous. As a result, we do not know if the "cost-plus" method is still the equilibrium rule in this type of markets. In fact, our results show that when producs are homogeneous, the equilibrium solution to the transfer pricing decision is to follow a "cost-minus" [3/] rule.

Second, these authors avoid mentioning most of the implementation problems that are present when strategically setting transfer prices. These problems are derived mainly from the unobservability of the characteristics and internal practices of companies by their competitors. Likewise, they do not pay attention to the kind of administrative mechanisms on which those practices are based. Our work provides a detailed analysis of the implementation problem, as well as the administrative forms that sustain such policies (i.e., the accounting treatment that is given to the departments in relation to their nature as responsibility centers and the implications resulting from this). In addition, comments are made about the possibility of communicating the internal aspects of the accounting system in order to facilitate a collusive behavior in the product market, something ignored in the management accounting literature. The reasons for this kind of behaviorur are clear: in order for an unobservable internal practice to have an effect on the competition, there has to be a credible flow of information towards the competing firms.

Section two presents the theoretical model, which is the basis for obtaining the main results about the equilibrium pricing rules in markets with homogenous products and in markets where products are differentate. The third section appraises and discusses the results, as well as the implicit assumptions on which they are supported.

3. THE THEORETICAL MODEL

Schematically, the exposition below models a decision process in two stages for two competing firms that sell a single prduct. These firms may be in a market where products are homogeneous or in a market with products are differentiated. We do not consider multi-product companies, because our goal is not to analyze the possibilities of crossed sbsidies between products, as in Alles and Datar (1998: 455).

In the first stage, general management implements a system for setting the transfer prices based on the cost. This means determining what the transfer prices are going to be for the resources transferred from the cost center, meaning the production unit, to the profit center, meaning the sales unit. In the second stage, the profit center determines the quantity (price) of the product in the final market, given that the internal price of the resources that it consumes is fixed by the general management. We assume complete information about all of the parameters, so that the general manager does not need to design mechanisms that incentivate the revelation of private information by the functional managers.

3.1 Quantity competition with a homogeneous product

Figure 1 illustrates the market conditions and the internal organization of the two firms which we will generically identify by *j* and *k*. For the sake of simplicity, we assume constant marginal costs, meaning constant returns. We also assume that there exists an inverse linear demand function, where α and β are positive and the first parameter is greater than the marginal costs in order for the business to be profitable:

Both companies organize their activities around two departments: production and sales. This is a simplified organizational structure in which the production department would be in charge of purchasing the inputs necessary for producing the good that the other department sells and distributes. The use of an internal accounting system would imply the identification of two responsibility centers. Thus, the production department would be a cost center that transforms inputs in outputs at a unit cost c_i $(i=j,k)$, and the output quantity would be determined by the sales department. Therefore, the decisions of the production unit would be to determine the best combination of inputs to minimize the production costs, and it would be evaluated starting from the deviation that occurs with respect to its budget. For its part, the sales department would be defined as a profit center, given that it would decide on the output quantity to launch onto the market or its corresponding price and it would be evaluated in term of differences with respect to the budget. The cost of the inputs for the sales department will be equal to the transfer price δ_i $(i=j,k)$. Finally, it should be added that the role of general management is to set the objectives of both departments , and to set the transfer price at which they exchange resources.

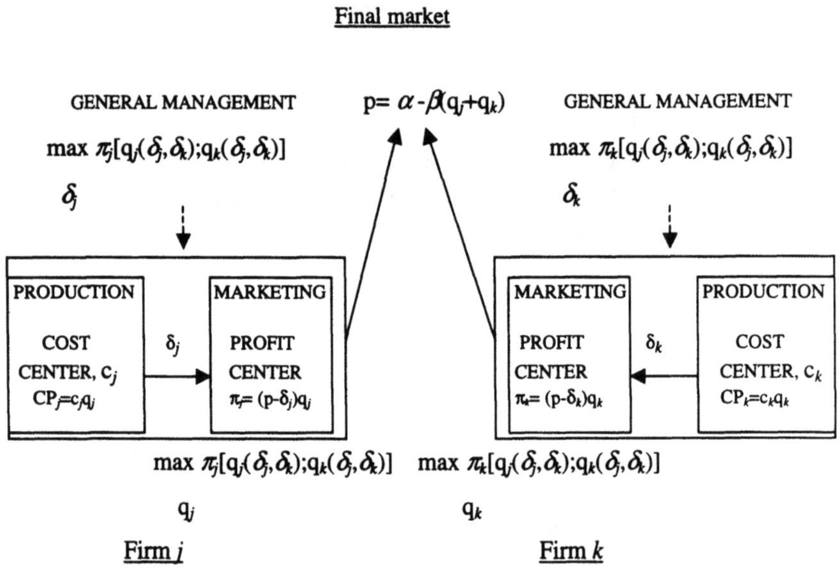

Figure 1. Structure of the decision problems: duopoly with quantity competition

The assumption of centralized trasfer pricing decision is consistent with the responsability centers that are considered in the organizational structure because, in the event of negotiation between the two, the cost center would be indifferent to the resulting transfer price, as profits do not enter into the evaluation of its performance. Conversely, the profit center would have incentives to negotiate the lowest possible price in order to achieve higher profits. Therefore, it is reasonable to think that the production manager could easily be "bribed" by the commercial manager, so that they might agree on a price for the intermediate inputs that would not maximize the joint profits. In reality, as pointed out by Dearden (1976: chapters 10 and 12), the production unit is nothing more than a captive supplier whose greatest responsibilities must be concerned with cost control, quality, and production schedules. It is for this reason that, within the framework that we have proposed, it would be evaluated according to its capacity to control costs. For its part, the fact that the marketing department is evaluated according to its budgeted profit implicitly means that it works on the bases of *rigid delegation*, so that the profit assigned to the department manager is considered as a firm commitment in relation to which it is going to be evaluated. Dearden indicates that this administrative mechanism will additionally require complete involvement by upper management, as well as the existence of expert personnel in accounting, budgets, and analysis. Likewise, evaluation and control will be performed through personal observation and non-financial information, in addition to strictly financial information [4/].

Under these premises, the Nash perfect equilibrium solution for the competition game between the two firms is summarized in the following proposition.

Proposition 1. If the firms compete in quantities, then, for positive output quantities:

a) In the equilibrium solution, the two firms set a price below the marginal cost.

b) In the equilibrium solution, the two firms produce a greater quantity of output and obtain lower profit than in the situation in which both set a price equal to the marginal cost.

c) In the equilibrium solution, the final price is less than in the case in which the two companies choose the marginal cost as the transfer price.

Proof: See appendix.

In the equilibrium solution, the general management of both companies "subsidize" the internal acquisition of resources by the sales departments, and therefore these departments behave aggressively, which will mean a lower sale price for the product they sell.

Figure 2 shows the reaction functions of the two sales departments when price is set equal to marginal cost and when price is set strategically (which means going from equilibrium situation A to B). The shift of both functions is parallel and to the right. All of this means a decrease in the final price of the product sincein the cost-minus solution both firms produce more than in the case of price equal to marginal cost.

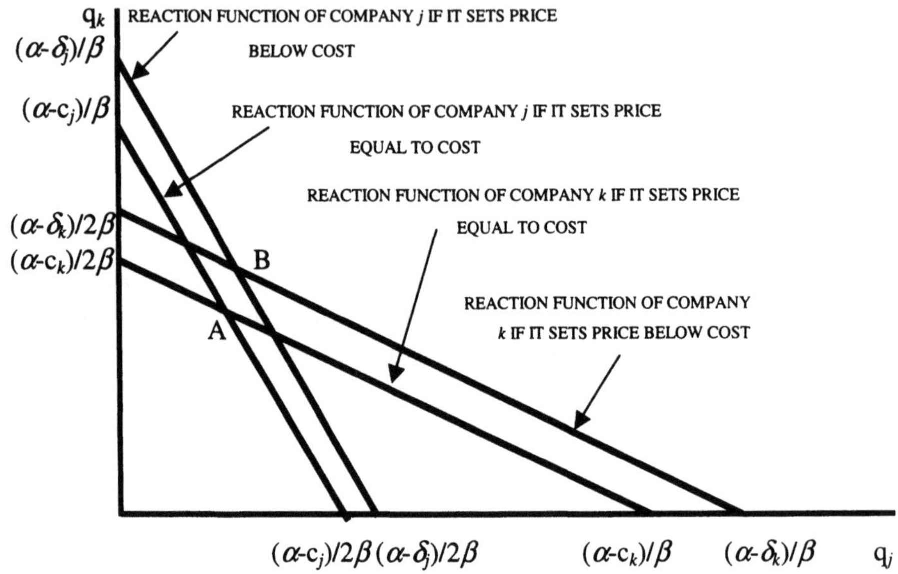

Figure 2. Nash equilibrium when j and k deviate from the rule price equal to marginal cost

The rational decisión of seting a transfer price bellow the marginal cost of production is very novel in this literature, in particular when one assumes symmetric information. Harris, *et al.* (1982: 604-620) obtain a result of price lower than unit cost but under conditions of asymmetric information . Ronen and Balachandran (1988: 310-311), under conditions similar to the previous paper, find that when communication is not feasible between general management and the functional area managers, there are cases where firms choose a price lower than marginal cost. In both cases, setting transfer prices that are lower than the marginal cost responds to the purpose of private information revelation, but not to strategic reasons. In fact, in both papers the internal price does not affect the price of the product in the final market. Finally, Ziss (1999: 1169-1171) proves, in a competitive environment different to the one posed here, that sometimes it is optimal to set prices that are less than the marginal cost.

3.2 Price competition with a differentiated product

The assumption now is that each of the two firms sells a symmetrically differentiated product in the final market. Therefore, the demand for firm *j* may be represented as $q_j=\alpha-\beta p_j+\gamma p_k$, where p_j would indicate the price of the product that company *j* sells. The parameter γ, positive, is lower than β, which means that the demand for the good that company *j* sells is more affected by its own price than by the price set by its rival. This demand function may be considered a generalization of the function used by Alles and Datar (1998).

Assuming the same two steps decision processes as in the case of homogeneous product, the new equilibrium solution is summarized as follows.

Proposition 2. If both firms compete in prices, for positive product quantities:

a) In the equilibrium solution, both firms deviate from the rule of transfer price equal to the marginal cost, and choose a price higher than the production cost.

b) In the equilibrium solution, both firms decide to sell their respective products at a price greater than the price in the case when they followed the rule of setting the transfer price equal to the marginal cost. Following this rule they obtain higher profits than in the case of price equal to cost.

c) In the equilibrium solution, the quantity sold by each company is less than in the case in which both companies chose a transfer price equal to the marginal cost.

Proof: see appendix.

Under price competition and diferenciated products both firms benefit from softening competition in the final markets. By choosing a transfer price from the production to the sales department higher than procuction costs, the general mangers force to the sales departments to reduce the intensity of competition. As a result, both firms sell their product at a higher price and obtains higher profits than in the case of price equal to cost.

The new equilibrium results are shown in Figure 3. The introduction of strategic considerations implies a parallel shift of the reaction functions of the sales departments of both companies, that is, to go from point A to point B.

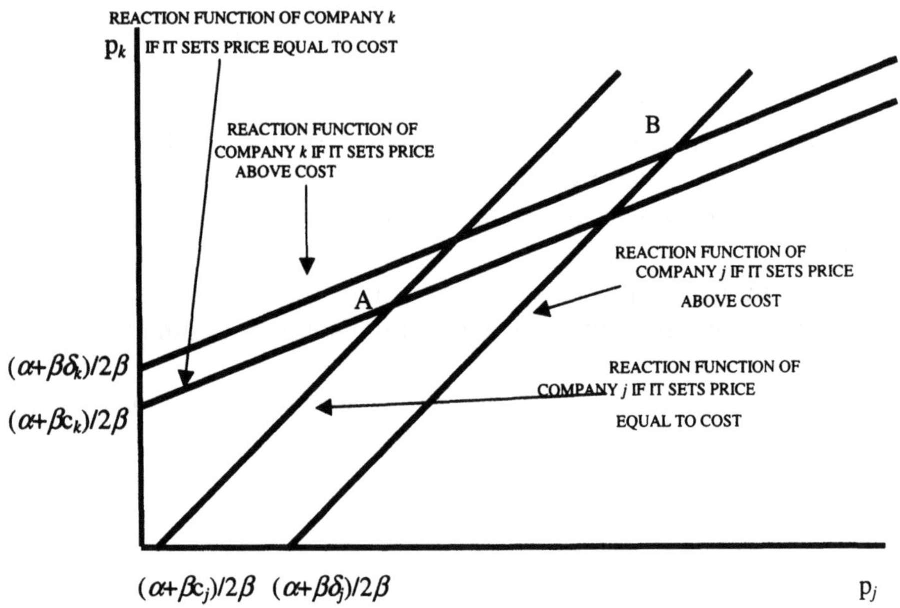

Figure 3. The Nash equilibrium solutions under price competition and differentiated products

4. DISCUSSION OF THE RESULTS

In this section, we will evaluate the results of section 2 and refer to an apparent weakness of the preceding model, which can be extended to the model of Alles and Datar. This consists of the fact that, in order to strategically use transfer prices, these prices must be known by the competitors, which at the start seems complicated. Alles and Datar assume from the beginning that the firms know the internal organization of the production and marketing departments (and therefore, the manner in which their respective managers are compensated) of their rivals. This is what allows the rivals to infer the internal equilibrium price, even when they do not know it directly. This supposition is clearly unsatisfactory.

In reality, it can be affirmed that the agency contract between general management and the corresponding functional managers influences the competition stage in the product market, in spite of being unobservable to the rival company. But, in order for this unobservable agreement to allow the managers to be credibly pre-committed when competing, as indicated by Katz (1991: 313-323)5/, it must have a series of characteristics that are all satisfied by the model, as long as contracts cannot be writen whereby the agent becomes the residual claimant.

The result that, in equilibrium, both firms end up with lower profits when they deviate from the price equal cost rule and final products are homogeneous, may be considered disturbing. Therefore it is likely that firms will try to find ways to avoid this undesirable situation. One possible way to proceed is to change the nature of the production unit from a cost center to a profit center. If the production manager maximizes profits and price is lower than marginal cost, then the output decision will be zero. If the firm wants to produce positive output it will have to set the transfer price equal to marginal cost. Our conjecture at this point is that both firms can credibly communicate to each other their commitment to set a profit center for the production department, and in this way avoid the lower profit equilibrium. That is, we could go even further than this paper and analyze whether or not the principals (that is, general management) have incentives to inform their rivals about the accounting practices of their own production and marketing departments. Technically, what we mean is considering a signaling game (specifically, a variation of so-called cheap talk games, for obvious reasons). This materializes into the introduction of a stage, prior to the decisions by general management about the transfer prices, whereby both companies simultaneously launch a non-binding message to their corresponding competitors. It then may be shown that, in certain relevant situations, there are incentives to credibly reveal beforehand practices of the production and commercial sub-units which yield Cournot oligopoly profits for both firms.

The situation changes when firms compete in prices and products are differentiated. Now, the choice of the transfer price by the general manager will not be affected by the decision of having a profit or a cost center in the production department. The reason is that in this case the equilibrium transfer price is higher than the unit cost of production and therefore the production unit will still produce positive output.

The final problem we consider is that, in spite of all this, a larger caveat persists, which has to do with the fact that each company lacks knowledge of its rival marginal costs. This drawback can be overcome if general management starts benchmarking programs which thereby permit each company to estimate the marginal costs of their competitors, (Alles and Datar [1998: 453]). Another way to take this problem into account would be assuming a probability distribution over marginal costs and applying the bayesian perfect equilibrium concept to solve the game.

5. APPENDIX

5.1 Quantity competition

For a given transfer price, the reaction function of the sales department in the second stage of the game is given by,

$$q_j = \left[\frac{(\alpha - \beta q_k)}{2\beta}\right] - \frac{\delta_j}{2\beta}$$

The equilibrium solutions in terms of transfer prices are,

$q_j = (\alpha + \delta_k - 2\delta_j)/3\beta$

$q_k = (\alpha + \delta_j - 2\delta_k)/3\beta$

Taking into account these functions, general managers choose the profit maximizing transfer prices, which in turn determine the quantities produced for the final product,

$\delta_j^{**} = (8c_j - 2c_k - \alpha)/5$ and

$q_j^{**} = (12c_k - 18c_j + 6\alpha)/15\beta$.

This means that the transfer price will be less than the marginal cost if, and only if, $q^{**}{}_j^{*} > 0$ (part a) of proposition 1). The final results regarding the market price of the product and the profit of firm j (symmetrical for *k*), would be:

$p^{**} = (\alpha + 2c_j + 2c_k)/5$ and

$\pi_j^{**} = (6\alpha - 18c_j + 12c_k)^2/450\beta$.

As regards section b) of proposition 1, it is computationally tedious to show that either firm, for example *j*, earns less profit ($\pi_j^{**} < \pi_j$) when the two of them deviate from the transfer price equal to marginal cost rule and set a lower price. In the special case where the two firms have the same cost (for a relatively complicated, similar demonstration, see Sklivas [1987: 455]):

$(6\alpha - 6c)^2/450\beta < (\alpha - c)^2/9\beta \Leftrightarrow 14(\alpha - c)^2 > 0.$

Furthermore, it is straightforward to show that, when firms deviate from price equal to marginal costs, the total output produced increases.

And regarding section c) of proposition 1, $p^{**} < p$ if, and only if, $\alpha > \max(c_j, c_k)$:

$(\alpha + 2c_j + 2c_k)/5 < (\alpha + c_k + c_j)/3 \Leftrightarrow 2\alpha - c_j - c_k > 0 \Leftrightarrow \alpha > \max(c_j, c_k).$

5.2 Price competition

When neither firm deviates from the rule price equal to marginal cost, the main results are:

$$p_j = \frac{(2\alpha\beta + \alpha\gamma + \beta\gamma c_k + 2\beta^2 c_j)}{(4\beta^2 - \gamma^2)},$$

$$q_j = \left[\frac{2\alpha\beta^2 + \alpha\beta\gamma + \beta^2\gamma c_k + (\beta\gamma^2 - 2\beta^3)c_j}{(4\beta^2 - \gamma^2)}\right],$$

$$\pi_j = \beta\left[\frac{2\alpha\beta + \alpha\gamma + \beta\gamma c_k + (\gamma^2 - 2\beta^2)c_j}{(4\beta^2 - \gamma^2)}\right]^2.$$

Now we introduce the strategic use of transfer prices. For this, we solve the game in the same way that we did previously. Thus, if the sales managers maximize the profit function ,

$\pi_j^{PC} = (p_j - \delta_j)(\alpha - \beta p_j + \gamma p_k)$,

we will obtain the reaction function ,

$$p_j = \left[\frac{(\alpha + \gamma p_k)}{2\beta}\right] + \frac{\delta_j}{2}.$$

The next step in order to obtain the sub-game perfect equilibrium, is to solve the problem that is presented in the first stage, regarding the determination of the transfer prices. If we consider the sales prices of the products as given- as well as the quantities -

$$p_j = \frac{(2\alpha\beta + \alpha\gamma + \beta\gamma\delta_k + 2\beta^2\delta_j)}{(4\beta^2 - \gamma^2)} \quad \text{and}$$

$$q_j = \left[\frac{2\alpha\beta^2 + \alpha\beta\gamma + \beta^2\gamma\delta_k + (\beta\gamma^2 - 2\beta^3)\delta_j}{(4\beta^2 - \gamma^2)} \right],$$

and we maximize the profit of company j (symmetrical for company k), we will obtain the transfer price that general management will set in equilibrium:

$$\delta_j^* = \frac{2\alpha\beta\gamma^2 + \alpha\gamma^3 + \beta\gamma^3\delta_k + (\gamma^4 + 8\beta^4 - 6\beta^2\gamma^2)c_j}{(8\beta^4 - 4\beta^2\gamma^2)}.$$

Due to the analytical complexity, we will assume that both companies are symmetric (whereby $c=c_k=c_j$ and $\delta=\delta_j=\delta_k$ is met), so that

$$\delta^* = \frac{\alpha\gamma^2 + (4\beta^3 - 2\beta^2\gamma - 2\beta\gamma^2 + \gamma^3)c}{\beta(4\beta^2 - 2\beta\gamma - \gamma^2)}$$

Performing the calculations, it is possible to show that this transfer price is greater than the marginal cost if firms produce positive output (section a) of proposition 2).

This implies sale prices, quantities sold, and profits for both companies equal to $p^* = \dfrac{2\alpha\beta + (2\beta^2 - \gamma^2)c}{(4\beta^2 - 2\beta\gamma - \gamma^2)}$

$$q^* = \frac{(2\beta^2 - \gamma^2)(\alpha + c)}{(4\beta^2 - 2\beta\gamma - \gamma^2)} \quad \text{and}$$

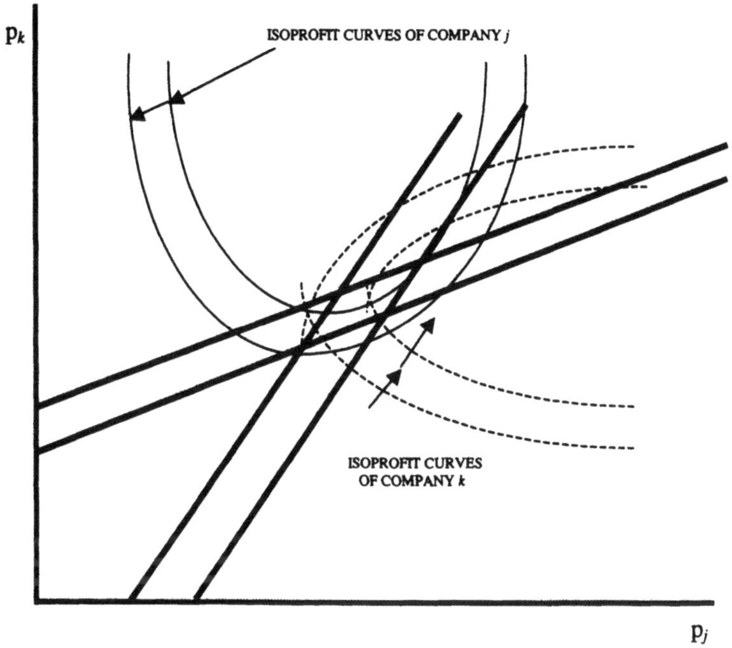

Figure 4. Isoprofit curves and equilibrium when j and k deviate from the internal price equal to marginal cost rule

$$\pi^* = \frac{2\beta(2\beta^2 - \gamma^2)(\alpha + c)[\alpha - (\beta - \gamma)c]}{(4\beta^2 - 2\beta\gamma - \gamma^2)^2}$$

In order to show that the profit that the companies earn is greater than the case in which they both set the transfer price equal to the marginal cost, section b) of proposition 2, we take into account figure 3. According to this figure, the reaction functions of *j*'s and *k*'s sales departments shift so that the final prices are greater for both companies. Likewise, we will consider the isoprofit curves that indicate the output combinations of the two firms which generate a constant profit level for each one of them. In general, *j*'s profit is $\pi_j = (p_j - c_j)(\alpha - \beta p_j + \gamma p_k)$ (the demonstration is symmetrical for *k*). Now, if we differentiate the profit with respect to the price of the rival company, we will obtain the expression $\gamma(p_j - c_j)$, which is greater than 0. This means that, for a final price already set by *j*, this company's profit will increase if the price set by its rival increases. Therefore, the further away an isoprofit curve is from the origin, the more profit that that price combination will mean for a company. Finally, it must be kept in mind that equilibrium is reached when the isoprofit curve of a company is tangent to the reaction function of its sales department. Graphically, the demonstration of section b) of proposition 2 would be (figure 4):

Finally, in order to demonstrate section c) of proposition 2, we differentiate the demand function, $q_j=\alpha-\beta p_j+\gamma p_k$, taking into account that $q=\alpha+(\gamma-\beta)p$ will be met due to the existence of symmetry:

$$dq=(\gamma-\beta)dp \Rightarrow dq/dp=(\gamma-\beta)<0.$$

6. NOTES

1/ In Ronen (1992: 125-136), the drawbacks that appear in Ronen and McKinney (1970: 99-112) are overcome due to the multiplicity of equilibriums. Thus, the efficient solution is obtained by introducing a penalty for lying, which prevents collusion between the divisional managers. For an experimental analysis that compares both predictions, see Avila and Ronen (1999: 689-715).

2/ The work of Zhao constitutes an extension of Alles' and Datar's work, mainly by the introduction of tax considerations since it focuses on multinational companies.

3/ As Alles and Datar (1998: 452) suitably point out, the article does not deal with the process of obtaining the most precise information possible about the marginal cost, so that it is assumed that the process concludes in a completely satisfactory way.

4/ Notice that we assume that there is no external market for the intermediate product. Hamilton and Mqasqas (1997: 220-234) model a transfer price decision where the marketing and production departments must consider the opportunity cost that is supported by not buying (selling) on the external market.

5/ In his paper, Katz shows how the rival firm infers the agent's behavior in various situations that have in common the fact that the principal-agent contract is unobservable, and there is no feasible contract in which the agent becomes the residual claimant.

REFERENCES

Alles, M. and S. Datar (1998). "Strategic transfer pricing", *Management Science*, 44, No. 4, pp. 451-461.

Avila, M. and J. Ronen (1999). "Transfer-pricing mechanisms: an experimental investigation", *International Journal of Industrial Organization*, 17, No. 5, pp. 689-715.

Dearden, J. (1976). *Sistemas de Contabilidad de Costos y de Control Financiero* (Ed. Deusto, S.A.)

Hamilton, J.L. and I.M. Mqasqas (1997). "Direct vertical integration strategies", *Southern Economic Journal*, 64, No. 1, pp. 220-234.

Harris, M., C.H. Kriebel and A. Raviv (1982). "Asymmetric information, incentives and intrafirm resource allocation", *Management Science*, 28, No. 6, pp. 604-620.

Holmstrom, B. and J. Tirole (1991). "Transfer pricing and organizational form", *The Journal of Law, Economics & Organization*, 7, No. 2, pp. 201-228.

Horngren, C.T. and G. Foster (1991). *Cost Accounting: a Managerial Emphasis* (7th edition, Prentice Hall).

Kanodia, C. (1979). "Risk sharing and transfer price systems under uncertainty", *Journal of Accounting Research*, 17, No. 1, pp 74-98.

Kaplan, R.S. and A.A. Atkinson (1989). *Advanced Management Accounting* (2nd edition, Prentice Hall).

Katz, M.L. (1991). "Game-playing agents: unobservable contracts as precommitments", *RAND Journal of Economics*, 22, No. 3, pp 307-323.

Ronen, J. (1992). "Transfer pricing reconsidered: reflections on Groves and Loeb's reflections", *Journal of Public Economics*, 47, No. 1, pp. 125-136.

—— and K. Balachandran (1988). "An approach to transfer pricing under uncertainty", *Journal of Accounting Research*, 26, No. 2, pp. 300-314.

—— and G. McKinney III (1970). "Transfer pricing for divisional autonomy", *Journal of Accounting Research*, 8, No. 1, pp. 99-112.

Salas, V. (1992). "Relative performance evaluation of management: the effects on industrial competition and risk sharing", *International Journal of Industrial Organization*, 10, No. 3, pp. 473-489.

Sklivas, S.D. (1987). "The strategic choice of managerial incentives", *RAND Journal of Economics*, 18, No. 3, pp. 452-458.

Whinston, A. (1961). "Price guidelines in decentralized organizations", in W. Coopers et al, New Perspectives in Organizational Research, Wiley.

Zhao, L. (2000). "Decentralization and transfer pricing under oligopoly", *Southern Economic Journal*, 67, No. 2, pp. 414-426.

Ziss, S. (1999). "Divisionalization and strategic managerial incentives in oligopoly under uncertainty", *International Journal of Industrial Organization*, 17, No. 8, pp. 1163-1187.

Chapter 3

Trading Mechanism Design for Swap Markets

Ming Fan: Xiaorui Hu: Han Zhang

University of Notre Dame:Saint Louis University:Georgia Tech

Abstract: This paper proposes an electronic market for swap exchange. We have designed a trading mechanism that allows multiple swaps, futures and forwards to be traded on the same market and guarantee that traders will get either the combination of assets or nothing.

Key words: swap market, trading mechanism

1. INTRODUCTION

The financial world has become more volatile in the last few decades. Corporations, individuals and even nations have been affected by the increased risks. Corporations are now exposed to more risks in interest rate, currency exchange rate and commodity prices than ever before. Those risks directly affect the value and the competitive position of a firm. For a long time, seeking solutions to financial problems and innovating new financial products have been the tasks of many financial managers (Stulz 1984, Johnson 1960, Ederington 1979, Miller1994). In order to manage and reduce financial risks, firms are looking for effective methods to hedge their financial positions. For those firms who are exposed to the volatile interest rate, foreign exchange rate, or commodity prices, they surely need to consider financial derivatives such as forward contracts, futures, swap and options to manage their risks (Hull 1997, Layard-Liesching 1986, Turnbull 1987).

The growth in the field of financial engineering has been increasing at an astonishing rate during the past two decades. A sharp acceleration in the pace of innovation, deregulation and structural changes has transformed the international financial system in many ways. A substantial amount of financial instruments have been invented and have dramatically increased their roles in the financial structure. The development of financial engineering can be categorized in two areas. First, financial engineering research shows that any complicated instruments can be broken down into a few simpler instruments, which can be decomposed further into small basic components. This is the building block of financial engineering. It allows banks and corporations, who can easily manipulate those basic components in their daily practice, to provide more complicated instrument to satisfy the needs of their clients. Second, through financial engineering, one can separate financial price risks from the underlying physical operations of a corporation and to manage them separately through the use of derivative products (Hull 1997). As we know that corporations can manage their risks either through changing the operating characteristics of firm itself or via an off-balance-sheet financial instrument – derivative products. The cost of changing operations characteristics is much higher and the flexibility is much lower compared to that of the off-balance-sheet management. Thus the greater the expected volatility of the financial environment, the greater the tendency will be to adopt the off-balance-sheet derivative products.

In this paper, we focus on the derivative products such as interest rate swap and currency swap. Interest rate and currency swaps have developed quickly since their birth in the 1980s. The swap contract is cleared based on privately negotiated bases. Most of the time, two counter-parties directly sign contracts with a commercial bank and pay 3% transaction fee to the bank. Until now, there is no exchange market for swaps and the bid and ask information on swaps are very limited.

The development of financial engineering has encouraged the creation of thriving new financial instruments. However, as more and more new financial instruments have been created and traded, it has become harder for the banks and corporations to get their financial instrument orders cleared. The difficulty is rooted in the organization of the traditional market trading system. First, the traditional market trading mechanism does not allow a combination of assets to be traded in one market simultaneously. It only allows each asset to be traded in its own market. In order to get the whole bundle of assets, one has to bid on different markets to get the whole combination of assets. As we know, the new financial instrument always exists in bundle format, and in order to fulfil the task of hedging, every single asset in the bundle must be bought or sold at the same time. This leads to the fact that traditional trading system cannot effectively fulfil the task. It is easy to get an incomplete bundle in the traditional market, and lose the position of hedging, thus exposing to market risks. Second, some financial instruments, such as interest rate swap and currency swap, are still traded on a privately negotiated basis. Market information for swaps' demand and supply is very limited. As the swap trading grows rapidly, the over-the-counter (OTC) trading mechanism cannot satisfy the worldwide swap transaction needs. Therefore, it is important to design a market for those traded financial instruments.

This paper proposes an electronic market for swap exchange. Due to the fact that swaps can be a very long-term commitment, we design a trading mechanism to achieve trading efficiency. We allow multiple swaps, futures and forwards to be traded on the same market and guarantee that traders will get either the combination of assets or nothing.

2. BACKGROUND INFORMATION

Interest rate and currency swaps have grown quickly. According to the International Swap and Derivatives Association (ISDA), global transactions of privately negotiated derivatives continued to reach new highs in the first half of 2000. Measured in notional principal outstanding amounts for the six months (ending June 30, 2000), the total currency & interest rate swap outstanding reached \$60.366 trillion, compared with \$58.265 trillion at the end of 1999. For the period ending June 30, 1999, the total currency & interest rate swap outstanding stood at \$52.711 trillion.[2]

The worldwide growth of transactions in privately negotiated derivatives is due to the worldwide volatility and expansion of international trade. The volatility continues to drive the wider use of privately negotiated derivatives. The volatility in interest rate and exchange rate has been great. The interest rate, whether it is the three-month T-bill or ten-year Treasury bond rate is volatile over a long period of time. So is the exchange rate.

Under a volatile financial environment, when a company is facing a tight cash flow payment every period and a huge penalty of not meeting the requirement, the firm has no choice but to seek a hedging position.

Swap contracting is a new phenomenon to the financial market. It was started in 1981 by Salomon Brothers. Swaps are private agreements between two companies to exchange cash flows in the future according to a prearranged formula. They can be regarded as portfolios or bundles of forward

[2] See http://www.isda.org/.

contract (Hull 1997). Until now, swap contracting is still traded on privately negotiated base. Banks usually take a position in the swap agreement, acting as an intermediary and signing contracts with two counter-parties. This OTC trading mechanism has contributed to the development of swap market for some time. With a rapid growth of swap activities, the OTC trading is less efficient and involves higher transaction cost and longer settlement time. An exchange market has many advantages. It can gather swap contracts, provide detailed trading information, and settle trades in real time. With the Internet, market information can be disseminated quickly. Traders can react to the changing market situation. Supply and demand in the market can be better balanced.

3. BUNDLE MARKET FOR SWAPS

Since swap contract can be viewed as a series of forward contracts with different settlement dates, a bundle market mechanism can be developed for the swap market. The swap contract can be decomposed as a combination of forward contracts. For example, a "plain vanilla" interest rate swap has the following structure. Two parties are in the contract, with party A paying fixed interest rate and receiving floating interest rate and party B receiving fixed interest rate and paying floating inters rate. Party A pays fixed rate and is the party who "bought" the swap.

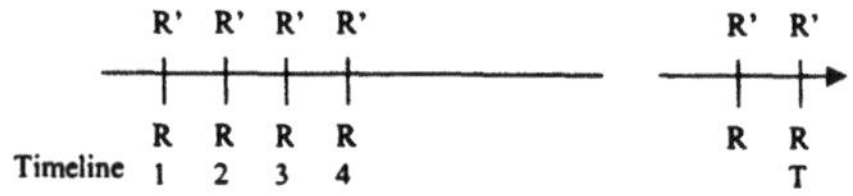

Figure 1. Interest Rate Swap

Every R and R' is a forward contract. Party A has total number of T forward contracts that pay a fixed rate to counter-party B and receive a floating rate from B in each time period 1, 2, 3 to T. Party B has a total number of T forward contracts that pay a floating rate to party A and receive a fixed rate from party A in every time period 1, 2, 3 to T.

As we study the swap contract time line, a swap contract can be decomposed into a large combination of forward contracts, forwards on swap and shorter period swap contracts. This unbundling mechanism gains opportunity for big swap contract that needs to be matched by several small swap contracts, forward contracts, or forward on swaps. Unbundling provides great advantage over the traditional privately negotiated OTC market, which must match the two swap contracts with the exactly same maturity, same notional principal amounts, and correspondent interest rate requirements etc. The bundle swap market idea provides the flexibility to swap contracts and opens the door to competitive swap market.

3.1 Trading Rules

We design the bundle swap market as a continuous double auction market. Buyers and sellers can submit their orders and the electronic trading centre automatically matches the incoming orders and notifies traders about their order status. Traders can get updated information on the last transaction price and volume as well as the historical trading data. All trades are anonymous and all orders are sealed. Traders can only communicate with the market.

Traders submit bundle orders to the market. An order contains the notional principal amount, maturity, and the exchange conditions.

The following trading rules are imposed on bundle swap market:

- A trade is executed only when buy order in the bundle has a matched sell order or orders for the same asset.
- The order can be matched only when the bidding price is higher or equal to the ask.
- Buyers and seller can withdraw their open orders.
- Buyers and sellers can view their open orders.
- The clearing mechanism is to maximize total trading surplus. When orders have the same volume, higher priced buy order has higher priority and lower priced sell order has higher priority. When orders have different volume and the same price, high volume order will get higher priority. For orders with the same price and same volume, execution follows the rule of first-come first-serve.

3.2 Market Properties

The valuation function at the bundle market is different from that in the traditional market, where each single asset is traded by its own. Even though in the traditional valuation function, people can express their preferences over bundles of assets. They acquire the bundle by trading in each individual asset market.

Consider an economy with N infinitely divisible assets. Let $\Omega = \{\omega_1, \omega_2, \omega_3, ... \omega_N\}$ denote the set of all assets in the economy. It follows that $\Omega \in R^N$. Any specified bundle is a subset of Ω. In general, we call the bundle of asset, Z, and the set of all possible bundles is the following: $2^\Omega := \{Z \mid Z \subset \Omega, \text{or } Z \subseteq \Omega\}$. The price vector for the bundle, $P \in R^+$, represents the price for each bundle in Ω, and is a singular. Trader only needs to specify the bundle price as a whole instead of specifying a vector of prices for all assets within the bundle.

Now we define the valuation function and the net valuation function, which represent the total trading value and net trading surplus for each bundle respectively. A map $V: 2^\Omega \to R$ is called the valuation function over Ω. A valuation function assigns a value to each bundle Z in Ω. With each specific valuation function V, we associated it with a net valuation function v, which is denoted as the difference between the valuation of the bundle and the price paid for the bundle. $v(Z, P \mid \xi) = V(Z, P \mid \xi) - P$, Where ξ denotes all other financial environment factors that will affect the valuation function.

The following are some properties of the bundle valuation function:

A bundle market valuation function $V: 2^\Omega \to R$

(1) is monotone, if $\forall\ X \subset Y \subset \Omega$,

$$V(X|\xi) \leq V(Y|\xi)$$

(2) is super-modular, if $\forall\ Z \subset \Omega$, and $Z=\{X,Y\}$, $X \cap Y = 0$,

$$V(Z|\xi) \geq V(X|\xi) + V(Y|\xi)$$

Or in general, $\forall\ Z \subset \Omega$, and $X \subset Z$ and $Y \subset Z$

$$V(Z|\xi) \geq V(X|\xi) + V(Y|\xi) - V(X \cap Y|\xi)$$

(3) has increasing marginal returns, if $\forall X \subset Y \subset \Omega$, and any element $e \in X$

$$V(Y|\xi) - V(Y/\{e\}|\xi) \geq V(X|\xi) - V(X/\{e\}|\xi)$$

(4) has perfectly complimentarily among assets, iff $Z \subset \Omega$, $\forall$ bundles X and Y where $\{X \cup Y\}=Z$, $X \subset Z$ *and* $Y \subset Z$

$V(Z|\xi)=M$, where M is a positive big number

And $V(X|\xi)=0$; $V(Y|\xi)=0$

(5) has strong complimentarily among assets, iff $Z \subset \Omega$, $\forall$ bundles X and Y where $\{X \cup Y\}=Z$, $X \subset Z$ and $Y \subset Z$, $X \cap Y = 0$

$M = V(Z|\xi) >> V(X|\xi) + V(Y|\xi)$

3.3 Market Model

In order to trade in swap market, the bundle needs to be pre-specified. The objective function of the bundle market is to maximize the total trading surplus subject to the market clearing conditions. The mathematical programming problem is as follows:

$$Max \sum_i r_i x_i$$

$$s.t. \sum_j SB_{ij} x_j \leq 0$$

$$\sum_i x_j \leq 1$$

$$x_i \geq 0$$

The objective function is to maximize the total trading surplus. The r is the price vector denoting the limited price s for the n bundle orders for each bundle, and x represents a particular order's proportion in the matched trade. Every x should be non-negative. Positive r means willingness to pay for the bundle, called a buyer position. While a negative r denotes the willingness to accept a bundle, called a seller position. Matrix SB can be written as a vector (B1,B2,B3,....,Bn), which contains n vectors, called n assets. The x vector represents the composition of a particular bundle submitted for trade. The first constraint guarantees that each individual buy order in a bundle could be matched with the seller order for the same asset from other bundles. The second constraint normalizes the matched trade to be a number less or equal to one.

Using the above linear programming model to solve this market-matching problem, we can achieve efficient outcome for the swap market. In addition, by solving the dual problem of our primary model, we can derive the efficient bundle pricing for the trade. The bundle-clearing program also provides the price discovery mechanism that is different from the traditional auction. The prices are the shadow prices for the assets that make up the bundles. The bundle-clearing price is always better than the limit price that traders submit (Fan et al. 1999).

The transaction price of the matched order (bundle) j can be calculated by the following formula:

$$t_j = \sum_{i=1}^{m} b_{ij} r_i^d$$

where r_i^d is the shadow price of the dual problem.

It can be proved that the transaction price t_j, for the matched bundle j is better than the submitted limited price r_j. For all matched bundle, the$r_j > t_j$.

4. TRADING PROCESS

To successfully trade in the bundle market, a standard swap contract needs to be specified. Different types of swap contract will need different specification. The following section discusses the standard contracts for interest rate and currency swaps.

4.1 Interest rate swap

Interest rate swap is an exchange of a cash flow of fixed interest rate with another of floating interest rate. As explained in the earlier example of plain vanilla swap, an interest rate swap is a portfolio of forward contracts with different maturity date. Now we need to set up a standard bundle that can manage all interest rate swap contracts. Interest rate swap contract contains four parts: notional principal, maturity, preference over fixed or floating interest rate, price for the bundle you bid or ask. The notional principal can be viewed as the scale of the standard contract. If the standard contract is set as notional principal of $1000, a swap contract writing $100,000 notional principal is equivalent to 100 standard contracts.

Maturity can be one year, two year, up to thirty years. Maturity determines the length of the swap contract. In other words, it affects the number of forward contracts contained in the swap contract. If the maturity is 10 years, there are 20 forward contracts with six-month period apart. So the maturity will be contained in the standard bundle. The number of asset contains in the bundle is equal to the maturity T times 2. We write the standard bundle for interest rate swap as the following: $(f_1, f_2, f_3, \ldots, f_{2T})$ where T can be 30 years, and each f_i is a forward contract and indicates how much the buyer is willing to pay for a fixed swap rate. A positive f means that a trader is a buyer and prefers a fixed interest payment, while a negative f means a trader wants to sell fix rate and prefers a floating interest rate.

When a trader submits the order (bundle), he needs to declare the willingness to pay (WTP) or willingness to accept (WTA) for the bundle that will be recorded in the limited price order *(r)*. Suppose you want a 10-year interest rate swap with a payment of fixed interest rate and $100,000 notional principal. Then the order you submit is 100 bundles of the following bundle *B1*=(1, 1, ..., 1, 0,...0), with 20 ones and others are zero. At the same time, your WTP will be submitted too. Our bundle market will not be restricted to posting equal weight on every forward contract within the bundle or holding a pure long or short position within the bundle. Traders can compose any kind of bundles and customize them by their interests. For example, you can submit a bundle *B1*=(3, -1, -2, 5, 0...0). This is a two-year interest rate swap, at the first six-month period, the trader wants to hold long position with 3 forward contracts, which trades fix interest rate with floating rate. The second component of this bundle shows that the trader wants to hold one forward contract but with a short position, which means he wants to trade the floating interest rate with a fixed interest rate payment, and so on. When traders write buy and sell order in one bundle, they need to set the WTP and WTA at the same rate, which is the bundle price. If traders need separate WTP and WTA, they should submit different orders. Traders are allowed to have swap and forward on swap in one contract order, such as *B1*=(1, 1, 1, 1, 0,...0, 1, 1, 1, 1, 0...0). This is a two-year swap contract plus a two-year forward on swap contract. By using the unbundling and re-bundling mechanism, we can easily divided a huge contract into several sub-contracts and matching them with small orders or subcontracts of other big orders. This allows a single contract to match with several counter-parties and the trade will be executed more easily and efficiently.

4.2 Currency swap

Currency swap is more complex than interest rate swap. First, the associated cash flows are denominated in different monetary units and the principal amount is always exchanged at the origination and maturity dates of the contract. Second, because two currencies are involved, the interest rate defining the transaction can be expressed on either fix-rate or floating rate basis in either or both currencies. This leads to four combinations: (1) fixed rate in foreign currency and fixed-rate in domestic currency (U.S. Dollars) (2) fixed rate in foreign currency and floating-rate in domestic currency (3) floating rate in foreign currency and fixed-rate in domestic currency (4) floating rate in foreign currency and floating rate in domestic currency.

Foreign Currency

		Fixed rate	Floating rate
Domestic Currency	Fixed rate	1	3
	Floating rate	2	4

In practice, the most popular quotation convention in the market is the second type: currency swap with fixed-rate foreign currency *vs.* floating rate U.S. dollar. We will start with type 2 currency market bundle set up, and all other three types can be composed as follows:

- Type 1 currency swap can be constructed by combining type 2 standard with a domestic currency swap, which trades the floating domestic interest payment to a fixed interest rate payment.
- Type 3 currency swap can be constructed by combining type 2 standard with two swap contracts. One is the domestic interest rate swap which exchanges the floating rate payment to fixed interest rate payment, the other is the foreign interest rare swap which exchanges the fixed interest rate payment to floating rate payment.
- Type 4 currency swap can be constructed by combining type 2 standard with a foreign interest rate swap which exchanges the fixed interest rate payment to a floating one.

As long as those four types of currency swap can be represented by type 2 swap and interest rate swap, we only need to analyse type 2 swap and all other types of currency swap can be composed accordingly.

One big problem in currency swap is the complex combination of currency exchanges. This is the main reason why currency swap is hard to be cleared and the total trading volume and value are much lower than the interest rate swap. Without a swap market, many currency swap contracts are unable to be matched. For example, if we have three currency swaps with U.S. dollar to Japan Yen, Japan Yen to Deutch Mark, and Mark to U.S. dollar, none of them can be cleared under the current OTC setting. Therefore, no contracts will change hand. With the swap market and the unbundling each contract to buy and sell components, we can mix these three currency swaps together and clear those three contracts together.

The currency swap has an outstanding feature that it usually exchanges the notional principal at the origination date and the maturity date. The exchange is based on the spot rate of exchange. In order to increase the computational efficiency, we need to solve the notional principal exchange first. We cannot add too many elements to the standard bundle, which will contain every currency's fixed-floating exchange rate forward of n years. As long as the notional principal is based on spot market, we can just use the exchange market to clear every matched order's principal requirement without adding those features to the standard bundle. Now our currency swap bundle is similar to the interest rate swap bundle with more currency in it. We assume there are k currencies in the exchange and each currency bundle can be viewed as the original interest rate swap bundle. Our currency swap bundle will look like the following vector:

$CSB=(CF_1, CF_2, \ldots CF_k)$ and each $CF_i=(\ cf_{i1},\ cf_{i2},\ \ldots,\ cf_{i2T})$ where T denotes years of contract, and each cf_{it} is a forward contract and represent how much the buyer is willing to pay for a fixed swap rate for the currency i. A positive cf_{it} means traders are buyers and prefer fixed interest payment; a negative cf_{it} means traders want to sell and prefer a floating interest rate. When traders submit the orders (bundles), they need to declare the WTP or WTA for the bundle that will be recorded in the limited price order r.

5. CONCLUSION

In this paper, we have proposed an electronic market for swap exchange with a bundle trading mechanism. We allow multiple swaps, futures and forwards to be traded at the same market and guarantee traders will get either the whole bundle of assets or nothing. We illustrated our mechanism with two examples: interest rate swap and currency swap. We will conduct experiments using the designed mechanism to evaluate the system in future.

REFERENCES

Ederington, L. H., "The hedging Performance of the New Futures Market", Journal of Finance, 34 (March 1979), 157-170

Fan, Ming, Jan Stallaert and Andrew B. Whinston "The Design and Development of a Financial Cybermarket with a Bundle Trading Mechanism," International Journal of Electronic Commerce 4 (1), 1999, 5-22.

Hull, J.(1997), Options, Futures, and Other Derivatives, 3rd ed., Prentice Hall, Englewood Cliffs, NJ.

Johnson, L.L., "The Theory of Hedging and Speculation in Commodity Futures Markets." *Review of Economics Studies*, 27 (October 1960), 139-151.

Layard-Leisching, R., "Swap Fever," *Euromoney*, Supplement (January 1986), 108-113.

Miller, M., and C.Culp, "Risk Management Lessons from Metallgesellschaft", *Journal of Applied Corporate Finance*, Fall 1994.

Stulz, R.M., "Optimal Hedging Policies," *Journal of Financial and Quantitative Analysis*, 19 (June 1984), 127-140

Teweles, R.J., and F.J.Jones (1987), *The Futures Game*. McGraw-Hill, New York

Turnbull, S. M., "Swaps: A Zero Sum game," *Financial Management*, 16 (Spring 1987), 15-21.

Chapter 4

Production Capacity for Durable Goods

R. Preston McAfee
University of Texas and University of Chicago

Abstract: A theory of manufacturing capacity choice for a durable good is provided. The remarkable conclusion is that efficient production may entail ten to fifty years before full market saturation is reached. The time to market saturation is increased as the good becomes less durable, and the size of the crash when saturation is reached falls as the durability decreases. The monopoly seller is efficient provided he doesn't ever undercut himself, a feature of some equilibria of the "no gap" case, where demand intersects marginal costs.

Key words: Coase, durable good, market saturation, production capacity, market penetration

1. INTRODUCTION

Compaq introduced the ipaq 3600 series handheld computer in mid-2000. Priced at $500, the device was rated as a best buy by C/Net, PC World and other industry sources. One year later, these devices are still in short supply, with resellers asking – and getting – $800.[3]

[3] There are actually two devices – the 3650 and the 3630. The distinction between these devices is the retail outlet – the 3630 is sold in "brick and mortar" stores while the 3650 is intended for sale over the internet. The initial plan, apparently, was to give different numbers to the devices so that customers who purchased the 3630 did not feel ripped off when they found out the 3650 was sold for less. However, the prices have actually inverted, with average internet prices for the 3650 being considerably higher than the physical store prices. Indeed, some sales of 3630 labeled devices are now transpiring on the internet.

The ipaq 3600 series stands out because we have become accustomed to rapid provision of high technology goods, with the products reaching market saturation in a very short period of time, a matter of a few months or years. But how much production capacity is desirable? Is it efficient for firms to install sufficient manufacturing capacity to saturate the market in a year or less? Should we expect the Compaq story to be normal, with extended shortages of popular devices, or is it reasonable to expect market saturation to occur rapidly? How much capacity should a durable good seller possess?

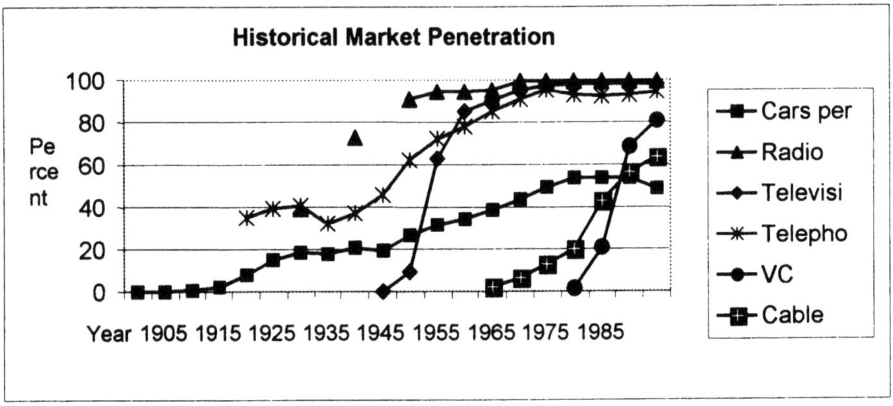

Figure 1. Historical market penetration

Figure 1 presents data on the rate of U.S. penetration for six major consumer durables over this century. For all of these items, full market penetration took place over a decade or more. The producers of these items experienced a "soft landing," in the sense that sales did not plummet, but instead converged to replacement level. In contrast, full market penetration of the Citizen's Band radio took place over approximately five years, leading to a crash in CB radio sales in 1977. Unlike the case of CB radios, Figure 2 shows that sales of color televisions in the U.S never fell, even during recessions – the growth rate was always positive. Should we expect durable goods to have a soft landing, as occurred with televisions, when market saturation is reached, so that the replacement market is sufficient to sustain industry sales, or is it more likely that the sellers will experience a collapse along the lines of the "CB radio craze?" How long should it take for manufacturers of durable goods to satiate the marketplace?

This paper introduces a simple model to address such questions. The basic theory concerns a monopolist with no threat of competition facing identical consumers, and abstracts from the learning curve, substitute products and other features of durable goods manufacturing and sales, many of which work to slow market penetration relative to the rate predicted by the theory. The main conclusion of the theory is that, for common interest rates and other parameters, we should expect full market penetration to require ten to twenty years or more. Moreover, when the goods are imperfectly durable, full penetration can require fifty years or so. The theory suggests that penetration requires a long time relative to the actual rate of penetration of cellular phones, VCRs, camcorders, palm computing devices and other imperfectly-durable consumer durables. In such cases, the crash is small, while fast penetration necessarily requires that a significant crash occurs around the time of full market penetration, when the market switches from new sales to replacement sales.

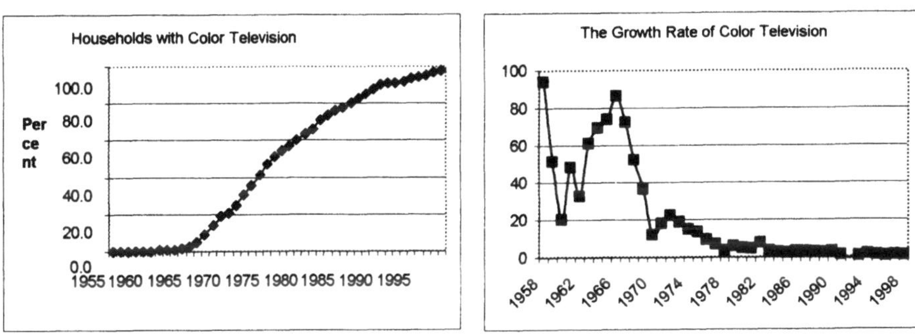

Figure 2. Households with colour television

The basic theory has the feature that market penetration is efficient, for the intuitive reason that the monopolist is capturing all the value of production, and thus desires to maximize that value and hence chooses an efficient capacity. Thus, the long times to market penetration are a feature of efficiency as well as monopoly. The time to market penetration is decreasing in the durability of the good, and tends to be U-shaped in the interest rate. For low interest rates, there is little gain from fast penetration, because everyone is patient, and thus it pays to use capacity over longer times to satiate the market. For very high interest rates, the profitability of the market is reduced, and the firm slows market penetration in response, converging to an infinite time to market penetration for a finite interest rate that makes the production unprofitable.

Does competition speed up market penetration? We will show that in one sense, the answer is yes – the more firms there are, the faster is the market penetration. However, this increase in speed will not be adequate to overturn the conclusions of the basic theory. The basic theory considered a seller who did not undercut itself over time, even when the market reached saturation. With competition, such a path becomes implausible, and prices will tend to converge to marginal costs over time, a feature of the theory known as the Coase conjecture. It turns out that while competition accelerates market penetration, penetration converges to the basic theory solution as the number of firms goes to infinity. This is quite sensible: a monopolist that can capture all the value of its sales produces efficiently, as does the perfectly competitive industry; an imperfectly competitive industry is slower to saturate the market as a means of propping up the price. The case of monopoly divides into two types – the efficient monopolist and the monopolist who competes, imperfectly, with future incarnations of itself. The former is efficient, the latter the slowest to market of all.

Most relevant economic theory has been focused on Ronald Coase's wonderful 1972 conjecture that a monopolist of a durable good will have an incentive to cut the price, and when the monopolist can cut the price sufficiently rapidly, the monopolist will price near marginal costs. For example, Gul, Sonnenchein and Wilson (1986) demonstrate that the Coase conjecture is a feature of stationary equililbria. Kahn (1986) demonstrates that increasing marginal costs insure that even the continuous time limits of discrete time games have positive profits, although these profits are lower than those which would arise on the commitment path. By positing a fixed, albeit endogenous, initial capacity, we sidestep the Coase conjecture, because the seller *cannot* sell the large quantities required by the Coase path.

In one sense the Compaq ipaq story is unusual because Compaq did not price the 3600 series to capture the high prices created by the shortage. Consequently, an important part of the analysis of pricing concerns the optimal price path. We are used to the rapid decline in prices of consumer electronics. Prices may start high, but rapidly fall to a small fraction of their initial levels as mass production and competition take hold.[4]

2. A BASIC MODEL OF MONOPOLY

If Consider the introduction of a new durable product by a monopolist. The product's durability, , is the rate at which the product fails; this is modeled for convenience as an exponential, so that a product sold at time t is

[4] It appears Compaq misjudged the popularity of its device, or perhaps was unable to obtain sufficient displays to meet the market projection, because it introduced a black and white version of the device after the initial introduction.

still operating at time s with probability $e^{-(s-t)}$. Let r be the rate at which future profits are discounted, so that profits received by the firm at time t have a present value of e^{-rt}.

Suppose that the flow value of the good to any customer is equal to the continuous consumption value of a competitively supplied non-durable good. This would be precisely the case if the durable good replaced a flow of a non-durable, such as an energy saving device. The expected present value of the cost of obtaining continuous use of the good, if the price is p, is the amount v satisfying

$$v = p + \int_0^{\infty} \delta e^{-\delta t} e^{-rt} v dt = p + \frac{\delta}{r+\delta} v,$$

as the probability density function of failure of the first purchase occurring at t is e^{-t}, at which point a new unit is purchased, incurring the discounted cost ve^{-rT}. This solves for a present cost:

$$v = \frac{r+\delta}{r} p.$$

The value v is determined by the pricing of an equivalent non-durable; let a constant infinite stream of a competitively supplied non-durable, such as labor, represent the numeraire good. If the non-durable is competitively supplied, the present value of cost of purchasing the non-durable will be $v = mc/r$, where mc is the marginal cost of the non-durable. Thus, setting this mc to \$1 without loss of generality, the maximum willingness to pay for the good is $\frac{1}{r+\delta}$. The flow value of benefits from the good is \$1.

Set marginal production costs to zero. If marginal costs are constant, then there is no loss of generality setting them to zero, because prices can be measured net of marginal costs.

The state variable of the system will be the proportion of the population that currently has the good, a variable denoted y. This variable has the equation of motion

(1) $y'(t) = x - \delta y,$

where x is the production of the firm. This equation arises because the increase in the number of consumers holding the good is the flow of production x minus the consumers whose good depreciates, the number y. Let c/r be the cost of the physical manufacturing facilities per unit of output;

a production plant that produces x units per day costs cx/r to build.[5] The value c is the flow cost of the manufacturing facility if it were completely financed with debt. Moreover, for small , c is approximately equal to the so-called payback period – the number of periods prior at which the total dollars received equals the expenditure on the plant. The firm is assumed to choose x initially and not augment it later; this situation is justified if there are fixed costs associated with adding capacity.

If $(r+\ )c$ 1, then it is not profitable to construct any manufacturing facility, because the present value of the proceeds is less than the cost of the facility. The present value of the proceeds from a plant of size x is, for sufficiently small x that the plant is fully utilized forever:

$$\frac{x}{r+\delta}\int_0^\infty e^{-rt}dt-\frac{cx}{r}=\frac{x}{r(r+\delta)}-\frac{cx}{r}.$$

Consequently, the interesting case is when

(2) $(r+\ )c<1$,

so that production is profitable, and this assumption is maintained for the remainder of the paper.

Given the nature of demand, the firm will buy all of its productive capacity initially at time 0 and produce at full capacity until the market is saturated, a time denoted T. After that time, the firm will only sell to the replacement market, which is the fraction of the total population. The equation of motion can be solved for T given the initial condition $y(0)=0$ and the capacity x by integrating and solving for $y(T)=1$. This calculation yields:

(3) $$T=\frac{Log(x/(x-\delta))}{\delta}$$

or

(4) $$\frac{\delta}{x}=1-e^{-\delta T}.$$

The firm's profits arise from sales of x for T periods, plus sales of for the remainder of time, minus the cost of capacity. (Recall that marginal costs of production were already subtracted from the payments of customers, so that the only remaining costs are capacity costs.) Thus the firm's profits are:

(5)

$$\pi=\frac{1}{r+\delta}\int_0^T e^{-rt}xdt+\frac{1}{r+\delta}\int_T^\infty e^{-rt}\delta dt-\frac{cx}{r}=\frac{x}{r(r+\delta)}(1-e^{-rT})+\frac{\delta}{r(r+\delta)}e^{-rT}-\frac{cx}{r}.$$

[5] The cost of the facility takes the form c/r to denominate it in terms of the labor or non-durable units used for the revenues; \$1/r purchases a fixed stream of non-durables, the numeraire.

In the expression for profits, T and x are related by equation (4). However, it will prove practical to think of the firm as choosing T, with equation (4) determining x. In this case, profits can be expressed as
(6)

$$r\pi = \frac{r}{r+\delta}\frac{\delta}{r}\left[\frac{1-e^{-rT}-(r+\delta)c}{1-e^{-\delta T}}+e^{-rT}\right]=\frac{\delta}{r+\delta}\left[\frac{1-e^{-(r+\delta)T}-(r+\delta)c}{1-e^{-\delta T}}\right].$$

This expression is maximized when the first order condition yields:

(7) $$c=\frac{\delta-(r+\delta)e^{-rT}+re^{-(r+\delta)T}}{\delta(r+\delta)}$$

The right hand side of this expression ranges from 0 to 1/(*r*+) as T ranges from 0 to and is increasing in T. Thus, there is a unique solution T^* to (7) if and only if (2) holds. Moreover, T^* increases in the cost of capacity – when capacity is more expensive, it takes longer for a monopolist to saturate the market. That the saturation time increases as capacity becomes more expensive is a feature of any reasonable model.

As depreciation rises, the optimal saturation time T increases, a fact that is demonstrated in Lemma A1 of the appendix. Consequently, the optimal value of T is minimized when =0. The case when =0 is the case of a perfectly durable good, and in this instance, T^* satisfies:

(8) $rc = 1 - e^{-rT^*}(1 + rT^*)$.

Equation (8) can be used to prove two interesting heuristics for the saturation of a market.

Theorem 1: The optimal time for market saturation, T^*, satisfies:

(9) $T^* \geq \frac{2.6}{r}(rc)^{0.718}$, and

(10) T^* 3.35 c.

Proof: It is simplest to work with (8), which gives a lower bound to T^*. Define $y=rT$ and $a=1/(e-2)$ 1.392. Rewrite (8) to obtain

(11) $$\frac{rc}{(rT)^a}=\frac{1-e^{-x}(1+x)}{x^a}\equiv h(x)\leq 1-\frac{2}{e}\approx 0.264241.$$

The inequality in (11) arises from maximization of h over x, a maximization that results in x=1. (In fact, a was chosen so that the maximization of h results in x=1. Because a<2, h(0)=0.) From (11),

$$T \geq \frac{(rc)^{1/a}}{r(1-2/e)^{1/a}} = \left(\frac{e}{e-2}\right)^{e-2} \frac{(rc)^{e-2}}{r} \geq 2.601 \frac{(rc)^{.718}}{r}.$$

The derivation of (10) is accomplished as follows. Rewrite (8) to give

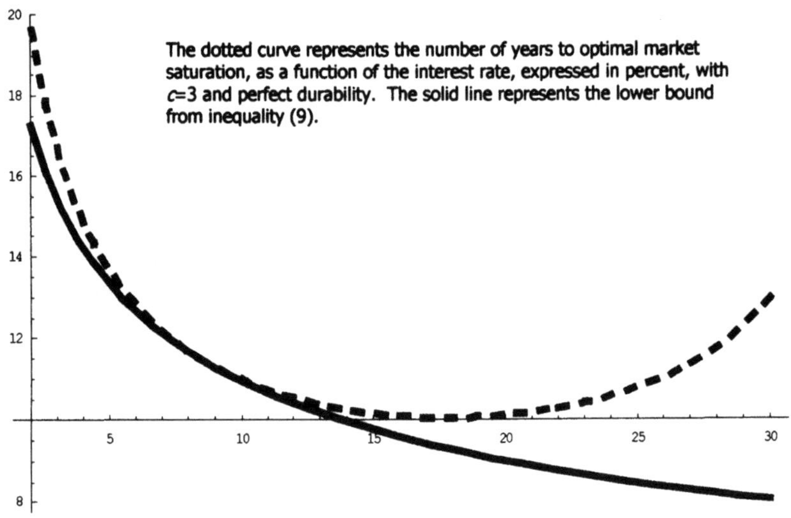

Figure 3. The dotted curve represents the number of years to optimal market saturation, as a function of the interest rate, expressed in percent, with c=3 and perfect durability. The solid line represents the lower bound from inequality (9)

$$\frac{rTc}{T} = 1 - e^{-rT}(1+rT).$$

Consequently,

$$(12)\ \frac{c}{T} = \frac{1-e^{-rT}(1+rT)}{rT} \leq 0.298427 \leq \frac{1}{3.3508}.$$

The inequality (12) readily proves (10). *Q.E.D.*

Theorem 1 provides two heuristics for the optimal time to reach market saturation for the case of a perfectly durable. Inequality (10) is the most straightforward, placing a lower bound on the time to saturation for any interest rate. The interesting fact about this lower bound is the absolute magnitude – the lower bound is quite large. Recall that c is the cost of a manufacturing facility per dollar of profit generated.

Thus, a value of c=3 corresponds to a pay-back period of 3 years.[6] In this case, the time to market saturation is at least a decade! In general, the time to market saturation is at least $3\frac{1}{3}$ times the undiscounted pay-back length of time. For moderate interest rates, the optimal length of time can be substantially longer, with two decades arising in the case of very low interest rates. These values are illustrated in Figure 3.

An interesting aspect of the problem is visible in Figure 3. For very low interest rates, the firm is patient, so that the value of fast market penetration is small. Thus, as the interest rate falls toward zero, the optimal penetration time converges to infinity. This is not a consequence of the increase in manufacturing costs, because the willingness to pay by consumers is rising at the same rate. Moreover, as the interest rate approaches $1/c$, the profitability of the project is declining, and the terminal time for saturation diverges.

Figure 4 explores the U-shaped optimal penetration time and illustrates the effect of various costs, for =0, as a function of the interest rate. For low interest rates, the optimal penetration time is high, because the seller is patient and doesn't care that it takes a long time to sell to the market. As the interest rate gets high, the entire projcct is becoming less and less worthwhile, thus increasing the time to penetrate the market, indeed sending it to infinity as r $1/c$.

[6] This is standard, if weird, usage – the payback period is the length of time until the number of dollars – undiscounted – received in return equals the investment. If =0, this value equals c.

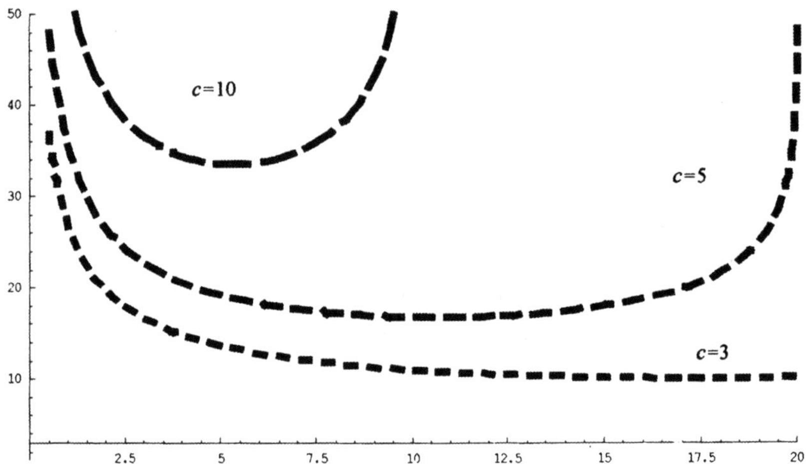

Figure 4. The number of years until market saturation for various costs of manufacturing as a function of the interest rate in percent, with d=0

Depreciation of the good reduces the profitability of sales by reducing the buyer's willingness to pay. However, depreciation also increases the ultimate demand, increasing the long-term profitability of a larger capacity. On balance, the former effect dominates, and the effect of depreciation is to increase the optimal time before full penetration is reached. Figure 5 illustrates this effect when $c = 3$ and $r = 0.05$ – a five percent interest rate. The terminal time rises slowly for modest depreciation rates, but as the depreciation rate rises to 25% – so that the good has an expected life of four years – the terminal time rises to fifty years.

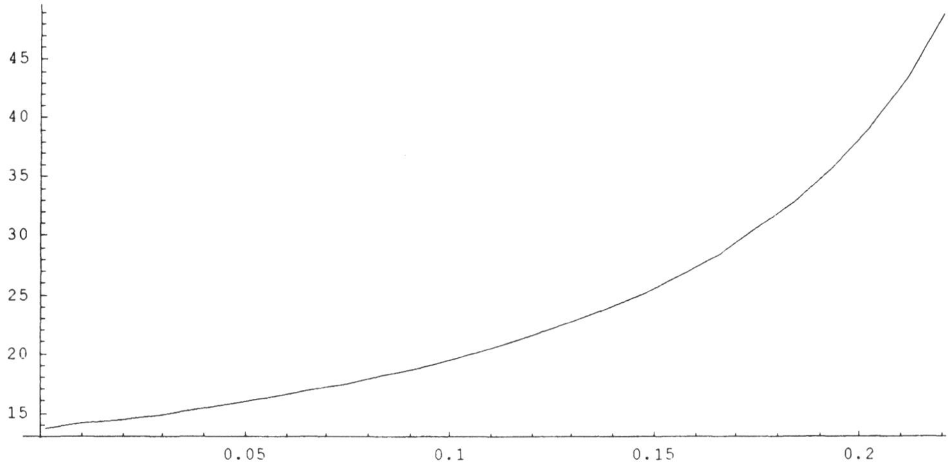

Figure 5. The effect of depreciation (in proportion that depreciates per year) on the optimal time T*, with a 5% interest rate and c=3

The implication of these numbers are very surprising. A monopoly seller of a fairly durable good, one that lasts four years, facing no Coase conjecture problems with price erosion, and $c = 3$, will take fifty years to penetrate the market. Part of the reason is that the pay-back period with a large depreciation rate, which reduces the willingness to pay, increases the payback period substantially, to eighteen years.

Capacity has an inverse relationship to market saturation, given by (4). Thus, capacity is upside-u-shaped in the interest rate, and decreases in the cost of capacity. For sensible parameters, it appears capacity increases in the depreciation rate of the good, in spite of the fact that the time to saturation also increases.

The main conclusion of the basic theory is that the optimal time for market saturation is quite long – substantially longer than the time to saturation usually observed in real-world durable goods. There could be several reasons for this. First, competition will increase the speed of market penetration by creating a race – the firm that brings more to market captures the lion's share of the rents. Second, even a monopoly will introduce good substantially faster if slow penetration is likely to attract entry– firms may increase market penetration to reduce the incentive of other firms to engineer competing solutions. In the subsequent section, we explore the former hypothesis – what is the effect of competition on the speed of market penetration?

3. THE BASIC MODEL WITH COMPETITION

Suppose there are n firms with the technology to provide the good to the market. We maintain the prevailing assumptions on the technology and demand, with the provision that there is no longer monopoly. Each firm will choose a capacity x_i, and will choose a quantity $q_i(t)$ to provide to the market, subject to the restriction that $q_i(t) \ \ x_i$. We will only consider equilibria in which all the firms engage in full production, given their capacities; this assumption is warranted by the analysis of Kreps and Scheinkman (1983). Firms are assumed to choose their initial capacities and not augment capacity later. This restriction is made for computability, but can be justified by positing some fixed costs associated with capital investment or a "putty-clay" technology that cannot be augmented.

In contrast to the monopoly analysis, if $\delta < \sum_{i=1}^{n} x_i$, then prices must be driven to zero (marginal cost) once the market is saturated, which occurs at time T given by (3), where x is replaced with the sum of the x_i. Let $p(t)$ represent the price charged to customers, so that $p(t)=0$ for $t \ \ T$. The prices are determined by the fact that consumers must be indifferent to waiting to purchase, which produces utility $e^{-rT}\left(\frac{1}{r+\delta}\right)$, because the present value of the good to the customer is $1/(r+\ )$. Thus, the prices are determined by the equation:

(13)

$$\frac{e^{-rT}}{r+\delta} = \int_t^T \delta e^{-\delta(s-t)}\left(\frac{e^{-rt}-e^{-rs}}{r}+\frac{e^{-rT}}{r+\delta}\right)ds + e^{-\delta(T-t)}\left(\frac{e^{-rt}-e^{-rT}}{r}+\frac{e^{-rT}}{r+\delta}\right) - e^{-rt}p(t).$$

The left hand side of (13) is the value of purchasing at T. This value arises by waiting until T to purchase for a price of zero. Alternatively, if the agent buys at t, the good survives until T with probability $e^{-\ (T-t)}$, and in this event, because of the exponential failure, the future value to the customer is the same as if they bought at time T, plus the customer has the flow value of the good from t to T. If the good fails in the interval $[t,T]$, at time s, which has density $e^{-\ (s-t)}$, the customer gets the flow value to date, plus the value of waiting to purchase at T. Equation (13) reduces to

$$(14)\quad p(t) = \frac{1}{r+\delta}\left(1-e^{-(r+\delta)(T-t)}\right).$$

Equation (14) provides the prices that make a customer indifferent between purchasing during the phase of production where production is constrained by capacity and waiting until production is unconstrained and prices fall to marginal cost, which was set to zero.

The profits earned by firm i, then, are

$$(15)\quad \pi_i = \int_0^T e^{-rt} p(t) x_i dt - \frac{cx_i}{r} = \frac{x_i}{r+\delta} \int_0^T e^{-rt} - e^{\delta t-(r+\delta)T} dt - \frac{cx_i}{r}$$

$$= \frac{x_i}{r}\left(\frac{1-e^{-rT}}{r+\delta} - \frac{re^{-rT}(1-e^{-\delta T})}{\delta(r+\delta)} - c\right) =$$

$$\frac{x_i}{r}\left(\frac{1-e^{-rT}}{r+\delta} - \frac{re^{-rT}}{(r+\delta)\sum_{j=1}^{n} x_j} - c\right)$$

where $X = \sum_{j=1}^{n} x_j$. Differentiating (4),

$$(16)\quad \frac{dT}{dX} = -\frac{e^{\delta T}}{X^2} = -\frac{e^{\delta T}(1-e^{-\delta T})^2}{\delta^2}.$$

Thus,

$$(17)\quad \frac{\partial \pi}{\partial x_i} = \frac{\partial}{\partial x_i} \frac{x_i}{r}\left(\frac{1-e^{-rT}}{r+\delta} - \frac{re^{-rT}}{(r+\delta)X} - c\right)$$

$$= \frac{1}{r}\left(\frac{1-e^{-rT}}{r+\delta} - \frac{re^{-rT}}{(r+\delta)X} - c\right) + \frac{x_i}{r(r+\delta)}\left(\frac{re^{-rT}}{X^2} + r\left(1+\frac{r}{X}\right)e^{-rT}\frac{dT}{dX}\right)$$

$$= \frac{1}{r(r+\delta)}\left[1-e^{-rT}-\frac{re^{-rT}}{X}-c(r+\delta)+\frac{x_i e^{-rT}}{X^2}\left(r-r\left(1+\frac{r}{X}\right)e^{\delta T}\right)\right]$$

$$= \frac{1}{r(r+\delta)}\left[1-e^{-rT}\left(1+\frac{r}{X}\right)-c(r+\delta)+\frac{rx_i e^{-rT}}{X^2}\left(1-\left(1+\frac{r}{X}\right)e^{\delta T}\right)\right]$$

Note that marginal profits are decreasing in the market share x_i/X, which implies that the only candidates for equilibria involving finite saturation time are symmetric – firms with larger market shares have strictly lower marginal profits. Thus, an equilibrium (with $X>$) must satisfy:

$$\text{(18)}\quad 0 = 1-e^{-rT}\left(1+\frac{r}{X}\right)-c(r+\delta)+\frac{re^{-rT}}{nX}\left(1-\left(1+\frac{r}{X}\right)e^{\delta T}\right).$$

Equation (18) reduces to:

$$\text{(19)}\quad 1-c(r+\delta) = e^{-rT}\left[\left(1+\frac{r(1-e^{-\delta T})}{\delta}\right)\left(\frac{n-1}{n}+e^{\delta T}\frac{r(1-e^{-\delta T})}{n\delta}\right)+\frac{1}{n}\right].$$

In the limit as n diverges, this expression replicates the solution to the basic monopoly problem. This sounds strange, however, it arises because consumers are identical, which makes the monopolist a perfectly price-discriminating monopolist. As is well-known, a perfectly price-discriminating monopolist is efficient about production, and consequently the monopoly solution and the zero-profits competitive solution coincide; the difference is in the prices charged in the two cases.

Theorem 2: If $r>$, the unique equilibrium is an interior solution to (19) with $T<$. If r and n 2, any equilibrium involves $X=$ and $T=$. If $r<$ and $n>2$, either kind of equilibrium is possible, depending on c. Finally, if $r=$, and $n>2$, the equilibrium is an interior solution to (19) with $T<$.

Proof: First note that X is decreasing in T, and moreover that profits are continuous in the limit as X . It is readily established that profits are increasing in x_i for $X<$, so the only candidates for equilibria involve T [0,]. Thus we can work with (19) to characterize firm's incentives globally. (What makes this a bit tricky is that (19) is expressed in terms of T, and T is decreasing in x_i.)

The right hand side of (19) is 1 at T=0. The slope of the RHS is given by

$$\frac{\partial RHS}{\partial T} = \frac{r(r+\delta)e^{-rT}(1-e^{-\delta T})}{\delta^2 n}((\delta - r)e^{\delta T} + r - \delta(n-1)).$$

Thus, if *r*> , the RHS converges to 0 as *T* , and there will be an equilibrium given that the maintained hypothesis (2) is satisfied. Moreover, note that any extreme point to RHS is a maximum – the second derivative, evaluated where the first derivative is zero, is proportional to -*r*, which is negative by hypothesis. The only valid candidates for equilibria involve a decreasing RHS – this corresponds to the second order condition of the maximization problem of the firm.

If *r*< , the RHS diverges as *T* . Moreover, every extreme point is a minimum. Thus, the RHS is always at least unity if it is nondecreasing at *T*=0, which occurs if *n* 2. In this case, profits are increasing in *T*, which is equivalent to profits decreasing in x_i when *X*> . Hence all equilibria involve *X*= and *T*= . If *r*< and *n*>2, there will be locally optimal (RHS decreasing) solutions to (19) when *c* is large enough, and won't when *c* is sufficiently small.

The final case arises when *r*= . If *n*=1, the RHS is increasing and the only solution involves *X*= . If *n*=2, the RHS is constant at 1 and thus any equilibrium involves *X*= . Finally, if *n*>2, the RHS falls monotonically to zero and thus is equivalent to the case when *r*> . *Q.E.D.*

Intuitively, when is large, it doesn't pay for any firm to increase capacity beyond the point where prices start to fall, because the replacement market is sufficiently large that a larger share of a market with lower prices doesn't pay. In contrast, when is small, firms will prefer to sell more even at the cost of lower prices terminating at zero. The more firms there are, the stronger the incentive to increase capacity beyond even if this leads to declining prices.

When *T*< , there are no asymmetric equilibria. In the case =*X*, however, there may be asymmetric equilibria – the requirement that a firm doesn't find it profitable to increase x_i is an inequality in market share that holds strictly around symmetry.

The case n=1 can be interpreted as a Coasian path. (See Gul, Sonnenschein and Wilson(1986) and Coase(1972).) Along this path, the monopolist cuts his price because buyers won't buy unless he cuts his price, eventually driving prices to zero. Profits are positive because the firm cannot satisfy all the demand instantaneously, and profits exceed competitive levels because the monopolist chooses to restrict capacity so as to influence beliefs by customers. Nevertheless, pessimistic conjectures imply decreasing prices.

$$\frac{\partial RHS}{\partial n} = -\frac{e^{-rT}(1-e^{-\delta T})^2 r(r+\delta)}{\delta^2 n^2} < 0.$$

Thus, under the circumstances that T is finite, T is decreasing in n – more competition decreases the time before market saturation. For example, if =0, the expression defining T reduces to

$$1 - rc = e^{-rT}\left(1 + rT + \frac{(rT)^2}{n}\right).$$

A plot of the solution to this equation, for various values of n is provided in Figure 6. It is striking how long full market penetration takes. In contrast to the basic monopoly model with monopoly prices (which encourage investment in capacity due to high prices), competition *increases* the time to full market saturation, equaling the monopoly only in the limiting case of perfect competition. On the Coasian path, the monopolist who succumbs to the temptation to cut prices winds up cutting capacity dramatically, as a means of committing to higher prices than arise with larger capacity. With no depreciation, a payback period of 3 years and a 5% interest rate, it takes fifty years for the market to reach saturation.

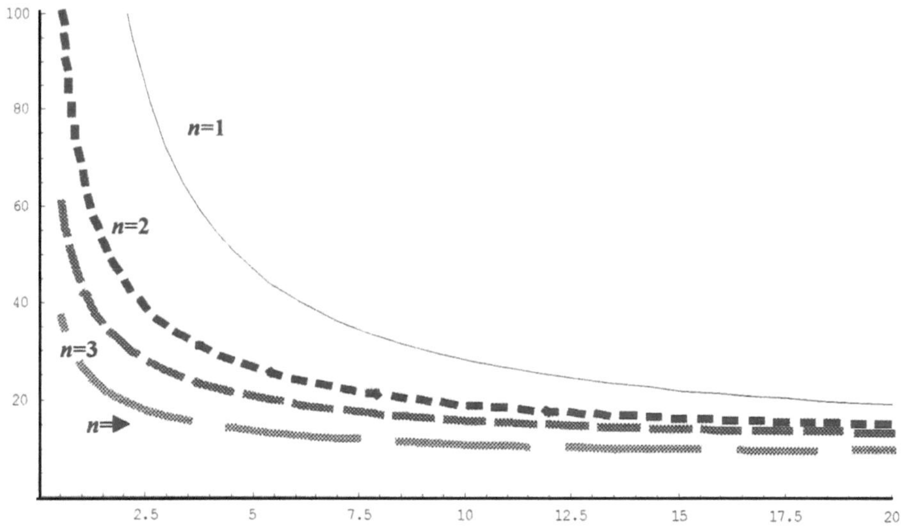

Figure 6. The penetration time for various interest rates expressed in percent, with a single firm, duopoly, triopoly and perfect competition, assuming no depreciation of the good and c=3

The value of *T* appears to increase in the failure rate , which is sensible given that the required capacity to saturate the market rises as rises. Figure 7 illustrates the saturation times with a 5% interest rate and $c=3$. The effect of an increase in is generally modest for five or more firms. However, with only a few firms, increasing increases the saturation time significantly.

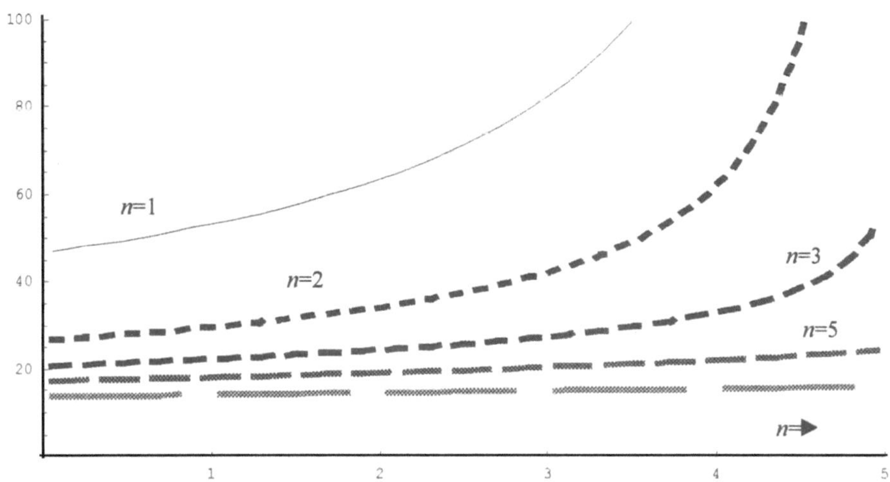

Figure 7. The saturation time as a function of d (in percent), with a 5% interest rate and c=3

4. CONCLUSION

This paper presents a theory of manufacturing capacity choice for a durable good. The remarkable conclusion is that efficient production may entail ten to fifty years before full market saturation is reached. The time to market saturation is increased as the good becomes less durable, and the size of the crash when saturation is reached falls as the durability decreases. The monopoly seller is efficient provided he doesn't ever undercut himself, a feature of some equilibria of the "no gap" case, where demand intersects marginal costs.

With competition, either on the Coase path for a monopolist, or with multiple producers, market penetration may arrive only in the limit as time diverges, with sellers producing only the amount that replaces a satiated market. This situation arises only if the depreciation rate of the good is larger than the interest rate, and may not arise when the number of competitors exceeds two, depending on the cost of capacity. In such a case, there is no crash, only a soft landing as the market is satiated, with a growth rate converging to zero.

Increases in the number of competitors speed product introduction, converging to the efficient level as the number of competitors goes to infinity. In addition, increases in the depreciation rate of the good also tend to increase the time to market saturation.

REFERENCES

Coase, Ronald, "Durability and Monopoly," *Journal of Law and Economics* v15 (1972): 143-9.

Gul, Faruk, Hugo Sonnenschein and Robert Wilson, "Foundations of Dynamic Monopoly and the Coase Conjecture," *Journal of Economic Theory* v39, n1 (1986): 155-90.

Kahn, Charles, "The Durable Goods Monopolist with Consistency and Increasing Costs," *Econometrica* v54, n2 (March 1986): 275-94.

Kreps, David and Jose Scheinkman, "Quantity Precommitment and Bertrand Competition Yield Cournot Outcomes," *Bell Journal of Economics* v14, n2 (1983): 326-37.

TECHNICAL APPENDIX

Lemma A1: T is increasing in .*

The value of T^* is determined by (7). It is readily established that the RHS of (7) is increasing in T, so it suffices to show that the right hand side of (7) is decreasing in Define a function by the right hand side of (7), that is,

$$\gamma(\delta,T)=\frac{\delta-(r+\delta)e^{-rT}+re^{-(r+\delta)T}}{\delta(r+\delta)}=\frac{1}{r+\delta}-\frac{e^{-rT}}{\delta}+\frac{re^{-rT}}{\delta(r+\delta)}.$$

Then

$$\frac{\partial\gamma}{\partial\delta}=\frac{-1}{(r+\delta)^2}+\frac{e^{-rT}}{\delta^2}-\frac{re^{-(r+\delta)T}}{\delta(r+\delta)}\left(\frac{1}{\delta}+\frac{1}{r+\delta}+T\right).$$

It is straightforward to show that / = 0 at T=0; indeed, (,0)=0. Thus, it suffices to show that / is decreasing in T to show that / 0. But

$$\frac{\partial}{\partial T}\frac{\partial\gamma}{\partial\delta}=-\frac{re^{-rT}}{\delta^2}+\frac{re^{-(r+\delta)T}}{\delta(r+\delta)}\left(-1+(r+\delta)\left(\frac{1}{\delta}+\frac{1}{r+\delta}+T\right)\right).$$

$$=\frac{1}{\delta^2(r+\delta)}\left[-(r+\delta)re^{-rT}+re^{-(r+\delta)T}\left(-\delta+(r+\delta)\left(1+\frac{\delta}{r+\delta}+\delta T\right)\right)\right].$$

$$= \frac{re^{-rT}}{\delta^2(r+\delta)}\left[-(r+\delta)+e^{-\delta T}\left((r+\delta)(1+\delta T)\right)\right]$$

$$= \frac{-(r+\delta)re^{-rT}}{\delta^2(r+\delta)}\left[1-e^{-\delta T}(1+\delta T)\right] \le 0. \qquad \text{Q.E.D.}$$

Simplification of (13): Rewrite (13) to obtain

$$0 = \int_t^T \delta e^{-\delta(s-t)}\left(\frac{e^{-rt}-e^{-rs}}{r}\right)ds + e^{-\delta(T-t)}\left(\frac{e^{-rt}-e^{-rT}}{r}\right) - e^{-rt}p(t)$$

, or

$$rp(t) = \int_t^T \delta e^{-\delta(s-t)}\left(1-e^{-r(s-t)}\right)ds + e^{-\delta(T-t)}\left(1-e^{-r(T-t)}\right), \text{ or,}$$

$$rp(t) = (1-e^{-\delta(T-t)}) - \frac{\delta}{r+\delta}(1-e^{-(r+\delta)(T-t)}) + e^{-\delta(T-t)}\left(1-e^{-r(T-t)}\right), \text{ or,}$$

$$rp(t) = 1 - \frac{\delta}{r+\delta}(1-e^{-(r+\delta)(T-t)}) - e^{-\delta(T-t)}e^{-r(T-t)} = \frac{r}{r+\delta}(1-e^{-(r+\delta)(T-t)})$$

Simplification of (18): Rewrite (18) and substitute (4) to obtain:

$$1-c(r+\delta)=e^{-rT}\left[\left(1+\frac{r}{X}\right)-\frac{r}{nX}\left(1-\left(1+\frac{r}{X}\right)e^{\delta T}\right)\right], \text{ or,}$$

$$1-c(r+\delta)=e^{-rT}\left[\left(1+\frac{r(1-e^{-\delta T})}{\delta}\right)-\frac{r(1-e^{-\delta T})}{n\delta}\left(1-\left(1+\frac{r(1-e^{-\delta T})}{\delta}\right)e^{\delta T}\right)\right]$$

, or,

$$1-c(r+\delta)=e^{-rT}\left[\left(1+\frac{r(1-e^{-\delta T})}{\delta}\right)\left(1+e^{\delta T}\frac{r(1-e^{-\delta T})}{n\delta}\right)-\frac{r(1-e^{-\delta T})}{n\delta}\right],$$

or,

$$1-c(r+\delta)=e^{-rT}\left[\left(1+\frac{r(1-e^{-\delta T})}{\delta}\right)\left(\frac{n-1}{n}+e^{\delta T}\frac{r(1-e^{-\delta T})}{n\delta}\right)+\frac{1}{n}\right],$$

as desired.

Chapter 5

Cost-Sharing For Pollution Abatement

An Informationally Decentralized Coordination Process

Edna T. Loehman : Rabih Karaky

Department of Agricultural Economics, Purdue University, West Lafayette, Indiana 47905, loehman@agecon.purdue.edu

Key words: cost-sharing, externality, coordination, decentralization, adjustment process

Abstract: This paper presents a method of ameliorating externality problems when polluters and sufferers would like to take a cooperative approach, sharing costs of abatement and jointly deciding expenditure for abatement and environmental goals. The method for solving this joint problem uses decentralized messages among the involved participants concerning willingness to pay and proposals about environmental quality. The iterative process starts from exogenously specified cost shares that are then adjusted through personalized prices (which can be taxes or subsidies). The process arrives at equilibrium through price adjustment rules. The equilibrium of the process satisfies social efficiency by design. A simulated example shows that the method can solve a complex problem in a relatively few iterations.

1. INTRODUCTION

Welfare economic literature has discussed the possibility of reducing externalities through alternative policies of taxes, standards, and subsidies, and the properties of these policy alternatives have been compared in theory and in practice (e.g. Baumol and Oates, 1990; Stavins, 2000). For example:

with a tax, if the cost abatement is too expensive for a polluter to undertake alone, a polluter could just elect to pay a tax, thereby not achieving an environmental improvement; with a technology standard, an environmental goal may not be achieved at least cost due if the mandated technology is not appropriate. Traditional economics treatment of pollution also embodies the non-cooperative paradigm, i.e. that each polluter would treat her own wastes individually if abatement were cheaper than paying a tax.

In contrast, Whinston with his colleagues have emphasized the importance of cooperation to achieve environmental goals (LPW, 1974). Because there are economies of scale (cost savings) that could be achieved by multi-user treatment of pollution (LOTW, 1979, applied to regional wastewater treatment), participants involved in pollution should seek a joint solution, minimizing total system costs and then sharing abatement costs with appropriate cost allocation. The concept underlying cost allocation was that of a cooperative game. (See also LW, 1970, for early discussion of cooperation in a temporal frame.)

1.1 Whinston's Influences

This paper extends several aspects of Whinston's work: the cooperative approach to externality problems, cost-sharing, and construction of pricing algorithms. The application is for water pollution, a focus of Whinston's applied work in the period 1969-79. Below we briefly review important themes in Whinston's work.

1.1.1 Bargaining and Cooperative Solutions for Externalities

Wellisz (1964) portrayed a dichotomy in welfare economics between the "modern" view and the "modern-old" view (basically the distinction between centralized and decentralized solutions for so-called market imperfections). In the modern view, market failure gave the imperative for government intervention, and the Pigouvian tax was the instrument of choice. The "modern-old" school (including economists Coase, Buchanan, and Davis and Whinston) expressed concerns with the Pigouvian solution on the grounds of cost of information requirements and appropriateness, and they presented alternative solutions to externality problems.

Coase (1960) described ideal conditions under which a bargaining solution between participants to the externality could reach a desirable outcome. Coase further proposed that the same socially efficient outcome could be achieved regardless which party was given priority rights. His work gave support to the ideas that participants to an externality could work out a mutually agreeable solution without need for government intervention, and that there need not be concern with the problem of determining rights.

Davis and Whinston (1962, 1966) further expanded the set of alternatives to government action. First, they presented the possibility of merger among firms involved in externalities, i.e. the idea that structure of production is endogenous. More importantly, they described a decentralized iterative computational procedure -- with adjustment of transfer payments -- to find an equilibrium outcome for firms involved in an externality. The proposed bargaining method would allow firms to find output levels satisfying joint maximization of profits without actual merger or firms having knowledge about each other. Thus, they distinguished between decentralization and non-cooperation.

Wellisz countered these arguments of bargaining alternatives to centralized Pigouvian taxes by pointing out that the cases in which bargaining would work (low transactions costs, small number of involved participants, etc.) may be a limited set. Nevertheless, these may be important cases!

The Coase hypothesis about property rights is now known to be limited to the case of quasi-linear utilities (Hurwicz 1999). A restatement of the Coase theorem is thus: direct bargaining of participants involved in externalities can lead to a socially efficient outcome, but different initial rights positions may lead to different efficient outcomes. Correspondingly, Davis and Whinston (1965) formulated a role for government in a bargaining context. Their idea originates from game theory of bargaining (Luce and Raiffa, 1957): "It may be that the proper role of the legal and/or thc judicial system is to choose a status quo point...so that the participants are free to determine a final settlement by bargaining methods..."

1.1.2 Cost Allocation and Cooperative Game Theory

Whinston with Loehman (LW, 1971, 1974, 1976) developed the idea of cooperative game theory and Shapley value for cost allocation for joint projects. This method of cost allocation was applied for regional pollution treatment and for public utilities. The idea was that certain reasonable tenets or axioms (e.g. that each user of a common facility should pay their incremental cost to the system, and that those with equal costs should be treated equally) would determine the formula for charging participants in such a way that costs are covered equitably. Following Buchanan (1969), Loehman and Whinston (1974) suggested for cost allocation that if a group agrees to a set of rules as a constitution, they may then agree to any outcome derived from executing the rules.

One limitation of the axiomatic approach is that an a priori size or scale for a shared facility must be specified exogenously, e.g. by minimizing joint cost. To address endogenous determination, LW (1971, 1974) suggested using the cost allocation formula as a pricing scheme in an iterative process to determine the equilibrium size of a shared facility.

Because there are many reasonable cooperative game solution concepts (see Loehman, 1995 for a comparison), the lasting importance of this work may be the framing of joint cost problems as cooperative.

1.1.3 Decentralization through Construction of Pricing Algorithms and Computational Economics

The employment of price as a coordination signal in a non-classical environment stems from Whinston's doctoral dissertation (for decision-making within a business firm, reported in Whinston 1964). He has continued to expand the application of economic theory for developing pricing algorithms (see for example MRW, 1994 and SW, 1994). Development and application of pricing algorithms is an important new sub-field of computational economics, a field that Whinston helped to initiate.

1.2 Coordination Process Design for Pollution Abatement Cost-sharing

Cost-sharing may be necessary to achieve environmental improvement when it is too costly for a polluter to undertake abatement alone. By *cost-sharing*, here we mean cooperative interaction between polluters and sufferers to determine a joint outcome, including mutually acceptable pollution emissions, expenditure for abatement, and arrangements among the participants to finance abatement costs. Of course, to be voluntarily adopted, such joint decision-making must lead to a situation in which all participants are better off compared to a status quo. The status quo may be a pollution standard that must be met. Thus, there may be a role for government to define the status quo even when the final outcome is determined through cooperative bargaining.

Sufferers can be made better off with cost-sharing for pollution abatement if the resulting quality is better than the standard. Polluters can become better off if their cost shares are less than in a noncooperative solution. The possibility of such an outcome was demonstrated by Loehman and Dinar, 1994.

In contrast, real world use of the term *cost-sharing* is rather non-interactive. It can refer to formula allocation of costs among government entities (e.g. Army Corps and state and local governments for water projects) or to pre-set government subsidies of pollution reduction (e.g. USDA payments for wetland restoration and buffer strips).

The externality/cost-sharing situation of this paper assumes that the participants involved in an externality desire to find a joint (cooperative) solution. It is a coordination problem because the externality-producing activity under the control of one party affects the other participants, and participants have limited information about each other's values and constraints. The cost of pollution abatement must be covered within the system of participants, and the participants may differ in their values and abilities to pay. A priori, it is desirable that any outcome be socially efficient, individually rational, and fair.

To this end, this paper develops an informationally decentralized method to address cost-sharing for pollution abatement. There are three reasons for decentralization: maintaining privacy of information, reducing information and coordination costs (for example, participants may not be located in such a way to make direct communication easy), and computation. Following Davis and Whinston (1966), the method uses a message exchange process to find an equilibrium outcome solving the joint problem. The computational method is based on price response -- with appropriate price adjustment rules -- to facilitate solving the joint decision problem.

The coordination process is an algorithmic method of solving the group decision problem. It is a set of rules, including iterative procedures, pricing, and allocation rules. A group desiring to solve an externality problem in a cooperative cost-sharing framework may agree to use the coordination process as a form of group decision support

This paper demonstrates a three-step design paradigm for a coordination process; the steps are:

1) describe Pareto optimality (the joint decision problem) and corresponding social efficiency requirements;
2) define a cost share instrument and corresponding decentralized equilibrium that satisfies efficiency requirements;
3) develop an iterative process using the cost share instrument.

The cost share instrument is defined in such a way that any equilibrium for the iterative process will solve the decision problem.

Using Pareto optimality to as a benchmark for equilibrium parallels the First Theorem of welfare economics. It is more general than Davis and Whinston's joint maximization of profits as a benchmark for firms involved in an externality. (Loehman, 2001, applied this paradigm to address a simpler local public goods problem.)

Below, we describe an externality situation such that polluter(s) and sufferer(s) jointly determine the level of pollution, abatement, and finance of abatement cost. A combination of policy instruments -- tax, transfer payment, and cost-sharing -- is used to solve the joint decision problem. The basis for the combined policy is the concept of cost share equilibrium (Mas-Colell and Silvestre, 1989), originally defined for public goods and here applied to an externality.

2. EXTERNALITY SITUATION

For the rest of the paper, we use an example situation to demonstrate the design paradigm. The situation involves pollution associated with food production that affects both farmers and consumers. We show that cooperation can achieve a better outcome than non-cooperation.

Nitrogen from fertilizer used to produce food is an important source of water pollution when excess -- not taken up by plants -- is carried by runoff into streams. Installing buffer strips between fields and streams has been shown to be highly effective in reducing pollution, because vegetation in the buffer takes up excess nitrogen; other local benefits (reduced soil erosion, wildlife habitat, improved stream ecology) are also provided.

Besides direct loss of net revenue from crops, establishing buffers has economic costs for the farmer for land treatment (such as for specialized plantings). To provide incentives for buffer adoption, there are several government programs offering published payment rates for establishment cost and annual rental to offset loss of crop returns. For example, the Conservation Reserve Program will pay at least 50% of the establishment costs for 10 to15 year contracts; the Wetland Reserve Program will pay 50-75% for thirty-year easements. Farmers apply to the USDA Natural Resources Conservation Service to propose their land for enrollment and may be accepted into the program. Criticisms (e.g. lack of targeting) have led to establishment of the Conservation Reserve Enhancement Program. The CREP program allows states to target watersheds in need of significant improvement and increase the incentives offered from state resources.

Potentially, state or local areas may wish to enhance buffers beyond federal guidelines, e.g. in terms of buffer size, location, and vegetation, thus entailing a greater cost of adoption at the farm. To identify appropriate and feasible incentives, local entities (farmers and beneficiaries of water quality improvements) could work together cooperatively for program development. Individualized arrangements could emerge with tailored cost-sharing packages. The mathematical description of the rest of this paper applies to how such arrangements could be worked out.

2.1 Economic Model

A partial economy consists of a farmer (f) and a consumer (c). Both like water quality Q that is degraded by nitrogen fertilizer N used to grow food. The farmer produces food F^s using inputs N and L. The farmer consumes some of his own food (F_f), and sells the rest (F_c) to the consumer. Each consumes a *numeraire* good x_f, x_c (representing all other goods besides F, Q, N and L) with price $p_x = 1$. We take the price (p_N) of nitrogen as being exogenous. The price of fertilizer and abatement cost are expressed relative to the *numeraire* good. The price of food is endogenous. Each has initial endowments M_f, M_c of the *numeraire* good used to purchase food and inputs and pay cost shares for abatement.

2.1.1 Cost of Pollution Abatement

The farmer is assumed to be the agent for improving water quality. Two relationships are combined to define a cost function $C(N,Q)$ for abatement cost for a given nitrogen use to achieve a desired environmental quality Q:

$c(N, r)$: The cost of removing nitrogen runoff increases in N and removal rate r.

$Q = g(N(1-r))$: The non-removed pollution causes a deterioration in water quality; $g'(.) < 0$.

To obtain the combined relationship $C(N,Q)$, we solve implicitly for r in terms of N and Q from the second relationship and substitute for r in $c(N, r)$. "No abatement" is represented by $C(Q, N) \equiv 0$ and $Q = g(N)$.

2.1.2 Farmer model

$U^f = U^f(x_f, F_f, Q)$: The utility function for the farmer based on all other goods, food, and environmental quality.

$F^s = f(L, N)$: The production function for food with nitrogen N and other inputs L.

$L \le \bar{L}$: There is a limit on input use (e.g. land).

$x_f + p_F F_f + p_N N + C(Q,N) \le M_f + p_F F^s$:
The budget constraint for the farmer in terms of the *numeraire*.

2.1.3 Consumer model

For the base case, Q is exogenous for the consumer.

$U^c = U^c\,(x_c, F_c, Q)$: The utility function for the consumer.

$x_c + p_F F_c \le M^c$: The budget constraint for the consumer.

2.2 Pareto Optimality

The Pareto optimality (or coordination) problem for the farmer-consumer economy is to determine a socially efficient allocation of outputs (food, environmental quality, and other goods) between the consumer and farmer sectors and allocate inputs for production of the outputs subject to constraints. The constraints include: feasibility relative to the combined budget constraint; production; input resource limits; and supply-demand balance. A socially efficient allocation is determined by Negishi weights α_f, α_c on utility for the farmer and consumer respectively.

$$\max_{N,Q,x_i,F_i,F^s,L} \quad \alpha_f U^f\,(x_f, F_f, Q) + \alpha_c\, U^c\,(x_c, F_c, Q)$$

s.t.

$$x_f + x_c + p_N N + C(Q, N) \le M_f + M_c$$

$$F^s \le f\,(L, N)$$

$$L \le \bar{L}$$

$$F_f + F_c \le F^s$$

For any given set of Negishi weights, an allocation satisfying first order (Lagrangian) conditions -- assuming concave utility, diminishing returns for inputs in production, and convex cost -- solves the optimality problem. For concave utility, diminishing returns for inputs in production, and convex cost, a Pareto optimum solution will exist (Takayama, 1985).

From first order conditions, optimality conditions for environmental quality and nitrogen use can be derived. These conditions have the same form for any choice of Negishi weights. (See Appendix 1 for details.) The optimality condition for Q corresponds to the well-known Samuelson condition for public goods: the sum of marginal rates of substitution between Q and the *numeraire* good should be equal to marginal cost of pollution abatement:

$$\frac{U_Q^f}{U_x^f}+\frac{U_Q^c}{U_x^c}=C_Q(Q,N)$$

For the optimality condition for nitrogen N, the value of the marginal product (marginal product f_N times the value of food F relative to the *numeraire*) should be equal to the total social cost of the input -- the price of N *plus* the marginal externality cost (MEC) due to N.

$$\underbrace{\frac{\lambda_2}{\lambda_1}f_N}_{VMP} = \underbrace{p_N}_{price} + \underbrace{C_N(Q,N)}_{MEC}\ .$$

2.3 Technical Efficiency with and without Pollution Abatement

As in the classical (non-externality) case, technical efficiency is necessary for Pareto optimality. That is, if an outcome is not on the technical efficiency frontier (boundary of the constraint set), it cannot be socially optimal. Technical efficiency is a vector maximization problem: at an efficient point, no output could be further increased without reducing another output. Given any prices for outputs, we can locate the corresponding efficient point (Takayama, 1985); constraints are the production functions and resource constraints.

With abatement, the vector maximization problem (I) is:

$$\text{Max}\quad (Q,\ x,\ F^S)$$

$$\begin{aligned} s.t.\qquad & Q \le g(N(1-r)) \\ & F^S \le f(N,L) \\ & x + p_N N + C(N,r) \le M \\ & L \le \bar{L} \end{aligned}$$

(x denotes the total output for the *numeraire* good. Without abatement, the vector maximization problem (II) has abatement cost and removal rate r constrained to be zero:

$$\text{Max} \quad (Q,\ x,\ F^s)$$

$$s.t. \qquad Q \le g(N)$$

$$F^s \le f(N, L)$$

$$x + p_N N \le M$$

$$L \le \bar{L}$$

Comparing (I) and (II), it is clear that any solution for (II) is feasible for (I) but may not be optimal. (Note that here may be output prices that give zero abatement as an efficient solution!)

3. A DECENTRALIZED EQUILIBRIUM WITH TAX, TRANSFER PAYMENT, AND COST-SHARING

Analogous to the First Theorem of welfare economics, we seek a decentralized exchange setting that has an equilibrium satisfying Pareto optimality (social efficiency). A policy will be called *satisfactory* if a resulting equilibrium outcome satisfies Pareto optimality. From the argument above, a policy that does not explicitly include covering abatement cost may not be satisfactory. For example, a tax on nitrogen without cost-sharing may not achieve a technically efficient outcome.

A satisfactory policy solution to the externality problem is described below. This policy solution combines three tools: a tax on N, a transfer payment on Q (which may be a tax or subsidy), and cost-sharing. It may be surprising that more than one of these policy tools should be necessary. In fact, cost-sharing alone without transfer prices is not satisfactory (see Appendix 1). Below, we explain the rationale for the policy combination in terms of the *cost share equilibrium.*

As defined by Mas-Colell and Silvestre (MCS), the cost share equilibrium is an outcome such that each participant cannot be made better off by any other level of the jointly chosen good for the given cost share system $T = \{T_1. T_2, \ldots. T_n\}$ such that the sum of cost shares for each participant T_i equals cost for the jointly chosen good (Weber and Wiesmeth, 1991; Mas-

Colell and Silvestre, 1989). For the *linear cost share system,* the personalized charge T_i is linear in personalized prices and share parameters s_i (Mas-Colell and Silvestre, 1991). With multiple shared goods, there are personalized prices for each participant for each good.

For the situation here, a *cost-sharing system* $T = \{T_1. T_2, \ldots T_n\}$ is a set of personalized charge functions (continuous and increasing) defined on Q and N, one for each farmer or consumer participant, such that the sum of personalized charges equals the cost of abatement:

$$\Sigma_i\, T_i(Q, N) = C(Q, N) \text{ for } N, Q > 0$$

and $T_i(0,0) = 0$. For the linear cost share system, personalized prices for the two goods Q and N are respectively denoted by $p_Q^{\,i}$ and $t_N^{\,i}$. The personalized charge function has the form:

$$T_i(Q, N; s_i, p_Q^{\,i}, t_N^{\,i}) = s_i\, C(Q) + p_Q^{\,i}\, Q + t_N^{\,i} N.$$

Balancing conditions necessary for optimality are that: $p_Q^{\,i}$ and $t_N^{\,i}$ should each sum to zero and s_i should sum to one. A *cost share equilibrium* based on T is a feasible state vector $(x^*, Q^*, F^*, N^*, F^{s*})$ that is preferred by all participants to all other feasible allocations under the cost-sharing system T.

MCS (Proposition 1, 1989) prove that for increasing utilities and increasing cost, any cost share equilibrium yields an optimal state. An alternative proof that the cost share equilibrium is optimal compares the quasi-saddle point (first order) conditions for the cost share equilibrium with the first order conditions (FOC) for the Pareto optimality problem. (See Appendix 1.) If the underlying utility and production functions are concave and cost is convex (Takayama, 1985), since the form of the FOC is the same for the two problems, a cost share equilibrium will provide a Pareto optimal solution.

One criticism (MCS, 1989) of the cost share equilibrium is that each agent would have to know the cost function in order to locate any equilibrium. However, for the coordination process below, only the coordinator has to know the cost function, and she presents group members with proposed personalized charge schedules that add up to total cost for any Q, N. (The coordinator's role could be carried out by a computer network and algorithm with the appropriate rules.)

3.1 Marginal Willingness to Pay

For the sake of interpretation, equilibrium conditions can be conveniently expressed in terms of the *marginal willingness to pay.* Define $MWTP^i_{Qx}$ for a given Q and x_i to be the marginal rate of substitution between shared and private goods for a group member:

$$MWTP^i_{Qx}(x_i, F_i, Q) \equiv \frac{U^i_Q(x_i, F_i, Q)}{U^i_x(x_i, F_i, Q)}.$$

At a given Q, F_i, cost shares, and corresponding x_i, marginal willingness to pay is approximately equal to the maximum that would be paid to increase Q to the next higher level with the given cost share system:

$$U^i(x_i - MWTP^i_{Qx}, F_i, Q + \Delta Q) \approx U^i(x_i, F_i, Q).$$

Then, an interior LCSE will satisfy the following condition for each group member (see Appendix 1):

$$MWTP^i_{Qx}(x_i, F_i, Q) = s_i C_Q(Q, N) + p^i_Q.$$

Thus, given personalized prices and share parameters satisfying the balancing conditions, the Samuelson condition is satisfied by an interior LCSE. The balancing conditions also imply that the optimality condition for the externality good N is satisfied (see Appendix 1).

3.2 Full Information Equilibrium Solution

Given the concept of a cost share equilibrium, the question is how such an equilibrium could be found in a real application: that is, how could cost share parameters, personalized prices, food prices, and other market prices be determined such that all participants unanimously agree to the level of externality and abatement cost, their cost shares, and related markets clear.

The following programming problem gives a method of finding an equilibrium solution for specified share parameters $\{s_i\}$. It includes as constraints all the first order conditions for the decentralized cost share equilibrium and budget conditions; see Appendix 1. (To simplify, we include only the nitrogen input in the following.)

$$\underset{p_Q, t_N, l, Q, N, F^s, F, x}{Min} \ \Sigma\, l_i^2$$

$$MWTP^i_{Qx} - s_i C_Q + p^i_Q = 0;$$

$$p_F f_N - p_n - s_f C_N - t^f_N = 0;$$

$$- s_c C_N - t^c_N = 0;$$

$$F^S = f(N);$$

$$F^S = \Sigma F_i;$$

$$\Sigma p^i_Q = 0;$$

$$\Sigma t^i_N = 0;$$

$$MWTP^i_{Fx} = p_f;$$

$$x_f + p_F F_f + p_N N - p_F F^S + s_f C(Q,N) + t^f_N N - p^f_Q Q + l_f = M_f;$$

$$x_c + p_F F_c + s_c C(Q,N) + t^c_N N - p^c_Q Q + l_c = M_c;$$

$$\Sigma l_i = 0.$$

The slack variables l_i for the budget constraints must sum to zero for feasibility. The objective function of minimizing the sum of squares allows for the possibility of zero slack variables. If the programming problem solution has these slack variables at exactly zero, then all conditions for an LCSE are satisfied; otherwise lump sum transfer payments would be needed.

This setup clarifies the role of the personalized prices and why both sets of prices p_Q^i and t_N^i are needed: these prices serve as slack variables, making it possible to find a solution. A solution with transfer payments p_Q^i all zero may not be possible.

Here, the use of taxes and subsidies is not a moral issue (e.g. "the polluter pays" principle) but a computational issue. Note that the first order condition for t_N^c implies that it is negative, and hence t_N^f is positive; thus t_N^f is a tax on nitrogen use by the farmer received by the consumer. The transfer payment p_Q^f for the farmer can be positive or negative depending on the cost share parameters. A negative p_Q^f for the farmer means there is a positive payment from the consumer to the farmer (a subsidy) for producing Q; this outcome is associated with a low consumer cost share parameter.

Conversely, a high consumer cost share can be associated with a positive p_Q^f paid by farmer and received by the consumer.

Table 2 shows solutions of the full information system obtained for several sets of cost share parameters $\{s_i\}$. We use one farmer and two consumers for this simulation, and take the price p_N to be exogenous. Empirical forms for utility, cost, and production functions are shown in Appendix 2. Since we employ nonlinear utility functions, the level of Q varies as the share parameters vary. (Many theorists use quasi-linear utility; then the solution will not vary with income.)

The solution of this problem (Q, N, prices, etc.) does not exhibit much variation as the cost share parameters are varied. Evidently, the range of possible equilibrium outcomes is relatively small. For the utility function specification, the implied Negishi weights for the Pareto optimality problem are approximately the relative shares $x_i / \Sigma x_i$.

A higher cost share for the farmer is accompanied by a higher equilibrium subsidy. The farmer is actually best off paying the full cost of abatement with a very high subsidy per unit Q produced and no tax on N! Conversely, the consumers are best off by paying the largest share (here 90%) of the cost of abatement and receiving payment for Q.

Table 1 shows a base case with no cooperation: the farmer pays the full cost of abatement, and personalized prices on Q and N are not used. In comparison, cost-sharing equilibria have about three times larger abatement cost and less than half as much N; the resulting level of Q is about 7 times greater. For a bargaining solution, any cost share equilibrium with a cost share parameter of at least 0.20 for the farmer would be individually rational, since all participants are better off than in the base case.

Table 1. Base Case

Shares	
s_f	1.0
s_{c_1}	0.0
s_{c_2}	0.0
Allocation	
Q	1.47
N	170.19
F^s	118.83
F_f	54.43
F_{c_1}	53.4
F_{c_2}	22.11
C	60.02
U^f	13.35

Shares	
U^{c_1}	21.50
U^{c_2}	11.63
Prices	
p_f	3.0

Table 2. Equilibrium for Different Cost Shares

Shares						
s_f	.10	.20	.33	.5	.8	1.0
s_{c_1}	.45	.40	.34	.25	.1	0.0
s_{c_2}	.45	.40	.33	.25	.1	0.0
Allocation						
Q	8.16	8.13	8.08	8.02	7.92	7.85
N	69.2	69.5	69.94	70.41	71.32	71.94
F^s	91.51	91.62	91.77	91.95	92.29	92.51
F_f	34.09	34.71	35.52	36.58	39.76	38.49
F_{c_1}	42.87	41.58	41.24	40.69	39.80	39.19
F_{c_2}	15.55	15.33	15.03	14.67	13.99	13.53
C	171.8	171.5	170.9	170.34	169.17	168.38
U^f	13.30	13.35	13.41	13.48	13.62	13.70
U^{c_1}	22.94	22.90	22.85	22.77	22.63	22.54
U^{c_2}	13.26	13.21	13.15	13.06	12.79	12.91
Prices						
p_f	3.02	3.02	3.015	3.01	3.00	2.99
t_N^f	0.74	0.66	0.55	0.41	0.16	0.
$t_N^{c_1}$	-0.37	-0.33	-0.28	-0.20	-0.08	0.
$t_N^{c_2}$	-0.37	-0.33	-0.27	-0.20	-0.08	0.
$-p_Q^f$	-3.95	-2.23	0 .01	2.96	8.20	11.73
$-p_Q^{c_1}$	1.17	0.30	-0.76	-2.34	-5.01	-6.81
$-p_Q^{c_2}$	2.78	1.94	0.75	-0.62	-3.19	-4.92
Implied Negishi Weights						
α_f	0.482	0.487	0.495	0.507	0.527	0.541
α_{c_1}	0.292	0.290	0.287	0.275	0.272	0.266
α_{c2}	0.227	0.223	0.218	0.216	0.200	0.193

4. MECHANISM DESIGN AND COORDINATION PROCESS FOR THE COST-SHARING SITUATION

The design of a coordination process for pollution reduction can be based on principles of mechanism design (Hurwicz, 1994) and organizational design (Reiter, 1995). Both literatures have focused on decentralization of information.

According to mechanism design principles, an institution is viewed as a game with allocation rules, and allocation rules become a variable of the design problem (Hurwicz, 1973). Players' strategies in terms of messages are influenced by the allocation rules. Allocation rules and behavior together determine a mapping from the message space to a social outcome. Allocation rules are selected on the basis of desirability of the resulting social outcomes.

Reiter (1995) defines an organization to consist of "(i) an algorithm for computing the decision rule, and (ii) an assignment to individual agents of the steps required to execute the algorithm". Following Reiter, a coordination process is an iterative decentralized message procedure based on an algorithm that solves the joint decision problem.

4.1 Coordination Process

Below coordination to find a group solution is achieved through a price adjustment process that locates a cost share equilibrium. For this process, personalized prices serve as *local controllers* to guide the voluntary decisions of individuals toward a unanimous group outcome about the environmental quality level, abatement cost, and cost-sharing. (See Loehman, 2001, for background and general description of a coordination process. Findeisen, W., F. N. Bailey, M. Brdys, K. Malinowski, P. Tatjewski, A. Wozniak, 1980, describe local controllers in an engineering context.)

For the process, cost share parameters s_i are exogenous while the personalized prices and price of food (p_F) are endogenous. (Price of fertilizer is also exogenous.) The process starts with initial cost shares s_i and zero prices. At equilibrium, the resulting equilibrium shares are $T_i/\Sigma T_i$.

For each iteration, each group member is given a personalized charge schedule, based on current personalized prices and current p_F. The iterative steps to find an equilibrium are as follows:

1. Given the cost share schedule, the farmer chooses N, F^s, and F_f and her proposed Q^f.
For these choices, the farmer also presents bids $MWTP^f_{Qx}$ and $MWTP^f_{Fx}$ for additional Q and F respectively.

2. Given the cost share schedule, the consumer chooses his proposed Q^c and F_c.
For these choices, the consumer also presents bids $MWTP^c_{Qx}$ and $MWTP^c_{Fx}$.

3. The Q proposals are averaged.

4. The coordinator computes new personalized prices as follows, where the functions are evaluated at the current N and average Q:

$$t^f_N = -s_f C_N + p_F f_N - p_n;$$

$$t^c_N = -s_c C_N;$$

$$p^i_Q = -MWTP^i_{Qx} + s_i C_Q.$$

The personalized prices are then normalized to sum to zero.

5. The price of food is computed as the weighted average of bids for food, weighted by the relative shares of food.

$$p_f = \Sigma MWTP^i_{Fx}\ (F_i / F^s).$$

The process repeats until the proposals for Q are the same, and all prices are no longer changing.

Step 5 is an alternative to a *tatonnement* rule that specifies price changing in proportion to excess demand, with a specified speed of adjustment. A *tatonnement* rule could be unstable unless a good speed of adjustment can be determined, a problem in itself. For the averaging rule here -- when demands for food and this condition are satisfied at the same price, then the supply-demand balance for food will also be satisfied. (Note that the averaging rules for Q and price of food may ameliorate any misrepresentation of bids.)

The adjustment rules for personalized prices in Step 4 are directly from the first order conditions for the cost share equilibrium. Note that the condition for the tax on fertilizer for the farmer looks like the traditional definition of the Pigouvian tax: the farmer is charged the difference between the value of the marginal product of nitrogen and its social costs. However here this tax formula is used in an iterative setting. (In contrast, the Pigouvian tax is computed at the social optimum, assuming that all the requisite information to determine the optimum is available to a social planner.)

Table 3 demonstrates the adjustment process for share parameters (.5, .25, .25). Although the process took 15 iterations to converge in the third decimal place, by iteration 11 the outcomes were stable and the same as the equilibrium outcome in the first two decimal places. This performance is quite spectacular, considering that there are seven prices and nine allocations to determine for the equilibrium!

There could be alternative rules for a coordination process, e.g. varying the message space and related adjustment rules, and different rules could interact differently with behavioral strategies. Smith (1980, 1989) proposed and demonstrated the usefulness of experimental economics as a tool to compare alternative institutions. Experimental economics testing to determine efficacious rules should be added as a fourth step for the design paradigm of this paper.

Table 3. Coordination Process (15 iterations to equilibrium) Shares (.5, .25, .25)

Iteration	**2**	**5**	**8**	**11**	**13**	**15**
Q avg.	5.67	7.76	7.98	8.02	8.02	8.023
Q_1	4.52	7.94	8.01	8.021	8.024	8.023
Q_2	6.59	7.55	7.96	8.015	8.021	8.023
Q_3	7.05	7.63	7.97	8.016	8.021	8.022
p_f	2.54	2.92	2.99	3.01	3.01	3.01
t_N^f	0.1955	0.3686	0.4001	0.4049	0.4054	0.4056
$t_N^{c_1}$	-0.0978	-0.1843	-0.2000	-0.2025	-0.2027	-0.2028
$t_N^{c_2}$	-0.0978	-0.1843	-0.2000	-0.2025	-0.2027	-0.2028
$-p_Q^f$	3.5078	3.1278	2.9871	2.9610	2.9589	2.9582
$-p_Q^{c_1}$	-3.0069	-2.4704	-2.3636	-2.3448	-2.3433	-2.3428
$-p_Q^{c_2}$	-0.5009	-0.6574	-0.6235	-0.6161	-0.6157	-0.6154

5. CONCLUSIONS

A coordination process is an algorithmic method to address a group decision problem through decentralized messages. This concept was demonstrated here for a joint solution for an externality situation with cost-sharing for abatement costs to ameliorate the externality. The process has characteristics similar to a decentralized market, namely price-taking behavior, privacy of individual preference information, individual rationality, and use of price as an equilibrating tool.

In general, processes based on price adjustment have great potential for solving complex group decision problems. A numerical simulation was given to show that a price adjustment process can solve the coordination problem in a relatively few steps. The numerical tractability of the problem is important for reasons of transactions costs. To alleviate information, geographical proximity, and group size limitations of group interaction, a coordination process can be operated on a computer network.

Incentive problems are a major concern in much of economic literature. Admittedly, incentive problems could reduce the efficacy of a coordination process for real applications. Simulation of a similar process for public goods showed that it was robust for certain kinds of misrepresentation (Loehman, 2001). Experimental economics testing compared alternative adjustment processes for a public good with a group size of three; results with price adjustment processes were 62-72% efficient in terms of the output level determined by the group (depending on the information rules of the process) even with some misrepresentation (Loehman et al, 2001).

REFERENCES

Baumol, W.J. and Oates, W.E. (1990). *The Theory of Environmental Policy.* Cambridge University Press.

Buchanan, J. M. (1969). *The Demand and Supply of Public Goods.* Rand McNally..

Buchanan, J. M. (1969). External Diseconomies, Corrective Taxes, and Market Structure. *American Economic Review* 59(1), 174-177.

Coase, R. (1960). The Problem of Social Cost. *Journal of Law and Economics* 3, 1-31.

Davis, O.A. and Whinston, A.B. (1962). Externalities, Welfare, and the Theory of Games. *Journal of Political Economics* 70(3), 241-262.

Davis, O.A. and Whinston, A.B. (1966). On Externalities, Information, and the Government-Assisted Invisible Hand. *Economica*_63(131), 303-318.

Findeisen, W., Bailey, F. N., Brdys, M., Malinowski, K., Tatjewski, P., Wozniak, A. (1980). *Control and Coordination in Hierarchical Systems*_ John Wiley and Sons, Chichester.

Ferrar, T.A. and Whinston, A.B. (1972). Taxation and Water Pollution Control. *Natural Resources Journal* 12(3), 307-17.

Graves, G.W., Hatfield, G.B., Whinston, A.B , (1969). Water Pollution Control using By-pass Piping. *Water Resources Research* 5(1), 13-47.

Graves. G. W., Hatfield, G. B., Whinston, A.B., (1972). Mathematical Programming for Regional Water Quality Management. *Water Resources Research* 8(2), 273-90.

Hurwicz, L (1972). Organizational Structures for Joint Decision Making: A Designer's Point of View. in *Interorganizational Decision Making.* ed., M. Tuite, R. Chisholm, and M. Radnor, Aldine Publishing Co., Chicago.

Hurwicz, L. (1973). The Design of Mechanisms for Resource Allocation. *American Economic Review* 63, 1-30.

Hurwicz, L. (1980). On Information Decentralization and Efficiency in Resource Allocation Mechanisms. in *Studies in Mathematical Economics*, ed. Stanley Reiter. Wiley Publishing Co., New York.

Hurwicz, L. (1994). Economic Design, Adjustment Processes, Mechanisms, and Institutions. *Economic Design* 1, 1-14.

Hurwicz, L. (1999). Revisiting Externalities. *J. of Public Economic Theory* 1(2), 225-45.

Hurwicz L. and Marshak, T. (2000). Comparing Finite Mechanisms with an Application to Exchange Economies. presented at NBER Decentralization Conference, St. Louis, April.

Luce, R. D. and Raiffa, H. (1957). *Games and Decisions.* John Wiley.

Loehman, E.T., and Whinston, A.B. (1970). The Welfare Economics of Water Resource Allocation Over Time. *Applied Economics* 2(2): 75-99.

Loehman, E.T., and Whinston, A.B. (1971). A New Theory of Pricing and Decision-Making for Public Investments. *Bell Journal of Economics and Management Science* 2(2): 606-625.

Loehman, E.T., and Whinston. A.B. (1974). Axiomatic Approach to Cost Allocation for Public Investment, *Public Finance Quarterly* 2(2): 236-250.

Loehman, E.T., Pingry, D. and Whinston, A.B. (1974). Cost Allocation for a Regional Pollution Treatment System, *Economics and Decision-Making for Environmental Quality*, ed. J.R. Connor and E.T. Loehman, Gainesville: University of Florida Press, pages 223-250.

Loehman, E.T., and Whinston, A.B. (1976). A Generalized Cost Allocation Scheme, *Theory and Measurement of Economic Externalities*, ed. Steven Lin, New York: Academic Press, pages 87-101.

Loehman, E.T., Orlando, J., Tschirhart, J. and Whinston, A.B. (1979). Cost Allocation for a Regional Wastewater Treatment System. *Water Resources Research Journal* 15(2): 193-202.

Loehman, E. T. and Dinar, A. (1994). Cooperative Solutions to Externality Problems: The Case of Irrigation Water. *J. of Environmental and Economic Management* 26, 235-256.

Loehman, E. T. (1995). Cooperative Solutions for Problems of Water Supply. in *Water Quantity/Quality Management and Conflict Resolution*, eds. A. Dinar and E. Loehman, Greenwood Press.

Loehman, E.T. (1998). Cooperation in Pollution Reduction: Design of a Policy Instrument. Chap 11 in *Designing Institutions for Environmental and Resource Management,* eds. E.Loehman and D. Marc Kilgour. Elgar Pub., Northampton, MA, pp 180-198.

Loehman, E. T. (2001). Cost Share Adjustment Processes for Group Decisions about Local Public Goods. Manuscript, Dept. of Ag. Econ., Purdue University.

Loehman, E.T., Kiser, R. and Rassenti, S. J. (2001). Cost Share Adjustment Processes for Local Public Goods: Exploring Alternative Institutions. Manuscript, Dept. of Ag. Econ., Purdue University.

Mas-Colell, A. and Silvestre, J. (1989). Cost Share Equilibria: A Lindahlian Approach. *J. of Economic Theory* 47, 239-256.

Mas-Colell, A. and Silvestre, J. (1991). A Note on Cost-Share Equilibrium and Owner-Consumers. *J. of Economic Theory* 54, 204-214.

Moore, J.C., Richmond, W.B., Whinston, A.B. (1994). Economic Decision Theory as a Paradigm for the Construction and Evaluation of Algorithms and Information Systems. in *New Directions in Computational Economics.* Advances in Computational Economics, vol. 4, Kluwer Academic Press.

Reiter, S. (1995). Coordination and the Structure of Firms. manuscript, Northwestern University.

Smith, V. L. (1980). Experiments with a Decentralized Mechanism for Public Good Decisions. *American Economic Review* 70, 584-599.

Smith, V. L. (1989). Theory, Experiment, and Economics. *J. of Economic Perspectives* 3, 151-169.Stahl, D.O. and Whinston, A. B. (1994). A General Economic Equilibrium Model of Distributed Computing. in *New Directions in Computational Economics*. Advances in Computational Economics, vol. 4, Kluwer Academic Press.

Stavins, R. N. (2000). *Economics of the Environment*, W.W. Norton.

Takayama, A. (1985). *Mathematical Economics*, Cambridge Press.

Weber, S. and Wiesmeth, H. (1991). The Equivalence of Core and Cost Share Equilibria in an Economy with a Public Good, *J. of Economic Theory* 54, 180-197.

Wellisz, S. (1964). On External Diseconomies and the Government-Assisted Invisible Hand, *Economica*, November, 3346-362.

Whinston, A. B. (1964). Price Guides in Decentralized Organizations, in *New Perspectives in Organization Research*, eds. W.W. Cooper, H. J. Leavitt, H. W. Shelly, John Wiley.

Whitcomb, D. K. (1972). *Externalities and Welfare.* Columbia Press.

APPENDIX 1: FIRST ORDER CONDITIONS FOR PARETO OPTIMALITY AND DECENTRALIZED EQUILIBRIA

A1.0 Pareto optimality problem

$$\max_{N,Q,x_i,F_i,F^s,L} \alpha_f U^f(x_f, F_f, Q) + \alpha_c U^c(x_c, F_c, Q)$$

s.t.

$$x_f + x_c + p_N N + C(Q, N) \le M_f + M_c \quad (\lambda_1) \qquad (1)$$

$$F^s \le f(L, N) \quad (\lambda_2) \qquad (2)$$

$$L \le \overline{L} \quad (\lambda_3) \qquad (3)$$

$$F_f + F_c \le F^s \quad (\lambda_5) \qquad (4)$$

First order conditions (FOC):

$$L_x^p: \ \alpha_f U_x^f - \lambda_1 = 0 \qquad (5)$$

$$L_Q^p: \ \alpha_f U_Q^f + \alpha_c U_Q^c - \lambda_1 C_Q(Q, N) = 0 \qquad (6)$$

$$L_N^p: \ -\lambda_1 C_N(Q, N) + \lambda_2 f_N - \lambda_1 p_N = 0 \qquad (7)$$

$$L_{F^s}^p: \ -\lambda_2 + \lambda_5 = 0 \qquad (8)$$

$$L_{F_f}^p: \ \alpha_f U_F^f - \lambda_5 = 0 \qquad (9)$$

$$L_x^p: \ \alpha_c U_x^c - \lambda_1 = 0 \qquad (10)$$

$$L_L^p: \ \lambda_2 f_L - \lambda_3 = 0 \qquad (11)$$

$$L_{F_c}^p: \ \alpha_c U_F^c - \lambda_5 = 0 \qquad (12)$$

A2.0 Decentralized Exchange Equilibrium (DEE) with Cost-sharing, a Tax on N, and a Transfer Payment on Q.

Exogenous cost shares s_f and s_c must sum to one. This policy is satisfactory.

Farmer's Problem

$$\underset{x_f,\, F_f,\, Q,\, L,\, F^s,\, N}{\text{Max}} \quad U^f\left(x_f, F_f, Q\right)$$

s.t.

$$x_f + p_F F_f + p_N N + s_f C(Q,N) + t_N^f N + p_Q^f Q \leq M^f + p_f F^s \quad (\mu_f) \qquad (13)$$

$$F^s \leq f\left(L_f, N\right) \qquad (\lambda_2) \qquad (14)$$

$$L_f \leq \overline{L} \qquad (\lambda_3) \qquad (15)$$

Consumer's Problem

$$\underset{x_c,\, F_c,\, N,\, Q}{\text{Max}} \quad U^c\left(x_c, F_c, Q\right)$$

s.t.

$$x_c + s_c C(Q,N) + t_N^c N + p_Q^c Q + p_F F^c \leq M^c \qquad (\mu_c) \qquad (16)$$

Equilibrium conditions:

$$p_F\left[F^s - \left(F_c + F_f\right)\right] = 0;$$

$$\Sigma p_Q^i = 0;$$

$$\Sigma t_N^i = 0.$$

First Order Conditions:

If s_i are exogenous, we can solve for the personalized prices from the following system plus equilibrium conditions:

$$L_x^f:\ U_x^f - \mu_f = 0 \tag{17}$$

$$L_Q^f:\ U_Q^f - \mu_f s_f C_Q(Q,N) - \mu_f p_Q^f = 0 \tag{18}$$

$$L_N^f:\ -s_f C_N(Q,N) - t_N^f + \frac{\lambda_2}{\mu_f} f_N - p_N = 0 \tag{19}$$

$$L_F^f:\ U_F^f - \mu_f p_F = 0 \tag{20}$$

$$L_{F^s}^f:\quad p_F - \lambda_2 = 0 \tag{21}$$

$$L_L^f:\ \lambda_2 f_L - \lambda_3 = 0 \tag{22}$$

$$L_x^c:\ U_x^c - \mu_c = 0 \tag{23}$$

$$L_F^c:\ U_F^c - \mu_c p_f = 0 \tag{24}$$

$$L_Q^c:\quad U_Q^c - \mu_c s_c C_Q(Q,N) - \mu_c p_Q^c = 0 \tag{25}$$

$$L_N^c:\ -\mu_c s_c C_N(Q,N) - \mu_c t_N^c = 0 \tag{26}$$

The Pareto optimality condition for Q is satisfied:

$$\frac{U_Q^f}{U_x^f} + \frac{U_Q^c}{U_x^c} = (s_f + s_c) C_Q(Q,N) = C_Q(Q,N)$$

The Pareto optimality condition for N is satisfied:

From

$$-s_f C_N(Q,N) - t_N^f + \frac{\lambda_2}{\mu_f} f_N - p_N = 0,$$

and

$$-s_c C_N(Q,N) - t_N^c = 0,$$

we obtain

$$\frac{\lambda_2}{\mu_f} f_N = C_N(Q,N) + p_N$$

Note that $t_N^c < 0$ if $s_c > 0$, so that $t_N^f > 0$ is implied. Thus t_N^f is a tax for the farmer while t_N^c is received as compensation per unit of nitrogen for the consumer. However, no signs are implied for p_Q^i; p_Q^i may be positive or negative depending on the shares s_i. If $p_Q^f < 0$, then $p_Q^c > 0$ which implies that the consumer pays the farmer for Q, as for any other commodity!

A3.0 Base Case: The Farmer is Solely Responsible for Pollution Abatement

This policy is not satisfactory in terms of achieving Pareto optimality.

Farmer's Problem

$$\underset{x_f, F^s, F_f, Q, L, N}{\text{Max}} U^f(x_f, F_f, Q)$$

$$\text{s.t. } x_f + p_f F_f + p_N N + C(Q, N) \leq M_f + p_F F^s \quad (\mu_f) \qquad (27)$$

$$(\lambda_2) \qquad (28)$$

$$F^s \leq f(L_f, N)$$

$$L_f \leq \overline{L} \quad (\lambda_3) \qquad (29)$$

Consumer's Problem:

Q is exogenous.

$$\underset{x_c, F_c}{\text{Max}} \quad U^c(x_c, F_c, Q)$$

s.t.

$$x_c + p_F F_c \leq M^c \quad (\mu_c) \qquad (30)$$

Equilibrium condition:

$$p_F\left[F^s-\left(F_c+F_f\right)\right]=0. \tag{31}$$

First Order Conditions:

$$L_x^f:\ U_x^f-\mu_f=0 \tag{32}$$

$$L_Q^f:\ U_Q^f-\mu_f C_Q(Q,N)=0 \tag{33}$$

$$L_N^f:\ -C_N(Q,N)+\mu_f\ f_N-p_N=0 \tag{34}$$

$$L_F^f:U_F^f-\mu_f p_F=0 \tag{35}$$

$$L_{F^s}^f:\ p_F-\lambda_2=0 \tag{36}$$

$$L_L^f:\ \lambda_2 f_L-\lambda_3=0 \tag{37}$$

$$L_x^c:\ U_x^c-\mu_c=0 \tag{38}$$

$$L_F^c:\ U_F^c-\mu_c p_F=0 \tag{39}$$

The Samuelson optimality condition for Q is not satisfied since only the farmer is involved in choosing Q. Although the form of the Pareto optimality condition for N is correct, its level N will not be at the optimal level because Q will not be optimal.

A4.0 DEE with Cost-sharing Only (No Personalized Prices)

This policy is not satisfactory.

Farmer's Problem:

$$\underset{x_f,\,F_f,\,Q,\,F^s,\,L_f,\,N}{\text{Max}}\quad U^f\left(x_f,F_f,Q\right)$$

s.t.

$$x_f+p_F F_f+p_N N+s_f C(Q,N)\le M^f+p_F F^s \quad \left(\mu_f\right) \tag{40}$$

$$F^s\le f(L,N) \qquad \left(\lambda_2\right) \tag{41}$$

$$L\le \overline{L} \qquad \left(\lambda_3\right) \tag{42}$$

$$N \leq \overline{N} \qquad (\lambda_4) \qquad (43)$$

Consumer's Problem:

N is exogenous, and Q is endogenous.

$$\underset{xc,\ Fc,\ Q}{\text{Max}} \quad U^c(x_c, F^c, Q)$$

s.t.

$$x_c + s_c C(Q,N) + p_F F^c \leq M^c \qquad (\mu_c) \qquad (44)$$

Equilibrium condition:

$$p_F\left[F^s - (F_c + F_f)\right] = 0$$

First Order Conditions:

Cost shares s_c $(s_f = 1 - s_c)$ can be determined endogenously from:

$$L_x^f:\ U_x^f - \mu_f = 0 \qquad (45)$$

$$L_Q^f:\ U_Q^f - \mu_f s_f C_Q(Q,N) = 0$$

$$L_N^f:\ -s_f C_N(Q,N) + \frac{\lambda_2}{\mu_f} f_N - p_N = 0 \qquad (47)$$

$$L_F^f:\ U_F^f - \mu_f p_f = 0 \qquad (48)$$

$$L_{F^s}^f:\ p_F - \lambda_2 = 0 \qquad (49)$$

$$L_L^f:\ \lambda_2 f_L - \lambda_3 = 0 \qquad (50)$$

$$L_F^c:\ U_F^c - \mu_c p_F = 0 \qquad (51)$$

$$L_x^c:\ U_x^c - \mu_c = 0 \tag{52}$$

$$L_Q^c:\ U_Q^c - \mu_c s_c C_Q(Q,N) = 0 \tag{53}$$

The Pareto optimality condition for N *is not satisfied because of the cost share. The Pareto optimality condition for* Q *is satisfied:*

$$\frac{U_Q^f}{U_x^f} + \frac{U_Q^c}{U_x^c} = (s_f + s_c) C_Q(Q,N) = C_Q(Q,N)$$

APPENDIX 2: EMPIRICAL SPECIFICATION OF FUNCTIONAL FORMS

$U^i(x_i, F_i, Q) = log\,(1+x_i) + \gamma_i\, log\,(1+Q) + \delta_i\, log\,(1+Q)$

$C(Q, N) = 2.41\ (1 + N/200)1.28\ \ (1 + 10Q).88$

$f(N) = 61 + .51\ N - .001\ N2$

$p_N = .30$

$p_F = 3$ (endogenous except in base case)

$\gamma_i:\ \ 1, 2, 2$

$\delta_i:\ \ 2, 4, 2$

$M_i\ :\ 0, 200, 100$

i = 1 denotes the farmer; i = 2, 3 denote consumers

The cost function is adopted from:
Dasgupta, S., M. Huq, D. Wheeler, and C. Zhang, Water Pollution Abatement by Chinese Industry: Cost Estimates and Policy Implications, draft paper, May 1996.

The production function is from:

Tauer, L.W, Determining the Optimal Amount of Nitrogen to Apply to Corn using the Box-Cox Functional Form, Working Paper 2000-06, Department of Agricultural, Resource, and Managerial Economics, Cornell University, April 2000.

Chapter 6

A Study on Coefficient Reduction of Binary Knapsack Inequalities

Gary J. Koehler
Department of Decision and Information Sciences, University of Florida, Gainesville, FL 32611

Abstract: In 1975, Bradley, Hammer and Wolsey characterized the minimal representation of binary knapsack problems. A linear programming formulation for this problem often gave integral solutions leading the authors to state "We know of no satisfactory explanation of why the large fraction of linear programming optimal solutions are integer for this problem." Here we provide a study of this phenomenum. We find these problems are close in structure to problems having a dual that is an integral, dynamic Leontief Substitution System. The duals of integral Leontief Substitution Systems have feasible sets with a least element so they have an integral solution for any objective having non-negative coefficients.
Key words: Knapsack program, Leontief substitution system, least element, integral solutions, integer programming, coefficient reduction.

1. INTRODUCTION

The binary knapsack problem is a key combinatorial optimization problem possessing the inherent complexity of such problems with a minimum of structure. Although the binary knapsack problem is NP-hard (Garey and Johnson, 1979), it is often easily solved by one of a host of solution strategies (e.g., see Martello and Toth, 1990, and Pisinger, 1995). A number of exact solution strategies are available for binary knapsack problems and for a variety of special cases. There are also near-optimal and probabilistic methods.

As is well-known, every bounded integer programming problem can be converted to an equivalent knapsack problem (Bradley, 1971). Initial enthusiasm for this result was tempered when it was realized that the new coefficients could grow exponentially. Prompted by this, Bradley et al., (1974) showed how the (normalized) knapsack inequality

$$\sum_{i=1}^{n} a_i x_i \le a_0 \quad x_i \in \{0,1\} \quad a_0 \ge a_1 \ge \ldots \ge a_n \ge 0$$

could be reduced to an equivalent one with minimal integer coefficients. By equivalent we mean one having the same 0-1 solution vectors. For example, below are two randomly generated knapsack inequalities satisfying Chvatal's criteria (Chvatal, 1980) with their equivalent minimal representation:

$93x_1 + 64x_2 + 59x_3 + 8x_4 \le 112$ is equivalent to $x_1 + x_2 + x_3 + 0x_4 \le 1$

$84x_1 + 59x_2 + 44x_3 + 21x_4 \le 104$ is equivalent to $2x_1 + x_2 + x_3 + x_4 \le 2$.

These minimal coefficients are found using an integer program (describe below).

Bradley, et al. (1974) noted that the straightforward linear programming relaxation often gave integer answers. And "We know of no satisfactory explanation of why the large fraction of linear programming optimal solutions are integer for this problem." They go on to show that an explanation offered in threshold logic was fallacious.

Even if one could rely on linear programming, their procedure might require an exponential number of constraints. Hence, these results became more valuable theoretically than practically.

This paper attempts to shed light on their observation that "The linear programming problems ... often have integer optimal solutions." We stick to using tools roughly available at the time of their work.

1.1 Ruminations on Andrew B. Whinston

This may seem a strange topic for a book dedicated to a top information systems scholar like Andy Whinston. However, I decided to focus attention on Andy's early years and on some areas that originally brought us together. By the time Andy and I published our first article in 1974 (with the now deceased Gordy Wright), Andy had already published 55 papers in refereed journals. By my count, 25 of these were in operations research areas, 14 in economics/finance areas and 16 miscellaneous applications (including papers on water resource management, school bus scheduling and even two on information systems topics)!

Andy's unique contribution to information systems has been his penchant for quantitative and/or economic modeling of problems. Of course, Andy has been extremely good at foreseeing new, important topics and bringing approaches from diverse disciplines to bear. His early work in economics and operations research rings throughout his career.

Under Andy, I explored solving linear programs using iterative methods – methods not requiring the simplex method, matrix inversion or other trappings found in such approaches. We focused on solving a large, important class of problems known as Leontief Substitution Systems that had been originally emphasized by Arthur F. Veinott, Jr. (1968). These problems include a host of special cases like the Markov Decision problem, transshipment problems, and many more (see Koehler, Whinston and Wright, 1975).

Interestingly, I received a request to contribute a paper to this book just as I was getting ready to spend six weeks of my 2001 Sabbatical at the University of Texas at Austin working with Andy. While there we explored topics generally related to solving distributed problems with an eye towards e-commerce applications. Surprisingly, this work brought us both back to our roots of management science/operations research. This only underscored my decision to contribute a work harkening back to our early involvement.

1.2 Organization of this Paper

This paper is organized as follows. In Section 2 we present our notation, background results and some preliminary results. Throughout we illustrate key results with examples. In Section 3 we give a potential insight into why so many Bradley problems have integer solutions. Section 4 continues with another viewpoint. In Section 5 we summarize and discuss our results.

2. NOTATION AND INITIAL RESULTS

Let e_i be the ith unit vector, e be a vector of ones, x' be the transpose of vector x, $N_n = \{1,\ldots,n\}$, $\mathcal{N}_n$ be the power set of N_n,

$B^n = \{0,1\}^n$ and Z^n be the n-dimensional space of integers. If $x \in B^n$, define $S^x = \{i : x_i > 0\}$ and, conversely, if $S \subseteq N_n$, x^S is the associated characteristic vector. Let $A^{n+1} = \{a \in Z^{n+1} : a_0 \geq a_1 \ldots \geq a_n \geq 0\}$. For $a \in A^{n+1}$ define

$$F(a) = \left\{ x \in B^n : \sum_{i=1}^{n} a_i x_i \leq a_0 \right\}.$$

We need the following three definitions modified from Bradley et al. (1974).

Definition 2.1 *(Ceiling Point)*
Let $a \in A^{n+1}$. $x \in B^n$ is a ceiling point and S^x a ceiling of $F(a)$ if

(a) $x \in F(a)$.

(b) $x + e_t \notin F(a)$ if $x'e_t = 0$.

(c) $x + e_t - e_{t+1} \notin F(a)$ if $x'e_t = 0$ and $x'e_{t+1} = 1$.

The set of all ceiling points of $F(a)$ is $\mathcal{C}(a)$.

Definition 2.2 *(Roof Point)*
Let $a \in A^{n+1}$. $x \in B^n$ is a roof point and S^x a roof of $F(a)$ if

(a) $x \notin F(a)$.

(b) $x - e_t \in F(a)$ if $x'e_t = 1$.

(c) $x - e_t + e_{t+1} \in F(a)$ if $x'e_t = 1$ and $x'e_{t+1} = 0$.

The set of all roof points of $F(a)$ is $\mathcal{R}(a)$.

Definition 2.3 *(Dual Knapsack)*
Let $a \in A^{n+1}$. The dual of $F(a)$ is

$$F_D(a) \equiv \{x \in B^n : e - x \notin F(a)\} = F(a + (a'e - 1 - 2a'e_0)e_0).$$

Lemma 2.1 *(Bradley, et al. 1974)*
Let $a \in A^{n+1}$. $x \in B^n$ is a roof(ceiling) point of $F(a)$ if and only if $e - x$ is a ceiling(roof) of $F_D(a)$.

Ceiling and roofs can be computed by a procedure given in the Bradley, et al. paper (restated here). The roof points of $F(a)$ are given by procedure Roof below. Ceilings are the complements of the roofs of the dual to $F(a)$.

Roof Candidate (a,x): Input $a \in A^{n+1}$, $x \in B^n$. Output a new candidate or stop.

Let $r = \max_{x_i=1} i$.

If $r < n$ do { if $x \in F(a)$ return $x + e_{r+1}$ otherwise return $x - e_r + e_{r+1}$ }.

Let $S^x = \{s_1 \le \ldots \le s_k\}$ and $t = \max_{s_{i+1}-s_i \ge 2} i$. If there is such a t, then return $x^{\{s_1,\ldots,s_{t-1},s_t+1\}}$.

Stop.

Roofs(a): Input $a \in A^{n+1}$. Output the set of all roof points $\mathcal{R}(a)$, of $F(a)$.

Let $\mathcal{R}(a) \leftarrow \phi$ and $x = e_1$.

do {

$x \leftarrow \text{RoofCandidate}(a, x)$

if x is a roof of $F(a)$, $\mathcal{R}(a) \leftarrow \mathcal{R}(a) \cup \{x\}$

}

Example 2.1: For $a' = [80 \quad 65 \quad 64 \quad 41 \quad 22 \quad 13 \quad 12 \quad 8 \quad 2]$.

$$\mathcal{C}(a) = \left\{x^{\{1,5,8\}}, x^{\{3,4,5,8\}}, x^{\{3,5,6,7,8\}}\right\}$$

$$\mathcal{R}(a) = \left\{x^{\{2,4\}}, x^{\{2,6,7\}}, x^{\{3,4,6,7\}}\right\}$$

We define the relation $\succ$ on $\mathcal{N}_n$ as follows. For the ordered set $\{s_1,\ldots,s_{|S|}\} = S \subseteq N_n$ let $\alpha(S) \in Z^n$ be defined by

$$\alpha(S)_i \equiv \begin{cases} s_i & i \le |S| \\ n+1 & \text{otherwise} \end{cases}.$$

Let $S, T \in N_n$. Then $S \succ T$, if $\alpha(S) \le \alpha(T)$. We say S dominates T. Equivalently, we say $x \succ y$ for $x, y \in B^n$ if $S^x \succ S^y$. For $x \in B^n$, we also use $\alpha(x)$ in place of $\alpha(S^x)$. Clearly, $\succ$ is a partial order on N_n. We say x strictly dominates y if $x \succ y$ and $x \ne y$. The following compendium is given without proofs since they are either easy to generate or follow from the normal properties of partially-ordered sets.

Remark 2.1: Some properties of the $\succ$ are given below. Let $x, y, z \in B^n$ and $S \subseteq B^n$. Then the following are true.

a. (antisymmetry) $x \succ y$ and $y \succ x$ implies $y = x$.
b. (reflexive) $x \succ x$.
c. (transitive) $x \succ y$ and $y \succ z$ implies $x \succ z$.
d. (directed) $e \succ x \succ 0$.
e. $x \succ y$ implies $e'x \ge e'y$.
f. $x \ge y$ implies $x \succ y$.
g. (confluent) $y \succ x \wedge z \succ x$ implies there is a $u \in B^n$ such that $u \succ y \wedge u \succ z$.
h. (bounds) The greatest lower bound of S is computed by setting each component z_k to one if $n \ge \max_{y \in S} \alpha(y)_k$ and zero otherwise. The least upper bound is computed similarly with "min" replacing "max". For example, for n = 5 and $S = \{x^{\{1,4\}}, x^{\{2,3,5\}}\}$, the greatest lower bound is $x^{\{2,4\}}$ and least upper bound is $x^{\{1,3,5\}}$.
i. (minimal and maximal element) A minimal(maximal) element of S is an $x \in S$ where no other $y \in S$ satisfies $x \succ y$ ($y \succ x$). All the points of $S = \{x^{\{1,4\}}, x^{\{2,3,5\}}\}$ are minimal and maximal since none are comparable except to themselves.

j. $x \succ y$ and $a \in A^{n+1}$ gives $\sum_{i=1}^{n} a_i x_i \geq \sum_{i=1}^{n} a_i y_i$. Hence $x \in F(a)$ for some $a \in A^{n+1}$ then $y \in F(a)$ and, conversely, if $y \notin F(a)$ then $x \notin F(a)$.

k. If $c \in \mathcal{C}(a)$ then $c \succ x \Rightarrow x \in F(a)$. $x \in F(a) \Rightarrow \exists c \in \mathcal{C}(a) \ni c \succ x$.

l. If $r \in \mathcal{R}(a)$ then $x \succ r \Rightarrow x \notin F(a)$. $x \notin F(a) \Rightarrow \exists r \in \mathcal{R}(a) \ni x \succ r$.

Bradley, et al., show that for $a, d \in A^{n+1}$, $F(a) = F(d)$ if and only if $\mathcal{C}(a) = \mathcal{C}(d)$ or, equivalently, $\mathcal{R}(a) = \mathcal{R}(d)$. They also give the following linear program. (They provide five alternative values for b, all having $b \geq 0$.)

$$\min b'd$$

st

$$d_0 \geq d_1 \ldots \geq d_n \geq 0 \qquad (1)$$

$$d_0 - \sum_{i \in S^x} d_i \geq 0 \qquad x \in \mathcal{C}(a) \qquad (2)$$

$$-d_0 + \sum_{i \in S^x} d_i \geq 1 \qquad x \in \mathcal{R}(a) \qquad (3)$$

If $d \in Z^{n+1}$ *solves this, then d is the minimal* $d \in A^{n+1}$ *such that* $F(d) = F(a)$. *Bradley, et al. (1974) noted "The linear programming problems ... often have integer optimal solutions." And "We know of no satisfactory explanation of why the large fraction of linear programming optimal solutions are integer for this problem."*

Example 2.1 (Continued): The solution to the LP above with b being a vector of ones is $d' = (5,4,4,2,2,1,1,1,0)$.

We will study this problem and put forward insights into why so many have integer solutions. We first need the following result.

Theorem 2.2

Let $a \in A^{n+1}$ and $r \in R(a)$. Then for each $k \in S^r$ there exists $c \in C(a)$ and $x \in F(a)$ with $c \succ x$ such that $(r-x)_k = 1$, $e_k \geq r-x$ and $(r-x)_j = -1$ implies $j > k$.

Proof:

$r \in R(a) \Rightarrow e'r \geq 2$ since $e_i \in F(a)$ for all i. Let $k \in S^r$. Then, from Definition 2.2(b), $r - e_k \in F(a)$. Hence, by Remark 2.1(k), there is a $c \in C(a)$ such that $c \succ r - e_k$. Clearly $c \not\succ r$ or else, by Remark 2.1(l), $c \notin F(a)$ a contradiction. Let $c \succ x \geq r - e_k$ with $x'e_k = 0$ where x is formed by performing the minimal number of increasing subscript shifts on c's positive components (and possibly setting some values to zero to get $x'e_k = 0$).

□

For each $r \in R(a)$ and $k \in S^r$, let $X(r,k)$ be the set of x's corresponding x to those derivable by Theorem 2.2.

***Example 2.1 (Continued)**: Theorem 2.2 gives the following (this is not a complete enumeration):*

For $r = x^{\{2,4\}}$,

$X(r,2) = \{x^{\{3,4,5,8\}}, x^{\{4,5,6,7,8\}}\}$ *and* $X(r,4) = \{x^{\{2,5,8\}}\}$ *from*

$x^{\{3,4,5,8\}}$ *comes from* $x^{\{3,4,5,8\}} \in C(a)$

$x^{\{4,5,6,7,8\}}$ *comes from* $x^{\{3,5,6,7,8\}} \in C(a)$.

$x^{\{2,5,8\}}$ *comes from* $x^{\{1,5,8\}} \in C(a)$.

For $r = x^{\{2,6,7\}}$,

$X(r,2) = \{x^{\{3,6,7,8\}}, x^{\{3,5,6,7,8\}}\}$ *and* $X(r,7) = \{x^{\{2,6,8\}}\}$ *from*

$x^{\{3,6,7,8\}}$ *comes from* $x^{\{3,4,5,8\}} \in C(a)$.

$x^{\{3,5,6,7,8\}}$ *comes from* $x^{\{3,5,6,7,8\}} \in C(a)$.

$x^{\{2,6,8\}}$ *comes from* $x^{\{1,5,8\}} \in C(a)$

For $r = x^{\{3,4,6,7\}}$,

$X(r,4) = \{x^{\{3,5,6,7,8\}}\}$ *and* $X(r,7) = \{x^{\{3,4,6,8\}}\}$ *from*

$x^{\{3,5,6,7,8\}}$ *comes from* $x^{\{3,5,6,7,8\}} \in \mathrm{C}(a)$

$x^{\{3,4,6,8\}}$ *comes from* $x^{\{3,4,5,8\}} \in \mathrm{C}(a)$.

Corollary 2.3

Let $a \in A^{n+1}$, $r \in \mathrm{R}(a)$ *and* $k \in S^r$. *Then the constraints*

$$d_0 - \sum_{i \in S^x} d_i \geq 0 \qquad \forall x \in X(r,k)$$

$$\sum_{i \in S^r} d_i - \sum_{i \in S^x} d_i \geq 1 \qquad \forall x \in X(r,k)$$

are redundant to (3).

Proof:

The first constraint follows since $c \succ x$, $x \in X(r,k)$, *for some* $c \in \mathrm{C}(a)$ *and (2). The second results from adding the first to a copy of the row of (3) corresponding to r.*

□

The following result follows directly from Theorem 2.2, Corollary 2.3 and (3).

Corollary 2.4

Let $a \in A^{n+1}$ *and if* $r'e_k = 0$ *for all* $r \in \mathrm{R}(a)$ *and* $k = s,\ldots,n$, *then (1) can be reduced by requiring* $d_k = 0$, $k = s,\ldots,n$.

Reduction will be accomplished by actually reducing the problem. This will entail setting $c_k = 0$, $k = s,\ldots,n$, *for each* $c \in \mathrm{C}(a)$.

Example 2.1 (Continued)*: Corollary 2.4 shows that (3) can be reduced by adding* $d_n = 0$ *since no* $r \in \mathrm{R}(a)$ *has* $r'e_n = 0$.

3. WHY INTEGRAL SOLUTIONS? AN INSIGHT

Let $X(r)=\bigcup_k X(r,k)$ *for* $r \in R\ (a)$. *A linear program equivalent to (1)-(3) can be specified by adding redundant constraints.*

$$\min b'd \tag{4}$$

s.t.

$$d_0 \geq d_1 \ldots \geq d_n \geq 0 \tag{5}$$

$$d_0 - \sum_{i \in S^x} d_i \geq 0 \qquad x \in c\ (a) \tag{6}$$

$$d_0 - \sum_{i \in S^x} d_i \geq 0 \qquad x \in X(r), r \in R\ (a) \tag{7}$$

$$-d_0 + \sum_{i \in S^r} d_i \geq 1 \qquad r \in R\ (a) \tag{8}$$

The inequalities of (7) are dominated by related (through the corresponding c's in the proof of Theorem 2.2) inequalities in (6). We only require one $x \in X(r)$ *for each* $r \in R\ (a)$. *Without loss of generality, we assume the rows of (7) and (8) are chosen using* $r \in R\ (a)$ *in the same order. Let the rows of this LP be described using respective matrices as in*

$$D'd \geq 0$$
$$C'd \geq 0$$
$$G'd \geq 0^{\cdot}$$
$$R'd \geq e$$

Clearly C, D and G have exactly one positive element per column. From Theorem 2.2, $G'+R'$ *has exactly one positive element per row. Furthermore, each positive element is a "1" and precedes (from the left) any negative element (-1's) in its row*

Let d^* *be a solution to (1)-(3) and* x^* *a solution to its dual. The redundant rows (7) can be replaced with* $G'd = G'd^*$. *Then, an equivalent problem to (1)-(3) via (4)-(8) and this replacement is:*

$$\min_d b'd$$

s.t.

$$D'd \geq 0$$
$$C'd \geq 0$$
$$G'd = G'd^*$$
$$(R'+G')d \geq e + G'd^*$$

Consider the lagrangian relaxation of this problem:

$$(LLP)\ z = -x^{*}{}'G'd^* + \min_d \left(b' + x^{*}{}'G'\right)d$$

s.t.

$$D'd \geq 0$$
$$C'd \geq 0$$
$$(R'+G')d \geq e + G'd^*$$

Clearly LLP has the same optimal, objective value, z^*, *as (1)-(3) although the solution vector may not be feasible to the original problem. Let*

$$(LLPt)\ z(t) = -x^{*}{}'G'd^* - t'D'd^* + \min_d \left(b' + x^{*}{}'G' + t'D'\right)d$$

s.t.

$$D'd \geq 0$$
$$C'd \geq 0$$
$$(R'+G')d \geq e + G'd^*$$

where t is chosen so that $b + Gx^* + Dt > 0$. *This is always possible. For example, let* $t = D^{-1}e - D^{-1}\left(b + Gx^*\right)$. *This gives the desired result since* $D^{-1} \geq 0$.

Let

$$A' = \begin{bmatrix} D' \\ C' \\ R'+G' \end{bmatrix} \qquad c = \begin{bmatrix} 0 \\ 0 \\ e + G'd^* \end{bmatrix}$$

Provided $b + Gx^* + Dt$ *is integral (which is trivial to enforce if b is integral), the dual of (LLPt) has three properties. It is an (a) integral (Veinott and Dantzig, 1971), (b) dynamic (Dantzig, 1955), and (c) Leontief*

Substitution System (see Veinott, 1968, and Koehler, et al. 1975 for related material). In particular, the dual of (LLPt) has an easily computed (from the dynamic property), integral solution (from the integral property). Furthermore, the constraint set of (LLPt) has a least element (from the Leontief property). The least element is less than or equal any other element of the feasible set. This latter point was shown by Cottle and Veinott (1972).

***Example 2.1 (Continued)**: One possible G is:*

$$G' = \begin{bmatrix} 1 & 0 & 0 & -1 & -1 & -1 & 0 & 0 & -1 \\ 1 & 0 & 0 & -1 & 0 & 0 & -1 & -1 & -1 \\ 1 & 0 & 0 & 0 & -1 & 0 & -1 & -1 & -1 \end{bmatrix}.$$

so

$$R' + G' = \begin{bmatrix} 0 & 0 & 1 & -1 & 0 & -1 & 0 & 0 & -1 \\ 0 & 0 & 1 & -1 & 0 & 0 & 0 & 0 & -1 \\ 0 & 0 & 0 & 1 & 0 & 0 & 0 & 0 & -1 \end{bmatrix}$$

Given A and $b \ge 0$ *consider* $Y(A,b) = \{y \ge 0 : Ay = b\}$. $Y(A,b)$ *is called a Leontief Substitution System if A has exactly one positive element per column and there is a* $y \ge 0$ *such that* $Ay > 0$. *Let* $\Delta_i = \{j : A_{i,j} > 0\}$, $\Delta = \bigtimes_{i=1}^{n+1} \Delta_i$ *and* A_γ *be the square submatrix of A composed of the columns listed in* $\gamma \in \Delta$. $Y(A,b)$ *is called a dynamic Leontief Substitution System if there is a permutation of the rows and columns of A such that each resulting* A_γ, $\gamma \in \Delta$, *is lower triangular. Finally,* $Y(A,b)$ *is called an integral Leontief Substitution System if every feasible basis is unimodular. Veinott (1968) showed that every feasible basis of a Leontief Substitution System is determined by (a permutation of)* A_γ *for some* $\gamma \in \Delta$. *Cottle and Veinott (1972) showed that, if A is Leontief, there is an* $\ell \in D(A',c) \equiv \{d : A'd \ge c\}$ *such that* $\ell \le d$ *for all* $d \in D(A',c)$. *Furthermore,* $\ell = A_\gamma^{-1} c_\gamma$ *for some* $\gamma \in \Delta$. *Clearly,* ℓ *minimizes* $b'd$ *over* $D(A',c)$ *for any* $b \ge 0$.

Turning to problem LLPt, we have that A has one positive element in each column, that A_γ, $\gamma \in \Delta$, *is lower triangular and unimodular (since the diagonal consists of ones and the strictly lower triangular part is composed of integers – zeros and negative ones). We only have to show that there is a* $y \geq 0$ *such that* $Ay > 0$. *Let*

$$y = \begin{bmatrix} D^{-1}\left(b + Gx^{*} + Dt\right) \\ 0 \\ 0 \end{bmatrix}.$$

Then $Ay > 0$. *In fact, here A is totally Leontief since every* A_{γ}, $\gamma \in \Delta$, *is Leontief. Now, since* $b + Gx^{*} + Dt > 0$, *the least element,* $\ell \in D(A',c)$, *solves LLPt uniquely*

***Example 2.1 (Continued)**: Number the rows of A' starting at one and columns starting at zero. The* Δ_i *'s are:*

$\Delta_0 = \{1,10,11,12\}$, $\Delta_1 = \{2\}$, $\Delta_2 = \{3,13,14\}$, $\Delta_3 = \{4,15\}$,
$\Delta_k = \{k+1\}$ *k=4,...,n.*

Using the dynamic property of Leontief substitution problems, we have the simple solution procedure for solving LLPt:

$$\ell_h = \max_{j \in \Delta_h} c_j + \sum_{A_{i,j}<0} \ell_i \qquad h = n,\ldots,0.$$

Unfortunately, LLPt is just a relaxation of (1)-(3). It is easy to show the following since D is non-singular.

Lemma 3.1
For any instance of LLPt, there exists a v such that changing $D'd \geq 0$ *to* $D'd \geq v$ *gives a solution to the original problem (1)-(3).*

Of course, this only shows that there is a close equivalent dual problem having an integral, dynamic Leontief Substitution System. In general, we don't know how to find v without solving the original problem.

4. LEAST ELEMENT

Section 3 gives a possible insight into the integrality property first noted by Bradley et al. We employed changes in the formulation to convert the problem to a relaxation having a dual that is an integral, dynamic Leontief Substitution System. It is always possible to tighten this relaxation to get a system having a solution to the original problem. Stepping back, one can posit that the original problem might have a hidden Leontief structure with an integrality property easily exposed by the Leontief structure. A system $Hx = b, x \geq 0$ *is called hidden Leontief if there is a non-singular matrix, B, where* BH *is Leontief and* $Bb \geq 0$. *These have been investigated by Saigal (1971), Cottle and Veinott (1972) and Koehler, et al. (1975).*

Ideally, one would show how to construct B for a class of problems. Koehler et al. (1975) actually show how to do this for a practical class of linear programming problems. However, in general, this is exceedingly hard to accomplish, even for a particular instance of a problem. An alternative is to show that a system has Leontief-like properties. Cottle and Veinott (1972) focus on this approach. We use this approach to give further insights into the Bradley problem.

Cottle and Veinott (1972) provide two useful results. Let $X(c) = \{d : A'd \geq c\}$.

Theorem 4.1 *(*Cottle and Veinott Theorem 1*)*
The following are equivalent.

(1) $\bar{x}$ *is the least element of* $X(c)$.

(2) $\bar{x} \in X(c)$ *and there is a matrix* $A^* \geq 0$ *such that* $A^*A' = I$ *and* $\bar{x} = A^*c$.

Theorem 4.2 *(*Cottle and Veinott Theorem 2*)*
Assume A has an identity submatrix. Then the following are equivalent.

(1) $X(c)$ *has a least element for each c where* $X(c) \neq \phi$.

(2) A is Leontief.

For a limited class of A matrices, these two theorems relate one type of property, having a least element, to being Leontief. Although we clearly don't have an identity submatrix in our problem, there is value in seeing whether our system (1)-(3) has a least element. Using

$$\begin{aligned} &D'd \geq 0 \\ &C'd \geq 0. \\ &R'd \geq e \end{aligned}$$

in place of (1)-(3) and $A = (D \quad C \quad R)$. *One can form a candidate matrix* $A^* \geq 0$ *by letting*

$$\begin{aligned} &\text{column } A_i^* \in \arg\max c'x \\ &\text{st} \\ &\qquad Ax = e_i \\ &\qquad x \geq 0 \end{aligned} \qquad (10)$$

Clearly $A^*A' = I$ *but it may not be the case that* $A^*c = \overline{x} \in X(c)$. *If it is, then it is a least element.*

***Example 2.1 (Continued)**: (10) gives us:*

$$A^{*\prime} = \begin{bmatrix} 0 & 5 & 0 & 1 & 0 & 6 & 3 & 0 & 6 & 5 & 0 & 1 & 1 & 4 & 0 \\ 0 & 4 & 0 & 1 & 0 & 4 & 2 & 0 & 4 & 3 & 0 & 1 & 1 & 3 & 0 \\ 0 & 3 & 0 & 1 & 0 & 4 & 2 & 0 & 4 & 3 & 0 & 1 & 1 & 3 & 0 \\ 0 & 2 & 0 & 1 & 0 & 2 & 1 & 0 & 2 & 2 & 0 & 0 & 1 & 1 & 0 \\ 0 & 2 & 0 & 0 & 0 & 2 & 1 & 0 & 2 & 2 & 0 & 0 & 1 & 1 & 0 \\ 0 & 1 & 0 & 0 & 0 & 2 & 1 & 0 & 1 & 1 & 0 & 0 & 0 & 1 & 0 \\ 0 & 1 & 0 & 0 & 0 & 1 & 1 & 0 & 1 & 1 & 0 & 0 & 0 & 1 & 0 \\ 0 & 1 & 0 & 0 & 0 & 1 & 0 & 0 & 1 & 1 & 0 & 0 & 0 & 1 & 0 \\ 0 & 0 & 0 & 0 & 0 & 0 & 0 & 0 & 1 & 0 & 0 & 0 & 0 & 0 & 0 \end{bmatrix} \quad A^*c = \begin{bmatrix} 5 \\ 4 \\ 4 \\ 2 \\ 2 \\ 1 \\ 1 \\ 1 \\ 0 \end{bmatrix}$$

Thus, for this instance, (1)-(3) has a least element.

As in Bradley et al's. (1974) paper, we turn to experiments to examine the polyhedron of (1)-(3). In part of their study, they focused on three groups of problems:

Group 1: Random coefficients in the range 1 to 200, 10-15 variables.
Group 2: Random coefficients in the range 150 to 200, 13-16 variables.
Group 3: Random coefficients in the range 5,000 to 10,000, 13-16 variables.

Their focus was on the number of roofs and ceilings. Here we wish to determine two things.

How many randomly generated problems have a least element in (1)-(3)? How often is the least element integral?

We present an experimental study similar to that given in Bradley et al. (1974). The details and results are given in Table 1. For each case, the process is as follows.

(1) For n given, randomly generate a set of integer coefficients $a_0 \geq \ldots \geq a_n \geq 0$ *from the allowed range with* $a_0 < \sum_{i=1}^{n} a_i$.

(2) Generate all roofs and ceilings. Due to limitations on our LP solver, we are limited to problems with $|C| + |R| \leq 1000$.

(3) Solve the n+1 linear programs of Equation (7) to form A^*.

(4) Compute $\overline{x} = A^* c$.

(5) Test if $\overline{x} \in X(c)$ *and record results. If true, test if* $\overline{x}$ *is integral. Record results.*

Table 2 shows problem parameters from the coefficient range of 1-200 that did not have a minimal element. Table 3 shows problems that did have a minimal element, but was not integral.

Two trends are apparent in Table 1. Most problems have a least element and these are usually integral. Deviations from this observation tend to occur as the number of coefficients and ranges increase. The roll played by the coefficient range is obfuscated. Ranges starting at one seem to have fewer least elements and integral solutions than those starting at 200 or 5,000.

Our results are somewhat filtered since we rejected any problem not satisfying $|C| + |R| \leq 1000$. *Table 4 shows the actual number filtered for n = 25. Only 4, in total, were filtered so our observations are probably fairly representative. Table 5 shows the coefficients for these filtered cases.*

5. SUMMARY AND DISCUSSION

In this paper we give some potential insights into why so many of the Bradley problems had integral solutions. It appears these problems are close in structure to problems having a dual that is an integral, dynamic Leontief Substitution System. The duals of Leontief Substitution Systems have feasible sets with a least element. After all, Bradley et al. (1974) are trying to determine the smallest, equivalent, integral coefficients for the knapsack inequality which is not inconsistent with being a least feasible choice from the set of all candidate coefficients.

We say "these problems are close in structure" since not all have a least element directly nor do all the LPs have integral solutions as discovered in Section 4. This latter point was noted by Bradley, et al., too. However, Section 3 shows that there is always a simple tightening of a relaxation of the Bradley LP problem that has an integral, least element. This too was hinted at in the Bradley paper when they observed that "Using branch and bound with branching on the smallest non-integer coefficient quickly yielded the minimum integer equivalent inequality."

Table 1: *Number of problems, out of 1,000, with a minimum element and, for these, the number with integral values.*

Number of Coefficients (n)	*Coefficient Ranges*	*Number with a Least Element*	*Number with Integral Least Elements*
5	*1-200*	*1000*	*1000*
	150-200	*1000*	*1000*
	5,000-10,000	*1000*	*1000*
	1-10,000	*1000*	*1000*
10	*1-200*	*1000*	*1000*
	150-200	*1000*	*1000*
	5,000-10,000	*1000*	*1000*
	1-10,000	*999*	*999*
15	*1-200*	*996*	*995*
	150-200	*1000*	*1000*
	5,000-10,000	*1000*	*1000*
	1-10,000	*993*	*991*
20	*1-200*	*993*	*983*
	150-200	*1000*	*1000*
	5,000-10,000	*1000*	*1000*
	1-10,000	*995*	*983*
	1-200	*981*	*977*
	150-200	*1000*	*1000*

25	*5,000-10,000*	*1000*	*1000*
	1-10,000	*982*	*955*

Table 2: *Coefficients for problems without a minimal element (coefficients in the range 1-250)*

n=15
192 189 160 137 118 113 100 98 77 71 69 67 57 46 39 1
193 191 184 177 167 160 137 99 98 90 86 44 27 25 15 1
174 152 152 132 125 100 97 92 91 73 73 58 55 38 37 24
193 179 167 164 138 134 102 93 76 76 64 63 62 51 49 40
n = 20
189 183 173 173 154 154 139 119 87 87 78 70 68 55 55 51 51 51 36 25 11
187 177 166 160 156 152 146 121 107 92 88 86 82 81 78 61 53 44 36 16 11
182 178 173 170 169 163 158 140 131 126 118 101 97 56 41 35 34 32 28 17 12
193 191 184 180 177 167 163 160 137 128 116 98 98 90 86 44 39 27 25 15 1
174 158 158 152 152 145 132 128 125 103 97 97 92 91 73 59 58 50 39 38 24
184 150 132 129 124 120 117 114 108 106 103 89 87 85 72 51 50 37 30 17 13
197 196 183 181 179 178 175 170 158 150 134 130 123 92 61 51 51 39 31 23 7
n = 25
196 192 181 168 165 143 134 132 130 127 124 123 118 115 113 110 85 69 66 56 38 22 16 11 9 5
196 186 182 164 160 158 149 138 135 132 131 111 100 96 92 88 79 77 77 67 56 39 29 16 15 14
183 182 175 174 163 143 138 138 131 130 127 125 119 111 110 89 88 83 71 69 59 46 42 34 27 3
194 191 187 187 178 170 170 146 128 127 125 123 119 111 108 104 104 96 91 83 78 62 62 54 45 18
193 189 184 179 157 147 127 125 109 101 98 97 90 88 84 81 78 57 46 46 44 40 31 26 4 2
198 194 190 190 187 182 176 174 161 153 146 145 127 108 98 90 81 61 58 48 36 34 34 31 21 21
197 194 172 159 155 154 150 145 139 137 133 128 99 94 91 83 74 70 69 55 51 43 38 20 20 15
198 195 191 181 161 160 159 149 132 110 99 98 97 88 84 67 67 57 55 38 31 30 25 13 5 5
199 191 177 172 171 166 150 145 139 138 121 114 113 103 96 81 77 74 65 65 33 29 20 11 5 2
195 175 159 155 154 152 150 142 123 118 109 105 104 101 100 99 87 83 80 79 79 67 60 49 43 28
187 185 175 147 145 132 130 126 125 115 111 96 95 87 80 74 74 73 71 60 60 48 40 38 16 11
176 165 159 152 150 141 135 135 131 126 109 106 98 98 96 92 91 70 66 66 56 55 43 37 32 4
195 189 189 181 179 177 174 169 162 160 148 143 134 131 129 117 114 110 100 100 95 90 41 12 11 10
185 175 175 170 146 145 139 139 132 124 118 111 106 93 93 86 83 80 79 73 68 67 66 61 48 23
200 197 181 177 167 163 160 146 143 138 130 122 116 100 99 96 94 79 73 70 69 69 58 56 55 34
200 196 192 182 174 158 156 150 147 143 127 122 118 97 95 78 70 70 66 61 59 58 37 29 28 18
200 180 174 173 168 166 155 153 143 136 134 127 124 123 122 96 88 77 77 68 41 37 33 25 23 15
200 188 173 166 147 142 139 128 126 116 116 112 93 84 80 78 73 69 62 58 56 48 45 31 30 7

195 188 185 181 178 178 173 171 164 160 150 136 128 124 116 92 87 81 75 70 62 52 22 20 4
3

Table 3: *Coefficients for problems with a non-integral minimal element (coefficients in the range 1-250)*

n = 15
199 186 175 171 150 121 105 101 85 74 57 41 37 30 22 5
n = 20
200 195 194 188 181 170 145 135 115 105 102 99 94 80 77 76 73 55 31 17 11
179 170 168 155 144 136 134 131 130 125 110 101 83 59 59 58 51 49 40 28 20
169 166 155 147 137 135 132 117 101 100 97 88 81 69 68 54 51 36 33 21 3
190 189 184 163 141 137 114 110 102 92 83 76 76 71 47 46 43 43 38 25 3
199 188 178 172 169 145 139 139 133 108 94 91 82 81 77 76 63 35 21 13 10
186 184 172 171 164 140 134 132 114 106 94 73 68 66 60 57 44 41 30 19 9
199 193 185 184 148 138 125 124 105 100 92 85 84 67 61 43 29 21 16 12 10
198 190 173 150 135 132 131 119 119 94 89 78 75 74 71 67 48 28 17 16 4
184 179 156 140 126 124 122 113 100 98 88 85 81 78 74 70 63 46 31 15 5
192 189 187 184 149 124 123 118 113 110 106 103 85 81 58 51 43 39 37 32 6
n = 25
182 178 173 170 169 164 163 158 140 131 126 125 121 118 101 97 84 56 41 35 34 32 28 20
17 12
199 178 178 155 150 148 143 128 126 112 101 101 92 92 88 87 80 74 68 65 52 44 32 25 17 9
198 182 182 177 172 171 156 156 155 128 120 112 105 87 86 82 78 72 63 53 47 44 41 30 25
22
196 194 189 171 166 162 159 158 151 144 130 112 95 93 92 87 85 82 80 74 63 47 26 24 21
15

Table 4: *Number of cases filtered when n = 25*

Coefficient Ranges	*Number Filtered*
1-200	*2*
150-200	*0*
5,000-10,000	*0*
1-10,000	*2*

Table 5: *Coefficients for problems filtered with n = 25.*

1-200
200 186 176 137 131 128 112 105 78 74 59 52 52 51 46 43 42 33 23 22 16 10 9 7 6 1
173 169 157 134 117 100 86 85 85 79 74 57 54 48 45 42 38 33 32 23 15 11 11 6 3 2
1-10,000
9968 9264 8790 6803 6524 6399 5570 5231 3898 3660 2911 2598 2592 2531 2287 2103 2083
1637 1110 1057 769 497 435 315 292 50
8630 8415 7849 6694 5827 4957 4289 4236 4205 3950 3676 2832 2688 2352 2231 2063 1881
1637 1571 1147 745 531 513 294 141 73

REFERENCES

Bradley, G. H. (1971). "Transformation of Integer Programs to Knapsack Problems," *Discrete Mathematics*, 1(1), pp. 29-45.

Bradley, G. H., P. L. Hammer and L. Wolsey (1974). "Coefficient Reduction for Inequalities in 0-1 Variables," *Mathematical Programming*, 7, pp. 263-282.

Chvatal, V. (1980). "Hard Knapsack Problems," *Operations Research*, (28)6, pp. 1402-1411.

Cottle, R. W. and A. F. Veinott, Jr. (1972). "Polyhedral Sets having a Least Element," *Mathematical Programming*, 3, pp. 238-249.

Dantzig, G. B., (1955). "Optimal Solution of a Dynamic Leontief Model with Substitution.", *Econometrica*, 23, pp. 295-302.

Garey, M. R. and D. S. Johnson (1979). Computers and Intractability: a Guide to the Theory of NP-Completeness, Freeman, San Francisco.

Koehler, G. J., A. B. Whinston and G. P. Wright (1975). Optimization over Leontief Substitution Systems, North-Holland/American Elsevier, New York.

Martello, S. and P. Toth (1990). *Knapsack Problems: Algorithms and Computer Implementations*, John Wiley & Sons, New York.

Pisinger, D. (1995). "Algorithms for Knapsack Problems," Ph.D. thesis, DIKU, Copenhagen, Denmark.

Saigal, R. (1971). "On a Generalization of Leontief Substitution Systems," No. CP-325, Center for Research in Management Science, University of California at Berkeley.

Veinott Jr., A. F. (1968). "Extreme Points of Leontief Substitution Systems," *Linear Algebra and Its Applications*, 1, pp. 181-194.

Veinott Jr., A. F. and G. B. Dantzig (1971). "Integer Extreme Points," *SIAM Review*, 10, No. 1, pp. 98-108.

Chapter 7

Qualitative Reasoning:
Theory and Applications

Aimo Hinkkanen[1] and Karl R. Lang[2]
[1]*Department of Mathematics, University of Illinois, 1409 W Green St, Urbana, IL 61801-2975, USA, aimo@uiuc.edu*

[2]*Department of Information and System Management, Hong Kong University of Science and Technology, Clear Water Bay, Hong Kong, Phone, klang@ust.hk*

Abstract: This paper presents a general theory of qualitative reasoning (QR) systems which includes, as special cases, reasoning methods that use representations of qualitative differential equations and qualitative difference equations. Based on set theory, our QR framework describes fundamental concepts such as qualitative models and solutions, and relates them to the quantitative analogues of its underlying quantitative reference system. Our motivation arises from the types of models found in the social sciences. Thus we emphasize the significance of discrete, dynamic models and optimization models in the management and economics fields, both of which have received less attention in current QR research. We discuss in detail rules constraint reasoning, a QR system based on qualitative difference equations. Finally, we extend on theoretical framework to include an approach to qualitative optimization.

Key words: qualitative reasoning, qualitative modelling, incomplete information, simulation

1. INTRODUCTION

More than a decade of research in qualitative reasoning has produced a vast amount of literature on modeling techniques and reasoning methods for predicting and explaining the qualitative behaviors of physical mechanisms, cf. Bobrow (1985), Weld and deKleer (1990), deKleer and Williams (1991) and Kuipers (1994). The main driving force behind this research has been problem solving in the engineering and physics domain (cf. Iwasaki 1997). The orientation toward tasks that arise typically in the engineering field has lead to the development of computational theories and the implementation of qualitative reasoning systems that are aimed at representing and solving/simulating continuous, dynamic systems which have normally been formulated as differential equation systems, for example, confluence systems (deKleer and Brown 1984), qualitative process theory (Forbus 1984), and qualitative simulation (Kuipers 1986). Qualitative reasoning systems are normally based on some sort of qualitative calculus and present a particular way of how to define qualitative operands and qualitative operations. Developing a qualitative algebra as the basis of qualitative reasoning systems is the focus of work like Simmons (1986), Raiman (1991), and Williams (1991).

While all those concepts have applicability beyond the engineering domain they were developed with that kind of application in mind, and although there is some research on actually applying qualitative reasoning technology to other areas, for example, economics (Farley and Lin 1990; Lang et al 1995), business management (Bailey et al 1991; Hinkkanen et al 1995), and medicine (Kuipers and Kassirer 1984), its success has been limited thus far to problems that are in line with the differential equations paradigm so characteristic for the engineering domain.

The potential of qualitative reasoning as a practical analytic tool that uses problem descriptions based on qualitative knowledge and/or incomplete quantitative information is much greater than modeling just differential equations type of problems. Difference equation systems, that is, discrete, dynamic systems, are traditionally a much more important mathematical tool in the social sciences in general, cf. Goldberg (1958), and economics in particular, cf. Allen (1956), than its continuous analog. Monge (1990) has observed that current research in the social sciences is suffering from the lack of computational systems for processing qualitative information. Essentially unaware of the work in the qualitative reasoning field, he calls for a mathematical representation language that provides a useful compromise between expressiveness and inferential power. Emphasizing the modeling of dynamic systems he describes crucial features of such a hypothetical language including provisions for continuous as well as discrete processes integrating qualitative and quantitative information. Providing qualitative reasoning systems that are apt at handling discrete systems would open a huge realm of new applications problems to the qualitative reasoning community. This new direction of qualitative reasoning research could attract many researchers from the social sciences to join the qualitative reasoning community. This could provide a new stimulus and foster interdisciplinary research which is necessary in order to advance the field to a state where qualitative reasoning becomes a standard modeling methodology in various application fields.

The purpose of this paper is to go a step in this direction by presenting a comprehensive theory for a set-based qualitative reasoning system that integrates the modeling of continuous and discrete systems. We present a qualitative analog to differential-difference equation systems, and give a theoretical account for this reasoning method in the spirit of Struss (1990) who introduced a general framework for analyzing qualitative reasoning methods. In related work, Dordan (1992) did a rigorous theoretical study of qualitative simulation. Following the common approach in qualitative reasoning which derives qualitative descriptions from quantitative reference models, we tacitly assume that each qualitative model can be related to a (collection of) quantitative models. Hence, a proper evaluation of any particular qualitative reasoning system makes sense only with respect to an underlying reference system which is usually derived from a well-known quantitative theory like the mathematical theory of differential equation systems. This paper is organized as follows. We first present Struss' general qualitative reasoning framework in Section 2. Then, in Section 3, we introduce the quantitative reference system, and define the concepts of a quantitative model and a quantitative solution to such a model. Likewise, Section 4 presents the related qualitative system, and defines the theoretical concepts of a qualitative model and a qualitative solution. The relationships between qualitative and quantitative systems are explored in Section 5. Section 6 concludes the paper with some remarks and suggestions for further research.

2. A FRAMEWORK FOR ANALYZING QUALITATIVE REASONING METHODS

Assuming a world in which physical, social, and economic phenomena are governed by deterministic mechanisms which can theoretically be described as some sort of mathematical equation system, but which are, in practice, only partially observable, qualitative reasoning is usually seen as an approach to reason about incompletely known systems. The true but hidden model which describes a real-world phenomenon at any desired level of detail in precise mathematical terms is called the underlying quantitative model. Finite cognitive capabilities and resources, on the other hand, limit science to discover incomplete models only. A qualitative model is an abstract characterization of the partially discerned real-world system in qualitative yet formal terms, that is, in terms of qualitative values and qualitative relationships. While quantitative models are tacitly assumed to be standard mathematical descriptions in the real number system, qualitative models are mathematical descriptions based on some qualitative quantity space whose representation might differ greatly among particular QR systems. In order to analyze and compare specific QR methods, Struss (1990) presents a rigorous framework which includes definitions of desired mathematical properties as well as definitions of relations between qualitative and underlying quantitative models. The remainder of this section summarizes Struss' framework for analyzing QR systems.

The basic link between a qualitative and its affiliated quantitative model is the notion of a qualitative variable as an abstraction of a real-valued variable which can take on qualitative values where qualitative values are an abstraction of the real numbers. Particular QR systems extend this basic abstraction into the development of some qualitative calculus with the precise specification of the representation of qualitative (functional) relationships and inference rules thereof. Struss stipulates various goals that ought to be pursued when devising such a qualitative abstraction.

Finiteness refers to the idea that a QR method should define qualitative variables on a finite set Q of qualitative values called the *quantity space* . *Coverage* means that there should exist a well-defined mapping, $q{:}\mathbf{R} \rightarrow Q$, that abstracts the entire range of numerical values into corresponding qualitative values. Inversely, there should also be an *interpretation,* that is, a mapping[7], $p{:}Q \rightarrow 2^{\mathbf{R}}$ that associates qualitative values with a set of

[7] The notation 2^X denotes the power set of X, that is, the set of all subsets of X.

numerical values that are consistent with the semantics of each particular qualitative value, that is, $\forall x \in \mathbf{R} : x \in p(q(x))$. Arithmetics of signs, for example, are based on the simplest quantity space $Q = \{-,0,+\}$ containing only three qualitative values which, nevertheless, cover the whole range of the real numbers. In this case, the mapping q would be defined as

$$q(x) = \begin{cases} -, & if \ \ x < 0; \\ 0, & if \ \ x = 0; \\ +, & if \ \ x > 0. \end{cases}$$

Likewise, one would define the interpretation p as

$$p(y) = \begin{cases} \{x | x < 0\}, & if \ \ y = -; \\ \{0\}, & if \ \ y = 0; \\ \{x | x > 0\}, & if \ \ y = +. \end{cases}$$

Exclusiveness requires that each qualitative value exclusively designates a particular range of numerical values, that is, the interpretations of qualitative values may not overlap, $\forall a,b \in Q$: $a \neq b \Rightarrow p(a) \cap p(b) = \varnothing$. *Ordering* refers to $(Q,\leq)$ being at least partially ordered, and that $\forall x, y \in \mathbf{R} : x < y \Rightarrow q(x) \leq q(y)$. Any particular qualitative calculus needs to define operations on Q which should include, at least, a qualitative analog to binary operations like addition, subtraction, multiplication, and division whose algebraic properties should resemble as closely as possible those of its quantitative counterparts.

Grounded on these basic concepts, figure 1 associates quantitative models and their solutions with qualitative analogs and also indicates essential relations between them. Notice, the inclusions such as $\mathbf{B} \subset 2^{\mathbf{B}}$ are understood so that if $B \in \mathbf{B}$ then the inclusion maps B onto the element $\{B\}$ of $2^{\boldsymbol{B}}$.

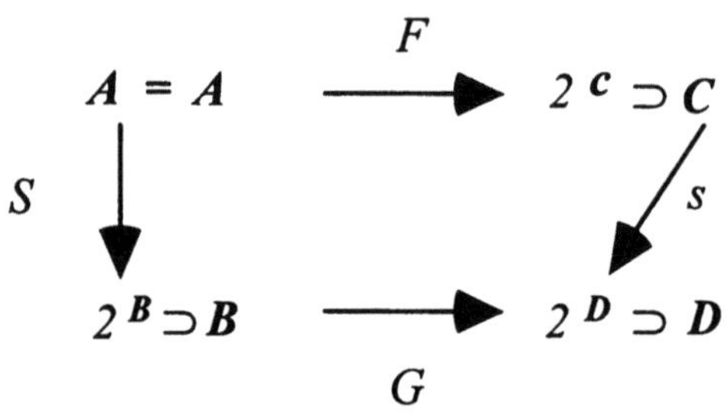

Figure 1 Basic Relationships Between Quantitative Models and Solutions and Qualitative Models and Solutions in the General Qualitative Reasoning Framework.

In order to establish meaningful relations between quantitative and qualitative models where both types of models, although from different perspectives, are supposed to describe the same real-world system, we need to clearly specify what kind of models we have in mind when we relate a qualitative model to a quantitative one. Struss calls $\boldsymbol{A}$ the space of quantitative descriptions which restricts the analysis to a specific class of models. Current QR systems are usually based on algebraic equation systems or differential equation systems as their quantitative reference systems, also commonly referred to as their gold standard. However, Struss' framework is actually more general and could also be adopted to treat difference equation systems, which we shall do in the subsequent sections of this paper, mathematical programs of various types, and others. For each particular class of models under consideration, one can presumably select a quantitative solution method S which produces the solution B to any completely specified quantitative model instance $A \in \boldsymbol{A}$ that is, S is formally being considered a mapping from the space of quantitative descriptions into the space of quantitative solutions $2^{\mathbf{B}}, S: \mathbf{A} \rightarrow 2^{\mathbf{B}}$. For example, one could choose Gaussian elimination to solve linear equation systems, the Runge-Kutta method to solve ordinary differential equations, and the Simplex algorithm to solve linear programs.

Likewise, there is a qualitative solution method $s, s: \mathbf{C} \rightarrow 2^{\mathbf{D}}$, which maps from the qualitative description space $\boldsymbol{C}$ into the qualitative solution space $2^{\boldsymbol{D}}$. Typically, $\boldsymbol{C}$ is specified as a qualitative analog to $\boldsymbol{A}$. Sign equations, for example, can be treated as a qualitative analog to algebraic equation systems, and confluence systems or qualitative differential equations might be associated with ordinary differential equation systems. To accommodate for multiple solutions, both quantitative and qualitative ones, solutions are usually specified as sets of n-tuples like tuples of numerical values as the solution to a quantitative algebraic system, tuples of qualitative values as the solution to a qualitative algebraic system, tuples of real-valued functions as the solution to a differential equation system, or tuples of functions that can only take on qualitative values as the solution to a qualitative equation system.

Struss assumes that, within any particular QR system, there exists, at least conceptually, a deterministic description mapping, *F,* which links a quantitative model to a corresponding qualitative model. If the true quantitative model were known, such a transformation would derive the corresponding qualitative model from a given quantitative description by replacing numerical parameters and operators with analogous qualitative terms. Since one of the main assumption of qualitative reasoning is the absence of complete knowledge, which prohibits the specification of complete, precise, quantitative models, the transformation mapping *F* has little practical value. Nevertheless, it constitutes an important theoretical part of the framework, because it is generally assumed that a true, complete model does exist, even when we don't know it. In a similar manner, Struss introduces mappings between quantitative solutions and qualitative solutions. The mapping *G* provides the coverage of quantitative solutions, and the mapping G^{-1} gives a quantitative interpretation of qualitative solutions.

For example, a QR method based on algebraic equations in *n* variables would construct the mapping *G* from the basic coverage mapping *q* by expanding it to *n* dimensions. In this case, the quantitative solution method *S* would be a mapping from the quantitative description space *A*, consisting of, say, all systems of linear equations in *n* variables and *m* equations, into its solution space $2^{\mathbf{B}}$ where $\mathbf{B} = \mathbf{R}^N$. Likewise, the qualitative solution method *s* would be a mapping from the qualitative description space **C**, which comprises all systems of qualitative algebraic equations of a certain kind, into its solution space $2^{\boldsymbol{D}}$ where $\boldsymbol{D} = Q_1 \; x \; Q_2 \; x ... \; x \; Q_n$ with Q_i being the quantity space of the *i*-th qualitative variable. Now, one would define *G* as a mapping that associates to a particular quantitative solution $S(A) = B$, where $A \in \mathbf{A}$, $B \in 2^{\mathbf{B}}$, its covering set of qualitative values *G(B),* with $G{:}2^{\mathbf{B}} \rightarrow 2^{\mathbf{D}}$. On the other hand, G^{-1} would provide a quantitative interpretation to a given qualitative solution $s(C) = D$, thus G^{-1} is a mapping $G^{-1} : 2^{\mathbf{D}} \rightarrow 2^{\mathbf{B}}$.

In Struss' framework, any particular QR method is to be defined by precisely specifying the qualitative description space **C**, the quantity space *Q*, the qualitative solution method *s*, the transformation mapping *F,* the coverage mapping G, the interpretation mapping G^{-1}, and the explicit specification of the quantitative reference model space A, which presumably implies a quantitative solution method S. In other words, Struss defines a QR method as a tuple $(A, Q, C, s, G, G^{-1}, F)$. Given such a detailed specification it is then possible to analyze the relations of qualitative models, qualitative solutions, and their qualitative counterparts with respect to particular QR methods. Especially interesting question to investigate are (a) *completeness,* that is, does the particular QR method under study produce some covering qualitative solution to all quantitative solutions of the underlying quantitative model, (b) *soundness,* that is, is the QR method at hand capable of eliminating all (potential) qualitative solutions that do not have a quantitative solution to the corresponding reference model, and (c) *stability,* that is, what degree of robustness does this QR method exhibit ?

3. QUANTITATIVE MODELS AND SOLUTIONS

In order to develop a completely formalized qualitative reasoning method we need to have a quantitative reference system from which we can derive qualitative descriptions. Since we want to model dynamic systems, both continuous and discrete, we choose differential-difference equation systems as the basis of our definition of a quantitative system. The next section gives a detailed definition of what we mean by a quantitative model, that is, we describe a specific space, A, of quantitative descriptions. This is then followed by a section that defines what is meant by a quantitative solution to such a quantitative model, that is, we introduce a particular $2^{\mathbf{B}}$ as our quantitative solution space.

3.1 Definition of a Quantitative Model

We shall take a *quantitative system* to be a *finite collection of equations* of a suitable kind. To define what kind of equations we want to consider, we need to specify what kind of *quantities* can appear in them, and what kinds of *operations* can be applied in them.

We allow the following quantities to appear in our equations: (1) Independent real-values variables, denoted for convenience by $x_1, x_2, ..., x_N$, and t, where t is intended to denote time; (2) dependent variables or functions $y_1, y_2, ..., y_M$, of the independent variables; and (3), the (ordinary or partial) derivatives of functions y, whenever the differentiation of y, is defined with respect to some x_i .

Next, we specify at which point(s) the functions y_i and their derivatives can be evaluated in an equation. In order to include difference equations we allow translations, and we assume that vectors of the form $(a_1, \ldots, a_N, a)$ with nonnegative real entries are given such that the functions y_i or their derivatives can be evaluated not only at the point $(x_1, \ldots, x_N, t)$ but also at a point of the form $(x_1 - a_1, \ldots, x_N - a_N, t - a)$. Furthermore, when the same function y_i appears several times in one equation or across several equations we need to specify independently at which points $(x_1 - a_1, \ldots, x_N - a_N, t - a)$ the function shall be evaluated. This covers differential equations, difference equations, as well as differential-difference equations like, for example, $(y(t))^5 = 2y''(t-1) - y'(t-2.3)$.

We said above that each of the variables $x_1, x_2, \ldots, x_N,$ *and* t will assume real values. This is not intended to mean that all real values, or all values on an interval, must be taken. Some of the variables might take discrete values, and others might be continuous, or taking values in an interval. Thus, we assume that a certain subset Ω of $\mathbf{R}^{N+1}$ is given such that each y_i is defined for all $(x_1, \ldots, x_N\ t) \in \Omega$. The set Ω classifies the variables as discrete or continuous, or possibly as constants, and also determines the existence of the derivatives of y_i with respect to the variables $x_1, x_2, \ldots, x_N,$ and t As an example, Ω might be defined as a Cartesian product of intervals. Then each of the $x_1, x_2, \ldots, x_N,$ *and* t varies on some interval, independently of the others.

Finally, we have to discuss what kind of mathematical relationships we want to allow for our equations, that is, we need to define a set of admissible operands and operators from which we can formulate proper equations. Above, we have already introduced the operands that we consider, namely, constants and variables x_i , and the functions y_j with their derivatives. Recall that the operations that we shall tentatively allow are addition, subtraction, multiplication, division, the y_j describe the dependent variables as functions of the independent variables x_i . Now, we need to define which operations we allow in the specification of functional relationships. For our discussion it shall be sufficient to use the standard arithmetic operations addition, multiplication, subtraction, division, and exponentiation, and the application of standard mathematical functions, say, exponential functions e^x and logarithms $\log x$. Obviously, this list of admissible operands could be extended to suit the needs of specific application problems.

Finally, in order to provide a link to corresponding qualitative models, we introduce a special kind of designator functions φ, whose only purpose in the quantitative model specification is to identify those (sub)expressions which are going to be abstracted into a qualitative expression in a corresponding qualitative model. We postpone a further discussion of this transformation process until section 4.1, where we define what we mean by a qualitative model. For now, it should suffice to define the φ as independent, context-free functions of variables, say $u_1,\ldots,u_P$, which are completely expressed in terms of operands and operators as described above, and are defined on a specified set, V, $V \subset \mathbf{R}^P$. In most cases we will encounter several designator functions, $\varphi_1,\ldots,\varphi_L$. For notational brevity we use the symbol φ whenever we talk about an arbitrarily chosen φ_i. Thus, the value of P depends on the particular φ that we are considering

In addition to equations where equality holds between the two sides, we also allow inequalities. For notational convenience, we don't distinguish between equalities and inequalities, and subsume both under the term equation. To summarize, a quantitative model specification comprises of a list of variables, functions, and their derivatives, the set Ω, and the equations themselves. Now we can define the set of all models A satisfying the above specification requirements as a particular quantitative model space $\mathbf{A}$, which is specifically intended to cover differential-difference equation systems.

3.2 Definition of a Quantitative Solution

Solving a differential-difference equation system means, that we need to determine the exact functional form of the unknown dynamic quantities, that is, the quantities which are functions of time. More precisely, given a particular quantitative system $A \in \mathbf{A}$, we shall say that the functions Y_1, ..., Y_M, each defined on Ω, define a *quantitative solution* of *A,* if all given equations are satisfied for all choices of $(x_1, \ldots, x_N, t) \in \Omega$ when we substitute Y_i for y_i for all i , where $1 \le i \le M$, and when we make the corresponding replacement for all of the derivatives of the y_i being considered. In particular, this means that if the equations involve any derivatives, then, for these particular functions Y_i, all of those derivatives must exist in the appropriate parts of the set Ω, so that the equations are meaningful after the substitution. For many totally unrelated systems might have the same solution we define the quantitative solution as the **pair** *(A,B)* where A denotes the quantitative system and B denotes the quantitative solution. Notice, that a quantitative system A can have multiple, possibly infinitely many, solutions. Since we will also talk about B alone, we call B a *candidate for a quantitative solution* . A candidate B becomes a solution once a particular system A is identified to which it actually provides a solution.

Note that a system might have no solution. In order to exclude trivial situations let us, from now on, restrict our attention to only those quantitative systems that have at least one quantitative solution.

4. QUALITATIVE MODELS AND SOLUTIONS

Qualitative reasoning is mainly motivated by the observation that the tremendous complexity of many real-world phenomena impedes us from specifying precise, quantitative models which would correctly describe a particular problem under study. This does not mean that a true, quantitative model does not exist, it rather means that our limited cognitive capabilities too often prevent us from discovering it. Hence, qualitative reasoning generally assumes the existence of true, quantitative model, but one which usually remains hidden. The purpose of formulating a model of real-world phenomenon is foremost to derive conclusions from it, which help us to understand and learn about the world. A precise model typically produces a precise answer, but then we have to ask to which question is this really the answer. Assessment of the quality of the quantitative model used becomes an utmost important part of quantitative analysis, a difficult task which is highly dependent on the specifics of the problem at hand. Qualitative reasoning suggests a different approach in which the information requirements for formulating a problem description are lowered, and adjusted to the qualitative, incomplete kind of knowledge that is predominant in many fields. Qualitative models are viewed as abstractions of a true, hidden model, an abstraction that relieves the modeler from the specification of details and exact relationships, whose validity are beyond her or his state of knowledge. Of course, weaker problem descriptions entail weaker, often ambiguous results, and the question arises what level of detail should be required in the specification of qualitative models? The idea of using qualitative models as an abstraction of a quantitative model implies not only a weaker, qualitative problem representation, but also a representation which is consistent with the underlying, quantitative formulation, that is, a representation that is analogous to a quantitative descriptions of a certain kind. Otherwise it would be impossible to relate quantitative and corresponding qualitative models and their solutions. Qualitative reasoning systems commonly abstract real-valued quantities into quantities that are defined on a coarser quantity space, and provide a qualitative calculus as an analog to the calculus on which their quantitative reference system is based on.

The precise way we define a qualitative system affects the type of questions we can successfully analyze, the generality of the situations that can be considered, and the degree of precision and ambiguity we can expect from our results. The quantity space, Q, constitutes the backbone of any qualitative reasoning systems, and different definitions have been proposed in the literature. The ENVISION reasoner, de Kleer and Brown (1984), is based on sign arithmetic and defines all quantities on the coarsest quantity space, $Q=\{-,0,+\}$. Qualitative simulation, Kuipers (1986), introduces ordinal landmark values which partition the real line, and abstract each interval into a symbolic value, that is, each quantity in a model is defined on a quantity space of the form $Q=\{-\infty,l_1,l_2,...l_k,0,l_{k+1},...,l_n,\infty\}$. Kuipers and Berleant (1990) present Q2 as an ex-post analyzer to qualitative simulation where numerical intervals can be associated with landmark values, thereby enhancing the preciseness of the results, and reducing ambiguity. Williams (1991) suggests a hybrid form of reasoning where some quantities are defined on the set of real numbers while the others are defined on a sign-based quantity space. Experience with current qualitative reasoning systems has shown that models based on sign information or ordinal information tend to create ambiguous predictions, which explode in a combinatorial manner even for moderately sized problems. Therefore, we suggest a qualitative reasoning framework based on set theory, which allows to adjust the model formulation to any desired level of preciseness, depending on the information requirements of a particular application. As a special case, it includes interval-based representations as a genuine form of reasoning, as opposed to Q2, which is merely a post-processor to qualitative simulation (QSIM), and can only be applied as a retrograde method when qualitative simulation was actually successful in solving a model. However, interval analysis is computationally more powerful than purely quantitative calculi,that are based on ordinal information and monotonicity properties, and can be applied to obtain qualitative characterizations of partially known mechanisms.

4.1 Definition of a Qualitative Model

We define a qualitative model analogous to the way we defined our quantitative reference system, and base it on the definition of a quantitative model as presented in the previous section. We need only one modification. We introduced designator functions φ, and said they identify those parts of the quantitative model that are intended for a qualitative abstraction. What we mean by that is, that the functions φ represent the hidden parts in the true, quantitative model. In other words, they are unknown functions for which only incomplete, qualitative knowledge is available. If they were known, one could simply specify a complete, quantitative model, and they would be no reason to resort to qualitative reasoning techniques.

We assume that the φ are functions of variables, say $u_1,\ldots,u_P$, where the value of P depends on the particular φ that we are considering. The functions φ are to be defined on completely and explicitly specified subsets V of $\mathbf{R}^P$. Given that the exact functional forms of the functions φ are unknown, we assume that our qualitative knowledge allows us to provide upper and lower bounding functions which envelope the unknown φ. There is no requirement on the tightness of the bounding functions, although the tighter they are the better the predictions we can expect to derive. Each φ in the underlying quantitative reference model is replaced by an abstraction, which yields a corresponding qualitative model. More precisely, the qualitative model represents the unknown functions φ as pairs of bounding functions $L(u_1, \ldots, u_P)$ and $U(u_1, \ldots, u_P)$, defined for all $(u_1, \ldots, u_P) \in V$, such that

(1) $L(u_1,\ldots,u_P) \le \varphi(u_1,\ldots,u_P) \le U(u_1,\ldots,u_P)$, for all $(u_1,\ldots,u_P) \in V$

Furthermore, the type of the functions L and U is restricted to the same kind of operators as described before, and without the possibility of applying other functions of the type φ. We could impose additional restrictions on the functions φ, to ease computational problems, for example. Thus, we could require that φ is monotone (either increasing or decreasing) separately with respect to each of its variables. For example, the statement that $\varphi(u_1, \ldots, u_P)$ is increasing with respect to u_1 means that for any fixed choice of $(b_2, \ldots, b_P)$ the function $\psi(u) = \varphi(u, b_2, \ldots, b_P)$ of one variable u is increasing on the set $V_1 = \{u \in \mathbf{R} : (u,b_2,\ldots,b_P) \in V\}$, that is, $\psi(u) \le \varphi(v)$ whenever $u, v, \in V_1$ and $u < v$. This completes our description of the functions φ, as well as our definition of a qualitative system.

Note that according to this definition, each qualitative system C arises from some, usually unknown, quantitative system A. In this case we say that C is **compatible in form** with A. We call C **compatible** with A if, in addition, for every specific φ in A that was abstracted into qualitative terms, (1) holds for all $(u_1, \ldots, u_P)$ in the appropriate set V. The system A may contain many functions φ, and the same function φ might occur several times, in the same equation or across equations. Each time when a function φ occurs in A we need to provide specific upper and lower bounds which, in general, cannot be determined uniquely. Thus, a generic A is compatible with infinitely many different systems C, which differ only in the particular specification of their bounding functions. Similarly, the same C can be obtained from different systems A. If a particular $C \in \mathbf{C}$ is compatible with both $A_1 \in \mathbf{A}$ and $A_2 \in \mathbf{A}$ then this does not imply that $A_1 = A_2$.

4.2 Definition of a Qualitative Solution

Now, we still need to define what we mean by a qualitative solution to a qualitative model, which we shall do in an analogous way to our definition of quantitative solution in section 3.2. Recall that we called *(A,B)* a quantitative solution if substituting the functions $B = (Y_1, \ldots, Y_M)$ for the quantities $y_1, \ldots, y_M$ satisfies all constraints of the quantitative system A. Given a precise, quantitative description A we were able to determine the exact functional forms, say f_j, of the Y_j such that they provide a solution to A[8]. The situation is different when looking at a qualitative model C that contains unknown functions for which only upper and lower bounds are given. Then we cannot expect to find precisely defined functions which would provide a solution to C in a meaningful fashion. Hence, we shall try to characterize the solution to C in qualitative terms, and propose a set-based definition of a qualitative solution. We introduce sets $\hat{E}_j$ in order to provide a qualitative description of the unknown quantities Y_j, that is, we define the $\hat{E}_j$ such that they envelope the functions f_j, in the solution B of the underlying, hidden model A. We say, the collection of sets $\hat{E}_j(x_1, x_2, \ldots, x_N, t)$ given for each $(x_1, x_2, \ldots, x_n, t) \in \Omega$ and for each j, where $1 \leq j \leq M$ defines a qualitative solution of C if and only if for any quantitative system A compatible with C and every quantitative solution *(A,B)* we have $f_j(x_1, x_2, \ldots, x_N, t) \in \hat{E}_j(x_1, x_2, \ldots, x_N, t)$ for all $(x_1, x_2, \ldots, x_n, t) \in \Omega$ and for each j. Furthermore, we require each set $\hat{E}_j(x_1, x_2, \ldots, x_N, t)$ to be as small as possible such that it still has this property. More precisely, for each $(x_1, x_2, \ldots, x_n, t) \in \Omega$ and each j we define

$$(2) \quad \hat{E}_j(x_1, x_2, \ldots, x_N, t) = \{f_j(x_1, x_2, \ldots, x_N, t) : f_j \in B \sim A \sim C\}$$

Here, this ad-hoc notation is intended to mean that given a particular qualitative model C; A runs through all quantitative systems A compatible with C; and for each such A, the quantity B runs through all quantitative solutions to A; and then for any such A and B, f_j denotes the appropriate (completely and explicitly defined) function in B.

[8] Of course, in complicated cases we might not be able to find a solution analytically, and might need to resort to numerical methods.

The minimality property of (2) guarantees a unique solution to any qualitative system C, that is, the sets $\hat{E}_j$ are uniquely determined. Now, in order to actually compute the sets $\hat{E}_j$ we need to embellish definition (2) with a particular specification of the form of the sets the sets $\hat{E}_j$. We discuss three possible ways of representing them: (i) as a single, closed interval; (ii) as the union of at most *K* disjoint, closed intervals, where *K* is a fixed number, and for each different choice of *K* one would get a different representation; and (iii) as the union of finitely many disjoined, closed intervals, where the number of intervals used is arbitrary. However, for all three cases, (2) in its current form does not serve as an appropriate definition of the sets $\hat{E}_j$, because it is, in general, not possible to find closed intervals consistent with (2), and even in the cases where it actually is possible, it might be computationally unreasonably hard to calculate them. Henceforth, when we discuss the context of computational systems, we modify definition (2), and say, that for all *j*, where $1 \leq j \leq M$ the sets $E_j(x_1, x_2, \ldots, x_N, t)$ are taken to be the smallest sets of a specific form for which

(3) $E_j(x_1, x_2, \ldots, x_N, t) \supset \{f_j(x_1, x_2, \ldots, x_N, t) : f_j \in B \sim A \sim C\}$
holds.

The general requirement that we consider only disjoint intervals for representing the sets E_j has the advantage of avoiding unnecessary ambiguity. The same set can usually be represented in many different ways, for example, [0,3] could be represented as the union of at most two intervals as [0,3], [0,1]≈[1,3], [0,2]≈[2,3], and so forth. Using sets of an unrestricted kind, definition (2) of a qualitative solution has the nice property of being unique, that every qualitative model has exactly one solution.[9]

Representational form (i), suggested above, requires that each $E_j(x_1, x_2, \ldots, x_N, t)$ has to be a single, closed interval. This specific form yields also a unique solution, because we demand that the $E_j(x_1, x_2, \ldots, x_N, t)$ have to be minimal, that is, the smallest closed intervals containing the unrestricted sets $\hat{E}_j(x_1, x_2, \ldots, x_N, t)$. This follows because any subset of **R** is contained in a unique minimal closed interval[10].

[9] Recall, that, in section 3.2, we excluded quantitative systems that have no solution from our consideration. Therefore, definition (2) excludes also all qualitative systems that have no solution.

[10] In case we deal with possibly unbounded sets, we consider sets of the form $(-\infty, b]$, $[a, \infty)$ and $(-\infty, \infty) = \mathbf{R}$ to be closed intervals; then if *E* is any subset of **R**

When discussing representational form (ii) notice that, in general, for a set E and for a given integer $K \geq 2$, there does not exist a unique minimal set I containing E such that I is the union of at most K disjoint closed intervals. Here, minimal means that if a set J is of the same type as I and $J \subset I \subset E$ then $J = I$. For example, let us take $E = [1, 2] \approx [3, 4] \approx [5, 6]$ and $K = 2$. We could take $I_1 = [1, 2] \approx [3, 6]$ or $I_2 = [1, 4] \approx [5, 6]$, and both I_1 and I_2 would be minimal. Each I also has the same (total) width, which shows that the attempt to ensure a unique solution by introducing this extra, and rather natural, criterion fails. In other words, the additional requirement of representing a set $E_j(x_1, x_2, \ldots, x_N, t)$ as the union I of at most K disjoint closed intervals, where I, has minimal width, does not necessarily lead to a unique solution, not even in rather simple cases. Choosing representational form (iii) entails another problem. For example, if

$$E = \{0\} \cup \left(\bigcup_{i=1}^{\infty} \left[\frac{1}{2i+1}, \frac{1}{2i} \right] \right)$$

and if E is to be represented as the union I of an unspecified, finite number of disjoint closed intervals, then there is no minimal solution at all, which means there are infinitely many solutions none of which being minimal, and no unique solution can be determined. Also, there does not exist a solution that would minimize the total length of I.

When defining qualitative solutions using representational forms (ii) or (iii), one forsakes the uniqueness of a solution for an increased preciseness of its representation. A unique qualitative solution is, albeit its appealing properties, by no means a mandatory requirement. Ambiguous inferences is actually a typical attribute of qualitative reasoning methods, see paper two of the thesis. Thus, judging which form of representing the sets $E_j(x_1, x_2, \ldots, x_N, t)$ of a qualitative solution might be most appropriate has to take specific application needs into account, and cannot be done generally. However, from a computational perspective, one would prefer a method based on the usage of single intervals, which could be implemented by applying standard techniques of interval analysis. Representational form (ii) and, especially, representational form (iii) are computationally much more difficult, and any implementation would have to make additional, operational assumptions on how to regulate the representation of the sets $E_j(x_1, x_2, \ldots, x_N, t)$ as union of intervals.

---

and $a = \inf E$ and $b = \sup E$, the smallest closed interval containing E is $[a, b]$ $\cap \leftrightarrow$ R.

We have defined what we mean by a qualitative system and a qualitative solution to it. We have seen that the ideal qualitative solution, as defined in (2), is hard to compute. Hence, in (3), we have suggested a weaker, more practical definition of a qualitative solution which contains the ideal solution as a subset, and which is intended to be used as the result of a computational procedure for solving qualitative systems. We have then shown, that the particular form of the sets $E_j(x_1,x_2, \ldots,x_N,t)$ we are going to obtain from solving a qualitative model depends on the way they are represented. The same qualitative model will yield a different solution, depending on which specific representational form is chosen. All of them will contain the ideal qualitative solution as a subset, but they will also contain spurious elements, that is, elements which are not part of a quantitative solution to any compatible quantitative system. Thus, we define the set of spurious elements of a qualitative solution as

(4) $\tilde{E}_j = \{e : e \in E_j \wedge e \notin \hat{E}_j\} = E_j \setminus \hat{E}_j$, for all j, where $1 \le j \le M$.

We can partition a qualitative solution in (3) such that we get $E_j = \hat{E}_j \cup \tilde{E}_j$ for all j. Ideally, when solving a given qualitative model we are seeking a minimal solution according to (2) where $\tilde{E}_j = \varnothing$ for all j, that is, a solution without any spurious elements. However, when designing an algorithm for solving qualitative models of the kind we have described above, we (a) have to decide which representational form to use, and (b) we have to devise a computational procedure which derives the sets E_j from a qualitative model description. We have already seen that the particular choice of representational form of the sets E_j, such as the three forms suggested above, affects the kind of solution we can obtain, in terms of preciseness and uniqueness. When choosing the simplest representational form (i) and applying standard interval analysis, we cannot expect to get minimal solutions, because of the multiple occurrence problem of interval analysis, see section 3.2 in paper two of the thesis, which creates spurious elements, that is, we get solutions where, at least some, $\tilde{E}_j \neq \varnothing$. Switching to representational form (ii) or (iii) increases the preciseness of a solution, that is, we can expect, for all j, $\tilde{E}_j^1 \supset \tilde{E}_j^2 \supset \tilde{E}_j^3$ where the superscripts refer to the particular representational form used. However, the finer the representation used the more complicated the computation of a solution.

Now, we shall define a qualitative solution method as a completely specified algorithm which finds, for any qualitative system $C \in \mathbf{C}$, sets

$E_j(x_1, x_2, \ldots, x_N, t)$, for each $(x_1, x_2, \ldots, x_n, t) \in \Omega$ and each j, with the property that for every quantitative system A compatible with C and every quantitative solution (A,B) to such an A, we have $f_j(x_1, x_2, \ldots, x_N, t) \in E_j(x_1, x_2, \ldots, x_N, t)$. Then we call the collection of these sets $E_j(x_1, x_2, \ldots, x_N, t)$ a *candidate* D for a qualitative solution, and we call the pair *(C,D)* the qualitative solution to C. By a completely specified algorithm we mean a specification that includes operational assumptions which (a) ensure an unambiguous model representation, (b) imply a particular form of representing the sets E_j, and (c) provide a rule that determines unique sets E_j, if unions of intervals are chosen to represent them. Now the qualitative solution exists and is unique, even though not minimal in general, since we demand that a solution method is so well defined that given any initial information, it works in only one way and produces a unique answer.

5. THEORETICAL RELATIONSHIPS BETWEEN MODELS AND SOLUTIONS

This section applies Struss' general framework for analyzing qualitative reasoning systems, as summarized in section two of this paper, to our specialized, set-theoretic approach of qualitative reasoning, which we presented in the foregoing two sections. Section three introduced the class of differential-difference equation systems as our quantitative reference system, and section four described a particular abstraction thereof as our qualitative description space. Using Struss' framework, we, first, discuss the properties of our interval-based quantity space, then relate quantitative models and solutions with their qualitative counterparts, and, finally, derive certain properties of these relationships. We will argue that some of Struss' stipulated properties for qualitative reasoning systems are too rigid, and we will then suggest certain modifications thereof.

5.1 Properties of the Quantity Space

At the core of any qualitative reasoning system is the quantity space for describing qualitative variables. In our case, we have the universal quantity space $Q = \{\bigcup_{i=1}[a_i, b_i] : a_i, b_i \in \mathbf{R}, a_i \leq b_i, K \in \mathbf{N}\}$ on which all qualitative variables can be defined. Important specializations arise by fixing K, for all or for some of the variables, and thereby restricting their representation to the union of at most K intervals. Of particular interest[11], especially when considering a computer implementation, is the case where K=1, that is, $Q = \{[a,b]: a,b \in \mathbf{R}, a \le b\}$, where all variables are represented as single intervals, and standard interval analysis can be applied to derive inferences from a qualitative problem specification. We could impose further, problem-specific restrictions, and define each system quantity on an individualized quantity space instance. For example, we might know that a certain quantity x can only take on nonnegative values. Thus, we could define x on an individual instantiation $Q_x = \{[0,b]: b \in \mathbf{R}_+\}$. In any case, and contrary to Struss, we don't demand that a quantity space needs to be defined as a finite set of qualitative values. Instead, we use infinite sets of certain kinds to describe qualitative values, which provides not only a more compact and general way of representing qualitative values, but also a flexible means of incorporating new information into qualitative model specifications. Suppose, for example, we are given a particular model where a quantity z was initially defined on an individualized quantity space, $Q_z = \{[a_0, b_0]\}$, with specific bounds a_0 and b_0 on the possible values of z. Now, we might be able to acquire better information, and learn that z can be more accurately bounded by a_1 and b_1, where $a_0 < a_1 < b_1 < b_2$. This sort of information can be incorporated into the model specification in an easy manner by simply replacing the initial bounds with the new ones while the structure of the model, including the structure of the quantity spaces, is retained.

Although we haven't explicitly provided a basic coverage mapping $q: \mathbf{R} \to Q$ which would abstract the entire range of numerical values into corresponding qualitative values, one could obviously map any arbitrary real value $x \in \mathbf{R}$ onto a corresponding value, say $[a,b]$, of our universal quantity space such that x would be covered, that is, $a \le x \le b$. On the other hand, the basic interpretation mapping $p: Q \to 2^{\mathbf{R}}$, which associates qualitative values with a set of numerical values that are consistent with the semantics of each particular qualitative value, follows immediately from our definition of a quantity space, that is, for any $[a,b] \in Q'$ we would get $p([a,b]) = \{x: a \le x \le b\}$. While a partial order $(Q, \le)$ could be defined for our interval-based quantity space, we have deliberately forsaken the exclusiveness property in order to better represent fuzzy, vague, and uncertain problem descriptions. Our framework allows qualitative values

[11] For the sake of simplicity, and without explicit mention, we use the simplified quantity space based on single intervals in some of our illustrative examples. However, it should be clear from the context to which particular form of the quantity space we refer to.

from the same quantity space to overlap; $\exists [a,b],[c,d] \in Q : [a,b] \neq [c,d] \not\Rightarrow p([a,b]) \cap p([c,d]) = \varnothing$.

5.2 Functions between Models and Solutions

This Section uses the generic diagram, figure 1 in section two, to characterize our framework as a specific qualitative reasoning approach. According to our definition in section 4.2, a qualitative solution *(C,D)* is always unique in our specialized qualitative reasoning framework. Hence, figure 2 shows a modified basic diagram, which reflects this important difference.

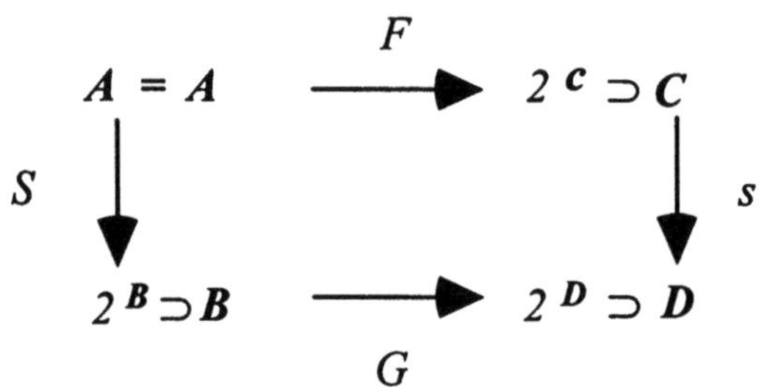

Figure 2. Basic Relationships in the Specialized Qualitative Reasoning Framework

Now, we tie this template to our specific definition of quantitative model and solution, and qualitative model and solution. Then, we complete the diagram by developing specific transformation, interpretation, and coverage mappings, and by introducing a few additional functions, which enable us to establish theoretical relationships and their properties of our suggested qualitative reasoning framework. As before, let $\boldsymbol{A}$ denote our quantitative reference system, the set of differential-difference equation systems A as defined in section three. Recall that we only consider quantitative systems that have at least one solution. Let $\boldsymbol{B}$ denote the set of all candidates for quantitative solutions B to the quantitative systems A of $\boldsymbol{A}$. Let $\boldsymbol{C}$ denote the qualitative counterpart of $\boldsymbol{A}$, the set of all qualitative differential-difference equations that arise from the systems in $\boldsymbol{A}$ as described in section 4.1. Let $\boldsymbol{D}$ denote the set of all candidates D for qualitative solutions to the qualitative systems C.

Next, we define specific functions that relate quantitative and qualitative concepts. We begin with the transformation mapping F which relates quantitative models to corresponding qualitative ones. Recall, that Struss assumes that there is, in principle, a deterministic way of transforming any given model from the quantitative model space into an analogous qualitative model. We propose a more general type of transformation mapping, and suggest a non deterministic, many to many relationship. Given $A \in \mathbf{A}$, there is no way to associate with A a unique C in a natural way and not by means of making arbitrary choices for each A separately. So, we define the function F as a mapping from $\mathbf{A}$ into $2^{\mathbf{C}}$ by taking F(A) to be the set of all qualitative systems compatible with A. Since A itself could be view as a degenerated qualitative system, where no abstraction is applied, we include A in the set of compatible qualitative models, thus we have $A \in F(A)$ for all $A \in \mathbf{A}$. Given any $X \in 2^{\mathbf{c}}$ (that is, $X \subset \mathbf{C}$), we have[12] $F^{-1}(X) \in 2^{\mathbf{A}}$. We further have $A \in F^{-1}(F(A))$ for all $A \in \mathbf{A}$, that is, $\{A\} \subset F^{-1}(F(A))$, and in general, $\{A\} \neq F^{-1}(F(A))$

We define the function S to be a mapping from the quantitative model space $\mathbf{A}$ into the quantitative solution space $2^{\mathbf{B}}$ by taking for any given $A \in \mathbf{A}$ the value S *(A)* to be the set of all B such that *(A, B)* is a quantitative solution of A, and call S the quantitative solution method. Again, for any $E \in 2^{\mathbf{B}}$, we have $S^{-1}(E) \in 2^{\mathbf{A}}$. We further have $A \in S^{-1}(S(A))$ for all $A \in \mathbf{A}$, that is, $\{A\} \subset S^{-1}(S(A))$, and in general, $\{A\} \neq S^{-1}(S(A))$. In other words, if A has *(A, B)* as one of its solutions, then usually there is some other $A_1 \in \mathbf{A}$ that has(A_1, B) as one of its solutions.

Similarly, we define the function s *to* be a mapping from the qualitative model space $\mathbf{C}$ into the qualitative solution space D by taking for any given $C \in \mathbf{C}$ the value $s(C)$ to be the unique D such that (C, D) is the qualitative solution of C, and call s the qualitative solution method. Note that$s$ need not be one-to-one. Again, for any $E \in 2^{D}$, we have $s^{-1}(E) \in 2^{c}$. We further have $C \in s^{-1}(s(C))$ for all $C \in \mathbf{C}$, that is, $\{C\} \subset s^{-1}(s(C))$, and in

12 Here, a word about notation. Let f be a function of a set X into a set Y. Even if f is not one-to-one, so that a (single-valued) inverse function of f (which would be denoted by f if it existed) need not exist, we write, for any subset Z of Y,

$$f^{-1}(Z) = \{x \in X: f(x) \in Z\} \subset X.$$

We also use the abbreviation $f^{-1}(y) = f^{-1}(\{y\})$ when $y \in Y$. The use of such notation is standard and does not imply that f has an inverse function. In the special case when f does have an inverse function, say f^{-1} = g, the notations f^{-1} *(Z)* and f^{-1} *(y)* then have the same meaning as the notations *g(Z)* and *g(y)* have for a function *g*.

general, $\{C\} \neq s^{-1}(s(C))$. In other words, if C has the solution (C, D), then there may be some other $C_1 \in \mathbf{C}$ that has the solution (C_1, D).

Next, we want to relate solutions of qualitative models with the solutions of their underlying quantitative reference models. We say that a candidate for a qualitative solution, D is compatible with a candidate for a quantitative solution, B, if they correspond in structure, that is, all functions in B and D can be put in one-to-one correspondence with each other so that the sets Ω are the same, there are equally many functions y_i and the same derivatives of the y_i, if any occur. The important difference, however, is the representation of the functions f_j, here the f_j denote the functions y_i and their derivatives. While the functions f_j are completely defined in B, there are only the sets $E_j(x_1, x_2, \ldots, x_N, t)$ in D, which provide a qualitative characterization of the functions f_j, and for which we require that $f_j(x_1, x_2, \ldots, x_N, t) \in E_j(x_1, x_2, \ldots, x_N, t)$ for all $(x_1, x_2, \ldots, x_N, t) \in \Omega$ and for each j. Then we say that D *covers* B. Clearly for each B there is at least one D that covers B. For if B is a solution to A then, for example, A itself is a (degenerate) qualitative system also, and its solution D covers the quantitative solution to A and thus covers B.

Now we can define the coverage function G as a mapping from $\mathbf{B}$ into $2^{\mathbf{D}}$ by taking $G(B)$ to be the set of all $D \in \mathbf{D}$ that cover B. Next, we define some composite functions and look at their relationships. We define a function F^* of $\mathbf{A}$ into $2^{\mathbf{D}}$ as a composite function *soF* by setting

$$F^*(A) = s(F(A)) = \{s(C)\colon\ C \in F(A)\}. \tag{5.4}$$

Note that $F^*(A)$ will contain a D that covers the solution B to A. Next, we define a function G^* of $\mathbf{A}$ into $2^{\mathbf{D}}$ as a composite function *GoS* by setting

$$G^*(A) = \cup\{G(B)\colon\ B \in S(A)\}. \tag{5.5}$$

Then we have

$$F^*(A) \subset G^*(A) \quad \text{for all } A \in \mathbf{A} \tag{5.6}$$

while usually one does not expect equality to hold here. Namely, if $D \in F^*(A)$ then D is the solution of some C that is compatible with A. So if

B is any solution of A then by (2), D covers B. Hence $D \in G(B)$ not only for some but for any solution B of A, that is, for any $B \in S(A)$. Hence $D \in G^*(A)$, and since D was an arbitrary element of $F^*(A)$, it follows that $F^*(A) \subset G^*(A)$. Since some $D \in G^*(A)$ could arise in a different way, we do not expect to have $F^*(A) = G^*(A)$.

Figure 3 extends the basic diagram shown as figure 2, and includes the composite functions F* and G* as new relationships which relate quantitative reference models with corresponding qualitative solutions.

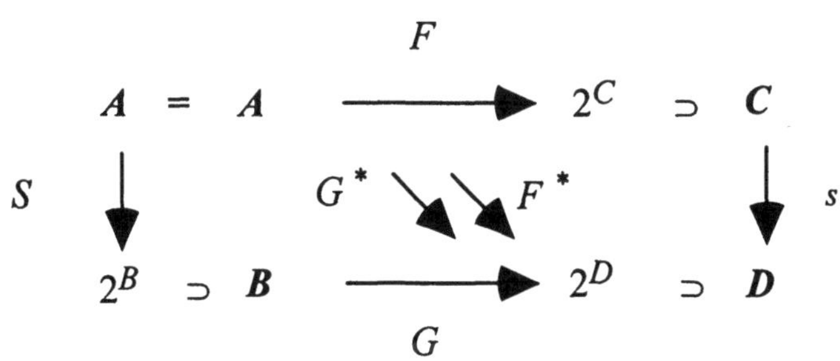

Figure 3: Extended Diagram for the Specialized Qualitative Reasoning Framework

5.3 Completeness and Soundness

We say a qualitative reasoning system is *complete* if the qualitative abstraction of each quantitative solution to any quantitative system from the quantitative model space forms a qualitative solution to the corresponding qualitative models. In the context of our framework, this means that, given an arbitrary $A \in \mathcal{A}$, then for all its solutions *(A,B)* there must be a corresponding qualitative solution *(C,D)*, that is, each B must be covered by D, and C must be compatible with A. Now, applying the quantitative solution S to a given $A \in \mathcal{A}$, we obtain $B^*=S(A)$, the set of all candidates B such that *(A,B)* is quantitative solution. Then we can apply the coverage mapping G to all $B \in B^*$, which gives us D^*, the set of all candidates D for a qualitative solution which cover the B. Thus, $D^* = (G \circ S)(A)$ which can be equivalently written as $D^*=G^*(A)$. Next, we need to show that the covering D actually arise from solutions of qualitative systems which are compatible with the original quantitative model A. Applying the transformation mapping F to the given quantitative systems A gives us $C^*=F(A)$, the set of all compatible qualitative models C, and applying the qualitative solutions method s to C^* yields $D^*=s(C^*)$, the set of all candidates for qualitative solutions D such that (C,D), is a solution of a qualitative system C which is compatible with the given A. Hence, $D^*=(s \circ F)(A)$ which can be equivalently written as $D^*=F^*(A)$. From (3) follows that every $D \in D^*$ covers all $B \in B^*$, thus they have to be contained in D^*, that is, $D^* \subset D^*$. This is equivalent to $F^*(A) \subset G^*(A)$ which follows also directly from (5.6). Thus, our qualitative reasoning framework is complete.

We say a qualitative reasoning method is sound if each qualitative solution to any given qualitative system, which is an abstraction of an underlying quantitative system, covers at least one of the quantitative solutions to the underlying quantitative system. Applied to our framework, this means that for any $C \in \boldsymbol{C}$ such that C is compatible with some $A \in \boldsymbol{A}$, there is $D \in (s o F)(A)$ such that $G^{-1}(D) \cap S(A) = \varnothing$. This is equivalent to $D \in G(S(A))$. Since this needs to be true for some $D \in (s o F)(A)$, we are requiring that $G(S(A)) \cap s(F(A)) \neq \varnothing$, or equivalently, $G^*(A) \cap F^*(A) \neq \varnothing$. This is true since we have $F(A) \neq \varnothing$ and, from (5.6), $F^*(A) \subset G^*(A)$. So our qualitative reasoning framework is sound, according to this definition. This result, however, depends on the way we have defined our qualitative values, which we have done, in section 4.2, by introducing the sets $E_j(x_1, x_2, \ldots, x_N, t)$ in (3), and by defining a qualitative solution as a uniquely determined collection of such sets. Since each of the sets $E_j(x_1, x_2, \ldots, x_N, t)$ contains, in general, spurious elements, we cannot derive soundness for particular selections from a qualitative solution.

6. CONCLUSION

In this paper, we have used Struss' general framework for analyzing qualitative reasoning systems, and presented a specific derivative from it, which is intended to serve as a theoretical foundation for qualitative reasoning about partially known differential-difference equation systems. We have precisely defined the nature of our quantitative reference system, that is, we have defined what constitutes a quantitative system, and what we mean by a quantitative solution. We then introduced a qualitative abstraction mechanism for transforming a quantitative system into a corresponding qualitative one, and defined what we mean by a qualitative solution thereof. Using unions of intervals as qualitative values, we were able to ensure uniquely determined solutions to such qualitative systems. This uniqueness property enabled us to establish, with respect to the quantitative reference system, completeness and soundness of our proposed qualitative reasoning framework. In this paper, we have not attempted to develop a computational procedure for actually computing a qualitative solution for a given qualitative model, that is, we have not specified a particular qualitative solution method. However, Kiang et al (1995) and Hinkkanen et al (1995') present rules constraint reasoning (RCR), an implementation of such a specific qualitative solution method. RCR is derived as a special case of the framework proposed in this paper, which restricts consideration to only difference equation systems and uses single interval representations of qualitative values.

REFERENCES

Allen, R.G.D. (1956), Mathematical Economics, MacMillan, London.

Bobrow, D.G., eds., (1985), Reasoning about Physical Systems, MIT Press, Cambridge, Ma.

Bailey, A.D., Y. Kiang, B. Kuipers, and A.B. Whinston (1991), Analytic Procedures and Qualitative Reasoning in Auditing, Applications in Management Science, JAI Press.

de Kleer, J., and J.S. Browne (1984), A Qualitative Physics Based on Confluences, Artificial Intelligence, **24**, 7-83.

Dordan, O. (1992), Mathematical Problems Arising in Qualitative Simulation of a Differential Equation, Artificial Intelligence, **55**, 61-86.

Farley, A.M., and K.P. Lin (1990), Qualitative Reasoning in Economics, Journal of Economic Dynamics and Control, **14**, 465-490.

Forbus, K.D. (1984), Qualitative Process Theory, Artificial Intelligence, **24**, 85-168.

Goldberg, S. (1958), Introduction to Difference Equations, John Wiley, New York.

Hinkkanen A., K.R. Lang, and A.B. Whinston (1995), On the Usage of Qualitative Reasoning as an Approach Towards Enterprise Modeling, Annals of Operations Research **55**, 101-137.

Iwasaki, Y. (1997), Real-World Applications of Qualitative Reasoning, IEEE Expert, **12**, May/June, 16-21

Kiang, M. Y., A. Hinkkanen, and A.B. Whinston (1995), An Interval Propagation Method for Solving Qualitative Difference Equations Systems, IEEE Transactions on Systems, Man, and Cybernetics **25**, 1110-1120.

Kuipers, B. (1986), Qualitative Simulation, Artificial Intelligence, **29**, 289-338.

Kuipers, B. (1994), Qualitative Reasoning, Modeling, and Simulation with Incomplete Knowledge, MIT Press Cambridge, MA.

Kuipers, B., and D. Berleant (1990), A Smooth Integration of Incomplete Quantitative Knowledge into Qualitative Simulation, Tech. Report AI90-122, Artificial Intelligence Laboratory, University of Texas at Austin.

Kuipers, B., and J.P. Kassirer (1984), Causal Reasoning in Medicine: Analysis of a Protocol, Cognitive Science, **8**, 363-385.

Lang, K.R., Moore, J.C. and Whinston, A.B. (1995), Computational Systems for Qualitative Economics, Computational Economics, **8(1)**, 1-26.

Monge, P.R. (1990), Theoretical and Analytical Issues in Studying Organizational Processes, Organization Science, **1**, 406-430.

Raiman, O. (1991), Order of Magnitude Reasoning, Artificial Intelligence, **51**, 11-38.

Simmons, R. (1986), "Commonsense" Arithmetic Reasoning, in: *Proceedings AAAI-86,* Philadelphia, PA., 118-124.

Struss, P. (1990), Problems of Interval-Based Qualitative Reasoning. In J. de Kleer, and D. Wald (Eds.), *Readings in Qualitative Reasoning about Physical Systems*, Morgan Kaufman, Los Altos, CA.

Weld, D.S., and J. de Kleer, eds. (1990), Reading in Qualitative Reasoning about Physical Systems, Morgan Kaufman, San Mateo, CA.

Williams, B.C. (1991), A Theory of Interactions: Unifying Qualitative and Quantitative Algebraic Reasoning, Artificial Intelligence, **51**, 39-94.

GLOSSARY[13]

attainable envisionment. The subset of states in the total envisionment reachable from a given initial state (or set of states).

behavior tree. The tree of qualitative states defined by the state completion, successor, and transition relations. Each path from root to leaf in this tree is a qualitative behavior.

comparative statics. The class of problems in which we attempt to find the relationship between an initial stable equilibrium state and the possible stable equilibrium state or states resulting from a small perturbation to the system.

corresponding value tuple. A tuple of qualitative values, one for each variable in a QSIM constraint, representing a consistent set of values for that constraint.

landmark. A qualitatively distinctive value in the range of a variable. A symbolic description of a particular number, whose numerical value may be unknown. The three predefined landmarks are minf, 0, and inf.

limit analysis. The act of determining which among a set of changing variables will reach the landmarks they move toward.

operation region. The domain within which the current QDE is valid. Usually characterized by bounding landmark values in the quantity spaces of some variables in the QDE. A region transition is invoked if the value of a variable is equal to a bounding landmark and moving out of the current operating region.

parameter. Exogenously determined variable. Usually a constant in QSIM QDEs. (Formerly, and incorrectly, used to mean "variable.")

QDE. Qualitative differential equation. A qualitative abstraction of an ordinary differential equation (ODE).

qdir. Qualitative direction of change. The sign of a derivative of a variable at given qualitative state.

qmag. Qualitative magnitude. A description of the magnitude of a variable in terms of the landmarks in a quantity space. A value is described as either equal to a landmark value, or in an interval defined by two landmarks, usually the open interval defined by two adjacent landmarks.

qplot. The output format representing the qualitative behavior of a variable in a graph with the quantity space for the variable on the vertical axis, the quantity space for time on the horizontal axis, and representing the value of the variable at each qualitative state by a symbol for the qdir either at or between adjacent landmarks.

[13] This glossary has been adopted from Kuipers (1994)

QSIM constraint. A qualitative abstraction of an algebraic, differential, or functional relation among reasonable functions. Determines which tuples of qualitative values for its variables are consistent.

Q2. The semi-quantitative reasoner that takes a behavior predicted by QSIM with interval bounds on landmark values, and derives tighter bounds on landmark values, or a contradiction refuting the behavior.

qualitative behavior. An alternating sequence of qualitative time-point and time-interval states describing the behavior of a reasonable function or set of reasonable functions. Often this set corresponds to a possible solution to a QDE model.

qualitative state. A description of the qualitative values for the variables in a QDE at a time-point or over a time-interval when that description remains constant. A *basic* qualitative state describes the values only with respect to the originally given landmark values.

qualitative value. A qualitative description of the value of a variable at a qualitative time-point or time-interval state. Consists of a qmag and a qdir.

quantity space. An ordered set of landmark values, defining the possible qualitative descriptions of the magnitude of a variable.

quasi-equilibrium assumption. The assumption that a system is always at, or very near, a point of stable equilibrium.

qval. Qualitative value.

reasonable function. A continuously differentiable function amenable to qualitative reasoning. It has only finitely many critical points over its domain, and its derivative approaches limits at the endpoints of the domain.

region transition. The point in a behavior when simulation stops because some variable has crossed the boundary of the operating region of the current QDE. The behavior either ends at that point or resumes a discontinuous change, in the same or a different QDE.

sign-valued operators. Mapping from the extended real number line $\Re^* = [-\infty,+\infty]$ to the extended domain of signs $S' = \{+,0,-,?\}$.

total envisionment. The set of all possible states of a given QDE, and all possible transitions among them.

variable. A real-valued function of time.

Chapter 8

An Architecture for Knowledge Management Featuring Metaknowledge

Roger Alan Pick: George P. Schell
University of Missouri - Kansas City & University of North Carolina - Wilmington

Abstract: In our tribute to Andrew B. Whinston, we return to our roots to examine an area that is important today but had not been described in the literature when we wrote our dissertations -- knowledge management. We briefly describe knowledge management, give an architecture for a general knowledge management system, and give examples to illustrate how metaknowledge could assist in a knowledge management system.
Key words: knowledge management, metaknowledge, model management.

1. INTRODUCTION

Our economy is an increasingly knowledge-based economy. According to *The Economist* (October 16, 1999, pp. 80-81), "Knowledge-based industries accounted for over half of rich-country business output in the mid-1990s, up from around 45% in 1985." The same article reported increasing business investment in knowledge-based intangibles as opposed to investment in physical goods. Furthermore, most forms of e-business are arguably knowledge-based (Holsapple & Singh, 2000). Spending on information systems has been found to contribute to output at the firm level (Brynjolfsson & Hitt, 1996). In sum, business is investing in knowledge in order to compete in today's economy. Generally, knowledge goes beyond data or information insofar as knowledge includes the ability to be applied within an organization's own processes.

The increasing level of investment in knowledge necessitates that the firm systematically manage this investment in order to preserve its value and in order to maximize the return from the investment. Initiatives to systematically manage knowledge generally fall under the term knowledge management (KM). KM initiatives have occurred in a diverse variety of organizations, ranging from consulting firms such as McKinsey (Bartlett, 1996) or Andersen Consulting (now called Accenture) (Davenport & Hansen, 1998), to the U.S. Army (U.S. Army TRADOC, 1997), to the World Bank (Knoop et al, 1997) to chemical companies such as Buckman Laboratories (Fulmer, 1999), and to basic steel companies such as NUCOR (Gupta & Govindarajan, 2000).

Knowledge management is a fairly amorphous area, meaning different things to different people. The field encompasses such areas as creativity enhancement, training, data mining, expertise directories, best practices, lessons learned, knowledge sharing, knowledge transfer, incentives for sharing, incentives for trusting others' solutions, research and development, management of patents, and management of intellectual property. In this paper, the term will be used to represent initiatives to capture, preserve, share, and spread knowledge throughout the organization.

Although it is commonly argued that knowledge management is more about organizational behavior than information technology (Cross & Baird, 2000; Davenport & Prusak, 2000; Dixon, 2000; Nonaka & Takeuchi, 1995; von Krogh et al, 2000), we argue that both ingredients, appropriate information technologies as well as organizational initiatives, are necessary. Information technology is necessary as an enabler of knowledge management within any organizations except the smallest; without the technology, it is not possible to scale capture and reuse of knowledge beyond internally within small workgroups. This paper discusses some information technology aspects of a knowledge management system. We will focus upon a system that holds both knowledge in some raw form (presumably unstructured text, but it could just as easily be multimedia content) and pointers to knowledge located outside of the system (either in people's heads, or in other information systems, or in other non-technology-based repositories). Depending upon the needs of the organization, that knowledge may be pushed to recipients via such mechanisms as e-mail or pulled by organizational members using a search mechanism, perhaps via a web-based interface.

2. KNOWLEDGE MANAGEMENT ARCHITECTURE

We propose a five-layer architecture for knowledge management, with each layer relying upon services provided by the one below it. Table 1 shows the layers.

Table 4. An Architecture for Knowledge Management

Name of Layer	Items Within Layer
Language System	Web browser
Transport	TCP/IP
Metaknowledge	Intelligent agent tools & documents describing KM system
Integration	Import tools and pointers
Repository	Multimedia documents

The five-layer architecture begins at the user's workstation, with a web browser to support the user's interaction with the system. Following the terminology of Bonczek et al (1981), we call that layer the language system. The web browser relies upon TCP/IP protocols to communicate with the remainder of the system; those protocols constitute the second layer or transport. The third layer is metaknowledge, knowledge about the system itself. This layer is analogous to a data dictionary facility for a database management system. There will be further discussion about this layer in the next section. The fourth layer is an integration layer, used both to access knowledge stored in the repository layer of the system and to bring in knowledge from outside of the system. This latter form of knowledge might be stored in pre-existing legacy systems, or it might be knowledge in the form of people's expertise, known to the system but never or not yet captured by it. The fifth layer or repository layer is an information storage and retrieval system for generalized documents containing knowledge.

The architecture supports the capture of knowledge, the storage of knowledge, and the retrieval and delivery of knowledge. Knowledge capture can occur in at least three ways.

In one form of knowledge capture, a document is added to the system and stored by the facilities in the repository layer. The document is entered via the web interface, transported by TCP/IP, scanned by the metaknowledge tools to extract metaknowledge about the document (third layer), and then stored by the document repository (fifth layer). The integration layer (fourth layer) would note that the document is to be found within the knowledge management system.

In a second form, the system is informed of the existence of expertise within the organization. This expertise arrives via a web interface, is transported, and the nature of the expertise is added to the metaknowledge (third) layer. Who possesses that expertise and how to contact them is stored in the integration layer.

In the third form, legacy knowledge is integrated into the system. That knowledge is not copied into the system. Instead, it is scanned for metaknowledge (third layer), and the location of the knowledge and access methods are stored in the fourth layer.

The fifth layer requires the storage of knowledge. Storage of knowledge is the transport of knowledge through time, from an occasion when the organization acquires it to a time when it is needed. The knowledge can be stored in a series of generalized documents. The documents might be unstructured text verbally describing lessons learned or best practices, but the notion of document should be generalized in this context to include multimedia documents, enhanced with graphics, sound, and video.

In some instances, a document will be in a computer-managed format. For example, a document could be a relational database; we believe that at least some knowledge management initiatives will continue to require storage of structured data such as is supported by a relational database. More generally, sometimes the relational database may be needed in the context of a larger document explaining how the data can be applied. As a second example of knowledge coded in a computer-managed format, some knowledge will be in the form of specialized expertise such as has been captured historically by expert systems. Such knowledge can be stored in a semantic, rule-based or frame-based expert system and can be considered as a document object.

Thus, the fifth layer needs to support knowledge coded in a variety of formats, ranging from legacy structured data through frames to multimedia documents. To be extensible and support the widest variety of formats, the fifth layer should be object-oriented; then, when a new document format is needed, it can be stored along with the software to store, manipulate, and display it. This would allow knowledge be available when and where needed again no matter what form the knowledge requires. A reasonable subset of the fifth layer could involve self-describing documents, using extensible markup language (XML). With XML, data structures are embedded in the web page code itself. Knowledge management systems will have to adapt to these new structures as they become more common. It is unlikely that the entire knowledge base of the system would be coded in XML, as many documents within the system are created for reasons other than use in the system, and are incorporated into the system incidently; such documents would be in whatever code or format is most amenable to their primary purpose.

Retrieval and delivery of knowledge involves the location of knowledge within the system and giving that knowledge to the user. This can be initiated by a proactive knowledge management system (push) or by proactive users (pull). Knowledge can be pushed via such technologies as e-mail, or it can be pulled via such technologies as search of documents on a web site. To push, a person entering knowledge into the system can indicate that it should be forwarded to certain individuals. Alternatively, pushing can be done by standing queries that are executed against each document entered into the system. If the document satisfies the conditions of the query, it is forwarded to the appropriate users.

Web technologies enable another approach to pushing knowledge. Web servers can take advantage of cookies created during web browsing to look for similar characteristics of users visiting the web server. For example, assume that an organization has a web server for internal use and various organization members visit web pages on the server at different times. If a user has a problem, visits a number of web pages on the server, but is unable to find a solution, the knowledge management system might be able to provide a list of other users with similar interests. One of the 'similar' users may have found a solution. The knowledge management system's ability to find similarities based upon web page access, sequence of access, duration of page view, and other characteristics helps the organization to introduce a user with a problem to another user who may have the solution.

3. METAKNOWLEDGE

The third layer of this architecture is metaknowledge. Broadly speaking, metaknowledge is knowledge about knowledge. It enables assisting in the retrieval and management of knowledge in a manner analogous to how a data dictionary/directory includes metadata which assists both a database management system and its users in locating and using data. It is typical practice for the data dictionary/directory for a relational database to be implemented using relations. Similarly, the metaknowledge for a knowledge management system is knowledge about knowledge and therefore will be coded in generalized documents. However, some of the knowledge about knowledge is structured and could be stored in a structured format such as a relational database.

It is fitting with the spirit of this book to discover that Andy Whinston was writing about metaknowledge (Chang et al, 1993; Chang et al, 1994) before we ever became interested in the topic. Andy and his coauthors used the term hyperknowledge rather than metaknowledge. However, the earliest use of the term metaknowledge we have been able to locate comes from Blanning (1987), who used the term to refer to an approach to improve inference in a knowledge-based decision support system. Other uses of the term prior to the present paper refer to an artificial intelligence application in the form of an expert system's self-awareness (Botten et al, 1989; Zahedi, 1987), model building in decision support (Chang et al, 1993; Chang et al, 1994) or in terms of a librarian□s knowledge about a subject (Connell, 1995). In all cases except Connell, the term is used to refer to knowledge about knowledge but is applied in a more specialized niche than occurs in the present paper. In the case of Connell, the metaknowledge is something which exists in librarians' expertise about a subject matter, rather than within an information system. We have not been able to locate in the journals any other research which has proposed the use of metaknowledge in the context of a knowledge management system.

Our conception of metaknowledge in the context of a knowledge management system is that it is knowledge. Such knowledge could be created and added to the system in at least two ways. First, it could be added to system by its own users to describe their own best practices in making use of the system in a way similar to how other contributions are made to the system. Second, it could be added to the system automatically.

Metaknowledge would be a series of documents created by people experienced in the use of the knowledge management system itself. They would create these documents to describe how to effectively make use of the system within the organization. When entered into the system, these documents would be identified as metaknowledge - knowledge about how to use the knowledge management system itself - rather than knowledge about organizational processes outside the knowledge management system. Thus, best practices about the use of the knowledge management system become encoded as part of the system's metaknowledge and stored in the metaknowledge layer.

Metaknowledge could also be created by the knowledge management system itself, as a by-product of its operation. When a new document is added to the system, the document is scanned, and knowledge about the document is added to the metaknowledge layer even as the document is added to the repository layer.

3.1 Metaknowledge: A Data Mining Example

In this paper we focus on the technology behind initiatives to capture, preserve, share, and spread knowledge throughout the organization. Organizations are increasingly using the corporate database for these tasks. From the point of view of knowledge management, the corporate database is a pre-existing legacy system. Access to the database will be via the fourth layer, the integration layer, which will include pointers and other access methods for the corporate database. The database is not just for data within the database management system itself, but for other data to which the database management may point or reference. The database, within and without the database management system, becomes the raw material upon which a knowledge management system can act.

Meta-data exists in a database management system in the form of table definitions, field definitions, table relationships, and other characteristics. Relational database structures are especially useful for enabling this type of knowledge management process in that the table relationships may define a first cut path for knowledge management systems to exploit. Relationships are formed by primary key and foreign key linkages between different tables. While these relationships are formed as part of the normalization process, most corporate databases will violate some normalization requirements in the pursuit of security and/or processing efficiency.

The key/foreign key feature of relational database structures allows the knowledge management system to discern records with similarities. For example, suppose a data request involved data from (or at least navigation through) five database tables. Navigation in relational database management systems proceeds when the values in primary keys/foreign keys match. It would be reasonable for the knowledge management system to relax the database rule and conclude that records where the primary keys/foreign keys match in four of the five tables to be somewhat related. This would allow the knowledge management system to branch out intelligently to closely related records if an exact match is not found.

If a guided approach were preferred, a knowledge management system could mine the database looking for similarities. Those similarities could be in the form of document titles, authors, recipients, date of document, key words, and other indices. If the sought data were not overtly in the database, the knowledge management system could search for data with a high degree of match on these indices and refer the user to the matches. Matches could be presented to the user in a hierarchy of 'approximate match' similar to those performed by web searching.

An example of a relational database that tracks customer complaints can demonstrate how database structure lends itself to knowledge management. Consider a database schema consisting of four relations:

- COMPLAINT (ID (key), ProductNumber (foreign key), CustNumber (foreign key), RepID (foreign key), Date, Description, Disposition),
- CUSTOMER (CustNumber (key), Name, Address, Phone, Email),
- PRODUCT (ProductNumber (key), Cost, NumberOnHand), and
- SERVICEREP (RepID (key), RepName, HireDate).

The four tables each have a single field key which uniquely identifies each row in the table. The COMPLAINT table has three foreign keys which allow records from the related tables to be joined when the key/foreign key values are the same.

Assume the Disposition field may contain on of four values: return for refund, return for store credit, return for replacement, and customer appeased. A knowledge management agent could be developed that searched the values of COMPLAINT table records for the Disposition value of customer appeased. From there it could navigate to related SERVICEREP records via RepID foreign key/key matching values. The name of the service representatives (RepName) could be extracted to find representatives who were adept at appeasing customers. These service representatives' names could be coded into an internal best practices directory. They could also create documents explaining their appeasement practices and procedures for entry into the knowledge management system.

A similar use of this database could suggest which service representative is best suited for a particular complaint. By linking both the SERVICEREP and PRODUCT tables from the COMPLAINT table, a knowledge management agent might be able to suggest which service representative should handle a complaint based upon a past ability to appease customers who purchased a particular product. The knowledge management system merely needs to use the structure of the relational database and simple rules for assessing association strengths.

3.2 Metaknowledge: A Model Management Example

We will now focus on a specific type of metaknowledge: modeling knowledge. Models constitute an intellectual asset of the enterprise. Models represent explicit knowledge. At the same time, the knowledge about the model is (unless documentation practices are exemplary) tacit. It is difficult to make people in an organization beyond the model-builder's workgroup aware that a model exists so that it can be more widely used. Muhanna and Pick (1994) describes some of the structured data needed for this kind of sharing. This includes the list of inputs and outputs for each model and the components that are combined to form a model. Other structured data for a model would include the type of model, the solution algorithm, and the name and contact information for the model formulator. We will describe further knowledge about modeling that is often tacit, and such knowledge could usefully be captured by the system for sharing.

Knowledge about models is often undocumented and is therefore tacit. How the model was built, what simplifying assumptions were made during the modeling process, and how the model results are interpreted are all examples of modeling knowledge that even if explicit are too complex to capture in a structured database. If knowledge about how to modify and reapply an existing model to new situations is to be made widely available, the modeler has to create a document that makes that knowledge explicit.

When that document is entered into the knowledge management system, the metaknowledge about the document is extracted in order to assist in finding it later when it is appropriate to do so. The metaknowledge about modeling will include information about how to find existing models, information about how to modify existing models, and a directory of employees who have model-building skills.

3.3 Metaknowledge: A Best Practices Directory Example

A common type of knowledge management system is an organization-wide best practices directory. Such a directory lists types of applications and people who have experience with each type of application, various skills and people who are known to have that skill, clients and people who have worked with that client, and so on. In our architecture, the best practices directory would reside at the fourth layer, the integration layer. The integration layer allows the comprehensive system to include how to locate expertise that exists outside of the system.

However, an indication of the existence of the best practices directory and the types of applications, skills, and clients that it includes would be stored in a document at the metaknowledge layer. Users searching for assistance would first find the metaknowledge, which in turn directs their inquiries to the best practices directory portion of the integration layer.

4. CONCLUSION

This paper has briefly outlined how metaknowledge might be used in an organization's knowledge management initiatives. We view knowledge as stored in generalized documents, stored in an extensible object-oriented repository at the bottom or fifth layer of a knowledge management system. Pointers to knowledge outside of the system would be stored in the fourth layer of the system. The third layer is metaknowledge. We see metaknowledge as itself specialized knowledge intended to guide the system in its own retrieval and to guide users in their interactions with the system. The second layer of the system is the Internet. The top layer of the system is the language system. We believe that metaknowledge would be a useful way of organizing a knowledge management system and would assist in later retrieving relevant knowledge.

REFERENCES

Bartlett, Christopher A. (1996). *McKinsey & Company: Managing knowledge and learning.* Boston: Harvard Business School Case 9-396-357.

Blanning, Robert W. (1987). The application of metaknowledge to information management. *Human Systems Management 7(1)*, 49-57.

Bonczek, Robert H., Holsapple, Clyde W., & Whinston, Andrew B. (1981). *Foundations of decision support systems.* New York: Academic Press.

Botten, Nancy, Kusiak, Andrew, & Raz, Tzvi (1989). Knowledge bases: Integration, verification, and partitioning. *European Journal of Operational Research 42(2)*, 111-128.

Brynjolfsson, Erik, and Hitt, Lorin (1996). Paradox lost? Firm-level evidence on the returns to information systems spending. *Management Science 42(4)*, 541-558.

Connell, Tschera Harkness (1995). Subject searching in online catalogs: Metaknowledge used by experienced searchers. *Journal of the American Society for Information Science 46(7)*, 506-518.

Chang, Ai-Mei, Holsapple, Clyde W., and Whinston, Andrew B. (1993). Model management issues and directions. *Decision Support Systems 9(1)*, 19-37.

Chang, Ai-Mei, Holsapple, Clyde, W., and Whinston, Andrew B. (1994). A hyperknowledge framework of decision support systems. *Information Processing & Management 30(4)*, 473-498.

Cross, Rob, & Baird, Lloyd (2000, Spring). Technology is not enough: Improving performance by building organizational memory. *Sloan Management Review*, 69-78.

Davenport, Thomas H., & Hansen, Morten T. (1998). *Knowledge management at Andersen Consulting.* Boston: Harvard Business School Case 9-499-032.

Davenport, Thomas H., & Prusak, Laurence (2000). *Working knowledge: how organizations manage what they know.* Boston: Harvard Business School Press.

Dixon, Nancy M. (2000). *Common knowledge: how companies thrive by sharing what they know.* Boston: Harvard Business School Press.

Fulmer, William E. (1999). *Buckman Laboratories (A).* Boston: HBS Case 9-800-160.

Gupta, Anil K. & Govindarajan, Vijay (2000, Fall). Knowledge management□s social dimension: Lessons from Nucor Steel. *Sloan Management Review*, 71-80.

Holsapple, Clyde W. & Singh, Meenu (2000). Toward a unified view of electronic commerce, electronic business, and collaborative commerce: A knowledge management approach. *Knowledge and Process Management 7(3)*, 151-164.

Knoop, Carin-Isabel, Valor, Josep, & Sasser, W. Earl (1997). *Information at the World Bank: In search of a technology solution (A).* Boston: HBS Case 9-898-053.

Muhanna, Waleed A., & Pick, Roger Alan (1994). Meta-modeling concepts and tools for model management: A systems approach. *Management Science 40*, 1093-1123.

Nonaka, Ikujiro & Takeuchi, Hirotaka (1995). *The knowledge-creating company: how Japanese companies create the dynamics of innovation.* Oxford: Oxford Univ. Press.

Knowledge gap. (1999, October 16). *The Economist, 353*, 80-81.

Sharda, Ramesh, Frankwick, Gary L, & Turetken, Ozgur (1999). Group knowledge networks: a framework and an implementation. *Information Systems Frontiers, 1 (3)*, 221-239.

U. S. Army Training and Doctrine Command (1997). *A Guide to the Services and the Gateway of CALL (Center for Army Lessons Learned).* Fort Leavenworth, KS.

Von Krogh, Georg, Kazuo, Ichijo, & Nonaka, Ikujiro (2000). *Enabling knowledge creation: how to unlock the mystery of tacit knowledge and release the power of innovation.* Oxford: Oxford University Press.

.Zahedi, Fatemeh (1987). AI and the management science practitioner: The economics of expert systems and the contribution of MS/OR. *Interfaces 17(5)*, 72-81.

PART II

MODELLING IN ELECTRONIC BUSINESS

Chapter 9

Multi Agent Enterprise Modeling

Riyaz Sikora: Michael J. Shaw
Department of Business Administration, University of Illinois @ Urbana Champaign, Champaign, IL 61820, rtsikora@uiuc.edu: *m-shaw2@uiuc.edu*

Abstract The advent of information technology has made today's enterprises increasingly distributed. To stay competitive organizations of today have to manage the different components of their technology by integrating and coordinating them into a highly efficient, effective, and responsive system. Rather than dealing with each component individually, it is necessary to have a new paradigm for management of enterprise systems, so that all the components and their operations can be managed in an integrated fashion. The multi-agent framework presented in this paper is such a paradigm for achieving enterprise integration. We specifically emphasize the coordination mechanisms needed for ensuring the orderly operations and concerted decision making among the components - i.e., agents - of an enterprise.
Keywords: Enterprise Integration, Agent-Based Information Systems, Multi-Agent Systems, Coordination Mechanisms, Coordination Theory.

1. INTRODUCTION

Intense competition on a global level is fast changing the way enterprises organize and manage themselves. To stay competitive organizations of today have to manage the different components of their technology by integrating and coordinating them into a highly efficient, effective, and responsive system. The spectacular growth of Information Technology (IT), especially the Internet, electronic commerce, and wireless communication, not only has an enormous potential for improving the performance and productivity of enterprises but is also shaping their structure and design. Electronic markets, powered by the Internet and the Web, are working as a catalyst for enterprise integration. Ubiquitous computing and mobile and wireless communication will be the key to tying together the diverse functions of many enterprises.

The problem of enterprise integration has been with us for a long time, but there have been some changes in the way that we think of the problem. Until recently, we operated under the assumption that large enterprises could be managed effectively by working on "reductionism" (the practice of decomposing a problem into smaller, more manageable pieces. Increasingly the research community has recognized the need for a new paradigm, which incorporates explicit treatment of integration. The evidence that something more is needed continues to accumulate driven mostly by the advent of communication technologies (including the Internet) and the increasing need for coordination in organizations and, especially, in information systems. There can be several objectives of enterprise integration, such as establishment of good communication and coordination procedures, promoting collaboration among a group of networked participants, sharing information among different entities across an enterprise, efficient management of the coordination between different information systems in an enterprise, and consolidating various business functions to make the processes more efficient.

In this paper we present a multi-agent framework for modeling the coordination and integration of enterprises. It models each stage or process as an autonomous agent. Message passing among these autonomous agents forms the control structure. Each agent has an internal behavior model, a functional component consisting of procedures/heuristics/strategies, and a protocol for interacting with other agents. The protocols specify what action an agent will take based on its local state and the messages received from other agents. Thus, the concurrent execution of the protocols by all the agents determines the coordination mechanism used by the agents and the resulting emergence of their behavior.

The development of the above multi-agent framework can be of utmost importance to the management of technology in an enterprise. For instance, the development and introduction of IT in enterprises has historically followed the "islands of automation" approach where many functional units or departments are independently equipped with local computing resources. The resulting enterprise-wide information infrastructure is typified by interconnected and interdependent information systems where both the information and control flows are highly complex. For a fully integrated information system it is extremely important that these interrelated system functions be mutually rationalized and completely coordinated via the application of a unified framework of system integration, such as the one being proposed in this paper.

Enterprise integration can be studied and implemented at various levels of granularity. For example, typical enterprise integration might involve: (a) Integration of heterogeneous information systems, data bases, or application software to facilitate the data flow between them and to make the overall system robust and efficient; (b) Integration of different physical stages in business processes to improve the internal performance metrics; and (c) Integration of subsystems into a well-coordinated, networked system. The basic requirement for achieving enterprise integration is coordination of the different components or sub-systems.

Coordination has been an intensely studied concept across different disciplines. For example: Ledyard (1993) provides an introduction to a theory of coordination mechanism design. Hewitt (1977, 1991) and Hewitt & Inman (1991) present the framework for the development of the Actor and Open Systems. Ferber and Carle (1991) present a reflective actor language for implementing Distributed Artificial Intelligence (DAI) systems that is based on the Actor model. There is, however, a lack of rigor and formalization in the Actor model. The key missing link is how to make the concepts presented in that model computational. Although the foundations of Open Systems are based on the Actor model, the connection is incomplete. As pointed out by Gasser (1991), the descriptive power of Actor model is limited. For example, the relation between the Actor model and concepts such as negotiation, coordination, and cooperation is not clear.

An intelligent agent framework for enterprise integration is presented in Pan and Tenenbaum (1991). The framework provides only a vision of how agent-based systems would look like in the future without providing a formal model that relates to such concepts as negotiation and cooperation that have been intensely studied in the coordination literature. Malone and Crowston (1994) present an interdisciplinary study of coordination, drawing from such diverse fields as computer science, organization theory, operations research, economics, linguistics, and psychology.

The concept of coordination has not been incorporated in information system design until recently. As the cost of communication is being significantly reduced, the framework of computer system design today is shifting from computing to communication. A growing function of information systems today is to allow people across the organization to share information and coordinate their respective activities. A large factor in driving companies to improve their organization coordination through information sharing is the Web.

Markets and hierarchies are two mechanisms traditionally used by organizations to coordinate their various functions. Information technology is facilitating transaction coordination and is making both markets and hierarchies more efficient. Electronic hierarchies coordinate the flow of materials through centralized information processing and decision making using centralized information systems, such as enterprise systems. To a large extent, enterprise systems follow simple design rules such as a maximum integration of information flows and standardization (Davenport 1998). In contrast, electronic markets coordinate the flow of materials through supply and demand forces and external transactions between different individuals and firms. Market forces determine the design, price, quantity, and target delivery schedule for a given product that serves as an input into another process. The buyer of the good compares its many possible sources and makes a choice based on the best combination of these attributes. While enterprise systems may be suitable for organizations with hierarchical structures, studies have shown that decentralizing information processing and decision making are valuable for organizations that have to deal with multiple markets, where local knowledge is indispensable in the decision making process (Anand and Mendelson 1997, Davenport 1998). In those situations, it becomes costly and nearly impossible for a hierarchical organization to gather and communicate timely information from the local office to the central headquarters (Tan and Harker 1999).

2. REVIEW OF RELATED RESEARCH

Multi Agent Systems (MAS) have been studied for more than a decade as a sub-discipline of the broader area of Distributed Artificial Intelligence (DAI) research. The MAS research is, for the most part, concerned with coordinating intelligent behavior among a collection of (possibly pre-existing) autonomous intelligent "agents", how they can coordinate their knowledge, goals, skills, and plans jointly to take actions or to solve problems (Bond and Gasser 1988). The underlying assumption in all of the MAS research is that it was applicable in areas that are distributed and have heterogeneous components that are (semi) autonomous. Although this discipline is not new, there has been a very strong revival of interest in recent times in agent-based applications because of the recognition that the core problems in MAS research are quite profound, ubiquitous, and impact many areas across different disciplines. This resurgence in MAS research can be tied to two phenomenon: (1) The spread of concurrent and distributed computing with the advent of the Internet and WWW and (2) a deeper integration of computing into organizations and the lives of people, which has led to increasing collaborations among large collections of interacting people and large groups of interacting machines.

One of the side effects of the increase in connectivity and collaboration has been the phenomenal increase in the magnitude and volatility of the available data. Intelligent agents are now emerging as a way to deal with this staggering variety and volume of data in distributed and heterogeneous environments (March *et al.* 2000). Agents and agent-related technologies are also becoming important because they let software components interoperate within modern applications like e-commerce and information retrieval. This has become especially relevant since most large-scale information systems applications of today assume that components will be added dynamically and that they will be autonomous (serve different users or providers and fulfill different goals) and heterogeneous (be built in different ways).

In the past, the use of agent-based concepts has been inhibited by limitations of process control structures in conventional computing languages. This is currently changing with the wide diffusion of object-orientation as a result of the success of the Web (for example, the Java 2 Platform, Enterprise Edition - J2EE). Object-orientation is a far better match with agent system characteristics than conventional software languages (Prietula *et al.* 1998).

One of the best examples of effective development of enterprise integration has been in the manufacturing domain. The increasing trend toward integrated manufacturing system began with the development of the MRP/MRP-II systems that tried to integrate the functions of forecasting, order entry, aggregate planning, and materials requirements. The increasing need for integrating cross-functional areas lead to the development of Computer Integrated Manufacturing (CIM) (Harrington 1975). The underlying philosophy behind CIM was that system integration can be achieved by providing a computer-based system to link the different advanced flexible production. However, it was pointed out by Duimering *et al.* (1993) and many others (Mize 1991, Wolfe and Settles 1989, Conaway 1985) that merely linking different systems does not lead to integration. For true integration, the actual activities performed by the different systems should be coordinated.

There has been a fair amount of work done in developing distributed systems for manufacturing control. Maley (1988) presents a system that uses a distributed negotiation procedure for managing physical parts' operations and the information flow within manufacturing. There have been many applications of contract net for distributed manufacturing control (Shaw 1987, Parunak 1987). Most of these assume the use of MRP II's functionality and use the contract net for lower level control. Baker (1988) presents a system that uses contract net to implement both MRP II and lower level control. Parunak *et al.* (1985) describe a factory control system that uses the actor model as its software architecture and a negotiation-based fractal hierarchical control structure. Fractal hierarchy refers to the notion that the formalism used to model the factory is the same at every level of the hierarchy.

The above-mentioned approaches of managing manufacturing systems utilize functional decomposition to specify the tasks to be completed by each component of the system. In contrast, the agent-based approach emphasizes the importance of information and control by utilizing the relationships and interdependencies between the agents as a fundamental part of the system. This point of view is shared by research in agent-based systems (Lee *et al.* 1993) and network organizations (Ching *et al.* 1993).

The framework presented here is based on rigorous analytical treatment (Sikora & Shaw 1998) characterizing different control structures in a multi-agent system that lead to a useful taxonomy of interdependencies and coordination mechanisms. The main advantages of using the framework presented in this paper are: (1) it provides uniformity of a general framework for the total system by treating the heterogeneous components in a homogeneous fashion, (2) it recognizes modularity by allowing different modules to be individually developed and implemented, (3) it underscores the importance of the capability to reconfigure the system easily, and (4) it represents distributed control by modeling the "agents" as having local control along with the capability for interacting and coordinating their activities through message-passing. In the next section we present the conceptual agent-based framework.

3. Agent-Based Framework for Enterprise Integration

Agents are the basic entities in our framework. Agents can model either physical components and processes of the system or decision modules. Each agent has it's own well-defined goals and objectives. Designing a *synthesis function*, which defines how the individual sub-goals of the agents or their performance measures are related to the performance of the system as a whole, is the crucial problem for the design (or analysis) of any multi-agent system. We can identify three important types of synthesis functions:

(1) *Competitive Synthesis:* This applies to the case where the agents are brought together to work asynchronously on the same problem, and the best solution from among them is chosen as the group solution. Since only one agent's solution is meant to be selected, it encourages competition among the agents, which in turn improves their individual performances. This concept

of 'survival of the fittest' is found not only in ecosystems but also in many social systems involving group deliberation or group problem solving. The Distributed Learning System (DLS) discussed in Sikora and Shaw (1996) incorporates a computational model of the above synthesis process.

(2) *Additive Synthesis:* In this case, the group performance is given by the sum of individual performances of the agents. This is the most common type of synthesis function found in multi-agent systems that are designed in a top-down approach. The goals of the system are decomposed into *independent* sub-goals and are then assigned to different agents. Distributed Artificial Intelligence (DAI) literature is rich in the work done on task or goal decomposition. Sometimes decomposition can be obtained by the transformation of problem representation (see for e.g., Amarel 1968, Simon 1969), or it can be obtained by using abstraction levels as the basis (see for e.g., Sacerdoti 1977, Erman and Lesser 1975, Wesson *et al.* 1981).

(3) *Cooperative Synthesis:* In this case the group or system performance is a more complicated function of the agent's individual performance measures. The complication arises because of interactions, possibly conflicting, among the sub-goals and activities of the agents. This type of synthesis mainly arises in the context of system integration, or bottom-up design of multi-agent systems where existing agents with different functional or operational perspectives have to be integrated into a whole.

The problem of ensuring cooperation among the agents to improve the performance of the system becomes important in this case. The important issues in this context of system integration are determining the types of interactions or interdependencies present among the activities of the agents, and developing coordination mechanisms that result in cooperative synthesis of the agents' performance measures into the system performance.

Figure 1 shows the conceptual model of an agent. The shaded blocks represent components that might not be present in all agents. Each agent is modeled as consisting of three important components: A *knowledge base*, a *control unit*, and a *functional component*. The knowledge base in turn consists of a list of acquaintances, which is a finite collection of agents that it directly knows about, and a knowledge base containing the domain knowledge and data. The control unit of the agent consists of protocols and in some cases a learning module. The functional component consists of computational procedures and in some cases a behavior model. Below we describe each component in detail.

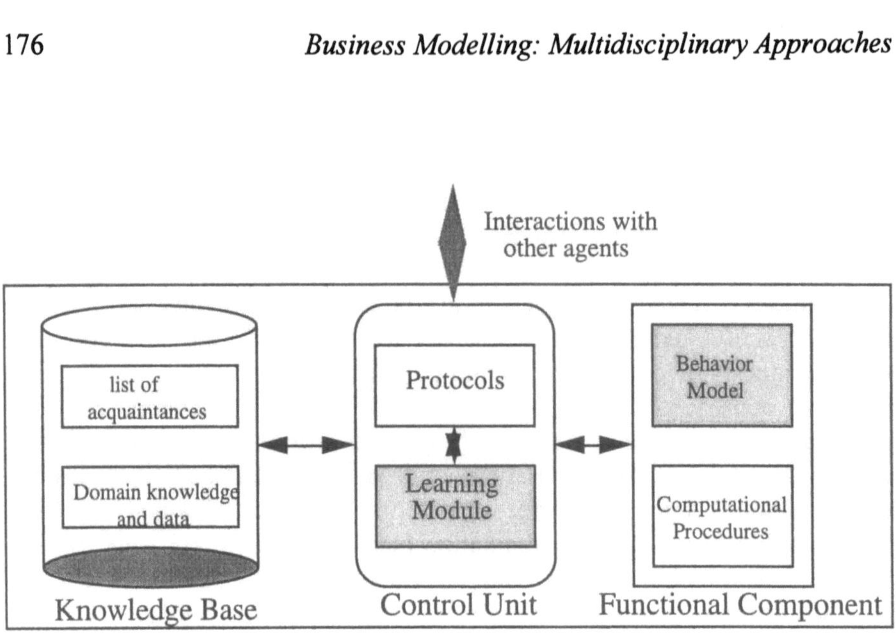

Figure 1. Conceptual Model of an Agent

(1) *Knowledge / Data*

Each agent has a knowledge base that contains the essential data and knowledge required by the agent to perform its activities. For example, in case of a manufacturing enterprise the data might include information about the manufacturing environment such as customer orders, production schedule, etc. An agent might also have knowledge about the capabilities of other agents. For example, it might know that Agent2 has the capability of manufacturing a specific sub-assembly. Note that unlike the data component, which for the most part remains static, the knowledge component of the knowledge base might be continuously updated either by the agent itself or by the system administrator.

(2) *List of Acquaintances*

Each agent has an acquaintance list that contains the list of agents that it directly knows about. An agent can communicate only with those who are in its acquaintance list. The acquaintance list determines the interdependency and control structure among the agents. For example, the activities of the agents might be interdependent due to the constraint of ordering them in a certain order (*temporal interdependency*), the agents might be using a common resource (e.g., money, storage space, or an agent's computation time) to perform their activities (*resource interdependency*), or the sub-goals of the agents resulting from task decomposition might be overlapping or interdependent (*sub-goal interdependency*). A taxonomy of interdependencies is discussed later.

(3) *Functional Component*

Each agent has a functional component that contains the computational procedures that the agent might need. The computational procedures can be optimization techniques or heuristic/search techniques. For example, an agent responsible for doing the short interval scheduling of a manufacturing line might have heuristic procedures for doing lot-sizing and sequencing. In some cases the agents might also have a behavior model of the corresponding system component. For example, a scheduling agent for a manufacturing line might contain a simulation model of the line in order to test and evaluate different production schedules.

(4) *Protocols*

Protocols provide the basic mechanism for the agents to communicate with each other. Protocols specify what kind of information sharing takes place between the agents and how the agents respond to messages they receive from other agents. Protocols can be specified in the form of *if-then* rules or in the form of a sequential algorithm that is executed by each agent.

The protocols of all the agents together constitute the coordination mechanism being used by the system. The concurrent execution of the protocols of the agents, therefore, determines the emergence of behavior for the agents and the resulting system performance.

(5) *Learning Module*

The learning module enables the agent to constantly update the knowledge component of its knowledge base based on the performance of its functional component and on the interaction with the other agents. For example, over time the agent might learn the best dispatching rule (a computational procedure) to use in a given scenario.

Figure 2 shows a general representation of the application of the agent-based framework. For example, the entities can be the different computer-based machines in a shop floor that have to be integrated. The physical links would correspond to the material handling system that interconnects the islands. The application of the agent-based framework for integrating the working of the islands of automation would then involve creating the agents corresponding to each island of automation and enabling them to interact and control the entities. Note that the agents do not necessarily have to correspond to physical entities (for e.g., Agent A in figure 2). They could be logical decision modules that also have to be integrated with the working of the physical entities. In such cases there would not be a behavior model in the functional component of the agent. Each agent can in turn be analyzed within the agent-based framework as consisting of sub-agents (for e.g., Agent 4 in figure 2).

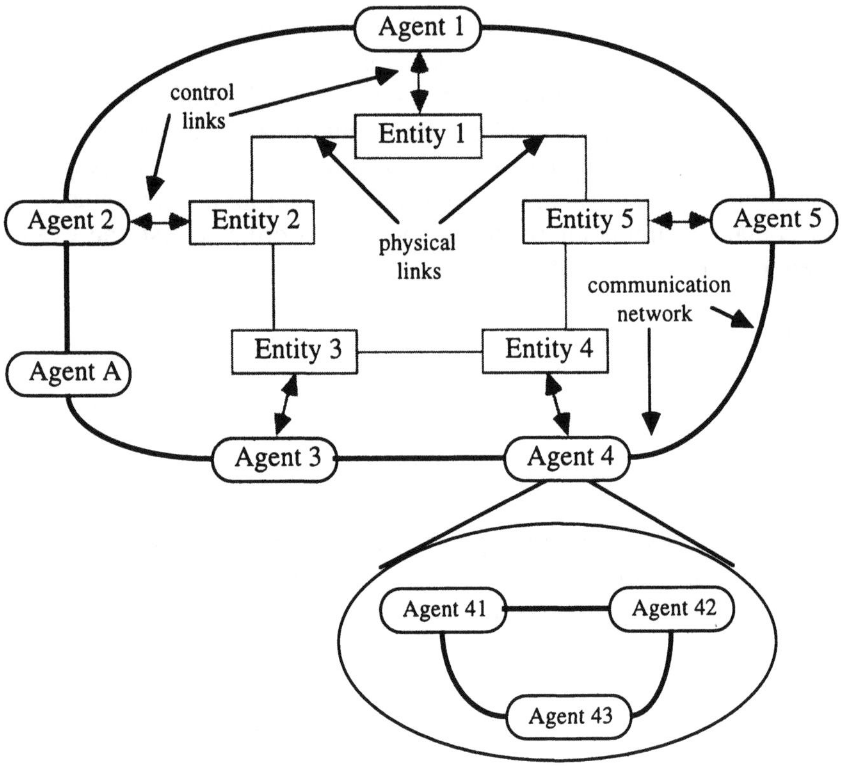

Figure 2. Multi-Agent Framework for Enterprise Integration

The most important problem faced by any multi-agent system is the problem of coordination that arises due to the interdependencies among the internal activities of the agents, represented by the interaction variables in our framework. The first step towards developing a framework of coordination should therefore be identifying the various kinds of interdependencies possible and discussing the different coordination mechanisms one can use. Below we give taxonomy of the kinds of interdependencies possible.

2.1 Taxonomy of Interdependencies

Interdependencies among the agents can be of various forms. Each requires a different kind of coordination mechanism. Based on the survey of the dependencies given in Malone and Crowston (1994), we can identify three main types of interdependencies.

(1) *Temporal Interdependency:* The activities of the agents might be interdependent due to the constraint of ordering them in a certain order. In some cases, certain activities cannot be started until others are finished (the problem of sequencing) or a certain group of activities have to be performed at the same time (the problem of synchronization).

Techniques from operations research, such as PERT charts and critical path methods are designed to manage the temporal interdependencies among the multiple activities in large projects. Problems of managing temporal interdependencies also arise frequently in computer science. For example, in order to effectively use the available technology of parallel computers one has to decide which activities can be done in parallel and which ones must wait for the completion of others (see for e.g., Peterson 1977, Arvind and Culler 1986, Krajewski and Ritzman 1987, Holt 1988).

(2) *Resource Interdependency:* The agents might be using a common resource (e.g., money, storage space, or an agent's computation time) to perform their activities. In such a case, the amount of resource that an agent can use for its activities is dependent on its usage by the other agents and hence coordination is required for resource allocation. The process by which the agents modify their individual utilizations would constitute the coordination mechanism.

There has been a good amount of work done in resource allocation in DAI. Several important approaches that have been used are resource allocation using specialist "sponsor" agents (Kornfeld and Hewitt 1981, DeJong 1988) that allocate fixed portions of resources in a manner analogous to research sponsors, resource allocation based on the criticality of the tasks (Lesser *et al.* 1988), and resource allocation via resource pricing (Chandrasekaran 1981, Kurose *et al.* 1985). Resource allocation has also been an important issue in the design of organizational structures. For example, Pfeffer and Salancik (1978) have investigated the effects that resource dependencies often have on entire organizational structures; Burton and Obel (1980) have studied various hierarchical resource allocation processes in organizations.

(3) *Sub-goal Interdependency:* The sub-goals of the agents resulting from task decomposition might be overlapping or interdependent. The agents have to exchange information about their partial results during the course of their problem solving or their partial solutions have to be integrated into the final

solution. The extreme case where all the agents are working on the same problem collaboratively also falls in this category.

More often the kind of interdependencies found are a combination of the above types. The classic mutual exclusion problem in computer science involving preventing two different processes from simultaneously accessing the same resource (Dijkstra 1968) also can be viewed as having two kinds of interdependencies. On one hand the above problem can be viewed as a problem involving temporal interdependency since the processes have to be ordered properly. On the other, this can also be viewed as resource interdependency problem since only one process can use the resource at a time.

In order to successfully handle the different kinds of interdependencies discussed above, the use of coordination becomes very important in any multi-agent system. Communication mechanisms play an important role in forming the control structure, which determines the possible types of interactions among the agents and subsequently defines the coordination mechanism. The design of communication channels and mechanisms has also been important in the design of organizational structure when viewed from an information-processing perspective. The key characteristic of organizational structure is that it links the elements of the organization by providing the channels of communication through which information flows (Duncan 1979). Consistent with this view is the concept of treating organizations as a collection of knowledge processing systems (Holsapple and Whinston 1987). In this paper we will treat message passing as the basic control unit of any coordination mechanism. In the next section we present taxonomy of the different control structures possible and discuss some of the coordination mechanisms found in the literature.

2.2 Taxonomy of Control Structures and Coordination Mechanisms

The following taxonomy gives the main kinds of control structures possible and the subsequent coordination mechanisms that can be used in multi-agent systems. Since, in our framework, communication based on message passing is treated as the basis for the control structure, the taxonomy given below is based on the different structures of communication links possible.

(1) *Centralized Control*: There is a central coordinator to whom everyone communicates their solutions. The agents cannot communicate among themselves. The coordinator therefore handles the interdependencies among the agents.

In terms of our framework, we can think of the coordinator as also one of the agents. The list of acquaintances of the coordinator would include all the other agents. The list of acquaintances of the agents, on the other hand, would only include the coordinator. The above centralized control structure can be generalized to a hierarchical structure where the list of acquaintances of any node (*agent*) consists of its immediate children nodes and its parent node. Most organization structures fall into this category.

(2) *Decentralized Control*: This is the most common form of control structure found in distributed systems. There is no coordinator or a single agent who has the global view of the problem. Instead, the agents have to interact among themselves, exchanging information and coordinating their interdependencies. In the extreme case of this control structure every agent can communicate with every other agent. In practice, however, due to the communication costs and overload of information, each agent is allowed to communicate only with a small subset of the agents. In most cases the list of acquaintances of any agent is determined by the set of agents with whom it has interdependencies.

There are several coordination mechanisms that use the decentralized control structure. The right kind of coordination mechanism depends on the type of interdependencies among the agents. Some of the representative coordination mechanisms widely used are coordination by negotiation (see for e.g., Davis and Smith 1983, Sycara 1989, Holsapple *et al.* 1995), coordination by constraint reasoning (Fox *et al.* 1992), coordination by group deliberation (Laughlin and Shippy 1983, Nunamaker *et al.* 1988, Hayes-Roth 1985, Watabe, Holsapple, and Whinston 1992), and coordination by synchronization (Georgeff 1983).

Another related work has been the development of a model of communication in a work environment by Winograd and Flores (1987). In their model every conversation is governed by some rules, which constrain the actions of the participants. Their model of communication is that of a finite automaton, with the automaton states corresponding to different states of the conversation. The Winograd and Flores coordinator can be easily implemented within our framework by designing the agent protocols based on the communication constraints. For example, requiring that each request received by an agent be followed by an accept or a reject.

3. CONCLUSIONS

In this paper we have presented a general multi-agent framework for understanding and analyzing the different issues involved in coordinating and integrating an enterprise consisting of a collection of stand alone units, each of which can be viewed as an "agent." The above framework can form the foundation for the development of a complete theory of coordination.

The main advantages of using the above framework are: (1) it provides uniformity of a general framework for the total system by treating the heterogeneous components in a homogeneous fashion, (2) it recognizes modularity by allowing different modules to be individually developed and implemented, (3) it underscores the importance of the capability to reconfigure the system easily, and (4) it represents distributed control by modeling the "agents" as having local control along with the capability for interacting and coordinating their activities through message-passing.

The multi-agent framework also has important implications for the system development issues. Broadly speaking one can consider two methods of achieving coordination in a system: Centralized and Distributed. In centralized approaches, one can either develop a large system to automate the coordination or one can develop smaller modules that can then be linked to form the centralized system. In contrast, in distributed approach one can develop modules that run independently of one another in parallel but interact with each other. Note that the individual modules may or may not correspond to the physical entities whose activities they are trying to coordinate. We outlined the drawbacks of the centralized approaches and the need for distributed approaches in the introduction section. One of the most important applications of the framework presented here can be the integration of various heterogeneous components, databases or software systems, at the organizational level.

REFERENCES

Amarel, S. 1968. "On Representations of Problems of Reasoning About Actions." In D. Michie (Ed.), *Machine Intelligence 3*, pp. 131-171.

Anand, K.S., H. Mendelson. 1997. Information and Organization for Horizontal Multimarket Coordination. *Management Science* **43** (12) 1609-1627.

Arvind and Culler, D. E. 1986. "Dataflow Architectures." In *Annual Reviews in Computer Science.*, vol. 1, Palo Alto, CA: Annual Reviews, Inc.

Baker, A. D. 1988. "Complete Manufacturing Control Using a Contract Net: A Simulation Study." *Proceedings of the International Conference on Computer Integrated Manufacturing (CIMIC)*, IEEE. pp. 100-109.

Bond and Gasser (Eds.). 1988. *Readings in Distributed Artificial Intelligence*, Morgan Kaufmann Publishers, Inc., San Mateo, CA

Burton, R. M. and Obel, B. 1980. "The Efficiency of the Price, Budget, and Mixed Approaches under Varying A Priori Information Levels for Decentralized Planning." *Management Science.* 26.

Chandrasekaran, B. 1981. "Natural and Social System Metaphors for Distributed Problem Solving: Introduction to the Issue." *IEEE Transactions on Systems, Man, and Cybernetics.* SMC-11(1):1-5.

Ching, C, Holsapple, C. W., and Whinston, A. B. 1993. "Modeling Network Organizations: A Basis for Exploring Computer Support Possibilities." *Journal of Organizational Computing.*

Conaway, J. 1985. "What's In A Name: Plain Talk About CIM." *Computers in Mechanical Engineering.*

Davenport, T.H. 1998. Putting the enterprise into the enterprise system. *Harvard Business Review* (July-August) 121-131.

Davis, R. and Smith, R. G. 1983. "Negotiation as a Metaphor for Distributed Problem Solving." *Artificial Intelligence.* 20(1): 63-109.

DeJong, P. 1988. The UBIK Configurator. *Proc. of the Conference on Office Information Systems.* ACM Press, New York. 309-315.

Dijkstra, E. W. 1968. "The Structure of the T. H. E. Operating System." *Communications of the ACM.* 11(5), pp.341-346.

Duimering, P., Safayeni, F, and Purdy, L. 1993. "Integrated Manufacturing: Redesign the Organization before Implementing Flexible Technology." *Sloan Management Review.* pp. 47-56

Duncan, R. 1979. "What is the Right Organization Structure? Decision Tree Analysis Provides the Answer." *Organizational Dynamics.* 7, no. 3, pp.59-80.

Erman, L. D. and Lesser, V. R. 1975. "A Multi-Level Organization for Problem Solving." In *Proc. of the International Joint Conference on Artificial Intelligence.* pp.483-490.

Ferber, J and Carle, P. 1991. "Actors and Agents as Reflective Concurrent Objects." *IEEE Transactions on SMC.* 21(6), pp. 1420-1436.

Fox, M. S., Finger, Gardner, Chandra, Safier, and Shaw. 1992. "Design Fusion: An Arch. for Concurrent Design." *Knowledge Aided Design.* 157-195.

Gasser, L. 1991. "Social Conceptions of Knowledge and Action: DAI Foundations and Open Systems Semantics." *Artificial Intelligence.* 47, pp.107-138.

Georgeff, M. P. 1983. "Communication and Interaction in Multi-Agent Planning." In *Proceedings of 1983 Conference of the AAAI.* pp. 125-129.

Harrington, J. 1975. *Computer Integrated Manufacturing.* Krieger Publishing Company, Malabar, Florida.

Hayes-Roth, B. 1985. "A Blackboard Architecture for Control." *Artificial Intelligence.* 26, pp.251-321.

Hewitt, C. 1977. "Viewing Control Structures as Patterns of Message Passing," *Journal of Artificial Intelligence.* 8(3), pp.323-364.

Hewitt, C. 1991. "Open Information Systems Semantics for Distributed Artificial Intelligence." *Artificial Intelligence.* 47, pp.79-106.

Hewitt, C and Inman, J. 1991. "DAI Betwixt and Between: From "Intelligent Agents" to Open Systems." *IEEE Transactions on SMC.* 21(6), pp. 1409-1419.

Holsapple, C. W., Lai, and Whinston, A. B. 1995. "Analysis of Negotiation Support Systems Research." *Journal of Computer Information Systems.* 35(3), 2-11.

Holsapple, C. W. and Whinston, A. B. 1987. "Knowledge-Based Organizations." *The Information Society,* Vol. 5, pp. 77-90.

Holt, A. W. 1988. "Diplans: A New Lang. for the Study and Implementation of Coordination." *ACM Trans on Office Info. Systems.* 6(2), 109-125.

Kornfeld, W. A. and Hewitt, C. 1981. "The Scientific Community Metaphor." *IEEE Transactions on Systems, Man, and Cybernetics.* SMC-11(1):24-33.

Krajewski, L. J. and Ritzman, L. P. 1987. *Operations Management: Strategy and Analysis.* Addison-Wesley Publishing Co., Reading, MA.

Kurose, J. F., Schwartz, M., and Yemini, Y. 1985. "A Microeconomic Approach to Optimization of Channel Access Policies in Multiaccess Networks." In *Proc. of the Fifth Intl. Symposium on Distributed Computing Systems.* pp.70- 80.

Laughlin, P. R. and Shippy, T. A. 1983. "Collective Induction." *Journal of Personality and Social Psychology.* vol. 45, pp. 94-100.

Ledyard, J. O. 1993. "The Design of Coordination Mechanisms and Organizational Computing." *Journal of Organizationl Computing.* 3(1), pp. 121-134.

Lee, K-C, Mansfield, W., and Sheth, A. 1993. "A Framework for Controlling Cooperative Agents." *IEEE Computer.* pp. 8-16, July.

Lesser, V. R., Pavlin, J., and Durfee, E. H. 1988. "Approximate Processing in Real Time Problem Solving." *AI Magazine.* 9(1):49-61.

Maley, J. G. 1988. "Managing the Flow of Intelligent Parts." *Robotics and Computer-Integrated Manufacturing.* Vol. 4, No. ¾. pp. 525-530.

Malone, T. W. and Crowston, K. 1994. "The Interdisciplinary Study of Coordination." *ACM Computing Surveys.* Vol. 26, No. 1, pp. 87 - 119, March.

March, S., Hevner, A., and Ram, S. 2000. An Agenda for Information Technology Research in Heterogeneous and Distributed Environments," *Information Systems Research* 11(4).

Mize, J. H. 1991. "Fundamentals of Integrated Manufacturing." In J. Mize (Ed.), *Guide to Systems Integration.* Industrial Engineering and Management Press, Institute of Industrial Engineers, Norcross, Georgia. pp. 27-43.

Nunamaker, J. F., Applegate, L. M., and Konsynski, B. R. 1988. "Computer-Aided Deliberation: Model Management and Group Decision Support." *Operations Research.* Vol.36, No. 6, pp. 826-848, Nov-Dec.

Pan, J. Y. and Tenenbaum, J. M. 1991. "An Intelligent Agent Framework for Enterprise Integration." *IEEE Transactions on SMC.* 21(6), pp. 1391-1408.

Parunak, H. V. D. 1987. "Manufacturing Experience with the Contract Net." In M. N. Huhns (Ed.), *Distributed Artificial Intelligence*, Pitman Publishing/Morgan Kaufmann Publishers, San Mateo, CA.

Parunak, H. V. D., Irish, B. W., Kindrick, J., and Lozo, P. W. 1985. "Fractal Actors for Distributed Manufacturing Control." *Proceedings of the Second IEEE Conference on Artificial Intelligence Applications.* pp.653-660.

Peterson, J. L. 1977. Petri Nets. *ACM Computing Surveys.* 9 (3) 223-252.

Pfeffer, J. and Salancik, G. R. 1978. *The External Control of Organizations: A Resource Dependency Perspective.* Harper and Rown New York.

Prietula, M. J., K. M. Carley, and L. Gasser (eds). 1998. *Simulating Organizations: Computational Models of Institutions and Groups.* The MIT Press: Cambridge, MA

Sacerdoti, E. D. 1977. *A Structure for Plans and Behavior.* Elsevier, New York.

Shaw, M. 1987. "Distributed Scheduling in Computer Integrated Manufacturing: The Use of Local Area Network." *International Journal of Production Research.* Vol. 25. pp. 1285-1303.

Sikora, R. and Shaw, M. 1996. "A Computational Study of Distributed Rule Learning." *Information Systems Research.* Vol. 7, No. 2, pp. 189 – 197. June.

Sikora, R., and M. J. Shaw. 1998. A Multi-Agent Framework for the Coordination and Integration of Information Systems. *Management Science* 44(11) (November): 65-78

Simon, H. A. 1969. *Sciences of the Artificial.* MIT Press, Cambridge, MA.

Sycara, K. 1989. "Multi-Agent Compromise via Negotiation." *Distributed Artificial Intelligence (Vol. II),* L. Gasser and M. Huhns (Eds.). Pitman, 119-137.

Tan, J.C., P.T. Harker. 1999. Design workflow coordination: centralized versus market-based mechanisms. *Information Systems Research* **10** (4) 328-342.

Watabe, K., Holsapple, C. W., and Whinston, A. B. 1992. "Coordinator Support in a Nemawashi Decision Process." *Decision Support Systems*. 8, pp. 85-98.

Wesson, R. B., Hayes-Roth, F. A., Burge, J. W., Stasz, C., and Sunshine, C. A. 1981. "Network Structures for Distributed Situation Assessment." *IEEE Transactions on SMC*. 11, 5-23.

Winograd, T. and Flores, C. 1987. *Understanding Computers and Cognition : A New Foundation for Design*. Addison-Wesley.

Wolfe, P. M. and Settles, F. S. 1989. "Computer Integrated Manufacturing from a Pragmatic Perspective." *Proc. of the IIE International Industrial Engineering Conference*.

Chapter 10

Designing IT-Supported Market Mechanisms for Organizational Coordination

Sulin Ba: Jan Stallaert
Marshall School of Business, University of Southern California

Abstract: Markets have always taken a prominent place in Professor Andrew Whinston's research. In his earlier work, for example, he concentrated on finding conditions under which resources can be allocated in a non-convex economy, although economists had raised questions about the applicability of markets in such an economy. In later research, he also applied the market idea to non-conventional application areas. Some of the most influential research is in the area of developing models and methods for real-time problem solving and resource management in computer networks. His most recent research, recognizing the potential opportunities the networked environment provides to companies, has taken the market idea to the internal economy of organizations: how to design IT-supported coordination systems for organizational resource allocation. In this essay, we discuss some issues that differentiate IT-supported internal markets from IT-supported commerce between different companies. We then draw on recent research by Dr. Whinston and his colleagues on market mechanisms to illustrate how such systems might be designed.
Key words: Market Mechanisms, Internal Market, Incentive Compatibility, IT Coordination Systems, Distributed Decision Support, Market Organizations.

1. INTRODUCTION

The rapid advance of information technology (IT) in the area of eCommerce allows us to drastically rethink and redesign organizational processes. IT now supports and drives forms of commerce that were previously not possible. Firms such as Amazon.com have brought online order taking to a new level by adding a one-to-one marketing feature: users' profiles are stored, and based on similarities with other users' profiles, a consumer is informed about new book offerings likely to please her. Online auctions such as eBay have added a new dimension to the age-old auction process by providing feedback on sellers' and buyers' past trading behavior and by introducing automated "agents" that will watch the auctions of interest. Drastically new forms of commerce have been created by the use of IT, such as the reverse auctions pioneered by priceline.com. The common characteristic of these new ways of trading is their absence of *posted prices*: the seller no longer posts sales prices which the buyer can take or leave. Rather, transaction prices are dynamically formed through the interaction of buyers and sellers.

At the same time, an evolution of organizational structure has taken place from the divisionalized firm that originated in the 1950s to network or market organizations that started to arise in the late 1980s and were introduced more frequently in the 1990s (Halal 1998, Halal et al. 1993). Market organizations are characterized by autonomous decentralized units that "sell" and "buy" goods and/or services to or from other units of the firm or outside firms. The literally thousands of "internal enterprises" that make up Asea Brown Bovari (ABB), a global corporation with operations in multiple industries, is an example of this new organizational structure. The management of such an organization is no longer done by directives or executive fiat, but is best summarized with Percy Barnivik's (former CEO of ABB) own words: "I don't sit like a godfather, allocating jobs. What I guarantee is that every member of the federation has a fair shot at the opportunities." (Halal 1994). In other words, task and resource allocation are no longer done hierarchically, but are established using (internal) market interactions. The new structure of market organizations explicitly recognizes that organizations are economic systems of their own, where the organization of labor and tasks is left to the entrepreneurial spirit of the workers within the organization. The allocation of tasks and resources is established exclusively by market forces: goods or services that take up too many resources or are produced with inferior quality standards will automatically disappear under the competitive pressure from other units that can use the organizational resources more efficiently.

The question that consequently arises for the IS community is: *How to design information systems needed to support the managerial decision making in such market organizations?* Clearly, the information systems of the past won't necessarily fit this new type of market organization. When only a single person is involved in the decision making (such as in purely hierarchical or very small organizations), the role of the information system is limited to providing the necessary and relevant information or analysis to the single decision maker. Present organizations, however, are more democratic and allow several members of the organization to participate in the decision. In this case of *collective decision making,* the information system has—apart from providing the necessary and relevant information to the individual decision makers involved—an additional role: the system needs to facilitate the formation of a collective decision based on the individuals' preferences.

In traditional hierarchical firms, Group Decision Support Systems (GDSS or in short GSS), systems that combine communication, computing, and decision support technologies to facilitate formulation and solution of unstructured problems by a group of people (DeSanctis and Gallupe 1987), have often been used to come to a consensus and to resolve conflicts where collective decision making was called for. In these types of organizations, ad hoc committees or advisory boards are set up before making important decisions (Mintzberg 1979). They are composed of persons (possibly from different divisions) who will be affected by the consequences of the decision, or have expert knowledge or specific information in the problem domain under consideration. The advice of the committees or advisory boards is not binding; a specific person within the organization has the final say and makes the final decision. Since the background of the group of people that constitutes these advisory boards is very different and their goals and incentives may conflict, an appropriate tool to come to a unanimous or consensual proposal is the use of a GSS.

When the organization is composed of very many autonomous units as in the case of a market organization, and the decisions (for example, production quantities, local capital investments) will be made as a result of market transactions, the GSS, which is consensus driven by nature, is no longer a suitable tool. Alignment of the organizational structure and processes dictates that the new information systems should be market-driven by design. In other words, the new market processes of eCommerce will see a radically new application, namely IT-supported coordination mechanisms *within a market organization.*

Markets have always taken a prominent place in Professor Andrew Whinston's research. In his earlier work, for example, he concentrated on finding conditions under which resources can be allocated in a non-convex economy (Moore, Whinston, and Wu, 1972), although economists had raised questions about the applicability of markets in such an economy. In later research, he also applied the market idea to non-conventional application areas. Some of the most influential research is in the area of developing models and methods for real-time problem solving and resource management in computer networks (e.g., Gupta, Stahl, and Whinston, 1997, Gupta, Jukic, Stahl, and Whinston 2000, Konana, Gupta, and Whinston 2000). His most recent research, recognizing the potential opportunities the networked environment provides to companies, has taken the market idea to the internal economy of organizations: how to design IT-supported coordination systems for organizational resource allocation (Fan, Stallaert, and Whinston, 2001, Ba, Stallaert, and Whinston 2001). The research is extremely timely given that many organizations are moving towards the market economy. However, many different resource allocation and decision-making problems can be tackled using IT-supported internal markets, and researchers have just begun to scratch the surface.

In this essay, we discuss some issues that differentiate IT-supported *internal* markets from IT-supported commerce between different companies. We then draw on recent research by Dr. Whinston and his colleagues on market mechanisms to illustrate how such systems might be designed.

2. BACKGROUND

2.1 The M-form and the *New Organization*

Between the two World Wars, firms such as General Electric and General Motors, growing bigger and adding new products and product lines to their existing ones, became aware that the information and coordination that were required to run an organization in a strict hierarchical form became overwhelming (Milgrom and Roberts 1992). For a centralized organization with a multiplicity of products and a variety of product lines serving very non-homogeneous markets, the decision-making problems became utterly complex. The information required to make sound decisions originated too far away from the decision makers and the information transferred was distorted, delayed and/or incomplete (Galbraith, 1973).

Chandler (1962) describes how four U.S. organizations (GM, Du Pont, Sears and Standard Oil) were the innovators of a new organizational form: the *multidivisional firm.* The multidivisional firm (the *M*-form) was created to have decisions made by the persons who had instant access and familiarity with the problem domain: the headquarters' responsibility was reduced to outlining an overall strategy for the firm and to allocating the firm's resources (such as capital) to the various divisions (e.g., in the form of budgets). The divisional managers are evaluated on the basis of their performance, which then becomes the basis for their own reward. The divisionalized firm has the advantage that the decision-making authority is now distributed, but the fact that the decisions are made based on local information not available to the headquarters creates a new problem: How can the performance of the division managers be judged objectively and how can their performance be compared to their peers? Consequently, with the decision-making authority came the financial responsibility: to the extent possible, divisions are converted into profit centers. As the decision rights get more decentralized, the headquarters require less information (Jensen 1998), which means that profit (or investment) centers — which, by nature, are more autonomous — lower the information costs for the firm. In today's turbulent and ever-changing environment and the ensuing increasing information needs, more and more companies are being run according to this model: large firms are disaggregated into smaller entrepreneurial units (Zenger and Hesterly 1997). Viewing a firm as an economic system of itself, there could be two choices of how to run it economically: centralized (hierarchically) or decentralized (using markets). It may be worthwhile to borrow a quote from Friedrich Hayek, written more than half a century ago (Hayek 1945):

> "Which of these systems [a centralized authority or a market approach] is likely to be more efficient depends mainly on the question under which of them we can expect that fuller use will be made of the existing knowledge. And this, in turn, depends on whether we are more likely to succeed in putting at the disposal of a single central authority all the knowledge which ought to be used but which is usually dispersed among many different individuals, or in conveying to the individuals such additional knowledge as they need in order to enable them to fit their plans in with the others."

In today's tumultuous economic environment, with ever-progressing technological innovations and changing customer needs, it becomes less and less possible that such "central authority," as Hayek called it, would be able to collect all knowledge necessary to come up with a plan of action, hence the inevitable evolution to market organizations.

2.2 Decision Support in Traditional Organizations

Organizational structure and processes often dictate what and how information technology is used to support those processes. In a purely hierarchical organization, information systems solely provide decision *support,* not decision *coordination.* Expert systems, data warehouses, optimization-based systems are examples of such *support* systems. When more than one person participates in the decision making process—which is almost always the case in today's organizations—the system should also provide mechanisms for decision *coordination.* Group Support Systems (GSS) are the most widely used tool for collective decision-making. They have been utilized in various organizational contexts to help facilitate decision-making.

Being one of the major information technology tools to support organizational decision making, GSS has been studied extensively (Benbasat and Lim 1993) by the IS community from a social, behavioral or technological perspective. For example, the literature has investigated issues such as end-user satisfaction, media choices, decision satisfaction, and usefulness of various technology features (McGrath and Arrow 1996, Burk and Aytes 1998, Davey and Olson 1998, Dennis and Valacich 1994, Ellis et al 1990, Gallupe et al 1988, to cite a few). The effectiveness of these systems, such as decision quality and productivity, is mostly evaluated by measures such as number of critical comments made and ideas or alternatives generated. Subjective satisfaction is often used to measure decision satisfaction. While the above research has laid the groundwork for IT-supported coordination systems, there is still a major gap in the literature: there is no objective measure of the quality of decisions made using GSS (Fjermestad and Hiltz 1999). Very rarely would the system be measured based on the potential economic outcomes of the decisions. Therefore, there is no guarantee that these mechanisms would accomplish certain ends such as the optimal allocation of resources or support internal market transactions where economic performances are crucial.

Many GSS implement a voting mechanism that allows users to vote on a set of alternatives. That is, the voting mechanism is used as a tool to coordinate the decision making process. The problem of casting a vote other than one's highest preference (which we will call the problem of *incentive compatibility* later) arises in the process. Gavish and Gerdes (1997) describe the attributes of different voting protocols and the susceptibility of the mechanisms to yield paradoxical behavior. Empirical evidence has shown that individual preference orderings do not necessarily converge to one group preference ordering after many iterations of interaction and evaluation among the participants (Chen et al. 1994, Briggs et al. 1998). Theoretically, it has been established that a social preference ordering, given the participants' individual preference rankings, does not always exist (Arrow 1963). Therefore, the usefulness of such systems for selecting projects among multiple choices is limited: *When users use the GSS to rank order their preferences, how to ensure that they are revealing their true preferences? What incentives should be in place so that the users of the GSS will be truthful in their evaluations of the alternatives?*

Under certain circumstances, individuals may derive a benefit from casting a strategic vote, which may cause a social choice that would be more to their liking than the one resulting from casting a sincere vote. There may be no incentive compatible and Pareto-optimal (or close to) solution when using the voting-based GSS.

Another significant aspect that needs to be considered in organizational coordination processes is that many times the projects being considered are complementary, meaning that each project alone may have only limited value, but together they are synergistic and deliver higher values to the organization because of their complementary nature (Topkis 1978, Milgrom and Roberts 1990, Barua et al. 1996). Although most GSS allow participants to express their opinions and to evaluate the proposed projects together so that they can gain benefits from complementarity, the tools currently available do not really support the convergence of these opinions at the computational level. In other words, exactly how should an organization select the projects that are complementary when opinions provided are different or even contradictory? How to maximize the total value these projects deliver to the organization? In the ideal case, a computational solution should be implemented in the coordination systems so that the decision is quantified.

In short, organizational coordination mechanisms such as GSS may no longer be appropriate in today's market organizations where economic outcomes are crucial. How can IT support the processes that enable transactions (or commerce) between the different divisions or centers in the firm? The issues of "internal commerce" from an economics standpoint have been well studied; the issues relating to the design of information systems to support and enable this new organizational form, on the contrary, have been left open for the most part. Fortunately, the advent of electronic commerce offers opportunities for exploring new forms of organizational coordination mechanisms that can be used to provide IT support in market organizations. For example, the computational power provided by network servers has not been exploited so far (Bayers 2000). With more companies becoming wired and implementing electronic commerce solutions, the possibility of introducing more computations in market clearing mechanisms opens a new door to market-based applications in situations that were previously thought to have to be coordinated only by hierarchical methods, such as organizational resource allocation when complementarities are present.

3. TOWARDS AN IT-SUPPORTED MARKET SYSTEM

Given the changed conditions of the organizational forms and the new types of markets created by electronic commerce, we are now in an era where the blending of both can transform the organizational processes even more. Economists, in their fairly abstract view of the functioning of markets, are slow to study the new forms of electronic commerce that the Internet has brought. Studies in organizational strategy, being more concerned than economists about the operation of internal markets within firms, still have not gone beyond traditional forms of commerce. The market mechanisms driving the internal markets that are studied are either posted price systems, negotiated prices, or prices determined in an external market (see, e.g., Poppo 1995). It seems that the area of introducing *new* markets *within* an organization, together with an information system that supports these transactions, is an under-developed, yet promising, area in Information Systems.

Running a divisionalized firm with profit centers introduces a new economic problem: how are *transfer prices* set between different divisions? One of the main design questions for an organizational coordination system is how to design a mechanism to promote value discovery of complicated, inter-related projects. It's also crucial to consider the properties of an information system that supports the management of such a firm. Economic theories in mechanism design should be looked at as a way of designing IT-supported organizational coordination systems, especially in resource allocation situations where individuals have private information/preference that is not directly observable. Mechanism design principles require that incentive constraints be considered in the formulation of an economic problem. In situations where individuals' private information and actions are difficult to monitor, the need to give people an incentive to share their true information may impose constraints on the economic system (Myerson 1989). A mechanism is incentive compatible when the participants involved in the process would not find it advantageous to violate the rules of the process (Hurwicz 1972, Ledyard 1989). In other words, in an incentive compatible mechanism, truth-telling is an equilibrium (in the game-theoretic sense) and no participants can gain by deviating from the rules.

The properties of an information system needed to support such an economic mechanism, however, have been mainly ignored by economists so far. Yet, no system can be operationalized without explicitly considering the interaction between the economic principles of the system and their informational requirements. For example, economists sometimes are satisfied with demonstrating that "a (properly-defined-depending-on-context) equilibrium exists," but they fail to show how it is attained, and even at times ignore whether the computational requirements are feasible or not in practice. In short, an operational economic mechanism should explicitly address information systems issues, such as computational feasibility and information requirements.

On the other hand, no information systems can be effective if economic principles such as incentives of end users are ignored. Implicitly, underlying *any* information system — be it in a market organization, divisionalized firm or strict hierarchy — economic principles are at play. For example, the issue of whether information will be shared or not (or whether someone is willing to do the effort to make it part of a knowledge repository), is partly an economic issue: without the proper economic incentives, people would be less motivated to participate in these efforts [14]. With mounting competitive pressures within the firm, and performance evaluations and reward systems that are more and more geared towards an individual's contribution to the overall organization's performance, the economic incentives embedded in the design or the use of an information system become more and more critical. Such issues are simply too important to be left to economists alone. It is the interplay between economics and information systems that creates both the challenges and opportunities for new research.

The critical research questions are: How do we construct organizational coordination systems that, at the conceptual level, take into account economic incentive principles to ensure that when an IT-supported coordination system is in use, the information provided by the economic agents into the coordination process is truthful to their best understanding? How to design IT systems that take advantage of the computational power that is provided (and mainly unused) in a networked environment to solve complicated coordination problems?

[14] A personal anecdote from a consultant from a well-known firm is pertinent. He argued that by hiring him as a consultant, you're actually hiring 5000 consultants, since he has access to the knowledge repository where others submit their knowledge or past experiences. When asked how often he himself contributes to the knowledge repository, he answered: "Well, actually, I am too busy for it."

To what extent can these new economic oriented mechanisms be developed, and in which areas of coordination can they be applied?

Professor Whinston has always been an advocate of market systems (Whinston, 1962). Recent research by Professor Whinston and his colleagues on IT-supported market mechanisms provides a solid starting point for developing the necessary IT support to efficiently run a market organization. In what follows, we summarize two such mechanisms and illustrate the design principles behind these mechanisms.

3.1 An Incentive Compatible System for Supply Chain Coordination

Suppose that a multi-division, multi-product firm faces a warehouse scheduling problem where warehouse space has to be allocated among three autonomous units, each with a separate product line. Each unit has its own local considerations, preferences and objectives. Assume their preferences are super-additive, i.e., there is complementarity among the preferences. For example, if warehouse space is obtained in location A for product X, then it is worth more to the unit to have location A also to store product Y (because, for example, most of the orders are for X and Y together). There are often conflicting interests over shared resources: in this case, other units may want to acquire storage space in the warehouse at location A also.

When the firm is operated as a collection of independent profit centers, economics tells us that potential problems may arise – if each profit center is allowed to set its own prices for the goods or services it provides, the quantities of the final goods and services produced by the firm are very rarely optimal (see, e.g., Jensen 1998). Letting the headquarters set the transfer prices between the divisions can be problematic as well (e.g., Jensen): the firm has been divisionalized because the headquarters do not have accurate information about all aspects, such as cost and demand figures, of the goods being produced by the divisions. Therefore, it is not realistic to assume that the headquarters have the knowledge to determine what this good or service is worth within the internal economy of their firm.

An attempt was made by Groves and Loeb (1979) to outline a method on how certain transfer prices can be calculated. In their approach, the allocation problem may be solved using an internal market structure in which the warehouse management auctions off the warehouse space and each unit bids on the space available. That is, the transfer price is calculated based on the bids for the goods or services reported by the different divisions such that an organizational optimum is reached. It is shown that a *dominant strategy* for the division managers is to reveal their best estimates of the true cost or benefit for the good.

However, this analysis, being economic and very abstract in nature, does not provide any guidelines as to how to implement such a system in practice. Moreover, the method only addresses a very isolated case of single commodities or services being exchanged, whereas in reality a combination of such things is often needed to run a division (such as warehouse space for BOTH product X and product Y).

The bundle auction mechanism designed by Dr. Whinston and his colleagues (Fan, Stallaert, and Whinston 2001) partially addresses the above problems. They propose a decentralized mechanism that allows the organizational units to demand a combination of warehouses and/or transportation capacity with a single bid price, and the headquarters simply acts as a market maker and allocates the warehouse space in a way that maximizes the organization's benefit. Each unit responds with a bid for resources based on its own managerial objective, and a bid can be in "bundled form", i.e., it may specify one price for a whole bundle of resources. For example, unit 1 may demand, at the price of b_1, space at warehouse A for product X AND product Y. The headquarter collects all the bids and its role is to maximize the value of the warehouses at the bid prices received from the units, subject to the limitation of available resource totals.

The competition between the organizational units will induce them to state the correct cost/value information, or their best estimate thereof. In Fan et al. (2001) it is proved how this system satisfies the incentive compatibility requirements: no party can be better off by misrepresenting the (private) information they have available, and the headquarters, by playing the role of market maker maximizing his profit, allocates the warehouse space in a manner that contributes to maximizing firm profit.

Unlike the voting mechanism where each autonomous unit has to decide a preference order over a huge set of alternative states (e.g., voting on whether unit 3 gets space in warehouse A, etc.), the auction mechanism is easier and more direct for the unit to make the decision. In addition, "bid price" is a more sensitive indicator than "preference" in an internal economy. What is also noteworthy about this bundle auction mechanism is that it takes advantage of the computational power provided by the network servers, making this auction mechanism a feasible real time procedure for supply chain coordination.

3.2 An Incentive Compatible Mechanism for Knowledge Investment

There are at least two types of resource allocation problems within the organization. The previous example outlined a mechanism to design an information system that supports allocation of warehouse space to different divisions and/or product lines. This class of problems involves the competition for resources that are exclusive, i.e., once a unit makes use of the resource, other units are excluded. Another very general class of problems involves resources that are *public* within an organization, i.e., once the investment in the *public good* has been made, anyone within the organization can benefit from it at (close to) zero cost. The Groves and Loeb method (1979) described previously addresses the situation in which the goods or services produced and exchanged between divisions are of a *private good* nature, i.e., these goods or services are excludable. Goods and services that have a *public good* characteristic (such as knowledge generated in a firm, or brand or quality reputation of the company) are not considered in the method.

In order to illustrate how economic incentive issues can play a different role depending on the problem to be solved, we give the example of how to decide on investments in information services or knowledge within a market organization.

The difference between a knowledge project, for example, a R&D project, and a capacity expansion project is that the output of the R&D project is knowledge which is normally considered a public good (i.e., non-depletable goods) within an organization (Arrow 1962, Radner 1986, Mas-Colell 1995, Adler 2001). Once knowledge is created, it can be freely disseminated to or shared by everybody in the organization. Consumption of such a non-depletable good by one employee does not preclude its consumption by anyone else. Being a public (non-excludable) good, knowledge is non-depletable and the use of it is non-excludable. The provision of public goods generates an externality – if one individual provides a unit of a public good, all individuals benefit. Therefore, knowledge is subject to the "free rider" problem, which is an example of a lack of incentive compatibility where individual organizational units may refuse to pay for the creation of knowledge even though they privately have a high value for the knowledge.

The public good aspect complicates the decision problem significantly and the information technology supporting this collective decision has to be designed accordingly. Due to the "public goods" nature of knowledge, corporate divisions, when asked to contribute to knowledge creation, tend to understate their true valuation of knowledge, hoping that they can use it without contributing much to its creation. The potential for under-contribution to a public good is particularly clear when contributions are voluntary (viewers of PBS will immediately recognize the problem). In this situation, a traditional GSS most likely will fail to elicit the decision participants' true opinion of the importance of each knowledge management projects and how to maximize the total value of the knowledge projects in the organization. The free-rider problem has typically been used as the reason for a hierarchical decision-making approach. A higher echelon decides on knowledge investment projects in order to maximize the net return on investment. At best, knowledge end users and knowledge providers are consulted to assist in deriving the net value of the knowledge projects, but in their consultative role they have no economic incentives to truthfully derive and reveal valuation information.

Another aspect frequently ignored in resource allocation processes for knowledge is that knowledge is often interrelated and interdependent. For example, a pharmaceutical company routinely has multiple research projects. Results from one project (e.g., investigating the effects of certain chemical substances), when combined with the results from another (e.g., the successful synthesis of a group of chemical compounds), can potentially lead to a new drug treatment (i.e., there is complementarity between the two research projects). When allocating the R&D budget, allowing the two projects to be supported at the same time as a bundle will deliver more value than funding one of the projects alone. This complementarity of knowledge calls for a resource allocation mechanism that explicitly allows the bundling of knowledge components.

A market mechanism to decide on the provision of a public good has been considered by Clarke (1971) and Groves (1973). It was commonly believed, prior to their seminal papers, that in economies with public goods it would be impossible to devise a decentralized process that would allocate resources efficiently since each participant would have an incentive to "free ride" on others' provision of those goods in order to reduce their own share of providing them. There is therefore a systematic bias to under-report valuations if the mechanism requires people to contribute according to their reported valuation. Clarke and Groves show that it is possible to generate an incentive-compatible market mechanism for investment in one public good. In these seminal works, however, no bundling of public goods is allowed, as is desired when there is complementarity among the goods.

In a groundbreaking work by Whinston and his colleagues (Ba, Stallaert, and Whinston 2001), an internal market is introduced in which knowledge providers offer knowledge projects and knowledge consumers place bids to acquire them. The mechanism is a Groves-Clarke type double auction that allows bundled knowledge goods to be traded so as to recognize complementarities between knowledge projects. The market mechanism is *incentive compatible*; i.e., it induces people to reveal their true valuation. In addition, it allows trades of knowledge bundles to determine which knowledge components are most valuable from the organization's viewpoint. Under mild assumptions, the mechanism is a computationally tractable solution to operating a market of bundled public goods. They prove that a market mechanism that does not allow bundle orders or does not address the free-rider problem yields a systematic *underinvestment* in knowledge.

This market mechanism is a combinatorial double auction for public goods. It addresses the free-rider problem associated with public goods, which is not present in any of the combinatorial auction mechanisms for private goods. Indeed, the mechanism is a practical way to handle the resource allocation problem for public goods in general.

4. CONCLUSION

The pioneering work by Professor Whinston and his colleagues is the first step to address the need for designing coordination systems that support market organizations. The need for these systems is confirmed by the trend in organizational structure: in the popular press, as well as during conversations with executives, it becomes clear that more and more organizations are run with some sort of internal market structure in place. Although mainstream IS design has lagged this evolution in creating methodologies of the new support systems needed to run this organization, we believe that IT enables the creation of novel market mechanisms and has the potential for shaping organizations where internal markets permeate the organizational structure at all levels.

REFERENCES:

Adler, P. (2001) "Market, hierarchy, and trust: the knowledge economy and the future of capitalism." Organization Science. March-April. 12(2): 215-234.

Arrow, K. (1962) "Economic Welfare and the Allocation of Resources for Invention," in *The rate and direction of inventive activity: Economic and Social factors*. Princeton University Press, Princeton NJ, 609—625.

Arrow, K. (1963) Social Choice and Individual Values. 2nd ed. New York: Wiley.

Ba, S., J. Stallaert, and A. B. Whinston (2001) "Optimal investment in knowledge within a firm using a market mechanism." Forthcoming in Management Science.

Barua, A., S. Lee, and A. B. Whinston (1996) "Calculus of reengineering," Information Systems Research, 7(4): 409-428.

Bayers, C. (2000) "The Bot.Com future: capitalist econstruction." Wired. March. Pg. 210-219.

Benbasat, I., and L.H. Lim (1993) "The effects of group, task, context, and technology variables on the usefulness of group support systems: a meta-analysis of experimental studies." Small Group Research, 24, 4: 430-462.

Briggs, R., J. Nunamaker, and R. Sprague (1998) "1001 unanswered research questions in GSS." Journal of Management Information Systems. 14(3): 3-21.

Buchanan, J.M. and Tullock (1962) The Calculus of Consent, Ann Arbor, University of Michigan Press.

Burk, K., and K. Aytes (1998) "A longitudinal analysis of the effects of media richness on cohesion development and process satisfaction in computer-supported workgroups." Proceedings of the Thirty-First Hawaii International Conference on Systems Sciences, 1: 135-144.

Chandler, A. Jr. (1962) Strategy and Structure: Chapters in the History of the American Industrial Enterprise, MIT Press, Cambridge.

Chen, H.; P. Hsu, R. Orwig, L. Hoopes, and J. Nunamaker (1994) "Automatic concept classification of text from electronic meetings." Communications of the ACM. 37 (10): 56-72.

Clarke, E.H. (1971) "Multipart pricing of public goods," Public Choice 11, 17-33.

Davey, A., and D. Olson (1998) "Multiple criteria decision making models in group decision support." Group Decision and Negotiation, 7, 1: 55-75.

Dennis, A.R., and J.S. Valacich (1994) "Group, sub-group, and nominal group idea generation: new rules for a new media?" Journal of Management, 20, 4: 723-736.

DeSanctis, G. L. and R. B. Gallupe (1987) "A foundation for the study of group decision support systems," Management Science (33:5). pp. 589-609.

Ellis, C.A.; G.L.Rein, and S.L. Jarvcnpaa (1990) "Nick experimentation: selected results concerning effectiveness of meeting support technology." Journal of Management Information Systems, 6, 3: 7-24.

Fan, M., J. Stallaert, and A. B. Whinston (2000) "Decentralized mechanism design for supply chain organizations using an auction market." Forthcoming in Information Systems Research.

Fjermestad, J. and S. Hiltz (1998) "An assessment of group support systems experiment research: Methodology and results." Journal of Management Information Systems. 15(3): 7-149.

Galbraith, J., (1973) "Designing complex organizations," Addison-Wesley Publishing Company, City, MA.

Gallupe, R.B.; G DeSanctis, and G.W. Dickson (1998) "Computer-based support for group problem-finding: an experimental investigation." MIS Quarterly,12, 2: 277-296.

Gavish, B. and J. H. Gerdes Jr. (1997) "Voting mechanisms and their implications in a GDSS environment." Annals of Operations Research, 71, pp. 41-74.

Groves, T. (1973) "Incentives in teams." Econometrica 41, 617-631.

Groves, T. and M. Loeb (1979) "Incentives in a divisionalized firm." Management Science 25, 221-230.

Gupta, A., B. Jukic, D. O. Stahl, and A. B. Whinston (2000) "Extracting Consumers' Private Information for Implementing Incentive-Compatible Internet Traffic Pricing." Journal of Management Information Systems, Vol. 17, No. 1, Summer 2000, pp. 9-29.

Gupta, A., D. O. Stahl, and A. B. Whinston (1997) "A Decentralized Approach to Estimate Activity Based Costs and Near-Optimal Resource Allocation in Flexible Manufacturing Systems." International Journal of Flexible Manufacturing Systems, Vol. 9, No. 2, April, pp. 167-194.

Halal, W.E. (1994) "From hierarchy to enterprise: Internal markets are the new foundation of management," Academy of Management Executive 8, 69-83.

Halal, W.E. (1998) "The infinite resource: creating and leading the knowledge enterprise," Jossey-Bass Publishers.

Halal, W.E., A. Geranmayeh and J. Pourdehand (1993) "Internal markets: bringing the power of free enterprise inside your organization." John Wiley and Sons.

Hayek, F. (1945) "The use of knowledge in society," American Economic Review 35, pp. 519-530.

Hurwicz, L., (1972) "On informationally decentralized systems." in: Decision and Organization, ed. by C.B. McGuire and R. Radner, North Holland. Amsterdam.

Jensen, M. C. (1998) Foundations of organizational strategy. Harvard University Press.

Konana, P., A. Gupta, and A. B. Whinston (2000) "Integrating User Preferences and Real-Time Workload in Information Services." Information Systems Research, Vol. 11, No. 2, June 2000, pp. 177-196.

Ledyard, J. (1989) "Incentive compatibility." In J. Eatwell, M. Milgate, and P. Newman (eds.), Allocation, Information and Markets. New York: Norton, pp. 141-151.

Mas-Colell, A., M. D. Whinston and J. R. Green (1995), Microeconomic Theory, Oxford University Press.

McGrath, J.E., and H. Arrow (1996) "Introduction: the JEMCO 2 study of time, technology and groups." Computer Supported Cooperative Work, 4, 2:107-126

Milgrom, P. and J. Roberts (1990) "Rationalizability, Learning, and Equilibrium in Games with Strategic Complementarities," Econometrica, 58(6): 1255-1277.

Milgrom, P. and J. Roberts (1992) "Economics, Organization and Management," Prentice-Hall.

Mintzberg, H. (1979) The structuring of organizations: a synthesis of the research. Prentice Hall. Englewood Cliffs, N.J.

Moore, J., A. B. Whinston, and J. S. Wu (1972) "Resource Allocation in a Non-Convex Economy." Review of Economic Studies, July 1972.

Myerson, R.B. (1989) "Mechanism design." In J. Eahtwell, M. Milgate, and P. Newman (eds.), Allocation. Information and Markets. New York: Norton. pp. 191-206.

Poppo, L. (1995) "Influence Activities and Strategic Coordination: Two Distinctions of Internal and External Markets," Management Science 41, pp. 1845-1859.

Radner, R. (1986) "The Internal Economy of Large Firms," The Economic Journal 96, Supplement: Conference Papers. pp. 1-22.

Topkis, D.M. (1978) "Minimizing a Submodular Function on a Lattice," Operations Research, April 1978: 305-321.

Whinston, A. B. (1962) "Control and Coordination of Complex Economic and Managerial Systems." Ph.D. Dissertation. Carnegie-Mellon University.

Zenger, T.R. and W.S. Hesterly (1997) "The Disaggregation of Corporations: Selective Intervention, High-powered Incentives, and Molecular Units," Organization Science 8, pp. 209-222.

Chapter 11

Congestion Based Pricing and Management of Distributed Computational Resources

Alok Gupta: Boris Jukic: Prabhudev Konana
University of Minnesota: George Mason University: The University of Texas at Austin

Abstract: Congestion based usage pricing for management of IT resources has been discussed for several decades. However, a whole array of fundamental issues plagued productive discussions about its feasibility in computing environments. Under Prof. Whinston's leadership, co-authors of this article have participated in several projects whose primary purpose was to move the discussion of economic modeling beyond normative discussion to real-time computability and implementation. The research has addressed some of the fundamental objections to externality based pricing, i.e., the problem of acquiring customers private information regarding their demand characteristics. The research agenda in the network and computing resources pricing has now moved to management of particular environments -- from corporate networks to distributed database environments. In this article we summarize the key ideas that were generated by the research group at CREC on theory and implementation of congestion based pricing. These include issues ranging from demonstration of computational feasibility of such prices based on transient system information to the issue of incentives of network infrastructure owners in the presence of multiple co-existing pricing paradigms. In addition, we will discuss and present other applications of this work and directions of future research.

Key words: Dynamic Pricing, Welfare Economics, Simulation, Internet Traffic, Real-time Databases, Distributed Computing Resources, Resource Allocation, Simulation.

PREAMBLE

We know it is highly unusual to have a preamble in a research article but in a book honoring Prof. Whinston, being predictable should be considered unusual. We (the 3 authors of this manuscript) are perhaps the most recent affiliates of Prof. Whinston, among the contributors of this book. We consider ourselves fortunate to have been his students and collaborators, and it is an honor to be part of this endeavor to recognize his contributions to various disciplines, particularly at the intersection of MIS, economics, and computer science. The stream of research presented in this article – congestion-based pricing – is perhaps like most of the other research streams Prof. Whinston has been involved in. We were fortunate to have been involved at the near inception of this research stream. All three of us feel that being involved in this research has provided us with the most critical of the research tools -- thinking beyond the obvious and focusing beyond what is easy -- very early in our careers. The longevity and relevance of this research in the fast paced and dynamic Internet environment is a testament to Prof. Whinston's vision even when at early stages of research we often felt safer beyond the reach of computer scientists who were ardently opposed to any pricing based approaches to manage the Internet traffic.

1. INTRODUCTION

Numerous books and articles have discussed the technology that supports and enables the emerging world of electronic commerce and the roles played by the various technology providers. There are numerous examples of the applications that already exist or are underdevelopment in areas such as banking, marketing and logistics. Despite the phenomenal growth in both the technology and applications areas and the feverish pitch of excitement fueling it, the ultimate and unrelenting goal of all businesses involved in electronic commerce must be to increase profits. The recent demise of dot-com sector is, if nothing else, a strong indication of a lack of economic thought in implementing technology oriented market structures.

At this time we still lack definitive answers to most of the fundamental economic issues underlying electronic commerce. In this paper, we will present research that has been conducted at Center for Research on Electronic Commerce (CREC), or by its close affiliates, to explore two of the wide-reaching basic topics: (i) network traffic pricing and surrounding issues such as its effect on infrastructure investment; and (ii) the need to design corporate computing systems by embedding economic considerations in its operational characteristics. Needless to say, Prof. Whinston's fingerprints are all over this research and the vision of electronic commerce generated at CREC in early to mid 1990's (at that time the center was named CISM -- Center for Information Systems Management), is still relevant and is undergoing a renewed push by computer scientists as is evident from virtually identical research being produced and presented at major computer science conferences (for example see Ganesh, Laevens, Steinberg, 2001; Marbach, 2001; and Wang and Schulzrinne, 2001). In another article in this volume (Pingry and Marsden, 2001), a case is made for considering Prof. Whinston as a reference discipline, we believe that the longevity, relevance, and cross-disciplinary adaptation of research issues presented in this article, and being dealt with at CREC under Prof. Whinston's guidance, is another case in point to support that argument.

One of the most exciting phenomena of the last decade is the dramatic transformation of the Internet from being an academic and research network into a part of American folklore, as a medium for fun, education, exploration, communication, propaganda, and, most of all, for doing business. The spread of the World Wide Web (WWW), Networked Computing (NC) and Electronic Commerce (EC) have been crucial factors in this change. These developments have been too fast for the evolution of the required infrastructure and protocols, leaving the cyber-economy in a chaotic state. The challenge is how to facilitate all this traffic, of a nature and volume not anticipated by the original design of the Net. Indeed, the inefficiencies in infrastructure investments and in handling traffic are showing up in widespread congestion, frustrating delays, and a lack of applications that require guaranteed Quality of Service (QoS). Congestion results in losses to the tune of billions of dollars to the economy every year, besides crippling network performance and discouraging infrastructure investments. Further, unpredictable performance inhibits EC investments.

These delays are due to several reasons:

- Traffic has been growing almost at double the rate of the number of users.
- The advances in high bandwidth technologies are not able to match this pace.
- New technologies are allowing richer multimedia information to be transferred over the Net, and to execute applications over the network.
- The providers face only fixed one-time costs of setting up the network, and are essentially unregulated.
- The providers also lack any incentives for managing congestion better.

Arbitrary pricing strategies of infrastructure owners and access providers complicate the issue. Infrastructure owners charge flat fees for access; access providers use either a price based on time of usage, or, as recent trends indicate, a flat monthly fee. Neither takes the volume of traffic into account. This leads to a total lack of any incentives for providers and users to optimize congestion. For instance, the provider of a slow network pays a flat fee for access to a fast network such as Sprint's regardless of usage; so this provider dumps all the traffic onto the fast network as quickly as possible, the so-called "hot potato" approach (The Economist, Oct. 19, 1996). The major network providers suffer for providing higher bandwidth, and have no incentive to invest in further infrastructure. At the user level, a curious teenager and a researcher pay the same flat rate for Internet access; the former downloads terrabytes of video clips, blocking the computations the latter may be trying to execute in a remote supercomputer. Mission critical applications have no guarantee of precedence over others, nor any on expected level of performance. Thus, users lack incentives to control misuse of resources, providers lack incentives to manage congestion, and to invest in new capacity. These are not merely problems with the current pricing administration. Rather, they follow from the inherent features of the way packet traffic is handled in the Internet; the best-effort, no guarantee delivery, and first-come first-served way of handling traffic at intersections.

New technological developments, such as next generation Internet Protocol IPv6 (Deerin and Hinden, 1995), are trying to address the performance issue by moving away from best- effort, first-come first-serve approach by differentiating traffic based on priority classes and associating priorities with different application classes. However, such solutions still do not consider the criticality of the usage context and still be prone to misuse. For example, just because a video stream requires better response time, it does not mean a recreational video should be preferred over a simple text stream being used for a stock purchase. Other technological solutions such as raising the bandwidth or building new networks to segregate traffic may work in the short term; but eventually congestion will catch up, even as new automobiles clog up new lanes or new highways. There is increasing recognition of the fact that the issue is one of resource allocation, and needs to be addressed by a convergence of the economic and technological viewpoints, so as to ensure the streamlined functioning of a virtual economy.

Economic theory can be gainfully applied to develop mechanisms for managing network resources in a manner that is incentive compatible for both users and providers. The focus needs to be on managing resources, rather than providing better resources while existing misallocation persists. The application of economic principles is not restricted to Internet; rather, they are applicable to allocating resources efficiently over computer networks in general, such as distributed computing systems. Indeed, recent research in Computer Science has been increasingly drawing from Microeconomic theory to design resource allocation schemes, otherwise referred to as load balancing schemes. Any such scheme trying to allocate network resources in a globally optimal fashion will incur prohibitive overhead costs. It will not be feasible to collect and process information over all the nodes in a huge network to neither allocate capacity for each request, nor will it be possible to model such a scheme. As such, we advocate decentralized mechanisms that yield significant increase in benefits and performance, and undertake to demonstrate their feasibility.

We would like to go a step further and argue that most computing system are not designed to operate under the economic environment they are deployed in. In other words, while the application base provides support for economic transactions, it has never been part of the economic process itself. We contend that time has come to change that. The computing environments and electronic business processes should become integral part of the transaction itself by incorporating the costs, savings, profits, and priorities due to the mechanism itself as a part of the business process. To this extent, we also applied pricing for controlling admission in real-time database environments and showed that such efforts not only result in higher economic benefits but also perform better according to traditional performance metrics such as miss ratio.

The rest of this chapter is arranged as follows. In section 2 we contrast our pricing oriented resource allocation approach for decentralized computing resources to other suggested/implemented approaches. In section 3, we highlight some of the key results and features of the pricing approach and its computational implementation developed at CREC. In section 4 we present the application of this work to real-time database environment to illustrate the flexibility and modularity of the approach. Finally, we conclude in section 5, with summary of the research presented in this article.

2. RESOURCE ALLOCATION IN COMPUTER NETWORKS

To put our approach in context this section discusses previous approaches towards resource management, both in centralized and distributed systems. Many resource management algorithms in centralized systems devise a benefit/cost equation to represent their service goals and resource requirements and then attempt to maximize the benefit/cost of their decisions. Examples include LRU cache replacement, which approximates the optimal policy of replacing the page that will not be used for the longest period of time, and decay usage CPU scheduling (Hellerstein, 1993), which approximates the optimal shortest job first policy. Although this approach can work well for small subsystems, it requires the system designer to understand the entire subsystem well enough to devise an optimization criterion. Unfortunately, criteria for different subsystems are not generally easy to formulate; if a system designer wants to manage resources shared by several different subsystems, she must devise the more complex optimization equations for the larger combined system.

Recently, several centralized resource management techniques have been borrowing concepts from microeconomic theory. These algorithms continue to take the approach of trying to optimize the benefit/cost of their resource usage, but the economic theory provides additional leverage. For example, phrasing the benefit/cost calculation in terms of a common currency that can be shared across subsystems makes it easier to compose the optimization criteria of different subsystems. Patterson and Gibson (1995) devised optimization criteria that balance the use of memory buffers by the prefetching and caching subsystems of a machine. In a similar vein, lottery scheduling (Waldspurger and Weihl, 1994) and stride scheduling (Waldspurger and Weihl, 1995) allow CPU cycles to be assigned according to tickets that could correspond to a revenue stream in an economic model.

Most load balancing approaches in distributed systems rely on three basic techniques: global knowledge, randomization, and feedback. Most global knowledge based process migration systems, including Amoeba (Mullender, Rossum, Van Renesse, and Van Staveren, 1990), Condor (Litzkow and Solomon, 1992), Charlotte (Artsy and Finkel, 1989), Sprite (Douglis and Ousterhout, 1991), and process lifetime algorithm (Harchol-Balter and Downey, 1996) send the load level of their machines to a central server that directs jobs to unloaded machines. This central server limits the scalability of this approach.

Randomization can reduce the amount of global knowledge needed to make good decision. For example, it is well known that after placing n balls uniformly randomly into n bins, the fullest bin holds O(log n/log log n) balls with high probability; a small amount of additional load information can improve this result to O(log log n) (see Azar, Broder, Karlin and Upfal, 1994; and Adler, Chakrabarti, Mitzenmacher and Ramussen, 1995). Systems have exploited either oblivious randomization or randomization plus localized load information both to balance load across processors (see Barak and Shiloh, 1985; and Eager, Lazowska and Zahorjan, 1986) and to distribute cache pages across memories (Dahlin, Wang, Anderson and Patterson, 1994; Feely, Morgan, Pighin, Karlin, Levy and Thekkath, 1995; and Sarkar and Hartman, 1996). Random early detection (RED) routers illustrate an additional advantage of randomization: it can help avoid performance oscillations sometimes caused by global synchronization from deterministic algorithms (Floyd and Jacobson, 1993).

The third common technique for distributed load balancing is feedback. This approach is exemplified by the Ethernet (Metcalfe and Boggs, 1976) and TCP (Jacobson, 1988) exponential backoff schemes to deal with network congestion. The load information used by some of the randomized algorithms listed above could also be characterized as feedback information.

A key question in distributed networking is how to partition resources between real-time and non-real time traffic. The most common current approach gives absolute priority to multimedia traffic at the expense of "best effort" traffic by transmitting multimedia traffic using IP and best effort traffic using TCP (Eriksson, 1994). A better approach is to partition bandwidth so that both real time and best effort traffic are guaranteed some fraction of the system's bandwidth (Goyal, Vin and Cheng, 1996), but for these algorithms to work well the system must determine a good partitioning of resources between the traffic classes.

The problem with most such work is that they do not view the resource allocation problem as a whole, and use economic rationale to address it; instead, isolated devices or techniques are borrowed from economic theory. For these to be sound, it is essential that there is theoretical support, and that participants have sufficient incentives to use the mechanisms, and that use of such mechanisms are shown to lead to sustainable equilibria. The research in computer science, for the large part, treats all service requests equally in allocating resources, and does not account for the value or precedence of individual jobs. Economics, on the other hand, lets the forces of supply and demand to operate over markets, in achieving equilibria with efficient resource allocation and maximized benefits. Such approaches are more relevant in the context of the privatization of the network infrastructure and the advent of EC. Load balancing in distributed systems will also need to maximize user benefits accounting for their preferences. In resource allocation issues in networked computing, the locality of computation is the crucial choice variable, and computing research has not really looked at how decisions on this would be made, and why.

Applying economic solutions to the Internet is complicated by various factors: one, since infrastructure investments are sunk, or one-time fixed costs, marginal cost of data transport is essentially zero; the equilibrium price suggested by economics would be based on marginal costs in a simple market. Indeed, infrastructure providers with flat-fee prices admit that they do not recover the capacity investments from users; rather, it is voice-line users that typically bear these costs. The access fees merely act as steady revenue, and are often dictated by competitive considerations in trying to survive with giants such as AOL, MSN, AT&T etc. (Lewis, 1996). Second, network resources are public goods in effect, and congestion is a potential negative externality. As no one has any incentive to reduce congestion, and as there is no limit on the utilization of resources, the capacity is misutilized, resulting in loss of social welfare, similar to say, air pollution. Thus, what is called a "Tragedy of the Commons" results. In such a case prices should include the marginal social cost of congestion, and the consumer will utilize the resource only if his value exceeds the social cost of usage plus his private cost of time. Multiple ownership, instead of improving the state of affairs by changing the public good to a private one, can still cause a Tragedy of the Commons (Gupta, Stahl and Whinston, 1997a).

One possible way to provide different classes of services is to provide different priority levels on demand. Bohn, Braun, and Wolff (1994) propose a voluntary choice of priority level for different applications, and penalize users if they don't make appropriate choices. This system lacks incentive for providers to implement such a system, as it will only mean increased overhead costs for them. Further, priority levels are based on the type of application, such as E-mail or FTP; the value of the job may vary regardless of the type of application. In any such system, individual providers should have incentives to match the service priority levels offered by other networks, as most requests have to be serviced by multiple networks.

The ideas of managing traffic from a resource allocation viewpoint, and that traffic should be differentiated according to the level of performance required by the users reflect current trends in Internet technology. IPv6 is providing for users to specify their priority by using a field in each packet. Router technology is moving in the direction where traffic can be differentiated at router level.

Pricing the different priority levels would provide the users with the incentive to make choices depending on the value of individual jobs: the economic solution would be to set the price equal to the incremental social cost of congestion; the optimal congestion toll. The users will compare value of a job with the total private cost (congestion toll + private cost of wait), and voluntarily make appropriate service level choices. Further, socially optimal pricing provides increased revenues for the provider and better capacity utilization. This viewpoint of pricing for services over the network is consistent with the emerging trends in EC, and would thus enable a more meaningful discussion of network management. Furthermore, pricing could be used as a mechanism to assign priority class in next generation Internet protocol IPv6, instead of using application based priority assignment. In pricing based priority assignment, the priority for a data stream is based on the value a user associate with it, rather then what application is associated with the data stream.

A pricing scheme for managing resources should have theoretical support; should be operational; should be able to adjust prices in real time to account for the transient demand; should have manageable overhead costs such as administration, accounting, monitoring, implementation costs; and should be adequately tested with models and experiments. The pricing scheme suggested by Cocchi, Shenker, Estrin and Zhang (1991) has fixed or static prices, assumes user demand is not affected by cost, and requires information on the entire network to compute prices, causing high overhead costs, and rendering implementation over large networks infeasible. MacKie-Mason and Varian (1995) address the congestion issue directly by a pricing mechanism based on spot auctions at each node, where each packet bids for the value of the job, and the bids are resolved so that the best strategy for users is to bid the correct value. Bidding is a static, one-shot process, and as such each auction will only account for packets present at that node, while packets arriving a nanosecond later can also cause congestion. More important, in TCP-IP networks, constituent packets of same job may pass through different routes, and the value of any individual packet clearing a node is contingent on the remaining packets of that transaction. The price paid at a node may go waste in many cases. Any attempts to address this would render the system infeasible. In the next section we present an overview of the dynamic pricing approach developed at CREC along with the characteristics of the computational approach to implement the theoretically derived prices.

3. A DYNAMIC PRIORITY PRICING APPROACH FOR INTERNET TRAFFIC

The traditional view of the non-commercial Internet has already been replaced by the realization that the Information Superhighway will entail complete reliance on a global network infrastructure owned and operated by private companies interested in making a profit. In this new profit-oriented world, telecommunication infrastructure companies will explore different ways of providing a variety of user services of the appropriate quality, taking care not to over-provision the network and thereby create excessive costs. To date, communication services have typically been divided into voice- and-video versus Internet services, and companies were for the most part equipped to handle one or the other. There are clear-cut differences between the two: The former requires an allocation of bandwidth from origin to destination, which we can call connection-oriented communications, while the latter is based on connectionless or "best effort" communication.

Network traffic management is complicated by the unique characteristics of this market. The data communications networks operate in a completely distributed environment with little or no precedence or inheritance relationships. Furthermore, the demand for services is highly irregular, and even if there were a central governing body, it would be impossible to centrally manage and allocate computing resources in this setting. Another important dimension is the need to manage the network traffic in real time, since by definition the data communication services are time constrained, and the demand structure is quite dynamic. One mechanism for facilitating efficient resource usage and allocation as well as the management of a multi-service, multi-protocol data communication network is the development of pricing schemes for information products and services such as business applications, entertainment and educational material. Gupta, Stahl, and Whinston (1997b) identified the following characteristics for a viable pricing approach:

a) it should reduce the excess load from the user end without wasting network resources (for example by congesting routers) when users can reschedule without any loss in their value;
b) it should take the impact of current load on the future arrivals into account;
c) it should preferably be coarser than packet level pricing so that it is easier and less-costly to implement;
d) the load status of the network nodes (routers, gateways) should be taken into account in users' decision making process;
e) it should be implemented in a completely decentralized manner thus not requiring any central governing body and allowing for interaction with other possible resource management schemes;
f) it should result in effective load management;
g) it should have multiple priorities to take into account the different qualities of service required by different applications and users; and
h) it should be implemented in such a way that users have incentives to make the right decisions and service providers have incentives to provide the right level of service.

As in virtually all areas, the development of appropriate pricing schemes for the electronic marketplace is in its fledging stage. Consumers, on the one hand, are only interested in obtaining the services/products, and could care less whether they are delivered through the airwaves or using ISDN or POT lines. As long as the products are delivered when required and in the correct form, they will be satisfied. Companies, on the other hand, must take into consideration the cost of network services (i.e. data transmission), the cost of the informational products/services themselves, and fixed costs for both the network service providers and the information providers. Appropriate pricing is also related to management of cross-traffic among different parts of the network that may be owned by different entities. Without being motivated by appropriate prices, infrastructure service providers will have little incentive to fulfill the requests of customers who do not subscribe to their network.

In Gupta et al. (1996a), we developed a model of the Internet as an economic system that provides a theoretical foundation for deriving priority prices that maximize net user benefits taken as a collective. Quite simply, the essential idea is to charge a user an amount that is proportional to his/her usage of the network. Specifically, we suggest charging as much as others on the network would have valued this use. Over and above this "base rate," in the case of real time or urgent applications, the need for faster access - and thus higher priority - is reflected in the use of priority pricing.

In the model a rental price, a priority premium, and an expected waiting time are associated with each processor. These prices are dependent upon the size of services desired, while user requests for these services will depend on the benefits to the user and the costs. Given the prices and the anticipated waiting times, a user evaluates and selects cost-minimizing service schemes. Figure 1 provides a schematic representation of the model. Optimal service demands are then translated into demands on individual processors. Research shows (Gupta et al., 1997c) that there is a generically unique welfare-maximizing allocation, and the rental prices are set at a level that supports this optimum as a "stochastic equilibrium." That is (i) user flow rates are optimal for each user given the rental prices and anticipated waiting times; (ii) the anticipated waiting times are the correct ex ante expected waiting times given the flow rates; and (iii) the aggregate average flow rates are equal to welfare-maximizing rates.

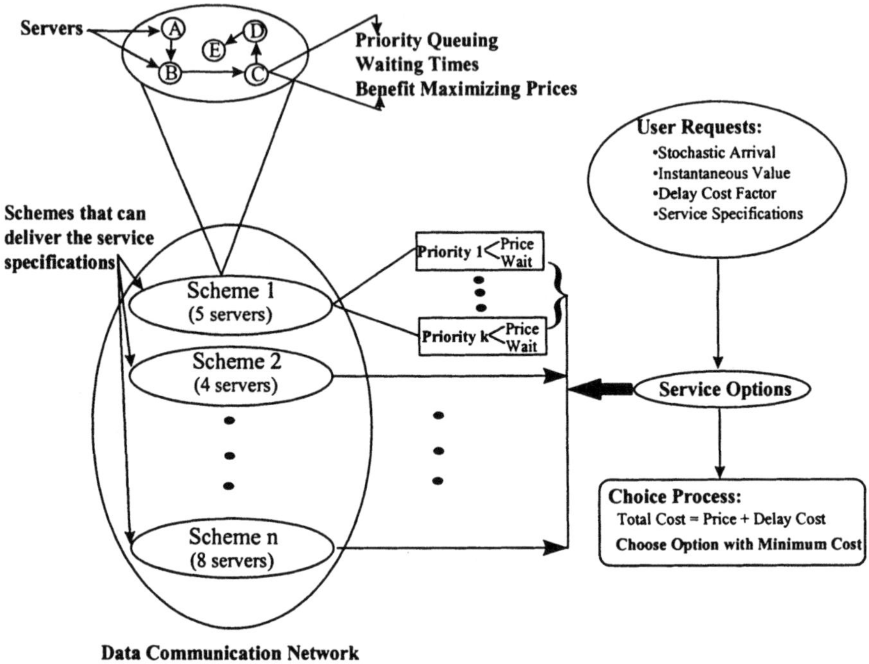

Figure 1. Schematic Representation of the Network Priority Pricing Model

The advantage of this model is that the pricing mechanism can be implemented in a decentralized manner with relatively little information overhead, since price calculations can be decentralized to each server and user decisions can be decentralized to their client machines.

With the addition to the model of a priority pricing capability, a rationale and mechanism exists to take into account the urgent needs of users. In fact, a priority pricing scheme is the only way to provide multiple levels of performance for different types of services in an interoperable network that will be able to delivery all types of service without significant deterioration in service quality (see Bohn et al., 1994; Gupta et al., 1997b; and Shenker, 1995 for more detailed discussion on multi-service class networks).

And, finally, in order to be able to adjust prices according to fluctuating demands and to provide automatic management of resources, a real-time pricing mechanism is an essential feature of the model. Although in a stochastic system prices may never be exactly equal to the optimum, if they converge quickly towards the optimum, significant benefits can still be realized. Since it will be practically impossible to predict or judge the service demands on global networks, a real-time pricing mechanism is key.

Although the area of real-time problem solving is still in its infancy, at CREC we developed pioneering simulation models that show how this can be accomplished (see Gupta et al. 1997b, 1997c for details of the simulation model). Note that many researchers, such as Marbach (2001), incorrectly infer that we are suggesting that prices should be changed every second. While its true that the maximal benefits would be reaped if optimal schedule of prices is available for each request, our approach provides complete flexibility in making the decision to change prices. For example, bounds can be established and price changed only when estimated prices go above or below these bounds. The key is that the robustness of the price computation mechanism provides flexibility to pick a system at any state and steer it towards optimal direction. While the focus of the following description is infrastructure pricing, it is also a valuable tool to explore the impact of other relevant issues such as regulatory policies, alternative product pricing strategies, capacity and design, and competition. Simulations can be used to evaluate the alternatives and may be extremely valuable in anticipating problems and devising solutions. In the next subsection, we briefly provide some key results from simulation study.

3.1 A Simulation of the Internet

The most important questions answered by our simulation of the Internet are: What are the benefits of a properly designed pricing approach, and who will benefit? The results presented here reflect two different information conditions. First, the results for the free access policy are based on perfect information regarding the waiting times. This is the "best case" scenario for implementation of the free access policy because users first check where they can get the fastest service and the information they receive is exact. However, providing perfect information is not practical in reality given the excessive cost involved in computing new information for each new request. Also, since several users can submit requests at virtually the same time, the waiting time information would still be invalid even if it was feasible from a financial perspective. However, it is virtually impossible to make good future predictions with free access if information is periodically provided, negating the realized benefits. Even though this in itself justifies the use of the model's pricing scheme, we are also interested in other performance measures, such as the benefits delivered by the network, all other things being equal. Because of this, our free access results are based on a perfect information scenario. We also looked at priority pricing under a periodic updating scenario.

Figure 2 below illustrates the results of comparison of a non-priority pricing scheme under a free access system and a fixed price scheme. Both the net and customer benefits are shown under varying load conditions, using the perfect information scenario. By "net benefits" we refer to the benefit to the system as a whole, which is equal to the aggregated users' value of the services rendered minus the loss of value due to the delay. By "customer benefits" we refer to the net benefit less the price charged by the service providers. (Note that in the case of free access net benefits = customer benefits.)

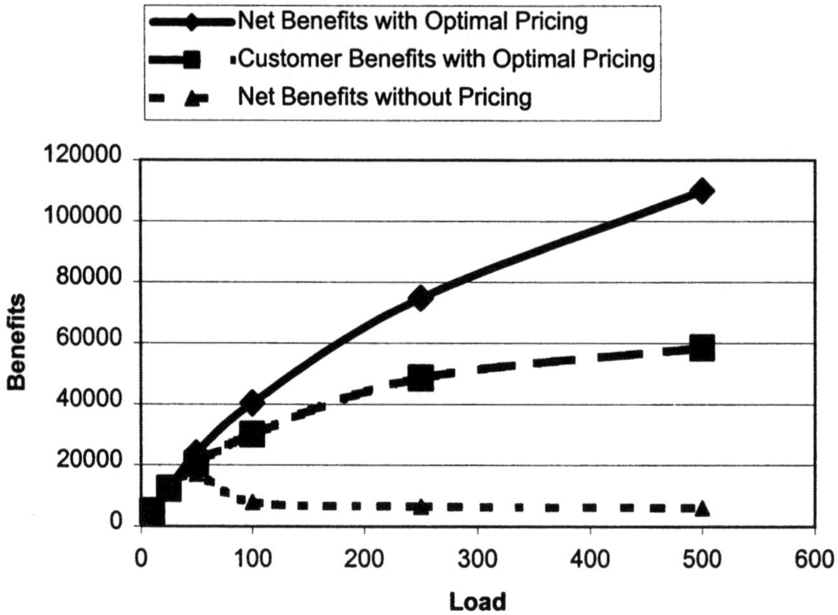

Figure 2. Net and Customer Benefits With and Without Pricing

Somewhat surprisingly our results suggest that this may be a win-win situation on the aggregate level. In other words, both consumers and service providers may benefit from using appropriate prices. Users benefit because their requests are delayed less, resulting in the availability of timely and hence useful information. Providers benefit because of the revenues generated and the optimal usage of the network.

When we take the simulation one step further and compare the benefits between a relatively simple two-priority system and a non-priority system, this time using the periodic update scenario (i.e., the information regarding the waiting time is not exact), the results clearly favor the two-priority system. As Figure 3 shows, this holds true as regards both net benefits and customer benefits and over varying load conditions.

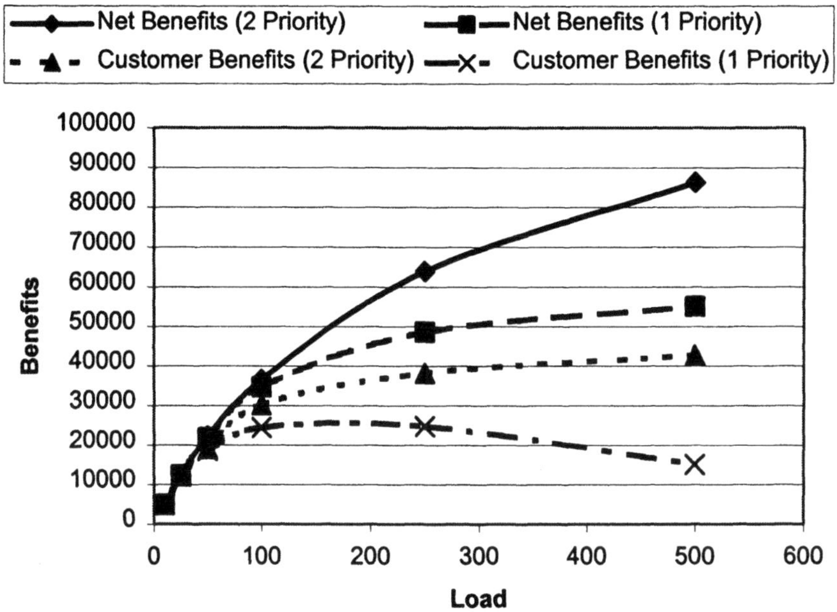

Figure 3. Net and Customer Benefits with Two-Priority Pricing Under Periodic Update

To explore the responsiveness of price adjustment process we varied the arrival process during the simulation and collected the data on how responsive price adjustment process was. In addition, we also explicitly modeled fractal demand (see Gupta, et al., 1999) by drawing each new arrival from a different distribution while keeping the long run average arrival rate fixed. Figure 4 presents results from such a simulation. Note that system responds very quickly to the changed demand patterns and the benefits from fractal demand are virtually indistinguishable from the case when demand is not explicitly modeled as a fractal demand.

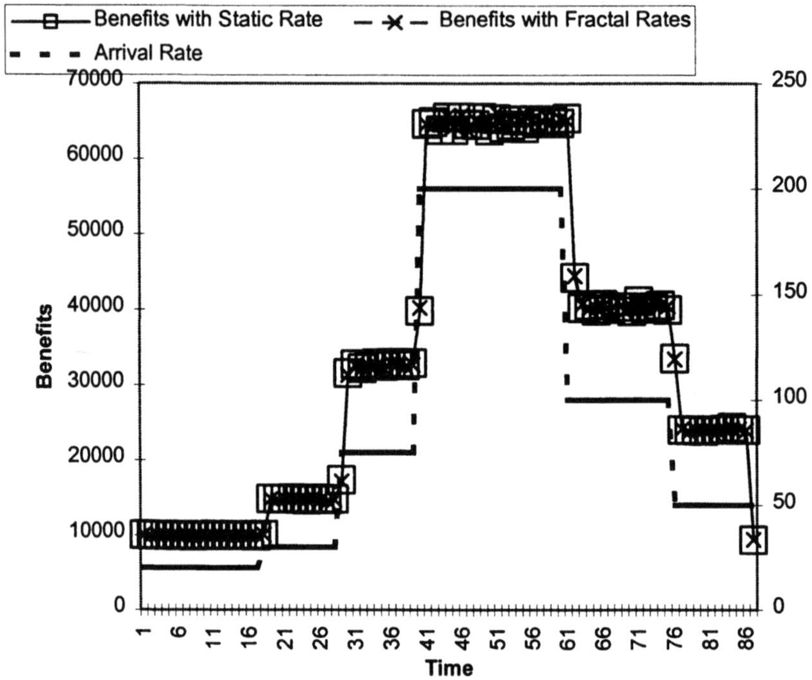

Figure 4. Responsiveness of Pricing Mechanism

Another related issue is the question of what effect competition will have on the pricing of products and services. Different parts of the public networks are or will be owned by different entities, and service providers already compete fiercely to win customers over. It is unlikely that all of these will use the same pricing scheme. Evaluating all the possibilities is a monumental task - and may not result in an analytic equilibrium anyway. In reality there may be many big service providers - we can think of them as electronic department stores - and the pricing strategies they employ may be complex, continuously evolving and inherently dynamic. If left unregulated, pricing strategies may emerge that create a monopolistic market and a single multi-service class network may turn out not to be feasible. On the other hand, hastily drawn legislation with little understanding of its impact may end up providing the same results.

We explored the effect of competition among networks. In Gupta, Linden, Stahl, and Whinston (2001), we modeled two identical networks that employ different pricing strategies. We explored 3 different cases: (i) where both competitors use optimal pricing policies; (ii) where both competitors use a fixed fee system; and (iii) where one competitor uses optimal prices and the other fixed fee. Among several other interesting results, we found that a while people who use network for smaller jobs benefit more with priced network, the people requesting larger jobs get less individual benefits at least at moderate level of congestion as shown in figures 5 and 6. At higher level of congestion the two extremes start converging for larger job sizes. However, in such cases a network environment where less time sensitive customers can go to fixed fee access and more time sensitive customers to priced part, i.e., the case (iii) described above, is more beneficial since the customers can self select the level of service they want.

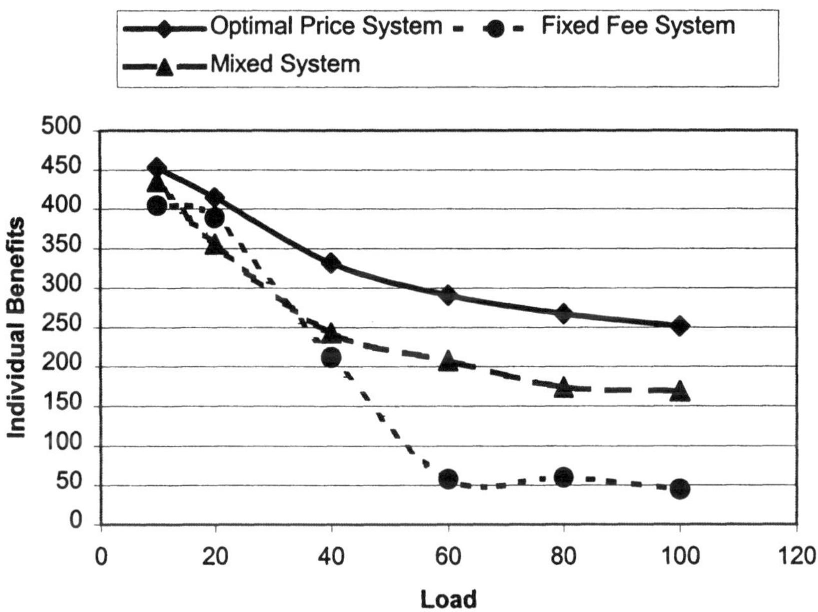

Figure 5. Benefits for Customer Requesting Smaller Jobs

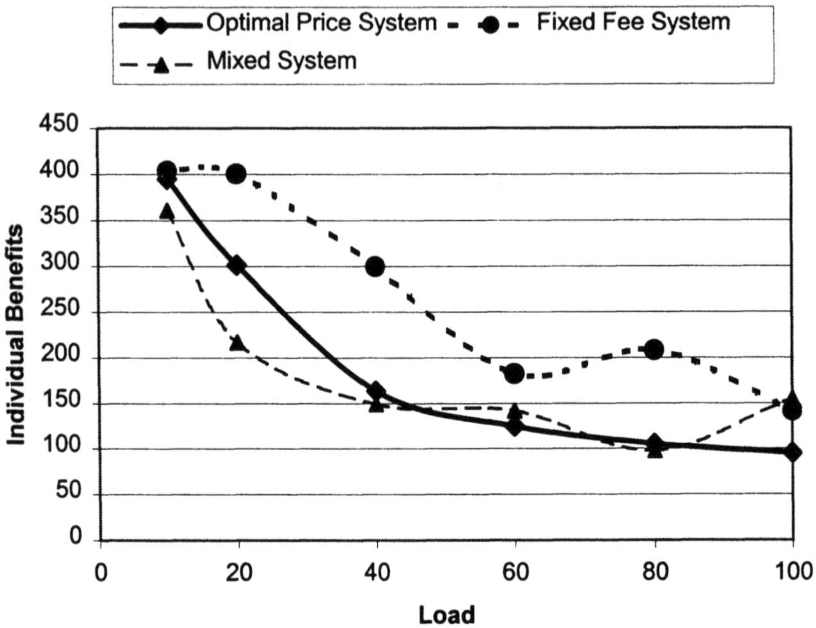

Figure 6. Benefits for Customer Requesting Larger Jobs

Another important investigation of this research was the question of network infrastructure investment. One of the main arguments from opponents of the implementation of any congestion regulating mechanisms for public computer networks is their belief that congestion on such networks is not a long-term issue. This belief is founded on the notion that a so called "bandwidth bonanza" is bound to happen within the next two to three years. It has also been implied that pricing mechanisms dealing with congestion are not only irrelevant (since they deal with a problem that will soon will not exist), but also that they would provide a disincentive for capital investment by discouraging usage. In Gupta, Jukic, Stahl, and Whinston (2001), we examined the incentives to invest in capacity with optimal pricing and with fixed fee pricing. In our research we concluded that:

Optimal level of system-wide capacity is higher under flat-rate pricing when per-unit cost of the capacity is lower than the average value of user's request. When that price/performance threshold is reached, building of a large system will be the optimal strategy under the zero based pricing. Congestion based pricing will result in an earlier deployment and a more gradual expansion of a system. In other words, until the users start putting high value for a service relative to the cost of its delivery, congestion based pricing is necessary for providing investment incentives. However, once a high valuation is attached to the network usage (as compared to capacity costs) fixed price access will provide sufficient incentives to expand the capacities as required.

It is interesting to note that in voice communications we are witnessing precisely this phenomenon. However, for data communication networks, we are traversing in the reverse direction and we believe is the root cause of delay in widespread, sustainable availability of broadband access and QoS guarantees. In this research we also found that the profit maximizing capacity will be lower than the social value maximizing levels of capacity-- where profits are zero.

One of the main contributions of this research stream is the demonstration of computationally feasible decentralized pricing approach and its robustness. Naor (1969), Mendelson (1985), Mendelson and Whang (1990), Westland (1992), Li and Lee (1994), Lederer and Lode (1997) have proposed that levying congestion-based tolls can result in optimal allocation of resources. However, none of these researchers discuss computational aspects of these pricing mechanisms. All these studies assume that consumers' demand characteristics (in terms of their delay costs) are known. However, Shenker, Clark, Estrin, and Herzog (1996) criticize these approaches and claim that the consumers' delay costs are fundamentally unknowable and even though, theoretically, these pricing mechanism are incentive compatible the consumers will not provide their delay costs. In Gupta, Jukic, Stahl, and Whinston (2000), we addressed the issue of estimating these (fundamentally unknowable) delay costs based on observed users' choice. Figure 7 presents results that compare the average real delay costs and the estimated delay costs. Note that while the estimated values are within the range of 3.8-4.17, which is less than 10% of the actual mean. In addition, we showed that using the estimated delay costs results in minimal efficiency loss in terms of system-wide benefits.

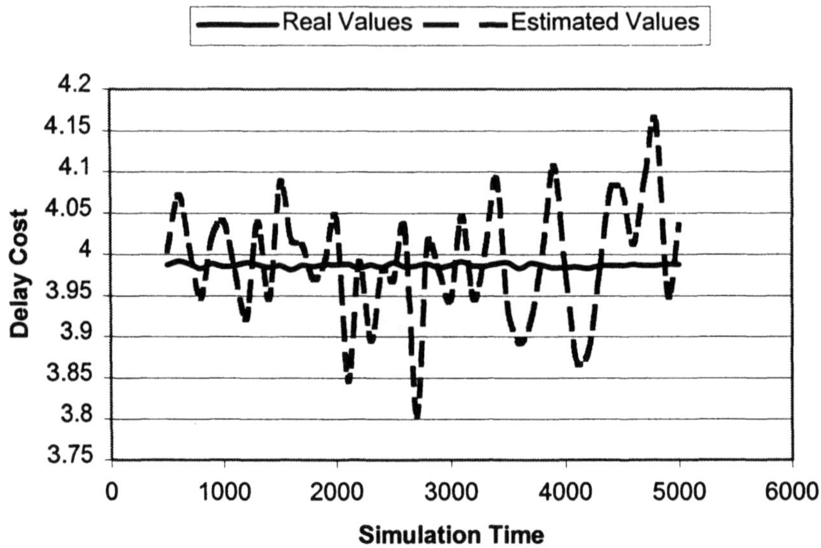

Figure 7. Estimating Delay Cost Based on Observed Consumer Choices

In the next section we discuss application of pricing in real-time service delivery via real-time databases.

4. ECONOMICS ORIENTED SYSTEM DESIGN

In Konana, Gupta, Stahl, and Whinston (1996) and Konana, Gupta, and Whinston (2000) we develop a model for delivery of real-time services through Real-Time Databases (RTDBs). The objective of this study was to explore the operational characteristics of a computing system under economic principles. We investigated whether the natural rationing imposed by pricing mechanisms perform adequately from the perspective of traditional system performance metrics, such as miss ratio. To this extent, we note that Mariposa, a research initiative from University of California, Berkeley, is unique in that it employs economic principles in an attempt to achieve resource allocation in a pragmatic manner in databases distributed over public networks (Stonebraker, Aoki, Litwin, Pfeffer, Sah, Sidell, Staelin and Yu, 1996). Recognizing that it is not viable to have the ideal consistent and integrated database distributed across nodes and serving a wide variety of users, Mariposa partitions the database and stores copies of different fragments at various nodes. A user query submits a "bid curve" along with the query, specifying the relation between delay of delivery and willingness to pay. The query is decomposed in accordance with the way the database is fragmented, and an intermediary asks individual servers to submit their bids for handling each subquery. These bid curves specify the relation between delivery time and the price they would charge. The broker looks through competing queries for each fragment, and comes up with a combination of bidders, so that the aggregate of prices and delivery times satisfy the user's willingness to pay and time requirements. Once a contract is made, the subqueries are executed and the results assembled to deliver the answer to the user query.

While the initiative to apply economic principles, in such a way, to what is largely a real world resource allocation issue is commendable, Mariposa raises questions as well. It assumes that the users and servers can quantify their bid curves, for each individual instance. Further, it assumes they have incentives to reveal such characteristics; both assumptions are unrealistic, and would defeat an economic framework. It is notable that our mechanism does not make any such assumptions whatsoever, and robustly estimates the demand characteristics from the only observable attributes as discussed earlier.

When an economic device for resource allocation is used in isolation with underlying characteristics of the users, where it is merely an artifact, and not part or consequence of an economic framework the results can be arbitrary and may not even provide normative guidance. In such systems, as each provider submits a bid, he may be submitting bids for delivering the same fragment to other clients, but not engaging in a commitment or contract. The crucial weakness in such proposals is that any individual server has no assurance that he will be contracted, and hence no incentive to exclude other clients and reserve his resources for a particular client. By the time the broker resolves competing bids, a participating provider may already have contracted with other clients, and may no longer be in a position to deliver the level of performance he claimed he could. Iterations of such sequences could rapidly lead to a breakdown of the bid-ask mechanism.

In contrast, we derive the strategies from contending economic forces seeking equilibria; these policies are adopted only because they are the best options for each participant, in view of incentive compatibility and optimal resource allocation. In our research we implemented the pricing approach in a simulation model of the RTDB to test the operational characteristics of the RTDB system, such as the number of jobs processed on time (or the number of jobs processed late), throughput and tardiness. These operational characteristics (performance metrics), typically used in computer science literature, are difficult to incorporate into microeconomic models. The simulation study evaluated the performance of RTDB under our economic theory based model against traditional performance measures used in computer science literature. We also use the simulation model to conduct comparative studies with first-come-first-served (FCFS) and two other well studied scheduling techniques in RTDB literature, namely, Earliest-Deadline First (EDF) and Least-Slack First (LSF) (Abbott and Garcia-Molina, 1992; and Haritsa, Carey and Livny, 1991). In addition we evaluated the robustness and the equilibrium conditions when certain theoretical assumptions are violated. For example, in theoretical model, we assumed that a job once accepted is executed until completion even when the performance requirements (e.g., timeliness requirements) cannot be satisfied. We tested the system performance and evaluate economic benefits by relaxing this assumption by dropping user requests from the queue during processing if the actual waiting times are higher than the expected waiting times.

Figure 8 presents results regarding the economic performance of RTDBs with dynamic prices. The model was operated under fixed multiprogramming levels (i.e., no new jobs are accepted if a certain number of jobs already exist in the system) as an admission control mechanism and the results for no pricing case is the best-case performance. No multiprogramming level was used with pricing as it provides a natural admission control mechanism with price sensitive demand. As expected system wide benefits are much higher with prices as opposed to without prices. Even more interesting is the case where users drop out if their timeliness requirement is not met. The results for net benefits are virtually indistinguishable from the case where there are no dropouts. At first glance this seems counter-intuitive since the loss due to delay of customers who wait but do not get serviced reduces net benefits. However, jobs that drop out reduce the waiting time (due to their processing time requirements) for all other jobs in the queue and thus they suffer less of a loss. In the equilibrium, these two factors, i.e. the loss of dropouts and the gain of jobs in the queue, should balance each other. Overall, we feel that these results enhance the robustness of the simulation and the confidence that the simulation and the price computation mechanism within it, indeed reach equilibrium.

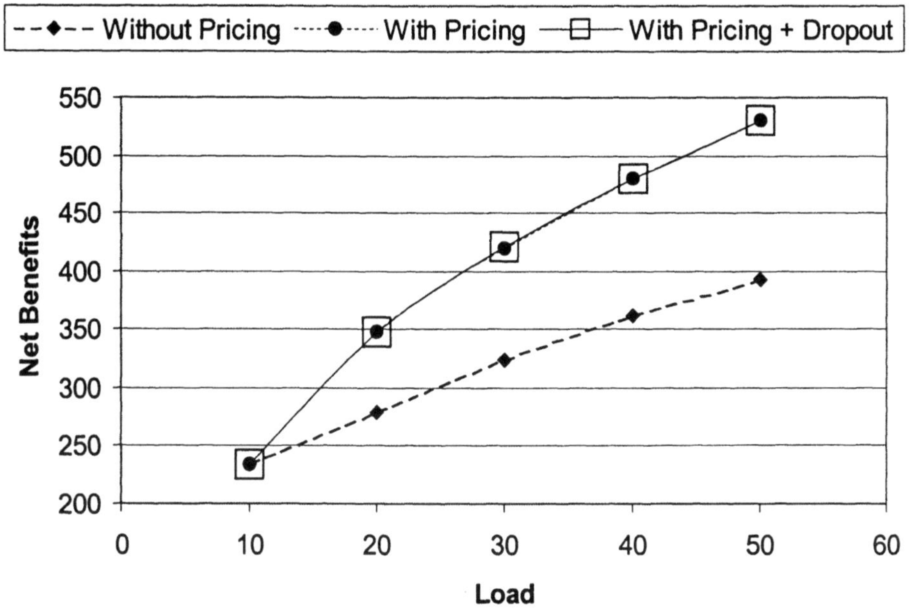

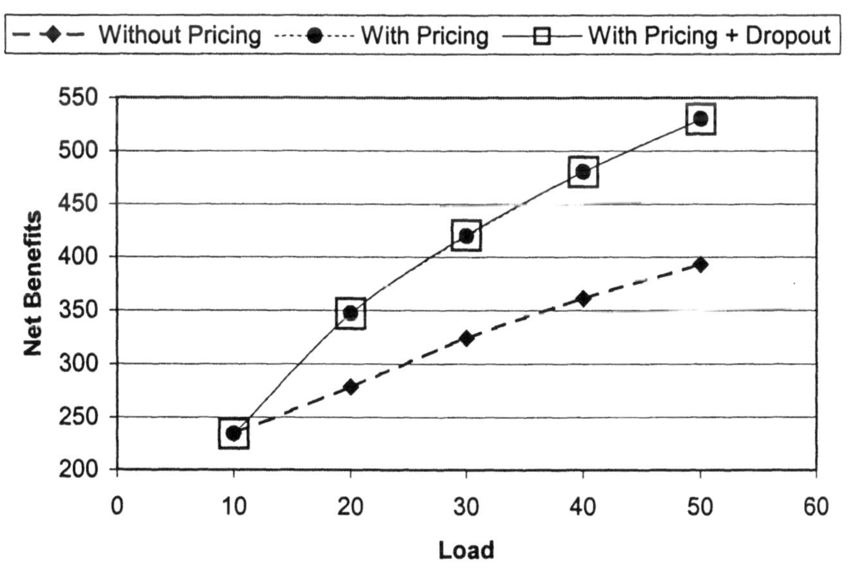

Figure 8. Net Benefits With and Without Pricing

Figure 9 presents results regarding the performance metric of miss ratio, i.e., the ratio of jobs for which the deadline wasn't met. Note that the pricing with no dropouts has a miss ratio of near zero for almost all loads. For the case with dropouts, the miss ratio increases because the overall reduction in expected waiting times lets a lot more marginal jobs in that may not eventually meet their deadlines and drop out themselves. For the case with no pricing at low levels of load all the jobs go in and do not meet the time expectations since it is difficult to accurately predict short run wait in near empty systems, however once the loads are little higher the combination of multiprogramming and more consistent queues allow better prediction of waiting times and the miss ratio stabilizes, however it is significantly higher than the cases with pricing.

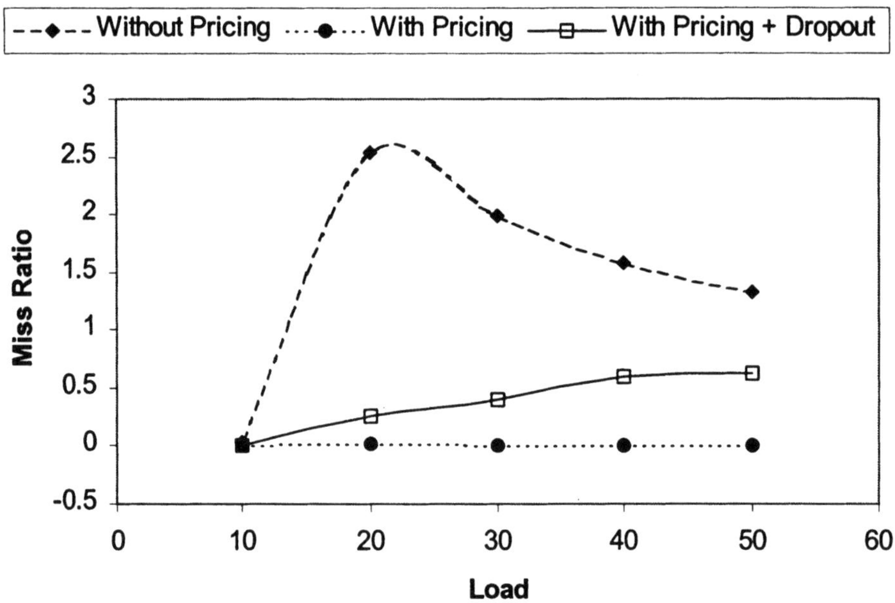

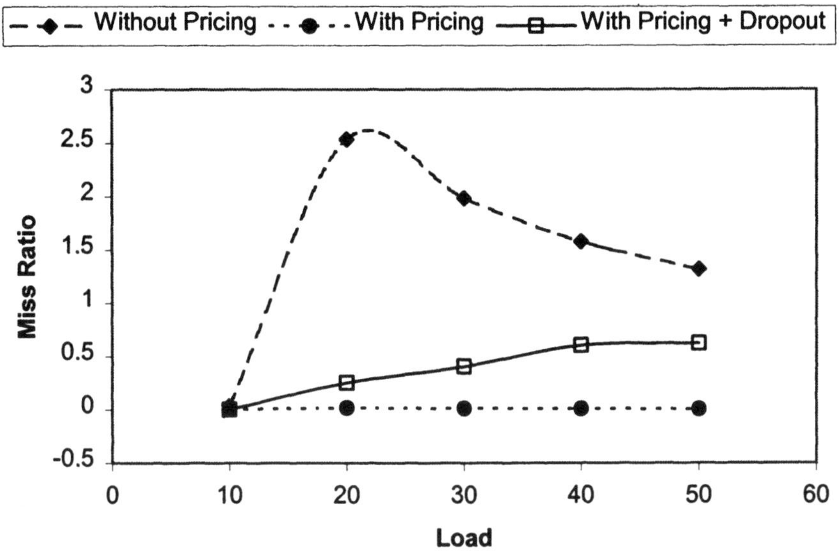

Figure 9. Miss Ratios With and Without Prices

We also examined the other scheduling approaches such as Least Slack First (LSF), Earliest Deadline First (EDF), and First Come First Serve (FCFS). We found that while LSF and EDF perform well under low load condition, pricing provides significantly and more importantly consistent and predictable performance in terms of Miss Ratio and Normalized Miss ratios. Overall, this study provided evidence that using economics oriented mechanisms for operations of computing systems is feasible and beneficial from both economic as well as performance perspectives.

5. CONCLUSIONS

In this chapter, we provided an overview of ongoing research and results on dynamic pricing at CREC. The research has yielded a rich set of original analytical, computational, and strategic results. Some specific examples of the contributions include:

- Development of theoretical economic model of decentralized network pricing.
- Development of an iterative price computation mechanism that converges quickly to near optimal prices.

- Development of prediction tools based on transient (non steady state) information.
- Development of demand estimation technique based on observed user choices -- proving solution for a key theoretical shortcoming of externality based pricing mechanisms in terms of actual implementation.
- Analysis of consumer incentives and choice under competitive scenarios.
- Analysis of incentives for capital investment in infrastructure.
- Application of economic principles in operational aspects of electronic processes.

Clearly, a lot more could and should be done before an actual implementation. In future, we hope to develop a testbed for pricing implementations and use real-world processes to price and manage.

REFERENCES

Abbott, R., & Garcia-Molina, H. (1992). Scheduling real-time transactions: Performance evaluation. ACM Transactions on Database Systems, 17 (3), 513-560.

Adler, M. Chakrabarti, M., Mitzenmacher, M., & Rasmussen, L. (1995). Parallel randomized load balancing. Proceedings of the Twenty-seventh ACM Symposium on Theory of Computing.

Anonymous (1996, October 19th). "The economics of the Internet: Too cheap to meter? The Economist, pp. 23-27.

Artsy, Y., & Finkel, R. (1989). Designing a process migration facility: The Charlotte experience. IEEE Computer, 22(9), 47-56.

Azar, Y., Broder, A., Karlin A., & Upfal E. (1994). Balanced allocations. Proceedings of the Twenty-sixth ACM Symposium on Theory of Computing, 593-602.

Barak, A., & Shiloh, A. (1985). A distributed load balancing policy for a multicomputer. Software Practice and Experience, 15(9), 901-913.

Bohn, R., Braun, H. W., & Wolff, S. (1994). Mitigating the coming internet crunch: Multiple service levels via precedence. Technical report, San Diego Supercomputer Center, University of California at San Diego.

Cocchi, R., Shenker, S., Estrin, D., & Zhang, L. (1991). Pricing in computer networks: Motivation, formulation and example. IEEE/ACM Transactions on Networking, 1 (6), 614- 627.

Dahlin, M., Wang, R., Anderson, T., & Patterson, D. (1994). Cooperative caching: Using remote client memory to improve file system performance. Proceedings of the First Symposium on Operating Systems Design and Implementation, 267-280.

Deerin, S., & Hinden, R. (1995). Internet protocol, version 6 (IPv6) specification. Technical Report [On-Line], IETF. Available Internet: http://www.globecom.net/ietf/rfc/rfc1883.shtml

Douglis, F., & Ousterhout, J. (1991). Transparent process migration: Design alternatives and the Sprite implementation. Software Practice and Experience, 21(7), pp.757-785.

Eager, D., Lazowska E., & Zahorjan, J. (1986). Adaptive load sharing in homogeneous distributed systems. IEEE Transactions on Software Engineering, 12(5), 662-675.

Eriksson, H. (1994). MBone: The multicast backbone. Communications of the ACM, 37(8), 54-60.

Feeley, M., Morgan, W., Pighin, F., Karlin A., Levy, H., & Thekkath, C. (1995). Implementing global memory management in a workstation cluster. Proceedings of the ACM Fifteenth Symposium on Operating Systems Principles, 201-212.

Floyd, S., & Jacobson, V. (1993). Random early detection gateways for congestion avoidance. IEEE Transactions on Networking.

Ganesh, A., Koenraad L., & Steinberg, R. (2001). Congestion pricing and user adaptation. Proceedings of IEEE Infocom [On-Line]. Available Internet: http://www.ieee-infocom.org/2001/

Gupta, A., Stahl, D. O., and Whinston, A. B. (1994). Managing the Internet as an economic system, Technical Report [On-Line], University of Texas at Austin. Available Internet: http://cism.bus.utexas.edu/ravi/pricing.ps.Z

Gupta, A., Stahl, D. O., and Whinston, A. B. (1996a). An economic approach to network computing with priority classes. Journal of Organizational Computing and Electronic Commerce, 6(1), 71-95.

Gupta, A., Stahl, D. O., & Whinston, A.B. (1996b). Economic issues in electronic commerce. In Readings in Electronic Commerce, Kalakota, R. and Whinston, A. B. (eds.), 197-227, Reading: Addison Wesley.

Gupta, A., Stahl, D. O. & Whinston, A. B., (1996c). A priority pricing approach to manage multi-service class networks in real-time. The Journal of Electronic Publishing [On-Line], 2 (1). Available Internet: http://www.press.umich.edu/jep/econTOC.html

Gupta A., Stahl, D. O., & Whinston, A. B. (1997a). A stochastic equilibrium model of Internet pricing. Journal of Economic Dynamics and Control, 21, 697-722.

Gupta A., Stahl, D. O., & Whinston, A. B. (1997b) Priority Pricing of Integrated Services Networks. In Internet Economics, McKnight L. and Bailey J. (eds.), 323-352, Cambridge, MA: MIT Press.

Gupta A., Stahl, D. O., & Whinston, A. B. (1997c). The Internet: A future tragedy of the commons? In Computational Approaches to Economic Problems, H. Amman, B. Rustem, and A. B. Whinston (eds.), 347 - 361, Dordrecht, The Netherlands: Kluwer Academic Publishers.

Gupta A., Stahl, D. O., & Whinston, A. B. (1999). The economics of network management. Communications of the ACM, 42 (9), 57-63.

Gupta, A., Jukic, B., Stahl, D. O., & Whinston, A. B. (2000). Extracting consumers' private information for implementing incentive compatible Internet traffic pricing. Journal of Management Information Systems, 17 (1), 9-29.

Gupta, A., Linden, L., Stahl, D. O., & Whinston, A. B. (2001a). Benefits and costs of adopting usage based pricing in a subnetwork. Information Technology and Management, 2 (2), 175-191.

Gupta, A., Jukic, B., Li, M., Stahl, D. O., & Whinston, A. B (2001b). Estimating Internet Users' Demand Characteristics. Computational Economics, forthcoming.

Goyal, P., Vin, H., & Cheng, H. (1996). Start-time fair queuing: A scheduling algorithm for integrated services packet switching networks. Proceedings of the ACM IGCOMM '96 Conference on Applications, Technologies, Architectures, and Protocols for computer Communication, 157-168.

Harchol-Balter, M., & Downey, A. (1996). Exploiting process lifetime distributions for dynamic load balancing. Proceedings of the SIGMETRICS Conference on Measurement and Modeling of Computer Systems.

Haritsa, J., Livny, M., & Carey, M. (1991). Earliest deadline scheduling for real-time database systems. Proceedings of IEEE Real-time Systems Symposium, 232-242.

Hellerstein, J. (1993, August). Achieving Service Rate Objectives with Decay Usage Scheduling. IEEE Transactions on Software Engineering.

Jacobson, V. (1988). Congestion avoidance and control. Proceedings of the ACM SIGCOMM '88 Conference on Applications, Technologies, Architectures, and Protocols for Computer Communication.

Konana, P., Gupta, A., Stahl, D. O., & Whinston, A. B. (1996). Pricing and real-time database applications for information services: A framework and economic justification. Proceedings of ICIS, 249-264.

Konana, P., Gupta, A., & Whinston, A. B. (2000). Integrating user preferences and real-time workload in information services. Information Systems Research, 11 (2), 177-196.

Lederer, P. J., & Lode, L. (1997). Pricing, production, scheduling, and delivery-time competition. Operations Research, 45, 407-420.

Lewis, P. (1996, December 17). "All You Can Eat" Price is Clogging Internet Access. New York Times.

Li, L., & Lee, Y. S. (1994). Pricing, and delivery-time performance in a competitive environment. Management Science, 40, 633-646.

Litzkow, M., & Solomon, M. (1992). Supporting checkpointing and process migration outside the UNIX kernel. Proceedings of the Winter 1992 USENIX Conference, 283-290.

MacKie-Mason,J., & Varian, H. (1995). Pricing the Internet. In Public Access to the Internet, B. Kahin and J.Keller (eds.), Englewood Cliffs, NJ: Prentice-Hall.

Marbach, Peter (2001). Pricing Differentiated Services Networks: Bursty Traffic. Proceedings of IEEE Infocom [On-Line]. Available Internet: http://www.ieee-infocom.org/2001/

Mendelson, H. (1985). Pricing computer services: Queuing effects. Communications of the ACM, 28 (3), 312-321.

Mendelson, H., & Whang, S. (1990). Priority pricing for the M/M/I queue. Operations Research, 38 (5), 870-883.

Metcalfe, R., & Boggs, D. (1976). Ethernet: Distributed packet switching for local computer networks. Communications of the ACM, 19(7), 395-404.

Mullender, S., van Rossum, G.,van Renesse, R., & van Staveren., H. (1990). Amoeba - a distributed operating system for the 1990s. IEEE Computer, 23(5), 44-53.

Naor, P. (1969). On the regulation of queue size by levying tolls. Econometrica, 37, 15-24.

Patterson, R., Gibson, G., Ginting E., Stodolsky, D., & Zelenka, J. (1995). Informed prefetching and caching. Proceedings of the ACM Fifteenth Symposium on Operating Systems Principles, 79-95.

Pingry, D. E., & Marsden, J. R. (2001). Reference discipline vs. nodding reference. Or Is Andy Whinston a reference discipline? In Business Modeling: A Multi-Disciplinary Perspective: Essays in Honor of Professor Andrew B. Whinston, C. Holsapple, V. Jacob and H. R. Rao (eds.), Dordrecht, The Netherlands: Kluwer Academic Publishers.

Sarkar, P., & Hartman, J. (1996). Efficient cooperative caching using hints. Proceedings of the Second Symposium on Operating Systems Design and Implementation.

Shenker, S. (1995). Service models and pricing policies for an integrated services internet. In Public Access to the Internet, Kahin B. and Keller J. (eds.), 315-337, Englewood Cliffs, NJ: Prentice-Hall.

Shenker, S., Clark, D., Estrin, D., & Herzog, S. (1996). Pricing in computer networks: reshaping the research agenda. Journal of Telecommunications Policy, 20 (3), 183-201.

Stonebraker, M., Aoki, P., Litwin, W., Pfeffer A., Sah, A., Sidell, J., Staelin, C., & Yu, A. (1996). Mariposa: A wide-area distributed database system. VLDB Journal, 5(1), 48-63.

Waldspurger, C., & Weihl, W. (1994). Lottery scheduling: Flexible proportional-share resource management. Proceedings of the First Symposium on Operating Systems Design and Implementation, 1-12.

Waldspurger, C., & Weihl, W. (1995, June). Stride scheduling: Deterministic proportional-share resource management. Technical Report TM-528, Massachusetts Institute of Technology Laboratory for Computer Science.

Wang, X., & Schulzrinne, H. (2001). Pricing network resources for adaptive applications in a differentiated services network. Proceedings of IEEE Infocom [On-Line]. Available Internet: http://www.ieee-infocom.org/2001/

Chapter 12

Pricing Virtual Private Networks - An Economic, Engineering and Experimental Approach

Zhangxi Lin: Peng Si Ow: Dale O. Stahl

College of Business Administration, Texas Tech University, Lubbock, TX 79409-2101, USA zlin@ba.ttu.edu, [2] Center for Research in Electronic Commerce (CREC), The University of Texas at Austin, Austin TX, 78712, USA phighnam@aol.com, [3] Department of Economics, The University of Texas at Austin, Austin, TX 78712, USA stahl@eco.utexas.edu

Abstract This chapter presents a network traffic-pricing model for virtual private network (VPN) deployed on packet-switching networks. A transaction-level pricing architecture based on proxy server technology is proposed for the implementation. Analytical expressions of pricing formulas for first-in-first-out and round-robin bandwidth are derived. Both agent-based simulations and the human subject based direct experiment have been conducted using real-time test data. The experimental outcomes strongly support that the pricing mechanism can effectively improve a VPN's transmission efficiency measured by the service welfare rate.

Key words: Network traffic pricing, virtual private networks, queueing model, agent-based simulation, direct experiment.

1. VIRTUAL PRIVATE NETWORKS AND THEIR TRAFFIC MANAGEMENT PROBLEM

The virtual private network (VPN) (Kosiur, 1998) is a value-added network built upon various types of network clouds, particularly on the Internet, with secured virtual paths for data transmission. The explosive growth of the Internet is also spilling over to Internet-based VPNs, so that VPNs are emerging as an important enterprise networking solution for corporations. The cost-effectiveness of Internet-based VPNs has stimulated the demand for VPN services. According to Infonetics Research, worldwide expenditures on VPNs should double annually through 2002 when they are expected to reach $20 billion. Yankee Group predicts that by the year 2003, VPNs will be used by 70 percent of all companies for up to 90 percent of their data communications needs.

Although the Internet-based VPN can reduce the monetary cost of network applications, Internet traffic congestion also reduces the benefit from the use of VPNs as a result of exponentially increasing traffic loads. In its "*Top 10 Discoveries About the Internet*" [http://www.keynote.com/measures/top10.html], Keynote Systems listed the Internet performance problem as the first among the ten. In one of its weekly reports, Keynote System's *Keynote Business 40 Internet Performance Index* showed that the best response time was about 1.5 seconds in a web site access and the worst average was about 15 seconds.

The history of Internet is in fact a recursive process of performance improvement and demand growth. The high demand urges better Internet service quality and the improved Internet services results in higher demand. In late 1980s, a group of flow-control algorithms such as *slow-start* and *congestion avoidance* were proposed and widely implemented today (Jacobson and Karels, 1988; Nagle, 1984; Stevens, 1997), which made Internet services stable from the collapse caused by network congestion. In addition, queue management algorithms for Internet transmission nodes have been designed to complementarily allocate bandwidth and deal with queue overflow for network nodes along data paths (Braden et al, 1998). Recent research in active queue management algorithms, such as *Random Early Detection* (RED) (Floyd and Jacobson, 1993) and *fair queuing* (FQ) (Demers, Keshav and Shenker, 1990), has led to more powerful networking products that can provide better quality of service (QoS).

The major idea behind these technical schemes to improve Internet services is feedback. With feedback in a flow control session, the sender and the receiver computers of an end-to-end connection dynamically exchange the information about available bandwidth and maintain an appropriate transmission bandwidth. Furthermore, heavily loaded nodes can send back alerts to the origins of data flows to trigger responses to the congestion. If the network communication software for the sender is responsive to these mechanisms, it will automatically reduce the data rate to avoid the congestion.

However, there are two problems with these non-incentive-compatible approaches. First, they are effective only if the network applications are responsive. Those data flows generated by "non-responsive" applications can get around the flow-control mechanism to obtain more bandwidth (Floyd and Fall, 1999), and therefore deteriorate the network performance. Because of the ever-increasing heterogeneity of Internet protocols, many of which do not comply with the traffic control algorithms, these traditional approaches are no longer working properly. Second, a pure technical scheme is unable to discriminate among different types of data flows in accordance with their values. The only constraint to the overexploitation of the network bandwidth resource is the throughput time when the network is overloaded. In this case, the data flows sensitive to the delay are affected more regardless of their value to users. Presently, there is no final solution for the Internet congestion problem. Hence traffic congestion control is still an important research topic (Allman, Paxson and Stevens, 1999).

Since the 1990's, there is an emerging consensus that the Internet traffic congestion problem is not merely an engineering issue, but a problem of allocating scarce network resources to users whose valuations of these resources vary. Increasingly research has been conducted on economic network resource allocation mechanisms that support usage-based pricing and incentive compatibility (Clark, 1996; Gupta, Stahl and Whinston, 1999). Examples are dynamic bidding for access *by MacKie-Mason and Varian (1995);* priority pricing *by Gupta, Stahl and Whinston (denoted as the GSW model) (Gupta et al, 1997; Gupta, Stahl and Whinston, 1997; Li et al 2000);* edge pricing *by Shenker et al (1996);* Paris metro pricing *by Odlyzko (1997); and* progressive second price auction *by Lazar and Semret (1998).*

Although researchers theoretically proved that the economic approach has the potential to solve Internet congestion problems, they also realized that a good traffic-pricing model must come with an implementation scheme that is proved to be practical. It must be convincing to computer scientists that a mathematically intensified economic approach would not disturb the operation of the current mechanism for network traffic management and congestion control, and would work well alongside the existing technologies.

Our research in VPN traffic pricing is focused on the implementation feasibility of the network traffic-pricing scheme. The reasons that the Internet-based VPN is chosen as the target network are:

- *The VPN's performance has become a significant issue in its business applications because the encrypted packets impose more traffic loads which reduce the benefits.*
- *The VPN possesses some useful business features such as user authentication and user account management that make the implementation of traffic-pricing feasible*

The model developed in this research follows the methodology used by the GSW model, which was initialized by Stahl and Whinston (1991) and enriched by Gupta, Stahl and Whinston (1997). The GSW model is a general equilibrium model with a resource-price structure that is incentive compatible for network resource allocation. It was tested under various scenarios by a simulation of a public network. The simulation indicated that traffic pricing can significantly improve network service benefits and the service prioritization will lead to better outcomes. In theoretical aspect, we have enhanced the GSW model to fit packet-switching networks that use either first-in-first-out (FIFO) or round-robin (RR) bandwidth scheduling. In practical aspect, we have developed the architecture and technology for a prototype of VPN traffic-pricing system. The experimental outcomes from the prototype system have conversely verified the correctness of the theoretical results.

2. A TRANSACTION-LEVEL TRAFFIC-PRICING SCHEME

Before a dynamic traffic-pricing model can be developed, we need to know how it is used and where it is enacted. In particular, the topology and data flow control scheme for a VPN may critically affect the form of the pricing formula. A typical Internet-based VPN can be built up with special network devices to connect geographically distributed LANs into a virtual intranet/extranet over the Internet. The constructive hardware includes firewalls, certificate authority servers, security gateways, etc., underpinned by the security technologies such as security transmission protocols (e.g. IPSec), user-authentication information management protocols (e.g. LDAP), key-management protocols (e.g. ISAKMP), etc. Logically, we refer to the hardware set supporting the VPN technology as the *VPN gateway*. Therefore, a VPN gateway is an enhanced network gateway between an application domain and the Internet. It can provide the required security functions such as:

- Wide-area network tunneling, i.e., establishing a secure network connection across the public Internet;
- Data encryption;
- Filtering/firewalling, i.e., security control of incoming and outgoing packets at network edges; and
- User authentication.

The application of encryption/decryption and related security protocols has added more traffic and processing overhead to VPNs and is blamed for the worsened congestion problem. Here, we define network traffic congestion as prolonged time for a data flow to get through the network compared with the time it would take to get through an idle network. By this definition, the congestion may result from the queue waiting time at network nodes as well as from queue overflow.

We propose a transaction-level pricing *architecture for the VPN traffic pricing to solve implementability and efficiency problems. We claim that it allows us to solve relevant issues for a network traffic-pricing system, such as: digital contracting; pricing system efficiency; logistic system operation (payments, accounting, etc.) irregularities; problems involved with the integration of the traffic-pricing system and existing traffic-control techniques; and user acceptability. Proxy server-based VPN traffic pricing is the underpinning infrastructure for transaction-level VPN pricing architecture (Figure 1). A proxy server is employed as the bandwidth broker to schedule the data flows with a pricing mechanism for an affiliated VPN gateway, which is called* traffic proxy server *(TPS). TPSs can be deployed somewhere between VPN security devices and application domains, for example, between VPN gateways and local area networks.*

The terms used in this chapter include: A Job *is a synonym for* Transaction *and is defined as a unit of a network service requested by a user, which may generate one or several data flows transmitted through a network. A* data flow *is a group of IP packets controlled by, for example, a TCP connection.* Job size *is referred to as the total volume of data flows incurred by a job. It is measured in the number of segments composed of several packets in the same data flow.* Throughput time *is used to describe the transmission time for a group of packets, e.g. a data flow, going through a section of transmission channel. The throughput time of a data flow includes its transmission time and waiting time at a given channel. It is determined by the traffic load conditions as well as routing and transmitting disciplines. Transaction-level pricing is to be implemented on top of transport layer protocols without looking into the internal mechanism at the lower layer for data flow delivery and control. With the transaction-level implementation, VPN gateways can schedule data transmission tasks in regard to the application needs and priorities.*

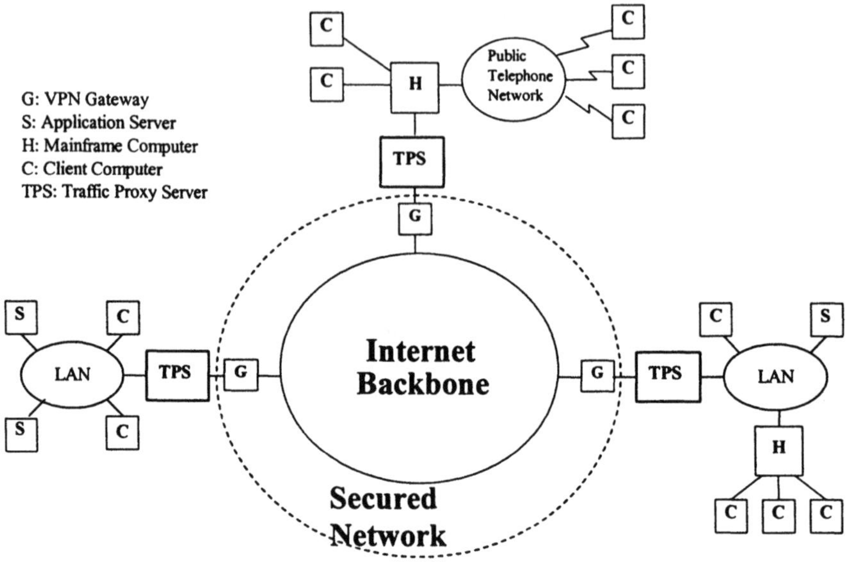

Figure 1. The infrastructure of proxy server-based VPN traffic-pricing system

We suggest a two-session interactive model for TPS operation. A similar model has been designed in practice for secure proxy servers (Oppliger, 1998). One of the sessions is designed for security control purposes and another for data transmission service. The following process provides an example for a data retrieval transaction:

- A remote client on a user's behalf requests a connection to the TPS with the user's ID and password.
- If the user's information is properly authenticated, the client is permitted to proceed to request information services from the application server that the TPS proxies. Meanwhile the TPS checks an active user list. If the user/client pair is not on the list, the TPS adds the user/client to the list. The TPS periodically sends pricing information to all active clients according to the active client list, so that users are able to make job submission decisions.
- The user may submit jobs after the primary control connection is properly processed. Only the jobs with positive net values are submitted, which are calculated by a smart agent using the expected throughput time and the price that the client received from the TPS through the primary connection. In this stage, the client establishes a secondary connection to the TPS.
- The TPS authenticates and authorizes each job request and relays it to a destination application server.

- The application server completes services and sends back flows of data to the TPS.
- The TPS schedules data transmission tasks for the affiliated VPN gateway and bills the services to the user's account according to the jobs' sizes and the user's QoS requisitions.
- The TPS forwards data flows to the client.

The major difference between the interaction model suggested for the TPS and the one used for the secure proxy server is that the TPS schedules data flows and accesses user accounts each time that an application server generates data flows, while the SPS function is accessed before a service starts. Some protocols, such as *Remote Authentication Dial-In User Service* (RADIUS) that has been used by some VPN solutions (Rigney and Livingston, 1999; Rigney et al, 2000), can be utilized for the TPS in user authentication and remote network connection administration.

3. A DYNAMIC TRAFFIC PRICING MODEL FOR VPN

Several restrictions are necessary to narrow down the VPN traffic-pricing problem. First, we focus our discussion on the data flows incurred by application service requests but neglect the traffic for the routing and addressing services, such as domain name service and routing information distribution, because they have relatively less impact on the network bandwidth. Second, in the main part of this paper we will discuss the traffic-pricing model based on the assumption that a job incurs a single data flow. We can extend the result to a general situation, where one job is related to multiple data flows. This strategy allows us to simplify the model derivation without losing the correctness of the outcome. Third, we do not consider traffic management in the backbone because it is out of the organization's control. We assume that Internet service providers assure the requested QoS on the Internet in accordance with the contracts, such as a service-level agreement. Finally, traffic control within LANs is not considered. This is because LANs normally have enough bandwidth. Therefore, we can concentrate on LANs' Internet connections, which could be the network bottlenecks because their bandwidth is restricted by an organization's networking budget.

3.1 The Characteristics of VPN Queueing Model

An Internet-based VPN can be defined as a set of $G = \{g_s\}$ gateways, $s \in S$, an equal number of channels $C = \{c_s\}$ connecting gateways to the Internet, providing that each gateway has only one Internet connection, and Internet tunnels that are dynamically established for secured transmissions. With the assumption of the assured QoS of Internet tunnels, the bottleneck of a VPN route, if it exists, is one of the two channels between VPN gateways and the Internet, not the Internet tunnel. Consider a route R^j carrying data flow j from a sender to a receiver. R^j is a set of nodes and channels. It can be denoted as $R^j = \{g_1^j, g_2^j, c_1^j, c_2^j, c_n\}$, where g_1^j is the gateway with a bottleneck Internet connection c_1^j, g_2^j is the gateway with a non-bottleneck Internet connection c_2^j, c_n^j is an Internet tunnel for data flow j. g_1^j and $g_2^j \in G$, c_1^j and $c_2^j \in C$. Here, we say channel c_s^j is a bottleneck in route R^j referring to a data flow j if the channel's cumulative available bandwidth capacity is always less than another channel's cumulative available bandwidth capacity in the time period servicing the data flow. If the data transmission request at a VPN gateway is a Poisson process with a general size distribution, the bandwidth allocation service becomes an M/G/1 queueing system because the capacity of a channel is deterministic but the size of the data flows varies (Kleinrock, 1975).

Generally, the above VPN route can be modeled as a three-stage queueing system (Figure 2): the first queueing server is the Internet connection channel c_1 for outgoing data flows from the sender; the second one is the Internet tunnel c_n; and the third one is the Internet connection channel c_2 for incoming data flows to the receiver. The traffic loads on channel c_1 also come from other computers in the LAN the sender locates. A major portion of outgoing data flows from channel c_1 is sent to other destinations than the receiver being discussed, and therefore they will not join the queue for channel c_2. In a similar way channel c_2 also transmits data flows from other sources to the LAN where the receiver locates without increasing the burden on channel c_1.

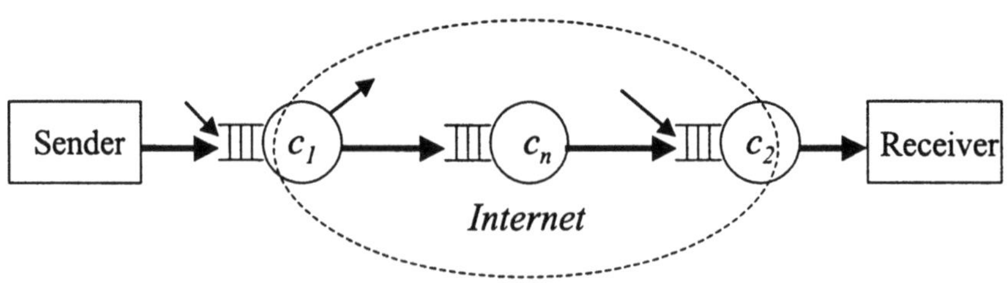

Figure 2. A three-stage queueing model for a VPN route.

Even though the capacity of the Internet connection channels is the main concern in traffic control, the channels are passive to traffic loads, and routers/gateways are actually allocating bandwidth for them. The traffic through channel c_1 can be observed and measured at gateway G_1 that maintains the queue for channel c_1 and allocates the bandwidth for c_1. Although the queue for channel c_2 forms at a router in the Internet, the traffic through channel c_2 can still be observed and controlled at gateway G_2. In this context, the VPN gateway and the transmission channel are equivalent in traffic control. If an Internet connection channel is the bottleneck in a route, we can also refer to the affiliated VPN gateway as the bottleneck gateway.

One of the important advantages of packet-switched networks is that the total delay a data flow encounters in a route is less than the summation of waiting and servicing times in all channels (or equivalently nodes) along the route. This feature allows packet-switched networks to provide better bandwidth efficiency than other types of network, such as circuit-switched networks. However, the "pipeline" effect in a packet-switched network adds complexity in setting up the price for traffic because the total throughput time is not a sum of the throughput times at each individual packet-forwarding device. The same effect is applied to VPNs built on the Internet.

Proposition:

In a packet-switched network, the total throughput time that a data flow is transmitted through a route can be expressed as the time spent at the bottleneck node plus a relatively trivial amount of delay on other nodes of the path.

The following is an intuitive explanation of the proposition:

When a data flow is transmitted through a route in a packet-switched network, packets are sent just like water flows through a pipe. Every node in the route forwards the packets through the channel to next node whenever it receives the packets and the channel has available bandwidth. Because of time overlapping, the total throughput time for the data flow is less than the summation of throughput times at each node. By intuition, the time that the data flow passes through the bottleneck node will almost overlay the throughput time at any other node. There is only a minor difference in transporting a unit of the data flow, which has been defined as a segment of packets. The number of packets in a segment depends on the flow control algorithm adopted by the network. Therefore, the total time of the data flow transmitted through the route can be expressed as the throughput time for the bottle node plus the time for a unit of packets to be sent through the route.

Applying the above proposition to the VPN, we can infer that the total transmission time for a data flow through a VPN route is the throughput time of the bottleneck Internet connection plus the time for a segment of packets, which is the processing unit of packets, to go through the other path.

3.2 VPN Traffic-Pricing Formulae

The VPN traffic-pricing model is assumed to comply with the following economic conditions:

- A job has an intrinsic value perceived by the user who generates it;
- A job's net value to the user depends on three factors: the intrinsic value, the price charged, and the delay cost which is proportional to the throughput time;
- Prices are set for the channel bandwidth consumption in accordance with the network traffic status;
- The information of both the bandwidth price and the expected throughput time are periodically disseminated to users;
- Users are rational, i.e., they submit their jobs only if expected net gains from job submissions are positive.

The protocol for VPN traffic pricing is a three-stage process:

1) *A TPS periodically decides the bandwidth usage price, based on its current traffic load status, for the bandwidth service between the local network and the Internet. The price and the traffic load status are disseminated to those client computers that are using the VPN transmission services.*
2) *A smart agent, i.e., a client side application, helps users estimate jobs' values and sizes, as well as the effects of delay on the jobs. It automatically makes job submission decisions according to the net values of the jobs by taking account of transmission service prices and throughput times. These decisions are imprecise, but statistically the errors are acceptable because users can update the rules for job size predictions and job value estimations, and therefore improve the smart agent's performance.*
3) *Once a job is submitted it will be charged with the price by the real size of total data flows serviced by the VPN. The costs are billed to the user's account.*

In the transaction-level pricing architecture, the TPS replaces the VPN gateway to allocate the bandwidth of Internet connections. We investigate three bandwidth-scheduling algorithms, prioritized FIFO bandwidth scheduling, non-prioritized RR bandwidth scheduling, and prioritized RR bandwidth scheduling.

The priority is one of the user's choices in data transmission services, which makes a difference to the delay cost. In prioritized FIFO scheduling, if the queue of a higher priority is nonempty the service for the queue of a lower priority will never begin. In another aspect, we assume there is no preemption once a data flow transmission has begun. That is, if a data flow at a lower priority is being serviced and another data flow at a higher priority arrives, the data flow at the lower priority is continued until completion.

The prioritized RR bandwidth scheduling adopts a preemptive policy. That is, a data flow at higher priority obtains bandwidth immediately after it arrives the server regardless the service status of jobs at the lower priority classes. A new data flow joins the tail of the queue for the requested priority class and is assigned a fixed-length time slice in its turn if there is no data flow in higher priority queues. With prioritized RR bandwidth scheduling, a VPN gateway allows all data flows being serviced in the same priority class to share Internet connection channels equally. The non-prioritized RR is the special case when there is only a single priority class.

From the user's viewpoint, we define *job type* to distinguish the characteristics of a job, such as job size and application type. Different users may submit the same types of jobs at different moments. However, jobs of the same type remain identical in size and application type, even though their values vary from user to user and from time to time. We model the demand for transmission services as determined by (i) an exogenous "potential" rate which would prevail if all costs were zero, and (ii) the monetary and time costs of obtaining the service. Let I denote the set of users, J the set of job types, and Q the set of job sizes. Let λ_{ij} be the exogenous potential service request rate of job type j from the user i. The total exogenous rate, i.e., the maximum potential job rate, for the VPN is $\lambda = \sum_{i=1}^{I}\sum_{j=1}^{J}\lambda_{ij}$, and the maximum potential data flow rate is $\sum_{j=1}^{J} q_j \sum_{i=1}^{I}\lambda_{ij}$, where $q_j \in Q$ is the size of a type j job measured in the number of segments. These two forms of exogenous rates are based on the aggregation of the demands when there are no costs—no transmission charges and no response delays that impose extra costs to services. A cost reduces a service's net value and hence prevents the submission of lower-valued jobs. Therefore, in reality, not every potential service request will be submitted because the costs from service delays are inevitable. The real demands in responding to the price and the delay time are the rates of jobs submitted to the network.

The above conditions allow us to setup a benefit maximization problem for VPN bandwidth service (Lin et al, 2000; Lin, Stahl and Whinston, 2000). By solving a VPN benefit-maximization problem, we can obtain a general expression of VPN bandwidth rental price for a given channel:

$$r_{qk}^{*} = \sum_{l \in I} \sum_{m \in J} \sum_{h \in K} \frac{\partial \Omega_{mh}}{\partial \varphi_{qk}} x_{lmh} \delta_{lm}$$, if the channel is the bottleneck of route R^j; *(3.1a)*

$$r_{qk}^{'} = \sum_{l \in I} \sum_{m \in J} \sum_{h \in K} \frac{1}{q} \frac{\partial \Omega_{mh}}{\partial \varphi_{qk}} x_{lmh} \delta_{lm}$$, if the channel is **not** the bottleneck of route R^j. *(3.1b)*

where Ω_{mh} is the expected throughput time—the time that a job gets through a VPN gateway—for type-m job submitted to priority-h service, x_{lmh} is data flow rate of type-m job submitted by user l for priority-h service, δ_{lm} is delay cost coefficient for type-m job submitted by user l indicating the impact of delay on user's benefit, and φ_{qk} is job rate for jobs of size q submitted to priority-k service. Size q is defined as $q = q_j$ for type-j jobs.

Generally, $q >> 1$, hence $r_{qk}^{*} >> r_{qk}^{'}$. Then we can approximately apply a single price r_{qk}^{*} to type-j job submitted by user i for service priority k neglecting the effect of the non-bottleneck price $r_{qk}^{'}$.

The total price paid for a job j at priority k of the channel can be expressed as:

$$r_{jk} \approx r^{*}_{qk} = \sum_{l \in I} \sum_{m \in J} \sum_{h \in K} \frac{\partial \Omega_{mh}}{\partial \varphi_{qk}} x_{lmh} \delta_{lm} \qquad (3.2)$$

With FIFO scheduling, the expected throughput time depends on the expected waiting time in the queue, w_k, which is invariant to a job's type, and the channel service time, which is invariant to priority class once the job is being serviced. Therefore, the queue waiting time w_k for a M/G/1 queueing system can be expressed in terms of job size q instead of job type j:

$$w_k = \frac{\sum_{h \in K} \sum_{q \in Q} \varphi_{qh} q^2}{2B^2 (1 - \sum_{h<k} \rho_h)(1 - \sum_{h \le k} \rho_h)} \qquad (3.3)$$

Then the throughput time:

$$\Omega_{jk} = w_k + q / B \qquad (3.4)$$

where B is bandwidth.

By using the above formula, we can obtain a pricing formula for a FIFO scheduling that is quadratic in job size:

$$r^*_{qk} = \sum_{h \in K} \varphi_h \bar{\delta}_h (a_{1h} q + a_{2h} q^2) \quad \forall q \in Q, k \in K \qquad (3.5)$$

where $a_{1h} = \dfrac{w_h (2 - \sum_{l<h} \rho_l - \sum_{l \le h} \rho_l)}{B\,(1 - \sum_{l<h} \rho_l)(1 - \sum_{l \le h} \rho_l)}$ when $k < h$, $a_{1h} = \dfrac{w_h}{B\,(1 - \sum_{l \le h} \rho_l)}$

when $k = h$, $a_{2h} = \dfrac{1}{2B^2 (1 - \sum_{l<h} \rho_l)(1 - \sum_{l \le h} \rho_l)}$, ρ_l is the bandwidth utilization

ratio for priority l service, $\bar{\delta}_h = \sum_{l \in I} \sum_{m \in J} \dfrac{x_{lmh}}{\varphi_h} \delta_{lm}$ is the mean of δ_{lm} over user l and job type m, weighted by the flow in priority h, and $\varphi_h = \Sigma_q\ \varphi_{qh}$ is job arrival rate at priority-h queue.

In a round-robin scheduling system, a job's throughput time is proportional to job size and the average number of jobs in the queue during servicing. The throughput time of a size q_j job in a non-prioritized queue is

$$t_j = t(q_j) = [(L^* + 1)\, q_j - \rho/2]/B,$$

where $L^* = \dfrac{\rho^2 E[q^2]}{(1-\rho)(E[q] + E[q^2])}$ is the average number of jobs being serviced, ρ is the bandwidth utilization ratio of the gateway, and $E[q]$ *and* $E[q^2]$ are the expected size and size-squared values for the gateway. We can derive the optimal unit price (Lin et al, 1999):

$$r_0 \approx \frac{\bar{\delta}}{B}\left(L^* + \frac{L^* - \rho}{1 - \rho}\right), \qquad (3.6)$$

where $\bar{\delta} = \sum_{l \in I} \sum_{m \in J} x_{lm} \delta_{lm} q_m / \sum_{l \in I} \sum_{m \in J} x_{lm} q_m$ is the mean of δ_{ij} over i and j, weighted by data volume rates. The approximate form for the pricing with RR scheduling indicates that the expected number of jobs in the queue is a critical factor in a job's price and the price is proportional to the size of a job.

In a prioritized RR bandwidth scheduling, the price for type-j job submitted to class-k is (see the Appendix in Lin, Stahl and Whinston, 2000):

$$r_{jk} = \sum_{m \in J} \sum_{h > k} \varphi_{mh} \bar{\delta}_m \frac{q_{mh} q_{jk} L_h^2 [2(1 - \sum_{l<h} \rho_l) - \rho_h]}{B^2 (1 - \sum_{l<h} \rho_l)^2 \rho_h}$$

$$+ \sum_{m \in J} \varphi_{mh} \bar{\delta}_m \frac{q_{mk} q_{jk} L_k^2}{B^2 \rho_k^2}$$

$$= \frac{q_{jk}L_k^{\;2}}{B^2\rho_k^{\;2}} \frac{2(1-\sum_{l<k}\rho_l)\rho_k - \rho_k^{\;2} + (1-\sum_{l<k}\rho_l)^2}{(1-\sum_{l<k}\rho_l)^2} \sum_{m\in J}\sum_{h>k} q_{mh}\varphi_{mh}\bar{\delta}_m \quad (3.7)$$

The unit price for priority k service is:

$$r_k = \frac{L_k^{\;2}}{B^2\rho_k^{\;2}} \frac{2(1-\sum_{l<k}\rho_l)\rho_k - \rho_k^{\;2} + (1-\sum_{l<k}\rho_l)^2}{(1-\sum_{l<k}\rho_l)^2} \sum_{m\in J}\sum_{h>k} q_{mh}\varphi_{mh}\bar{\delta}_m$$

$$= \frac{L_k^{\;2}}{B\rho_k^{\;2}} \frac{(1-\sum_{l\le k}\rho_l)^2 - 2\rho_k^{\;2}}{(1-\sum_{l<k}\rho_l)^2}\rho\bar{\delta} \quad (3.8)$$

where $\rho = \sum_{k\in K}\rho_k$, $\bar{\delta}$ is the flow rate weighted delay cost coefficient.

4. TRAFFIC PRICING EXPERIMENTS

4.1 Experiment Design

We developed a prototype system named *VPN Traffic-Pricing Experiment System* (VTPES) (Lin et al, 1999) to test the transaction-level pricing architecture and to conduct experiments for the pricing model. VTPES is built on a small network platform in the Center for Research in Electronic Commerce (CREC) at UT Austin. Currently, it has six major distinctions from the previous GSW model simulation system:

1) It is a real-time system. Both data traffic generation and bandwidth allocation are implemented on a real-time basis.
2) It is a scalable distributed system. VTPES runs with a real network consisting of several computers. The configuration of the network can be varied to test the performance of VPN traffic pricing under certain definable conditions.
3) It has a dual-queue structure. In addition to a regular queue structure for bandwidth services, an extra queue is configured as a benchmark system. By using a shared traffic generation source, we can test different experimental schemes and compare the outcomes with that of a standardized scheme.

4) It can carry out both agent-based simulations (Tesfatsion, 2000) and human subject based direct experiments.
5) It can record data flow patterns generated in a direct experiment and replay the data flow patterns later using agent-based configuration. In this way, assessing a traffic-pricing scheme's performance in a real environment becomes possible.
6) Only non-priority bandwidth scheduling is implemented that already satisfies the purposes of the experiment.

Implementation of the experimental system that allows comparison of performance between human subjects and computer agents provides a good means for us to move the research closer to a real world. It becomes possible to bridge the gap between the economic approach and behavioral approach particularly in the network traffic-pricing area (Sterman, 1987). Logically, VTPES consists of four modules (Figure 3):

1) *A virtual bandwidth server allocating bandwidth with a round-robin scheduling method for service requests;*
2) *A set of user-oriented applications operating on the web browser to generate service requests and display network status for request submission decisions;*
3) *A web-based application module as an intermediary between users and the virtual bandwidth server; and*
4) *A traffic load generator, which is an agent for generating or regenerating network data flows.*

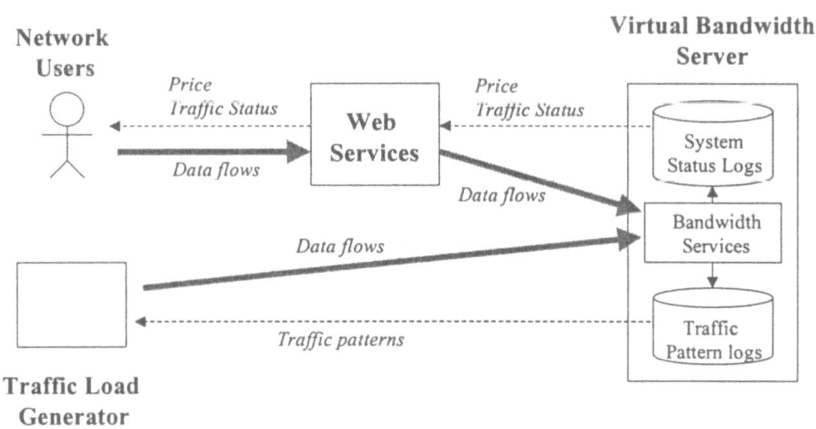

Figure 3. Current VTPES Logical Structure

VTPES can operate in three operation modes: agent-based, direct experiment, and mixed, i.e. computer agents and human subjects work together. When working in the agent-based simulation mode, VTPES can be configured with five components representing a network route: a client computer, a client-side VPN gateway, a server-side VPN gateway, a TPS, and an application server (Figure 4). The client computer generates jobs and submits those jobs that are expected to create net benefits after taking out all costs. The client-side VPN gateway routes the jobs to the destination application server via the server-side VPN gateway. The application server services the jobs relayed by the TPS and generates data flows back to the client computer. The TPS performs pricing, bandwidth scheduling and user-access accounting, etc.

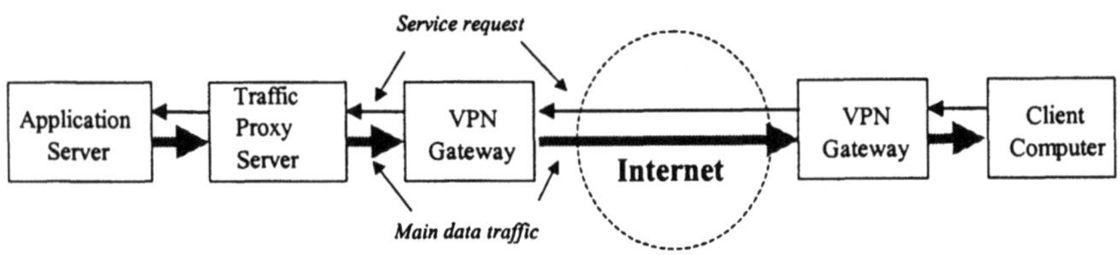

Figure 4. A unit VPN traffic-pricing system

This 5-tier pricing system can be reduced to a smaller scale to ease the experiment without losing the desired experimental features. The client-side gateway is "transparent" to data flows and can be ignored. The server-side VPN gateway's bandwidth scheduling function can be merged to the TPS because the TPS and the gateway can be logically considered as an integrated subsystem. Thus, the server-side gateway can also be ignored, handing over its functions to the TPS. In fact, the terms, VPN gateway and TPS, are exchangeable when referring to the experiment components.

4.2 Pricing Effectiveness

We mainly examined the welfare rate, i.e., per-second service welfare that is the output being monitored, to evaluate the effect of different scheduling schemes for non-priced and priced systems on VPN bandwidth service performance. The network load parameters for the experiment, i.e., the input, include the distributions of job size, the job value, and the delay cost coefficient. The job value and delay cost are random variables depending on the user's timely preferences and can be generated by the computer. Job size can be predefined in a profile.

In order to test whether the performance from the experiment based on a real network is the same as that from the GSW software-based simulation, we intensively used the same parameter values for most experiment schemes as those used in the GSW simulation. Although we also designed experiments with different job parameter distributions, using GSW experiment parameter values allows us to compare the data obtained from our experimental schemes with the ones from GSW model experiments.

The job value distribution used in the GSW model simulation has a normal distribution with a mean of 500 dollars and a standard deviation of 150 dollars, i.e., job value ~ $N[500, 150^2]$. It is independent of job size. The delay cost coefficient distribution is also independent of job size. The GSW model uses a normal distribution for the delay cost coefficient with the mean of 4 dollars and the standard deviation of 1 dollar, i.e., job delay cost~ $N[4, 1]$. The absolute levels of the job value and the delay cost coefficient are not important, but the relative levels and their correlation to job size are critical. Therefore, in addition to this basic set of distributions, we also tested two diversities: a set of job parameters with different standard deviations, and a set of the parameters that are relevant to the job size.

We conducted this group of experiments in four steps:

1) Verify the consistency of the outcome from a network-based experiment and the one from the GSW model simulation using FIFO scheduling;
2) Test the performance of the VPN using non-priced RR scheduling;
3) Compare the outcomes of priced schemes between RR scheduling and FIFO scheduling; and
4) Test the priced schemes using different job parameters.

The outcome from the simulation running on VTPES using the FIFO scheduling matches that from the GSW model simulation very well. VPN traffic pricing significantly improves network welfare rate in FIFO scheduling (Figure 5a). The curve of the welfare rate from the non-priced FIFO scheme starts to decline when exogenous traffic rate increases and approaches capacity, while that from the priced FIFO scheme keeps going up as the traffic rate increases. This is exactly the same result as the GSW model simulation revealed.

The experiment shows that priced FIFO scheduling performs better than non-priced RR scheduling (Figure 5b). The welfare rate yielded from a non-priced RR scheme increases with the augmented traffic rate. This is because the expected throughput time for a job in RR scheduling is proportional to the job's size. This provides the incentive for users not to submit the jobs with lower unit values. Since the submission decision is based on the comparison between the unit job value and the unit waiting cost, the efficiency of the network is better than that of non-priced FIFO. However, the increase rate of the welfare rate from a non-priced RR scheduling scheme is much lower that that from a priced FIFO scheme. The gap widens when the traffic rate goes up.

The experiment demonstrates that pricing is also effective in the RR scheduling scheme with approximately the same welfare rate as that from priced FIFO scheduling (Figure 5c). Pricing on FIFO and RR scheduling systems results in almost the same job submission ratio distributions (Figure 5d). In the chart, the *x*-axis is the job size index with larger numbers for larger job sizes and the *y*-axis is the percentage of jobs having been actually submitted in terms of an exogenous job rate. Both the submission ratio distributions consistently drop when the job size is getting larger.

Although it is necessary to make the outcome of VTPES-based experiments comparable to the previous results from the GSW model, a thorough and complete experimentation should cover more variable factors to provide strong evidence in supporting our conclusions. There are two versions of schemes in this step. The first experiment version uses the parameters with new job value distribution ~ $N\ [500,\ 200^2]$ and job delay cost coefficient ~ $N\ [4,\ 2^2]$. As the chart in Figure 6 shows, the welfare rate obtained from the scheme using the new job value and delay cost distribution has only a negligible difference from that using the parameter values designed for the GSW model simulation.

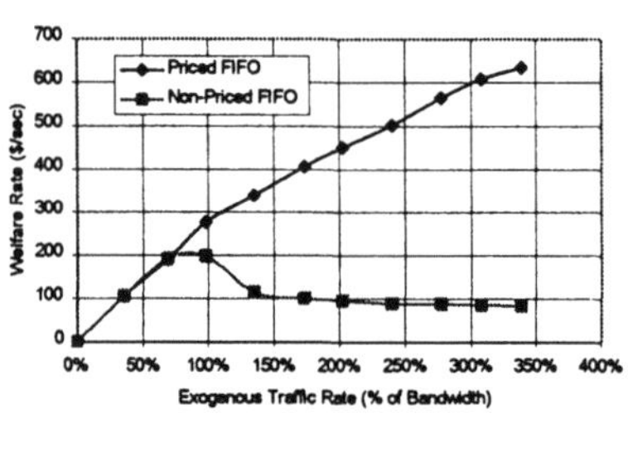

(a) Priced FIFO versus non-priced FIFO

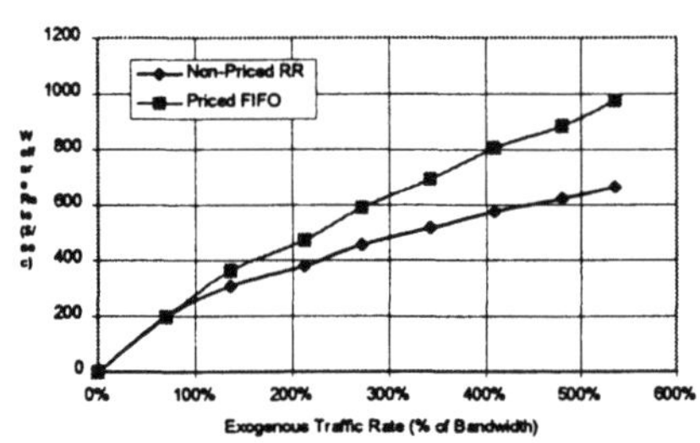

(b) Non-priced RR versus priced FIFO

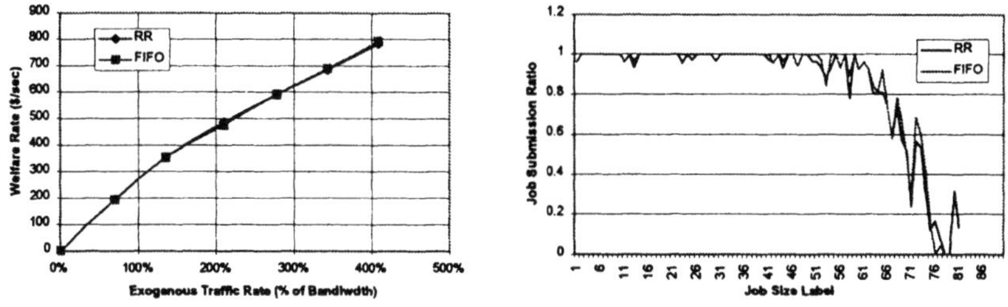

(c) Welfare rate comparison between priced RR scheduling and priced FIFO scheduling

(d) Job arrival distribution comparison between priced RR and priced FIFO schemes (exogenous traffic rate: 4 Mbps)

Figure 5. Effectiveness of VPN traffic pricing

The second experiment version uses a variable delay cost distribution and job value distribution that are relevant to the job size. We use the following conversion formula to make delay cost or job value relevant to job size:

$$X^{\wedge} = X * (J / B)^{s*0.5}$$

where J is job size, B is bandwidth, $s = 1$ when a job value is converted and $s = -1$ when a delay cost coefficient is converted, X is a regular value of the delay cost coefficient or a regular job value, and $X^{\wedge}$ is the converted value. The rationale behind the above conversion formula is that the larger a job's size is, the higher the job's gross value could be or the lower the delay cost coefficient could be.

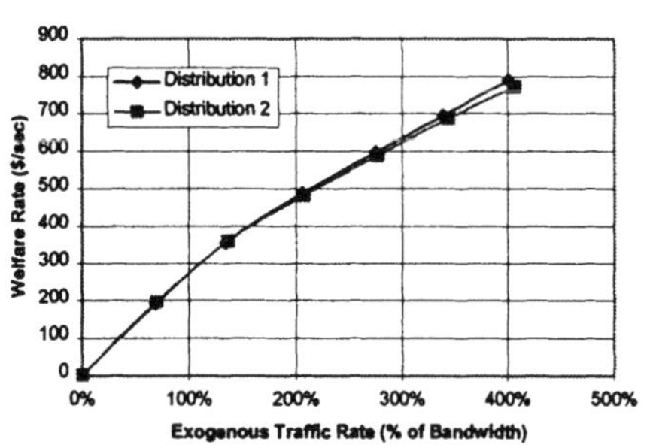

Figure 6: Welfare rates differentiated in standard deviations of job value and delay cost

The experiment demonstrated that there is no significant difference when using a variable job value or a delay cost coefficient correlating to job size. Welfare rate curves from two differentiated schemes in delay cost coefficient, one with a fixed distribution and the other with a variable mean correlating to job size, match well (Figure 7a). The same outcome is obtained from the scheme using variable job value correlating to job size. The curvature of welfare rate curves from the schemes using variable job value is more concave compared to previous welfare rate curves (Figure 7b).

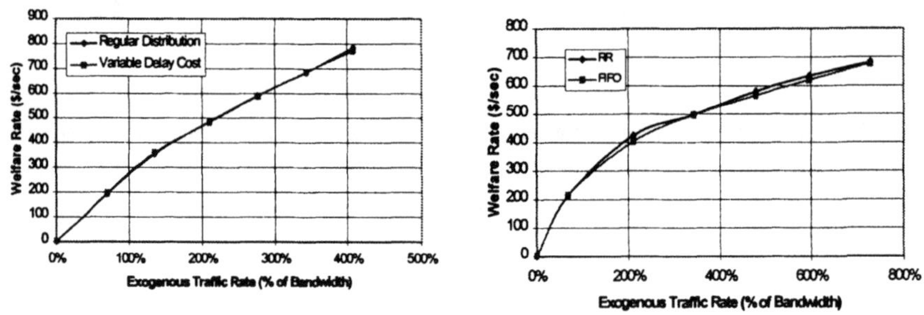

(a) Welfare rates from two schemes differentiated in the delay cost correlating to the job size.

(b) Welfare rates from FIFO and non-prioritized RR scheduling schemes using variable job value correlating to the job size.

Figure 7: Welfare rates from the schemes using variable parameters correlating to job size

In summary we can conclude that traffic pricing can effectively improve VPN bandwidth service benefits for a wider range of schemes using different job values and delay cost distributions.

4.3 Human Subject Based Experiments

The direct experiments using human subjects allows us to test the performance of traffic pricing system closer to real environment and also verify the parameters used in agent-based experiments. The experiments are performed in two steps: first, subjects are used to access the experiment system using both pricing and non-pricing schemes; then, the data flow patterns recorded during the process are replayed in agent-based experiment mode. All experiments in this phase use non-prioritized RR bandwidth scheduling. Figure 8 shows the outcomes from different setups of experiments. Curves *Agent_Pricing*, and *Agent_Non_P* are the welfare rates - total service benefits per second - from experiments using the agent-based traffic generation. The curves indicate that dynamic pricing improves bandwidth service welfare. This is the same result as the one from previous experiments. Similarly, welfare rates, with regard to different levels of traffic arrival rates, obtained from direct experiments using pricing (curve *Human_Pricing*) are relatively higher than the welfare rates from direct experiments without pricing (curve *Human_Non_P*). This strongly suggests the consistency between direct experiments and agent-based experiments.

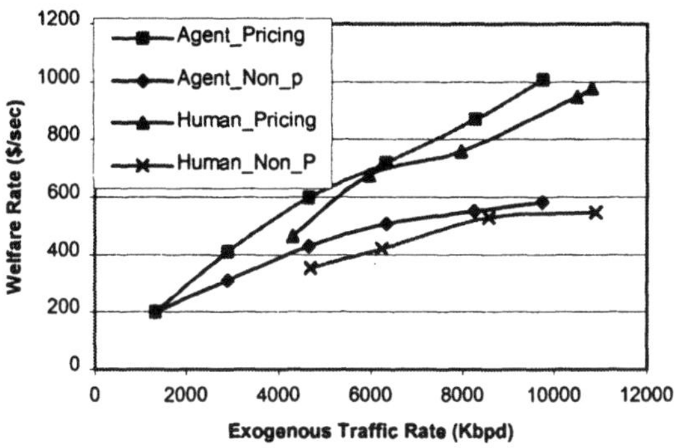

Figure 8. Welfare Rates (Bandwidth: 1544 Kbps)

It is noticeable that direct experiments show relatively lower welfare rates than the welfare rates from the same schemes as conducted in agent-based experiment. Nevertheless, curve *Human_Pricing* is almost parallel to *Agent_Pricing,* and *Human_Non_P* is also almost parallel to *Agent_Non_P*, indicating the compatibility of the outcomes from two types of experiments. Two possible reasons may cause the welfare rate observed from direct experiments lower than that from agent-based experiments: 1) the human errors and occasional irrationality, and 2) the different exogenous flow of potential traffic between two types of experiments. Roth (1996) commented "that human behavior deviates in systematic ways from the idealized behavior attributed to expected utility maximizers in particular, and to 'rational economic man' in general". A direct experiment using human subjects is closer to the real world, but may introduce errors caused by subjects' misbehaviors.

To investigate the issue, a group of simulations are carried out using the same exogenous traffic generation process as the direct experiments. The difference is in that the experimental system with the replaying setup makes optimum submission decisions to maximize the expected user utility for every request. The service welfare rates from these replay experiments are as good as those from experiments using agent-generated network traffic, and are better than those from direct experiments producing these exogenous traffic patterns (Table 1). The last column of the table shows that the welfare rate ratio between a direct experiment and the agent-based experiment replaying its traffic pattern, both using traffic pricing scheme, is about 86%. The same ratio for the experiments without using pricing is higher, being 93.3% in a sample case. Thus, we can conclude that this loss is due to user mistakes rather than exogenous traffic differences.

Table 1: ***Welfare Rate Comparison***

Schemes		Exog. Traffic Rate (kbps)	Welfare Rate ($/sec) (Direct)	Welfare Rate ($/sec) (Replay)	Welfare Rate Ratio (Direct / Replay)
Dataset (Pricing)	1	10601	948	1098	86.4%
Dataset (Pricing)	2	7750	763	893	85.4%
Dataset (Non_pricing)	3	4695	361	387	93.3%

In checking the size distribution of data flows that are incurred by submitted requests it is impressive that human subjects sometimes tend to make "regrettable" request submission decisions: submitting a request having a positive expected net value but realizing a negative outcome, or dropping a request because of its negative expected net value which would be actually positive if the request were serviced. Each individual subject's performance, in sense of the surplus ratio in two types of experiments, varies from as high as 91.4% to as low as 71.3%, indicating the existence of a subjective factor affecting subjects' performance. In another aspect, as a consequence of the imprecise information available to human subjects and more precise information for computer agents to make decisions, human subjects have a higher average surplus forecasting error with a much higher standard deviation of the error rate, where error rate is the ratio between the error of the estimated user surplus and the average user surplus.

5. SUMMARY

This chapter studies the VPN traffic-pricing problem targeting at the practical application with three foci: a transaction-level pricing architecture with a traffic proxy server-based implementation scheme, a dynamic traffic-pricing model for the VPN, and VPN traffic-pricing experiments using a prototype system called VTPES. The transaction-level pricing is proposed for the implementation of the VPN pricing system, taking advantage of VPN's user-account management features. This job-oriented basis is exploited to derive the dynamic VPN traffic-pricing model. The theoretical work is based on the GSW model with two important extensions for the VPN—it is tailored to fit packet-switched networks, typically the Internet, and it uses round-robin bandwidth scheduling in addition to FIFO bandwidth scheduling. The pipeline effect of packet-switched networks results in the dominance of the bottleneck Internet connection in a VPN route over total throughput time as well as the bandwidth price, which can be controlled by the TPS.

In a simplified case, the total price a job pays for bandwidth services can be approximated by a single price at the bottleneck gateway to reduce the complexity of implementation. We revealed that RR scheduling possesses useful implementation features such as allowing a consistent unit price for different types of jobs. The experimental outcomes from both direct experiments and simulations strongly support the theoretical result. The three aspects of the research in VPN traffic pricing jointly provide a complementary set of solutions for the VPN traffic control problem.

There are four apparent limits of our model and implementation scheme. The first one is that a practical gateway may use more than one scheduling algorithm for its bandwidth allocation tasks, for example, a mixed FIFO and RR scheduling. Deriving an analytical form of the price formula for a real gateway is very difficult. Even though the TPS-based solution proposed in this paper may bypass this problem, the mutual effect between the TPS and the VPN gateway in data flow control remains untouched.

The second limit is that the proposed VPN pricing model is designed for the problem of elastic traffic where the optimal objective function counts the total throughput time as the only QoS feature. In pricing real-time traffic, the important factors for evaluating service quality include jitter, i.e., the variation of available bandwidth; committed minimum bandwidth; and maximum allowable bandwidth. Quantifying these features is difficult and more dimensions will hence need to be introduced into the model.

The third limit is inherent in the assumption that the job arrival is a Poisson process. Paxson and Floyd (1995) revealed that the packet arrival pattern in the Internet is not a Poisson process. It is apparent that even if the interval of any two consecutive jobs is exponentially distributed the arrival of packets is not necessarily a Poisson process because the number of packets in a job is a random variable and these packets come in batches. Nonetheless, Alok, Stahl, and Whinston (1999) reported that the pricing formula based on Poisson arrivals works well even when arrivals are fractal.

The fourth limit is also very critical: we calculate the service delay as a linear function of traffic load at a network node without considering the non-linear effect when congestion happens. Once a network node's buffer overflows, it tosses some packets. This will stimulate reactions of the flow control mechanism to resolve the problem. In this case, the delay of an affected data flow will no longer be linear with its size. Since our experiments have shown that a VPN with the pricing mechanism performs better than a non-pricing VPN when the infinite queue is assumed, the former must also be superior to the non-pricing system with limited queue capacity. In the next research phase, we may let the model cope with the congestion in two aspects.

The above limits reflect the gap between a theoretical research and the practical application. As long as we have a suitable traffic-pricing architecture, the issue raised from the practical system can be solved accordingly with proper patches.

Acknowledgement

This research has been sponsored by Intel Corp., Lucent Technologies Inc., and Mannesman Ag.

REFERENCES

Allman, M., V. Paxson, and W. Stevens. "TCP Congestion Control," Internet RFC2581 (1999), http://www.ietf.cnri.reston.va.us/rfc/rfc2581.txt.

Blake, S. et al, "An Architecture for Differentiated Services," Internet RFC2475 (1998), http://www.ietf.cnri.reston.va.us/rfc/rfc2475.txt.

Braden B. et al. "Recommendations on Queue Management and Congestion Avoidance in the Internet," Internet RFC2309 (1998), http://www.ietf.cnri.reston.va.us/rfc/rfc2309.txt.

Clark, D. D. "Adding Service Discrimination to the Internet," *Telecommunication Policy* 20 (1996) 169-181.

Demers, A., S. Keshav, and S. Shenker. "Analysis and Simulation of a Fair Queuing Algorithm," *Internetworking: Research and Experience* 1 (1990) 3-26.

Floyd, S. "TCP and Explicit Congestion Notification," *ACM Computer Communications Review* 24 (1994) 10-23.

Floyd, S., and Kevin Fall, "Promoting the Use of End-to-End Congestion Control in the Internet," *IEEE/ACM Transactions on Networking* 7:4 (1999) 458-472.

Floyd, S., and V. Jacobson. "Random Early Detection (RED) Gateways for Congestion Avoidance," *IEEE/ACM Transactions on Networking* 1:4 (1993) 397-413.

Gupta, A. et al. "Streaming the Digital Economy: How to Avert a Tragedy of the Commons," *IEEE Internet Computing* 1 (1997) 38-46.

Gupta, A., D. O. Stahl, and A. B. Whinston. "A Stochastic Equilibrium Model of Internet Pricing," *Journal of Economic Dynamics and Control* 21 (1997) 697-722.

Gupta, A., D. O. Stahl, and A. B. Whinston. "The Economics of Network Management," *Communications of the ACM* 42 (1999) 57-63.

Jacobson, V., and M. J. Karels. "Congestion Avoidance and Control," *SIGCOMM'88*, (1988).

Kalyanaroman, S., T. Ravichandran and R. Norsworthy. "Dynamic Capacity Contracting: A Framework for Pricing the Differentiated Services Internet," (1998), http://www.ecse.rpi.edu/Homepages/shivkuma/research/papers/icepaper.html.

Kleinrock, L. *Queueing Systems*, Vol. I & II, John Wiley & Sons, 1975.

Kosiur, D. *Building and Managing Virtual Private Netowrks*, John Wiley & Sons, 1998.

Lazar, A. A., and Nemo Semret. "Design, Analysis and Simulation of the Progressive Second Price Auction for Network Bandwidth," *8th International Symposium on Dynamic Games and Applications* (1998).

Li, Mingzhi et al. "Estimating Internet Users' Demand Characteristics," forthcoming in *Journal of Computational Economics* (2000), http://crec.bus.utexas.edu/works/articles/demand.pdf.

Lin, Z. et al. "Exploring Traffic Pricing for the Virtual Private Network," *The Proceedings of WITS'99*, (1999).

Lin, Z. et al. "Exploring Traffic Pricing for the Virtual Private Network," forthcoming in *Information Technology and Management*, (2001).

Lin, Z., D. O. Stahl, and A. B. Whinston. "A Traffic-pricing Model for the Packet-switching Network with Prioritized Round-robin Queueing," *INFORMS-CIST'00*, (2000).

MacKie-Mason, J., and H. Varian. "Pricing the Internet in Public Access to the Internet," In B. Kahin and J. Keller (eds.), Englewood Cliffs, NJ:Prentice-Hall, 1995.

Nagle, J. "Congestion Control in TCP/IP Internetworks," Internet RFC 896 (1984), http://www.ietf.cnri.reston.va.us/rfc /rfc896.txt.

Odlyzko, A. M. "A Modest Proposal for Preventing Internet Congestion," *DIMACS Technical Report 97-68* (1997), http://www.dimacs.rutgers.edu/TechnicalReports/.

Oppliger, R. *Internet and Intranet Security*, Artech House, 1998.

Paxson, V., and S. Floyd. "Wide-Area Traffic: The Failure of Poisson Modeling," *IEEE/ACM Transactions on Networking* 3(3) (1995).

Rigney, C. et al. "Remote Authentication Dial In User Service (RADIUS)," Internet-draft (2000), http://www.ietf.org/internet-drafts/draft-ietf-radius-radius-v2-06.txt.

Rigney, C., and Livingston. "RADIUS Accounting," Internet RFC 2139 (1997), http://www.ietf.org/rfc/rfc2139.txt.

Roth, A. E. "Comments on Tversky's 'Rational Theory and Constructive Choice'," *The Rational Foundations of Economic Behavior*, K. Arrow, E. Colombatto, M Perlman, and C. Schmidt (eds.), Macmillan, (1996) 198-202.

Shenker, S. et al. "Pricing in Computer Networks: Reshaping the Research Agenda," *Telecommunication Policy* 20 (1996) 183-201.

Stahl, D. O., and A. B. Whinston. "A General Economic Equilibrium Model of Distributed Computing," in W. W. Cooper and A. B. Whinston (eds.), *New Decisions in Computational Economics* (1994) 175-189.

Sterman, J. "Testing Behavioral Simulation Models by Direct Experiment," *Management Science* 33(12), 1987, 1572-1592.

Stevens, W. "TCP Slow Start, Congestion Avoidance, Fast Retransmit, and Fast Recovery Algorithms," Internet RFC2001 (1997), http://www.ietf.cnri.reston.va.us/rfc/rfc2001.txt.

L. Tesfatsion, "Agent-Based Computational Economics: A Brief Guide to the Literature," January, 2000. http://www.econ.iastate.edu/tesfatsi/aceintro.pdf

Chapter 13

Knowledge Representation: A Classification with Applications in Telecommunications and the Web

Prudence T. Zacarias Kapauan: Eugenia Fernandez
Lucent Technologies, Naperville, IL 60566: Indiana University-Purdue University Indianapolis, Indianapolis, IN 46202

Abstract: Knowledge representation is often treated as an integral part of artificial intelligence (AI), robotics, machine learning, formal languages and other research areas. However, knowledge representation applications can be found today in different sectors of industry, including e-commerce, manufacturing, and telecommunications. This paper reviews knowledge representation schemes found in the AI literature, and identifies commonalities in perspectives and underlying philosophies of the various representation schemes. A close examination of the different schemes reveals that they can be classified under one or more of the four major knowledge representation philosophies: objects, networks, frames, and logic. Newer knowledge representation applications of these philosophies, specifically XML, UML and ontologies, are discussed and examples of their use in telecommunications and Web applications are given.
Key words: knowledge representation, telecommunications, UML, XML, ontology

1. INTRODUCTION

Knowledge representation is traditionally seen as a field of artificial intelligence (AI), robotics, machine learning, formal languages and other research areas. However, applications of knowledge representation abound in different sectors of industry, including e-commerce, manufacturing, and telecommunications. Often different knowledge representation techniques are disguised as everyday forms for organizing or storing data, or intrinsic in commonly used object-oriented programming languages.

There are many different knowledge representation schemes reported in the AI literature. For each distinct knowledge representation, there is usually an underlying philosophy from which one obtains a model of the application domain and its elements. The implicit models obtained can in turn be applied to a variety of activities, including simulation, natural language processing, and problem solving.

Bundy's *Catalogue of Artificial Intelligence Tools* (1986) is a handy reference to terminology found in the AI literature. Its purpose is "to promote interaction between members of the AI community ... by announcing the existence of AI techniques... and acting as a pointer to the literature". This paper is similarly motivated and hopes to foster discussion among members of the information systems community, especially those in the areas of knowledge representation, telecommunications, and the Web. It goes further than Bundy's catalogue by identifying commonalities in perspectives and underlying philosophies of the traditional representation schemes, and discussing newer representation models used in telecommunications and the Web.

A close examination of the different schemes reveals that they can generally be classified under one or more of the four major knowledge representation philosophies: *objects*, *networks*, *frames*, and *logic*. The following section provides a review of traditional knowledge representations organized by their underlying philosophy. In the final section, this paper describes newer knowledge representations currently used in telecommunications and the Web and presents examples of their use.

2. TRADITIONAL KNOWLEDGE REPRESENTATION

2.1 Object-Oriented Schemes

A scheme of this type can be characterized as one where information is organized around objects that communicate with each other. An object possesses private properties (attributes), and methods (procedures) that cannot be directly accessed by other objects. Objects communicate by passing messages to each other - this is the only way an object can invoke another object's methods.

Object-oriented schemes provide computational models that are useful in problem solving, design, and planning. Three object-oriented schemes are presented in this section: Smalltalk, actors, and contract nets.

2.1.1 Smalltalk Objects

Smalltalk (Bundy, 1986; Goldberg & Robson, 1983) is a programming environment developed by members of the Learning Research Group (now known as Software Concepts Group or SCG) at Xerox Palo Alto Research Center, as "a vision of the ways different people might effectively and joyfully use computing power" (Goldberg & Robson, 1983). SCG's strategy for realizing this vision has been to concentrate on two principal areas of research: a language of description (a programming language) which serves as an interface between models in the human mind and those in computing hardware, and a language of interaction (a user interface) which matches the human communication system to that of the computer. Several editions of Smalltalk have emerged over the years, starting with Smalltalk-72, which appeared around 1976 and culminating with Smalltalk-80, announced in 1981. Many new dialects based on Smalltalk-80 have emerged, e.g., VisualWorks, Squeak, VisualAge Smalltalk and Smalltalk X. Some are commercially available while others are freeware.

The fundamental philosophy of Smalltalk was developed from Simula (Franta, 1977) and, although the different editions differ in syntax, all share the view of a programming system as a collection of active objects communicating by passing messages. In addition, Smalltalk adopted Simula's class concept, and has extended and refined it considerably. The power of the Smalltalk system arises mainly from the modularity enforced by packaging declarative and procedural knowledge into individual objects. If the services of an object are required, messages are sent to invoke that object to perform internal actions. For example, to access the value of a certain location in an array, a message is sent to the array object from the object that is interested in accessing it. The message will specify all pertinent information regarding the request and will prompt a response that should contain the value of the requested location. A major contribution of Smalltalk is that it inspired a number of languages including STROBE (Smith, 1983) and LOOPS (Bobrow & Stefik, 1983) that are used in building knowledge-based AI systems.

2.1.2 Actors

The actor model of computation (Bundy, 1986; Hewitt, 1979; Hewitt & Baker, 1977a, 1977b) was developed in order to explore the fundamental issues involved with computation via message-passing. Actors are objects that know about other actors and can receive messages from other actors. Each actor is specified by detailing what kind of messages it can receive, and the sequence of actions it will take should it be sent one of these messages. Everything in an actor-based programming system is an actor. For example, to increment a value, a message would be sent to the actor representing the number, asking the actor to increment itself. The essential difference between the actor model of computation and the Smalltalk-80 language is that the sequencing of computations by actors depends critically on the concept of a continuation. A continuation is an actor that is prepared to accept an intermediate value as a message and continue the computation. In Smalltalk-80 an object (actor) will instead return a message to the object that triggered the computation in much the same way that a Pascal function will return a value to the routine that called it.

Kornfeld and Hewitt (1981) extended the principles of actor theory to provide what they call the scientific community metaphor. They claim that scientific communities behave as highly parallel systems, with scientists working on problems concurrently with other scientists. Scientists can work on the same problem or on different problems, in cooperation with others or independently. They may or may not know of the work of other scientists. However, they are able to communicate their ideas with each other. To model this behavior, Kornfeld and Hewitt developed a variant of ETHER, a pattern-directed invocation language designed to create highly parallel problem solving systems. In the variant, communication is modeled by disseminating messages. Messages can serve to communicate results (or assertions) of one's research. At any time, the system has certain goals, either to demonstrate the validity of a proposition or to find a method to solve a given problem. Messages are used to communicate the goals to other parts of the system that embody the necessary expertise to achieve them. While object computation is modeled by parallel problem solvers, actor computation is implemented by parallel problem solving systems where the nodes use result-sharing.

2.1.3 Contract Nets

A contract net (Smith, 1977; Smith & Davis, 1978) is a collection of interconnected processor nodes whose interactions are governed by a problem solving protocol that uses an announcement-bid-award communication sequence. Contracts are instances of the execution of individual tasks. A node that generates a task advertises it via a task announcement and then acts as the task's manager until its completion. A node can signify its interest in a task by issuing a bid. Each bid includes capabilities of the bidder; based on the information from the bids, the manager selects one or several nodes (or contractors) through an award message. The basic difference between contractors and actors is that contractors engage more in task-sharing, i.e., they divide the workload among themselves and work independently on large-grained subproblems, while actors are more appropriate for result-sharing, i.e., working with fine grained problems and periodically reporting partial results.

Contract nets are the basis for parallel problem solving systems where nodes engage in task-sharing, rather than result-sharing. Smith and Davis (1981) have implemented a contract net system motivated by the metaphor of manager-contractor linkage. The Multi-Agent Computing Environment (MACE, Gasser, Braganza & Herman, 1987) is an experimental system that can be used to model lower-level parallelism (several distributed production rule systems) and build higher-level problem-solving architectures like contract-net schemes.

2.2 Networks

Under this philosophy, a knowledge representation scheme is visualized to be a network of interconnected nodes, representing different entities that have various relationships. Networks have been used in automatic problem solving and natural language processing applications. The following sections discuss four network-based schemes: discrimination nets, semantic nets, conceptual graphs, and conceptual dependency.

2.2.1 Discrimination Nets

A discrimination net (D-net) (Bundy, 1986; Charniak, Riesbeck & McDermott, 1980) is a mechanism used in natural language processing for allocating an input data item to its class by applying successive tests for different individual predicates. The terminal nodes of the net represent the results to be returned for the various possible sequences of predicates. It is a nest of IF...THEN...ELSE tests all applicable to one data item, or more formally a binary, directed acyclic graph with unary predicates at non-terminal nodes. An example of the use of discrimination net of this basic kind in natural language generation is choosing an output word for an input meaning representation.

The basic mechanism can be extended by, for instance, using n-ary rather than binary graphs, with the corresponding replacement of simple feature tests by more complex branch selection functions, by the use of variables in the data item descriptions and net patterns, and by the use of sophisticated means of indexing. With such extensions, a net can be used, for example, to implement a PLANNER-style database (Hewitt, 1972; Sussam, Winograd & Charniak, 1971) optimized for retrieving individual assertions (i.e. invocation is pattern-directed). Discrimination nets have an obvious attraction when the set of classes involved is large. A prerequisite for their effective application is being able to identify clear test sequences for data items.

2.2.2 Semantic Nets

A semantic net (Bundy, 1986; Findler, 1979; Brachman, 1985, 1988) is a principle for the large scale organization of knowledge emphasizing the multiple associations of individual concepts. Concepts, objects, and entities are represented as nodes in a graph, and relationships between these are represented as labeled arcs. The range of possible network structure types is infinite. Semantic nets should properly be based on definitions of the net structure (the syntax and semantics of the nodes and links), and the configurations of these and of net operations (the syntax and semantics of node-node transitions), but too frequently are not. Nets have been found an attractive descriptive device and are popular in natural language understanding programs, especially for representing lexical (dictionary) information. However, the emphasis of concept association introduces difficulties in representing any partitioning or grouping of net elements. For example, it is difficult to represent quantified propositions, clusters of similar entities, etc. An ISA hierarchy (Bundy, 1986; Ullman, 1982; Fahlman, 1979) is strictly a straightforward manifestation of class membership, found useful in knowledge representation because property specifications for classes need only be explicitly indicated once (at the highest level) since they are automatically inherited by subclasses. ISA relationships are often found in a semantic net.

KL-ONE (Bundy, 1986; Brachman & Schmolze, 1985; Kas, Katriel & Finin, 1987) is a system for representing knowledge in AI programs, in the same tradition as semantic nets and frames. It provides a language for the explicit representation of conceptual information based on the idea of structured inheritance networks. The principal element of KL-ONE is the *structured conceptual object* or *concept*. KL-ONE uses a small, fixed set of underlying object and relation types for knowledge structuring as primitives for representing a broad spectrum of concepts. Classes are represented by *concepts* (similar to object and frames) and their properties are represented by *roles* (similar to the slots of frames). Concepts and roles are organized into separate taxonomies based on the relation of subsumption (similar to ISA), giving a notion of sub-concepts and super-concepts, as well as sub-roles and super-roles. There is a system of inheritance by which concepts (and roles) acquire attributes of their super-concepts and super-roles and an algorithm called *classification* that discovers appropriate subsumption relationships that are not explicitly stated. The advantage of a hybrid scheme such as KL-ONE is that it provides the combined expressiveness of frames and semantic nets.

2.2.3 Conceptual Graphs

A conceptual graph (Sowa, 1984) is a form of knowledge representation where concept nodes represent entities, attributes, and events, and relation nodes show how the concepts are interconnected. Conceptual graphs are used in natural language processing applications. Under conceptual graph theory, perception is defined as "the process of building a working model that represents and interprets sensory input" (Schank, 1975). Percepts are "fragments of images that fit together like pieces of a jigsaw puzzle" (Sowa, 1984). The interpretation of a percept is called its *concept*. A conceptual graph describes the way the percepts are assembled. Conceptual relations specify the role that each percept plays. Referents denote individuals, values, or sets explicitly mentioned in the world and in the universe of discourse.

Concept types are denoted by a concept type label inside a box. Conceptual relations are denoted by a relation label inside a circle. Arcs (arrows) link boxes (concept types) to circles (conceptual relations). A sample conceptual graph is given in Figure 1. This graph represents the statement "John Smith sent an email to Mary Doe". In this example, the concept types are Person, Send and Form. Past is a unary time relation, while Agent, Recipient, and Object are binary relations. John Smith and Mary Doe are referents of the person concept type.

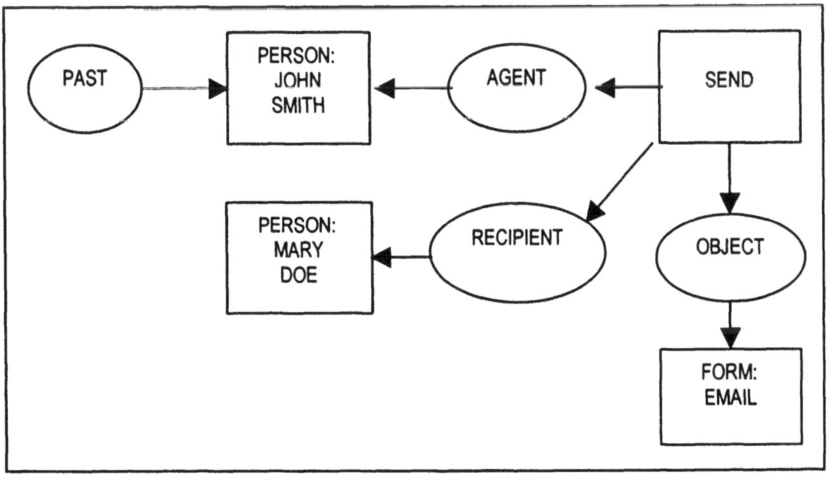

Figure 1. Conceptual graph - graphic form

A linear form with square brackets to represent concept types and rounded parentheses to represent conceptual relations provides a compact notation for conceptual graphs. The linear form of the previous example is shown in Figure 2. Each concept implicitly asserts the existence of some entity of the corresponding type. Thus concepts and concept types are often used interchangeably.

```
(AGENT) → [PERSON: JOHN SMITH]
            ↑
(PAST) → [SEND] → (OBJECT) → [FORM: EMAIL]
            ↓
(RECIPIENT) → [PERSON: MARY DOE]
```

Figure 2. Conceptual graph - linear form

2.2.4 Conceptual Dependency

Conceptual dependency (Bundy, 1986) is a theory of natural language meaning representation developed by Schank (1975) and extensively exploited at Yale. It relies on deep "conceptual" *semantic primitives* (Charniak & Wilks, 1976) and case frames (discussed in a later section) and provides a detailed decomposition of word and text meaning. The emphasis on key primitive acts and required properties of the fillers based on obligatory roles drives the primarily semantic expectation-based parsing of natural language. Under this theory, if two sentences have the same meaning, then there should be only one representation of that meaning.

Semantic primitives are general concepts underlying words. They are used for the determination and representation of textual or propositional meaning, e.g., MOVE underlies 'walk' and 'run'; THING, 'vase' and 'book'. Semantic primitives are used to define selection criteria for sense identification, and to define key properties, e.g., of case frame role fillers. Primitives, which should in principle be drawn from a closed set, may be shallow or deep, i.e., more or less fine-grained, domain-independent or domain-dependent, or categorical or relational. The characterizations of word (senses) may be by single primitives, primitive sets, or structured formulas, and the primitive characterizations of sentences may be regarded as elements of a distinct meaning representation language, or as selected elements of the language under description. Though primitives universally figure in some form or another in language understanding systems, they are more frequently adopted ad hoc, than systematically motivated, with the exception of those used by Charniak and Wilks (1976) and Schank (1975).

2.3 Frame-Oriented Schemes

The basic philosophy of frame-oriented schemes is that all information pertinent to an entity or scenario should be organized together in one structure associated with that entity or scenario. Schemes under this category are often used in natural language processing and in modeling planning and goal analysis. Frame-oriented schemes are considered the correct style of representation for prediction-based tasks, such as reading a paragraph or story, and have seen some application in representing Web-based data. Frames, scripts and case frames are discussed here.

2.3.1 Frames

Frames were first introduced by Minsky (1975) as a principle for the large-scale organization of knowledge, originally in connection with vision, but also more generally applicable. Frames (Bundy, 1986; Brachman, 1988) may be arbitrarily complex and have procedures attached to the slots. Default values for the slots are helpful when frames are exploited in the absence of full instantiation (i.e., when the slots were not initialized). The character of frames suggests a hierarchical organization of sets of frames, but non-hierarchical filling of one frame slot by another is possible.

Frame Representation Language (FRL) (Bundy, 1986; Roberts & Goldstein, 1977) is a knowledge representation language based on frames developed at MIT. FRL extends the traditional property list representation scheme by allowing properties to have comments, defaults and constraints, to inherit information from abstract forms of the same type, and to have attached procedures triggered by adding or deleting values, or if a value is needed. Each frame has a number of *slots* and each slot has a number of *facets*. The overall structure of a frame is shown in Figure 3.

Facet names conventionally have a "$" prefix, labels a ":" suffix. Each datum (facet entry) can have attached a list of comments, where each comment consists of some label or keyword followed by a list of messages. FRL provides procedural attachment; three of the six standard facet names being $IF-ADDED, $IF-REMOVED and $IF-NEEDED. FRL is implemented as an interpreter written in LISP.

```
(frame1
(slot1  ($facet1     (datum1        (label1 message1 message2 ... messageN)
                                    (label2: ...) ... (labelM ...))
                     (datum2        (label1: message1 ...)..)
        ...
                     (datumJ        (label1: message1 ...)..)..)
        ($facet2 ...) ... ($facetL ...))
(slot2  ($facet1     (datum1        (label1: ...) ...)
        ...
(slotK  ($facet1     (datum1        (label1: ...) ...))
```

Figure 3. Overall frame structure

A Knowledge Representation Language (KRL) (Bobrow & Winograd, 1977; Bundy, 1986) was developed by researchers at Stanford and Xerox PARC in the late 1970s. The researchers developed a set of INTERLISP programs that embodied many of the ideas of frames, together with facilities for matching structures against each other and for controlling multi-processing. Unfortunately, the software did not stabilize into a single programming language in the normal sense and was a continually evolving research tool within a small community for a short time, before it fell into disuse.

KRYPTON (Brachman, Fikes & Levesque, 1985) is a hybrid reasoning system that integrates a frame-based description language and a first-order resolution theorem prover. It provides a first-order language for composing sentences expressing beliefs and supports the definition of complex predicates (via frames) to be used in those sentences. It overcomes some of the difficulties (e. g. ambiguities) in knowledge representation systems based on frames and semantic networks by using the frame-based language only for forming descriptive terms and the logic-based language for making assertions.

Frameworks (Smith, Harris & Simmons, 1987) is a knowledge representation system that unifies concepts found in frame-based, rule-based and object-based systems. Frameworks consists of two basic parts: the knowledge structure and the inference mechanism. Frames are organized into a hierarchy of data types or "classes" that specify both the valid attributes of an instance of a particular class, and the set of legal operations that an instance may respond to. In this way, Frameworks is object-oriented and inherits many of the features of conventional object-oriented systems such as message passing and daemons. Concepts of inheritance, default values, function evaluation, and method application are integrated into an object-oriented inference engine. Inference is performed by sending messages to clauses to perform backward chaining, assertion or retraction.

2.3.2 Scripts

A script is a structure for the large-scale organization of knowledge, adapted by Schank and Abelson (1977) primarily as a support for natural language understanding, and uses conceptual dependency as the primary form of knowledge representation. Scripts define the normal character and sequence of events as a temporal incident, for example, in a restaurant visit. They can thus be used to assign an order to language data that do not give temporal information explicitly, and may also be used to indicate underlying causal relationships. The need for explicit inference to determine temporal or causal relations between data instances is therefore reduced if we assume that a script is available for filling us in with the details. The important components of a script are defined as (Rich, 1983):

1. *Entry conditions* are conditions that must be satisfied before the events described in the script can occur.
2. *Results* are conditions that are true after the events described in the scripts have occurred.
3. *Props* are slots representing objects that are involved in the events described in the script. The presence of these objects can be inferred (by default) even if they are not mentioned explicitly.
4. *Roles* are slots that represent people involved in the events described in the script. The presence of these people can be inferred (by default) even if they are not mentioned explicitly; if specific persons are mentioned they can be inserted into appropriate slots.
5. *Tracks* are specific variations on a more general pattern that is represented by a particular script. Different tracks of the same script will share many but not all components. For instance, the script for driving will have different tracks for manual and automatic transmission vehicles.
6. *Scenes* are actual sequences of events that occur. The events are represented in conceptual dependency formalism.

Scripts have been applied to a wide variety of language processing tasks chiefly by the Yale group. In Schank's view the event orientation of scripts distinguishes them from other frames, but they share many properties of frames, like defaults and attached procedures, and forms of set organization, and present similar problems of definition and use. Frame structures are often not assumed to imply temporal or causal relations between their slots, and are thus contrasted with scripts; community usage in this respect is very inconsistent: one person's frame is another person's script and vice versa. In general the usage of the term script is less variable than that of frames but it is still applied with a good deal of freedom.

2.3.3 Case Frame

A case frame (Bundy, 1986; Bruce, 1975; Rich, 1983) is a widely used device for the determination and representation of text meaning, based on the organization of information primarily around verbs, or actions, or by case roles, e.g., Agent, Instrument, Location. It predates all the other work mentioned in this paper and supports inference in natural language processing. Conceptual graphs are very similar to case roles. However, case frames are not built up to form graph networks. Case frames are ordinarily small-scale structures oriented towards linguistic units like sentences, as opposed to the typical large-scale structures oriented to world knowledge represented by frames.

Consider for example the sentences *Mary hit John.* and *John was hit by Mary.* Although the semantic roles of Mary and John are identical, their syntactic roles are reversed, i.e., each is the subject of one and the object in the other. Using a case grammar, the interpretation of the two sentences would both be

(Hit (Agent Mary)

(Dative John))

where Agent is the instigator of the action (hit), and Dative is the entity affected by the action. Though reference to Fillmore's linguistically-motivated ideas is conventional, there is great variation in the treatment of every aspect of case frames, for example, their relation to features of the surface text (is the sentence subject the Agent?), their number (ten or thirty?), their status (obligatory or optional?), the constraints on their fillers (is the Agent HUMAN). Conceptual dependency, for example, uses a small number of deep cases referring primarily to underlying rather than surface relations.

2.4 Logic

This section deals with representation schemes based on logic. Applications of logic are seen in natural language processing, automatic problem solving, and expert systems. Schemes based on organizing knowledge using logic include clausal forms, first-order predicate logic (including Horn Clauses), temporal logic, and non-monotonic logic.

2.4.1 Clausal Form

Clausal form (Bundy, 1986) is a normal form for predicate calculus formulas of mathematical logic much used in automatic theorem proving. It consists of applying prenex normal form, skolemization and conjunctive normal form transformations, in succession (Chang & Lee, 1973). Skolemization is a technique for removing quantifiers from predicate calculus formulas. The resulting formula has a model if and only if the original formula does. A formula in clausal form consists of a conjunction of clauses. Each clause is a disjunction of literals. Each literal is either an atomic sentence or the negation of an atomic sentence, where an atomic sentence is a predicate applied to some terms. For example, let α, β and γ be atomic sentences. Then, the following are examples of formulas in clausal form: α, $\alpha \ \& \neg \beta$, and $(\alpha \vee \neg \beta) \ \& \ \gamma$. The advantage of translating predicate calculus expressions into clausal form is the simplicity of the resulting formulas. Clausal forms are easy to represent and manipulate internally and lend themselves to automatic theorem proving used in problem solving systems.

2.4.2 Horn Clauses

Horn clauses (Bundy, 1986; Kowalski, 1979) make up a subset of first order logic of the form:

$$A_1 \ \& \ A_2 \ \& \ \ldots \ \& \ A_n \rightarrow A$$

or

$$A_1 \ \& \ A_2 \ \& \ \ldots \ \& \ A_n \rightarrow$$

where each of the A_i and A are atomic formulas of the form $R(C_1, C_2, \ldots, C_n)$ where R is a relation, each C_j is a term, and $n > 0$. They have several important properties when viewed from the point of view of mathematical logic. In addition, they form the basis for the logic programming language Prolog (Clocksin & Mellish, 1981; Kluzniak & Szpakoqica, 1985). Each predicate in a Prolog program has a Horn clause definition. The above formula could be written

$$A \text{ :- } A_1, A_2, \ldots, A_n$$

and

$$?\text{- } A_1, A_2, \ldots, A_n.$$

respectively as Prolog programs. Thus expressing knowledge as Horn clauses is similar to programming in logic.

2.4.3 Temporal Logic

Temporal logic is concerned with representing and reasoning about time. In the predominant approach of using state variables and state spaces, time is represented as a sequence of instantaneous time slices, where each time slice is described by a set of facts that hold at that time. This is successful in applications where a single agent is operating in a simple discrete world (e.g., the blocks world).

Allen (1981) proposes an interval-based temporal model for dealing with multiple agents where each agent acts not only on what is true now, but also on what each expects to be true in the future. There are thirteen relations that can hold between time intervals, listed in Table 1 (Allen, 1983). Allen also discusses algorithms for maintaining knowledge about temporal intervals and strategies for controlling propagation.

Table 5. Temporal Relations

Relation	Symbol	Inverse	Pictorial Example
X *before* Y	<	>	XXX YYY
X *equal* Y	=	=	XXX YYY
X *meets* Y	m	mi	XXXYYY
X *overlaps* Y	o	oi	XXX YYY
X *during* Y	d	di	XXX YYYYY
X *starts* Y	s	si	XXX YYYYY
X *finishes* Y	d	di	XXX YYYYY

2.4.4 Non-Monotonic Logic

In non-monotonic logic systems (Doyle, 1979; McCarthy, 1980; McDermott & Doyle, 1980; Reiter, 1980; Winograd, 1980) the introduction of new axioms can invalidate old theorems. The difference between classical and non-monotonic logic systems stems from the following. In classical logics, well-formed formulas and inference procedures are *abstractions* that *may* be mapped on to the real world; this mapping is called *interpretation*. At any given time, the logic is correct if the axioms are consistent and well-formed formulas are either "true" or "false" regardless of when they were derived and regardless of interpretation. Non-monotonic logic extends classical logic by introducing notions of consistency constraints and default reasoning. These logic systems can handle incomplete, missing, or new information. They are especially concerned with interpretation and revising the axiom sets to maintain consistency within the logic system. If the results of the interpretation are unsatisfactory, then one revises the abstract system by adding, deleting, or modifying axioms, thus changing the set of true well-formed formulas, or by including default values.

Classical symbolic logic lacks tools for describing how to revise a formal theory to deal with inconsistencies caused by new information, due to the recognition that the general problem of finding and selecting among alternate revisions is very hard. There are at least two different problems involved: world-model reorganization and routine revision. World-model reorganization is the problem of revising a complex model of a situation when it turns out to be wrong. Much of the complexity of such models is due to having parts of the model relying on descriptions of other parts of the model, such as inductive hypothesis, testimony, analogy and intuition. Routine revision is the problem of maintaining a set of facts that, although expressed as universally true, have exceptions. For example, a program may have the belief that all animals with beaks are birds. Telling this program about the platypus will cause a contradiction, but not a serious enough contradiction to cause reorganization. McDermott and Doyle (1980) give a proposal for avoiding the routine revision problem by expanding the notation in which rules are stated such that statements provide advice about belief revision. For example, to reconcile a rule stating that all animals with beaks are birds and the fact that a platypus has a beak but is not a bird, the rule can be expressed as "if something is an animal with a beak, then *unless proven otherwise*, it is a bird." McDermott and Doyle (1980) further discuss the problem of coordinating sets of rules of this form and providing a system where all the pieces of advice determine a unique revision.

2.5 Comparing the Philosophies

One can argue that the four knowledge representation philosophies described above are equally expressive and that one can define a mapping to show equivalence between their elements. However, it should be observed that in structuring information for a particular problem, it is critical to choose a knowledge representation scheme that closely models the application domain and lends its power of expression in the most natural way to support the solution of the problem.

Semantic nets are commonly used to show relationships between entities, while frame-oriented schemes are generally used to group information into units and define default values for fields. Semantic nets seem to emphasize very small and primitive units and their relations to one another. Frame systems emphasize much larger and complicated units of knowledge.

Objects are often used for applications where the different entities are independent and autonomous processors that can exchange information while keeping private information structures and procedures. Scripts are preferred for structuring information about predetermined, stereotypical behavior of interacting entities in sequences of everyday events. The object view emphasizes the static nature of 'things', while the script view emphasizes the series of transactions among different 'things'.

Logic schemes are used for expressing information in symbolic or mathematical statements for ease of computer manipulation. Logic-based schemes are useful in building natural language processing systems, expert systems and other problem solving systems where knowledge about the application domain is preferably expressed as facts and rules that can be manipulated.

3. KNOWLEDGE REPRESENTATION FOR TELECOMMUNICATIONS AND THE WEB

In AI applications, the knowledge representation schemes discussed in the previous section have been used to represent "closed world" knowledge bases so as to provide highly expressive inferences. Heflin, Hender & Luke (1999) contend that "this fundamental philosophical underpinning of knowledge representation is brought into question in dealing with the Internet, and particularly the World Wide Web." The Web is a massive open-world knowledge base whose contents are extremely dynamic. Because of this, the knowledge on the Web has reliability, availability and consistency problems, and the old techniques no longer serve. New applications of the traditional knowledge representation schemes are emerging for Web and telecommunications data. We discuss three of them here, XML, UML, and ontologies, and examine their use in telecommunications and the Web.

3.1 XML

The Extensible Markup Language, or XML, is a metalanguage that provides a hybrid frame/object-like structure to semi-structured data (generally referred to as documents). Structured documents contain both content and meaning. A markup language is a mechanism to identify structure in a document (Walsh, 1998). The XML specification, specified by the World Wide Web Consortium (W3C) (Bray, Paoli, & Sperberg-McQueen, 1999), defines a standard way of adding markup (or structure) to documents. It has become a defacto standard for representing data on the web.

In XML knowledge is represented in a document as a series of objects. Each object can contain one or more elements. Each element can contain one or more attributes that further describe the element. Objects may also contain child objects thus forming a hierarchy of objects. This nested hierarchy forces XML documents to take on a tree structure (Bosak & Bray, 1999). Thus a well-formed XML document has one root. Currently most of the content in an XML document is textual although elements of the document may point to other resources such as images or applications.

XML is similar to other object-oriented schemes in that it is used to represent objects within a document. However unlike object-oriented schemes, XML objects do not use message-passing for processing. XML is more frame-like. Just as frames have slots and each slot has facets, XML objects have elements and each element has attributes. Like frames, XML is a hierarchical collection of objects with just one root.

Like HTML (Hypertext Markup Language), XML uses a set of markup tags. While in HTML tags are used to describe how the data should be presented, in XML tags are used to describe the structure and meaning of the data. Figure 4 shows the markup of a postal address using both HTML and XML.

HTML

```
<html>
<b>101 Main St.<br>
Chicago, IL 60661</b>
</html>
```

XML

```
<?xml version="1.0" encoding="UTF-8"?>
<address>
    <street>101 Main St.</street>
    <city>Chicago</city>
    <state>IL</state>
    <zip>60661</zip>
</address>
```

Figure 4. Postal address in HTML and XML

XML data is self-describing and has no presentation information. This separation of presentation from meaning provides a "write once and publish everyone" capability and is one of the strengths of XML. Another strength of XML is its extensibility – it allows you to create your own tag names

(Walsh, 1998). This extensibility is fuelling its growth in many areas such as EDI, business, healthcare and telecommunications.

Because XML separates presentation from content, the same content can be represented in many ways. Current Web browsers can interpret XML and present it as HTML. Cascading style sheets may also be used for this transformation. For other presentation of XML data, an Extensible Style Language (XSL) is used. XSL is a W3C specification for a styling language used for creating style sheets that operate on XML documents. A typical use of an XSL style sheet is to transform an XML document into HTML. However, multiple XSL style sheets an be created to transform the same data into multiple formats, such as a bank teller interface or interactive voice response system (Klein, 1999).

In order for different applications to make use of a set of user-defined tags, the application need to know what the tags are and in which order they should appear. Enter the Document Type Definition or DTD. A DTD formally identifies the relationships between the objects that form a document (Bryan, 1977) and defines the syntax for a particular type of XML document. For our postal address example, the DTD might look like this (Conallen, 2000) :

```
<?xml version="1.0" encoding="UTF-8"?>
<!DOCTYPE address [
<!ELEMENT address (street, city, state, zip) >
<!ELEMENT street  (#PCDATA)>
<!ELEMENT city (#PCDATA)>
<!ELEMENT state (#PCDATA)>
<!ELEMENT zip (#PCDATA)>
]>
```

A drawback to using DTDs is that all data elements are specified as PCDATA. Because of this, DTDs are slowly being replaced by XML schemas which allow for more detailed element specifications. Both DTD and schemas essentially describe a vocabulary for a particular type of document. Industry groups are banding together to define DTDs and schemas for their specific industries, commonly referred to XML vocabularies. A number of common XML vocabularies have been established (van den Hoven, 2000). Examples include Microsoft's BizTalk for business-to-business commerce (http://www.biztalk.org/), Financial Products Markup Language in finance (http://fpml.org), Health Level Seven in healthcare (http://www.hl7.org/Library/standards_non1.htm). For a more complete list, see XML Standards (2000).

3.1.1 Wireless Applications

XML has spawned many telecommunications applications. Two widely used XML telecommunications vocabularies have been developed: Telecommunications Interchange Markup (TIM, http://www.atis.org/atis/tcif/ipi/dl_tim.htm) and Wireless Markup Language (WML, http://www.wapforum.org/what/technical.htm). TIM is a DTD for describing the structure of telecommunications and other technical documents, using SGML (Standard Generalized Markup Language), XML's parent. WML is used with the Wireless Application Protocol (http://www.wapforum.org) to create and deliver content to wireless devices.

Saha, Jamtgaard & Villasenor (2001) have developed Relational Markup Language (RML), an XML application, as a middleware solution to the proliferation of transformations required by the wide range of wireless devices. RML uses relational hierarchies of content composed of atomics and groups. Atomics are discrete pieces of data such as a word, sentence or link. These atomics are encapsulated into relational groups. Groups can themselves be part of larger groups. Developers can use RML's customized atomics to add structural context to websites. This context enables multiple presentation formats. An RML interpreter applies predefined rule sets to the contextualized atomics and groups to create an information hierarchy optimized for a particular device. Converting existing information to a normalized RML format modularizes the data, as shown in Figure 5, and facilitates the addition of use of new devices since only the module to optimize RML to the new device need be added (Saha, Jamtgaard & Villasenor, 2001).

3.1.2 Service Creation Environments

Service creation environments (SCE) provide a means for different telecom customers to customize services to suit individual end user needs. For example, the special add-on service call forwarding can be customized so that at different times of the day, the call is forwarded to different phone numbers. A customer may want to have the following call forwarding pattern: during office hours, between 8 a.m. to 5 p.m., the phone is forwarded to an office number, between 7 a.m. to 8 a.m. and 5 p.m. to 6 p.m. to a mobile phone, and after 6 p.m. through 7 a.m. to their home number.

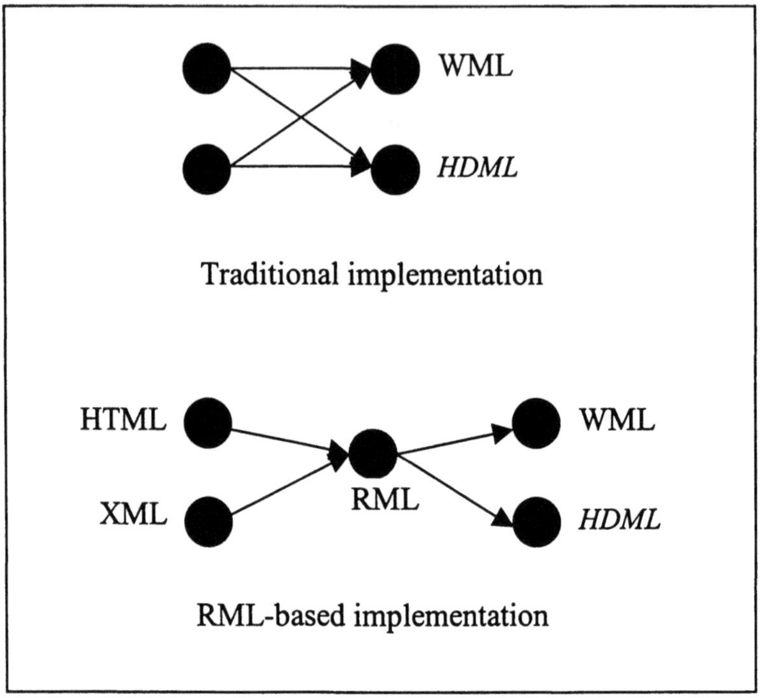

Figure 5. Creating a modular architecture using RML

XML can be used to represent the customer data indicating how incoming phone calls are handled. With XML, the customer can define different intervals and the service provider need not customize the data structures or program logic for each customer. For example, data for the call forwarding pattern can be represented as follows, with the corresponding DTD given in Figure 6.

```
<?xml version="1.0" encoding="UTF-8"?>
<!DOCTYPE call_forwarding SYSTEM "forwarding.dtd">
<call_forwarding>
    <customerID>312-123-4567</customerID>
    <routing day="mon">
        <begin_time>00:00</begin_time>
        <to_phone type="home">312-123-4567</to_phone>
    </routing>
    <routing day="mon">
        <begin_time>07:00</begin_time>
        <to_phone type="cell">312-254-8542</to_phone>
    </routing>
```

```
    <routing day="mon">
        <begin_time>08:00</begin_time>
        <to_phone type="office">312-547-8521</to_phone>
    </routing>
    <routing day="mon">
        <begin_time>17:00</begin_time>
        <to_phone type="cell">312-254-8542</to_phone>
    </routing>
    <routing day="mon">
        <begin_time>18:00</begin_time>
        <to_phone type="home">312-123-4567</to_phone>
    </routing>
</call_forwarding>
```

```
<!-- A call forwarding DTD -->
<!-- parameter entries -->
<!ENTITY % basic.content '#PCDATA'>
<!-- main elements -->
<!ELEMENT call_forwarding    (customerID, routing+)>
<!ELEMENT routing            (begin_time, to_phone)>
<!ATTLIST routing            day
          (mon | tues | wed | thurs | fri | sat | sun) #REQUIRED>
<!-- basic elements -->
<!ELEMENT customerID         (%basic.content;)>
<!ELEMENT begin_time         (%basic.content;)>
<!ELEMENT to_phone           (%basic.content;)>
<!ATTLIST to_phone           type NMTOKENS #IMPLIED>
<!-- end of call forwarding DTD -->
```

Figure 6. A DTD for the call forwarding pattern. See Ray, 2001, chap. 5 for an explanation of these terms.

3.2 Unified Modeling Language

Unified Modeling Language (UML) is a object-oriented language for specifying, visualizing, constructing and documenting the artifacts of software systems. (OMG UML Specification, 2000). UML is owned and managed by Object Management Group (OMG) which adopted UML 1.1 as an international standard in November 1997. UML 1.3, the current specification, was adopted in November 1999. The next minor revision, UML 1.4, is planned to be adopted in mid-2001 with a major revision UML 2.0 due to be completed in 2002 (Introduction to UML, 2001).

The basic building blocks of UML are elements, relationships and diagrams. Core elements include class, interface, component, node, and constraint. A class is a description of a set of objects that share the same attributes, operations, relationships, and semantics. An interface is a named set of operations that describe the behaviour of an element. A component is a modular, replaceable part of a system that packages implementation and exposes a set of interfaces. A node is a run-time physical object that represents a computational resource. A constraint is a semantic condition or restriction. (Introduction to UML, 2001). Like all object-oriented schemes, objects in UML communicate with each other via message-passing.

Core relationships include association, aggregation, generalization and dependency. Association is a relationship between two or more classes. Aggregation is a special form of association that defines a whole-part relationship between classes. Generalization describes inheritance between a general element and a more specific element. Dependency is a relationship between two modeling elements in which a change to one (the independent element) affects the other dependent element. (Introduction to UML, 2001).

UML is primarily a visual representation of knowledge used in object-oriented design. This knowledge is embodied by the various core elements and relationships and is modeled using one or more of the graphical diagrams listed in Figure 7 (UML Specification, 2000).

Structural diagrams:

- class diagram
- implementation diagrams:
    - component diagram
    - deployment diagram

Behavioral diagrams:

- use case diagram
- statechart diagram
- activity diagram
- interaction diagrams:
    - sequence diagram
    - collaboration diagram

Figure 7. Graphical Diagrams in the UML

3.2.1 Scenarios

UML is gaining popularity as a technique for capturing the characteristics of switching objects and relationships among objects and moving from behaviour specification to code generation. It can be used to represent the temporal and behavioural specification of switching objects, called scenarios. Scenarios are used to describe and specify interactions between switch subsystems and other telecommunications components. As new switching features are developed, messaging between switching objects are specified as fence post diagrams (a type of sequence diagram) where vertical lines depict the switching objects and rays depict messages sent from one object to another, as shown in Figure 8.

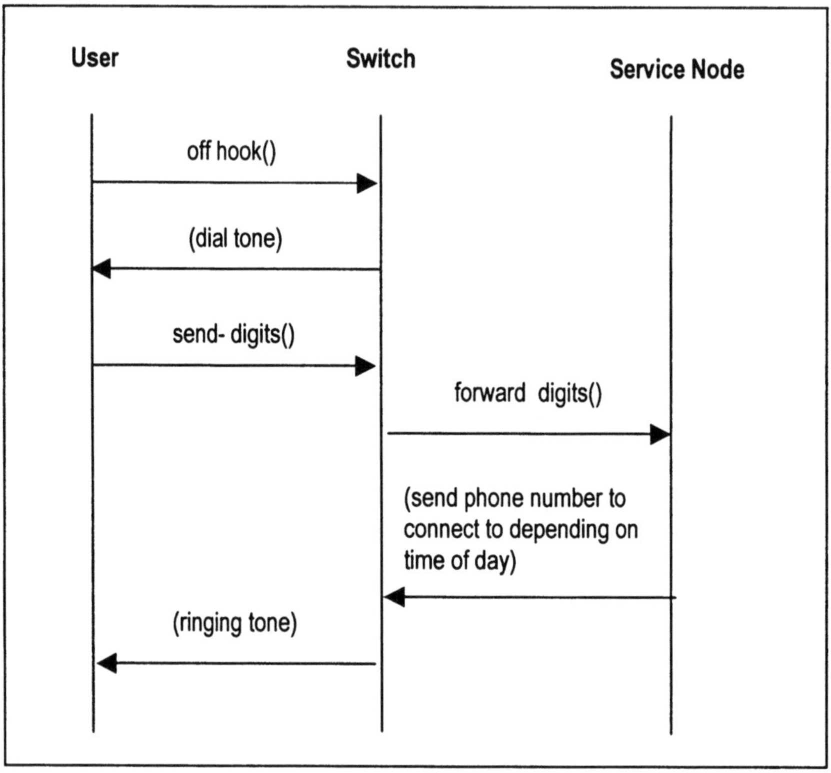

Figure 8. Fence Post (sequence) diagram showing a user interacting with a service

Scenarios are highly temporal and time is represented on the vertical direction. Scripts would be the technique of choice for representing these interactions, possibly with some extensions to support some of the highly parallel messaging that may occur.

Scenarios are not sufficient documentation for development. In Lee & Tepfenhart (1997), events are abstracted and the following aspects are specified: *meaning, source, destination, label* and *event* data. An event list can be generated listing all events and their aspects. In this example, off-hook is an event, the source is the user, and the destination is the switch. Next each object is represented as a finite state machine, with all possible states and events documented in a state transition table. The state transition table can then be used to create state diagrams and scenarios used to check the state diagrams.

3.2.2 Specifications and Requirements

Examples of specifications and requirements are statements like "The switching system shall support 4000 erlangs." or "The switching system shall be able to detect high bit errors from the far end and report this fault within 100 milliseconds after the condition is detected." This type of information appears to call for a representation scheme that is heavily rule-based. However, specifications and requirements also document interactions between system components. These interactions are best captured in an object-oriented scheme. Thus a hybrid system, such as an object-oriented scheme combined with logic or a rule-based system addresses this need. Regular characteristics of the system can be stored in the object representation while the behavioural aspects and constraints can be expressed by rule-based methods.

UML is predominantly an object-oriented representation though it has provisions for specifying rules given in the form of requirements. Switching requirements, like the two examples in the previous paragraph, are declarative statements in contrast to procedural statements that are always part of a specified sequence, e.g. an activity, task or procedure. As provided in (Lee & Tepfenhart, 1997), when a requirement is written as a declarative statement, it is best to specify it as a rule using structured English. However, representing requirements in UML is not always natural or straightforward. The rules generated are not production rules but rather linked to the object-oriented model to provide a meaningful and useful model for implementation. The sample requirement "the switching system shall support 4000 erlangs" intuitively should be translated to a service precondition and captured as part of the entrance criteria for whether the service requested is provided or not. In this case, service is to be provided by the system if the total capacity, i.e., the current calls being handled plus new calls, does not exceed 4000 erlangs. However, according to the mapping guidelines, the service precondition should be guaranteed by the calling object (the one requesting the service) instead of the object providing the service. Mapping declarative requirements in this manner does not accurately capture the spirit of the requirement, since this precondition check should be done by the called object. Thus, a richer form of expressing these types of rules is needed for UML to satisfactorily cover this area.

This is an example of an inadequacy in the UML specification. According to Rumbaugh (2000), the biggest hole in the original specification was the lack of an defined execution model. While the static structure of UML models was precisely defined, the run-time of these models were vague. The first version of proposal for an extension has been submitted.

It contains an execution model that supports highly concurrent actions without the overspecification of control necessary in major programming languages. The intent of this proposal is not to invent yet another programming language, but to serve as the semantic base on top of the effect of programming languages can be precisely defined in UML.

3.3 Ontologies and the Semantic Web

Most of the content of the Web is designed for people to read, not computers. Human users of the Web provide their own context to the material. While useful, this has limited potential for automated processing of Web resources. Enter the Semantic Web, an extension of the current Web championed by Berners-Lee, Hendler & Lassila (2001). The Semantic Web attaches meaningful structure to the content of web pages, creating an environment in which software agents, programs designed to carry out tasks for a user, can work.

For the Semantic Web (and software agents) to work, computers need structured data and inference rules in order to conduct reasoning, the area of traditional AI work. However, traditional AI applications were based on a centralized, limited knowledge base whereas data on the Web is decentralized and essentially limitless. New knowledge representation schemes are needed for developing the Semantic Web. Fortunately, two useful technologies already exist: XML and Resources Description Langue (RDF). A previous section discussed how XML allows users to add structure to their data. Meaning, or context, for this data is added using RDF.

RDF encodes meaning as sets of triples like the subject verb object of a sentence. These triples, which are a variation of horn-clause rules, can be written using XML tags. RDF is used to make assertions about the data in a document. For example, RDF can specify that (<phone type="home"/>) (is a field of type) (telephone number). Each subject, verb and object can be identified by a Universal Resource Identifier or URI. A URI defines an entity on the web. A familiar example is the Uniform Resource Locator (URL). Use of URIs ensure that concepts in a document are tied to a unique definition that can be found somewhere on the Web.

The basic RDF data model consists of three object types: *resources, properties* and *statements*. All things being described by RDF are called resources. Resources are always named by URIs. Properties are attributes or relation that describe a resource. Each property defines its permitted values, the types of resources it can describe and its relationship to other properties. A resource together with a property and the value of that property for that resource is an RDF statement. These three individual parts of a statement are called, respectively, the subject, the predicate, and the object. (Resource Description Framework (RDF) Model and Syntax Specification, 1999)

XML and RDF alone are not sufficient for the Semantic Web. Ontologies are the third basic component needed for the Semantic Web. Ontologies are collections of information used to aid communications between two sets of data. It is a document that formally defines the relationships among terms found in the XML and RDF. For the Semantic Web, an ontology contains a taxonomy, which defines classes of objects and the relations among them, and a set of inference rules, which provide reasoning power. The taxonomy is similar to an XML schema in that it defines the allowable classes and their interrelationships. Taxonomies, like other object-oriented schemes, make use of classes, subclasses and inheritance. Inference rules in ontologies provide for deductive reasoning. For example, a rule may exist which states "If an area code is associated with an city code and a phone number uses that city code, then the phone number has that area code." Then a program could deduce that a customer who lives in Indianapolis would have an area code of 317.

A parallel use of ontologies can be found in the development of Simple HTML Ontology Extensions (SHOE). SHOE is a knowledge representation (KR) language that "allows ontologies to be designed and used directly on the World Wide Web" (Heflin, Hendler & Luke, 1999). SHOE is a compliant extension of HTML and is available in XML as well. The basic structure of SHOE includes *ontologies* and *instances*. An ontology defines what kinds of assertions may be made and what kinds of inferences may be drawn from them. Instances are entities which make assertions based on those rules.

SHOE ontologies contains *basic data sets*, *category definitions*, *relational definitions* and *inferential declarations*. Four basic data types are defiened in SHOE: strings, numbers, dates and Boolean values. Category definitions specify categories under which varisou instances can be classified. Relational definitions define the relationships between instances, and inferential declarations specify the additional inferences that can be made.

SHOE and RDF share a conceptual base. However, RDF is a data model of metadata instances while SHOE is a KR language, which more easily supports the development of query engines and other tools. Examples of these are given in Heflin, Hendler & Luke (1999).

The use of ontologies, whether via RDF or SHOE, can enhance the web in many ways. They can be used, for example, to improve the accuracy of Web searches; to catalogue the content and content relationships available at a particular Web site; and for describing intellectual property rights of Web pages. The real power of ontologies will come when intelligent software agents are created to facilitate knowledge sharing and exchange, leading to more automation on the Web.

In telecommunications, many companies are banding together to promote the use of ontologies on the Internet. For example, Ontology.Org has formed an alliance with CommerceNet to address the formation and sustainability of large Internet trading groups. The standardisation of business models, processes, and knowledge architecture is critical for the development of next generation Internet commerce (Ontology.org, 1998).

4. CONCLUSION

Knowledge representation, an area traditionally seen as a sub-field of artificial intelligence, has many practical applications in e-commerce, automatic speech recognition, and telecommunications. This paper started with a review of the major existing knowledge representation philosophies. Four major philosophies were identified, namely object-oriented, network, frame-based and logic. Traditional knowledge representation philosophies can be classified under one of these four schemes. The paper continued with a look at newer knowledge representation applications for the Web and the telecommunications industry. These knowledge representation philosophies are generally hybrids of the traditional schemes.

This paper is by no means exhaustive. Not all the available implementations were described, nor were all the descriptions complete. The authors' intent was to highlight the emerging knowledge representation used for telecommunications and the Web.

According to the knowledge representation hypothesis espoused by Levesque (1986), [machine] intelligence is best served by explicitly representing in the data structures of a program as much as possible of what a system needs to know. The ability to reason depends on the ability to capture information and represent knowledge. Different applications require different knowledge representation choices. Each knowledge representation philosophy provides a model of the world and the entities to be represented. The appropriateness of a knowledge representation scheme to a particular application is dependent on whether its underlying philosophy supports the model for the application. Different knowledge representation schemes may be combined to support different aspects of an application domain, as seen in the telecommunications and Web examples.

REFERENCES

Allen, J. F. (1981). An interval-based representation of temporal knowledge. In Proceedings of the Seventh International Joint Conference in Artificial Intelligence (pp. 221-226). Vancouver, British Columbia, Canada: IJCAI.

Allen, J. F. (1983). Maintaining knowledge about temporal intervals. Communications of the ACM, 26(11), 832-843.

Berners-Lee, T., Hendler, J., & Lassila, O. (2001). The semantic web. Scientific American, May 2001. Retrieved June 19 2001 from http://www.sciam.com/2001/0501issue/0501berners-lee.html

Bobrow, D., & Winograd, T. (1977). An overview of KRL, a knowledge representation language. Cognitive Science, 1, 263-285.

Bobrow, D. G., & Stefik, M. S. (1983). The LOOPS manual. Xerox Corporation

Bosak, J. & Bray, T. (1999). XML and the second-generation Web. Scientific American, May 1999, 7p. Retrieved June 19, 2001 from http://www.siam.com/1999/0599issue/0599bosak.html

Brachman, R.J. (1985). On the epistemological status of semantic networks. In R. J. Brachman & H. J. Levesque (Eds.), Readings in knowledge representation (pp. 191-215). Cambridge, MA: Morgan Kaufman.

Brachman, R.J. (1988). The basics of knowledge representation and reasoning. AT&T Technical Journal, 67(1), 7-24.

Brachman, R. J., Fikes, R. E., & Levesque H. J. (1985). KRYPTON: A functional approach to knowledge representation. In R. J. Brachman and H. J. Levesque (Eds.), Readings in knowledge representation (pp. 411-429). Cambridge, MA: Morgan Kaufman.

Brachman, R. J., & Schmolze, J. G. (1985). An Overview of the KL-One knowledge representation System. Cognitive Science, 9, 171-216.

Bray, T., Paoli, J., & Sperberg-McQueen, C. M. (Eds.) (1998). Extensible markup language (XML) 1.0. Retrieved April 12, 2001 from http://www.w3.org/TR/1998/REC-xml-19980210

Bryan, M. (1997). An introduction to the extensible markup language (XML). The SGML Centre. Retrieved April 12, 2001 from http://www.personal.u-net.com/~sgml/xmlintro.htm

Bruce, B. (1975). Case systems for natural language. Artificial Intelligence, 6, 327-360.

Bundy, A. (Ed.). (1986). Catalogue of artificial intelligence tools (2nd rev. ed.). New York: Springer-Verlag.

Charniak, E., Riesbeck, C. & McDermott, D. (1980). Artificial intelligence programming., Hillsdale, NJ: L. Erlbaum Associates.

Charniak, E., & Wilks, Y. (1976). Computational semantics. Amsterdam: North-Holland.

Chang, C. L., & Lee, R. C. (1973). Symbolic logic and mechanical theorem proving. New York: Academic Press.

Clocksin, W. F., & Mellish, C. S. (1981). Programming in Prolog, New York: Springer-Verlag.

Conallen, J. (2000). XML in Building web applications with UML (pp. 54-59). Reading, MA: Addison Wesley.

Doyle, J. (1979). A truth maintenance system. Artificial Intelligence, 12, 231-272.

Fahlman, S. E. (1979). NETL: A system for representing and using real-world knowledge. Cambridge, MA: MIT Press.

Findler, N. V. (Ed.). (1979). Associative networks : representation and use of knowledge by computers. New York: Academic Press.

Franta, W. R. (1977). The process view of simulation. New York: North-Holland.

Gasser, L., Braganza, C., & Herman, N. (1987). Implementing distributed AI systems using MACE. In Proceedings of the Third Conference on Artificial Intelligence Applications (pp. 315-320). Kissimmee, FL: IEEE Computer Society.

Goldberg, A., & Robson, D. (1983). Smalltalk-80: The language and its implementation. Reading, MA: Addison-Wesley.

Heflin, J., Hendler, J., and Luke, S. (1999). SHOE: A knowledge representation language for Internet applications. Technical Report CS-TR-4078 (UMIACS TR-99-71), Dept. of Computer Science, University of Maryland at College Park. Retrieved June 19 2001 from the World Wide Web: http://www.cs.umd.edu/projects/plus/SHOE/pubs/techrpt99.pdf

Hewitt, C. (1972). Description and theoretical analysis (using schemata) of PLANNER: a language for proving theorems and manipulating models in a robot. (MIT Artificial Intelligence Laboratory TR-258).

Hewitt, C. (1979). Control Structure as Patterns of Passing Messages. In P.H. Winston & R. H. Brown (Eds.), Artificial Intelligence: An MIT Perspective: Vol. 2 (pp. 433-465). Cambridge, MA: MIT Press.

Hewitt, C. & Baker, H. (1977a). Actors and continuous functionals. In E. J. Neuhold (Ed.), Proceedings of IFIP working conference on the formal description of programming concepts (pp. 367-387). St. Andrews, New Brunswick, Canada: North-Holland.

Hewitt, C., & Baker, H. (1977b). Laws for communicating parallel processes. In B.Gilchrist (Ed.), Information processing 77; Proceedings of IFIP Congress 77 (pp. 987-992). Toronto, Canada: North-Holland.

Introduction to UML: Structural modeling and use cases. (2001, March). Object Management Group. (Updated UML Lecture 1). Retrieved April 4, 2001 from ftp://ftp.omg.org/pub/docs/omg/01-03-02.pdf

Kass, R., Katriel R., & Finin, T. (1987). Breaking the Primitive Concept Barrier. In Proceedings of the Third Conference on Artificial Intelligence Applications (pp. 67-73). Kissimmee, FL: IEEE Computer Society.

Klein, B. (1999, June 28). XML makes object models more useful. Information Week, pp. 1A-6A.

Kluzniak, F., & Szpakowicz, S. (1985). Prolog for programmers. New York: Academic Press.

Kornfeld, W. A., & Hewitt, C.E. (1981). The scientific community metaphor. IEEE Transactions on Systems, Man and Cybernetics, SMC-11 (1), 24-33.

Kowalski, R. A. (1979). Logic for problem solving. Amsterdam: North-Holland.

Lee, R. C. & Tepfenhart, W. M. (1997). UML and C++: A practical guide to object-oriented development. /Upper Saddle River, NJ: Prentice-Hall.

Levesque, H. L. (1986). Knowledge representation and reasoning. Annual Reviews of Computer Science, 1, 255-287.

McCarthy, J. (1980). Circumscription – a form of non-monotonic reasoning. Artificial Intelligence, 13, 27-39.

McDermott, D., & Doyle, J. (1980). Non-monotonic logic I. Artificial Intelligence, 13, 41-72.

Minsky, M. (1975). A framework for representing knowledge. In Winston, P. (Ed.), The Psychology of Computer Vision (pp. 211-277). New York: McGraw-Hill.

OMG Unified Modeling Language specification: version 1.3. (2000, March). Object Management Group. Retrieved April 3, 2001 from http://cgi.omg.org/cgi-bin/doc?formal/00-03-01

Ontology.org (1998, October 9). ONTOLOGY.ORG and CommerceNet form strategic alliance. Retrieved July 9, 2001 from http://www.ontology.org/main/press/091098.html

Ray, E.T. (2001). Learning XML. Sebastopol, CA: O'Reilly & Assoc.

Resource Description Framework (RDF) Model and Syntax Specification. (1999). W3C. (Updated 2 February 1999). Retrieved July 5, 2001 from http://www.w3.org/TR/1999/REC-rdf-syntax-19990222/

Reiter, R. (1980). A logic for default reasoning. Artificial Intelligence, 13, 81-132.

Rich, E. (1983). Artificial intelligence, New York: McGraw-Hill.
Roberts, R. E., & Goldstein, I. P. (1977). The FRL manual. (MIT AI Lab, AI memo 409 edition).
Rumbaugh, J. (2000, December). Trends in UML and e-Development. The Rational Edge. Retrieved July 9, 2001 from http://www.therationaledge.com/content/dec_00/f_uml.html
Schank, R. C. (1975). Conceptual Information Processing. Amsterdam: North-Holland.
Schank, R. C., & Abelson, R. (1977). Scripts, plans, goals, and understanding : an inquiry into human knowledge structures. Hillsdale, NJ: L. Erlbaum Associates.
Smith, R.G. (1977). The Contract net: A formalism for the control of distributed problem solving. In IJCAI-77, Proceedings of the Fifth Joint Conference on Artificial Intelligence (p. 472). Cambridge, MA: Morgan Kaufman.
Smith, R.G. (1983). STROBE: Support for structured object knowledge representation. In Proceedings of the International Joint Conference on Artificial Intelligence (pp. 855-858). Karlsruhe, Germany: Morgan Kaufman.
Smith, R.G., & Davis, R. (1978). Distributed problem solving: The contract net approach. (Computer Science Department Report No. STAN-CS-78-667). Stanford, CA: Stanford Heuristic Programming Project Memo HPP-78-7.
Smith, R.G., & Davis, R. (1981). Frameworks for cooperation in distributed problem solving. IEEE Transactions on Systems, Man and Cybernetics, SMC-11(1), 61-69.
Smith, H. R., Harris, W. H., & Simmons, D. (1987). Frameworks: A uniform approach to knowledge representation for natural language processing. In Proceedings of the Third Conference on Artificial Intelligence Applications (pp. 74-80). Kissimmee, FL: IEEE Computer Society.
Sowa, J.F. (1984). Conceptual structures: Information processing in mind and machine. Reading, MA: Addison-Wesley.
Sussman, G. J., Winograd, T. & Charniak, E. (1971). Micro-PLANNER reference manual. (MIT Artificial Intelligence Laboratory AI Memo 203A)..
Ullman, J. (1982). Principles of database systems (2nd ed.). Rockville, Md: Computer Science Press.
Van den Hoven, J. (2000). XML – Rosetta stone for data. Information Systems Management, 17(4), 55-58.
Walsh, N. (1998). A technical introduction to XML. ArborText. Retrieved April 12, 2001 from http://nwalsh.com/docs/articles/xml/
Winograd, T. (1980). Extended inference modes in reasoning by computer systems. Artificial Intelligence, 13, 5-26.
XML Standards in Effect or In Process. (2000, December). Geneer. Retrieved April 12, 2001 from http://www.geneer.com/report/xmlstandards.htm

Chapter 14

Quasi-naturally Occurring Experiments With Electronic Markets and Digital Products

Anitesh Barua: Ramnath K. Chellappa

Center for Research on Electronic Commerce, Department of Management Science and Information Systems, Graduate School of Business, The University of Texas at Austin, Austin, TX 78712: ebizlab, Department of Information and Operations Management, Marshall School of Business, University of Southern California, Los Angeles, CA 90089

Abstract: Organizational design includes the technology infrastructure, business processes, decision rules, incentive systems and control mechanisms. However, a key question facing managers and researchers alike is whether many of the theories regarding traditional markets, products and services are applicable to digital product businesses as well. Digital products are unique in that they can be instantly delivered to the customer and they also exhibit significant economic, marketing, production and technology related differences from their physical analogs. Thus, what can be a pragmatic yet conceptually sound basis for assessing alternative design of digital product companies? To address these issues, we developed a new approach at the Center for Research in Electronic Commerce at the University of Texas under the guidance of Prof. Andrew Whinston, that we call "quasi-naturally occurring experiments" and make the case that in the absence of well-developed and tested theories in the area of digital products and markets, such experiments will be critical to testing underlying design assumptions and rationale. This chapter presents our experience during two semesters.

Key words: digital products, electronic markets, experiments, business value

1. INTRODUCTION

Any commercial organization should be designed to contribute maximally to the bottom line, e.g., profitability or other financial metrics like shareholder value. The rapid proliferation of Electronic Commerce (EC) and electronic markets makes it an imperative for companies to re-examine and restructure their design, which includes strategies, information technology (IT) infrastructure and applications, business processes, decision rules, incentive systems and control mechanisms. Companies are investing heavily in these design decisions in order to do business in the new digital economy. However, a key question facing managers and researchers alike is whether many of the theories, beliefs and assumptions regarding traditional markets, products, services and business strategies and processes hold in the new world of EC.

A large section of EC activities are beginning to evolve around digital products like information and software goods [6], which are delivered to the customer directly over the network, and which have significant economic, marketing, production and technology related differences from their physical analogs. For example, digital products exhibit a declining average cost property which implies that firms should not provide much variety in these products. Yet the diverse preferences of consumers regarding digital products may force companies to "mass customize" their offerings [6]. Companies entering these uncharted territories of EC need systematic guidance and deep insights into the nature of investments in technology, processes and other design factors that can help them exploit maximum return.

To address these issues, we develop a new approach we call "quasi-naturally occurring" experiments, and make the case that given the absence of well-developed and tested theories in the area of digital products and markets and the scarcity of relevant data, such experiments will be critical to testing organizational design assumptions and rationale, as well as their impact on profitability. The methodology for these experiments involves (i) developing analytical models of the digital products market of interest, (ii) deriving testable hypotheses regarding processes, technologies and strategies for selling digital products, (iii) using a mix of real-world and experimenter created artifacts (e.g., infrastructure applications, transaction rules, etc.) to create the desired marketplace, (iv) setting participant incentives to parallel those found in the real world, (v) running the experiment for a sufficiently extended period of time to allow for market dynamics, and (vi) checking for potential validity biases. After providing a methodological foundation for our approach, we summarize three experiments we have conducted with a digital goods market within an educational setting, and present some preliminary but promising results.

2. THE MOTIVATION FOR EXPERIMENTATION WITH ELECTRONIC MARKETS

The literature on digital product electronic markets is thin [6], and traditional economic models of undifferentiated products tell us little about how businesses can succeed in an electronic world [10]. EC brings forth new opportunities and challenges, and old approaches to addressing new issues may prove unsatisfactory [9]. One approach to generating insights into what will and will not work in an electronic market is to obtain data from the real world along the tradition of field studies. While highly desirable from the standpoint of realism, this approach faces major obstacles. First, the field of EC is so new that the very existence of systematic data on investments, strategies, processes and products may be questionable. Second, with a few exceptions like Dell Computer, Cisco Systems and Amazon.com, EC success stories are hard to come by, while failures abound in the marketplace. Unfortunately, the handful of successful organizations are unlikely to part with any EC related information, while unsuccessful companies may not provide detailed information on why their initiatives failed. Yet senior managers need to know what type of product, marketing and pricing strategies they should adopt, what business processes they should design, and what type of IT applications will help them exploit the fullest potential of EC. In addition, models used in field studies are often limited by the nature of data the researcher hopes to collect. That is, the availability of data rather than unfettered theories starts driving the model building process, which is counter-productive for an emerging field like EC.

2.1 Quasi-naturally occurring experiments

A "quasi-naturally occurring" (QNO) experiment has the following characteristics:

- It is closer to field studies than to traditional laboratory experimentation in terms of the complexity and realism of the experimental setting.
- The researchers provide certain artifacts (e.g., software applications, transaction rules, transaction instruments, etc.) which are used by the experimental units (subjects).
- The time period involved is significantly longer than those in laboratory experiments in the social sciences to allow for the evolution of market dynamics.
- Through appropriate incentives, the degree of realism in QNO experiments parallel occurrences in the real world.

2.2 Experimental artifacts

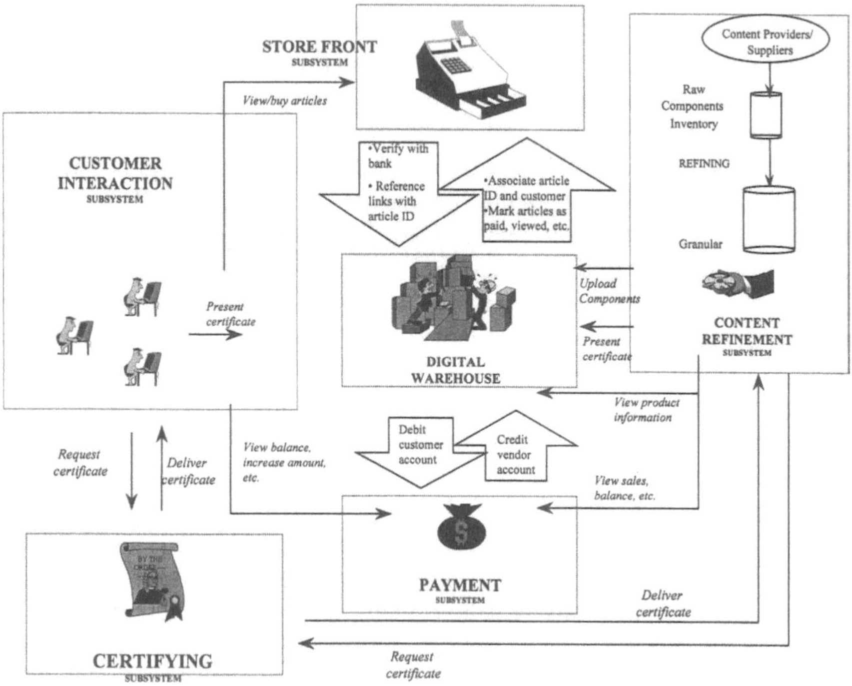

Figure 1. Experimental Artifact: Electronic Market for Digital Products

In QNO experiments, we create an electronic marketplace where buyers and sellers engage in transactions using certain transaction instruments according to rules set by us. We make available to buyers and sellers a technological infrastructure that is used to support certain basic activities in the electronic market. For example, in our QNO experiments, our offering to each digital products company includes a "digital warehouse" to store annotated information content, a product bundling/pricing system to create and price a variety of information product bundles, an electronic banking system, a virtual community building system [1] to bring potential buyers and sellers together, and a collaborative document filtering system for refining raw digital content (see Figure 1). While these infrastructure applications are made available to all companies, each company designs and creates its own storefront and links it to our artifacts. In this regard, we play the role of an electronic mall for digital goods, as indicated in Figure 1.

2.3 Setting rules in the marketplace

We provide a set of transaction rules to the players. For example, buyers and sellers are allowed to communicate only through electronic means. Buyers cannot resell or share digital products they buy. Further, the only valid transaction is the electronic cash that buyers receive as an endowment from us. A valid transaction must be executed through our electronic banking system. Financial penalties are assessed for violations of the above and other prescribed rules.

2.4 Setting incentives

A key limitation of MIS experiments arises from the fact that subjects are often rewarded for participation rather than their performance. The internal validity related question is whether the subjects have the incentive to apply any effort toward the experimental task, given that free riding and shirking behavior result from rewarding all participants equally [4]. In a QNO experiment, incentives are provided for sellers to participate actively in the electronic market. For example, the course grades of students selling digital products depend on their profits, and cash prizes and award certificates from a top-six consulting organization are given to the winning company from each seller class (see sidebar I).

2.5 Real Markets?

We believe that using student subjects instead of "real" managers does not jeopardize the external validity of our QNO experiments. A real market is one where there is real demand and real supply, and where products and services are exchanged based on their value to buyers and sellers. A real market does not even have to use real money as long as the transaction instrument is valuable to both buyers and sellers. By tying incentives to the electronic cash and by creating an environment where demand and supply are naturally created (based on the nature of the course projects), our experimental electronic market is a real one, albeit simpler than markets in the natural world.

3. GENERATING HYPOTHESES

The hypotheses to be tested in QNO experiments are derived from analytical models of a firm's business value, competition and channel relationships in an electronic market. For example, business value complementarity (BVC) [2, 3] appears well suited for generating hypotheses regarding a firm's EC design choices and how such choices affect its financial performance. In our market, a company makes choices pertaining to its product, marketing and pricing strategy, business processes, and IT applications. These are drivers of financial measures like profitability. Further, BVC suggests that there is complementarity or synergy between these choices whereby certain combinations of choices are more attractive than others. The choice of business value drivers and the complementarity between the drivers lead to a set of testable hypotheses. However, what is the motivation for bringing in a business value model? There are numerous combinations of choice variables, each leading to a design configuration for the organization. Rather than evaluate all possible design configurations, the BVC approach helps reduce the choices to a manageable few, whereby the impact of a particular design on profitability becomes the basis for reducing the admissible set of choices.

For the sake of illustration, a few hypotheses derived from the business value model are listed below, while a complete set of hypotheses can be found elsewhere [5].

H1: *For a given digital product, a company using a pull strategy will have a larger number of products as well as higher product variety than one using a push strategy.*

With a pull strategy, a company expects customers to visit its electronic store-front and select products that best suit their requirements. The company does not engage in collecting information from individual customers prior to designing and manufacturing products; as a result, it must offer a relatively large number and variety of products to meet diverse customer needs. A push strategist should use a more focused approach to create a relatively limited number of products targeted for specific customers.

H2: *For a given digital product, a company using a push strategy engages in higher levels of market research and interactions with potential customers prior to product design and manufacturing than one using a pull strategy.*

Examples of unfocused push abound on the Internet, where one's electronic mailbox gets filled with irrelevant product and service offers. Thus a necessary condition for success with a push strategy involves a high level of market research and interaction with potential customers before product design.

H3: *For a given digital product, a company using a push strategy will offer more customized products than one using a pull strategy.*

While customization is feasible with both push and pull strategies, a push strategist should use customer requirements as inputs at the product design stage, so that the product choices that are eventually offered are already targeted and partly customized.

On the other hand, with a pull strategy, customization may involve an assembly of more "generic" components, i.e., it involves a lower level of customization relative to a push strategy, where customization starts before the products are designed.

4. EXPERIMENTS AT THE UNIVERSITY OF TEXAS AT AUSTIN, THE UNIVERSITY OF SOUTHERN CALIFORNIA AND MONTEREY TECH, MEXICO CITY

The common theme across three experiments we have conducted is the creation of companies by 5-7 advanced level information systems and computer science students (per company) in "Advanced Data Communications" and "Electronic Commerce" courses at the University of Texas at Austin (UT). The companies' objective are to sell information goods (e.g., information on costs, market trends and other aspects of networking and computing technologies) and "original" software to students in basic "Data Communications" courses, who can incorporate these products in their course projects. Of course, a requirement is that buyers must add "significant" value to any material they buy from the market. The buyers' incentive to buy high quality contents in a timely fashion is provided by a relatively high percentage of the course grade (about 30%) attached to group projects. As shown in Figure 1, the sellers obtain their "raw materials" from public domain repositories and, more importantly, from IT managers and developers in real organizations, and add value through refinements, enhancements and integration. While buyers can also get access to these sources in principle, their "transaction cost" of doing so may be high, analogous to consumers producing raw food items rather than buying from a supermarket.

4.1 Experiments during Spring 1997

During Spring 1997, three companies, InfoEasy, E-Wizz and Custom Information Architects, were set up to sell products to 30 buyer groups (approximately 120 students) in two Data Communications classes at UT. In Fall 1997, the experiment involved five seller organizations and over forty buyer groups (approximately 160 students) from UT and the University of Southern California (USC). During Spring 1998, 18 companies were created across three classes at UT to sell to about 80 buyer groups in five classes at UT, USC and Monterey Tech, Mexico.

35 - 50% of the sellers' course grade was dependent on their profits. In Fall 1997, the sellers were given additional incentives through a $500 cash reward and award certificate from Ernst and Young for the winner. The runner-up company would also receive a certificate. In Spring 1998, there were companies in multiple classes, and the overall winner received an additional "grand prize" of $500 and a special certificate.

Each buyer group is endowed with $10,000 electronic cash, which immediately raises the question: What is the incentive of a buyer group not to spend this accounting money? This could lead to behavior which would be unlikely to be observed when the buyers deal with real money which always has an opportunity cost. In the spirit of experimental economics [11], the electronic accounting money is made valuable to the buyers by making it equivalent to bonus grade points. This scheme provides a balancing disincentive to the buyers to buy content, and encourages them to seek content on their own [8].

4.1.1 Preliminary Findings

While the number of observations from our experiments to date is insufficient for statistical testing of the above and other hypotheses, they provided many insights regarding critical success factors in a digital market. We found that companies using a "pull" product strategy would offer greater variety and number of products than one using a "push" strategy. For example, the total number of products offered by E-Wizz (a push strategist) was 90, of which there were only 12 unique offerings. This implies a high degree of common component sharing. By contrast, InfoEasy (a pull strategist) offered a total of 157 products, of which there were 48 unique offerings. We also found that successful push strategists engaged in higher levels of interaction with their potential customer base prior to their product offering than successful pull strategists.

Push strategists offered more customized products than pull based companies. For example, 11% of E-Wizz's offerings were customized products meant for specific buyer groups, while Info-Easy customized less than 1% of their offerings. This is explained by the rationale that unless a push strategist creates products that are targeted for specific buyer group, it runs the risk of buyer groups rejecting its products on grounds of not meeting their requirements.

Pull strategists provided more decision aids for potential buyers in their electronic storefronts including free previews, outlines, and content indices. By contrast, push strategists did not provide free previews, and did not modify the generic mall store-front technology to suit their needs.

Push strategists offer more bundled products (e.g., 16.6% of E-Wizz's products were bundled as opposed to 7.6% of InfoEasy's offerings). Since a successful push strategist knows its customers' specific requirements better than a pull strategist, it can create a bundle that is made up of components which are all useful to the buyer. Note that while a monopolist can extract consumer surplus by bundling unrelated components, our experimental market was competitive in nature.

Bundled products accounted for about 97% of all sales in the electronic market. This is due to the type of the goods being sold in the market. Given that the information and software components assembled by the companies were of a highly related nature, the buyers found the "whole to be worth more than the sum of its parts". Push strategists also charged more per product than pull strategists. For example, InfoEasy's average price per product offering was $100.89, which was significantly lower than E-Wizz's average of $271.18.

InfoEasy provided 17 free previews and 11 summaries and indices for 157 products. By sharp contrast, E-Wizz did not provide any means for the buyers to assess the quality and contents of their offerings. However, successful push strategists like E-Wizz generated most of their revenues from customized bundles, which they did not even, offer to the entire customer base. One of the most important factors that distinguish digital products from their physical analogs is the uncertainty associated with the content of the product. This is further complicated for information products which are consumed as soon as the customer "looks" at the content for the first time. Accordingly, sellers of this type of digital products should enable sampling of the contents without giving away the product. Pull strategists, however, will provide more information regarding the content of their products than push strategists because there is less upfront interaction between customers and pull strategists.

To summarize, we found that both push and pull strategies can succeed, provided they are accompanied by their complementary set of design choices: Higher levels of customer interactions, more bundling, customization, higher prices, etc. with a push strategy, and higher product variety and technology based decision aids with a pull strategy. Using the analogy of a set of dials, setting the position of one dial should not be done in isolation from the settings of the other dials. For example, we found from one of the companies that a push strategy without a high degree of customer requirements assessment fails to generate a high volume of business.

4.1.2 Market dynamics: From pull to push

In all three semesters, some of the most successful companies shifted their strategy from a pull to a push mode over time. For example, in the first half of the Spring semester, less than 5% of E-Wizz's products were customized bundles; however, in the second half, 80% of their offerings were customized bundles. In their own words, "after discussing the benefits and risks of different pricing strategies, such as bundling goods and pricing individual bits of information, E-Wizz concluded that the market would react most favorably to offering a dual-product strategy. The bundle included all the related articles to a particular topic as well as follow-up research according to their individual needs. The bundle strategy was so much more popular that individual article (component) sales were completely de-emphasized by the end of the exercise". That is, as they got to know the market requirements better, they felt that they should adopt an exclusive push strategy along with its complementary choices such as customization, higher prices, etc.

4.2 Experiments during Fall 1997

Some of the most innovative strategies and applications design came from Robby Hampton Enterprise (RHE), the winning company in Fall 1997 (see Sidebar II). This company was unique in the way it built credibility, trust and loyalty with its customers, how it handled product returns and customer service as well as dynamic personalization of storefront views.

4.2.1 Robby Hampton Enterprise – A winner's profile

The winner for Fall 1997 was Robby Hampton Enterprises (RHE). Its members selected the company name based on the fact that Robby Hampton, a member, was the past president of the MIS Association at UT. They felt that the name would help them create credibility among potential buyers at UT. RHE demonstrated a high level of innovativeness in the way they designed their electronic storefront. When customers logged on to their storefront with usernames and passwords, a customized display of the storefront would be provided, whereby customers would only see information products that were relevant for their specific project. Since each company could also browse its competitors' storefronts, RHE's strategy regarding customized views prevented its competitors from seeing its product descriptions and prices. In fact, one of the competing companies posted negative advertisements in the virtual community forum suggesting that RHE had no products to sell. In reality, RHE had many high quality products for sale, and the products would get listed based on the identity of the storefront visitor.

RHE also distinguished itself in its attempt to retain existing customers, and offered customers heavy discounts once they reached a preferred level of purchases. This is analogous to frequent flier programs, which help airlines achieve customer loyalty. To signal product quality, after the end of each project, RHE made available all its products for that project to all customers for free. Even though the products were no longer valuable to the customers, this action enabled them to assess the product quality.

Lastly, recognizing the time criticality of their business, RHE designed and implemented a special help desk facility, which would forward any customer query to all company members. This would maximize the probability of the customer getting a prompt response from the company. With all the above design related choices, RHE's net profit was over $69,000, while their closest competitor earned under $37,000.

4.2.2 Introducing an expert consultant

In Spring 1998, the level of competition was very high. With 18 companies in the market and with over 2000 products listed for sale, buyers had a wide choice and bargaining power. In an attempt to recreate winning strategies in one semester in subsequent semesters, we hired Gabriel Eapen, one of the key members of RHE as a Research Associate, and delegated to him a consultant's duty whereby he would provide consulting services to companies for a certain fee (electronic cash) to be negotiated depending on the type of consulting. One company "Your Project Starts Here!" (YPSH) hired Eapen for 10 percent of their net profit. Eapen communicated to YPSH what business strategies, processes and IT applications his company adopted, and YPSH followed Eapen's recommendations closely. At the end of the semester, YPSH emerged as the overall winner with a total profit of $59,000 (after paying Eapen 10 percent) and was ahead of their nearest competitor by over $30,000, a rather significant margin.

Eapen's consulting with YPSH can be considered as a business chain coming into a new market. YPSH worked hard to create early visibility and market presence; like RHE, they moved from a pull to a push strategy as they came to learn about their customers' requirements. Even though their storefront did not provide dynamic views based on customer profiles, they manually created multiple sites with customized content [7]. The effect for the customers is the same (even though it was laborious for YPSH to create multiple sites). Their help desk facility was the same as that of RHE, and based on Eapen's advice, their advertisements enabled the customers to directly enter their requirements in a concise and structured manner.

4.3 Experimental insights: Ten Commandments for digital products companies

Our observations in the electronic market over three semesters have led to the following insights regarding digital business strategies:

1. **Create early visibility**: YPSH contacted its Mexico City buyer segment even before the projects were distributed to the buyers. Successful companies like YPSH got started quickly with simple but functional storefronts, while others were late entrants in the market, being busy creating highly sophisticated sites. Others delayed offering products in the early part of the semester. Unfortunately when these sellers finally offered some products, buyers had already settled with the early movers.
2. **Invest in building trust**: Both RHE and YPSH were able to establish trust and rapport with their buyer base. For example, some buyers trusted YPSH to an extent where they would share their discontent over other companies with YPSH members. Even after the semester ended, multiple buyers contacted YPSH members regarding their whereabouts and career choices. This trust is absolutely critical for pure Internet companies since they initially lack the credibility enjoyed by established companies.
3. **Don't make it difficult for buyers to assess you and your products**: In order to avoid competitors from obtaining information on pricing and products, some companies protected their sites with registration procedures. Another key motive driving this strategy was the ability to personalize storefront and product views based on customer profiles. However, given the large number of suppliers, buyers were not willing to take the time to register and provide information about their requirements.
4. **Provide signals about product quality**: Since digital products are more difficult to assess in terms of quality and fit with requirements, companies must be able to help buyers make informed buying decisions. Indeed top companies in our market took the time to clearly describe each product they offered without actually giving the product away.
5. **Make it easy for buyers to express their needs**: While most companies relied on plain electronic mail for communication with buyers, RHE and YPSH deployed automated help desks with highly structured forms which clearly identified the buyers, their projects and needs. These forms also helped RHE and PSH quickly classify and store customer profiles for offering customized products.
6. **Don't forget product quality**: Since the ultimate consumer of the products (the professors in the buyer classes) emphasized originality and novelty, product quality in our market was synonymous with exclusivity (e.g., an original interview with a networking manager in a high profile organization) and uniqueness. The successful sellers created original

products, and were able to command a significant premium over those who used the Web as a primary source of raw material for low priced products. In fact, buyers spent most of their money on high priced products, implying that they took price as a signal for quality.

7. **Customize content and presentation**: Most of the money in the market was made from "big ticket" items which were all customized for specific buyers. Given the value of exclusivity as well as the diverse buyer preference of topics and issues, companies that recognized and acted on this opportunity were able to extract as much as $10,000 in a single transaction.
8. **Be nimble, be quick**: In an electronic medium, buyers expect immediate response from sellers. Automated help desks like the ones created by RHE and YPSH route customer requests in a predetermined way, enabling fast turnarounds like the "7x24 1-hour response" touted by YPSH, compared to the 1 day average for companies using basic electronic mail.
9. **Don't treat customers with a one-size-fits-all strategy**: Even though "money back" or warranty are not particularly meaningful for information products, YPSH refunded the purchase price of $1000 to one of their "important" customers, who came back for a subsequent purchase of $5000. Along similar lines, both RHE and YPSH treated their special customers differently by offering deeper discounts for their loyalty and high purchase volume.
10. **Offer bundled products in a world of complementarity**: Since the digital goods in our experimental context were highly complementary (e.g., a buyer seeking information on the market share of frame relay providers was likely to look for information on competing technologies as well), companies which carefully bundled related information and software items were able to generate top revenues with just a few transactions.

4.4 Observations on subject behavior

Apart from the above findings, we were convinced about the realism that can be achieved in a QNO experimental setting. For example, one company cracked another's passwords to enter their digital warehouse and intra-company workspace in order to access strategic information. Guessing and trying passwords are tedious chores, and without a strong sense of involvement in the task, it is unlikely that members of a company would try to find out confidential information about their competitors. In another development, InfoEasy had a problem where one of their customers got charged twice for some product due to a bug in our electronic accounting system. InfoEasy credited back the customer's account, tendered their apologies, offered a large discount on the customer's next purchase, and sent a note to us (the electronic mall provider) demanding an apology to the customer for the inconvenience caused. Without an intense level of realism, the "employees" of InfoEasy would not take such matters so seriously.

5. CONCLUSION

While billions of dollars are being invested in EC, little is known or understood regarding successful marketing, product, pricing and customer service aspects of online business. There is an acute paucity of systematic empirical evidence to test theories and assumptions, which makes it an imperative to consider experimentation as a valuable means to generating deep insights into phenomena in the digital marketplace. Our QNO experiments let us record in-depth observations on how successful companies create trust and reputation within their buyer base, how they select product bundles and prices, how they gather market intelligence and profiles on individual customers and use such information in deciding their business strategies, and how they alter such strategies over time with naturally occurring changes in the electronic business environment.

While it may appear that some of the "critical success factors" we discovered in our electronic market are the same ones that would drive performance in a physical market, factors like customer responsiveness take on a new meaning in an electronic world, and pose major challenges for organizations that do not redesign their strategies, processes and technologies for the new world. Our experimental setting enables us to observe how some companies in a digital market organize themselves to meet such challenges, and how others make inappropriate design choices leading to poor financial performance.

REFERENCES

[1] Barua, A., Chellappa, R., and Whinston, A.B., "Design and Implementation of Internet and Intranet Based Collaboratories," International Journal of Electronic Commerce, Vol 1, No. 2, Winter 1996-97.

[2] Barua, A., Kriebel, C.H., and Mukhopadhyay, T., "Information Technologies and Business Value: An Analytic and Empirical Investigation," Information Systems Research, Vol. 6, No. 1, pp. 3-23, March 1995.

[3] Barua, A., Lee, S., and Whinston, A.B., "The Calculus of Reengineering," Information Systems Research, Vol. 7, No. 4, December 1996.

[4] Barua, A., Lee, C-H S., and Whinston, A.B., "Incentives and Computing Systems for Team Based Organizations," Organization Science, Vol. 6, No. 4, pp. 487-504, July-August 1995.
[5] Chellappa, R., "Electronic Commerce for Digital Products Companies," Ph.D Dissertation, the University of Texas at Austin, December 1997.
[6] Choi, S.Y., Stahl, D.O., and Whinston, A.B., "The Economics of Electronic Commerce," MacMillan Technical Publishing, Indianapolis, IN, 1997.
[7] Gallaga, O., "Virtual reality check: UT project gives students insight into world of electronic commerce," Austin American Statesman, Technology Monday section, May 23, 1998, http://www.austin360.com/news/004biz/05may/25/25utecommerce.htm.
[8] Glasser, P., "An EC Grade," CIO Magazine, Trendlines section, January 15, 1998, http://www.cio.com/archive/011598_trendlines.html.
[9] Kalakota, R., and Whinston, A.B., "Electronic Commerce: A Manager's Guide," Addison-Wesley, 1997.
[10] McAfee, R.P., and McMillan, J., "Electronic Markets," in Readings in Electronic Commerce, R. Kalakota and A.B. Whinston (eds.), Addison-Wesley, 1997.
[11] Plott, C.R., "An Updated Review of Industrial Organization: Applications of Experimental Methods," in the Handbook of Industrial Organization, Volume II, R. Schmalensee and R.D. Willig (eds.), Elsevier Science Publishers, B.V., 1989.

Chapter 15

Finding the Right Products and Devising Marketing Strategies for E-Tailing

Melody Kiang; Robert T. Chi; and Kar Yan Tam
Information Systems Department, College of Business Administration, California State University, Long Beach; Department of Information and Systems Management, HKUST Business School, Hong Kong University of Science and Technology

Abstract: The tremendous growth of the Internet has created opportunities for consumers and firms to participate in an online global marketplace. It is conceivable that in the future every person with access to a computer will interact with firms marketing on the Internet. The potential of the Internet as a commercial medium and market has been widely documented in a variety of media. In this research, we focus on the use of the Internet as a virtual storefront where products are offered directly to customers. Our contention is that both product characteristics and consumer purchase behaviors play major roles in the successfulness of its marketing on the Internet. If we can identify the factors that impact the use of on-line marketing approach, we can build a framework to help evaluate the chance for a company to succeed in e-commerce.

Key words: Internet marketing, consumer purchase decision, e-tailing, marketing strategy, product category.

1. INTRODUCTION

The Internet has provided a rare opportunity for firms by moving beyond the physical limits of their traditional channels and creating a world-wide virtual community of competition. The potential of the Internet as a commercial medium and market has been documented in a variety of publications [Haffman et al., 1995; Jarvenpaa &Todd 1997]. A recent survey projects a threefold boom in the number of Internet users from today's 300 million to more than a billion by 2003, and new technologies coming online, such as wireless-application-protocol-enabled phones and digital TV [Waters 2000]. A complete report about measuring Internet economy can be found at http://cism.bus.utexas.edu [Barua et al., 1999] that discusses Internet economy layers, assumptions, methodology and findings. Despite the overwhelming statistics regarding the Internet development, both successful and unsuccessful cases of the Internet marketing have been reported. Previous research has identified common problems of e-marketing strategies, including failure to classify product characteristics and inappropriate channel selection, pricing, and promotion strategies [Larson 1998]. We contend that both the product characteristics and the purchasing behaviors of on-line shoppers play important roles in the success of e-marketing. If we can identify the factors that impact the use of an on-line marketing approach and the factors that influence the consumer's buying decision, e-tailers can design their marketing strategy accordingly to maximize customer satisfaction and hence increase total sales.

The objective of this paper is to provide a framework to identify factors that influence consumer buying behavior on different product/service categories over the Internet. The rest of this paper is organized as follows: Section 2 reviews the advantages of using the Internet as a new distribution channel for retailing verses traditional distribution channels. This is done through an analysis of characteristics of the Internet and its three channel functions: communication, transaction, and distribution functions. Our contention is, properly designed marketing strategies that enhance the three channel functions can increase the perceived value of a product. In Section 3, we extend current literature on channel functions and discover possible factors that could maximize the three channel functions. We categorize these factors based on fundamental objectives that consumers intend to achieve when making a purchase online. Section 4 gives the classification of retailing on the Internet. Then, we determine the product characteristics that can benefit the most from those e-commerce advantages and devise marketing strategies accordingly. Section 5 concludes the research and suggests directions for future research.

2. ADVANTAGES OF E-MARKETING APPROACH

Channel selection is a complex task for both researchers and practitioners in marketing. Although Internet marketing has boomed in recent years, most companies have used it mainly for advertising or promoting corporate images. Not many companies have fully utilized the power of Internet marketing as a new channel for making transactions on the Internet. Besides the various technical obstacles, issues such as security of online trading, authentication, tax policies, etc., have yet to be overcome, the main reason that has prevented companies going online is the uncertainty involved as the Internet is an entirely new transaction channel. In the following, we identify the key advantages of Internet marketing recognized by companies participating in Internet marketing.

Marketing activity occurs through three types of channels: communication, transaction, and distribution channels [Peterson 1997]. Although this study focuses on using the Internet as a new transaction and/or distribution channel, there are substantial interactions and overlapping among the activities performed by the three types of channels. Therefore, we need to consider the effect of Internet marketing on all aspects of marketing activities to be able to recognize the true benefits of Internet marketing. The extant literature in Electronic Commerce has documented various advantages for companies to sell directly on the Internet. These advantages can be classified into those three channels based on the functions performed. Table 1 summaries the advantages of the Internet grouped by the three channel functions.

Table 1. Advantages of the Internet marketing approach grouped by the three channel functions

Channel Functions	Advantages
Communication	Improved product information
	Improved price information
	Availability of service, 24 hours a day, 7 days a week
	Lower cost of communication
	Interactivity and the ability to provide information on demand (Peterson et al, 1997; Connolly 1998)
	Real-time inventory update
	On-line technical support
	Quick response of inquiries (Isaac 1998)
	Customized orders (Gardner and Roos 1997; Davy 1998; Marks 1998)
	Post-sale service
	No personal contact
Transaction	Virtual storefront can be reached by all Internet users (Long 1997)
	Lower cost of transaction (Andrews and Trites 1997; Long 1997; Sandilands 1997; McKim 1997)
	Cross-selling opportunities (Eichhorn and Helleis 1997)
	Allow microtransactions (Choi et al., 1997)
	Reduce human errors
	Reduce procurement cycle time
	Possible to customize promotion and sales to individual customers (Hawn 1996)
	Flexible pricing (Hawn 1996)

Channel Functions	Advantages
	Relatively low entry and establishment costs (Peterson et al., 1997)
Distribution	Reduced waiting time to receive product for digital products/services Lower cost of delivery for digital products/services (Edwards et al., 1998) Eliminate huge inventories and overheads (Avery 1997)

3. FACTORS THAT ENHANCE CHANNEL FUNCTIONS

Based on the advantages identified in Table 1, we reviewed and summarized the literature in e-commerce to determine the relevant design and marketing strategies that may enhance the three channel functions. Table 2 shows the 27 factors that were identified from existing research in e-commerce. The factors were again grouped according to the three channel functions. We classified the post-sale service factor into both the communication and the distribution channels to cover both the informational and physical (return or exchange) types of post-sales activities. For example, a well-designed Web site takes advantage of the improved product information and interactivity and the ability to provide information on demand capabilities of e-marketing to enhance the perceived value of products for the communication channel function. On the other hand, the purchase price of product factor can take advantages of the lower cost of transaction and lower inventory level and other related overhead of e-tailing and is relevant to the transaction channel function. Also, some factors can increase the perceived value through multiple channel functions. The 27 factors can be further grouped in a few fundamental objectives as shown in column 3 of Table 2.

Table 2. Factors that enhance channel functions

Channel Functions	Relevant Factors	Fundamental Objectives
Communication	Layout of Website (Richmond 1996) Entertainment (Richmond 1996) Animation (Richmond 1996)	Shopping Enjoyment
	Product Information (Aspinwall 1962; Lilien 1979) Availability of Products (Stewart 1999; Wilder 1996; Corey et al. 1989) Product Quality Assurance (Miracle 1965; Corey et al. 1989) Customized Orders (Kiang et al., 2000; Cohn 1999)	Product Quality
	Price Information (Richmond 1996)	Cost

Channel Functions	Relevant Factors	Fundamental Objectives
	Low Cost of Communication (Hibbard 1998)	
	Interactive Intelligent Applications (Steward and Videlo 1998) Ease of Obtaining Information (Selene 1997; Stewart 1999; Grahl 1998) User Friendliness (Yesawich 1998) Post-purchase Evaluation (Peter and Olson 1996) Post-sale Service (Miracle 1965)	Convenience
	Real-time Inventory Update (Fraone 1998) On-line Technical Support (Wilder 1998) Quick Response to Inquiries, FAQ (Selene 1997)	Time Spent
Transaction	Security (Dye 1998; Larson 1998) Personalized Payment Account; Privacy (Keeney 1998)	Privacy
	Purchase Price of Product (Richmond 1996; Selene 1997) Cost of Transaction (Brack 1998; Choi et al., 1997)	Cost
	Order Complexity (Richmond 1996; Brack 1998; Wilder 1996; Kiang et al., 2000) Reducing Procurement Cycle Time (Carbone 1997)	Time Spent
Distribution	Cost of Delivery (McGovern 1998)	Cost
	Time to Receive Product (Keeney 1998)	Time Spent
	Post-sale Service (Miracle 1965)	Convenience

Fundamental objectives are the fundamental reasons for customers to purchase on the Internet. The overall fundamental objective is to maximize customer satisfaction. We referenced Keeney's means-ends network model [1999] and identified six fundamental objectives: shopping enjoyment, product quality, cost, convenience, time spent, and privacy. Shopping enjoyment is about making shopping a social event, inspiring customers, minimizing worry, disappointment and regret, and maximizing customer confidence. Product quality includes issues such as maximizing price/quality relationship, ensuring quality of product, and maximizing functionality of purchased item. The cost objective looks at all types of costs associated with Internet shopping, which include product cost, tax cost, shipping cost, Internet cost, and travel cost. For maximizing convenience, the issues considered include purchasing convenience, time flexibility in purchasing, quality after-sales service, easy return process, shopping effort, personal hassle, and ease of finding product. The time factor concerns purchase time, processing time, payment time, queuing time, time to find product, communication time, search time, time to order product, time to gather information, and time to select a product. It also considers the delivery, shipping, and dispatch time that it takes for the customer to actually receive the product. The privacy issue addresses avoiding being placed on electronic mailing lists and no face-to-fact contact.

The importance of each channel function to the marketing of a product is greatly affected by the type of product. For example, for commodity goods, shopping enjoyment and product quality will be less important then reducing the overall transaction cost of the product. However, for specialty goods, the opposite may be the case. In the following section, we discuss the classification of product/services selling on the Internet

4. CLASSIFICATION OF PRODUCTS/SERVICES SELLING ON INTERNET

There is a broad range of products and services marketed on the Internet that range from consumable goods to durable goods. Services marketed on the Internet also range from on-line newspapers to business-wide consultation. Instead of modeling the problem at individual product level, we group the products into categories and analyzing the advantages of Internet marketing along each product group. This will provide a general picture regarding the effect of each factor (advantage) to the particular type of product. Once the classification grid is established, it can be used as the basis for analyzing individual product.

We follow Peterson et al. [1997] to classify products selling on the Internet based on three dimensions: tangibility of products (Digital or Tangible), frequency of purchase (Frequent or Infrequent), and degree of differentiation (High or Low differentiation). Tangibility specifies whether the value proposition of a product is physical or informational. For example, we define music CDs and software packages as intangible goods since they can be stored and transmitted digitally. The second dimension is the frequency of purchase. Generally speaking, frequently purchased products cost less, while infrequently purchased products tend to be more expensive. The third dimension is the degree of differentiation in the current e-market. If many e-tailers carry the same product, we categorize this product as being in a more competitive market, whereas specialty goods that have few or no substitutes are considered to be in a less competitive market. We use this classification to examine the relationships between optimal channel function strategies and purchase behavior of online shoppers in the next section.

In order to maximize the product perceived value through the three channel functions, it is important that we understand the differences in customers' needs for different categories of products. We label each product group using a three-letter acronym that represents the values of the three dimensions. For example, the first category, DHF, stands for digital, high differentiation, and frequently purchased products, and TLI stands for tangible, low differentiation and infrequently purchased products. Table 3 is a framework that links the product characteristics with the relative importance of each channel function. A check mark (x) in the box means marketing effort to improve that fundamental objective is important for that product group. Among the three dimensions, value proposition has the dominant effect because digital products can take advantages of using the Internet for all the three channel functions. The second important factor is the product customization potential of the products or services, and that is followed by frequency of purchase. From Table 3, we can derive the implications of marketing strategies according to the importance of each fundamental objective to the product group. For example, in the segment of tangible, frequently purchased, and competitive markets, products are likely to be familiar to targeted consumers. Therefore, the efforts to enhance shopping enjoyment, provide convenience, and assure product quality are less critical, while reducing total cost, shortening the lead time, and offering an easy return process are more essential. Therefore, e-tailers can improve the distribution channel function by shortening delivery time and reducing price (including shipping and handling) to improve the overall perceived channel value. For improving post-sales services, it will be harder for online-only retailers such as Amozon.com to compete with companies like BarnesandNoble.com that have retail stores nationwide to allow easy return or exchanges of books purchased online. Generally speaking, for specialty goods or in a less competitive market, the communication channel function will be pertinent in providing product information, quality assurance, and shopping enjoyment. On the other hand, for commodity products that are highly competitive, issues such as how to reduce cost and procurement cycle time will be more important to the customers. Quick response in the communication function is important to all categories. In general, the communication channel function is less important for frequently purchased products but becomes more important for less frequently purchased and more expensive products. For digital products, the distribution of the product is through the Internet. Thus it will take no time for the customer to receive the products and the delivery cost is negligible. Therefore, the distribution channel function becomes less of a concern for e-tailers providing digital products/services. However, for e-tailers selling tangible or physical products, especially for frequently purchased goods, how to reduce delivery cost and minimize the time to receive product are important issues when devising their marketing strategies. The convenience of post-sales services is important for all types of products, especially for products in a highly competitive market, but is less of a problem for digital products.

Table 3. Characteristics of products and corresponding marketing strategy implications

Channel Functions	Fundamental Objective	DHF	DHI	DLF	DLI	THF	THI	TLF	TLI
Communication	Shopping Enjoyment				X				X
	Product Quality				X				X
	Cost			X	X			X	X
	Convenience				X				X
	Response Time			X	X			X	X
Transaction	Privacy	X	X	X	X	X	X	X	X
	Cost			X	X			X	X
	Time Spent	X		X		X		X	
Distribution	Cost	X		X		X		X	
	Delivery Time	X		X		X		X	
	Post-Sales Services			X	X			X	X

D – Digital, T - Tangible, H – High differentiation, L – Low differentiation, F – Frequently purchased, I – Infrequently purchased.

The framework presented in Table 3 is not intended to provide universal rules for all e-tailers to develop their marketing strategies. Based on different classification schemes, the product categories can be further refined or modified. Each table cell's entry will support more discussion and is bound to change with the evolution of e-commerce. The fundamental objective of this research is to propose a framework that can help e-tailers to position their companies and to identify key success factors on which to focus their marketing efforts.

5. CONCLUSIONS AND FUTURE RESEARCH DIRECTIONS

The rapid developments of on-line computing technology make it imperative for business to seriously consider the Internet to avoid losing competitive advantage. A Web site gives direct contact between the organization and the consumer. However, product characteristics play an important role in whether the organization may benefit from utilizing the Web as a means of direct sales.

The structure of the consumer market depends on a variety of factors, but in general it evolves from the decision-making process of market participants. In this study, we emphasize the importance of fundamental objectives of online shoppers and derive implications for e-marketing strategies, especially in channel-function strategies. The objective of this research is concentrated on practical decision problems that impact a wide range of companies. Due to the complexity of the problem, in this research we have limited the scope to focus only on the product characteristics and their effects on the success of Internet marketing. When making channel selection decisions, we need to consider all the factors in the marketing mix – product, promotion, price, and distribution – as a whole. Other factors that may impact the performance of Internet marketing include: 1) the firm's current distribution structure and channel relationships, 2) the size of the company, 3) the promotion strategies, and 4) the pricing structure, etc., that are specific to individual companies. Future research can study the cases of individual companies to evaluate and design channels that would help with the successful launch of new products. In our future research, we also plan to justify the recommendations suggested in Table 3 through the application of the Delphi technique, a qualitative forecasting method that helps to consolidate multiple expert opinions to arrive at a consensus estimate. The Delphi technique involves repeated iterations of subjective estimates by multiple experts. Experts respond to a sequence of questionnaires. After each iteration, answers from experts are summarized and incorporated in the next round questionnaire. Multiple experts in the area of e-tailing marketing strategies will be asked to provide opinions on the implications of marketing strategies on different product categories. The results from the Delphi method will be used to validate or adjust the recommendations presented in Table 3 regarding the importance of each fundamental objective to the different product categories.

REFERENCES

Andrews, Jonathan; Trites, Gerald, "Net Sales." CA Magazine v130, n6 (Aug 1997):12-15.

Aspinwall, L. V., The Characteristics of Goods Theory, Managerial Marketing: Perspectives and Viewpoints, IL: Irwin 1962: 633-643.

Avery, Susan, "Online tool removes costs from process.", Purchasing v123, n6 (Oct 23, 1997):79-81.

Barua, A, J. Pinnell, J. Shutter, and A.B. Whinston, "Measuring the Internet Economy," Research Report, Center for Research in Electronic Commerce, 1999.

Brack, K., "Source of the future," Industrial Distribution (Oct 1998): 76-80.

Carbone, J., "Purchasing tools for the Internet toolbox," Purchasing (Dec 11, 1997): S26-S30.

Choi, S.-Y., D.O. Stahl and A.B. Whinston, "Cyberpayments and the Future of Electronic Commerce," presented at ICEC Cyberpayments '97.

Cohn, M., "Back-end Web developments," Catalog Age (Feb 1999): 75.

Corey, E.R., Cespedes, F.V., and Rangan V.K., "Going-to-Market," Harvard Business School Press (1989): 43-59.

Dye, P., "Online buyers turn to Net for product information," Marketing week (Oct 8, 1998): 43.

Edwards, Nick; Handcock, Sarah; Mullen John, "Electronic commerce: reality bytes.", Supply Management v3, n8 (Apr 9, 1998):32-34.

Eichhorn, Ole; Helleis, Sylvia, "Cyberspace cross-selling." Credit Union Management v20, n9 (Sep 1997):28.

Fraone, G., "Going once, going twice...," *Electronic Business* (Jun 1998): 28.

Garden, A., "Knowing when to trust a Website," *New Zealand Management* (Nov 2000): 104.

Grahl, C., "Shopping on the Internet: A beginner's guide," *Nursing Homes* (Jul 1998): 22-25.

Haffman, D.L., T.P. Novak, and P. Chatterjee, "Commercial Scenarios for the Web: Opportunities and Challenges," JCMC special issue on Electronic Commerce, M. McLaughlin and S. Rafaeli (eds.), Dec. 1995.

Hibbard, J., "Supply-side Economics," InformationWEEK (Nov 1998): 85-87.

Jarvenpaa, S.L. and Todd, P.A., "Consumer Reactions to Electronic Shopping on the World Wide Web," International Journal of Electronic Commerce, winter 1996-97, v 1, n 2, pp.59-88.

Keeney, R. L., "The Value of Internet Commerce to the Customer," *Management Science, Vol. 45, No. 4, April* 1999.

Kiang, Y. M., T.S. Raghu, and K.H. Shang, "Marketing on the Internet- Who can benefit from an on-line marketing approach?," Decision Support Systems, 27, (2000): 383-393.

Larson, M., "Search for the secure transaction; Barriers to E-Commerce falling," Quality (Aug 1998): 61-63.

Lilien, G. L., "ADVISOR 2: Modeling the Marketing Mix Decision for Industrial Products," Management Science (Feb 25, 1979): 191-204.

Long, Johnny, " E-COMMERCE: Doing What's Best for Business," Data Communications v26, n16 (Nov 21, 1997): 77-80.

McGovern, J Michael, "One-Stop Shopping," Transportation & Distribution, May 1998, 39(5): 39-42.

Miracle, G. E., "Product Characteristics and Marketing Strategy," Journal of Marketing (Jan 29, 1965): 18-24.

Peter, J.P. and Olson J.C. *Consumer Behavior and Marketing Strategy*. 4th Edition, Irwin 1996: 196-197.

Peterson, R.A., Balasubramanian, S. and Bronnenberg B.J., "Exploring the Implications of the Internet for Consumer Marketing," Journal of the Academy of Marketing Science, Vol. 25, No. 4, PP. 329-346, 1997.

Richmond, A., "Enticing on-line shoppers to buy- a human behavior study," *Computer Network and ISDN systems* (May 1996): 1469-80.

Sandilands, Ben, "The Internet: A tool of the trade?" Australian Accountant v67, n11 (Dec 1997):14-17.

Selene, I., "Are customers buying into technology?," *LIMRA's MarketFacts*, V16, n4, (Jul/Aug 1997): 36-40.

Stewart, T. A., "Larry Bossidy's new role model: Michael Dell," *Fortune* (Apr 12, 1999): 166-168.

Steward, S and Videlo J., "Intelligent on-line purchasing," *British Telecommunications Engineering* (Apr 1998): 36-42.

Waters, C Dickinson, "Second Coming: 'Passing' of Internet One Give Birth to Internet Two," Nation's Restaurant News, Dec. 11, 2000, 34(50): 29.

Wilder, C., "E-commerce emerges," Informationweek. (Jun 17, 1996): 14-15.

-　　, "Intermediaries Must Meet the Internet Challenge," Informationweek, n680, (May 4, 1998):3ER.

Yesawich, P. "More Cyberspeculation," *Lodging Hospitality* (Jul 1998): 20.

Chapter 16

To Surf Or To Ride

An Analysis of Channel Competition Between Electronic and Retail Stores

Beomsoo Kim and Byungtae Lee

Information and Decision Sciences Department, University of Illinois at Chicago 601 S. Morgan St. MC294, Chicago, IL 60607-7124 USA beomsoo@uic.edu: Information and Decision Sciences Department, University of Illinois at Chicago 601 S. Morgan St. MC294, Chicago, IL 60607-7124 USA blee@uic.edu

Abstract We study the competition between two shopping channels, i.e. electronic stores and retail stores, to focus on the profitability and expansion strategies of these channels as a function of consumer characteristics and store cost structure. A consumer's choice of a store is determined by price differences, perceived risk in online buying, network comfort level, and retail discomfort level (logical distance between a consumer and a retail store). Based on Hotelling's model of spatial competition, we find that the number of retail stores has no effect on the optimal pricing strategies of either the electronic store or the retail store. The result holds even when the retail stores belong to one chain. The optimal prices of the two channels move in the same direction at different rates with changes in the importance of network comfort level.

Key words: Channel Competition, Transaction Cost, Network Comfort Level, Perceived Risk

1. INTRODUCTION

The proliferation of the Internet and related technologies and applications has led to a new form of market place known as the electronic store. By reducing the time and transaction cost elements inherent in commerce, electronic stores are experiencing rapid growth and are in the process of securing an important niche in the business world. In a traditional retail channel, a producer sells to a wholesaler, who sells to a retailer, who then sells the product to consumers. By contrast, the electronic store sells by publishing product information on the Internet and other public data networks, taking orders, and using different distribution channels to get the product to the consumer. This research focuses on the competition between an electronic and one or more retail stores. We examine the proposition that differences in consumers' retail discomfort level, perceived online shopping risk, and network comfort level explain the selection of a marketing channel. Besides frequent references to these factors, we choose them to explain how relentless technical progress and diffusion may shape the future of marketing channels.

We show that the number of retail stores has no effect on the optimal pricing strategies of either the electronic or the retail stores. This result does not change even when the retail stores belong to one chain. This finding suggests that a retail store cannot compete with an electronic store simply by opening more identical outlets for a larger geographical coverage. We also find that the optimal prices of the two channels move in the same direction as, but at different rates from, the cost associated with consumers' network comfort level. Given that the unit "surfing" cost is declining due to technological advances, this result suggests that both stores will reduce their prices[15] over time; however, the demand faced by the electronic store increases, while that of the retail store decreases.

The remainder of the paper is organized as follows. Relevant prior literature and the motivation for the study are discussed in Section 2. Section 3 describes the basic scenario analyzed in the paper. The model assumptions and their justification are also provided in this section. Section 4 examines the question of whether a geographically limited physical retail store can compete with an electronic store through the deployment of multiple identical outlets. Future research directions and the conclusion are presented in Sections 5 and 6 respectively.

[15] The price reduction by the retail store is shown to be higher than that of the electronic store.

2. MOTIVATION AND PRIOR RESEARCH

Since the advent of the World Wide Web, "the Internet has emerged as a shopping channel with undeniable power to facilitate and increase sales of a growing range of products" (Ernst & Young, Special Report 1998; 1999). With commercial activity on the Internet gaining momentum, and with technological developments involving more secure means of making payments, sending documents, and verifying the identity of the consumer, electronic stores are opening up a new vista of opportunities (Hoffman and Novak, 1996; Margherio, 1998). However, Hoffman, Kalsbeek and Novak (1996) suggests "tapping the enormous potential of the Internet as a commercial medium and market is proving to be challenging." As indicated by the Ernst & Young Special Report (1998), only 7 percent of U.S. households have purchased products or services over the Internet to date. Further, a majority of retailers and manufacturers have no immediate plans to start offering products online (Ernst & Young, 1998; 1999). We view the current situation as a transient period where consumers are facing a new way of organizing economic activity in the form of electronic markets.

This research considers relevant trends in consumer demographics and store cost structures, and analyzes whether one channel is likely to dominate over the other in the near future. For example, if electronic stores are expected to enjoy significant economic advantages over traditional retail stores, then those retailers and manufacturers who are not considering the electronic medium as a marketing and selling channel may face a serious disadvantage in coping up with Internet based competitors. Further, we analyze how changes in consumer demographics are likely to affect the demand, pricing policy, investment priorities and business expansion strategies of electronic and retail stores.

Since the electronic and the traditional retail stores represent two different marketing channels, we turn to transaction cost theory to understand and explain the existence of the two structures, and to analyze the potential dominance of one over the other. Transaction cost economics (e.g., Coase, 1937; Williamson, 1989) has been deployed to explain changes in the organization of economic activity. This theory identifies two coordination mechanisms for economic transactions: market and hierarchy, and a continuum of hybrid forms between these two extremes. The transaction cost of an economic exchange determines the most desirable form of coordination mechanism from this spectrum. Malone, Yates, and Benjamin (1987) studied the impact of Information Technology (IT) on economic coordination mechanisms, and predicted the emergence of electronic hierarchies, electronic hybrid forms and the electronic market.

In characterizing channel selection behavior, we focus on factors such as price, retail discomfort level, perceived risks, and merchandise characteristics, which are also identified by Lusch (1982) as important attributes that consumers use to choose retail stores. A *Wall Street Journal* article (April 25, 1994) pointed out factors such as time, traffic and parking problems, which discourage shopping at retail stores. Similarly, the 1998 Ernst & Young report suggests that consumer perceptions about security constitute a significant hindrance to Web commerce.

Spence et al. (1970) and Cox and Rich (1964) find that the risk perceived in an indirect shopping situation is higher than that experienced in a corresponding in-store setting. Spence et al. confirm that consumers perceive less risk in buying from a store or salesperson than in buying from other marketing channels such as mail order or cable shopping. Given these findings, it is reasonable to assume that perceived risk is a deterrent to shopping on the Internet. The uncertainty generated by the inability to examine the item and to interact with the seller, as well as security-related fears, might be sufficiently high to keep many shoppers away from buying on the Internet. This study examines consumer's behavior and retailing strategies by comparing the level of perceived risk in buying from electronic versus traditional retail stores.

In terms of modeling the competition between the two channels, the Bertrand model assumes that two firms produce identical goods which are "non-differentiated" in that they are perfect substitutes in the consumers' utility function (Tirole, 1988). Consequently, consumers buy from the producer who charges the lowest price. If the firms charge the same price, each firm faces a demand schedule equal to half of the market demand at the common price. Hence, price is the only variable of interest to consumers, and no firm can raise its price above marginal cost without losing its entire market share. In practice, such an assumption is ill-founded. Some consumers will prefer buying a product even at a small premium because it is available at a closer store, can be delivered faster, or comes with superior post-sale service; other consumers will remain faithful to the high-price firm because they are unaware of the existence of other shopping channels and brands, or are not familiar with using electronic systems for shopping; still other consumers will be concerned that alternative brands do not have the same quality, or that the alternatives will not satisfy their preferences as well.

Hotelling's (1929) two-stage model of spatial competition is an extension of the Bertrand model. Hotelling uses location and price as strategic variables to find an equilibrium. We extend the simple price competition model to include other factors that affect consumers' choice. We assume that the two types of stores offer the same products. The net utilities derived by consumers in buying the same product from the two channels may differ due to a variety of factors including perceived risk of electronic shopping, network comfort level, retail discomfort level, and price differences (which are determined endogenously within the model). The questions addressed in the paper include the following: When will consumers use an electronic store rather than a retail store, and vice versa? What are the critical factors that give each type of store comparative advantages and effective marketing strategies? How much and in what way does the consumers' network comfort level or experience with information technology, especially the Internet, impact store strategies? What is the impact of the perceived risk of online shopping on the strategies of the stores? How will technological progress and emerging cyber-intermediaries (electronic stores) change the nature of the competition?

3. THE BASIC MODEL

We consider a market with two supply agents (an electronic store and a traditional retail store) and many consuming agents (consumers). Each agent wants to trade at least one unit of an identical commodity. The minimum requirement to be considered as an electronic store in this paper is that consumers of such a store discover and order products electronically so that price discovery and price setting are at least partially conducted through electronic media. While an electronic store on the Web is our primary concern in this paper, other forms of electronic channels, such as mail order, shopping TV channels, and toll-free telephone order systems, seem to share similar characteristics. The unique factor incorporated in our model is the customer's skill in using the computer network and network availability due to a premature stage of technology diffusion. Mail order and telephone shopping may not exhibit such problems.

3.1 Model Assumptions

3.1.1 Consumer Transaction Costs

From often-cited differences between electronic and conventional trading, we identify different types of transaction cost factors associated with the two competing organizations. As manifested in comparative analysis, we select the transaction cost elements because they differ in the degree of the firm's control. Some factors are of a rather macro-economic level beyond a firm's control. For example, the demography of computer (Internet-surfing) skills may be the product of technology diffusion and technological innovation.

As the original Hotelling's model describes, in retail store shopping, transportation cost is a major component of the transaction cost. This refers to the time and dollar costs incurred by a consumer as she travels a distance t to purchase a product. Due to these costs, consumers prefer a closer store to a more remote one, all other conditions being equal. Economides and Siow (1988) show that there is a tradeoff between market liquidity and the distance between market and consumer, *ceteris paribus*.

3.1.2 Network Comfort Level

An electronic store does not come without its transaction cost elements (Sarkar et al., 1995). Sometimes even locating an electronic store takes time. While recent Web applications have increased the public's network comfort level, searching for relevant information in cyberspace can involve significant effort (Ravindran et al., 1996; Barua et al., 1997). The time and resources a consumer spends on locating and ordering products over the Internet may depend on various factors such as the consumer's Internet literacy, network traffic, computer power, network connection speed, etc. Collectively, these factors constitute a consumer's "network comfort level", and are denoted as α, which lies between 0 (unable to use the Net) and 1 (the greatest Net savvy).

3.1.3 Perceived Risks

We postulate other opportunity costs of shopping in cyberspace stores. They result from two sources: quality discovery costs and a risky business environment. Malone et al. (1987) relate transaction costs to the complexity of a product – the higher the product complexity, the higher the associated transaction cost. According to Nelson (1970), a consumer's sources of information can be divided into three categories – description, inspection, and experience (Nelson, 1970). Some attributes of a product can be collected from a description in words, sounds, or pictures. Other attributes can be determined only upon inspection of the product – by physically handling and examining the object. Finally, some attributes can be determined only by experience (experience goods), by actually using the product. These three information sources cause differences in perceived risks of buying from electronic and retail stores, because each store provides different information through different media. Unless the product is well known or completely standardized, consumers using an electronic store are likely to perceive higher risks in terms of quality discovery since they cannot fully examine or experience the product.

Another source of risk arises from the potentially unsafe nature of electronic trading. Suspicion regarding the business ethics of electronic store operations and the non-secure nature of payment systems on the Net result in a higher perceived risk for many consumers.

In our model, for a given product, x represents the differences in perceived risk between electronic and traditional channels. We assume that electronic stores generally have higher opportunity costs because of the reasons cited above. Of course, there may be a correlation between the network comfort level α and the perceived risk difference x. For example, a novice user may incur a higher surfing cost, and s/he may perceive a higher risk-related opportunity cost due to a lack of experience and confidence in electronic shopping. For simplicity, however, we assume that the electronic store *search costs* and *risk opportunity costs* are independent. It is conceivable that consumers derive different utilities from different experiences with various distribution channels. Shopping can be an entertainment activity beyond an economic one for trading. Such psychological aspects are beyond the scope of this research. Consumers' choice of a store is based on the utilities they perceive. These utilities are denoted by functions $U_e(\alpha, x)$ and $U_r(t)$ for electronic and retail store shopping respectively.[16]

The following shows the factors which determine the levels of utility when a customer buys a product from one of the marketing channels. With normalized t and α,

$$U_e(\alpha,x) = U_0 - \{Pe + (1-\alpha)\, C_\alpha + x\, C_x\}$$
$$U_r(t) = U_0 - \{P_r + tC_t\},$$

where

U_0 : consumer surplus from consuming a product
P_i : price of a product at a store i ($i = e$ or r)
α : network comfort level ($0 \leq \alpha \leq 1$)
C_α : search cost coefficient ($C_\alpha > 0$)
x : risk level ($0 \leq x \leq 1$)
C_x : risk opportunity cost coefficient
t : discomfort level ($0 \leq t \leq 1$) for retail store
C_t : logical transportation cost coefficient

[16] Throughout this paper, subscripts *e* and *r* denote the electronic and physical retail stores respectively.

3.1.4 Channel Costs

For given demand d_i for channel i, a generalized total cost function is given by:

$c_i = a_i + b_i d_i^k$
a_i = fixed cost, where $a_i \geq 0$
b_i = variable cost, where ($b_i \geq 0$)

Note that the parameter k represents economies of scale. For the sake of analysis and without sacrificing generality, we first use an affine cost function ($k = 1$) in this section. However, different returns to scale are also examined later.

3.2 Analysis and Results

In order to find the optimal strategies of each store, we use the concept of a pure-strategy non-cooperative Nash equilibrium. From the profit function below, we derive the best response functions of each store. A Nash equilibrium in price, a Bertrand equilibrium, is determined from the intersection of the best response functions of the stores.

3.2.1 Demand Analysis

For a given logical distance t to a retail store, we describe a *marginal* consumer who is indifferent about shopping between an electronic and a retail store:

$$U_e(\alpha{:}x) = U_r(t)$$

$$\alpha^*(t) = \frac{P_e - P_r + C_\alpha - tC_t + xC_x}{C_\alpha} \qquad (1)$$

Figure 1 shows how channel choice depends on the attributes, α and t. The unit square for the case in this figure represents the total demand. The demand for each channel is determined by how $\alpha^*(t)$ divides the total demand. Let $\tilde{t}_1 = \{t{:}\ \alpha^*(t) = 1\}$ and $\tilde{t}_0 = \{t{:}\ \alpha^*(t) = 0\}$. Based on the levels of $\tilde{t}_0$, $\tilde{t}_1$, $\alpha^*(0)$, and $\alpha^*(1)$, the demand in this duopoly market has four cases as shown in Figure 1.

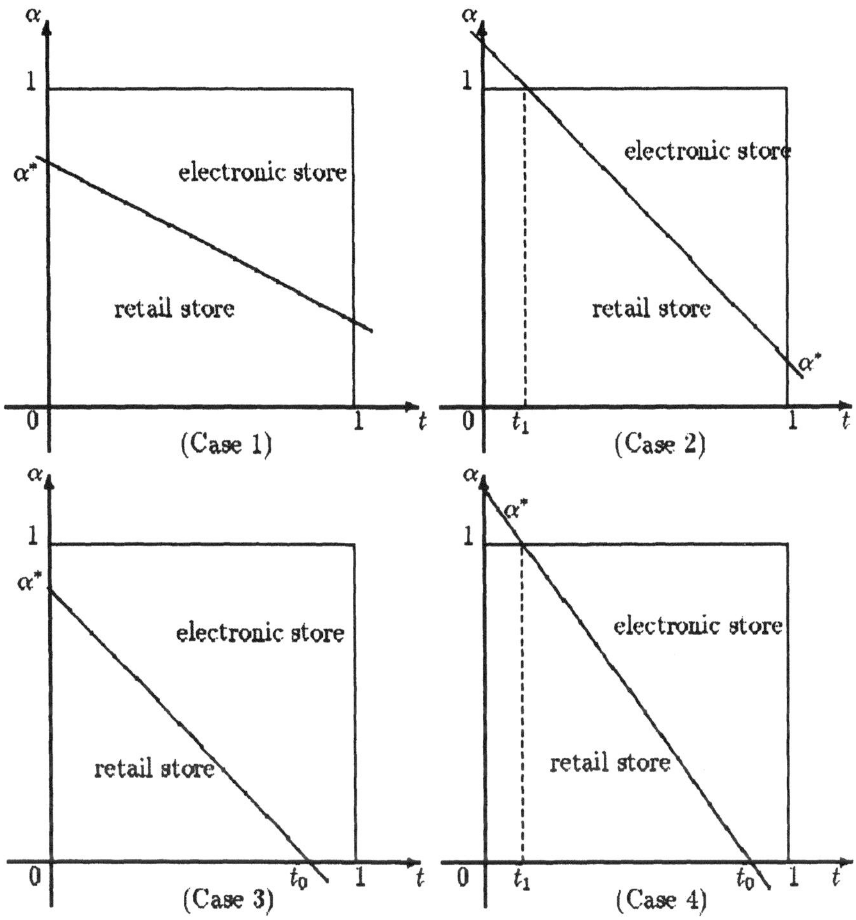

Figure 1. Demand Analysis for Electronic and Retail Stores

From the above, we have the following conditions for price differences:

Case 1: $x\,C_x \leq P_r - P_e \leq C_a + x\,C_x - C_t$, *where* $C_a \geq C_t$ (2)
Case 2: $xC_x - C_t \leq P_r - P_e \leq min\{x\,C_x, x\,C_x + C_a - C_t\}$ (3)
Case 3: $max\{x\,C_x, x\,C_x + C_a - C_t\} \leq P_r - P_e \leq C_a + x\,C_x$ (4)
Case 4: $x\,C_x + C_a - C_t \leq P_r - P_e \leq x\,C_x$, *where* $C_t \geq C_a$ (5)

Case 1 is a fairly competitive situation where the two stores will split the demand, regardless of the logical distance *t* and network comfort level, α. In Case 2, an electronic store cannot bring consumers who are closer than $\tilde{t}_1$ to the retail store. In Case 3, the electronic store has its advantage where consumers with longer travel distance ($t \geq \tilde{t}_1$) to the retail store are locked up. Both stores have some guaranteed demand in Case 4. Consumers with a shorter distance than $\tilde{t}_1$ have to be loyal to the retail store, while those with distances greater than $\tilde{t}_0$ shop from the electronic store.

Note that if $\tilde{t}_1 > 1$, i.e., $P_e + x\,C_x \geq P_r + C_t$, then the retail store becomes a monopoly. On the other hand, if $\tilde{t}_0 \leq 0$, i.e., $P_e + x\,C_x + C_a \leq P_r$, the retail store cannot compete any more. These facts, along with the conditions defined in Figure 1, depict that price differences and cost structures of surfing and transportation determine various cases of competition, as depicted in Figure 2.

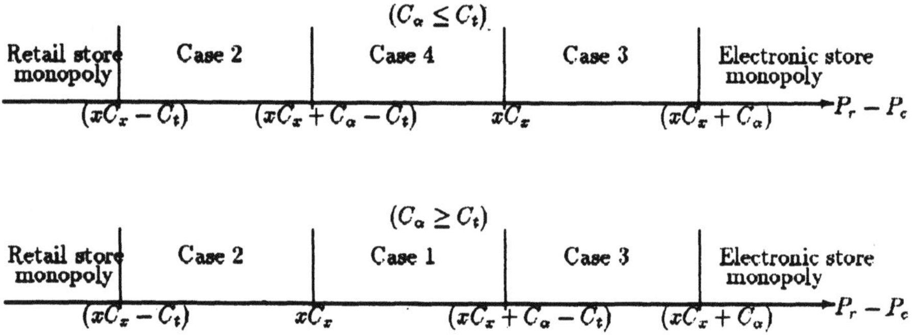

Figure 2. Monopoly and Four Competitive Market Conditions

Of course, differences in prices under head-to-head competition are ultimately constrained by the marketing costs of the channels. In the next section, with Nash equilibrium prices, competition structures are defined by the difference in marketing costs (b_r - b_e), as summarized in Equations in Section 4.

Without sacrificing generality, we assume a uniform distribution of α, and the derived demands of the two stores are shown in Table 1.

Table 1. Demands of the Two Channels

Cases	Retail Store Demand (d_r)	Electronic Store Demand ($d_e = 1 - d_r$)
Case 1	$\frac{P_e - P_r + C_a - C_t/2 + xC_x}{C_a}$	$\frac{P_r - P_e + C_t/2 - xC_x}{C_a}$
Case 2	$1 - \frac{(P_e - P_r - C_t + xC_x)^2}{2C_tC_a}$	$\frac{(P_e - P_r - C_t + xC_x)^2}{2C_tC_a}$
Case 3	$\frac{(P_e - P_r + C_a + xC_x)^2}{2C_tC_a}$	$1 - \frac{(P_e - P_r + C_a + xC_x)^2}{2C_tC_a}$

Cases	Retail Store Demand (d_r)	Electronic Store Demand ($d_e = 1-d_r$)
Case 4	$\frac{P_r - P_e - C_\alpha/2 + C_t - xC_x}{C_t}$	$\frac{P_e - P_r + C_\alpha/2 + xC_x}{C_t}$

3.2.2 Nash Equilibrium

For given market demand in Table 1 and cost in Section 3.1.4, firms maximize their profits as shown in Equation 6. In the competitive environment, firms have to make decisions considering their competitor's strategies. The *best response function* in Equation 7 shows this competitive strategy set.

$$\max_{P_i} \Pi_i(P_i, P_j) = P_i d_i(P_i, P_j) - c_i = (P_i - b_i)d_i + a_i \tag{6}$$

$$\frac{\partial \Pi_i}{\partial P_i} = d_i + (P_i - b_i)\frac{\partial d_i}{\partial P_i} = 0 \tag{7}$$

where j denotes i's competitor. The resulting Nash equilibria are summarized in Table 2. This competitive equilibrium shows the optimal strategy for each firm and relationship among strategic factors in the market environment.

Table 2. Nash Equilibrium Prices

Case	Electronic Store (P_e^*)
1	$(C_\alpha + C_t/2 - xC_x + 2b_e + b_r)/3$
2	$\{(C_t - xC_x + 7b_e + b_r) + \sqrt{(xC_x - C_t + b_e - b_r)^2 + 8C_tC_\alpha}\}/8$
3	$\{(-5C_\alpha - 5xC_x + 3b_e + 5b_r) + 3\sqrt{(C_\alpha + xC_x + b_e - b_r)^2 + 8C_\alpha C_t}\}/8$
4	$(-C_\alpha/2 + 2C_t - xC_x + 2b_e + b_r)/3$
Case	**Retail Store (P_r^*)**
1	$(2C_\alpha - C_t/2 + xC_x + b_e + 2b_r)/3$
2	$\{(5xC_x - 5C_t + 5b_e + 3b_r) + 3\sqrt{(xC_x - C_t + b_e - b_r)^2 + 8C_tC_\alpha}\}/8$
3	$\{(C_\alpha + xC_x + b_e + 7b_r) + \sqrt{(xC_x + C_\alpha + b_e - b_r)^2 + 8C_\alpha C_t}\}/8$
4	$(C_\alpha/2 + C_t + xC_x + b_e + 2b_r)/3$

3.2.3 Reaction Functions: Strategic Complements

In this section, we discuss the characteristics of price competition between the two stores. Equation 8 involves the second derivative of profits with respect to price.

$$\frac{\partial^2 \Pi_i}{\partial P_i^2} = 2\frac{\partial d_i}{\partial P_i} + (P_i - b_i)\frac{\partial^2 d_i}{\partial P_i^2} = 0 \qquad (8)$$

From demands in Table 1 and price ranges defined in Equations 2-5, it can be shown that $\frac{\partial^2 \Pi_i}{\partial P_i^2} < 0$ and $\frac{\partial^2 \Pi_i}{\partial P_i \partial P_j} > 0$. This leads to the following proposition:

Proposition 3.1 The optimal pricing strategies of the two stores are strategic complements.

This proposition is in conformance with the findings of Bulow et al. (1985). That is, a store tends to set a high price in relation to its competitor if the latter's price is low, while a store will lower its price relative to the competitor's price if the competitor sets a higher price. In this manner, a store will optimally increase its market share through pricing when the opponent increases its price because the demand of the store is a decreasing function of the difference between its own price and the competitor's price.

3.2.4 Comparative Statics

Table 3 summarizes the comparative statics for Case 1. Using rationale based on transaction cost economics, Malone et al. (1987) predicted that electronic markets may easily trade goods with less complexity in their description. Our comparative statics support this claim. As perceived risk (x) increases,[17] an electronic store has to lower its price at the rate of $\frac{C_x}{3}$. Further, its demand decreases at the rate of $\frac{C_x}{3C_a}$. Thus, an electronic store loses its profit, not only from reducing its price, but also from losing market share when the perceived risk increases. The electronic store can adopt various measures to mitigate this problem: building reputation, advertising to establish credibility, providing a money-back guarantee, and offering an assortment of products with low risk. In addition, the improvement of transaction security through encryption, cryptography practices such as digital signatures and certificates, and legal regulations (Kalakota and Whinston, 1996) will also reduce the risk-related cost (C_a).

[17] Perceived risk can increase due to various reasons, including increasing product complexity.

Several recent studies show that there are some markets where consumers are growing disenchanted with traditional retail stores. Fear of crime and concerns about personal safety and convenience keep a growing number of shoppers away from suburban stores and urban retail areas (Hickey 1994). As the logical transportation cost (C_t) changes, the demand also changes in the same direction as prices. Since the discomfort level increases, the profit of a retail store decreases, and an electronic store has a chance to increase profit by raising prices and expanding market share. It is well documented that increased transportation costs adversely affect retail store business. For example, in Chicago and San Francisco, where this cost factor is very high because of traffic and parking, Peapod, an electronic store, delivers groceries, liquor, prescriptions, and even subway tokens. This company focuses on consumers with a high discomfort level. These consumers spend five times more than consumers in a retail store, and pay an extra 12 percent for the service from Peapod (Kalakota and Whinston 1996). By understanding its consumer characteristics and competitive advantages, Peapod has been successful in its online business.

Table 3. Comparative Statics (Case 1)

$\partial X \setminus \partial Y$	d_e^*	d_r^*	P_e^*	P_r^*
X	$-\frac{C_x}{3C_a}$	$\frac{C_x}{3C_a}$	$-\frac{C_x}{3}$	$\frac{C_x}{3}$
b_e	$-\frac{1}{3C_a}$	$\frac{1}{3C_a}$	2/3	1/3
b_r	$\frac{1}{3C_a}$	$-\frac{1}{3C_a}$	1/3	2/3
C_t	$\frac{1}{C_a}$	$-\frac{1}{C_a}$	1/6	1/6
C_α	$\frac{(xC_x-C_a-C_t/2-b_r+b_e)}{3C_a^2}$	$\frac{(C_a+C_t/2-xC_x+b_r-b_e)}{3C_a^2}$	1/3	2/3

It is interesting to observe that each store can increase its price as the surfing cost increases. This result may not seem intuitive since a low network comfort level only reduces the utility of consumers when they shop at electronic stores. However, note that the change in unit surfing cost (C_α) does not affect all consumers uniformly. The surfing costs for a consumer with skill level α is $(1-\alpha)C_\alpha$. That is, users with lower surfing skill suffer more than those who have the right equipment and experience. Figure 3 illustrates this point. Line *(A,B)* denotes the indifference curve α_t defined in Equation 1. If the cost of surfing, C_α, is reduced, line *(A,C)* becomes the new indifference curve, so that retail store loses demand as much as ΔABC. If possible, the retail store will lower its price to re-capture its demand, which moves the indifference curve to line *(D,E)*. If the price reduction is not high enough compared to its demand prior to surfing cost change, the demand recovered through price reduction *(ΔADF)* may be much smaller than the lost demand *(ΔBEF)*.

The above finding underscores the importance of many on-going improvements in the conduct of electronic commerce. The World Wide Web and related applications have lowered Internet usage barriers, and the exponential performance/price improvements in desktop computers and low flat-fee schemes adopted by Internet Service Providers are responsible for 40 and 20 percent of U.S. households having at least one personal computer and Internet access, respectively (Ernst & Young, 1998). Combined with a rapid shift in the distribution of a Net-literate population, electronic stores are gaining momentum. The accelerated diffusion of the Internet and computer education, as well as technical progress such as more user-friendly Web browsers, more efficient search engines and services to reduce search time by cyber-intermediaries are lowering C_a at no additional costs to electronic stores. This can be highly advantageous to electronic stores in competing against retail stores, as implied by our comparative statics.

There are also factors offsetting the favorable movements discussed above. Over-population and ineffective use of resources on the Internet may result in negative network externalities in two ways: the problems of network congestion (Gupta et al., 1997) and increased search costs due to larger search space for consumers. This calls for careful and active management of advertising and network resources. For instance, targeted banner advertisements (Ernst & Young, 1998), a careful mix of "push" technologies (Chellappa et al., 1996), and optimal performance tuning of servers by mirroring (Wagner, 1998) are some of the technical solutions to address the negative externality-related problems.

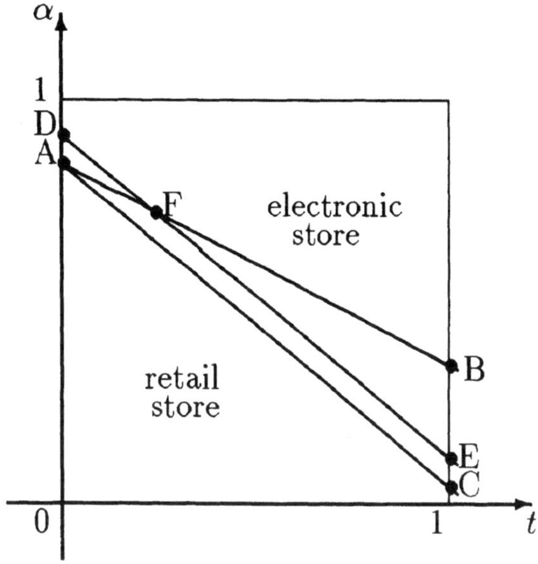

Figure 3. Comparative Statics of C_α

4. ECONOMIES OF SCALE: DIVIDE AND CONQUER?

It is well known that a firm becomes a monopoly if it has economies of scale while others do not (Varian 1984). In the previous section (Figure 2 and Equations 2-5), we showed that price advantages beyond certain threshold levels lead to a monopoly situation. It has often been observed that IT investment in a retail market typically requires large capital investments, but once in place, the new retail systems offer substantial economies of scale and scope (Bakos, 1991). Bagwell and Ramey (1994) note that declining marginal retailing costs are salient in retail markets, due to the prevalence of manufacturer quantity discounts in these markets. In order to investigate the role of marketing cost structures in competition, we note that the Nash Equilibrium prices in Table 2 which satisfy the conditions in Equations 2-5 can be re-written as follows:

Case 1: $x\,C_x - C_\alpha + C_t \leq b_r - b_e \leq x\,C_x + 2(C_\alpha - C_t)$, *where* $C_\alpha \geq C_t$

Case 2: $x\,C_x - C_\alpha + C_t \geq b_r - b_e$, *where* $C_\alpha \geq C_t$, or
$x\,C_x - 2\,(C_\alpha - C_t) \geq b_r - b_e$, *where* $C_\alpha \leq C_t$

Case 3: $x\,C_x + 2\,(C_\alpha - C_t) \leq b_r - b_e$, *where* $C_\alpha \geq C_t$, or
$x\,C_x - C_\alpha + C_t \leq b_r - b_e$, *where* $C_\alpha \leq C_t$

Case 4: $x\,C_x - 2\,(C_t - C_\alpha) \leq b_r - b_e \leq x\,C_x + (C_t - C_\alpha)$, *where* $C_t \geq C_\alpha$

In the short run, cost parameters such as C_t, C_x, and C_α are often exogenous to firms. Therefore, the number of decision variables in distribution channels often reduces to one, lowering marketing costs. This provides an incentive for the stores to invest in better technology, service systems, and efficient advertising programs to reduce variable costs in retailing. It also explains what makes quantity discounts a widespread and significant feature of the retail market (Bagwell and Ramey, 1994). If each manufacturer gives different discounts, a store may sell products that involve higher manufacturer volume discounts. This intensifies the competition between manufacturers who produce similar goods. From the results above, we anticipate that this trend will continue even in electronic commerce.

One distinction between the electronic and the retail store may be geographical coverage. While a well-established electronic store sells products in a global market, retail stores are geographically limited. In the previous discussion, we maintained that a lower cost structure is a key to winning this competition (or at least to remain in business.). Then, can a small and geographically-restricted retail store compete with a global player like an electronic store?

In order to address the above question, we relax an assumption that there is only one retail store, and assume that *n* retail stores are competing with an electronic store in a market. For simplicity of analysis, we assume *identical* markets in terms of cost structure and size. Further, we assume that stores are evenly distributed so that consumers go to the closest retail store to buy products. We are not interested in the competition among retail stores in this analysis. Hence, we also assume that retail stores do not compete with each other and that they do not overlap geographically.

We assume that fixed investment in electronic marketing does not vary significantly according to the number of users. Then, if d_e denotes the electronic store demand in one market, the total demand of an electronic store is given by $d_e' = n\ d_e$, and consequently its total cost is $c_e' = a_e + n\ b_e d_e$. Using these revised numbers in Equation 6, we obtain Nash equilibria which are the same as the ones previously derived. This implies that the competition and strategies of "an electronic store and a retail store" and "an electronic store and *n* retail stores" are identical. In other words, an electronic store has no additional cost disadvantage when it is competing with *n* retail stores in the same market, compared to the 1:1 competition case if the cost functions are linear. This leads to the following proposition:

Proposition 4.1 The number of independent retail stores, n, in a market has no effect on the strategies of either an electronic store or retail stores unless it changes unit variable costs.

This result holds for both constant and decreasing returns to scale. How does this result change if the multiple retail stores are under one ownership? Like the electronic store above, the total demand of the retail store chain becomes $n\ d_r$, and we can think of two extreme cases of the total cost:

$$c_r = a_r + n\ b_r d_r \quad \text{or} \tag{9}$$
$$c_r = n\ (a_r + b_r d_r) \tag{10}$$

Equation 9 represents a case where increasing the number of stores does not increase the fixed investment. In the other case (Equation 10), n stores require a fixed investment of na_r. From this modification, we obtain the following proposition:

Proposition 4.2 The number of retail stores, n, in a market has no effect on the strategies of either an electronic store or retail stores when the n retail stores belong to a chain.

This proposition shows that the number of retail stores in the chain does not make any difference in the competition, unless their cost structure changes as the number of retail stores increases or decreases. This also implies that an electronic store that competes with a chain of retail stores may not have to prepare several different strategies to compete with each retail store. For example, a retail store chain may consider building a new store to compete with an electronic store to overcome the geographical limitation in a markct. This business strategy, however, does not give any advantage to the store when the new store has the same technology and strategies as the incumbent. Furthermore, if the setup cost is high enough to have an impact on its prices, the store may lose its competitive edge.

From the retail store management's perspective, adding another store in a geographically new market does not bring competitive advantage to a retail chain over an electronic store. By virtue of doing business in a virtual market, electronic stores do not have geographic limitations. Therefore, we suggest that retail stores should focus on strategies which can change consumer utility and/or their cost structure in order to compete with electronic stores. The above proposition also shows that there is an incentive for retail stores belonging to a chain to deviate from the price and competition strategies of the chain in order to maximize their profits and secure their competitive edge in their respective markets.

5. FUTURE RESEARCH

Up until now, competition between electronic stores has not been severe because of the high risks involved in electronic transactions. However, once security, reputation and trust issues in electronic shopping are addressed, electronic stores will experience explosive growth and competition. Furthermore, retail shopping centers will have an increasingly higher discomfort level as the population grows (*Wall Street Journal*, April 25, 1994), which will cause consumers to choose the electronic channel. Thus, future research in this area should focus on key issues in competition between electronic stores. For example, suitable homepage positioning can provide many strategic advantages to an electronic store. Well-publicized and reputed homepages are easily accessible and lower a consumer's perceived risk in electronic shopping.

An important issue not addressed in this paper involves the competition between electronic stores and catalog businesses. In many ways, electronic stores are very similar to catalog businesses. Neither channels, for instance, require middlemen nor have retail stores to sell products, and both enable consumers to shop at home. In future research, we will focus on the differences between electronic stores and catalog businesses and analyze the optimal strategies of each channel.

Yet another issue not considered in this paper involves the use of an electronic channel for product research and information gathering, where a consumer still buys the product from a physical retail outlet (Ernst & Young, 1998, 1999). For traditional retailers this raises the issue of whether they should at least provide detailed product information through their Web sites, even if they do not have immediate plans to sell such products online. For pure electronic stores, this observation raises questions as to whether they can persuade consumers to actually buy products online through various strategies such as wider product mix and "money back" guarantees.

6. CONCLUSION

We developed a stylized framework to explore equilibrium pricing and demand strategies in the channel competition between traditional retail and electronic stores. The model made it analytically tractable to analyze the endogenous nature of retailers' incentives as well as consumers' selection behavior. We focused on markets where the demand for a good is dependent upon prices, network comfort level, perceived risks, and retail discomfort level. We addressed business strategies based upon different economies of scale.

A key advantage of an electronic store is the ability to overcome the geographical limitations of a retail store. An electronic store can compete with one or many retail stores which are both geographically limited and distributed. We investigated this issue under different marketing cost structures in order to identify the best channel structure.

We found that the number of retail stores has no effect on the optimal pricing strategies of either the electronic store or the retail store. Further, this result holds even when the retail stores belong to one chain. Another interesting finding is that the optimum price strategies of the channels move in the same direction at different rates as the importance of the network comfort level changes. Both these findings put an electronic store at a strategic advantage over a retail store as consumer demographics shift gradually in favor of the electronic medium. Finally, we showed that business expansion in retailing can create more profits due to complementarity or can decrease the profit because of diseconomies of scope. Given the trends in the level of retail discomfort level and perceived risk of online shopping, we suggested that traditional retail channels should consider expanding their business to the electronic medium but not vice versa.

For management, this research presents conceptual guidelines for making strategic decisions regarding electronic commerce. For electronic store managers, the paper provides pragmatic implications for store design as well as for prioritizing an investment agenda.

REFERENCES

Bagwell, K. and G. Ramey. (1994). Coordination economies, advertising, and search behavior in retail markets. American Economic Review. 84 (3) 498-517.

Bakos, J. Y. (1991). A Strategic Analysis of Electronic Marketplaces. MISQ. 295-310.

Barua, A., S. Ravindran, and A.B. Whinston. (1997). Efficient Selection of Suppliers Over the Internet. JMIS. 13 (4) 117-137.

Bulow. J., J. Geanakoplos, and P. Klemperer. (1985). Multimarket Oligopoly: Strategic Substitutes and Complements. Journal of Political Economy. 93. 488-511.

Chellappa. R., A. Barua, and A. B. Whinston. (1996). Electronic Publishing Versus Publishing Electronically: The Case of EC World. Proceedings of the International Conference on Information Systems (Technologies in Action Track).

Coase. R. (1937). The Nature of the Firm. Economica. 4. 386-405.

Cox. D. F., and S. J. Rich. (1964). Perceived risk and consumer decision making. Journal of Marketing Research. 1. 32-39.

Economides, N., and A. Siow. (1988). The division of markets is limited by the extent of liquidity. American Economic Review. 108-121.

Ernst & Young LLP. (1999). Internet Shopping Study: The Digital Channel Continues to Gather Stream.

Ernst & Young LLP. (1998). Internet Shopping: Ernst & Young Special Report.

Gupta, A., D. O. Stahl, and A. B. Whinston. (1997). A Stochastic Equilibrium Model of Internet Pricing. Journal of Economic Dynamics and Control. 21. 697-672.

Hickey, M. (1994). Shopping at home: one modem line, no waiting. HomePC. 6. 307-310.

Hoffman, D.L., and T. P. Novak. (1996). Marketing in Hypermedia Computer-Mediated Environments: Conceptual Foundations. Journal of Marketing. 60. 50-68.

Hoffman, D.L., W. D. Kalsbeek, and T.P. Novak. (1996). Internet and Web Use in the United States: Baselines for Commercial Development. Special Section on "Internet in the Home". Communications of the ACM. 39. 36-46.

Hotelling, H. (1929). Stability in Competition. Economic Journal. 39. 41-47.

Kalakota, Ravi, and A. B. Whinston. (1996). Frontiers of Electronic Commerce. Addison-Wesley Pub. New York.

Lusch, R. F. (1982). Management of Retail Enterprises. Kent pub. Boston.

Malone, T. W., J. Yates., and R. I. Benjamin. (1987). Electronic Markets and Electronic Hierarchies. Communications on ACM. 30 (6) 484-497.

Nelson, P. (1970). Information and consumer behavior. JPE. 78. 311-329.

Ravindaran, S., A. Barua, B. Lee, and A. B. Whinston. (1996). Strategies for Smart Shopping in Cyberspace. Journal of Organizational Computing and Electronic Commerce. 6 (1). 33--49.

Sarkar, M., B. Butler, and C. Steinfield. (1995). Intermediaries and Cybermediaries: A Continuing Role for Mediating Players in the Electronic Marketplace. Journal of Computer-Mediated Communication. 1 (3). Available Internet: www.ascusc.org/jcmc/vol1/issue3/sarkar.html

Spence, E. H., J. F. Engel, and R. D. Blackwell. (1970). Perceived risk in mail-order and retail store buying. Journal of Marketing Research. 7. 364-369.

Tirole, J. (1988). The Theory of Industrial Organization. Cambridge, Mass. MIT Press.

Varian, H. R. (1984). Microeconomic Analysis. (2nd ed.). Norton & Company, New York.

Wagner, M. (1998). Playing In Heavy Traffic. InternetWeek. 9.

Williamson, O. E. (1989). Transaction cost economics. The Handbook of Industrial Organization. Elsevier Science Publishers B.V.

Chapter 17

Organizational And Economic Mechanisms For Buyer-Supplier Contracts

Seung Kyoon Shin: R. Ramesh: H. Raghav Rao
Department of Management Science and Systems, State University of New York at Buffalo, Buffalo, New York 14260-4000, ss27@acsu.buffalo.edu; rramesh@acsu.buffalo.edu; mgmtrao@acsu.buffalo.edu

Abstract: In this paper, we present an overview of the nature of contracts in a buyer-supplier business environment, and identify factors that affect the contract relationships. Concepts from transaction cost theory and agency theory as well as the resource-based view are applied to develop an outline for mechanisms that can govern buyer-supplier contracts.

Key words: Buyer-supplier contracts, organizational economic theory, resource-based view, information sharing, long-term relationship.

1. INTRODUCTION

Contracting typically refers to the situation where an agency procures an item or service from another for the purpose of enabling an economic production in the contracting agency's own facilities. This requires the contracting agency to make specifications available to a contracted agency (Day, 1956; Katz, 1989; Tirole, 1988). Contracts in such outsourcing situations occur because a firm may find it less profitable or infeasible to have all required capabilities in house. Often firms concentrate on core competencies and strategically outsource other activities (Quinn and Hilmer, 1994). In economic literature, theories generally focus on the structure of equilibrium contracts, under the assumption that agents designing contracts are rational. Such approaches are useful in clarifying the conditions under which economic efficiency can be improved through the distribution of property rights and corresponding incentives (Grossman and Hart, 1986). However, a study of alternate literatures is needed to deepen our understanding of the nature of buyer-seller contracts, especially in emergent areas such as supply chains.

In this article, concentrating on the important role of information in contracts, we suggest contract issues that need to be scrutinized in buyer-supplier contracts in the context of supply chain networks. In the following sections, we investigate various phenomenon of contracts occurring between organizations, based on three established organizational economic theories; Transaction Cost Theory (TCT), Agency Theory, and Resource-based View (RBV). We believe that contracts need to be consistent with the perspective from these theories.

2. CONTRACTS AND ORGANIZATIONAL ECONOMICS

In this section, based on transaction cost theory, agency theory and the resource-based view, we identify variables that would have critical impacts on a buyer-supplier contract. Subsequently, we develop an influence diagram to project relationships among variables. We begin with a discussion on the objectives of contracts.

2.1 Objectives of Contracts

To understand what motivates parties to pursue certain contract structures, consider a simple supply chain relationship between a manufacturer and a retailer. There are three general objectives of contracts; risk-sharing, channel coordination, and long-term partnership (Tsay, et al. 1999). In a supply chain relationship, central control refers to the situation that all decisions are made by a single decision maker with access to all available information, while decentralized control refers to one where neither the manufacturer nor the retailer is in a position to control the entire supply chain, and each has his own incentives and states of information. If the expected profit from decentralized control is less than the expected profit from central control, then supply chain coordination mechanisms are considered inefficient. The first objective of contracts arises in that it provides means for the buyer and supplier to share the risks arising from various sources of uncertainty such as market demand, selling price, process yield, product quality, delivery time, and exchange rates. The risk-sharing motive caused by uncertainty is common in various contracts (Pick and Whinston, 1989; Richmond, et al., 1992). Contracts also provide mechanisms for increasing expected profit under different channels, for example, central control vs. decentralized control, a scenario. This is referred to as the channel coordination objective (Tsay, et al. 1999). Channel coordination may be achieved by first identifying intra-chain dynamics which cause inefficiencies, then modifying the structure of the relationship to more closely align individual incentives with global organization.

The third objective of contracts relates to long-term relationships between contract parties. There are gaps between the incentives (or interests) of contract parties, which generally result from and also lead to information asymmetry. Mutual trust among contracting parties enhances coordination by lowering administrative costs (McAllister, 1995). Trust also has emerged as an important component of alliances, and several studies confirm the importance of trust and coordination in long-term cooperative relationships such as supplier alliance or partnership (Pilling and Zhang, 1992; Smith, et al., 1995). Long-term relationships based on mutual trust provide benefits such as economic efficiency, committed personal relationship, and cultural affinity between buyers and suppliers (Dwyer, et al., 1987). Long-term partnerships have been regarded as a critical factor of nontraditional contracts in the perspective of strategic alliances (Yoshino and Rangan, 1995).

In this paper, we provide an organizational economic view of the various aspects of contracts, focusing on the role of information in buyer-supplier contracts. Based on organizational economic theory, we illustrate how the objectives of contracts may be focused on risk sharing, channel coordination, and long-term relationships, and what are the factors that impact contract objectives and execution.

2.2 Organizational economic view of contracts

We attempt to characterize the key differences among the three theories in terms of their orientation, focus, resource, and constructs as shown in Table 1.

Table 1. The key concepts from three theories

Orientation	Theory	Focus	Resource	Main Constructs

Organizational Economic View	Transaction Cost	Cost Efficiency	Production cost Transaction cost	Asset Specificity Uncertainty
	Agency Cost	Principal-Agent Relationship	Monitoring Cost Bonding Cost Residual Loss	Uncertainty Risk aversion Moral Hazard Length of relationship
Strategic Management View	Resource Based	Internal Slack Resources	Physical Capital Human Capital Organizational Capital	Value Rareness Imperfect Immutability Non-substitutablility

Although there are distinctions among the theories, they seem to have two things in common (Barney, 1991). The first is an abiding interest in firms. Unlike the traditional economics that merely focuses on structure, functioning, and implications of markets, organizational economics focuses on the structure, functioning and implications of firms. Organizational economics can be utilized to explain contracts that occur between firms. Second, most organizational economists have an interest in the relationship between competition and organizations. They believe that organizations exist in competitive environments, where other firms, individuals, institutions, and governments are seeking to obtain some part of the success that a particular firm may enjoy (Barney, 1986; Wernerfelt, 1984). The cause-effect relationship and phenomena occurring in the buyer-supplier contractual environment can be investigated in terms of three notable concepts of organizational economics; Transaction Cost Theory (TCT), Agency Theory, and Resource-based View. Williamson (1975) and his followers have presented a wealth of evidence supporting the idea that equilibrium organizational arrangement aligns transactions and incentives in a cost-minimizing way. TCT explains the conditions under which economic exchanges can be most efficiently managed using hierarchical forms of governance. If a firm is a bundle of interrelated transactions managed through hierarchical forms of governance, then transaction cost economics is a theory to explain why and how a firm cooperates with others. Agency theory extends this theory of the firm by enabling a more detailed examination of the linkages among these different transactions. This entails focusing attention on the effects of compensation, corporate governance, capital structure, and other attributes of firm governance on agency problems within the firm, and between a firm and its external stakeholders. While both theories assume that firms are essentially homogeneous in their transactions and agency governance skills, the resource-based view provides a different perspective of contracts based on the assumption that resources and capabilities can vary significantly across firms. In Figure 1, based on the organizational economic theories and the objectives of contracts, we present a framework that identifies contract issues. This could be utilized to build guidelines for contract execution. In the following sections, we will attempt to understand the nature of contract information in buyer-supplier relationships

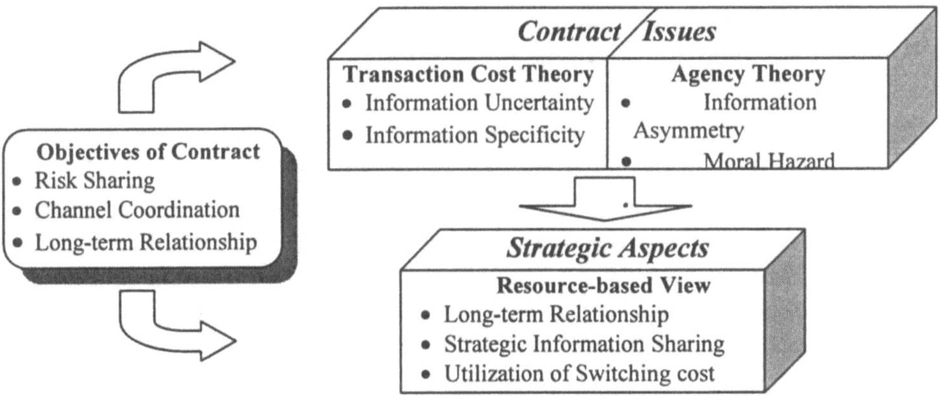

Figure 1. A Multi-viewed Perspective of Contract Issues

3. THE TRANSACTION COST THEORY PERSPECTIVE

In this section, we investigate contract variables that affect buyer-supplier contracts based on transaction cost theory (TCT) perspective. TCT helps explain the conditions under which economic exchanges can be most efficiently managed using hierarchical forms of governance. Transaction cost economics also offers a rationale for the potential benefits of contracting out excess resources (incentive intensity) and suggests circumstances in which such resources will be better spun off from a firm (Teece, 1982; Williamson, 1985).

TCT distinguishes between two governance structures, market and hierarchies (Coase, 1937; Williamson, 1975). As the market becomes more efficient, increasing the size and organizational complexity of a firm becomes uneconomical, since firms exist only to the extent that they reduce transaction costs more effectively. Thus,

TCT explains that firms exist because the cost of managing economic exchanges across markets is greater than the cost of managing economic exchanges within the boundaries of an organization (Coase, 1937). TCT rests on two essential behavioral assumptions about economic actors engaged in transactions: bounded rationality, and opportunism (Simon, 1975; Williamson, 1985) Most real-world contracts are incomplete (Tirole, 1999; Williamson, 1975). The main argument for incomplete contracts rests on the behavioral assumption of bounded rationality: Not all relevant future contingencies can be foreseen by exchange participants. Bounded rationality has an effect on the ability of economic actors to design contracts, and on the content of contracts. TCT also assumes the possibility of self-interest seeking with guile, called opportunism (Williamson, 1975). Opportunism includes lying, stealing, and cheating, but it more generally refers to the incomplete or distorted disclosure of information in order to confuse' partners in an exchange. The threat of opportunism is important because in a world without opportunism, all economic exchange could be done on the basis of promise, and parties in such a contraction would simply pledge at the outset to perform their part of an exchange fairly.

Contractors will choose the form of governance, contracting out or internalization, that reduces the cost of any potential exchange problems created by bounded rationality and by the threat of opportunism. If a contract enables parties to an exchange to reduce potential exchange then a contract will be preferred over a hierarchical form. However, if a contract cannot be executed without these exchange problems, then more costly forms of internalization may have to be employed. Given this characterization of the governance decisions facing economic actors and critical roles of information exchange between contract parties, it is important to understand the attributes of transactions that will make bounded rationality and opportunism problematic. Notably, two attributes of transactions have been widely seen as creating the most problems for economic actors in transactions: uncertainty and transaction specific investment (Barney, 1991; Williamson, 1991).

3.1 Uncertainty

Without cognitive limits, all exchanges could be conducted through planning (Williamson, 1975). However, given bounded rationality, complex contracting breaks down in the face of uncertainty. Contractors simply cannot foresee all possible outcomes in a contract, or cannot formulate optimal contracts or other responses to those eventualities. Uncertainty triggers the need to continually update contracts and incur the considerable costs of renegotiations. More importantly, constant change means that during extensive periods of negotiation, contracts are misaligned, and, in most cases, they fail to reflect this environmental change (Williamson, 1991). The greater the degree of uncertainty, the more frequent the misalignment of contracts and the costlier these resulting renegotiations (Williamson, 1991). From this perspective, one of the most problematic phenomena that cause a great uncertainty in a supply chain net is the bullwhip effect. Two typical sources that increase uncertainty in buyer-supply contracts are exploration and the bullwhip effect.

3.1.1 Exploration Cost

Exploration refers to the search and trial phase in a contract (Dwyer, et al., 1987). In this phase, the contract parties first attempt to gather information in relation to obligations, benefits and burdens, and the possibility of exchange. Potential exchange partners first consider obligations, benefits and burdens, and the possibility of exchange. The exploration phase may be very brief, or it may include an extended period of testing and evaluation. The exploration cost is highly uncertain and contract-specific because the output from this stage is neither guaranteed nor useful for other contract. Thus, contractors attempt to minimize this cost. This evaluation may result in a trial purchase, but the exploratory relationship is very fragile in the sense that minimal investment and interdependence make for simple termination. The exploration phase is conceptualized in five subprocesses (Scanzoni, 1979): (1) attraction, communication and bargaining, (3) development and exercise of power, (4) norm development, and (5) expectation development. Through such processes, each contract party attempts to gauge and test the goal compatibility, integrity, and performance of the other parties. The ultimate goal of these processes is to enable contract parties to share information and values that support joint investment in the relation (Dwyer, et al., 1987).

3.1.2 Bullwhip Effect

The bullwhip effect is one of the many complexities involved with supply chain contracts that are related to uncertainty factors (Lee, et al., 1997). In certain cases, contractors push the high risk onto subcontractors by having them carry a disproportionate share of market uncertainties (Van Bruggen, et al., 1998). Most complexities involved with SCM contracts are related to factors such as uncertainty in the supply or demand of products, forecasting and the possibility of revising those forecasts, constrained production capacity, and penalties for overtime and expediting (Tsay, et al., 1999). This kind of uncertainty evolves from bounded rationality. In general, the greater the level of uncertainty in a transaction, the more difficult it will be to use contracts and other forms of market governance to manage that transaction, and the more likely that hierarchical forms of governance will be adopted.

The bullwhip effect refers to amplification of demand variance. It is undesirable propagation in a supply chain since the supplier's costs generally increase with the order variance. This is due to the increased need for inventory buffers and/or the more tentative scheduling of machine and labor capacity that may result. Even when the buyer's demand is certain, the supplier's production costs may be lower when the order is larger than what the buyer may consider to be optimal. One response to this conflict is an agreement in which the buyer agrees in advance to accept delivery of at least a certain quantity of stock, either in each individual order or cumulatively over some period of time. Depending on the relative strategic power of the parties, the seller may offer the buyer some forms of inducement, the most natural of which is a lower unit cost on items purchased under the contract.

3.1.3 Transaction Specificity

The financial costs of subcontracting include decreased scale economies to the contractor, and the transaction costs resulting from the initiation and management of the contracting relationship (Nam, et al., 1996; Quinn and Hilmer, 1994). From a financial perspective, the main reported benefits of contracting out are lower operating costs and lower investment requirements for the contractor, and the spreading of risk between the two parties (Van Bruggen, et al., 1998). It is often the case that parties in a transaction will need to make investments in that transaction in order to facilitate its accomplishment. These investments can take many forms. Certain investments in a transaction are only valuable in that particular transaction and have little or no value in any other transaction. Such investments are transaction specific. Thus, an asset that has lower asset specificity can be used elsewhere without difficulty. Client firms can obtain less specific assets immediately without difficulty from the market (Nam, et al., 1996). That is, contracts for these assets are likely to be complete.

Williamson (1975) refers to two concepts: asset specificity in terms of durable investments that are undertaken in support of particular transactions, and the opportunity cost in terms of which investments are much lower with respect to best alternative uses or by alternative users. Transactions that are supported by high levels of asset specificity should be governed by hierarchical structures whereas transactions that require only general purpose investments will most efficiently be contracted out. However, the criteria for contract decision making does not end here. A decision maker should consider that the existence of transaction specificity increases the threat of opportunism. Thus, in general, the greater the level of transaction specific investments in an exchange, the greater the threat of opportunism. In turn, the greater the threat of opportunism, the less likely that market governance will effectively reduce this threat and the more likely that hierarchical forms of governance will be chosen. We discuss the details of opportunistic behavior of contractors in the following section.

Table 2 presents primary sources of contract information costs that are illustrated by Transaction Cost Theory and Agency Cost Theory. In TCT, high asset specificity is presumed to increase the potential threat of opportunism, thereby increasing the behavioral contractual costs of market-based exchange. The contractual costs include the ex-ante costs of drafting, negotiating, and safeguarding a contract, and the ex-post costs of enforcing the contract (Choudhury and Sampler, 1997). The cost of acquiring knowledge about contracting is also a major feature of the contract design process. Not only are contractors highly heterogeneous with respect to management talent and the quality of ideas, but also are differentially endowed with specific information regarding contracting. While additional information can be acquired from lawyers, academics, or consultants, different initial endowments will entail search costs that differ greatly across entrepreneurs (Stigler, 1961). This issue will be magnified if prior knowledge frames new information in ways that reduce the cost of recognizing its value (Cohen and Levinthal, 1989). In the following sections, we illustrate the problems of transaction specificity, search cost and information/knowledge specificity, related to supply chain contracts, focusing on the importance of information and knowledge associated with contracts.

Table2. Sources of Contract Information Costs

	Contract Information Costs	
	Transaction Cost Aspects	Agency Cost Aspects
Primary Sources of Contract Costs	➢ Uncertainty ▪ Bullwhip effect ▪ Exploration Cost ➢ Transaction Specificity ▪ Search Cost ▪ Cost of Awareness ▪ Information Specificity ▪ Contractual Solidarity	Information Asymmetry Information transfer cost Moral Hazard Contract interpretation Measurement Development Monitoring cost Verification cost

3.1.4 Switching Costs

Switching costs are created when customers make investments that are contract-specific to a particular supplier. An investment is said to be specific when its value in a particular exchange, with particular exchange partners, is significantly greater than its value in any alternative exchange (Williamson, O.E., 1985). In this sense, the redeployment of contract-specific information or knowledge in a new contract, with new contract partners, has the effect of destroying much of the value of that investment. Given these switching costs, the supplier is able to keep customers despite the extra value suppliers are able to extract from their relationship with their captured customers. These investments might include the costs of employee technical training to use a supplier's unique product, management experience working with a particular supplier's sales and support staff, and information or knowledge regarding a particular supplier's business policies and procedures. All these transaction-specific investments can be very valuable for firms in a contract, as long as they continue a contract with the same supplier. However, these investments have little or no value in facilitating contracts with other suppliers.

A principal argument in this line of reasoning is that the creation of significant customer switching costs in the acquisition of services or products from particular suppliers creates an economic opportunity for suppliers (Klemperer, 1987a). Once these switching costs are created, suppliers can increase the price, reduce the level of service, or in other ways extract additional value out of their relationships with their "captured" customers. As long as the cost to customers of switching suppliers is less than the extra value that is being extracted from this relationship by a supplier, customers will continue the contract with a supplier. Prescriptively, suppliers should attempt to create unique values of their product that requires specific investments by customers, to be used by customers (Shapiro and Varian, 1999).

3.1.5 Search Cost

Significant technological advances involving electronic commerce have created an enormous surge of interest among businesses eager to buy or supply products and services over the information superhighway. However, in the presence of an electronic network, the time and costs of potential supplier identification are still too high for a buyer organization to consider a large pool (Barua, et al., 1997). Search cost is one of the important dimensions of switching costs, and it constitutes a major portion of overall contract costs. When a decision-maker utilizes all the useful information related to a complex task like a contract decision, search is exhaustive because it has to deal with all available alternatives and all dimensions that might be relevant to the overall quality of an alternative (Minch and Sanders, 1986). Search cost is a transaction cost whose value is restricted to its use and/or acquisition by specific individuals or during specific time periods. Cost of awareness is a situational contractual element that increases search cost in contract development stage. Awareness refers to a party's recognition that another party is a feasible exchange partner (Dwyer, et al., 1987). In general, the more complex information required by the contract, the more expensive the cost of awareness.

Shavell (1998) argues that search effort is one of most important aspects regarding the formation of contracts. Parties expend effort in finding contracting partners, and it is apparent that their search effort will not generally be socially optimal. On one hand, they might not search enough. It is the case when the private return to search may be less than the social return because the surplus gained when one party locates a contract partner would ordinarily be divided between them in bargaining. On the other hand, parties might search more than socially desirable because of a negative externality associated with discovery of a contract partner (Diamond and Maskin, 1981). This implies that, when one party finds and contracts with the other, other parties are thereby prevented from contracting with that party.

3.1.6 Information/Knowledge Specificity

There are many different forms of asset specificity, such as human specificity, site specificity, physical specificity, and time specificity (Williamson, 1985). From the contract perspective, information or knowledge regarding a contract can be specific. Contract information specificity is defined as the extent to which the value of information is restricted to its use and/or acquisition by each party or during specific contract time periods. In the context of information, two forms of specificity are defined: knowledge specificity and time specificity (Choudhury and Sampler, 1997). Knowledge and time are both important influences on the way information is acquired and used in the context of decision making.

Contract knowledge is separate from contract information in that, while contract information is regarded as a flow of messages, contract knowledge is created and organized by the very flow of contract information, anchored on the commitment and beliefs of its beholders (Nonaka, 1994). This implies that, while contract information is the regular, ongoing flow of data to which each party is exposed, contract knowledge is the stock of contract information possessed by each party, based on previous contract experience. There are two forms of specific knowledge: (a) scientific or technical knowledge, and (b) knowledge of context, or knowledge of particular circumstances of time and place (Hayek, 1945). Specific knowledge has two attributes: (1) in most cases, it is possessed by a very limited number of individual in parties and (2) it is expensive to transfer (immobility of knowledge). Thus, while specific knowledge can be a type of transaction cost for a contract, it also can play a critical role in creating a strategic resource of a firm. (We will discuss issues related to utilization of contract information in the following section.) In general, the more costly the knowledge is to transfer, the more specific it is. The less costly the knowledge is to transfer, the more general it is (Jensen and Meckling, 1992). Specific knowledge is costly to transfer because it cannot be aggregated meaningfully in a different business relationship or a different environment (Hayek, 1945) and because there is no common vocabulary or procedure for transferring it. This is similar to the difficulties in transferring tacit knowledge (Nonaka, 1994). Knowledge is codifiable and easy to transfer if it can be structured into a set of identifiable rules and relationships (Kogut and Zander, 1992). However, not all knowledge is amenable to codification. An example is experiential knowledge acquired by an individual as a byproduct of doing his/her job.

4. AGENCY THEORY

Another organizational economic theory that illuminates the factors impacting contractual mechanisms and relationships among those factors is agency theory. In fact, many researchers agree that contracts are central in agency theory. While transaction cost theory is of little help in analyzing conflicting goals of individuals associated with a firm, agency theory seeks to understand the causes and consequences of goal disagreements in an organization. Like TCT, agency theory assumes that humans have bounded rationality, are self-interested and are prone to opportunism (Eisenhardt, 1989). The theories are also similar in their emphasis on information asymmetry problems in contracting and on efficiency as the engine that drives the governance of economic transactions (Barney, 1991; Eisenhardt, 1989). However, agency theory differs from TCT in its emphasis on the risk attitudes of parties of transactions (Eisenhardt, 1989).

Agency relationships occur whenever one partner in a transaction (the principal) delegates authority to another (the agent) and the welfare of the principal is affected by the choices of the agent (Arrow, 1974). The delegation of decision-making authority from principal to agent is problematic in that: (1) the interests of principal and agent will typically diverge; (2) the principal cannot perfectly and costlessly monitor the actions of the agent; and (3) the principal cannot perfectly and costlessly monitor and acquire the information available to or possessed by the agent. These conditions constitute the agency problem that hampers coordinated action directed at mutual objectives, and increases the possibility of opportunistic behavior on the agent's part that works against the welfare of the principal.

There are two essential sources of agency problems: moral hazard, which he equates to hidden actions, and information asymmetry, which he equates to hidden information (Arrow, 1974; Blair and Lewis, 1994). Moral hazard involves situations in which much of the agent's actions are either hidden from the principal or are costly to observe. Thus, it is either impossible or costly for the principal to fully monitor the agent's actions. In adverse selection, the agent possesses information that is, for the principal, unobservable or costly to obtain. Consequently, principals cannot fully ascertain whether or not their interests are best served by agent's decisions. This disadvantage is only exacerbated as the number of agents with similar incentives and advantages multiplies.

4.1 Information Asymmetry

An important consideration in initiating a contract is the existence of information asymmetry between contract parties or between customers and suppliers. While theories based on individual behavior in organizations highlight some important benefits such as better commitment and team spirit, agency theory points to another potential gain – beneficial resolution of information asymmetry from a contracting perspective.

Although efficiency can be achieved under certain types of asymmetry of information only using a relatively complicated mechanism in the contract, when parties are asymmetrically informed, contracts are less efficient or not successful in general (Richmond, et al., 1992). In any contract, informational asymmetries are bound to develop as parties gain more knowledge of their work environments and acquire more expertise. Welfare improvements of each party can be attained by encouraging participation in the setting of long-term contract relationship and by measuring performance in relation to mutual goals (Sivaramakrishnan, 1994).

Some recent works have proceeded under the realization that localization of decision-making authority may be necessary for large enterprises operating in complex environments. This creates a different set of challenges. Conflicts in the interests of the different parties may lead to inefficiency. In a setting of information asymmetry, a key decision may be under the purview of a party with inferior information. Yet, shifting control to the better-informed party may engender opportunistic behavior since self-interested actions might be undetectable. Hence, careful consideration of information and incentives is central to all attempts to improve contract relationship by reconfiguration of decision rights.

The supply chain transaction we are concerned with in this article, is the acquisition of information that is commonly accepted as an asset (King and Epstein, 1983). All organizations face uncertainty in their information requirements. All managers are boundedly rational (Simon, 1975) and it is widely accepted that individuals frequently engage in opportunistic behavior by deliberately misrepresenting information or restricting others' access to information for personal gain (Feldman and March, 1981; Zmud, 1990). Just as asset specificity defines the extent to which the value of an asset is restricted to specific transactions, information specificity is defined as the extent to which the value of information is restricted to its use and/or acquisition by specific individuals or during the contract time periods.

From a contracting perspective, researchers suggest that information asymmetry can be resolved in two alternative ways (Grover, et al., 1996; Rumelt, et al., 1991). One way is to encourage participation in the setting of long-term goals. Long-term plans can be drafted based on inputs from relevant parties and used to assess their performance over that horizon. An alternative approach is to wait till the relevant future period, and set appropriate short-term incentives through a participative process in that period. However, it is generally more efficient to utilize long-term strategy in contractual environment.

4.2 Interpretation of contracts

Although, completely enforceable contracts are desirable, they are mostly observed to be substantially imperfect (Shavell, 1998), and this nature of contract triggers opportunism or moral hazard of contract parties. There are two main reasons for the incompleteness of contracts. The first is that, in order to specify most details to avoid divergence of each party's interests, the cost of writing more complete contracts is expensive. The second reason for the incompleteness of contracts is that the expected consequences of incompleteness may not be very harmful to contracting parties, or even could be mutually beneficial to both parties. However, due to the possibility of opportunism by parties, it may be worthwhile elaborating the contract somewhat by viewing contract interpretation more formally, as a function that transforms the individuals' contract writing into an effective contract that a tribunal may enforce. Given a method of interpretation, parties will choose contracts in a constrained efficient way.

Notably, if an aspect of their contract would not be interpreted as they want, the parties would either bear the cost of writing a more explicit term that would be respected by the tribunal, or else they would not bear the cost of writing the more explicit term and accept the expected loss from having a less than efficient term. The best method of contract interpretation will take this reaction of contracting parties into account and can be regarded as implicitly minimizing the sum of the costs the parties bear in writing contracts and the losses resulting from inefficient enforcement.

4.3 Contract Problems from an Agency Theory Perspective

At the most general level, principals and agents resolve agency problems through monitoring and bonding (Eisenhardt, 1985; Mahoney, 1992). Monitoring involves observing the behavior and/or the performance or agents. One way that principals can try to monitor agents is by collecting relatively complete information about an agent's decisions and actions – an agent's behavior. From this behavioral information, principals can then form judgments about the underlying goals and objectives of agents. In particular, principals can attempt to judge how similar their agents' goals and objectives are to their own goals and objectives. As an alternative (or supplement) to monitoring agent behavior, principals can also monitor the consequences of agent behavior. In general monitoring performance is more efficient when tasks are not highly programmable (Eisenhardt, 1985; Mahoney, 1992). Bonding refers to arrangements that penalize agents for acting in ways that violate the interests of principals or reward them for achieving principals' goals. The contracts between customers and suppliers specify the monitoring and bonding arrangement. Jensen and Meckling (1986) argue that most organizations are simply legal fictions that serve as a nexus for a set of contracting relationships among individuals. Within this nexus firms adopt rules about monitoring and bonding.

5. RESOURCE-BASED VIEW

We have identified factors that have impacts on contractual relationship based on TCT and agency theory. These factors can be utilized in developing buyer-supplier relationships if they can operate as resources in contracts. In this section, we expand this idea based on the resource-based view. The resource-based view is based heavily on Penrose's theory of firm growth (1980). Penrose implicitly assumes that exploitation of excess resources necessitates their use within the firm. The resource-based framework suggests that the firm is best viewed as a collection of sticky and imperfectly imitable resources or capabilities that enable it to successfully compete against other firms (Barney, 1986; Wernerfelt, 1984).

The resource-based view builds on two basic assumptions about a firm's resources and capabilities: (1) that resources and capabilities can vary significantly across firms (resource heterogeneity), and (2) these differences can be stable (resource immobility) (Barney, 1991; Wernerfelt, 1984). A resource is mobile if firms without a resource (or capability) face no cost disadvantage in developing, acquiring, and using that resource compared to firms that already possess and use it. In this case, that resource (e.g., mobile resource) can only be a source of temporary competitive advantage at best. On the other hand, if a firm without a resource or capability does face a cost disadvantage in obtaining, developing, and using it compared to a firm that already possesses that resource (i.e., resource immobility), then the firm that already possesses that resource can have a sustained competitive advantage (Barney, 1991). These assumptions significantly differ from those of TCT and agency theory, where firms within an industry are assumed to be essentially identical, and where any differences that do emerge are quickly destroyed as firms without certain resources and capabilities move quickly to acquire or develop them (Scherer, 1980). However, not all firms are assumed to be heterogeneous with respect to their resources and capabilities, nor is it assumed that all these differences will be sustained over time. Barney (1991) suggests that, in order for a firm's resources and capabilities to be sources of superior performance, they must be (1) valuable, (2) rare among its current or potential competitors, (3) costly to imitate, and (4) without close strategic substitutes. Imitability is an important component of the resource-based view of the firm. Barney (1991) divides the reasons why a firm's resources and capabilities may be costly to imitate into three categories: the role of history, the role of casual ambiguity, and the role of socially complex resources and capabilities. Rumelt, et al. (1991) found that the unique attributes of a firm are more important determinants of its performancc than the industry within which it operates.

Long-term partnerships have been regarded as an important resource of a firm as well as a critical factor of contracts in the perspective of strategic alliance (Yoshino and Rangan, 1995). Resources of a firm can be physical such as unique equipment or innovations protected by patents, and intangible such as brand equity or operating routines. Long-term relationships can create a competitive advantage through the strategic sharing of organizations' key information. Switching costs that enable one party of a contract to extract a sustainable rent stream from these assets often make it nearly impossible for the other party of the contract to transplant them or utilize them effectively in a new context.

In the following section, long-term partnership and strategic utilization of switching costs as buyer and supplier's strategic resource are discussed. An influence diagram summarizing the discussion is presented in Figure 2.

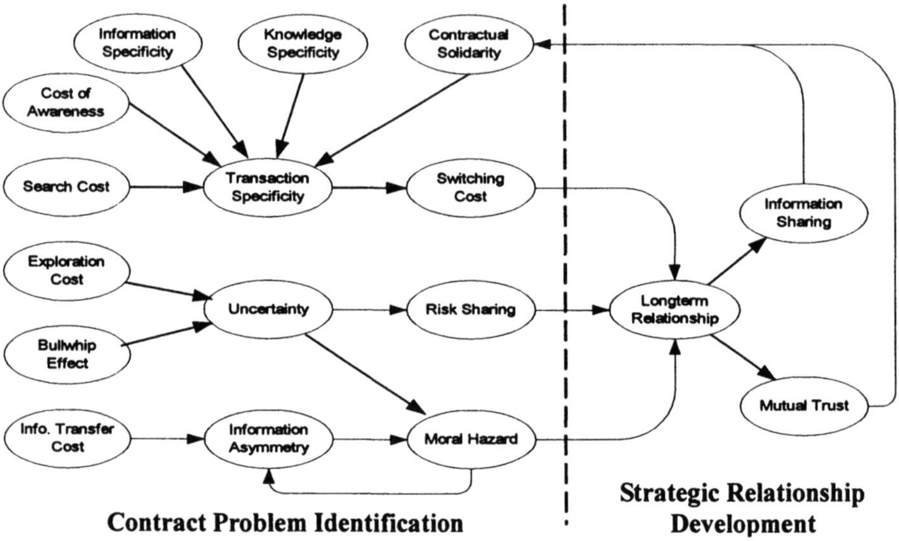

Figure 2. Contract Factor Influence Diagram

5.1 Long-term Partnership

Tsay, et al (1999) find that long-term partnerships are one of the major objectives of contracts in supply chain contracts. Long-term relationships also provide not only an economic benefit, but also social benefits such as committed personal relationship and cultural affinity between buyers and suppliers (Dwyer, et al., 1987). Long-term partnerships have been regarded as a critical factor of nontraditional contracts in the perspective of strategic alliance (Yoshino and Rangan, 1995). A contract facilitates long-term partnerships by delineating mutual concessions that favor the persistence of the business relationship, as well as specifying penalties for non-cooperative behavior. The lengthening of the time horizon may encourage parties to engage in activities that are unfavorable in the short term but have substantial payoffs over time.

A partnership is defined as an interorganizational relationship to achieve the participants' shared goals. Mohr and Spekman (1994) defined partnerships as purposive strategic relationships between dependent firms who share compatible goals, strive for mutual benefit, and acknowledge a high level of mutual interdependence. That is, partnership means a long-term relationship and is based on mutual recognition and understanding between the contract parties whose success is intrinsically dependent on each other. Partnership has been studied in various areas in management. Marketing and Management information systems research has explored relationships between customer and vendor, buyer and seller, manufacturer and distributor, or auditor and client, and so on (Chaudhury, et al., 1995; Moore, et al., 1997; Rao and Chaudhury, 1995). A number of different views have emerged concerning interorganizational relationships. Previous research classified the relationship between organizations into two types: transactional style and partnership style (Fitzgerald and Willcocks, 1994; Grover, et al., 1996; Henderson, 1990). A transactional style relationship develops through the formal contract in which rules of the game are well specified and the failure to deliver on commitments by either party should be resolved through litigation or penalty clauses in the contract. In contrast, the requirements of a partnership style relationship include risk and benefit sharing, the need to view the relationship as a series of exchanges without a definite endpoint, and the need to establish a range of mechanisms to monitor and execute its operations (Henderson, 1990).

Van der Meer-Kooistra and Vosselman (2000) distinguish three patterns of transactional relationship based on the TCT and trust-based social approach. They particularly emphasize the role of trust in transaction and outsourcing relationship. In the trust-based pattern, trust between the contracting parties is the dominant control mechanisms. Therefore, in the contract phase, suppliers are selected on the basis of trust stemming from friendship, previous contractual relationship, and/or reputation of trustworthiness. Thus, there is more risk sharing between the parties. The control mechanisms are process oriented and culture based. In the execution phase, control devices are aimed at the development of competence trust and goodwill trust. Under this situation, it is important that the parties involved should establish a trust-based commitment to each other.

Strategic partnerships are about building long-term relationships that in turn become the base of a strong strategic resource of both contract parties. Strategic partnership can become a strategic resource of a firm in that the partnership is valuable to contract parties, and rare among its current or potential competitors, costly or even impossible to imitate, and strategically non-substitutable. A strategic partnership is formed when two business partners agree to act together as a single strategic unit. In fact, it has been observed that the most important outcome of the contract negotiation is not the finished contract, but the deepened understanding of important issues that naturally arise in working out the contract. Thus, one of most advantages of long-term relationship is that contract information/knowledge with a certain party is more valuable as the duration of relationship become longer. In turn, long-term relationship decreases the risks caused by information/knowledge specificity.

5.2 Information Sharing

One of the optimal solutions to information asymmetry is strategic information sharing through stable long-term relationship. Information sharing refers to the extent to which critical, often proprietary, information is communicated to one's partner. Huber and Daft (1987) argue that closer ties result in more frequent and more relevant information exchanges between high performing partners. By sharing information and by being knowledgeable about each other's business, partners are able to act independently in maintaining the relationship over time. The systematic availability of information allows people to complete tasks more effectively (Guetzkow, 1965), is an important predictor of partnerships success (Devlin and Bleackley, 1988), and is associated with increased levels of satisfaction to each party that shares information (Schuler, 1979).

As described by (Konsynski and McFarlan, 1990), partnerships can create a competitive advantage through the strategic sharing of organizations' key information. Many researchers report that closer relationships result from more frequent and relevant information exchanges among high-performance partners (Henderson, 1990; Konsynski and McFarlan, 1990). In turn, partnerships sustain more effective relationships over time by sharing information and by being knowledgeable about each other's organization.

5.3 Utilization of Switching Costs

Switching cost has been presented earlier as a factor that generates transaction-specific costs to contract parties. There can be dynamic contract policies that take advantage of pros and cons of switching cost to avoid information asymmetry problem (Moore, et al., 1997). In this section, we propose that switching cost as a positive factor on contracts that enhance long-term relationship between contract parties. Also, we illuminate the strategic characteristics of switching cost that can be a strategic resource of contract parties. According to the resource-based view, resources of a firm can be physical such as unique equipment or innovations protected by patents, or intangible such as brand equity or operating routine. The application specificity inherent in such resources is particularly of importance. The same characteristics that enable a firm to extract a sustainable rent stream from these assets often make it nearly impossible for the firm to transplant them or utilize them effectively in a new context (Silverman, 1999). Thus, a firm that has developed an advantageous resource position is protected to the extent that its resources are specific to certain applications; at the same time, this specificity constrains the firm's ability to transfer these resources to new applications (Montgomery and Wernerfelt, 1988).

The study of strategic implications of switching costs has emerged as an active field in industrial economics (Klemperer, 1987a; Klemperer, 1987b; von Weizsacker, 1984). Switching costs can be strategically used to increase the mutual benefit of both parties of a contract. It is often argued that firms deploying a contract may face substantial costs if they decide to switch to an alternative party of contract. Such switching costs are a central element of the strategic contractual environment.

In order to create switching costs, suppliers attempt to create a unique property in their product that requires specific investments by customers, to be used by customers (Shapiro and Varian, 1999). However, the number of options for customers to obtain the same type of the product has generally increased over time. Perhaps the only way that customer switching costs could be a source of competitive advantage for a supplier is if the product is absolutely unique or costly to imitate, if it is absolutely essential to the customer, to a customer's business operations, and if there are currently no other substitutes or suppliers.

Switching cost can become a more strategic resource of a firm, especially when the base of switching cost is information- or knowledge-specific (Choudhury and Sampler, 1997). It is because these kind of switching costs are valuable to contract parties (mostly to suppliers), and rare among its current or potential competitors, costly or even impossible to imitate, and strategically non-substitutable. Analytic models of switching costs tend to predict aggressive behavior of early movers, who try to build a locked-in customer base that can be subsequently exploited. The actual results depend on the specific assumptions about technological evolution, arrival of new potential contracting parties, and economic benefits accruing to both parties of contracts.

However, customers will usually be able to anticipate the risk of being captured by a supplier if investments specific to that supplier are made. Typically, customers will only be willing to make these kinds of specific investments if they receive some form of guarantee that a supplying firm will not take unfair advantage of these investments. For example, the effort to avoid significant switching costs has led many hardware firms to insist on second sources for key hardware components. Rather than designing an entire hardware system around a component supplied by a single firm, these firms insist that suppliers license other firms to act as second suppliers. Second sources have the effect of reducing a customer's switching costs, and they act as a credible guarantee against suppliers exploiting customers. If switching costs were a significant problem in a contract, a similar second-source strategy could be used.

If guarantees cannot be made in a credible way, then customers will attempt to avoid the creation of significant switching costs by pursuing alternative suppliers or perhaps by supplying their own needs. Whether customers neutralize the threat of switching costs by receiving guarantees up front or by seeking alternative suppliers, the effect of these actions will be to reduce the ability of suppliers to extract extra value from their relationships with captured customers. In an important sense, these customers are not really captured, even if specific investments are made. In this context, the existence of switching costs will not be a source of competitive advantage for a firm selling IT.

Also, suppliers that opportunistically exploit their customer's switching costs will often gain a reputation for being untrustworthy. The effects of this type of reputation can be devastating. While firms may gain large profits from their currently captured customers, they will be unable to attract future customers. The value of opportunities lost because of a bad reputation for exploiting captured customers can be much larger than the value extracted from those captured customers. In this setting, rational suppliers will not find it in their best interest to exploit their captured customers, despite the existence of significant customer switching costs. For this reason, significant customer switching costs cannot be a source of competitive advantage for a firm supplying IT.

6. CONCLUSIONS

In this paper, we overview various organizational and economic perspectives to understand the nature of contracts in buyer-supplier business environments, and identify factors that have significant effects on the contract relationships. Transaction cost theory (TCT) and agency theory has been applied to identify information-related factors that cause costs and problems in buyer-supplier contracts. TCT and Agency Theory suggest that most contract-related problems are caused by each party's opportunism and bounded rationality. Those theories also show that information asymmetry in buyer-supply contracts results in contract costs, and decrease the efficiency of contract relationships. Developing long-term relationships, based on the resource-based view, has been suggested as a strategic solution to those problems that have been identified in terms of transaction cost theory and agency cost theory. Resource-based view proposes that most problems caused by those inherited characteristics of contractors and information asymmetry between them can be resolved through contract parties' trust-based long-term relationships. Contract implications in the context of three perspectives are summarized in Table 3.

Table 3. Implications for contracts

THEORY	IMPLICATIONS FOR CONTRACTS
Transaction Cost Theory	▪ Contract information can be a valuable resource of each contract party. ▪ Most contract information is highly contract-specific. ▪ Uncertainty is nature of information related to contracts.
Agency Cost Theory	▪ Contract relationship is greatly explained by agency cost theory. ▪ Moral hazard between contract parties endangers contract relationship. ▪ There exists information asymmetry between contact parties.
Resource-based View	▪ Most contract problem can be resolved by long-term relationship. ▪ Long-term relationship based on trust is a valuable strategic resource.

While quite a few models offer a variety of insights into supply chain behaviour, they fail to address durable perspectives of buyer-supplier contracts. This paper may provide a perspective for developing strategic buyer-supplier relationships so as to improve contract efficiency. Information asymmetry has been regarded as the root of contract costs and problems in buyer-supplier contracts. A few critical factors, switching cost and information sharing, that may stabilize long-term relationships have also been discussed. Although switching costs can generate transaction specific costs, they also can be regarded as strategic resources of contractual relationships. Identifying the precise characteristics of the switching costs imposed by different types of contracts on their participants and integrating these results with the theory of switching costs is an interesting path for future research in this area. Finally, we outline a series of potential questions for future research.

- Empirical research to test various kinds of relationships among attributes and constructs discussed in this article would help in crystallization of concepts in contract theory for the supply chain.
- Identifying the precise characteristics of each construct and attribute in different types of contracts and integrating these results with the theories is an interesting path for future research in this area.
- Competition, either between multiple buyers or multiple suppliers is an important but often neglected aspect of contract research. Most literature considers the relationship between two companies, the supplier and buyer. Buyers that share a common supplier and compete in the same consumer market might behave in ways that obstructs their competitors' access to suppliers. In turn, the supplier might consider playing the buyers off against one another to obtain price or purchase commitments. Multiple suppliers to a common buyer might need to alter their price, service, lead-time, and flexibility offerings in the light of the competitive environment.
- Another concern is regarding how the benefits from and strategic coordination of information and sharing information ought to be divided among the parties.

We believe that these issues offer a set of exciting future research opportunities on contracts in electronic supply chains.

REFERENCES

Arrow, K.J. *The Limits of Organization*, W. W. Norton, New York, 1974.

Barney, J. "Firm Resources and Sustained Competitive Advantage," *Journal of Management* (17:1), 1991, pp. 99-120.

Barney, J.B. "Strategic Factor Markets: Expectations, Luck, and Business Strategy," *Management Science* (32:10), 1986, pp. 1231-1241.

Barua, A., Ravindran, S. and Whinston, A.B. "Efficient selection of suppliers over the Internet," *Journal of Management Information Systems* (13:4), 1997, pp. 117-137.

Blair, B.F. and Lewis, T.R. "Optimal retail contracts with asymmetric information and moral hazard," *The Rand Journal of Economics* (25:2), 1994, pp. 284-296.

Chaudhury, A., Nam, K. and Rao, H.R. "Management of information systems outsourcing: A bidding perspective," *Journal of Management Information Systems* (12:2), 1995, pp. 131-160.

Choudhury, V. and Sampler, J.L. "Information specificity and environmental scanning: An economic perspective," *MIS Quarterly* (21:1), 1997, pp. 25-53.

Coase, R.H. "The Nature of the Firm," *Economica* (4), 1937, pp. 386-405.

Cohen, W.M. and Levinthal, D.A. "Innovation and Learning: The Two Faces of R&D," *The Economic Journal* (99:397), 1989, pp. 569-596.

Day, J.S. *Subcontracting policy in the Airframe Industry*, Harvard University, Boston, MA, 1956.

Devlin, G. and Bleackley, M. "Strategic Alliances: Guidelines for Success," *Long Range Planning* (21:5), 1988, pp. 18-23.

Diamond, P.A. and Maskin, E.S. "An Equilibrium Analysis of Search and Breach of Contract II. A Non-Steady State Example," *Journal of Economic Theory* (25:2), 1981, pp. 165-195.

Dwyer, F.R., Schurr, P.H. and Oh, S. "Developing Buyer-Seller Relationship," *Journal of Marketing* (51:2), 1987, pp. 11-27.

Eisenhardt, K.M. "Control: Organizational and Economic Approaches," *Management Science* (31:2), 1985, pp. 134-149.

Eisenhardt, K.M. "Agency Theory: An Assessment and Review," *Academy of Management Review* (14:1), 1989, pp. 57-74.

Feldman, M.S. and March, J.G. "Information in Organizations as Signal and Symbol," *Administrative Science Quarterly* (26:June), 1981, pp. 171-186.

Fitzgerald, G. and Willcocks, L.P. "Contract and partnerships in the outsourcing of IT," *Proceedings of the Fifteenth International Conference on Information Systems*, Vancouver, British Columbia, 1994, pp. 91-98.

Grossman, S.J. and Hart, O.D. "The Costs and Benefits of Ownership: A Theory of Vertical and Lateral Integration," *The Journal of Political Economy* (94:4), 1986, pp. 691-719.

Grover, V., Cheon, M.J. and Teng, J.T.C. "The effect of service quality and partnership on the outsourcing of information systems functions," *Journal of Management Information Systems* (12:4), 1996, pp. 89-116.

Guetzkow, H. "Communications in organizations," In *Handbook of organizations*, J. G. March (Ed.), Rand McNally, Chicago, IL, 1965, pp. 534-573.

Hayek, F.A. "The Use of Knowledge in Society," In *The economics of information*, D. K. Levine and S. A. Lippman (Ed.), 1, Elgar, Aldershot, U.K., 1945, pp. 3-14.

Henderson, J.C. "Plugging Into Strategic Partnerships: The Critical IS Connection," *Sloan Management Review* (30:3), 1990, pp. 7-18.

Huber, G.P. and Daft, R.L. "The Information environment of organizations," In *Handbook of organizational communication: an interdisciplinary perspective*, F. M. Jablin (Ed.), Sage Publications, Newbury Park, CA, 1987, pp. 130-164.

Jensen, M.C. and Meckling, W.H. "Theory of the Firm: Managerial Behavior, Agency Costs and Ownership Structure," *Journal of Financial Economics* (3:2), 1986, pp. 305-360.

Jensen, M.C. and Meckling, W.H. "Specific and General Knowledge, and Organizational Structure," In *Contract Economics*, L. Werin and H. Wijkander (Ed.), Blackwell, Cambridge, USA, 1992, pp. 251-274.

King, W.R. and Epstein, B.J. "Assessing Information System Value: An Experimental Study," *Decision Sciences* (14:1), 1983, pp. 34-45.

Klemperer, P. "The Competitiveness of Markets with Switching Costs," *Rand Journal of Economics* (18:1), 1987a, pp. 138-150.

Klemperer, P. "Markets with Consumer Switching Costs," *The Quarterly Journal of Economics* (102:2), 1987b, pp. 375-394.

Kogut, B. and Zander, U. "Knowledge of the Firm, Combinative Capabilities, and the Replication of Technology," *Organization Science* (3:3), 1992, pp. 383-397.

Konsynski, B.R. and McFarlan, F.W. "Information Partnerships - Shared Data, Shared Scale," *Harvard Business Review* (68:5), 1990, pp. 114-120.

Lee, H.L., Padmanabhan, V. and Whang, S. "Information distortion in a supply chain: The bullwhip effect," *Management Science* (43:4), 1997, pp. 546-558.

Mahoney, J.T. "The Choice of Organizational Form: Vertical Financial Ownership versus Other Methods of Vertical Integration," *Strategic Management Journal* (13:8), 1992, pp. 559-584.

McAllister, D.J. "Affect- and cognition-based trust as foundations for interpersonal cooperation in organizations," *Academy of Management Journal* (38:1), 1995, pp. 24-59.

Minch, R.P. and Sanders, G.L. "Computerized Information Systems Supporting Multicriteria Decision Making," *Decision Sciences* (17:3), 1986, pp. 395-413.

Mohr, J. and Spekman, R. "Characteristics of Partnership success: Partnership Attributes, Communication Behavior, and Conflict Resolution Techniques," *Strategic Management Journal* (15:2), 1994, pp. 135-152.

Montgomery, C.A. and Wernerfelt, B. "Diversification, Ricardian Rents, and Tobin's q.," *Rand Journal of Economics* (19:4), 1988, pp. 623-632.

Moore, J.C., Rao, H.R., Whinston, A.B., Nam, K. and Raghu, T.S. "Information acquisition policies for resource allocation among multiple agents," *Information Systems Research* (8:2), 1997, pp. 151-170.

Nam, K., Rajagopalan, S., Rao, H.R. and Chaudhury, A. "A two-level investigation of information systems outsourcing," *Communications of the ACM* (39:7), 1996, pp. 36-44.

Nonaka, I. "A dynamic theory of organizational knowledge creation," *Organization Science* (5:1), 1994, pp. 14-37.

Penrose, E.T. *The theory of the growth of the firm*, M.E. Sharpe, Inc., White Plains, N.Y., 1980.

Pick, R.A. and Whinston, A.B. "A Computer Charging Mechanism for Revealing User Preferences within a Large Organization," *Journal of Management Information Systems* (6:1), 1989, pp. 87-100.

Pilling, B.K. and Zhang, L. "Cooperative Exchange: Rewards and Risks," *International Journal of Purchasing and Materials Management* (28:2), 1992, pp. 2-9.

Quinn, J.B. and Hilmer, F.G. "Strategic outsourcing," *Sloan Management Review* (35:4), 1994, pp. 43-55.

Rao, H.R. and Chaudhury, A. "Modeling team processes: Issues and a specific example," *Information Systems Research* (6:3), 1995, pp. 255-285.

Richmond, W.B., Seidmann, A. and Whinston, A.B. "Incomplete Contracting Issues in Information Systems Development Outsourcing," *Decision Support Systems* (8:5), 1992, pp. 459-477.

Rumelt, R.P., Schendel, D. and Teece, D.J. "Strategic Management and Economics," *Strategic Management Journal* (12), 1991, pp. 5-29.

Scanzoni, J. "Social Exchagne and Behavioral Interdependence," In *Social Exchange in Developing Relationships*, R. L. Burgess and T. L. Huston (Ed.), Academic Press, New York, 1979.

Scherer, F.M. *Industrial Market Structure and Economic Performance*, Houhton Mifflin, Boston, MA, 1980.

Schuler, R.S. "A Role Perception Transactional Process Model for Organizational Communication-Outcome Relationships," *Organizational Behavior and Human Performance* (23:2), 1979, pp. 268-291.

Shapiro, C. and Varian, H.R. *Information Rules: A Strategic Guide to the Network Economy*, Harvard Business School Press, Boston, MA, 1999.

Shavell, S. "Contracts," In *The New Palgrave Dictionary of Economics and the Law*, P. Newman (Ed.), 1, Stockton Press, New York, 1998, pp. 436-445.

Silverman, B.S. "Technological resources and the direction of corporate diversification: Toward an integration of the resource-based view and transaction cost economics," *Management Science* (45:8), 1999, pp. 1109-1124.

Simon, H.A. *Administrative behavior: a study of decision-making processes in administrative organization*, Free Press, New York, 1975.

Sivaramakrishnan, K. "Information asymmetry, participation, and long-term contracts," *Management Science* (40:10), 1994, pp. 1228-1244.

Smith, K., Carroll, S. and Ashford, S. "Intra- and Interorganizational cooperation: Toward a research agenda," *Academy of Management Journal* (38), 1995, pp. 7-23.

Stigler, G.J. "The Economics of Information," In *Price theory and its applications*, B. Saffran and F. M. Scherer (Ed.), 89, Elgar, Northampton, MA, 1961, pp. 543-555.

Teece, D.J. "Towards an Economic Theory of the Multiproduct Firm," *Journal of Economic Behavior & Organization* (3:1), 1982, pp. 39-63.

Tirole, J. "Incomplete Contracts: Where Do We Stand?," *Econometrica* (67:4), 1999, pp. 741-781.

Tsay, A.A., Nahmias, S. and Agrawal, N. "Modeling Supply Chain Contracts: A Review," In *Quantitative Models for Supply Chain Management*, S. Tayur, R. Ganeshan and M. Magazine (Ed.), Kulwer Academic Publishers, Boston, MA, 1999, pp. 299-336.

Van Bruggen, G.H., Smidts, A. and Wierenga, B. "Improving decision making by means of a marketing decision support system," *Management Science* (44:5), 1998, pp. 645-658.

Van der Meer-Kooistra, J. and Vosselman, E.G.J. "Management control of interfirm transactional relationships: The case of industrial renovation and maintenance," *Accounting, Organizations and Society* (25:1), 2000, pp. 51-77.

von Weizsacker, C.C. "The Costs of Substitution," *Econometrica* (52:(5)), 1984, pp. 1085-1116.

Wernerfelt, B. "A Resource-Based View of the Firm," *Strategic Management Journal* (5:2), 1984, pp. 171-180.

Williamson, O.E. *Markets and hierarchies, analysis and antitrust implications: a study in the economics of internal organization*, Free Press, New York, 1975.

Williamson, O.E. *The Economic Institutions of Capitalism*, Free Press, New York, 1985.

Williamson, O.E. "Comparative Economic Organization: The Analysis of Discrete Structural Alternatives," *Administrative Science Quarterly* (36), 1991, pp. 269-296.

Yoshino, M.Y. and Rangan, U.S. *Strategic alliances : an entrepreneurial approach to globalization*, Harvard Business School Press, Boston, Mass, 1995.

Zmud, R.W. "Opportunities for Strategic Information Manipulation Through New Information Technology," In *Organizations and Communication Technology*, J. Fulk and C. Steinfield (Ed.), Sage Publications, Newbury Park, CA, 1990, pp. 95-116.

Chapter 18

The Intelligent Internal Accounting Control Model Under E-Business Environment

Kyeong Seok Han: James H. Gerlach
Soongsil University, Seoul, 156-743, Korea : University of Colorado at Denver, P.O. Box 173364, Denver, CO, 80217, USA

Abstract: This paper reviews the history of the development of TICOM (The Internal Control Model), a computer-assisted method for designing and evaluating accounting internal control systems. Early research on TICOM primarily addressed the development of a modeling language and analytical procedures for evaluating the effectiveness of the modeled system of controls. Later research sought to enhance the capabilities of TICOM through knowledge management and natural language processing. This research demonstrated the potential to develop a computer-based tool for internal control evaluation that could support a high-level of interaction with the auditor, improving both the user interface and the reasoning capabilities of TICOM. The latest proposed model, TICOM-V, is based on a logical specification of an auditing domain problem under e-Business environment and utilizes artificial intelligence and logic programming language concepts in computer science. A number of benefits are derived from this interdisciplinary approach: (1) TICOM-V is a more natural representation for the internal accounting control description than previously available under e-Business environment; (2) PROLOG is closer to natural language systems based on a declarative programming language in computer science than the PASCAL language used in the old TICOM; (3) The result improves on the previous TICOM models by providing a more convenient means of delivering the analysis benefits of TICOM, in particular, the contraction algorithm for identifying pre-conditions before a particular process. These factors help produce a system that offers greater auditability and maintainability under e-Business environment than previously possible.

Key words: TICOM (The Internal Control Model), computer-assisted method, designing and evaluating accounting internal control systems

1. INTRODUCTION

Internal control in any business organization is important to assure the accuracy and reliability of accounting information. Bailey et al. [1985] have presented a computer-assisted model for the design, analysis, and evaluation of internal accounting control systems. The model, called The Internal Control Model (TICOM), was originally designed for Office Information Systems (OISs). Experience with using TICOM to model and analyze typical accounting information systems has demonstrated that this approach is suitable to analyzing complex OISs, with speed, rigor, and accuracy. This technique compares favorably to the outmoded method of flowcharting and desk review, which auditors often use for evaluating accounting internal control systems.

However, the rigidity of the TICOM implementation and the modeling language prevented it from being widely accepted by auditors. TICOM analysis was derived from principles of formal program verification, which disregards the fact that internal control evaluation is more than deductive reasoning; it is also a social process. [De Millo et al., 1979, Bailey et al., 1989]. In an effort to advance the capabilities of TICOM, extensions and improvements have been proposed that incorporate Natural Language Processing (NLP), knowledge management, and artificial intelligence. The ultimate goal is to produce a computer-assisted tool for internal control evaluation that operates at the level of an expert auditor. The TICOM project provides the most comprehensive solution to internal control evaluation to date.

Wallace, a fore thinker in the auditing field, speculated that a TICOM-type solution would eventually be needed for dealing with increasingly complex accounting systems and organizations [Wallace, 1995, pp. 616]. e-Business is the manifestation of that prophecy. e-Business has led to the development of technically sophisticated, complex accounting systems and organization structures, which interconnect consumers to business and business to business. Although the original TICOM was created for the OIS environment of the 1980's, the fundamental principles of the original TICOM are still applicable today, and, as demonstrated in this article, can be used in evolved form to model and analyze e-Business systems.

This article reviews the original TICOM model and other extensions and improvements that have been proposed. The newest proposal is TICOM V. It offers a logic-based formulation that offers a better fit between how auditors naturally perceive accounting systems and the presentation and action languages. The PROLOG-based implementation makes it possible for auditors to perform traditional system walk-throughs and selected code checking at varying levels of detail. Auditors can also utilize the analytical techniques of the original TICOM to formally analyze the system of internal controls. In this manner, auditors can augment their own inductive reasoning by harnessing the deductive reasoning capacity of the computer.

2. TICOM

Research on Office Information Systems (OISs) during the early 1980's projected a shadowy image of the future office environment. Electronic mail and teleconferencing improved office communications. Word processors and document filing systems sped up clerical work. Besides automating office devices, research focused on automating office procedures as well. Innovations included office procedure development languages that integrated data base queries, spreadsheet calculations, electronic mail actions, and word processing operations. Supposedly, office workers would construct semi-automated office tasks for distributed document processing that would perform a variety of basic accounting functions such as loan processing and travel expense reporting [Bailey et al., 1985].

TICOM [Bailey et al., 1981] was originally proposed as a mechanism for addressing accounting security and control issues in an OIS environment. The fundamental concept was to model the formal flow of electronic form processing and analyze it for internal control reliability. TICOM provided a specification of a modeling language for describing office tasks and analytic procedures for assessing internal control reliability.

2.1 The Theoretical Basis of TICOM

The types of questions posed by auditors during internal control evaluation are diverse. Many of the questions concern state achievability. For example, the release of a payment to a supplier. For each state the modeled accounting system can achieve, TICOM analysis establishes a precondition for entering that state and a postcondition that is necessarily true when the state is achieved. The former permits analysis of the strength of safeguards in the system, while the latter allows the identification of the internal control system components to examine in regard to identifying the perpetrator when control circumvention is suspected.

Internal control systems are modeled using the Internal Control Description Language (ICDL). ICDL was based on the concept of abstract data type used in the programming language Pascal. Abstract data types could be defined for office worker roles, tasks, electronic forms, and data repositories. Office processing is defined by the concept of transaction: a series of interrelated, asynchronous tasks that specify how office objects (i.e., documents) move from their source repositories (i.e., new work) to their destination repositories (i.e., finished work). The rigid specification facilitated mechanical recognition, but lacked the human engineering needed to please the general office worker. A model specification resembled a large, but relatively simple, Pascal computer program. Figure 1 shows the ICDL task specification for a verification check made by a clerk in the stores department. The complete model would include task descriptions for vendor, receiving department, purchasing department and cash-disbursements department.

Precondition and postcondition evaluation of accounting models is closely related to the formal analysis of programs [Dykstra, 1975]. In TICOM, the ICDL specification for an accounting system is mapped into an internal representation that corresponds to a bilogic-directed graph, which resembles a flowchart. In this precedence model, each node represents a conditional action taken by an office worker. Node i is described by: $PC_i = ((n_1, \ldots, n_k), r_1, \ldots, r_m)$ if an only if node i follows nodes $n_1, \ldots, n_k$ under the condition $r_1, \ldots, r_m$.

The fundamental analytical algorithm for calculating preconditions and postconditions is known as contraction and simplification. Contraction and simplification enables the removal of a node from the graph without destroying the relationships of the original graph. By eliminating all nodes except the one representing the state that is of interest to the auditor, the precondition and postconditions can be determined. Figure 2 shows the steps to reduce a graph of several nodes to one. In each reduction, the actions of the eliminated node are incorporated into the other nodes that immediately depend on it. The coalesced nodes, which represent the serialized actions of many, are simplified using rules of logic.

2.2 The Implementation of TICOM

Early work on TICOM developed the underlying principles. Under a grant from the Peat, Marwick, and Mitchell Foundation, a prototype of TICOM was implemented. The objective was to enhance the theoretical development of TICOM and demonstrate the feasibility of computer-assisted internal control evaluation.

The implementation consisted of a parser for reading internal control systems described in ICDL and a query analyzer for answering questions posed by the auditor. The parser performs standard functions such as type checking and syntax checking. It also maps the textual model into an internal representation that could be further analyzed by computer methods that implement contraction and simplification. A query analyzer controls the analytical procedures. Queries identify the critical instruction(s) of interest to the auditor. The query analyzer uses contraction and simplification to reduce the internal control system to only those precedent conditions governing the critical instructions. For example, the query processor could determine the conditions under which a payment is made to a supplier.

The TICOM prototype demonstrated that computer-assisted methods have the advantage of speed, accuracy, and reliability [Bailey et al., 1985]:

a. The evaluation can be more rigorous and exhaustive.

b. The documentation of the system can be more thorough because of automated completeness and consistency tests.

c. The modeler may probe and test controls by using the query-processing portion of TICOM.

Although the prototype demonstrated that the theoretical principles of TICOM are sufficient for answering search, status, and what-if types of questions about the described internal control system; it also revealed other deficiencies. The implementation of TICOM was based on the then contemporary techniques for parsing and compiling third generation programming languages. By today's standards, the implementation of the ICDL was rigid and non-extensible. Furthermore, the ICDL was a textual language rather than a graphical language; textual specifications are not preferred by auditors who are accustomed to reviewing system flowchart specifications and both verbal and written system documentation. Lastly, TICOM requires a human expert to search for potential exposures, evaluate the strength of the controls based upon the precondition analysis, and combine the results of many queries into an overall evaluation. It was unknown whether the analytical approach to evaluating internal control systems is compatible with the auditor's cognitive processes.

2.3 Knowledge Representation Theory and TICOM

The early experience with TICOM revealed that without an accepted normative model for internal controls the evaluation capabilities of TICOM are too restrictive for field use. Auditors are used to asking "if the segregation of duties in the purchasing system is adequate?" They are not accustomed to translating that question into a request for the preconditions regulating the receipt of purchased assets and then examine that set of conditions for adequate separation of duties. Further, auditors are accustomed to working with fragmented and incomplete documentation of the internal control system; TICOM requires a full and complete description to operate. Furthermore, TICOM analysis relies solely on deductive, forward reasoning; but auditors also employ proof by contradiction.

Bailey, Whinston and Zacarias [1989] extended and redefined TICOM using artificial intelligence and knowledge management techniques. Natural Language Processing (NLP) was proposed as a solution to addressing the problems of the auditor interface. NLP would allow auditors to communicate with the system more easily, simplifying query processing and knowledge acquisition. The NLP approach emphasizes a script-based representation of the internal control model and accounting concepts that could be utilized by a Prolog-like inference mechanism for answering queries posed by the auditor.

Accounting scripts contain the audit expertise for familiar concepts as "segregation of duties" and "purchasing subsystem." For this example, the relevant scripts would specify that the purchasing activities of authorization, recording the transaction, and receipt of the purchased assets should be performed by separate departments or personnel. Scripts would also be used to represent details of the accounting internal control system. Each accounting task would be encoded as a script capturing originator, receiver and effect (e.g., Purchasing agent would send a cash distribution if the invoice items matched the items listed on the receiving report). A purchasing system would be described as a collection of purchasing scripts that would collectively describe the various ways of purchasing assets.

A dynamic knowledge base was envisioned for the storage and retrieval of scripts by the inference engine. The reasoning mechanism would identify relevant scripts stored in the knowledge base and use them to resolve the query. Nested scripts (i.e., one script referencing more detailed scripts) provided organization to the knowledge base that facilitated script retrieval for semantic understanding and deduction. The theoretical example presented demonstrated how the knowledge base of scripts could be utilized to answer the query, "Is segregation of duties in the purchasing subsystem adequate?" The inference engine would utilize the nested scripts describing segregation of duties, adequate, and purchasing activities. The inference mechanism would then construct a proof by contradiction by first assuming that the controls are not segregated and then finding that this assumption contradicts the knowledge base.

The intent of this line of research was on establishing a foundation for representing accounting knowledge and internal control system descriptions that could support a high-level of interaction with the auditor. The knowledge approach proved more powerful than the original TICOM theory in that it utilized semantic knowledge of accounting that TICOM did not have. Further, the knowledge representation could capture details of the timing of accounting events and incomplete information (i.e., uncertainty as a three-valued truth system that includes undefined). Last, the knowledge representation was sufficiently expressive to support a reasoning mechanism that can construct proofs by method of counter examples, as well as calculate pre- and post-conditions.

The study established a foundation that will guide future development of computer-based support for accounting internal control design, modeling and evaluation. However, demonstration will not be easy since the proposed system would need to utilize three different knowledge representations and corresponding translation mechanisms. Also, a vast array of basic accounting knowledge would have to be encoded in order for the system to reflect human understanding and judgment.

3. THE INTELLIGENT TICOM (TICOM V)

In order to incorporate artificial intelligence and to extend the ICDL, major implementation changes are required. PROLOG (PROgramming in LOGic) [Clocksin and Mellish, 1984] was chosen as the fundamental implementation language since it is more natural and more easily understood in this context. An important motivating factor in the selection of PROLOG is that the processes of "contraction and simplification", important in the original TICOM analyses, is very similar to problem reduction processes using an AND/OR graph [Bratko, 1986] based on the resolution refutation system in PROLOG. PROLOG-based TICOM-V retains the advantages of the original TICOM in terms of consistency of data entry, completeness of analysis, and simplification of process conditions, but improves on TICOM's analytical capabilities gaining insight into the implication of contraction and simplification, thus providing greater convenience, flexibility, and rigor than available in earlier formulations. The resulting model is a part of an ongoing research effort, which combines the internal control system based on PROLOG and the accounting reporting system based on Meta Language (ML) [Bailey et al., 1989] in a unified accounting model based on SEMLOG [Stansifer et al., 1989]. SEMLOG is a new language combining aspects of ML and PROLOG. The resulting system based on PROLOG is much more user-friendly and consistent with the auditors' view of auditing and the auditors' need for verifiability of the internal control structure.

The old TICOM relied on four unique methods of analysis beyond standard data base concepts in supporting auditor queries: consistency checking of data entry, completeness of analysis for any well specified input, simplification processes, and contraction processes. PROLOG is a better language to support these capabilities than was PASCAL. After representing an internal accounting control system in PROLOG, syntactic analysis is used to establish the consistency of data entry and system data flow. Semantic analysis helps to establish the completeness of the control system description and analysis. The model of TICOM-V based on e-Business is shown as Figure 3.

In this section, we describe a segment of purchasing cycle implemented in PROLOG. The flowchart of Figure 4 presents the flows in a directed graph in keeping with its translation to PROLOG. All interesting information in the flow chart can be represented in PROLOG. In TICOM-V, syntactic analysis is performed to check the consistency of data entry and system data flow in accordance with auditing systems, as discussed in previous section. Once the system is found to be syntactically correct, we can analyze whether or not it is a semantically correct from the viewpoint of auditors.

We represent the basic flowchart information using PROLOG predicates. PROLOG programs consist of facts and rules. Set off acts stated in PROLOG for the basic information form the data base. For example, the predicate, dept(node(X),Y), represents that the department of node(X) is Y. In our purchasing cycle example, dept(node(3),receiving) represents that the department of node 3 is a receiving department. In a similar way, process(node(X),Y), represents that the process of node(X) is Y. For example, process(node(7),transfer(rr2,stores)) represents the process of node(7) is "transfer a receiving-report-2 to a store department." The functor, transfer(rr2,stores), corresponds to TRANSFER RR-2 TO STORES in the Internal Control Description Language (ICDL) of the old TICOM. The restatement of the PASCAL-based the old TICOM to a PROLOG-based TICOM-V progresses by a similar mapping throughout.

Activity flows represented by arrows in the flow chart can be classified into three categories based on their unique properties. First, arrows within a department are named path arrows (pa). For example, pa(node(X),node(Y)) represents the path arrows from node(X) to node(Y) within a department. Second, arrows between departments are called transfer arrows (ta). For example, ta(node(X),node(Y)) represents the transfer arrows from node(X) to node(Y) between departments. Third, arrows related to decision-making are called decision arrows (da). For example, da(node(X),node(Y),node(Z),cond(C)) represents the decision arrows from node(X) to node(Y) if the condition C is true, or to node(Z) otherwise.

Syntactic analysis is used to check the consistency of data entry. The role of syntactic analysis is similar to that of type checking in programming languages. Unexpected data entries are subjected to syntactic analysis. The syntactic analysis enforces or constrains the system in selected ways. For example, the control system description accepts only one process per node. In other words, only one process can be associated with a node in our system. This condition is enforced by the predicate cknpc(N). Convenient consistency checking facility through PROLOG is an advantage over existing auditing expert systems using expert system shells. For instance, a process "transfer [Receiving Report 2] to STORES" must correspond to a process "wait for [Receiving Report 2]" in STORES and it will be checked out in the TICOM-V system.

Once we made the following predicates based on auditors' viewpoints, auditors can get the interesting information about an accounting system during execution of the PROLOG program. Several example queries are discussed in this section and next section.

"To which department are the vendor's invoices sent?" The entire program of the predicate is as follows:

```
ven_s_inv(D) :-
    dept(node(X), vendor),
    process(node(X), transfer(L,D)), member(invoice,L).
```

where, ven_s_inv(D) is the predicate for the query to be answered. An English translation follows: "The department of node x is vendor, the process of node x is 'transfer a list of documents, L, to a department D', and the invoice is on the document list, L." Using a set of well-formed formulas (wff's) in predicate logic, we can represent the program of the predicate as follows:

$\forall x\ \forall L\ \exists D$ dept(node(x),vendor) $\wedge$ process(node(x),transfer(L,D)) $\wedge$ member(invoice,L) -> ven_s_inv(D). The answer obtained in the execution is D = Purchasing.

We can explain the theorem proving process for the answer from the program execution segment using a technique called problem reduction in the AI literature [Nilsson, 1980] based on the resolution refutation system in PROLOG. The problem reduction replaces the main or ultimate problem with a set of sub-problems. If the sub-problems are solved, the main problem is also solved. The main problem, ven_s_inv(D), is solved, when the sub-problems, dept(node(X),vendor), process(node(X),transfer(L,D)), and member(invoice,L) are solved. The sub-problems are investigated based on a depth-first search algorithm until all of the sub-problems related to the main problem are solved. By the pattern matching process in PROLOG illustrated in Figure 5 we could obtain X=2, L=[invoice], D=purchasing. Details of the resolution refutation process appear in Figure 5.

"Under what conditions will a company distribute a check or cash to a vendor based on a valid voucher signed by the authorized personnel?" The program code for this query is as follows:

```
cond_voucher(C,MaxDepth) :-
    process(X, assign(voucher,amt,payee,authorized-person)),
    condition(X,C,MaxDepth).
```

where, cond_voucher(C,MaxDepth) is the predicate to be answered by the query, i.e. the conditions for payment of a voucher.

We can explain the meaning of the program segment using the same argument. The main problem, cond_voucher(C), is solved, when the subproblems, process(...) and condition(X,C), are solved. By the pattern matching process in PROLOG we could obtain x=node(23) from the predicate process(X,assign(...)), and the predicate condition(X,C) becomes condition(node(23),C). The role of predicate condition(node(23),C) is to collect conditions from the predefined decision nodes from the starting node to node(23) in Figure 4. Additional examples of queries and their related predicates are:

(1) A predicate to answer the query "What condition is required for Stores department to send the receiving report-2 to Cash Disbursement department ?" is cond_s_rr(C,MaxDepth).

(2) A predicate to check whether or not duties in the departments are segregated to protect company assets is segregation_duty. In the purchasing cycle example, we assume that at least the process of assigning amount and payee of voucher, the process of comparing items on an invoice with items on receiving-report-1, and the process of comparing items on a purchasing order with items on receiving-report-2 should be done in separate departments.

(3) A predicate to answer the query "Will a voucher be prepared after goods are received from the vendor?" is pay_with_receiving_goods. We get node numbers of the two processes and check a path between the two nodes.

The discussion to this point does not include feedback loops. TICOM-V supports a graph with any feedback loop in the accounting system. The old TICOM used a heuristic loop elimination procedure during path analysis[Gerlach, 1982]. We put some constraints on the process to permit solvability, e.g. the maximum depth (MaxDepth) of a search limits the number of feedback attempts in the feedback loop. In other words, we keep trace of the current depth of the search and prevent the program from searching beyond some depth limit [Bratko, 1986]. The predicates, solve and condition, include the MaxDepth operator to handle the feedback loops. The predicates and their execution results are shown as follows:

```
/* -- Path Analysis with AND/OR Graph (below) -- */
.....
solve(Node, [Node|Tree],MaxDepth) :-
   MaxDepth > 0, Node -- or : Nodes,
   Depth1 is MaxDepth-1, member(Node1, Nodes),
   solve(Node1, Tree, Depth1).

solve(Node, [Node|Trees],MaxDepth) :-
   MaxDepth > 0, Node -- and : Nodes,
   Depth1 is MaxDepth-1,
   solveall(Nodes, Trees, Depth1).

/* Semantic Analysis from Auditors' Viewpoint (below) */
.....
condition(N2,L,MaxDepth) :-
   solve(N2,X,MaxDepth), findcond(L,X).
.....
/* ---------------- Execution ------------------*/

| ?- solve(node(25),L,24).

L =
[node(25),node(23),node(22),node(21),node(20),[node(12),node(11),
node(10),node(9),node(7),node(6),node(5),node(4),node(3),node(1)],
[node(17),node(16),node(15),[node(2),node(1)],[node(6),node(5),
node(4 ),node(3),node(1)]]] ;

L =
[node(25),node(23),node(22),node(21),node(20),[node(12),node(11),
node(10),node(9),node(7),node(6),node(5),node(4),node(3),node(1)]
,[node(17),node(16),node(15),[node(2),node(1),node(19),node(16),n
ode(15),[node(2),node(1)],[node(6),node(5),node(4),node(3),node(1
)]],[node(6),node(5),node(4),node(3),node(1)]]] ;
```

.....

| ?- condition(node(25),L,25).

L = [Amount >= $100 for Vouchers Assigned by Authorized Persons,[Items in PO = Items in RR2],[Items in Invoice = Items in RR1,[],[]]] ;

L = [Amount >= $100 for Vouchers Assigned by Authorized Persons,[Items in PO = Items in RR2],[Items in Invoice = Items in RR1,[not Items in Invoice = Items in RR1,[],[]],[]]] ;

.....

The underlined portions of the above program results are related to the feedback loop. In the purchasing cycle example as shown in Figure 4 the path arrow from node(19) to node(1) is the feedback loop. As we can see in the above output, the path goes from node 1 to node 19 instead of terminating at node 1. It can not become an infinite loop, because we limit the number of feedbacks. As we can see in this section, PROLOG-based TICOM-V offers significant improvements over PASCAL-based the old TICOM.

4. SUMMARY AND CONCLUSIONS

The TICOM project represents a stream of research on computer-based support for accounting internal control evaluation that has spanned twenty years and involved over nine researchers. TICOM is an advanced computer-assisted method of designing, analyzing, and evaluating internal control systems. Compared to the outmoded method of flowcharting and narratives, which are still the auditor's tool of choice for internal control evaluation, the TICOM project provides the most comprehensive solution to internal control evaluation to date. TICOM makes it possible for auditors to perform traditional system "walk-throughs" and selected code checking at varying levels of detail. The internal control model can be checked extensively for consistency and completeness. Auditors can also query the system for the preconditions (controls) that must be satisfied prior to executing a transaction or an event and thus identify those controls that may warrant testing. The analytical procedures provide an exhaustive search of the problem space, identifying only the relevant controls that regulate accounting events. These factors should enhance both the effectiveness and efficiency of the audit.

Continued research on the basic TICOM concept has demonstrated theoretically that the capabilities of TICOM can be greatly enhanced using knowledge management and artificial intelligence techniques. Such a system might be capable of internal control analysis and judgment like that of a human expert.

The most recent research on TICOM has developed a new technology base for TICOM to extend its use to more complex systems, such as e-Business. The PROLOG basis makes it much more easy to implement the analytical procedures and extend the instruction set of the ICDL beyond data processing type activities of the original OIS model. The declarative form of the ICDL and the logic-based implementation of the analytic procedures reduce the conceptual gap between the auditor and the system; allowing the auditor to use the deductive reasoning power of the computer to enhance his/her own inductive reasoning. Furthermore, the artificial intelligence basis should facilitate the integration of expert system technology for automated internal control evaluation in the future. A goal that has been proposed by auditing experts decades ago but is yet to be realized. The new open system architecture of TICOM V should prove useful in this regard [Meservy et al., 1986, Holsapple and Whinston, 1987, Jacob and Bailey, 1989]. Combining TICOM-V with auditing expert systems would allow for an automated evaluation of internal accounting controls within the modeled accounting system and provide an overall architecture for integrating fragmented expert systems.

Future research is planned to further develop the TICOM model as a knowledge-based system. Han et al. intend to combine the processing system (TICOM-V) using PROLOG, and the reporting system using ML (Meta Language) to support the Formal Algorithmic Accounting Model (FAAM) based on high level programming languages [Bailey et al., 1989]. ML is a functional programming language whereas PROLOG is a logic programming language. Each of these languages has its own advantages. Han et al. are designing a high level programming language, SEMLOG (Semantic Logic) [Stansifer et al., 1989]. SEMLOG is suitable for supporting decision-making in an accounting environment. SEMLOG is a language with powerful capabilities based on the idea of logic (PROLOG), functional (ML), and object-oriented (Smalltalk) programming languages. In our proposed internal control model we could make good use of the SEMLOG typing system which is not available in PROLOG. Moreover, the inheritance capability in SEMLOG would make it possible to inherit the supertype information in the subtype elements. Using modularity concepts in object-oriented programming languages, we will be able to handle "transactions" more conveniently. For example, when an item is sold, all of the data related to the transaction have to be updated as one package. In order to obtain greater capabilities based on the inheritance and modularity, the object-oriented database model can be considered for the representation of auditing processes and accounting data.

Another research direction includes support for end-user communications. Users want information to be available in various formats such as flowcharts, forms, tables, etc. We will be able to develop a user interface model based on direct manipulation of the internal control model, TICOM, using visual programming implemented by user interface management systems. It will eventually be possible to create programs internally by producing flowcharts externally. We call this kind of programming process-visual programming. For example, end-users may use graphical flowcharts on a computer screen for documentation, manipulation, and evaluation of the internal accounting control system based on direct manipulation user interfaces [Schneiderman, 1983]. The graphical flowcharts can be converted into PROLOG or SEMLOG internally and automatically. Figure 6 illustrates a possible screen using current graphic software for drawing. The future user interface internal control model will be user-friendly [Bailey et al., 1987].

REFERENCES

Bailey, Andrew D., Jr., Gerlach, James.H. and Whinston, Andrew B (1985). Office Systems Technology and Organizations, Reston Publishing Co., 251 pages.

Bailey, Andrew D., Jr., Gerlach, James. H., McAfee, R.Preston and Whinston, Andrew B (1981) "Internal Accounting Controls in the Office of the Future," IEEE Computer, May, pp. 59-70.

Bailey, Andrew D., Jr., Whinston, Andrew B and Zacarias, P.T. (1989) "Knowledge Representation Theory and the Design of Auditable Office Information Systems," Journal of Information Systems, Spring, pp. 1-28.

Amer, T., Andrew D. Bailey, Jr., and Prabuddha De. (1987). A Survey of Computer-Information Systems Research in Accounting and Auditing, *Journal of Information Systems*, Fall.

Bailey, Andrew. D., Jr., Kyeong S. Han, Ryan D. Stansifer, and Andrew B. Whinston. (1992). A Formal Algorithmic Model Compatible with Conceptual Modeling in Accounting Information Systems, *Accounting, Management, and Information Technology, Vol.2, No.2*, 57-76.

Bailey, Andrew. D., Jr., Kyeong S. Han, Ryan D. Stansifer, and Andrew B. Whinston. (1989). A Formal Algorithmic Model Compatible with Conceptual Modeling in Accounting Information Systems, *Working Paper, Dept. of Accounting and MIS, Ohio State University.*

Bailey, Andrew. D., Jr., Kyeong S. Han, and Andrew B. Whinston. (1987). Technology, Competition, and the Future of Auditing, *In Proceedings of the Arthur Young Professors' Roundtable at Ohio State University*, October.

Bailey, A. D. Jr., G. L. Duke, J. Gerlach, C. Ko, R. D. Meservy, and A. B. Whinston. (1985). TICOM and the Analysis of Internal Controls, *The Accounting Review*, April.

Barber, G. (1983). Supporting Organizational Problem Solving with a Work Station, *ACM Trans. on Office Information Systems, Vol.1, No.1*, January.

Biggs, S. F., T. J. Mock, and P. R. Watkins. (1988). Auditor's Use of Analytical Review in Audit Program Design, *The Accounting Review*, January.

Biggs, S. F., W. F. Messier, Jr., and J. Hansen. (1987). A Descriptive Analysis of Computer Audit Specialists' Decision-Making Behavior in Advanced Computer Environments, *Auditing: A Journal of Practice and Theory*, Spring.

Biggs, S. F. and T. J. Mock. (1983). An Investigation of Auditor Decision Processes in the Evaluation of Internal Controls and Audit Scope Decisions, *Journal of Accounting Research*, Spring.

Bratko, I. (1986). *PROLOG Programming for Artificial Intelligence*, Addison-Wesley.

Chen, K-T and R. Lee. (1988). On Formal Modeling of Accounting Control Systems, *Working paper, Department of Management Science and Information Systems, University of Texas at Austin.*

Clocksin W. F. and C. S. Mellish. (1984). *Programming in Prolog (2nd edition)*, Springer-Verlag.

De, Prabuddha and Arun Sen. (1988). Semantic Modeling of Internal Controls in Database Design, *Journal of Management Information Systems, Vol.5, No.2*, Fall.

De Millo, R. A., R. J. Lipton, and A. J. Perlis. (1979). Social Processes and Proofs of Theorems and Programs, *Communications of the ACM*, May, 271-280.

Einhorn, H. and R. M. Hogarth. (1981). Behavioral Decision Theory: Processes of Judgment and Choice, *Journal of Accounting Research*, Spring.

Ellis, C. A. (1979). Information Control Nets: A Mathematical Model of Office Information Flow, *ACM Proceedings Conference Simulation, Modelling and Measurement of Computer Systems*, August, 225-240.

E.W. Dijkstra, "Guarded Commands, Nondeterminancy and Formal Description of Programs," Communications of the ACM, Vol. 18, August 1975, pp. 453-457.

Gerlach, J. H. (1982). Internal Accounting Control Design, Evaluation and Implementation in Automated Office Information Systems, *Unpublished Ph.D. Thesis, School of Management, Purdue University.*

Harrison, W. and B. Adrangi. (1986-87). The Role of Programming Language in Estimating Software Development Costs, *Journal of Management Information Systems, Vol.III, No.3*, Winter.

Holsapple, Clyde W. and Andrew B. Whinston. (1987). *Business Expert Systems*, Irwin.

Jacob, V. and A. D. Bailey, Jr. (1989). A Decision Process Approach to Expert Systems in Auditing, *2nd International Workshop on Artificial Intelligence in Economics and Management, Singapore*, January , North-Holland, forthcoming.

Meservy, R., A. D. Bailey, Jr., and P. E. Johnson. (1986). Internal Control Evaluation: A Computational Model of the Review Process, *Auditing: A Journal of Practice and Theory*, Fall, 44-74.

Nilsson, N. J. (1980). *Principles of Artificial Intelligence*, Springer-Verlag.

O'Leary, Daniel E. (1987). Validation of Expert Systems - with Applications to Auditing and Accounting Expert Systems, *Decision Sciences, Vol.18, No.3*, Summer.

Peterson, J. L. (1981). *Petri Net Theory and the Modeling of Systems*, Prentice-Hall Inc., Englewood Cliffs, N.J.

Ryu, Y. U. and R. Lee. (1988). Event Nets: A Formalism for Specifying Organizational Procedures, *Working Paper, Department of Management Science and Information Systems, University of Texas at Austin*, September.

Schneiderman, B. (1983). Direct Manipulation: A Step Beyond Programming Languages, *IEEE Computer*, August.

Stansifer, Ryan, Chul Y. Jung and Andrew Whinston. (1989). SEMLOG: A Multiparadigm Programming Language For Knowledge Engineering, *Working paper, Department of Computer Science, Purdue University.*

Tversky, A. and D. Kahneman. (1974). Judgment Under Uncertainty: Heuristics and Biases, *Science*, September.

Wallace, W. A. Auditing, South Western, 1995, 1146 pages.

Zisman, M. D. (1977). Representation, Specification and Automation of Office Procedures, *Doctoral Dissertation, University of Pennsylvania.*

```
WAIT FOR RECEIVING-REPORT2:
GET PURCHASE-ORDER FROM ONORDER-FILE;
IF (PURCHASE-ORDER.ITEMS = RECEIVING-
REPORT2.ITEMS)
   TRANSFER RECEIVING-REPORT2 TO CASH-
DISBURSEMENTS;
ELSE
   REVIEW;
PUT PURCHASE-ORDER INTO RECEIVING-FILE:
```

Figure 1. An ICDL Task Description for a Purchasing Activity Performed by a Clerk in Stores

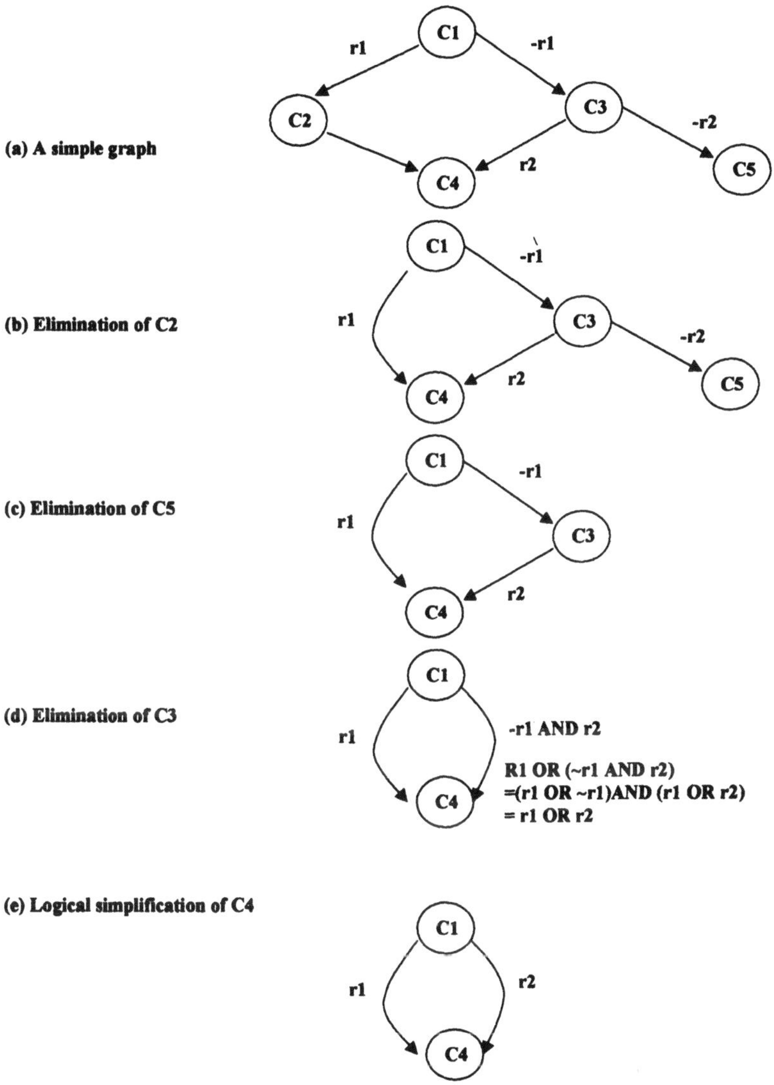

Figure 2. Contraction and Simplification

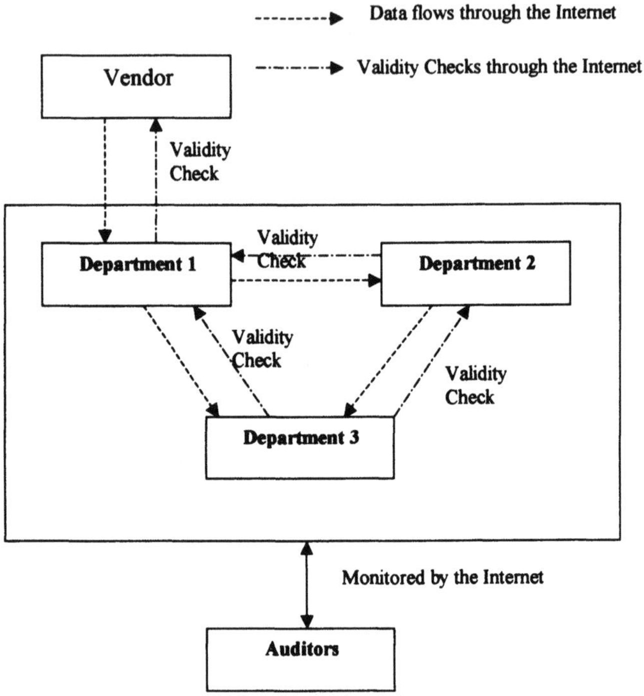

Figure 3. The Model of TICOM-V Based on e-Business

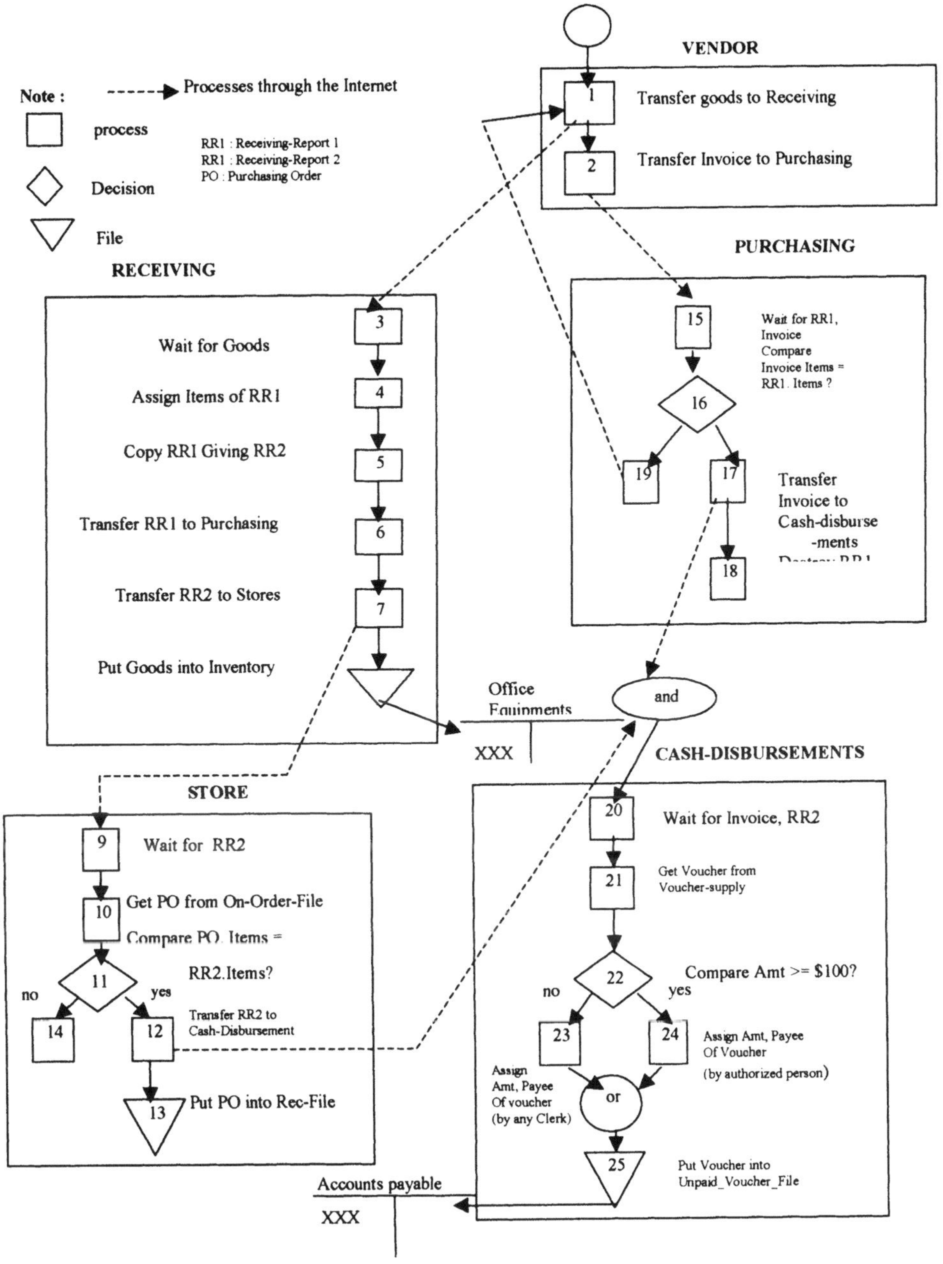

Figure 4. A Part of Purchasing System for Internal Accounting Control

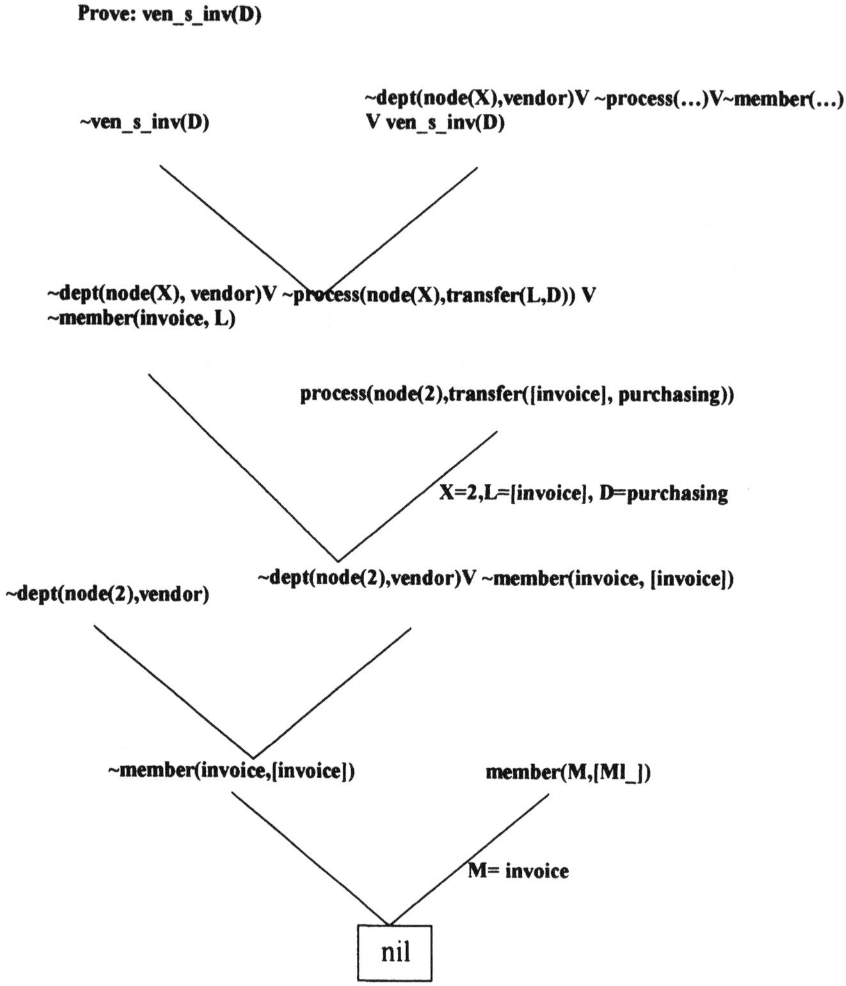

Figure 5. A Resolution Proof Process for the Predicate, ven_s_inv(d)

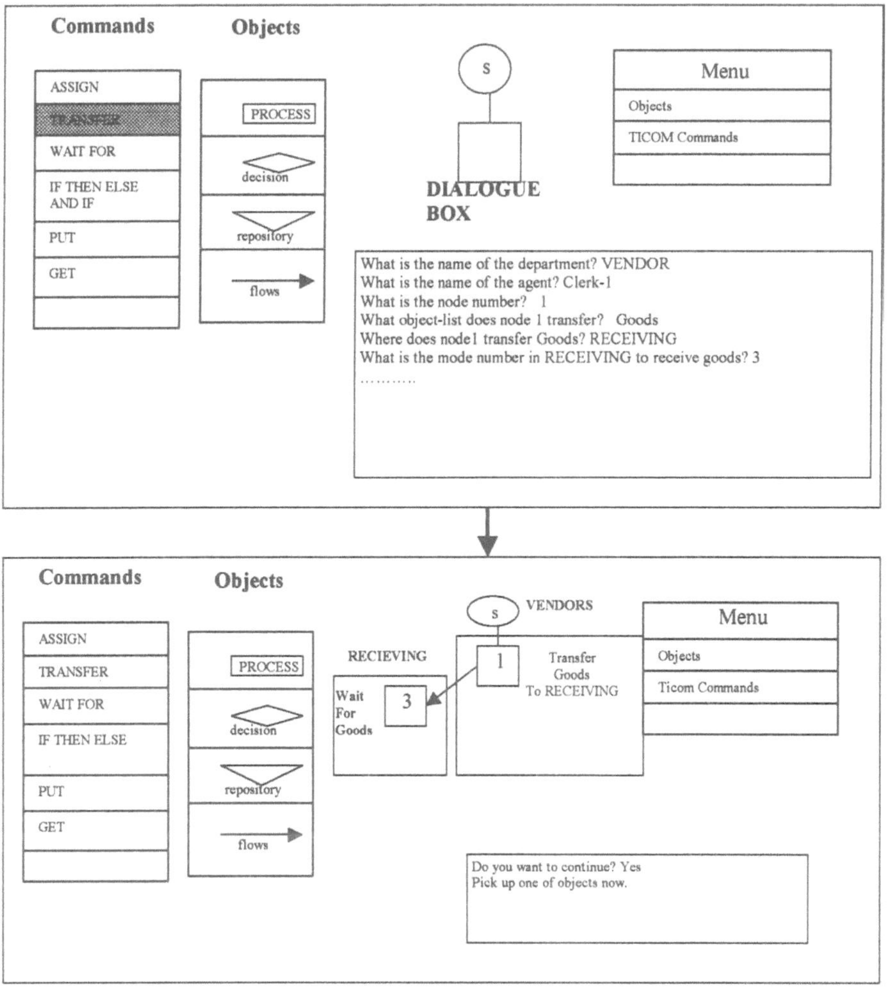

Figure 6. A Possible Window for the Documentation for Flowcharts for Internet Control

Chapter 19

Internet Diffusion In Developing Countries

A Socio-Technical Model

Amitava Dutta: Rahul Roy
School of Management, George Mason University, 4400 University Drive, Fairfax, VA 22020, USA. adutta@som.gmu.edu: MIS Group, Indian Institute of Management Calcutta, PO Box 16757, Alipore PO. Calcutta 700027, INDIA rahul@iimcal.ac.in

Key words: Internet diffusion, developing country, simulation, systems dynamics.

Abstract: Whinston and Kalakota have proposed a layered architecture for E-commerce, analogous to the 7-layer OSI model. Some of its components are purely technical while others involve social and political elements. It explicitly recognizes that E-commerce is a socio-technical activity and suggests certain building blocks with which to structure the same. In this article we report initial efforts to develop a model, which takes a systems view to analyzc how social and technical drivers are likely to interact and drive Internet diffusion in developing countries. These countries, in particular, need to understand the complex mechanics of this diffusion process in order to realize their potential for growth in the new world of E-Commerce based trade and business. The systems dynamics methodology is used to develop the model allowing for simulation of different growth scenarios and policy alternatives.

1. INTRODUCTION

The impact of the Internet on economic, social and political activity is well established. The impact is so significant that the Internet is now widely considered to be an integral part of national infrastructure, just as telephone networks were decades ago. In fact, a new term - "the digital-divide" - has been coined, to reflect the growing concern that digital have-nots will be left behind in the new economy. This concern is particularly acute in the case of developing countries, which are starting low on the economic ladder and where telecommunications infrastructure has been plagued by chronic and acute shortage of capacity, lack of reliability and obsolete technology. However, this situation also has a silver lining in that it offers these countries the opportunity to leapfrog intermediate generations and adopt cheaper and more effective technologies. For instance, wireless technologies have matured substantially in recent times, both in terms of performance and costs. Therefore, an examination of the diffusion of Internet infrastructure in developing countries is of some interest from the standpoint of global business. Further, since the achievement and maintenance of equitable economic growth is part of the development strategies of these countries, the diffusion of Internet infrastructure has been identified as an important national policy issue by the ITU [ITU99a] because of its potential to advance critical objectives such as health and education.

In two pioneering books [KaW96a], [KaW96b], Kalakota and Whinston propose a layered architecture for E-commerce, analogous to the 7-layer OSI model. The architecture specifies components that build on top of each other to support E-commerce. It contains technical components such as transmission media, protocols, encryption systems, electronic wallets and shopbots. One driver behind the diffusion of EC infrastructure anywhere, be it developing or industrialized countries, is advances in these technology areas. However, there are also non-technical components in the architecture. Examples include intellectual property and privacy laws, regulatory policy and trade laws. The proposed architecture explicitly recognizes the socio-technical nature of E-commerce. Unless the non-technical infrastructure components also mature, the diffusion of E-commerce will be restricted. The diffusion of E-commerce results from the interplay between the demand for and supply of its technical and non-technical elements.

Developing countries, in particular, need to understand the mechanics of this diffusion process in order to realize their potential for growth in the new world of E-commerce based trade and business. Diffusion will depend on several factors, most important of which will be their physical infrastructure for E-commerce, both physical (the telecommunication network), the financial and legal framework, and a business and trade environment conducive to E-commerce. It will also depend on the availability and price of hardware (computers, routers, switches etc.) and software, as well as availability of properly qualified human resources and the education standards of the country.

In this article, we make an initial effort to model this socio-technical diffusion process by taking a 'systems thinking' approach. The essence of systems thinking is that the individual structural elements of a system, and their interaction, leads to system behaviour. For the context of Internet diffusion, the system is a socio-technical rather than a purely physical one. The systems thinking approach would dictate that we represent the interactions among the technical, economic and social components in order to understand the mechanics of diffusion. The methodology of systems dynamics [Ste00] will be used to formally represent these structural interactions and examine diffusion behaviour generated by this structure.

2. SYSTEMS DYNAMICS

A variety of methods are available for representing dynamic processes. We have chosen systems dynamics [Ste00] to represent the Internet diffusion process for the following reasons. The main structural element in a systems dynamics (SD) model is the feedback loop, making it well suited for capturing the interaction among different drivers of diffusion over time. It can capture quantifiable as well as "soft" variables, which is useful given that the diffusion context has both social and technical aspects. Delays can also be modeled, and this is useful in representing certain social mechanisms. Moreover, SD models can be simulated, providing a platform on which to test various scenarios for policy determination. Of course, SD models can also be used for forecasting.

The basic premise in SD is that system structure causes system behavior. Behavior results from interaction among feedback loops in the system. Developing an SD model consists of identifying the feedback loop structure of the system and validating the simulated behavior through comparison with observed behavior. Model building begins with development of a 'cause and effect' graph that consists of a collection causal links, each having a certain polarity. A positive link implies a reinforcing relation where a positive change in the causing variable results in a positive change in the effect variable and vice versa. A negative link implies a balancing relationship where a positive change in the cause brings in a negative change in the effect and vice versa. Sometimes the change in the effect variable occurs after a delay. A small double-line intersecting the causal link perpendicularly, depicts this. A causal loop is formed by a closed sequence of causal links, and loop polarity can be easily determined from the individual link polarities. The cause effect graph leads to development of a mathematical model wherein relationships are depicted by means of time varying difference equations. System behavior is analyzed by simulating the mathematical model under different parametric or structural alternatives.

3. SOCIAL CULTURAL DIMENSIONS OF DIFFUSION

Data on Internet diffusion from different countries establishes that, although the Internet has experienced enormous growth in aggregate, the growth has been uneven across the world [Min00]. Several socio-economic factors have been cited to explain this difference in diffusion, and while the suggested impact of each factor is plausible, their collective impact remains ill understood. One recent overview may be found in [Pet98]. We draw on this literature to build a systems model that incorpoates interactions among these different factors.

We first summarize some of these explanations to be found in the literature and then follow that with a detailed presentation of the systems dynamics model. One explanation that has been put forward is economic output. Many earlier studies have confirmed a strong correlation between a country's economic outputs, measured by say per capita GDP, and its telecommunications infrastructure [CCI68]. The same correlation appears to hold for Internet infrastructure [Har98]. Also, since the Internet had grown in a way that favoured the use of English as the language of expression [Taw99], it has been suggested that language is also a factor in Internet diffusion – countries where English is well understood and used are likely to see more rapid diffusion of the Internet. In many countries where English is not widely used, lack of content in the local language has been cited in surveys as an impediment to Internet diffusion. In fact, the preponderance of Western culture based content has been seen as a threat in some countries, spurring efforts by their governments to legislate restrictions that present more barriers to diffusion[Hog99].

Internet diffusion is also affected by the population's ability to utilize the Internet. In other words, users must have awareness of the kinds of activities supported over the Internet and then be reasonably adept in the mechanics of carrying them out over a personal computer. In most western countries, this Internet ability and awareness has been associated with youth, although that is trend is changing. For developing countries, these two factors act in opposite directions. In general, their populations are younger, but literacy levels can be quite low. Besides, even when literacy levels are satisfactory, knowledge about IT and the Internet may be limited.

4. A SYSTEMS DYNAMICS DIFFUSION MODEL

Figure 1 show our systems dynamics model for Internet diffusion in developing countries. It has been represented as a causal loop diagram as described earlier in section 2. The model is an initial effort to represent the interactions among different diffusion mechanisms in an integrated manner. It is coarse grained in its structural components, made necessary by the diversity of mechanisms that need to be captured. As with any model, it is necessary to define model scope. Fortunately, causal loop diagrams make it easy to visually represent the boundaries of the model.

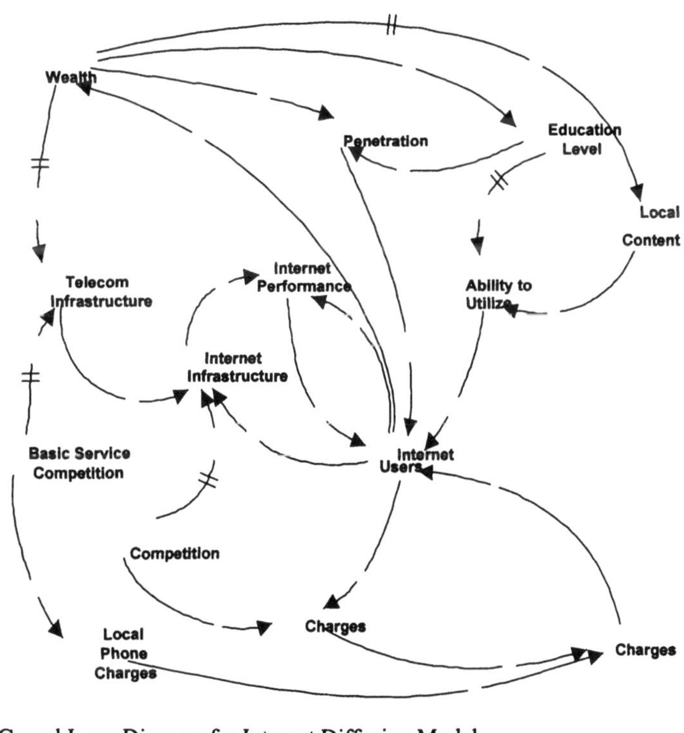

Figure 1. Causal Loop Diagram for Internet Diffusion Model

Different metrics have been used to quantify Internet diffusion, with number of users or number of hosts being the most common ones. The latter can be measured more reliably and statistics are available from different sources. However, some would argue that the first measure, however difficult to determine reliably, is a more meaningful indicator of diffusion. The difference between the two may be more pronounced in developing countries, where access to PCs and Internet connectivity is limited. In Figure 1, we have represented both indicators, represented by 'Internet Infrastructure' and 'Internet Users', respectively. Earlier, we alerted the reader to the coarseness of the causal model being developed. 'Internet Infrastructure' is one example. In Figure 1, this variable represents not only Internet host computers, but also the digital hardware and software infrastructure that supports Internet activity. Once the complete model is described, it will be seen that this level of aggregation may not be overly coarse for the diffusion phenomenon being studied.

The social and economic factors discussed previously are represented in Figure 1, but clearly those are not the only drivers of diffusion. As we continue to present the causal model, we will present and discuss these additional drivers and their impact on the diffusion process. The variable 'Internet Users' is directly driven by at least the following variables– ability of the population at large to use the Internet, the charges faced by users and the quality of the network, broadly interpreted. In industrialized countries, the diffusion of PCs is taken for granted. However, PCs are not as commonly deployed in developing countries. Prices have, until recently, remained high due to a variety of reasons including tariffs and lack of a local manufacturing base. For developing countries therefore, it is necessary to factor in the growth in PCs as a driver of Internet diffusion. These factors are represented by the following variables in Figure 1 – 'Ability to Use Internet', 'Internet Performance', 'PC Penetration' and 'Charges'. Note that the polarity of causal links from all these variables, except 'Charges', to 'Internet Users' is positive (refer to definition of link polarity provided in an earlier section).

One can now proceed in a top-down manner by examining the drivers of variables discussed above. The ability to use the Internet is certainly driven by general education levels. However, for developing countries where English is not the first language, presence of content in the local languages is also a driver of the population's ability to use the Internet. Again, as a first approximation, we are choosing not to distinguish among different types of education, particularly technical education, in representing the drivers of usage ability. In Figure 1, therefore, the two drivers of 'Ability to Use Internet' are 'Education Level' and 'Local Content'. Turning next to the variable 'Charges', it is necessary to distinguish two separate drivers of the charges faced by users. One component, of course, is the 'ISP Charges' levied by Internet providers. Unlike most industrialized countries however, the telephone provider in many developing countries is government owned and operated, and there is a per-minute charge for local calls as well. In fact, the local charge component may equal or exceed ISP charges in most circumstances. Hence, we have represented two drivers of 'Charges', namely 'ISP Charges' and 'Local Phone Charges'.

The regulatory environment in the telecommunications sector is also an important driver of Internet diffusion. Most developing countries have recognized that private funds must be brought into the telecommunications sector in order to make the massive investments needed to address chronic and acute deficiencies in infrastructure. Hence, deregulation of the telecommunications sector is underway in most of these countries. However, in developing an Internet diffusion model, it is necessary to recognize one important characteristic of this deregulation. While competition is being rapidly introduced in data communications, basic service has not been privatized in most developing countries and competition is being introduced very slowly to this major segment of the telecommunications sector [ITU99]. Therefore, there are two separate variables – 'ISP Competition' and 'Basic Service Competition' - in the model of Figure 1, so as to capture the distinctly different pace with which competition is being introduced in these two segments. Competition is generally accompanied by a reduction in charges. In India for instance, after the ISP market was deregulated in 1997, ISP charges dropped by 60% within a year. Hence, link polarity of 'ISP Competition' to 'ISP Charges' and of 'Basic Service Competition' to 'Local Telephone Charges' is negative.

The remaining causal links in Figure 1 follow from observations that have already appeared in the literature, or follow from the physical workings of network technologies. The link from 'Internet Users' to 'Internet Performance' has negative polarity reflecting the physical fact that, other parameters remaining constant, an increase in users will increase network load and reduce network performance. There is a positive link from 'Telecom Infrastructure' to 'Internet Infrastructure'. This link captures the reality that the Internet, in large part, rides over basic telecommunication infrastructure components, be it leased lines for carriers or twisted pair lines to the home. The lack of basic infrastructure in developing countries is a major bottleneck in Internet diffusion. Introducing competition in the ISP market, without simultaneously expanding basic infrastructure, will not have the desired impact on Internet growth. Just as competition in the telecommunications sector results in reduced prices, it also spurs infrastructure expansion and modernization. There is ample evidence from both developing and industrialized countries to support this linkage. In many developing countries, for example, telephone line density has increased dramatically as a result of competition, as has the number of cellular subscribers [ITU01]. In the United States, the telecommunications act of 1996 introduced, among other things, competition in the local services market. This event spurred the growth of several technologies such as ADSL, LMDS etc. that have become important elements of the Internet infrastructure. In Figure 1, therefore, there are positive links from 'Basic Service Competition' and 'ISP Competition' to 'Telecom Infrastructure' and 'Internet Infrastructure', respectively.

The remaining links are from 'Wealth', used to denote the economic output of a country, to selected variables mentioned thus far. The strong correlation between economic output and telecommunications infrastructure has been cited earlier in the paper and causality effects have been tested recently [Dut01]. Based on these findings, there is a positive link from 'Wealth' to 'Telecom Infrastructure' and one from 'Internet Users' back to 'Wealth'. 'Wealth' is positively linked to 'PC Penetration' and with 'Education level'. The positive link from 'Wealth' to 'Local Content' is based on the premise that higher levels of economic output foster higher levels of local content. This has been demonstrated repeatedly in many developing countries where content developers find it more and more viable to put up local content as the economy improves and consumerism, as well as Internet awareness, increases.

To conclude our discussion of the causal model, notice that a few links in Figure 1 indicate delayed causal effects (indicated by a double line drawn through the causal links). Most causal effects in this socio-technical model have some delay associated with them, but only the more significant ones are shown. The effect of education levels on ability to use the Internet clearly involves significant delay as does the impact of wealth on telecom infrastructure. Similarly, an increase in competition does not immediately impact infrastructure levels. It takes substantial time to install physical infrastructure, particularly wire based ones, resulting in significantly delayed effects.

5. MODEL VALIDATION AND DIFFUSION BEHAVIOR

A systems dynamics model is usually validated in stages, with the first stage consisting of setting forth the justifications for its different structural components. The previous section provided explanations for the different components that constitute this diffusion model. The next stage consists of replicating what are called reference behaviours. Here, the model is simulated to see if observed behaviours can be replicated [Ste00]. The simulation model is developed by representing the causal loop diagram of

Figure 1 using the standard stock-flow constructs of systems dynamics [Ste00]. Reference behaviour tests on an Internet diffusion model for the United States may be found in [DuR01]. Reference behaviour tests on this developing country model are in progress. Hence, in the remainder of the paper, we will present sample simulations only to illustrate the kinds of analyses that can be carried out with the systems model, and also point out the importance of taking an integrated socio-technical view of the diffusion process. Before proceeding with these presentations, it is worthwhile to point out the boundaries of this model. Notice from Figure 1 that drivers of 'Wealth' other than Internet usage, are considered to be external to this model. Also, the evolution of competition in basic telecommunications services and in Internet services is considered to be exogenous to the model.

Figure 2 shows comparative runs of Internet Diffusion over a duration of 120 periods with levels of competitiveness in the two telecommunications segments set as shown.

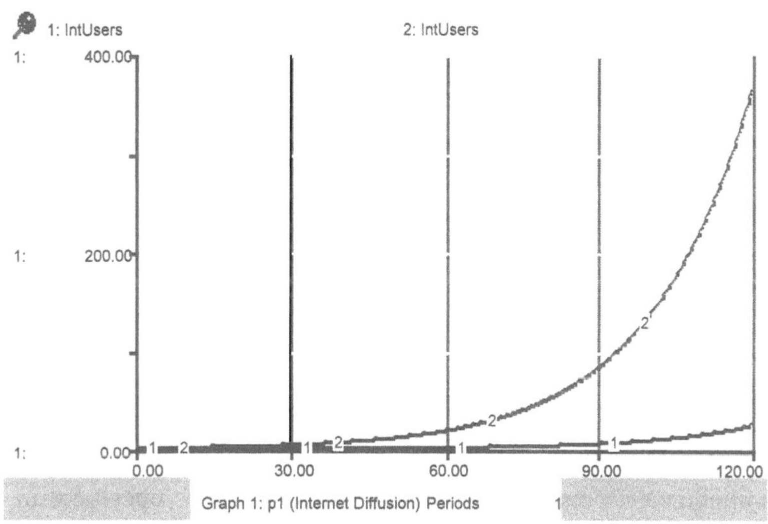

Figure 2. Internet Diffusion over 120 periods

The number of users at the end of the two runs was 24 and 365, respectively. While the exact numbers are not relevant here, the comparative runs demonstrate the importance of basic infrastructure for Internet diffusion. Figure 3 shows the same two comparative runs, this time with high level of competition in ISP services. Notice that, as expected, the shape of the diffusion curves is the same as in Figure 2. However, what is particularly interesting in Figure 3 is that the ending value for the number of users in the two runs is 24 and 3357, respectively. Comparing Figures 2 and 3, one can see that increased competition in ISP services had no effect on diffusion when competition in basic services is low. The reasons for this behaviour are clear from the causal loops present in Figure 1. Low levels of competition in basic services leads to low growth in basic service infrastructure, which in turn limits growth in Internet infrastructure. This acts as a restraint to infrastructure expansion that would follow from the increased competition in the ISP segment. In the same manner, notice how increased competition in the ISP segment has a dramatic impact on diffusion when there is adequate basic infrastructure. In this case, the number of users at the end of period 120 rose from 365 to 3357, almost a tenfold increase.

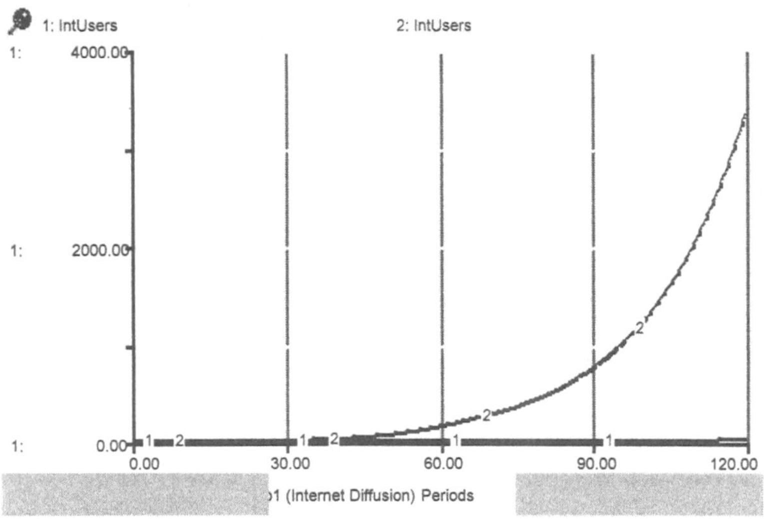

Figure 3. Internet Diffusion with High Level of ISP Competition

For political and cultural reasons, the basic service segment of telecommunications is still a government monopoly operation in many developing countries, while the ISP segment is being rapidly made competitive. The simulation results just discussed would suggest that this policy posture is not conducive to rapid Internet diffusion. These initial results give an indication of the kinds of analyses that can be carried out using the simulation model being constructed. In each case, behaviour can be traced back to interaction among causal loops, thus providing some insights into the mechanisms driving diffusion.

6. CONCLUSIONS

The diffusion model developed in this article is quite coarse grained, a necessity generated by the wide diversity of diffusion mechanisms that need to be represented. Nevertheless, we submit some claims based on this aggregate model. First, it reemphasizes the need to incorporate social as well as technical factors in any analysis of Internet diffusion, particularly in developing countries. Second, it shows how systems dynamics may offer a methodology to go beyond qualitative analysis and study the mechanics of Internet diffusion more rigorously. Since systems dynamics models are simulation based, a diffusion model based on this methodology can serve as a platform on which to examine the impact of different policy actions.

As mentioned earlier, the model is under development and these results are preliminary. We intend to use the model to explain differences in Internet diffusion across developing countries. It may be necessary to introduce structural refinements to the model of Figure 1 for this purpose. For example, level of competition is not the only regulatory factor affecting Internet diffusion. Licensing fees, interconnection policies and views on universal service are additional parameters affecting diffusion. In other words, the degree to which telecommunications regulation is 'Internet friendly' is also important. Based on the results of applying this model to multiple developing countries, we expect to identify the major causal loops that govern diffusion behaviour and thereby provide some guidance for policy-making purposes.

REFERENCES

[CCI68] CCITT. GAS-5 Handbook: Economic Studies at The National Level in the Field of Telecommunications. Geneva: CCITT (1968).

[DuR01] Dutta A. and Roy R., Anticipating The Internet's Diffusion: A Socio-technical Approach, forthcoming Communications of The ACM, 2001.

[Dut01] Dutta A., Telecommunications and Economic Activity: An Analysis of Granger Causality, Journal of Management Information Systems, vol. 17, no. 4, 2001 pp71-96.

[Har98] Hargittai E., Holes in the Net: The Internet and International Stratification , ***Proceedings INET 98***, Internet Society.

[Hog99] Hogan S.B., To Net or not to Net: Singapore's Regulation of The Internet, Federal Communications Law Journal, vol. 51, no. 2, 1999, pp429-447

[ITU01] International Telecommunications Union, Telecommunications Information on ITU Member States, http://www7.itu.int/bdt_cds/CDS/CDSHome.asp, 2001.

[ITU99a] International Telecommunications Union, Challenges to The Network: Internet for Development, ITU Geneva, October 1999.

[ITU99b] Intenational Telecommunications Union, Trends in Telecommunications reform 1999: Convergence and Regulation, ITU, Geneva, October 1999.

[KaW96a] Kalakota R., and Whinston A.B., Frontiers of Electronic Commerce, Addison-Wesley, 1996.

[KaW96b] Kalakota R., and Whinston A.B., Electronic Commerce: A Manager's Guide, Addison-Wesley 1996.

[Min00] Minges M., Counting The Net: Internet Access Indicators, Proceedings INET 2000, Internet Society, July 2000.

[Pet98] Petrazzini B.A., Explaining Variations in Internet Deployment Across Developing Countries, Proceedings INET 98: Internet Society.

[Ste00] Sterman J., Business Dynamics: Systems Thinking and Modeling for a Complex World, Irwin, 2000.

[Taw99] Tawfik M., Is the World Wide Web Really Worldwide?, http://www.unesco.org/webworld/points_of_views/tawfik_1.html,UNESCO 1999.

PART III

MULTIDISCIPLINARY BUSINESS MODELLING PROGRESS

Chapter 20

Advances In Business Problem Solving: Bridging Business And Computing Disciplines

Clyde W. Holsapple
University of Kentucky

Abstract: Fifty years have passed since the first business computing system began regular operations in 1951. Today, business computing systems in their may manifestations are important and often essential for the competitiveness or even survival of most organizations. This spectacular leap has been fueled by unrelenting advances in computer and communications technologies. It has been driven by the need to effectively deal with relentless growth in the volumes and complexity of knowledge produced and confronted by organizations in the course of their business activities. It has been guided by the successful bridging of computing and business disciplines in the interest of business problem solving. This chapter examines the exceptional bridging work of a remarkable contributor to the business computing field: Professor Andrew Whinston. It does so by way of a framework for appreciating both the multidisciplinary nature of the field and Andy's significant global contributions to it. The still unfolding legacy of Andy's work provides an outstanding role model and inspiration for both seasoned colleagues and beginning students throughout the business computing field.
Key words: business computing systems, business problem solving, modeling, multidisciplinary research, systems

1. INTRODUCTION

In November, 1951, the Lyons Electronic Office (LEO) began operations. An electronic computer system for weekly valuation of bakery products, LEO was a milestone that marked the beginning of the business computing field (Caminer et al., 1998). This is a field concerned with devising, applying, administering, and evaluating computer technologies for solving business problems. As such, the business computing (BC) field has expanded by building intellectual bridges that connect the many-faceted discipline of computer science (a basic source of technology) with various disciplines on the business side (basic sources of problems and solution methods). These business disciplines include organization science, accounting, economics, operations management, operations research, and so forth. Each presents BC challenges and each is a field for applying BC advances.

The tremendous growth over the past half century in using computers to solve business problems has been fueled by continuing technology advances rooted in computer science. This growth has been driven by the need for increasingly effective means of managing knowledge-rich business activities. An organization's knowledge assets give rise to problems, some of which are candidates for computer-based solutions. Knowledge assets also form a basis for solving business problems, in some cases via computer-based approaches. The fuel rooted in computer science and the drivers rooted in business needs are insufficient by themselves. There must be connections and maps to enable and guide deployments of technology to meet business needs. Advances in the BC field over the past 50 years have created bridges that connect technologies with business needs, expanding the maps available for guiding implementations and operations of BC systems.

The early emphasis was on BC systems that handled large volumes of transactional data (i.e., data processing systems). A subsequent BC emphasis was on systems that provide various reports giving managers information about predefined aspects of an organization's status (i.e., management information systems). By the 1980s, the BC domain had grown to include systems that could select and/or generate knowledge on demand (or when triggered by events) to satisfy the knowledge needs of individuals engaged in decision making (i.e., decision support systems, performance support systems). A further BC expansion into the realms of organizational computing and electronic commerce includes systems for sharing knowledge among multiple participants in a task (e.g., decision making) and for coordinating their interrelated knowledge manipulation activities. These may be participants in traditional organizations, or in organizations that are temporary and/or virtual.

Interestingly, the progression of systems encompassed by the BC field reflects a series of refinements in the states of knowledge with which the systems deal: from the lowest state of knowledge (i.e., data), to a more refined state (i.e., information), to a high value-added state of knowledge (i.e., solutions, decisions), to a state of knowledge transcending individual system users (i.e., collaborative creations, interrelated solutions, multiparticipant decisions). Today, the main thrust of business computing systems is concerned with handling the latter two states of knowledge in the course of solving problems.

This chapter examines advances in business problem solving related to the bridging of business and computing disciplines. It does so by tracing the work of BC's most prolific researcher along the broad business-computing frontier: Professor Andrew Whinston. This body of work is representative of the many kinds of multidisciplinary connections established in the BC field. It is the epitome of thought leadership that has directly enlarged the BC field in many directions and has stimulated much additional growth in its wake. It can serve as a suggestive template for succeeding generations of BC researchers aiming to launch new investigations that connect and integrate disciplines. Giving a clear picture of the wide-ranging breadth and substantial depth of this large body of work is certainly a challenge. The approach taken is to sketch out selected highlights organized in terms of a framework for appreciating the multidisciplinary nature of the BC field. Rather than aim to be exhaustive (a necessarily futile aim), the characterization that follows strives to capture the essence and spirit of Andy Whinston's remarkable career of significant contributions to the BC field and to the disciplines it connects. The result is a tribute to his accomplishments.

2. OVERVIEW

Dr. Andrew Whinston holds the Hugh Roy Cullen Centennial Chair in Business Administration at the University of Texas where he is founding Director of the Center for Research in Electronic Commerce and where he is Professor of Information Systems, Library & Sciences, Economics, and Computer Science. He is the Jon Newton Centennial Fellow of George Kozmetski's IC^2 Institute and Co-Director of the International Center for Electronic Commerce based in Seoul, Korea. Andy is the founder and editor-in-chief of two prominent BC journals: *Decision Support Systems* published by Elsevier and *Journal of Organizational Computing and*

Electronic Commerce published by Erlbaum. He also serves on more than a dozen editorial boards.

Andy holds a Ph.D. (1962) and M.S. in Industrial Administration from Carnegie-Mellon University and a B.A. from the University of Michigan. He has previously held faculty positions at Yale, Virginia, and Purdue (where he was the Weiler Distinguished Professor of Management and Economics). He has been honored as a Sanxsay Fellow at Princeton, as a Pre-doctoral Fellow and Post-doctoral Fellow of the National Science Foundation, with the Alexander Hamilton Award for Excellence in Economic Theory, as a Ford Foundation Faculty Research Scholar, and as the 1994 Distinguished Information Systems Educator by the Data Processing Management Association.

Andy's publication credits include 25 books and over 250 articles in journals and books. His research has been funded by the National Science Foundation, Office of Naval Research, Army Research Office, IBM, NCR, HP, Intel, Sun, and Shell Development. One perspective on Andy's work is to recognize that it revolves around the fundamental question ofhow systems can be made to be more productive. This includes systems that are economic, mathematical, organizational, environmental, manufacturing, and computer-based. He has made notable contributions in addressing all of these and his results for one have often turned out to be applicable to others. Another perspective, which is focused on business computing, is portrayed in Figure 1.

The five bridging arrows shown in Figure 1 depict major lines of investigation in the BC field. Each of these interdisciplinary bridges connects computer technology with a business discipline: organization science, economics, accounting, operations research, and operations management. While these are distinct disciplines, each with its own journals and heritage, they are collectively concerned with the study of systems for administration. Business computing exists as field of study because of the advances in business problem solving that accrue from integrating systems of computing with systems of administration, using the former to facilitate or enable the latter. As an analysis of the publication outlets for BC research indicates, the BC field has a clear identity as a distinct discipline in its own right, with many specialties, in addition to many reference disciplines (Holsapple et al., 1994).

The ongoing evolution of BC expands and reshapes the business disciplines themselves – advancing both the theory and practice of management, with enormous socio-economic impacts on organizations and individuals throughout the world. Perhaps the best known example of this can be found in electronic commerce, which not only embodies Internet-based and Web-based technologies for solving business problems, but is also profoundly impacting every one of the traditional business disciplines. Thus, the five interdisciplinary thrusts of Andy's work depicted in Figure 1 span a very significant field. Jim Cash, Harvard's James E. Robison Professor of Business Administration, writes, "I can think of no individual who has done as much the past quarter of a century to foster the integration of computer science into the realm of business, management, and economics. This ongoing integration has had profound, practical, and far-reaching impacts on improving the productivity of organizations and individuals." (personal communication, November 24, 1993).

The following characterization of Andy's contributions to business problem solving (in general) and the BC field (in particular) is organized into four major parts: a) research qualities/style, b) the general nature of his interdisciplinary contributions in terms of their breadth, depth, and pioneering character, c) the more specific nature of contributions along the five bridges in the reference disciplines, and in the overarching arena of electronic commerce, d) his work at fostering/facilitating/enabling the whole interdisciplinary movement unfolding between CS and business.

3. *RESEARCH QUALITIES/STYLE*

Consideration of Andy's research qualities and style is important because of the insight it provides into the modus operandi underlying his accomplishments. Andy leverages a brilliant, creative, agile, intellect by working very, very hard with unceasing dedication. He actively tackles research questions that run the gamut from theory into practice. He is open to and interested in research that is conceptual, analytical, technical, or empirical – recognizing that each has its place. He does not chain himself to any particular research method. Rather, his research is driven by asking questions and then choosing appropriate methods for addressing them.

Andy's work revolves around a single fundamental question: how can we make systems better? It makes no difference whether these are economic, mathematical, financial, organizational, manufacturing, environmental, symbolic, or computer systems – Andy deals with them all. His results for one often turn out to be transferable to others. He is a master of using and adapting one kind of system to address productivity issues in other systems. Specifically, in the BC field, this involves the use/adaptation/creation of computer systems to improve systems of interest in the business disciplines, and vice versa.

Nobel Laureate in Economics, Dr. James Buchanan states, "...I can say that in more than four decades of academic experience, Andrew Whinston was one of two best colleagues I have had...[He] was a fine colleague because of his continued willingness to adjust his intellectual-professional tools to fit the problem at hand, rather than the vice versa of most of his peers...His vita attests to the qualities that I noted, a continued willingness to explore and develop cross-disciplinary applications of analysis, along with a genuinely original and creative intelligence." (personal communication, October 27, 1993). Preston McAfee, Editor of the flagship *American Economic Review*, University of Chicago Business School Professor, and Murray S. Johnson Professor of Economics at the University of Texas describes Andy as "... perhaps the most creative researcher I have ever met..." (personal communication, November 18, 1993).

John Rice, W. Brooks Fortune Distinguished Professor of Computer Science at Purdue University, writes that "I have had many technical discussions with Whinston and I am very impressed by his broad knowledge about and deep insight into computing. His prolific research record reflects this talent plus his almost boundless energy...Whinston epitomizes the broad thinker and doer in computing." (personal communication, November 8, 1993). From AT&T Laboratories, Dr. WenLing Hsu has written "I was fortunate to have had the pleasure to work with two prominent researchers...great thinkers, inspiring...Professor Andrew Whinston [and]...Professor Allen Newell...From both of them, I learned what a true genuine researcher is like...that there is no boundary for science, not in any dimension – this is reflected in their lifestyle as well as their research style. Both of them work *constantly*...in multidisciplinary areas." (personal communication, November 17, 1993).

Lynda Applegate, Distinguished Professor of Business Administration at Harvard notes that Andy "...has also successfully bridged...academic and practitioner audiences with publications in *Computerworld, Datamation, Byte*, and others...Dr. Whinston is one of the most respected, dedicated, and important scholars of our time." (personal communication, November 24, 1993). From the University of Connecticut, OPIM Department Head and Chair of E-Business, Professor James Marsden observes "I know of no other individual that has so effectively cut across traditional discipline boundaries, created synergistic approaches, and, through these efforts, pushed out our knowledge frontiers...He approaches problems as problems, not as problems in a discipline." (personal communication, November 18, 1993).

Professor Tibor Vamos, Chairman of the Board of the Computer and Automation Institute of the Hungarian Academy of Sciences, says that "His basic quality is the early realization of interdisciplinary possibilities and requirements, ingenious stimulations of new direction..." (personal communication, October 29, 1993). Purdue's NEC Professor of Industrial Engineering and founding Editor of the *International Journal on Human-Computer Interaction*, Gavriel Salvendy concludes that "His publications are characterized by creativity and being at the cutting-edge and integrating the scientific know how from a variety of diversified disciplines...computer science, applied mathematics, accounting, economics, and engineering science. His contributions in germinating a new scientific framework in these disciplines by the integration of interdisciplinary areas of science and technology is so significant that if Nobel prizes would be awarded for interdisciplinary studies and for significant contributions for bringing together...a variety of different disciplines and germinating new theories and practical utilities, then Andy Whinston would be a prime candidate for receipt." (personal communication, November 4, 1993).

As a personal note, I have known Andy for over twenty-five years. Collaborating with Andy on a research project is invariably an adventure in creativity, learning, and discovery. His research qualities are beneficially complemented by an unassuming nature, great generosity, impeccable personal and professional integrity, and inclusive goodwill.

4. General Nature of Interdisciplinary Contributions

Andy's interdisciplinary contributions go far beyond bridging computer science with a single discipline or establishing a single stream of research. His work has great breadth. In addition, it has great depth, creating research foundations still in use today and rigorously probing issues in technical and analytical detail. Andy is also widely recognized for the pioneering nature of his research across the spectrum identified in Figure 1, and within and across several of the reference disciplines themselves.

The Chair of Georgetown University's Computer Science Department, Professor Dorothy Denning relates that "...I had the privilege of working with Andy while we were both on the faculty at Purdue...I was very impressed with the depth and breadth of his work then, as I am now. Andy has made pioneering contributions that bridge computer science, business, and economics, and his work has had a lasting and powerful impact on the field." (personal communication, October 27, 1993). From the opposite side of the BC frontier, John Henderson, the Richard C. Shipley Professor of Information Systems and Director of the Systems Research Center in Boston University's School of Management, reaches a similar conclusion: "I view Dr. Whinston's contributions to the field of Computer Science and its application in the field of Management Science as exceptional in terms of both breadth and depth. Few scholars have been able to produce such consistently outstanding work in areas that cross disciplinary fields. His contributions directly to Management Science, Computer Science, Economics and Management are significant in their own right. However, his ability and demonstrated record in integrating across these fields are rare." (personal communication, November 23, 1993).

Alumni Professor of Decision Support Systems at SUNY-Buffalo, Stan Zionts comments that "Andy is a professor's professor; he has worked in many areas, has produced an enormous number of publications in many diverse fields." (personal communication, October 26, 1993). Professor Andrew Philippakis, Director of Information Technology at Arizona State University, observes that "The extent of his contributions and achievements defies any attempt at parsimonious commentary...Dr. Whinston stands as the single most respected researcher and educator in decision oriented and organizational computing." He elaborates that "During the last three decades, Whinston's research has been a leading force and an intellectual catalyst in interdisciplinary studies that integrate conceptual foundations in computer and organization science with problems in management...[the] extent to which his publications are cited...confirms the pioneering and foundational nature of his research." (personal communication, 1993). Professor David Pingry former head of the Department of Management Information Systems at the University of Arizona, concurs that Andy's "contributions in computer-related areas has become immense, ranging over decision support, expert systems, organizational computing, manufacturing systems, etc." (personal communication, November 15, 1993).

Father of mathematical programming, Stanford University's Professor George Dantzig reflects that "Whinston has impressed me with the broad scope of his interests...he made important contributions to Economic Theory and Mathematical Programming...his focus and expertise has broadened to include the development of tools and techniques for building computer systems, distributed processing, computer integrated manufacturing, user interface languages, etc." (personal communication, November 22, 1993).

The University of Illinois Hoeft Distinguished Professor in Information Technology, Michael Shaw, says that "I am most impressed by his ability to identify emerging developments in computer science, creating new research fields and important applications to other disciplines along the way...[including] major impacts in fields such as organizational theory, management science, economics, accounting, and industrial engineering...I have met researchers from all over the world that are influenced by his thoughts...[They] come from every different disciplines ranging from business administration, manufacturing, to computer science and, especially, management information systems." (personal communication, November 15, 1993). An example is given by Ramyya Krishnan, the W. W. Cooper and Ruth F. Cooper Professor of Information Systems in Carnegie-Mellon University's Heinz School of Public Policy and Management. Referring to Andy, he indicates that "...it was his seminal work on developing the foundations of the interdisciplinary field of decision support systems that led to my own interest in the topic." (personal communication, 1993).

From the University of Colorado's Graduate School of Business in Denver, Professor James Gerlach points out that "...challenges that lay before us are not limited to improving the computer, but...include how to apply it effectively to...factory automation, office automation, accounting, production management, and economics. The work of Dr. Whinston spans this array and provides approaches and ideas...[that are] theoretically sound...[for] addressing real problems...Undoubtedly, he is the primary leader of academic research in management information systems." (personal communication, November 14, 1993).

Andrew Bailey, University of Illinois Ernst and Young Professor of Accountancy who has served as accounting department head at Illinois, Arizona, and Minnesota, writes that "There can be no question that Andy has contributed significant works in a variety of areas. More important, perhaps, is the fact that he has pioneered a number of areas...I have attended a variety of conferences where the major names in MIS and Computer Science have appeared...Andy's contributions have been publicly recognized on many occasions...[He] is clearly one of the major players in the field...most impressive is his breadth of interest and viewpoint." (personal communication, October 15, 1993).

According to Ka Yan Tam, Professor of Information and Management Systems and Associate Business School Dean at the Hong Kong University of Science and Technology, "...Andy's interdisciplinary contributions can hardly be matched by anyone in his age group...[He] is an international authority on management information systems – a discipline that bridges computer science with business management." (personal communication, November 14, 1993). Professor Hasan Pirkul, Dean of the Business College at the University of Texas at Dallas, concurs that Andy "has made significant contributions to the field of information systems that has evolved as a bridge between computer science and business disciplines...Andy's work clearly goes beyond any other academician in the field of information systems...Andy's efforts to provide a theoretical foundation for much of the work in information systems constitute the most significant attempt in this area." (personal communication, November 15, 1993).

Similarly, the University of Rochester's Xerox Professor Abraham Seidmann finds that Andy's "...pioneering work in the general area of business information systems is second to none. His numerous ideas and contributions have inspired all of us, and established the foundation for many of the leading research programs." (personal communication, November 22, 1993). Prabuddha De, the University of Dayton's Standard Register-Sherman Distinguished Professor of MIS and former Chair of the TIMS College on Information Systems, adds that Andy has "often been the first to study important problems in a discipline from a computational standpoint...[He] has also produced a large cadre of researchers who have continued to work toward the same goal...He is a source of insight and encouragement to many." (personal communication, November 16, 1993).

Summing up the general nature of Andy's interdisciplinary contributions, Harvard's Jim Cash states that "Andy's contributions to this integration of computer science with business, management, and economics are remarkable in several respects...[The] sheer breadth of his interdisciplinary efforts...range from the creation of tools for building various kinds of business computer systems (especially those involving database management and AI), to the development of computer models and solvers for socio-economic and physical systems, to studies of the economics of systems and computing, to revolutionary approaches for designing and evaluating accounting information systems, to designing computer information systems that support flexible manufacturing operations, to studies of organizational computing issues...Andy invariably plays the role of a pioneer. He consistently identifies, frames, and works toward solving previously unrecognized or unexamined issues emanating from the central question of his scientific work...[The] magnitude of quality work is unequaled by other researchers contributing to the bridging of computer science with management." (personal communication, October 15, 1993).

5. Observations on Specific Research Contributions

Having recognized the depth, breadth, and pioneering nature of Andy's research, the groundwork is laid to appreciate that work in a more detailed way. To begin to do so, one might carefully examine the titles of the more than 400 publications and presentations cited in his vita. They are indicative, in very specific ways, of the diversity of his interdisciplinary research all along the frontier between CS and the business disciplines (and, secondarily, among and within the reference disciplines themselves – for his research life has not been constrained by discipline boundaries).

While examining the publication titles, the diversity and high quality of journals in which his articles appear should also be noted. They include top journals in business disciplines, business computing, and computer science Examples for business disciplines include ten articles *in Management Science*, six in *Accounting Review*, four each in *Decision Sciences*, *Operations Research*, *Journal of Economic Theory*, and *IIE Transactions*, plus multiple papers in many other journals such as *Organization Science*, *Econometrica*, *American Economic Review*, *Naval Research Logistics*, and the *International Journal of Flexible Manufacturing Systems*. At least twenty of his articles have appeared in the five most influential journals devoted to business computing: *Decision Support Systems*, *Information and Management*, *Information Systems Research*, *Journal of Management Information Systems*, and *MIS Quarterly*. Many others appear in top BC specialty journals such as *Group Decision and Negotiation*, *Information Systems, International Journal of Electronic Commerce*, and *Journal of Organizational Computing and Electronic Commerce*. In the CS realm, there are over fifteen papers in *IEEE* journals, nearly ten more in *ACM* journals, and two in the British Computer Society's *Computer Journal*. The high quality of journal placements is one measure of the rigor, significance, and impact of Andy's published research.

The following sections summarize some of Andy's research contributions along each of the five bridges in Figure 1. Sound bridge building, of course, depends on establishing solid platforms in the disciplines being bridged. When applicable, Andy has adopted or adapted existing disciplinary platforms. In other cases, he has created new platforms from which to launch the bridging efforts. Examples of these more disciplinary contributions are briefly noted, after considering the five areas of interdisciplinary work. Finally, we highlight some of the contributions to electronic commerce which spans CS, business computing and all of the other business disciplines.

5.1 Organizational Computing and Multiparticipant Support Systems

One interdisciplinary thrust has its roots in Andy's work in the mid-1960s concerned with theoretical and computational problems in organizational decision making (e.g., pubs. 1-5 in Table 1). Two trend-setting publications appeared in 1979. One, concerned with flexible contracting theory (pub. 6), was the forerunner of Andy's seminal work on the important topic of computer support for coordination in so-called network or virtual organizations (e.g., pubs. 19, 25, 28-30, 33). The other (pub. 7) was the first to identify the issue of computer support for organizational (as opposed to individual) decision making. It led to a book (Bailey et al., 1985) and a large number of works concerned with the use of computers for supporting multiparticipant work (e.g., pubs. 8-18, 20-24, 26, 27, 31, 32, 34, 35). This includes computer-based support for team decisions, negotiated decisions, structured argumentation, organizational learning, organizational decisions (e.g., Nemawashi processes), and knowledge-based organizations. The latter (pub. 9) presented a very early view of the technology possibilities for implementing knowledge management in organizations, a view that is being actualized today.

Table 4. Example Publications in Organizational Computing and Multiparticipant Support Systems

Pub. No.	Title (co-authors)	Journal/Book/Proceedings	Year
1	Price Guidelines in Decentralized Organizations	*New Perspectives in Organizational Research,* Wiley	1964
2	Economics of Complex Systems (Davis)	*Kyklos*, Sep.	1964
3	Some Notes on Equating Private and Social Costs (Davis)	*Southern Economic Journal*, Oct.	1965
4	Theoretical and Computational Problems in Organizational Decision Making	*Operational Research and Social Sciences*, Tavistock	1966
5	Design of a Corporate Computer System (Nunamaker)	*Management Informatics*, 2, 4	1973
6	Flexible Contracting: Theory and Case Examples (Salas)	*European J. of Operational Research*, 3	1979
7	Computer Based Support of Organizational Decision Making (Bonczek, Holsapple)	*Decision Sciences*, Apr.	1979
8	On Optimal Allocation in a Distributed Processing Environment (Dutta and Koehler)	*Management Science*, 28, 8	1982

Pub. No.	Title (co-authors)	Journal/Book/Proceedings	Year
9	Knowledge-Based Organizations (Holsapple)	*The Information Society*, 5, 2	1987
10	Distributed Decision Making: A Research Agenda (Holsapple)	*ACM SIGOIS Bulletin*, 9, 1	1988
11	Concurrent Problem Solving and Organizational Learning (Ching and Holsapple)	*Proceedings of the 22nd Annual Hawaii International Conference on System Sciences*, Jan.	1989
12	A Model of Decision Making Involving Two Information Processors (Jacob, Moore)	*Computer Science in Economics and Management*, 2	1989
13	Organizational Computing: Definitions and Issues (Applegate, Ellis, Holsapple, Radermacher)	*Journal of Organizational Computing*, 1, 1	1991
14	Issues and Obstacles in the Development of Team Support Systems (Busch, Hamalainen, Holsapple, Suh)	*Journal of Organizational Computing*, 1, 2	1991
15	Negotiation Support Systems: Roots, Progress and Needs (Holsapple, Lai)	*Journal of Information Systems*, 1, 4	1991
16	CATT: An Argumentation Based Groupware System for Enhancing Case Discussions in Business Schools (Hashim, Rathnam)	*Proceedings of the Twelfth International Conference on Information Systems*, Dec,	1991
17	A Framework for Distributed Decision Support Systems (Chi, Rathnam)	*Proceedings of the 25th Hawaii International Conference on System Sciences*, Jan.	1992
18	Coordinator Support in a Nemawashi Decision Process (Watabe, Holsapple)	*Decision Support Systems*, 8, 2	1992

Pub. No.	Title (co-authors)	Journal/Book/Proceedings	Year
19	eputation, Learning, and Coordination n Distributed Decision-Making ontexts (Ching, Holsapple)	*Organization Science*, 3, 2	1992
20	oncensus Based Group Decision upport Method (Watabe, Holsapple)	*Transactions of Information Processing Society of Japan*, 33, 6	1992
21	valuation and Stability Analysis of eamwork (Geitner, Peng, Hu)	*Proceedings of IFAC Workshop on CIM in Process and Manufacturing Industries*, Nov.	1992
22	he Socially Acceptable Solution of a am and Stability Analysis (Le, Geitner, u)	*Preprints of the 12th IFAC World Congress*, July	1993
23	odeling and Evaluation of Teamwork Le, Geitner, Peng, Hu)	*Advances in Factories of the Future*, Elsevier Science	1993
24	omputer Support of Organizational esign and Learning (Holsapple, Rein)	*Journal of Organizational Computing*, 3, 1	1993
25	odeling Network Organizations: A asis for Exploring Computer Support oordination Possibilities (Ching, olsapple)	*Journal of Organizational Computing*, 3, 3	1993
26	nterprise Modeling and Decision upport (Ba, Lang)	*Sun Yat-Sen Management Review*, 2, 1	1994
27	nalysis of Negotiation Support System esearch (Holsapple, Lai)	*Journal of Computer Information Systems*, 35, 3	1995
28	ncentives and Computing Systems for eam-Based Organization (Lee, Barua)	*Organization Science*, 6, 4	1995
29	acilitating Coordination in Customer upport Teams: A Framework and Its mplications for the Design of	*Management Science*, 41, 12	1995

Pub. No.	Title (co-authors)	Journal/Book/Proceedings	Year
	Information Technology (Mahajan, Rathnam)		
30	Toward IT Support for Coordination in Newtork Organizations (Ching, Holsapple)	*Information and Management*, 30, 4	1996
31	Computationally Modeling Organizational Learning and Adaptability as Resource Allocation: An Artificial Adaptive Systems Approach (Paul, Butler, Pearlson)	*Computational & Mathematical Organization Theory*, 2, 4	1996
32	Implications of Negotiation Theory for Research and Development of Negotiation Support Systems (Holsapple, Lai)	*Group Decision and Negotiation*, 6, 3	1997
33	Coordination in Information Exchange Between Organizational Decision Units (Barua, Ravindran)	*IEEE Transactions on Systems, Man, and Cybernetics*, 27, 5	1997
34	A Formal Basis for Negotiation Support System Research (Holsapple, Lai)	*Group Decision and Negotiation*, 7, 3	1998
35	Collaborative Decision Making: A Connectionist Paradigm for Dialectical Support (Raghunathan, Chang)	*Information Systems Research*	2001

Vincente Salas, Professor of Managerial Economics at the Universitad Autonoma de Barcelona, points out that the "...paper on price guidelines in decentralized organizations...[is] one of the first papers in the field of economics of organization and management...MIS was much closer to Whinston's prior areas of interest than it may appear at first glance. Organizations exist because the price system operates with positive transaction costs...Therefore, organizations are closely related to information creation, storage, transmission and transformation (in the decision making process). The advances in Computer Science could not be ignored by those interested in organization design, at the same time that Computer Science would benefit from what had been learned by economists interested in the problems of organization decision making. Computer Science and Organization Science were from the beginning viewed as overlapping fields by Whinston...[who] designed most of his later work under this assumption...twenty years later it is clear that his approach proved to be the correct one." (personal communication, November 5, 1993). From the other side of the world, Hong Kong University of Science and Technology, Professor Tam sees Andy as "...a pioneer to offer inspiring and innovative perspectives...Among these...[seeing the] computer as a mediating instrument which integrates different functions of an organization has greatly improved our understanding of the structure of organizations." (personal communication, November 14, 1993).

Professor John Henderson of Boston University comments that "...Dr. Whinston's work on Database Management Systems, Management Science, and Economics enabled him to provide theoretical rigor in the area of Decision Support...[He] extends this pattern of theoretically grounded research with his current treatment of how Information Technology impacts a firm's ability to effectively coordinate its actions...Dr. Whinston's work is unique in its rigorous treatment of this topic." (personal communication, November 23, 1993). Dr. WenLing Hsu notes that "His recent work in coordination theory and organizational computing has created a theoretical framework for computer-supported multiparticipant work...an area of research that attracts tremendous attention nowadays." (personal communication, November 17, 1993). In referring to Andy's exploration of coordination in network organizations, Professor Erik Brynjolfsson of the Center for eBusiness at MIT's Sloan School of Management indicates that "...his research on how information and reputations are transmitted in the newly emerging networked organizations is influencing a whole cadre of researchers in this rapidly evolving area..." (personal communication, July 10, 1993).

Dr. David King, Chief Technology Officer and Vice President of Product Development at Comshare, notes that "Organizational computing began to emerge...in the mid to late 80s...Dr. Whinston has moved to the forefront of the field and carried a number of scholars and practitioners in his wake...he established the leading journal in the field...[and] instituted an annual conference...I have attended all...and their content has had a substantial impact on my own design and development work." (personal communication, November 19, 1993). From Japan, Professor Kazuo Watabe of the University of Shizuoka observes that "His work on decision support systems and groupware is well-known even in Japan...[and] often referred to in Japanese journals...[He] studied the Japanese way of group decision making...[and] formalized this approach mathematically as a basis for implementing computer systems for decision support...[He] visited our laboratory at NEC and...helped us to develop a multimedia desktop conferencing system called MERMAID...Dr. Whinston is admired and recognized for his interdisciplinary work even from the Far East." (personal communication, November 17, 1993).

5.2 Computational Economics

Andy's research that bridges computer science with economics and decision theory has many facets, but has collectively established him as the prime mover in establishing the area of computational economics as an identifiable area of study (Cooper and Whinston, 1994; Amman et al., 1997). He is the leader in exploring formal decision theoretic bases for building decision support systems. His initial work on this bridge dates to the early 1970s involving computer-based economic modeling, especially with respect to resource allocation problems (e.g., pubs. 1-4, 6-11 in Table 2). During this time, he was also the first researcher to apply pattern recognition methods to problems in economics (e.g., pubs. 5, 7, 10, 12, 14). Later, he conducted novel studies of the connections between social choice theory and formal language theory, database management, and optimization modeling (e.g., pubs. 8, 9, 13, 15, 16, 29).

Spanning the last decade is a substantial body of work that offered formal economic models of problem solving and decision making as a basis for DSS design (e.g., pubs. 17, 18, 23, 24, 26, 30, 31, 33-35, 42), economic analyses of human-computer decision making capabilities (e.g., pubs. 22, 27, 32), a decision theoretic basis for expert systems (pubs. 19. 20), applications of AI in economics (e.g., pubs. 21, 25), and decision theoretic approaches to information storage and retrieval (e.g., pubs. 28, 36). His work has also involved an integration of information economics and organizational computing (e.g., pubs. 36-41).

Table 5. Example Publications in Computational Economics

Pub. No.	Title (co-authors)	Journal/Book/Proceedings	Year
1	The Welfare Economics of Water Resource Allocation Over Time (Loehman)	Applied Economics, *2*	1970
2	Resource Allocation in a Non-Convex Economy (Moore, Wu)	*Review of Economic Studies*, Jul.	1972

Pub. No.	Title (co-authors)	Journal/Book/Proceedings	Year
3	Taxation and Water Pollution Control (Ferrar)	*Natural Resources Journal*, 12, 3	1972
4	A New Approach to Water Allocation Under Uncertainty (Thomas, Wright)	*Water Resources Research*, Oct.	1972
5	Pattern Recognition and Micro-Economics (Fu, Blin, Moberg)	*Proceedings of the International Conference on Cybernetics and Society*, Oct.	1972
6	Production Function Theory and the Optimal Design of Waste Treatment Facilities (Marsden, Pingry)	*Applied Economics*, 4	1972
7	Pattern Recognition and Quantitative Political Theory (Blin, Fu, Moberg)	IEEE Transactions on Decision and Control	1972
8	Optimization Theory and Social Choice (Blin, Fu, Moberg)	*Transactions of the Sixth International Conference on System Sciences*, Jan.	1973
9	Social Choice and Formal Language Theory (Piccoli)	*Journal of Cybernetics*, 3.2	1973
10	Application of Pattern Recognition of Some Problems in Economics (Blin, Fu)	Techniques of Optimization	1974
11	Cost Allocation for River Basin Planning Models (Pingry, Loehman)	*Economics and Decision Making for Environmental Quality*	1974
12	Fuzzy Set and Automata Theory Applied to Economics (Piccoli, Fu)	*Proceedings of IEEE Systems, Man and Cybernetics (Conference)*, Oct.	1974
13	Choice Functions and Social Preference Orderings Modeled by Heuristic Grammatical Inference (Piccoli, Fu)	*Proceedings of the Second European Meeting on Cybernetics and Systems Research*, Apr.	1974

Pub. No.	Title (co-authors)	Journal/Book/Proceedings	Year
14	Pattern Recognition in the Social Sciences (Blin)	Pattern Recognition – Theory & Application, *Sijthoff International Publishers*	1975
15	Sophisticated Voting with Information for two Voting Functions (Adelsman)	Journal of Economic Theory, *15, 1*	1977
16	The Equivalence of Three Social Decision Functions (Adelsman)	*French Journal of Operations Research*, 11	1977
17	A Formal Model of Problem Solving (McAfee)	*International Journal of Policy Analysis and Information Systems*, 4, 3	1980
18	Optimal Design of a DSS System (McAfee)	*International Journal of Policy Analysis and Information Systems*, 6, 4	1982
19	The Theory of Expert Systems (Hall, Moore)	*Proceedings of the 15th Symposium on the Application of Expert Systems in Emergency Management Operation*, Apr.	1985
20	A Theoretical Basis for Expert Systems (Hall, Moore)	*Artificial Intelligence in Economics and Management*, Elsevier	1986
21	Artificial Intelligence in Economics – Expert Systems Modelling of Microeconomic Systems (Hoffman, Jacob, Marsden)	Artificial Intelligence in Economics and Management, *Elsevier*	1986
22	A Decision Theoretic Perspective of the Integrated Human-Machine Information Processor (Jacob, Moore)	*Proceedings of the IFAC Conference on Economics and Artificial Intelligence*, Sep.	1986
23	A Model of Decision-Making with Sequential Information-Acquisition	*Proceedings of the Fourth Army Conference on Applied*	1986

Pub. No.	Title (co-authors)	Journal/Book/Proceedings	Year
	with Application to the File Search Problem (Moore, Richmond)	*Mathematics and Computing*, May	
24	A Model of Decision-Making with Sequential Information-Acquisition (Part 1) (Moore)	*Decision Support Systems*, 2, 4	1986
25	Development, Use, and Verification of Expert Systems in Modelling Microeconomic Systems (Holsapple)	Decision Support Systems: Theory and Application, *Springer-Verlag*	1987
26	A Model of Decision-Making with Sequential Information-Acquisition – Part II (Moore)	*Decision Support Systems,* 3, 1	1987
27	Artificial Intelligence and the Management Science Practitioner: Rational Choice and Artificial Intelligence (Jacob, Moore)	*Interfaces*, 18, 4	1988
28	A Decision Theoretic Approach to File Search (Moore, Richmond)	*Computer Science in Economics and Management*, 1	1988
29	Choice Theory and Data Base (Moore, Richmond)	Mathematical Models for Decision Support, *Springer-Verlag*	1988
30	Mathematical Basis for Decision Support Systems (Moore, Richmond)	Mathematical Models for Decision Support, *Springer-Verlag*	1988
31	An Economic Framework for Computing (Moore, Richmond)	*Proceedings of the 22nd Annual Hawaii International Conference on System Sciences*, Jan.	1989
32	A Model for an Intelligent Operating System for Executing Image Understanding Tasks on a Reconfigurable Parallel Architecture	*Journal of Parallel and Distributed Computing*, 6	1989

Pub. No.	Title (co-authors)	Journal/Book/Proceedings	Year
	(Chu, Delp, Jamieson, Siegel, Weil)		
33	A Model of Decision Making Involving Two Information Processors (Jacob, Moore)	*Computer Science in Economics and Management*, 2	1989
34	Optimal Decision Processes and Algorithms (Moore, Richmond)	*Journal of Economic Dynamics and Control*, 14, 2	1990
35	A Preference Theory Approach to Decision Analysis in Resource Allocation (Rao, Moore)	*Computer Science in Economics and Management*, 3	1990
36	A Decision-Theoretic Approach to Information Retrieval (Moore, Richmond)	*ACM Transactions on Database Systems*, 15, 3	1990
37	A Total and Partial Information Acquisition for Resource Allocation among Partial Agents (Rao, Moore)	*IEEE Transactions on Systems, Man, and Cybernetics*, 24, 7	1994
38	Multi-Agent Resource Allocation: An Incomplete Information Perspective (Moore, Rao)	*IEEE Transactions on Systems, Man, and Cybernetics*, 24, 8	1994
39	Claims, Arguments and Decisions: Formalisms for Representation, Gaming and Coordination (Ramesh)	*Information Systems Research*, 5, 3	1994
40	On the Usage of Qualitative Reasoning as an Approach Towards Enterprise Modeling (Hinkkanen, Lang)	*Annals of Operations Research*, 55	1995
41	Computatioal Systems for Qualitative Economics (Lang, Moore)	*Computational Economics*, 8	1995
42	Information Processing for a Finite Resource Allocation Mechanism (Moore, Rao)	*Economic Theory*, 8	1996

Pub. No.	Title (co-authors)	Journal/Book/Proceedings	Year

"One of the reasons for the diversity of his research," explains Professor Preston McAfee, Editor of the *American Economic Review*, "is that he takes central ideas and concepts from one field and finds applications for them in other fields. In many cases, he can do this in both directions...he has written two papers that use computer-based decision making as a means of finding economic allocations with desirable properties, and then in reverse, using the economic theory of auctions to improve the way computer resources are allocated in a distributed computer network." (personal communication, November 18, 1993).

5.3 Accounting Information and Managerial Control Systems

The computerization of business transactions and record keeping led to the emergence of accounting information systems as a specialty subject area shared by the accounting and business computing disciplines (arrow 3 in Figure 1). Andy was an important early contributor to building this bridge (e.g., pubs. 1-4 in Table 3). His recognition of the importance of control and evaluation methods for these systems led to the landmark TICOM work (e.g., pubs. 5, 8, 10). University of Colorado Professor James Gerlach comments that "In accounting research circles, the work on TICOM is indisputably recognized as a classic...This work directly affected the development and design of Peat, Marwick, and Mitchell's SEACAS, a computer-based system for accounting system evaluation; it revolutionized auditor's approaches to evaluating computer-based information systems...His work on accounting data base issues and decision support systems for auditors...can be characterized as progressive and creative." (personal communication, November 13, 1993).

Table 6. Examples of Publications in Accounting Information and Managerial Control Systems

Pub. No.	Title (co-authors)	Journal/Book/Proceedings	Year
1	A Unified Approach to the Theory of Accounting and Information Systems (Colantoni, Manes)	*Accounting Review*, Jan.	1971

Pub. No.	Title (co-authors)	Journal/Book/Proceedings	Year
2	Structuring of an Events-Accounting Information System (Lieberman)	*Accounting Review*, Mar.	1975
3	Design of Multidimensional Accounting Information Systems (Haseman)	*Accounting Review*, Jan.	1976
4	A Survey of Techniques for Auditing EDP Based Accounting Information Systems (Cash, Bailey)	*Accounting Review*, Oct.	1977
5	The TICOM Model – A Network Data Base Approach to Review and Evaluation of International Control Systems (Cash, Bailey)	Proceedings of the National Computer Conference	1977
6	An Application of Complexity Theory to the Analysis of Internal Control (Bailey, McAfee)	Auditing: A Journal of Practice and Theory, 1, 1	1981
7	Internal Accounting Controls in the Office of the Future (Bailey, Gerlach, McAfee)	*IEEE Computer*, May	1981
8	The Theoretic and Analytic Capabilities of TICOM-II (Bailey, Gerlach, McAfee)	*Proceedings of the Second International Workshop on Office Information Systems*	1981
9	An OIS Model for Internal Control Evaluation (Bailey, Gerlach, McAfee)	*ACM Transactions on Office Information Systems*, 1, 1	1983
10	TICOM and the Analysis of Internal Controls (Bailey, Duke, Gerlach, Ko, Meservy)	*Accounting Review*, Apr.	1985
11	Technology Competition and the Future of Auditing (Bailey, Han)	Auditor Productivity in the Year 2000, *Council of Arthur Young*	1988

Pub. No.	Title (co-authors)	Journal/Book/Proceedings	Year
		Professors	
12	Knowledge Representation Theory and the Design of Auditable Office Information Systems (Bailey, Zacarias)	*Journal of Information Systems*, 3, 2	1989
13	Analytical Procedure: Qualitative and Causal Reasoning in Auditing (Bailey, Kiang, Kuipers)	*Applications of Management Science*, Vol. 6, JAI Press	1991
14	The Use of Qualitative and Causal Reasoning in Analytical Review Proceduers (Kiang, Bailey, Kuipers)	*Recent Developments in Decision Support Systems*, Springer-Verlag	1993
15	Multi-Auditor Cooperation: A Model of Distributed Reasoning (Chang)	*IEEE Transactions on Engineering Managements*, 4, 4	1993
16	A Distributed Knowledge-Based Approach for Planning and Controlling Projects (Chang, Bailey)	IEEE Systems Man Cybernetics, *23, 6*	1994

Professor Preston McAfee remarks that "Whinston sees applications of ideas well before others. His applications of artificial intelligence and expert systems to management and accounting preceded others by several years, for example." (personal communication, November 18, 1993). These novel approaches to accounting come from such angles as qualitative reasoning and office automation. Summing up the overall presence of Andy's work on the accounting bridge, University of Illinois Ernst and Young Professor of Accountancy, Andrew Bailey, reflects that "As an accountant and past editor of an auditing journal, I can tell you that it has been difficult to place information systems-related work in the top accounting journals...Andy has managed this on a number of occasions." (personal communication, October 15, 1993).

5.4 Model Management and Decision Support Systems

Having made fundamental contributions to the operations research discipline (see Section 5.6 below), Andy had a very substantial base for bridging it with the CS discipline. This thrust began in the early 1970s with Andy's development of computer aspects of pollution control and waste management (e.g., pubs. 3, 4, 6, 8, 10, 12, 13 in Table 4). In tackling these problems, he recognized the need to integrate large scale database management capabilities with OR algorithms (i.e., solvers) in support of decision making. With the GPLAN system, Andy took a generalized approach to addressing this need, resulting in perhaps the first shell for constructing DSSs (pubs. 5, 7, 9, 11).

In the latter half of the 1970s, Andy worked on several important advances beyond the GPLAN system. These included means for automatically interfacing solvers with each other and with data, a generalized non-procedural mapping language for data transformation, a transformational-grammar-based query processor for handling both database retrieval and/or solver execution from a single request, extensions and corrections to DBTG network concepts, and the integration of logic programming with database management, introducing the concept of artificially intelligent DSSs (e.g., pubs. 14-19). At the same time, he founded a company that implemented and marketed the first viable DBMS for microcomputers – having a number of innovative (physical and logical) data structuring features that did not exist in mainframe counterparts of the day (Bonczek et al., 1984) (e.g., pubs. 20, 22-24).

In 1981, Andy's classic book, *Foundations of Decision Support Systems* was published (Bonczek et al., 1981). This work advanced a theoretical framework that guides DSS researchers to this day. It demonstrated for the first time how AI techniques could be integrated with databases and solvers for model management purposes. In the book's forward, Nobel Laureate Herbert Simon wrote "A few years from now, a single book will be too small to even sketch out the uses of AI techniques in management – just as no single book can any longer do that for OR. But this volume takes an important step in this new direction, and can provide us with a valuable guide to the art in its present state – until the research and development work that it helps to stimulate causes its own obsolescence. This is all we can ask of a pioneering book."

This assessment proved to be on the mark. The decade of the 1980s witnessed an explosion of DSS research, in which Andy actively participated, especially in the areas of model management, software integration, and DSS user interfaces (e.g., pubs. 25, 26, 28-31, 36-45). A citation analysis by Professors Sean Eom and Sang Lee (the University Eminent Scholar and Regents Distinguished Professor, University of Nebraska) identified Andy as the most frequently cited researcher in decision support systems over a 19 year period (Eom and Lee, 1993).

Ideas in the book related to the notion of a Generalized Problem Processing System were successfully implemented by Andy's company. The initial 1983 rendition of the DSS development tool did not have an AI capability. The 1985 version, called GURU, constituted the first commercial system to integrate all of the common business techniques of knowledge management (relational database, spreadsheet, structured programming, forms management, text processing, etc.) with a full scale rule management capability – all within the confines of a single problem processing system (e.g., pubs. 21, 27, 32-35). The net effect was the first expert system development tool geared specifically toward business applications, along with the first substantial book about business expert systems (Holsapple and Whinston, 1986).

Table 7. Decision Support Publications

Pub. No	Title (co-authors)	Journal/Book, Proceedings	Year
1	Application of Nonlinear Programming to Water Quality Control (Marsden, Pingry)	*Water, Air, and Soil Pollution*, 2	1973
2	A Multi-goal Water Quality Planning Model (Pingry)	*Journal of the Environmental Engineering Division, ASCE*, Dec.	1973
3	Regression Analysis Applied to the Wastewater Treatment Plants (Marsden, Pingry	*Journal of the Water Pollution Control Federation*, 45, 10	1973
4	Data Base Management System for Pollution Control (Phaseman, Nunamaker)	Proceedings of the 7th Annual Symposium on the Interface	1973
5	Specifications for the Development of a Generalized Data Base Planning System (Nunamaker, Swenson)	*AFIPS Conference Proceedings*	1973
6	Cost Allocation for River Basin	*Economics and Decision*	1974

Pub. No	Title (co-authors)	Journal/Book, Proceedings	Year
	Planning Models (Pingry, Loehman)	*Making for Environmental Quality*	
7	Automatic Interfacing of Application Software in the GPLAN Framework (Nunamaker, Pomeranz)	*Information Sciences and Organizational Structure*	1975
8	Water Quality Management and Information Systems (Haseman, Lieberman)	*Journal of Hydraulics Division*, Mar.	1975
9	Security for the GPLAN Systems (Cash, Haseman)	*Information Systems*, 1	1975
10	O.R. Data Base Interface – An Application to Pollution Control (Haseman, Holsapple)	*Computers and Operations Research*, 3,1	1976
11	A Partial Implementation of the CODASYL DBTG Report as an Extension to FORTRAN (Haseman, Nunamaker)	*Management Datamatics*, Sep.	1975
12	Picture Processing and Automatic Data Base Design (Bonczek)	*Computer Graphics and Image Processing*, 5	1976
13	Implementation of a Large Scale Water Quality Data Management System (Haseman, Holsapple)	*Socio-Economic Planning Sciences*, 10, 1	1976
14	Extensions and Corrections for the CODASYL Approach to Data Base Management (Bonczek, Holsapple)	*Information Systems*, 2	1976
15	Automatic Program Interface (Haseman)	*The Computer Journal*, 20, 3	1977
16	A Generalized Mapping Language for Network Data Structures	*Information Systems*, 2	1977

Pub. No	Title (co-authors)	Journal/Book, Proceedings	Year
	(Bonczek)		
17	A Transformational Grammar-Based Query Processor for Access Control in a Planning System (Bonczek, Cash)	*ACM Transactions on Data Base Management*, Jan.	1978
18	Information Transferal Within a Distributed Data Base via a Generalized Mapping Language (Bonczek, Holsapple)	*The Computer Journal*, 21, 2	1978
19	The Integration of Data Base Management and Problem Resolution (Bonczek, Holsapple)	*Information Systems*, 4, 2	1979
20	The Significance of Data Base Management for Micros (Holsapple)	Datamation, *27, 4*	1981
21	Development Tools for Decision Support Systems (Bonczek, Holsapple)	*Computerworld*, 15, 37	1981
22	Data-Base Manager Fits Microsystems, Avoids Application Dependency (Gagle, Koehler)	Electronics, *Nov.*	1981
23	Data-Base Management Systems: Powerful Newcomers to Microcomputers (Gagle, Koehler)	*Byte*, Nov.	1981
24	Data Base Management: A Comparative Study (Holsapple, Shen)	*Handbook of Industrial Engineering*, Wiley	1982
25	A Consulting System for Data Base Design (Holsapple, Shen)	*Information Systems, 7, 3*	1982
26	The DSS Development System	*Proceedings of the National*	1983

Pub. No	Title (co-authors)	Journal/Book, Proceedings	Year
	(Bonczek, Ghiaseddin, Holsapple)	*Computer Conference*	
27	Software Tools for Knowledge Fusion (Holsapple)	*Computerworld,* 17, 15	1983
28	Specification of Modeling Knowledge in Decision Support Systems (Bonczek, Holsapple)	*Processes and Tools for Decision Support,* North-Holland	1983
29	Semantic Representations for Natural Language Query Processing (Burd, Pan)	*Proceedings of the IEEE Workshop on Languages for Automation*	1983
30	Developments in Decision Support Systems (Bonczek, Holsapple)	*Advances in Computers,* Vol. 23, Academic Press	1984
31	A Formal Approach to Decision Support (Pan, Pick)	*Management and Office Information Systems,* Plenum	1984
32	Aspects of Integrated Software (Holsapple)	*Proceedings of the National Computer Conference*	1984
33	Integrated Software for DSS Development (Holsapple)	*Proceedings of the Conference on the Impacts of Microprocessors on Operations Research*	1985
34	Expert System Integration (Holsapple, Tam)	*Expert Systems for Business,* Addison-Wesley	1987
35	Artificially Intelligent Decision Support Systems – Criteria for Tool Selection (Holsapple)	*Decision Support Systems: Theory and Application,* Springer-Verlag	1987
36	Temporal Semantics and Natural Language Processing in a Decision Support System (De, Pan)	*Information Systems,* 12, 1	1987
37	Mathematical Basis for Decision	*Mathematical Models for*	1988

Pub. No	Title (co-authors)	Journal/Book, Proceedings	Year
	Support Systems (Moore, Richmond)	*Decision Support,* Springer-Verlag	
38	The Environment Approach for Decision Support (Holsapple)	*Mathematical Models for Decision Support,* Springer-Verlag	1988
39	Flexible User Interfaces for Decision Support Systems (Holsapple, Park, Stansifer)	*Proceedings of the 21st Annual Hawaii International Conference on System Sciences*	1989
40	Solving Complex Problems Via Software Integration (Watabe, Holsapple)	*The Journal of Computer Information Systems,* 31, 3	1991
41	Information Issues in Model Specification (Balakrishnan)	*Information Systems Research,* 2, 4	1991
42	Decision Support Systems (Holsapple)	*Handbook on Industrial Engineering,* Wiley	1992
43	Generating Structure Editor Interfaces for OR Procedures (Holsapple, Park)	*Zeitschrift fur Operations Research,* 36, 3	1992
44	Framework for DSS Interface Development (Holsapple, Park)	*Recent Developments in Decision Support Systems, Springer-Verlag*	1993
45	A Hyperknowledge Framework for Decision Support Systems (Chang, Holsapple)	*Information Processing and Management,* 30, 4	1995

Referring to the fourth bridge in Figure 1, Comshare's Dr. David King contends that Andy "...was instrumental in changing the direction of the field of decision support to encompass the emerging fields of expert systems, knowledge bases, and logic programming...[He] outlined a new framework for the field of decision support that combined the thinking of

Simon and Newell...framework came to dominate the field and set the direction of decision support research during the 80s and continues to do so." (personal communication. November 19, 1993). Carnegie-Mellon's Dr. Krishnan remarks that "...his ability to meld together ideas from artificial intelligence, database systems, operations research and economics injected rigor and scientific discipline into what had been up until then a muddied academic debate..." (personal communication, 1993).

In assessing Andy's activities, Vanderbilt University Professor of Management Robert Blanning states that "He is the leading scholar in the world in bridging the gap between computer science and MIS/DSS...and also in bridging the gap between computer science and the fields of economics and operations research...in the mid-70s...he applied...network database systems to model management systems...was able to address the question...are algorithms for the retrieval of stored data equivalent, from a user perspective, to algorithms for decision analysis? His answer...provided a graph-based foundation for the emerging discipline of model management systems...this work was a precursor to Art Geoffrion's work on structured modeling...[It] was the first solid development in model management systems...he began to examine the application of AND/OR graphs and logic programming to model management. This paralleled Green's (and later Minker's, etc.) work on logic programming and databases, but it examined a much more general issue...[and] led to a flurry of articles and a couple of books that established Andy as the founder of a major component of the field of DSS...he continues to explore technical issues in DSS...[and is] also examining economic issues...and organizational issues..." (personal communication, October 25, 1993).

Harvey Greenberg, Professor of Mathcmatics at the University of Colorado at Denver and founding Editor of the *ORSA Journal on Computing*, characterizes Andy's work as "...a lifetime of professional commitment to the interfaces between computer science and the decision sciences embodied in operations research...His work in decision support systems is widely recognized. These not only apply sound principles and methods of computer science, but also some of his works contribute to the advancement of some areas of computer science." (personal communication, October 27, 1993). Frazier Family Professor of Computer Information Systems at the University of Louisville, Brian Dos Santos, adds "Dr. Whinston's contributions over the past three decades have had a tremendous impact on theory and practice...His pioneering work bridging computer science, management and economics has attracted many others to work on problems that bridge these areas...His book on decision support systems...[is] required reading for doctoral students...[and] has had a profound impact on the DSS field, being as relevant today, as it was fifteen years ago…" (personal communication, October 14, 1993).

Comshare's Dr. King again comments: "Dr. Whinston helped re-direct the field through his leadership of…a company specializing in database and decision support software for personal computers…[It was] one of the first companies to offer PC software…[and the] first company to offer a decision support product…combining expert system, model and database components" (personal communication, November 19, 1993). Similarly, Dean Hasan Pirkul comments that "One area where he has done and continues to do pioneering work is Decision Support Systems and its links to artificial intelligence…resulting in the tool GURU…one of the first to provide a comprehensive environment for expert system development…[This] illustrates the fact that his work is not purely theoretical but also has a significant practical side…" (personal communication, November 15, 1993).

Professor James Courtney reflects that "As management science matured…Professor Whinston, as usual, was among the first to realize the importance of good data management…Dr. Whinston's work in integrating data management, knowledge management and modeling has been instrumental in the development of the decision support systems concept…*Foundations of Decision Support Systems* is without question the most important theoretical work in the area…[It was] published in 1981, but I still use it in my doctoral seminar. I believe it is a classic that should be read by all students in the field. His accomplishment in developing a successful software product built on this framework attests to Dr. Whinston's ability to bridge the gap from theory to practice…" (personal communication, November 12, 1993).

5.5 Production and Manufacturing Systems

Although his early work on this interdisciplinary bridge involved computer systems for vehicle scheduling, water quality planning, production functions, and process analysis (e.g., pubs. 1-6, 9 in Table 5), Andy is primarily known for his explorations of the uses of artificial intelligence in manufacturing systems to address operational planning and scheduling problems (e.g., pubs. 7, 8, 10-17). This work opened a new dimension for research into flexible manufacturing systems and computer integrated manufacturing. Today, this AI dimension is an active research area for industrial engineering and operations management investigators, and has a new journal devoted to it.

Table 8. Publications in Production and Manufacturing Systems

Pub. No.	Title (co-authors)	Journal/Book/Proceedings	Year
1	An Information System for Vehicle Scheduling (Noonan)	*Software Age*, Nov.	1969
2	Computer-Assisted School Bus Scheduling (Angel, Caudle, Noonan)	*Management Science*, 18, 6	1972
3	Production Function Theory and the Optimal Design of Waste Treatment Facilities (Marsden, Pingry)	*Applied Economics*, 4	1972
4	An Alternative Approach for Deriving Production and Cost Functions (Pingry, Marsden)	*Transactions of the Sixth International Conference on System Sciences*	1973
5	Engineering Foundations of Production Functions (Marsden, Pingry)	*Journal of Economic Theory*, 9, 2	1974
6	Process Analysis: A Comment (Marsden, Pingry)	*American Economic Review*, Sep.	1974
7	Control and Decision Support in Automatic Manufacturing Systems (Nof, Bullers)	*AIIE Transactions*, 12, 2	1980
8	Artificial Intelligence in Manufacturing Planning and Control (Bullers, Nof)	*AIIE Transactions*, Dec.	1980
9	Point Estimation and Process Models – The Spline Function Alternative (Bever, Marsden)	*Environmental Policy*, 3	1984
10	Applications of Artificial Intelligence to Planning and Scheduling in Flexible Manufacturing (Shaw)	*Flexible Manufacturing Systems: Methods and Studies*, North-Holland	1986

Pub. No.	Title (co-authors)	Journal/Book/Proceedings	Year
11	A Framework for Integrated Problem Solving in Manufacturing (De)	*IEEE Transactions*, Sep.	1986
12	Knowledge Representation for Decision Support in Computer Integrated manufacturing Systems (Shaw, Wang)	Artificial Intelligence – Implications for CIM *IFS Ltd.*	1987
13	New Directions in Decision Support for Manufacturing (Chaudhury, Nof)	*Computer Integrated Manufacturing: Current Status and Challenges,* Springer-Verlag	1988
14	An Artificial Intelligence Approach to the Scheduling of Flexible Manufacturing Systems (Shaw)	*IIE Transactions,* 21, 2	1989
15	Document-Centered Information Systems for Supporting Reactive Problem-Solving in Manufacturing (Balakrishnan, Kalakota, Ow)	*International Journal of Production Economics*, 38	1995
16	Information Technology for Automated Manufacturing Enterprises: Recent Developments and Current Research Issues (Shaw, Seidmann)	*The International Journal of Flexible Manufacturing Systems,* 9, 2	1997
17	A Decentralized Approach to Estimate Activity Based Costs and Near-Optimal Resource Allocation in Flexible Manufacturing Systems (Gupta, Stahl)	*International Journal of Flexible Manufacturing Systems,* 9, 2	1997

"The influence of his research..." says Professor Shaw, has had "...major impacts in...industrial engineering." (personal communication, November 15, 1993). Harvard's Lynda Applegate remarks that Andy's

"...publications have made important contributions within...flexible manufacturing." (personal communication, November 24, 1993). Professor Vamos adds that "Using patterns, applying them in flexible manufacturing and by this why connecting manufacturing with business administration added much to the avenues of practical usage of these fields' academic progress." (personal communication, October 29, 1993). Professor Marsden refers to Andy's "...noteworthy, even landmark contributions" to many areas, including "...computer integrated manufacturing, flexible manufacturing." (personal communication, November 18, 1993).

Purdue Professor of Industrial Engineering, Shimon Nof, relates how "Andy approached me with his brilliant ideas of applying concepts of artificial intelligence in manufacturing. Indeed, our joint interdisciplinary work has led to the first publication on applying Petri Nets to manufacturing operation systems...and later on to the pioneering article on applying AI to manufacturing." (personal communication, November 23, 1993).

5.6 Reference Disciplines

Andy has made major research contributions in reference disciplines linked to the five interdisciplinary bridges – especially in economics and the mathematical programming area of operations research. Recall the words of Professor George Dantzig, National Medal of Science recipient and Co-Director of Stanford's Systems Optimization Laboratory, recognizing that "Whinston...made important contributions to Economic Theory and Mathematical Programming." Economist Dr. Preston McAfee points out that "His paper on the theory of the second best is considered a classic in the economics literature." (personal communication, November 18, 1993). Professor James Courtney remarks that "I first became familiar with Dr. Whinston's work...in the early 1970s. His work in mathematical programming was highly regarded even then, and required reading in management science courses..." (personal communication, November 12, 1993).

Hiroshi Konno, Professor of Industrial Engineering and Management at the Tokyo Institute of Technology, reflects that "As a mathematical programmer, I was deeply impressed by his works in quadratic programming...and by a finite cutting plane algorithm for solving concave minimization problems developed jointly with Majthay. In fact, the idea of facet cuts enabled them to construct a finitely convergent cutting plane algorithm for the first time in history. Cutting plane algorithm for concave minimization problems was first introduced by H. Tuy in 1964...however, it lacked finite convergence property. Many researchers, including myself, tried in vain to establish finite convergence of this method in the early 70's. To my knowledge, Majthay and Whinston were the first to establish this property...Concave minimization (or in other words global optimization) is now developing rapidly and Andy's work should be counted as one important step toward the success of this new field..." (personal communication, November 11, 1993).

University of Texas Professor Emeritus in Accounting, Management Science and Information Systems, William Cooper, offers the following analysis: "In his early work, Andy combined both economics and operations research in..."Price Guides in Decentralized Organizations" which explored limits to uses of prices (in the presence of externalities). This thesis raised questions of fundamental importance by setting precisely established limits to what could be accomplished by a price system under such conditions. The results became a centerpiece for much subsequent research which attempted unsuccessfully to find flaws in the limits that Andy established or at least to find ways around these limits by introducing various assumptions. Not only did Andy's results stand up but they were also extended when Whinston (in collaboration with O. Davis) introduced concepts from non-zero sum game theory. In fact it is now accepted that situations like those associated with Prisoner's Dilemma and like considerations, produce these results and the fact that this is no longer identified with Andy does not detract from Andy's contributions...Similar remarks apply to Andy's work with Naslund in developing quadratic programming algorithms for use with chance constrained programming approaches to portfolio selection. This work combined operations research with finance after which Andy went on to develop and apply similar concepts to accounting and auditing. Andy began to turn his attention to computer-based information and decision support systems which he combined with his earlier work and interests. This expanded these topics in new directions and also provided new approaches and new directions for research on uses of computers and data bases for management as well as economics and other social and management sciences." (personal communication, October 28, 1993).

5.7 Electronic Commerce

The principal thrust of Andy's investigations since the mid-1990s has been in the realm of electronic commerce, which is in the process of reshaping the landscape of business to deal with and benefit from dramatic technical innovations. Electronic commerce (EC) involves approaches to achieving enterprise goals in which technology is used to manage knowledge in order to enable or facilitate execution of activities within and across value chains, as well as the decision making that underlies those activities (Holsapple and Singh, 2000). As such, the business computing field is at the core of emerging EC phenomena, which span the computing and business disciplines. EC, thus, represents a natural extension of Andy's past multidisciplinary work into the Internet/Web world.

Characteristically, Andy was an early mover in EC research and has been a prolific contributor to the literature of the field through a host of interdisciplinary explorations. In rapid succession, he has produced a series of cutting edge books on EC topics (Kalakota and Whinston 1996, 1997a, 1997b; Choi et al. 1998; Choi and Whinston, 2000). Table 6 cites examples of his recent EC research papers. They examine EC in relation to such disciplines as economics (e.g., Internet pricing), finance (e.g., electronic markets), operations management (e.g., supply chain automation), accounting (e.g., e-process control), organization science (e.g., agent coordination), marketing (e.g., online auctions), and business computing (e.g., Web-based decision support).

Table 9. Example Publications in Electronic Commerce

Pub. No.	Title (co-authors)	Journal/Book/Proceedings	Year
1	Electronic Commerce:Buildling Blocks of New Business Opportunity (Applegate, Holsapple, Kalakota, Radermacher)	*Journal of Organizational Computing and Electronic Commerce*, 6, 1	1996
2	Worldwide Real-Time Decision Support Systems for Electronic Commerce Applications (Kalakota, Stallaert)	*Journal of Organizational Computing and Electronic Commerce*, 6, 1	1996
3	Strategies of Smart Shopping in Cyberspace (Ravindran, Barua, Lee) An Economic Approach to Network	*Journal of Organizational Computing and Electronic Commerce*, 6, 1	1996
4	Computing with Priority Classes (Gupta, Stahl)	*Journal of Organizational Computing and Electronic Commerce*, 6, 1	1996
5	Knowledge-Based HTML Document Generation for Automating Web Publishing (Liu, Hämäläinen)	*Expert Systems with Applications*, 10, ¾	1996
6	Pricing Internet Services (Gupta, Stahl)	*IMPACT: How IC^2-Research Affects Public Policy and Business Markets*	1997

Pub. No.	Title (co-authors)	Journal/Book/Proceedings	Year
7	A Priority Pricing Approach to Manage Multi-Service Class Networks in Real-Time (Gupta, Stahl)	*Journal of Electronic Publishing*	1997
8	Using Client-Broker-Server Architecture for Intranet Decision Support (Ba, Kalakota)	*Decision Support Systems*, 19, 3	1997
9	A Stochastic Equilibrium Model of Internet Pricing (Gupta, Stahl)	*Journal of Economic Dynamics and Control*, 21	1997
10	Economic Issues in Electronic Commerce (Gupta, Stahl)	Readings in Electronic Commerce, *Addison-Wesley*	1997
11	Efficient Selection of Suppliers over the Internet (Barua, Ravindran)	*Journal of Management Information Systems*, 13, 4	1997
12	Enterprise Decision Support Using Intranet Technology (Ba, Lang)	*Decision Support Systems*, 20, 2	1997
13	Electronic Commerce: A Shift in Paradigm	*IEEE Internet Computing, E-Commerce*, 1, 6	1997
14	Streamlining the Digital Economy: How to Avert a Tragedy of the Commons (Gupta, Jukic, Parameswaran, Stahl)	*IEEE Internet Computing, E-Commerce*, 1, 6	1997
15	The Internet: A Future Tragedy of Commons? (Gupta, Stahl)	*Computational Approaches to Economic Problems,* Kluwer	1997
16	Intermediation, Contract and Micropayments in Electronic Commerce (Choi, Stahl)	*Electronic Markets Newsletter*, 4	1997
17	Marketing Information on the I-WAY: Data Junkyard or Information Gold Mine? (Kanna, Chang)	*Communication of the ACM*, 41, 3	1998
18	Implementing Real-Time Supply Chain Optimization Systems (Kalakota, Stallaert)	*Global Supply Chain and Technology Management, POMS Series in Technology and Operations Management*, 1	1998
19	The Design and Development of a Financial Cybermarket with a Bundle Trading Mechanism	International Journal of Electronic Commerce	1999

Pub. No.	Title (co-authors)	Journal/Book/Proceedings	Year
	(Stallaert, Fan)		
20	The Future of E-Commerce: Integrate and Customize (Choi)	*IEEE Computer*, Jan.	1999
21	A Web-Based Financial Trading System (Fan, Stallaert)	*IEEE Computer*, Apr.	1999
22	The Economics of Network Management (Gupta, Stahl)	*Communications of the ACM*, 42, 9	1999
23	Benefits and Requirements for Interoperability in the Electronic Marketplace (Choi)	*Technology in Society*, Dec.	1999
24	Markets for Everything in the Networked Economy (Parameswaran, Stallaert)	Mastering Information Management, *Prentice Hall*	2000
25	Financial Markets at the Time of the information Technology Revolution (Fan, Srinivasan, Stallaert)	The Future of Financial Services – Winning in the Age of Technology,Technology Publishing Ltd.	2000
26	Value and Productivity in the Internet Economy (Barua, Yin)	*IEEE Computer*, 33, 5	2000
27	Extracting Consumers Private Information for Implementing Incentive-Compatible Internet Traffic Pricing (Gupta, Jukic, Stahl)	*Journal of Management Information Systems*, 17, 1	2000
28	Emerging Market Structures in the Digital Supply Chain (Susarla, Parameswaran)	*IEEE IT Professional*, Sept./Oct.	2000
29	E-Process Control and Assurance Using Model Checking (Wang, Hidvegi, Bailey)	*IEEE Computer*, Oct.	2000
30	The Internet and the Future of Financial Markets (Fan, Stallaert)	*Communication of the ACM*, 43, 11	2000
31	Making E-Business Pay: Eight Key Drivers for Operational Success (Barua, Konana, Yin)	*IEEE IT Pro*, Nov./Dec.	2000
32	Radically New Product Introduction	*International Journal of*	

Pub. No.	Title (co-authors)	Journal/Book/Proceedings	Year
	Using Online Auctions (Geng, Stinchcombe)	*Electronic Commerce*	2001
33	Virtual Field Experiments for a Digital Economy: A New Research Methodology for Exploring an Information Economy (Kim, Anitesh)	*Decision Support Systems*	2001

Andy's EC research spans a host of issues including impacts on business protocols and processes, impacts on organizational structure and corporate networks, electronic publishing, systems for electronic education, complementarity of convergent computational paradigms, and creation of business value. Specific examples of this EC work include the following: A paradigm for corporate networks in virtual organizations has been introduced, and a prototype is being developed with emphasis on the reengineered business processes and protocols and workflows. This extends prior work on collaborative systems over the Internet. Usage-based priority pricing mechanisms for network access have been advanced and a simulated behavior of the Internet as an economy is being studied to analyze the underlying market structures and welfare implications. Various attributes and consequent market mechanisms of digital products in a virtual economy are being investigated. Prototype electronic education environments are being used to study a framework for virtual universities of the future. The protocols, standards, and design of intelligent agent organizations for coordinating and optimizing various tasks in global networked corporate entities are being studied in the context of supply chain management.

True to form, Andy is employing principles of management, economics, business computing, and computer science in analyzing evolving trends in electronic commerce and in laying out guidelines for future EC initiatives. His writings are required reading for anyone wanting to keep a thumb on the Internet Economy's pulse. Consider one of his latest EC books, for instance (Choi and Whinston, 2000). For those seeking an introductory grasp of EC, it offers a well-organized and highly insightful treatment of concepts, practices, and technologies. For those already deeply engaged in the Internet Economy, this book offers a wealth of provocative, stimulating ideas and perspectives. Central themes include the pervasive nature of the Internet Economy, the migration from value chains to value webs, the rise of knowledge-based products, and the emergence of a Smart Economy.

In lucid terms, Andy and co-author Choi make a compelling case for the pervasive expanse and pervasive effects of the Internet Economy, furnishing numerous examples and a discussion of the implications for individuals, organizations, and society. They observe that value chains are being replaced by value webs involving network organizations. Ample examples are given, as well as guidance about what this means for competitiveness. The book provides penetrating coverage of knowledge-based products, as a basis for clarifying the relationships between (and convergence of) electronic business and knowledge management. Building on the Internet Economy, the authors sketch out the boundaries and structure of a Smart Economy that will increasingly characterize the new century. The hallmarks of this Smart Economy are flexibility and real-time interactive responsiveness. Using these two concepts, they give an analysis of what to expect and how to be positioned in this new era. In all, the book reveals Andy's deep understanding of the Internet Economy based on his years of leading-edge work in the electronic commerce realm.

6. CULTIVATING THE INTERDISCIPLINARY BRIDGES

Andy's work toward fostering and facilitating the interdisciplinary movement linking CS with managerial disciplines is just as important and extensive as his direct research efforts. It complements his direct research to yield a fully developed, complete scholar. Three major aspects of his interdisciplinary cultivation work are a) mentoring/educating his own students and bright junior researchers, b) extensive editorial service and founding of two significant journals (*Decision Support Systems* and *Journal of Organizational Computing and Electronic Commerce*) that promote the integration of CS and managerial disciplines, and c) the founding and organizing of conferences on decision support systems, computational economics, and organizational computing.

Over the years, Andy's books have helped countless students around the world better appreciate the dynamic business computing field. They have been adopted for BC courses across the entire spectrum of universities, from regional schools to those with high international reputations. They also serve as basic reference works for instructors in developing course content. For instance, MIT's Professor Brynjolfsson writes that "I have referred to his books frequently when I teach my AI and expert systems courses." He goes on to observe that "The depth and breadth of his work is self-evident...yet where he is making his greatest contribution is in helping the research communities...journals he has established have provided a unique forum for...interdisciplinary work...and have already eclipsed many older...journals. He has mentored many of the current and future leaders of the field and has been instrumental in bringing them together at conferences he has unselfishly organized...Andy has also found time to make practical some of the research to which he has contributed by founding and advising numerous successful businesses." (personal communication, July 10, 1993).

Harvard's Professor Cash opines that "...the many indirect contributions that Andy has made to this bridging work...may even outweigh the impacts of his more direct efforts...[They] have enabled or facilitated a legion of other researchers in making their own interdisciplinary contributions...[They] include founding quality journals as forums for scholarly discourse...organizing numerous conferences for the sharing and stimulation of ideas...cultivating a host of emerging researchers as a dissertation chair and as a mentor of young faculty, interacting with and offering insights to numerous established researchers...[and delivering] personal classroom instruction of a multitude of students at all degree levels." (personal communication, November 24, 1993).

6.1 Mentoring and Education

Tokyo Institute of Technology's Professor Konno refers to "...the remarkable number of Ph.D. students who completed their works under his supervision. To my understanding this number is well over one hundred, which I believe is a record in the field of computer science as well as in management science." (personal communication, November 11, 1993). Dr. Hsu of AT&T Labs recalls how Andy "...inspired me to choose a research career that focuses on bridging the gap between management science and computer science...[and] also advised me on my doctorate dissertation on designing a programming language system for decision support systems." (personal communication, November 4, 1993).

John M. Olin Distinguished Fellow at George Mason University's Center for Study of Public Choice, Dr. James C. Miller, reflects that "In the fall of 1965...I took a course from Dr. Whinston and also his follow-on course the second semester. Under his auspices I began a project...which eventually formed the basis for my Ph.D. dissertation (Scheduling and Airline Efficiency) and a lead article in the journal, *Transportation Science* ("A Time of Day Model for Aircraft Scheduling")...Professor Whinston was an early inspiration in my career...as he has been for many others...here is one of the American academy's most prolific, innovative researchers. Also, a legion of students and colleagues will attest to his broad, positive influence." (personal communication, November 4, 1993). Dr. Miller's career has included service as Chairman of the Federal Trade Commission, Director of the U.S. Office of Management and Budget, and member of the

National Security Council. He is also a senior fellow of the Hoover Institution at Stanford University.

Professor McAfee of the Universities of Chicago and Texas points out that "In 1979, Whinston had fifteen concurrent (doctoral) students, and by this time, the number he's supervised must be in the hundreds. Whinston accomplishes this by dreaming up feasible research projects for most of them. He supplies ideas – lots of ideas – and students choose topics...Many of his students have gone on to become outstanding researchers themselves..." (personal communication, November 18, 1993).

Professor Pingry of the University of Arizona notes that Andy "has produced a large number of successful Ph.D. students. I have no idea how many, but I meet them everywhere...Andy has a high rate of success in transferring his interdisciplinary skills to his students...I believe that this ability is quite rare. First, Andy teaches his students to link theory to practice. Second, Andy teaches ideas, not disciplines...[The] major motivation is to solve problems...ideas that are appropriate may come from many literatures...[The] interdisciplinary view that Andy affords his students gives them the ability to relate ideas that are expressed in very different styles and jargons...He has trained an army of students that are truly an international resource in computer-related interdisciplinary research..." (personal communication, November 15, 1993).

Professor Henderson of Boston University comments that "His students serve as leading faculty at major universities...[Andy] has, over the years, been a consistent and critical voice in support of those that seek to make scholarly contributions in the field of Information Systems." (personal communication, November 23, 1993). Professor Blanning of Vanderbilt University observes that Andy "...has organized a large number of conferences...the NATO conferences were remarkable...[The] computational economics conference...provided a splendid opportunity to address pressing technical...and technology-related political and bureaucratic issues essential to this growing field." (personal communication, October 25, 1993).

6.2 Forums for Interdisciplinary Exchange

The University of British Columbia's Professor Izak Benbasat, who is Canada Research Chair in Information Technology Management and Editor of *Information Systems Research,* observes that "Dr. Whinston's research work and publications attest to his long time interest in bridging computer science related disciplines...[His] two journals...have provided high quality outlets...a home for the diverse reference disciplines which have to exist together...to advance the science and practice of the discipline of computer science...[It is] highly praiseworthy that Dr. Whinston, with his expertise and interests in so many diverse areas, has promoted linkages among these disciplines through his extensive editorial work." (personal communication, November 18, 1993). "His journals have been quickly recognized for their quality and have played a catalytic role in encouraging research that spans several disciplines," notes Carnegie-Mellon's Professor Krishnan (personal communication, 1993).

Professor Blanning of Vanderbilt explains that Andy "...established two journals that fill important gaps in the organizational applications of computer science. *Decision Support Systems* is a pioneering and leading journal on the technical (as opposed to behavioral) aspects of DSS. For example, much of the model management literature is formed in this journal. *Organizational Computing* addresses more general behavioral and managerial issues but in an analytically solid way...[Its] special issue on the application of AI to organizational modeling is the first...to appear in any journal." (personal communication, October 25, 1993).

Citation analyses have shown Decision Support Systems to be one of the top journals devoted to the BC field. It has bee recognized with the Anbar Golden Page Award for "most original content." Comshare's Dr. King affirms that "*Decision Support Systems*...is one of the premier journals...[It] has always promoted rigorous interdisciplinary research, especially research combining knowledge-base systems, logic programming, and decision support..." (personal communication, November 19, 1993). The *Journal of Organizational Computing and Electronic Commerce* was the first journal to be published with an explicit EC orientation. Andy saw early on that EC was a transorganizational computing phenomenon.

The editorial boards and authors for Andy's journals come from practically all regions of the planet, helping to make them global in terms of published perspectives and readership impact. From Hungary, Professor Vamos remarks that "...periodicals started and shaped by him create a massive force of knowledge dissemination. As a person who comes from the Central-Eastern European region I specially owe a debt of gratitude for his many years of beneficial activity, distributing advanced knowledge in these countries, tutoring young scientists to keep up with world's progress in years of separation." (personal communication, October 29, 1993).

7. *Conclusion*

This is a relatively lengthy chapter. However, given the magnitude of Andy's career accomplishments it could not be otherwise. Although, the chapter falls far short of an exhaustive in-depth presentation of Andy's work, it gives a substantial overall portrayal of an individual who has had an immense and unsurpassed creative impact on bridging computing and business disciplines in the interest of improved problem solving through business computing. Other chapters in this book give more in-depth insights into various aspects of the work overviewed here. In addition, the reader is advised to always remain alert for the next publication in the ongoing flow of innovative work from this remarkable scholar.

REFERENCES

Amman, H., Rustem, B., & Whinston, A., eds. (1997). *Computational approaches to economic problems*. Dordrecht, Netherlands: Kluwer.

Bailey, A., Gerlach, J., & Whinston, A. (1985). *Office systems technology and organizations*, Reston, VA: Reston Publishing Company.

Bonczek, R., Holsapple, C., & Whinston, A. (1981). *Foundations of decision support systems*. New York: Academic Press.

Bonczek, R., Holsapple, C., & Whinston, A. (1984). *Micro database management*. New York: Academic Press.

Caminer, D., Aris, J., Hermon, P., & Land, F. (1998). *LEO: The incredible story of the world's first business computer*. New York: McGraw-Hill.

Choi, S., Stahl, D., & Whinston, A. (1998). *The economics of electronic commerce*. New York: Macmillan.

Choi, S. & Whinston, A. (2000). *The Internet economy: Technology and practice*. Smart Econ.com Publishing.

Cooper, W. & Whinston, A., eds. (1994). *Computational economics: Theory and practice*. Dordrecht, Netherlands: Kluwer.

Eom, S. & Lee, S. (1993). Leading U. S. universities and most influential contributors in decision support systems research (1971-1989): A citation analysis.*Decision Support Systems*, 9, 3.

Holsapple, C., Johnson, L, Manakyan, H., & Tanner, J. (1994). Business computing system research: Structuring the field. *OMEGA: The International Journal of Management Science*, 22, 1, 69-81.

Holsapple, C. & Singh, M. (2000). Electronic commerce: From a definitional taxonomy toward a knowledge management view. *Journal of Organizational Computing and Electronic Commerce*, 10, 3.

Holsapple, C. & Whinston, A. (1996). *Decision support systems: A knowledge-based approach*. St. Paul, MN: West.

Holsapple, C. & Whinston, A. (1988). *The information jungle: A quasi-novel approach to managing corporate knowledge*. Homewood, IL: Dow Jones-Irwin.

Holsapple, C. & Whinston, A. (1986). *Manager's guide to expert systems using Guru.* Homewood, IL: Dow Jones-Irwin.

Kalakota, R. & Whinston, A. (1996). *Frontiers of electronic commerce.* Reading, MA: Addison-Wesley.

Kalakota, R. & Whinston, A. (1997a). *Readings of electronic commerce.* Reading, MA: Addison-Wesley.

Kalakota, R. & Whinston, A. (1997b). *Electronic commerce: A manager's guide.* Reading, MA: Addison-Wesley.

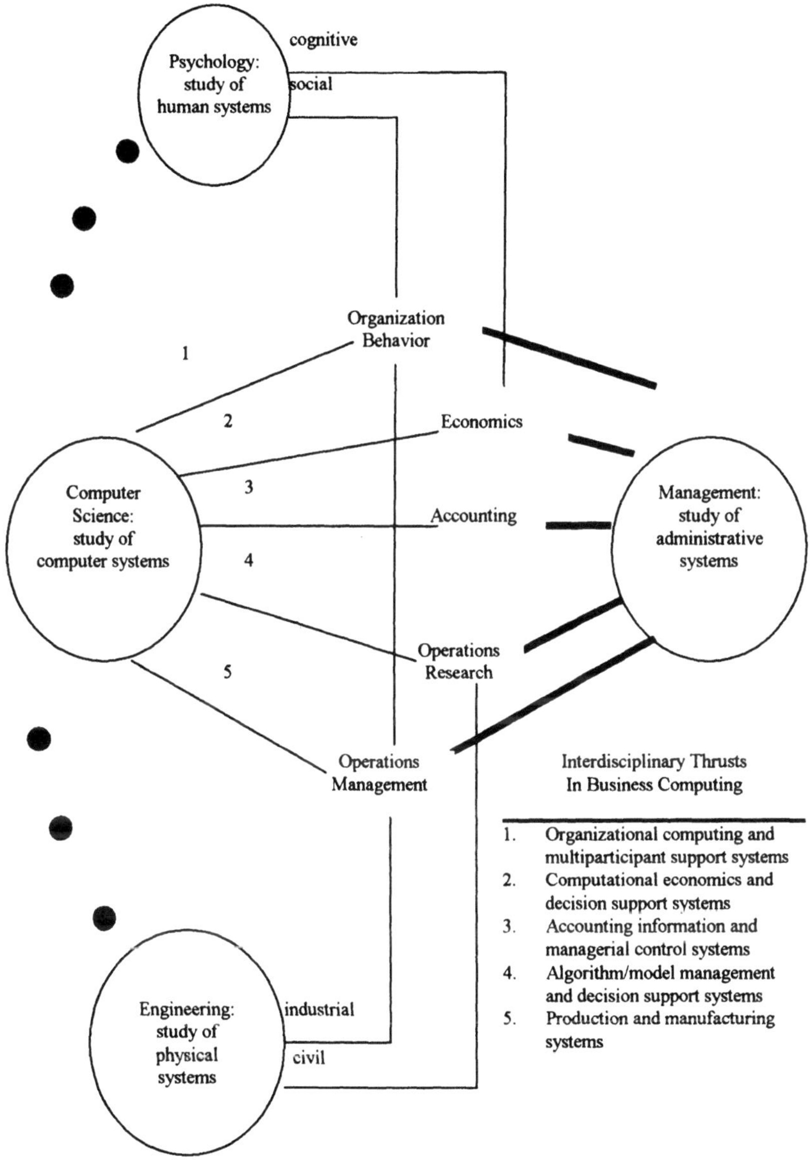

Figure 1. Business Computing Bridges

Chapter 21

The Intellectual Contribution Of Professor Andrew B. Whinston To The Field Of Information Systems In The Past Two Decades:

A CITATION ANALYSIS

Hsiangchu Lai: Yen-Ching OuYang: Ting-Peng Liang

Department of Information Management, National Sun Yat-sen University, Kaohsiung, Taiwan, ROC hclai@mail.nsysu.edu.tw: Department of Information Management, Fortune Institute of Technology, Kaohsiung, Taiwan, ROC lina@center.fjtc.edu.tw.:Department of Information Management, National Sun Yat-sen University, Kaohsiung, Taiwan, ROC tpliang@mail.nsysu.edu.tw.

Abstract: The purpose of this article is to explore professor Andrew B. Whinston's intellectual contribution to research in information systems in the past two decades. Information Systems is a young and fast growing field. In the past two decades, professor Whinston has pioneered in Decision Support Systems, Electronic Commerce, and many other research areas. We performed a citation analysis to explore the distribution of professor Whinston's publications and articles that cited them. A total of sixty-eight professor Whinston's articles and books have been collected in the Science Citation Index and Social Science Citation Index since 1980. The total number of citations is 357, which shows his significant contribution to the growth of this important field.

Key words: Citation Analysis, Information Systems Research, Electronic Commerce.

1. INTRODUCTION

In the past several decades, professor Andrew B. Whinston has pioneered many research areas. His distinguished contribution spreads over many disciplines from economics and operations research in early years to information systems later on. Numerous young researchers have benefited from his seminal work and insightful perspectives. He is not only a pioneer in Decision Support Systems and Electronic Commerce, but also innovators in economics, computer science and other related areas. It is virtually impossible to assess the value of his contribution.

However, we all know that information technology is supposed to solve problems that seem to be impossible. Recent development of citation databases is changing the way academic productivity is assessed. Therefore, we decided to try this new technology and used professor Whinston as a test case. This allows us to use a quantitative approach to explore the insight of professor Whinston's research and how his intellectual work has contributed to the research and development of other researchers. In this paper, results from a citation analysis that analyzes the frequency and distribution of articles and citations are reported. The citation data in the Social Sciences Citation Index (SSCI) and Sciences Citation Index (SCI) database were surveyed and analyzed.

The remainder of the article is organized as follows. First, the scope and method of the research are presented. This is followed by the analysis of professor Whinston's publication and the articles that citing Professor Whinston's publications. Due to the availability of the citation databases, the analysis is focused on the publications in the recent two decades. Although the coverage is after 1980, the findings do highlight professor Whinston's great contribution to the development of information systems and related areas.

2. SCOPE AND METHOD OF THE RESEARCH

Professor Whinston has published more than 250 articles and books in the past 40 years. These publications spread over many different academic disciplines. Due to the availability of data, it is hard to perform a complete analysis of their impact. Since professor Whinston has spent most of his time and energy in information systems research in the recent two decades, the scope of the study is defined to cover publications after 1980, with a focus on information systems and related research.

The research method adopted in the study was citation analysis. Although it is hard to fully quantify the contribution of a scholarly work, citation analysis provides a means to explore at least the popularity of a publication. A frequently cited article is generally more popular than a rarely cited one. SCI and SSCI are two major databases that keep track of article publication and citation data in major journals. SCI covers more than 3500 leading journals in 150 science and engineering areas, whereas SSCI covers around 1700 leading journals in 50 social sciences areas. Therefore, the citation data in the databases are reasonably comprehensive and reliable in indicating the impact of academic publications.

The study includes two stages. In the first stage, we intend to identify professor Whinston's article that has been collected in SCI and SSCI. All articles and books authored or co-authored with professor Whinston were identified. A comprehensive survey of SCI and SSCI databases was performed to locate those that were included in each year. The findings at this stage allowed us to have a clear profile of professor Whinston's publication.

In the second stage, we intend to locate all publications that cited professor Whinston's publications. This is much more difficulty than the first one because the SCI/SSCI databases do not have complete index of all citations. Since citation records of an article can only be retrieved by name of the first author, we had to code all publications by their first author. Then, separate database searches were conducted on each publication, including journal papers and books. The resulting citation data were then aggregated and analyzed.

Usually, the SCI/SSCI database lists authors, title, full source, year, language, address, author keywords, keywords plus, abstract, references and so on. However, not every record keeps complete information. Some records do not list author keywords, keywords plus and abstracts in the database. Therefore, more than one search is sometimes necessary to complete a citation record.

The amount of data collected from SCI and SSCI is very large. We adopted the method adopted by Black to process the data we obtained (Black, 1999). All data collected from SSCI and SCI were transferred into a Microsoft Excel spreadsheet and then analyzed

3. PROFILE OF PROFESSOR WHINSTON'S PUBLICATIONS

The result from the SCI and the SSCI search shows that, among the 176 articles and books published after 1980, sixty-eight of them have been collected in the databases. Among these, fourteen were in SCI, thirty-nine in SSCI and fifteen in both (as shown in Table 1). The distribution of these articles and books is shown in Table 2. We can see that the number of publications increase from twenty-two in 1980-1984 to eighty-six after 1995, which shows professor Whinston's increasing productivity over the years.

Table 1. Number of articles and books Collected in SCI/ SSCI (1980-2001)

Data base	SCI	SSCI	SCI&SSCI	Others*	Total
Number	14	39	15	108	176

* *Including 23 books.*

Table 2. Number of publications after 1980

	1980-1984	1985-1989	1990-1994	After1995	Total
Count	22	29	39	86	176

Figure 1 shows the annual number of publications after 1980. The top two years in which professor Whinston published twenty-five and seventeen articles were 1997 and 2000, respectively. Year 1995 tied with year 1996 for the third place, with thirteen articles in each year. In fact, these are the years when electronic commerce began to gain attention and grew exponentially. Professor Whinston's work has evidenced the development of this exciting age. On average, professor Whinston published eight papers a year since 1980.

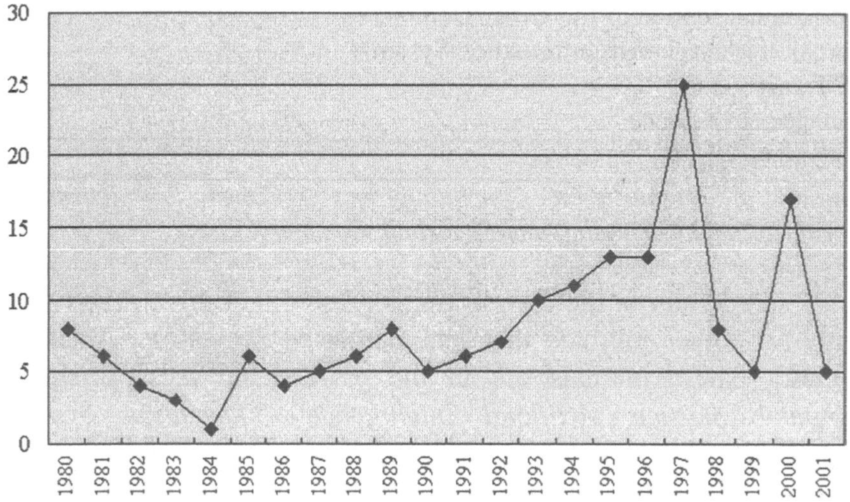

Figure 1. Yearly publication distribution after 1980

Professor Whinston's publication outlets have been very broad academically and geographically. The articles were published in ninety-three different journals. Table 3 shows the most frequently published journals for professor Whinston. Not surprisingly, Decision Support Systems was the journal in which professor Whinston published the most, followed by the *Journal of Organizational Computing and Electronic Commerce, Computers, IEEE Transactions on Systems, Man and Cybernetics,* and the *Communications of the ACM.* Other journals include *Information Systems Research, Group Decision and Negotiation, International Journal of Electronic Commerce, Journal of Management Information Systems, IIE Transactions,* and *Management Science.*

Table 3. Articles published in different journals

Journal	No. of articles
Decision Support Systems	11
J. Org. Computing and EC*	8
Computer	6
IEEE Trans. on Systems Man and Cybernetics	6
Communications of the ACM	5
Information Systems Research	4
Group Decision and Negotiation	3

International Journal of Electronic Commerce	3
Journal of Management Information Systems	3
IIE Transactions	3
Management Science	3
82 other journals, 23 books	

**Journal of Organization Computing was renamed the Journal of Organizational Computing and Electronic Commerce.*

In addition to the eleven journals listed in Table 3, there were eighty-two other journals that had published professor Whinston's articles. These journals are in the professional areas, including *Computer Science, Artificial Intelligence, Information Systems, Organizational and Behavior Science, Engineering, Education,* and *Medicine.* This shows diversity in professor Whinston's knowledge. These journals also cover several countries, such as European countries, Korea, Japan and Taiwan.

Unlike some senior faculty members, professor Whinston has been very supportive of students, and worked collaborative with colleague to get the research done. In the past two decades, professor Whinston has co-authored with more than 100 researchers. Table 4 shows his major co-authors. Professor Whinston's long-time partner, Clyde had co-authored thirty-five articles with professor Whinston. The next two co-authors were Dr. Moore and Dr. Barua, with eighteen and fifteen co-authored articles, respectively. In addition to the listed co-authors, there were 106 others who co-authored less than five articles with professor Whinston.

Table 4. Major Co-authors of Dr. Whinston after 1980

Author Name	No. of articles
Holsapple-CW	35
Moore-JC	18
Barua-A	15
Srinivasan-S	13
Stallaert-J	12
Kalakota-R	12
Applegate-L	12
Gupta-A	11
Chang-AM	8
Fan-M	7
Watabe-K	6

Rao –HR	6
Choi-S	6
Richmond-WB	5
McAfee-RP	5
Lang-KR	5
Jacob-VS	5
106 other co-authors	

In addition to the number of publications and the diversity of the publication outlets, professor Whinston's intellectual contribution can also be found by the diversity of the issues studied in his articles. We performed a classification analysis based on key words of the published articles. The keywords were identified from the titles or the abstracts of papers. The results, as shown in Table 5, indicate the diversity of professor Whinston's research contribution. We can see from the table that, although DSS and electronic commerce are professor Whinston's major areas of research (with sixty-five and fifty-two papers in these categories, respectively), his interests cover the following areas:

(1.) Information systems: Issues include database management, distributed computing, object-oriented approach, system analysis and design, IS evaluation, and IS applications;

(2.) Management: Issues include the interface between information and management, general management, internal control, business process reengineering, workflow management, and virtual organizations;

(3.) Artificial Intelligence: Issues include artificial intelligence, expert systems, and agent-based systems.

Table 5. Subject areas of professor Whinston's research, 1980-2001

Research Area		No. of papers	Total
IS	IS applications	14	50
	DBMS	11	
	Distributed computing	10	
	Information theory & management	5	
	SA&D	4	
	IS evaluation & IT Management	4	
	Objected-Oriented approach	2	
Management	Business & General Management	12	35

	Manufacturing	10	
	Internal control	7	
	BPR	4	
	Workflow	1	
	Virtual organization	1	
AI	AI	16	29
	ES & Knowledge based system	10	
	Multi-agent	3	
DSS	DSS	51	65
	GDSS	10	
	NSS	4	
EC/KM/E-learning		52	52
Economics		27	27
MIS research		2	2
Others		6	6
Total			266

4. IMPACT OF PROFESSOR WHINSTON'S RESEARCH: THE CITATION ANALYSIS

Another way to explore the impact of a research is to examine its citation, i.e., a paper cited by other papers. A frequently cited article means that it is referenced by many other papers. Again, we had to rely on the SCI and the SSCI databases to generate the citation profile.

A survey of the SCI and the SSCI databases after 1980 shows that professor Whinston's publications have been cited 357 times in the past two decades, among which 59 times in SCI, 256 times in SSCI, and 42 times in both. The distribution of these citations is shown in Table 6.

Table 6. SCI/SSCI citations after 1980

Data Base	SCI	SSCI	SCI&SSCI	Total
Citations	59	256	42	357

Table 7 shows the distribution of citing articles. Similar to the distribution of professor Whinston's publication, the period after 1995 had the highest number of citations (198). The next highest period was between 1990 and 1994, which had 95 citations. The increasing trend indicates that the impact of professor Whinston's publications increased over time. If we look at the number of citations per year as shown in Figure 2, the year 2000 had forty-nine citations and was ranked first. Years 1997 and 1999 were ranked second and third, respectively. On average, there were about eighteen citations per year.

Table 7. Distribution of citations after 1980

	1980-1984	1985-1989	1990-1994	After1995	Total
Citations	15	49	95	198	357

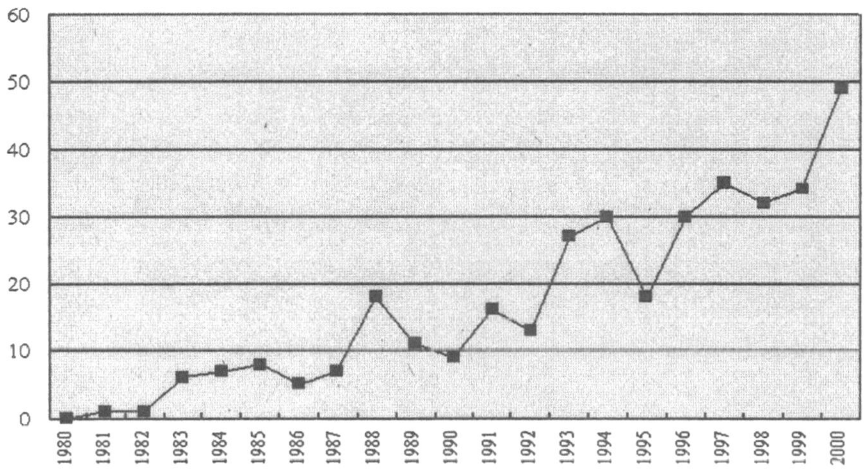

Figure 2. Distribution of citation by year (1980-2000)

Table 8. Analysis of professor Whinston's articles and citations

			Frequency of Citations																						Avg. citations per article	Avg. citations per year
			1980	1981	1982	1983	1984	1985	1986	1987	1988	1989	1990	1991	1992	1993	1994	1995	1996	1997	1998	1999	2000	Total		
Dr. Whinston's Articles	1980	8		1	1	2	1	5	3	5	8	4	3	4	3	8	9	5	4	1		3	2	72	9.00	3.60
	1981	6				3	4	2	1		4	1		3	3	4	3	1	2	2	1			34	5.67	1.79
	1982	4				1					2		1		2				1	2				9	2.25	0.50
	1983	3					2	1				1					1					1		6	2.00	0.35
	1984	1																						0	0.00	0.00
	1985	6							1	2	2	5	3	4	2	7	2				1		1	30	5.00	2.00
	1986	4									2										1			3	0.75	0.21
	1987	5																						0	0.00	0.00
	1988	6											1	2		2	2		1					8	1.33	0.67
	1989	8											1	2	2	2	4	1	3	2	2	2		21	2.63	1.91
	1990	5												1		1	2			1	1			6	1.20	0.60
	1991	6													1		4	3	4	3	1		3	19	3.17	2.11
	1992	7														2	2	4	5	5	2	3	2	25	3.57	3.13
	1993	10														1	1	4	5	4	3	1	4	23	2.30	2.88
	1994	11																	2		1		2	5	0.45	0.83
	1995	13																	3	6	7	3	3	22	1.69	4.40
	1996	13																		6	5	8	15	34	2.62	8.50
	1997	25																		3	7	13	11	34	1.36	8.50
	1998	8																					3	3	0.38	1.50
	1999	5																					3	3	0.60	3.00
	2000	17																						-	-	-
	2001	5																						-	-	-
Total		176	0	1	1	6	7	8	5	7	18	11	9	16	13	27	30	18	30	35	32	34	49	357		

In order to have a better understanding of paper citations in different years, a yearly analysis is shown in Table 8. The row in the table shows the citation distribution of the papers published in a particular year. The column shows the total number of citations in a particular year. Therefore, the numbers in the first row indicate that eight articles were published in 1980 and these articles were cited once in 1981 and 1982, twice in 1983, once in 1984, five times in 1985, ..., and twice in 2000. The total number of citations for these eight articles is 72. Similarly, the number of publications in 1998 is eight and the total number of citations on these eight articles is three times in the year of 2000.

Actually, Walstrom and Leonard (2000) argued that a work is unlikely to be cited until at least one year after its publication. Therefore, it is normal that there would be no citation in 1980 for articles published in 1980. We can see that articles published in nearly every year were cited except for articles published in 1984, 1987 and 2000. Articles published in 1980 were ranked first in citation frequency. The articles published in 1981, 1996 and 1997 were in a tie for second.

Two indices can be used to measure the citation performance: one is the average citations per article and the other is the average citation per year. The average citations per article are the number of citations divided by the total number of articles published in a particular year. The larger the number means that the impact of the research papers in that year is larger. The average citation per year is the number of citations divided by the total number of years available for citation. The larger the number means that the article is cited more often in every year.

The average citations per article shown in Table 8 indicate that articles published in 1980 were cited most frequently, followed by articles in 1981. This implies that articles published in 1980 have a lengthy impact on future research. In addition to these two years, the publications in 1985 and 1992 are also well-cited.

The average number of citations per year, as shown in Table 8, indicates that professor Whinston's articles published in 1996 and 1997 had the highest average citation frequency (8.50 each). This means that, on average, the papers published in that year were cited 8.5 times every year for the available years. In fact, 1996 and 1997 happen to be the years in which electronic commerce began to emerge.

This implies that Professor Whinston's publications in electronic commerce have a significant impact on the later research in the area.

Table 9. Journal that publishes the citing articles after 1980

Journal	Frequency
Decision Support Systems	39
European Journal of Operational Research	14
IEEE Trans. on Systems Man and Cybernetics	13
IIE Transactions	12
Omega-International Journal of Management Science	12
Decision Sciences	11
Information Systems Research	10
Management Science	10
Auditing-A Journal of Practice & Theory	8
Expert Systems with Applications	8
Group Decision and Negotiation	8
Communications of the ACM	7
Journal of Information Technology	6
Journal of The Operational Research Society	6
Other journals	96

Table 10. Research areas where professor Whinston's articles were cited (after1980)

Subject Areas	Frequency		Total
IS	IS applications	36	119
	IS evaluation & IT Management	28	
	Distributed computing	19	
	SA&D	16	
	Information theory & management	7	
	Object-Oriented approach	7	
	DBMS	6	
Management	Manufacturing	43	97
	Business & General Management	21	
	Internal control	17	
	Virtual organization	8	
	BPR	6	
	Workflow	2	
AI	ES & Knowledge based system	40	82
	AI	34	
	Multi-agent	8	

DSS	DSS	113	138
	GDSS	20	
	NSS	5	
EC/KM/E-learning		55	55
Economics		17	17
MIS research		3	3
Others		8	4
Total			519

Tables 9 and 10 show where the citing articles were published and the subject area of the citing articles. Again, the results show the diversity of professor Whinston's impact. The total number of journals in which citing articles were published is 110, which is very diversified. The journals that published articles that cited professor Whinston's work include *Decision Support Systems*, *European Journal of Operational Research*, *IEEE Transactions of Systems, Man, and Cybernetics*, *IIE Transactions*, *Omega*, *Decision Sciences*, and *Information Systems Research*.

If we review all 110 journals, they include disciplines such as Computer Science, Artificial Intelligence, Management Information Systems, Business and Management, Organizational and Behavior Science, E-commerce, Engineering, Education and Medicine (as shown in Table 10). Table 11 lists the most frequently cited papers, we can see that most of them are related to the development of Decision Support Systems, which clearly indicates professor Whinston's leading role in the field. Another supportive evidence is that professor Whinston's book, *Foundation of Decision Support Systems* was cited forty-six times between 1980 and 1990 by articles in the SSCI.

In fact, professor Whinston's recent work also leads the development of electronic commerce. For example, his book *Frontiers in Electronic Commerce*, co-authored with Kalakota, et. al., has been cited more than forty times by articles in the SSCI in the past these years. In the year of 2000, the book was cited nineteen times, which is pretty high by any standard.

Table. Most frequently cited articles after 1980

Titles	Frequency

1	"A Generalized Decision Support System Using Predicate Calculus and Network Data-Base Management"(with R.H. Bonczek, C.W. Holsapple), Operations Research, 1981, Vol. 29, Issue 2, pp. 263-281.	26
2	"Future Directions for Decision Support" (with R.H. Bonczek and C.W. Holsapple), Decision Science, Vol. 11, No. 4, October 1980	22
3	"Control and Decision Support in Automatic Manufacturing Systems"(with S.Y. Nof, W.I. Bullers), AIIE Transactions, 1980, Vol. 12, Issue 2, pp. 156-169.	17
4	"The Calculus of Reengineering"(with A. Barua C.H.S. Lee), Information Systems Research, 1996, Vol. 7, Issue 4, pp. 409-428.	16
5	"Model Management Issues and Directions" (with A.M. Chang, C.W. Holsapple), Decision Support Systems, Vol. 9, No. 1, January 1993, pp. 19-37	16
6	"Artificial-Intelligence in Manufacturing Planning and Control",(with W.I. Bullers, S.Y. Nof), AIIE Transactions, 1980, Vol. 12, Issue 4, pp. 351-363.	15
7	"Ticom and the Analysis of Internal Controls",(with A.D. Bailey, G.L. Duke, J. Gerlach, C.E. Ko, R.D. Meservy), Accounting Review, 1985, Vol. 60, Issue 2, pp. 186-201.	14
8	"Incomplete Contracting Issues in Information-Systems Development Outsourcing", (with W.B. Richmond, A. Seidmann), Decision Support Systems, 1992, Vol. 8, Issue 5, pp. 459-477.	14
9	"Organizational Computing: Definitions and Issues" (with L. Applegate, C. Ellis, C.W. Holsapple and F. Radermacher), Journal of Organizational Computing, Vol. 1, No. 1, 1991, pp. 1-10	13
10	"An Artificial-Intelligence Approach to the Scheduling of Flexible Manufacturing Systems", (with M.J. Shaw), IIE Transactions, 1989, Vol. 21, Issue 2, pp. 170-183.	9
11	"On Optimal Allocation in a Distributed-Processing Environment",(with A. Dutta, G. Koehler), Management Science, 1982, Vol. 28, Issue 8, pp. 839-853.	9
12	"Incentives and Computing Systems for Team-Based Organizations",(with A. Barua, C.H.S. Lee), Organization Science, 1995, Vol. 6, Issue 4, pp. 487-504	8

13	"Management Support Through Artificial-Intelligence",(with C.W. Holsapple), Human Systems Management, 1985, Vol. 5, Issue 2, pp. 163-171.	8
14	"Reputation, Learning and Coordination in Distributed Decision-Making Contexts",(with C. Ching, C.W. Holsapple), Organization Science, 1992, Vol. 3, Issue 2, pp. 275-297.	8

5. CONCLUDING REMARKS

As a pioneer in Decision Support Systems, Electronic Commerce, and many other areas, professor Whinston has contributed significantly toward our knowledge. In the past two decades, he has published 176 articles and books. His publications have been cited 357 times in SCI and SSCI databases. His intellectual contributions can be portrayed in several ways. First, his continuous investigation and publication demonstrate the spirit of pursuing frontier knowledge and scientific excellence. Second, the large number of co-authors shows his effort in helping students and collaborating with colleagues in the knowledge discovery process. Third, his diversity of professor Whinston's publication shows the breadth of his knowledge and inter-disciplinary capabilities. His scholastic work has generated significant impact on knowledge accumulation in multiple areas.

Although we have analyzed the data available in SCI and SSCI databases, there are a lot of other contributions that cannot be measured by counting numbers. For instance, numerous students and practitioners have benefited from reading the popular books, such as Frontiers of Electronic Commerce and Decision Support Systems. The results reported in the article, however, do provide valuable evidence for other researchers to follow.

REFERENCES

Black, S., "An assessment of social sciences coverage by four prominent full-text online aggregated journal packages," Library Collection, Acquisitions, & Technical Services 1999; 23:No.4, 411-419

Holsapple, C.W., "An empirical assessment and categorization of journals relevant to DSS research," Decision Support System 1995; 14:359-367

Ridley, D.D., "Citation searches in on-line databases: possibilities and pitfalls," Trends in analytical chemistry 2001; 20:No.1, 1-10

Walstrom, K.A., Leonard, L.N.K., "Citation classics from the information systems literature," Information & Management 2000; 38:59 -72.

Chapter 22

IT Reference Disciplines - Andy Whinston, A Case Study

James R. Marsden: David E. Pingry
Department of Operations and Information Management, 368 Fairfield Road U41-IM, School of Business, University of Connecticut, Storrs, CT 06269-2041, jimm@sba.uconn.edu : Department of Management Information Systems, Eller College of Business and Public

Key words: reference discipline, management information systems, research paradigms, methodology, Andy Whinston

Abstract: This work results from the support, collegiality, and synergies so characteristic of the Center for the Study of Unique Non-Convex Technologies, a circa '70's unofficial but very productive K-school (name deleted to protect the innocent) research center. Andy Whinston's written contributions to this current manuscript arc idcntical to his writtcn contributions to thc numerous papers generated at the center. It is important, however, to remember that those of us who can think and conceptualize, do actually think and conceptualize. Those of us who cannot, ***write***.

1. INTRODUCTION

In MIS's search for identity during its short history, much has been made of the notion of reference disciplines. In part, this emphasis may have arisen early on, since MIS was centered on technology rather than scientific research paradigms. Perhaps this has resulted in insecurity that has led certain MIS researchers to argue linkages to more familiar fields.

The lack of a unifying paradigm has been viewed both negatively and positively. On the negative side, it has been argued that MIS researchers sacrifice the reference paradigms for relevance and, as a result, lose the power of the reference discipline. Further, it is argued that there is no cohesion or "tradition" in the MIS literature, that it is too diverse and scattered. The literature is said to be full of pseudo social psychology or pseudo economics. On the positive side, it has been argued that power of MIS research is that it brings the best from diverse reference disciplines to bear on an important set of IT-related managerial, economic, and social issues. This argument suggests that the power and relevance of the MIS research occurs precisely because of the diversity and integration of the reference disciplines.

No one can deny that there are many examples of reference disciplines being abused badly by MIS researchers. It is easy to throw stones (or nodding references). However, it is not so easy to develop a body of research that balances the special circumstances required to deal with IT issues with the intellectual integrity of the reference discipline. To do this well requires a deep understanding of technology as well as insight and expertise in the reference discipline. Still, this is not enough. The successful researcher must often go beyond simply applying theorems of the reference disciplines and actually interpret and modify such theorems in the IT problem context.

Yet another complication arises from the fact that often multiple reference disciplines are relevant and theories on the boundaries of these disciplines are virtually nonexistent. This requires the researcher to possess the ability to "interface" methodologies, theories, and empirics from multiple disciplines. Thus, the "ideal IT researcher" is:

i) one with an intimate knowledge of many disciplines;

ii) one with the ability to morph within and among the knowledge sets of many disciplines;

iii) one with the ability to understand the applicability of existing knowledge sets to the IT-domain; and,

iv) one with the ability to develop new theories to deal with unique IT-related problems.

As the song says, "who you gonna call?" Andy. Andy. Andy. Andy. (even though he doesn't write!)

But what is a reference discipline? It easy to say, for example, "Economics is a reference discipline for MIS." However, this statement raises a number of important questions. How is the relation "is a reference discipline for" (RefD) defined? Does RefD exist and, if so, does it exist between all disciplines? If RefD exists, how can it be leveraged to create good research in the target discipline? Is the relationship RefD transitive or reflexive?

Although these questions could be approached from the point of view of philosophy of science, it seems to us that another approach is to evaluate some of the contributions of someone whom everyone agrees has utilized multiple reference disciplines well -- a case study approach which we label, ***Andy Whinston - the case study***. Our goal in presenting "Andy Whinston - the case study" is to help clarify the meaning of a reference discipline for MIS while demonstrating that Andy indeed possesses all of the qualities of the ideal researcher listed above.

In the sections that follow, we first briefly examine the views of several MIS authors on "reference disciplines" and on the status of MIS as a discipline. We then examine Andy as a case study of a reference discipline and argue that the establishment of MIS as a discipline is occurring because researchers like Andy are making MIS a reference discipline for other areas. It is, we argue, critical for MIS to reach the status of reflexive reference discipline if it is to continue in a central position rather than as distributed pockets of knowledge in the various disciplines. We focus on a few key pieces of Andy's earlier work and its morphing into the IT terrain. This work took place as Andy himself was transitioning from being primarily an economist to being primarily an IT person. During this period, Andy was trying to define the relation RefD between economics and MIS. Of course, at the same time he was trying to define the RefD relationships between many other disciplines (operations research, management science, computer science, artificial intelligence, chemical engineering, accounting, environmental engineering, etc).

2. NODDING REFERENCE TO MIS INSECURITY

In the early days of MIS, there seemed to be a constant struggle to stake a claim, to identify a unique piece of academic turf, to gain respect from peers in other disciplines. These were key themes in Keen's 1980 ICIS article on MIS reference disciplines and a "cumulative tradition." Keen argued that MIS was at that time a "theme rather than a substantive field." He suggested that a reference discipline is "an established field to which one looks to get an idea of what good MIS research would look like." Keen called upon individuals to try and link their work, to clearly identify the reference disciplines utilized, and to build from where others left off. He suggested that reference disciplines should "link into the core MIS field but not be the core." Interestingly, he had little kind to say about information economics but nevertheless saw the area's potential as a reference discipline:

> Information economics, though largely impractical, trivial, and at times fatuously overassertive, may be an excellent R.D. for those concerned with a theory for MIS, since it demonstrates how to approach the issue of defining information and presents an analytic strategy for developing and applying theory.

A decade later, Alavi et al analyzed the MIS research articles appearing over the 1968-1988 period in seven outlets that they selected: ***Communications of ACM, Data Base, decision Sciences, Harvard Business Review, Management Science, MIS Quarterly,*** and ***Sloan Management Review***. They found 792 articles that addressed an "aspect of research, management, design, implementation, operation, use or impact of MIS or MIS components." The authors indicated a shifting focus from conceptual to empirical work. They also found only 15 theoretically oriented articles in the entire sample, commenting:

> We find the paucity of MIS oriented theories alarming because of the potential implications for quality, experimental design, and value of MIS research. Baroudi and Orlikowski (1986) have reported problems with MIS empirical research.... In the absence of MIS theories, this can result in important relationships going undetected...theories are needed to guide empirical work.

In a 1989 ***CACM*** article, Banville and Landry chided a variety of MIS authors' calls for an "**MIS** research paradigm" and careful identification of proper reference disciplines. Banville and Landry argued that a multitude of approaches was important for continued development of a young discipline, espousing a free-enterprise approach. The authors cited Herbert Simon's view that:

> ...confusion, by another name, is progress to which we have not yet become accustomed... Science, like all creative activity, is

> exploration, gambling, and adventure. It does not lend itself very well to neat blueprints, detailed road maps, and central planning. Perhaps that's why it's fun!

In their concluding remarks, Banville and Landry suggest that MIS researchers should not "refuse any help from other disciplines....There is room for the indispensable free enterprise will." We will argue and demonstrate below that Andy Whinston epitomizes the ***"free enterprise will"***. Rather than classify and categorize, arguing what reference disciplines are or are not "appropriate," isn't more to be gained by delivering research that adds value, that leads to demonstrable real gains? We argue below that this typical of Andy's work. In short, is he a defining theme, a reference discipline, not in the limiting sense, but in the free-enterprise, open minded sense.

It seems that Banville and Landry's arguments fell on many deaf ears. In 1994, Teng and Galletta were still lamenting fragmentation in the field and lack of a cumulative research tradition. The authors seemed to mourn that reference disciplines "prescribed and identified" by Keen, Swanson, and others were not widely relied upon by researchers.

Robey's 1996 ***ISR*** supported the pluralism approach in MIS research espoused by Banville and Landry. He stressed the benefits of diversity in methodology, but also noted the need for collaboration across methodologies as crucial to avoiding destructive clashes. Robey argued:

> Rather than resorting to the political tactic of unification in order to build institutional legitimacy, the measures described in this paper are focused on the maintenance of a diverse and vital field.

In fact, as we argue below "collaboration across methodologies" is just another term for "Andy Whinston".

Authors will continue to debate the efficacy of MIS methodologies. Some will continue to call for unification, for standardization. We, rather, focus on contribution and impact. In the next section, we demonstrate how Andy Whinston is, indeed, a reference discipline and how this particular, real reference discipline has made important contributions by following the free-enterprise, methodological pluralism approach we refer to as "Andyism."

3. ANDY WHINSTON AS A REFENCE DISCIPLINE - A CASE STUDY

3.1 The Formulative Methodology - Andy in Productionland

Like most first generation MIS academics, Andy was trained in a reference discipline -- namely economics. Unlike many economists of his day, he was also well-versed in operational research and management science techniques. Andy was steeped in the "quantoid" as opposed to the "cognate" or "techweenie" view of the world.[1] Of historical interest, this was in stark contrast to the emerging MIS discipline that consisted mainly of "techweenies" becoming "cognates." It is only in the past 3-5 years that "quantoids" have emerged as big players in the world of MIS research.

For our case study, we choose to begin by considering a set of Andy's contributions to production theory in economics and the impact that his understanding of this theory had on his subsequent contributions in other areas, including IT. Production theory is a critical link in the economists understanding of the world. It is the theory that links what we have -- inputs like capital (computers) and labor (manual systems) -- to what we want (information, water, automobiles, etc.) It defines the possibilities for the design of artifacts and is the critical link between the physical world and human needs and wants.

In an important paper (***Journal of Economic Theory***, 1974), Andy and two co-authors (whose names are very similar to the authors of this article) articulated a view of production theory that acts as a baseline for articulating how many of Andy's contributions in IS, water resources, and other areas turn on this reference discipline.

At the time of the ***JET*** paper, there were two common themes in production theory. One involved the continual addition of subscripts (e.g., the creation of new variables) in what was termed the "development and estimation of flexible functional forms." In this approach, data from multiple firms or even multiple industries was fitted to the various functional forms (Cobb-Douglas, CES, translog, etc.) that had no theoretical link to the underlying production processes. Instead, these functional forms were selected for their economic properties and their arguments were selected because of their economic links, that is, they were priced in the market.

[1] Dave first heard the terms "quantoid," "cognate," and "techweenie" used by Gary Dickson at the AACSB Faculty Institute at the University of Minnesota in 1983. Jim claims to not understand the terms. Obviously, Dave is the writer here.

A second approach directly modeled the production process. In this approach the variables were selected because they were necessary to describe how the production process worked. The functional forms were selected because they could describe underlying physical constraints and could be interpreted in such a way that the production process could actually be constructed and operated. This approach was independent of the market prices or any economic description of the process. This approach is in the tradition of the textbook definition of a production function.

It was argued by "Andy et al" that rather than estimating functional forms that embodied economic characteristics, which may or may not reflect the underlying characteristics of the production process, that it would be useful to derive the production functions to be estimated from the process based model. This would allow for the direct testing of hypotheses about the economic characteristics of these functions, rather than the imposition of those characteristics by the selection of the functional form. The variables of the production function would have a technological interpretation and they would either be priced in the market or they could be linked to market priced items.

Further, in the ***JET*** paper, it was argued that for most "real-world" production processes it is likely that, when it is possible to derive the production function from a process description, the resulting function will be much more complex than the typical flexible functional forms. This was argued by demonstrating that a very simple chemical engineering production process could be shown to have the most complex flexible form as its associated production function. In another paper (Marsden et al, 1972) this same methodology was applied to a wastewater treatment plant. In fact, the methodology was used as the basis to assign pollution allocations for a significant piece of the Northern Indiana industrial complex in the Calumet Harbor and canal area.

In another set of papers (Bever et al, 1982 a, b) Andy and his co-authors developed and demonstrated techniques for directly "estimating" (actually, approximating by developed epsilon bounds) the true cost and production functions using data directly generated from process models. This provided an alternative to the indirect estimation based on empirical data which might or might not accurately represent production relations. As with the ***JET*** paper, the approach allowed the direct testing of hypotheses about the production process. Characteristics were not imposed by the selection of an assumed functional form. The approximations have direct technological interpretation and can be linked to market priced items.

There is a key insight threaded through the papers described so far. Even in theory construction, Andy was concerned with the implications for substitutability of inputs. In standard economic analysis utilizing assumed flexible functional forms, inputs are fully substitutable. In problems such as school bus scheduling, substitutability is limited by underlying constraints. For areas like IT, standard economic analysis would still treat labor as a substitutable input for all other inputs. In highly technical processes, including IT, the reality is that labor is no longer necessarily a substitutable input. Andy's early understanding of this issue held great portent for his later work in IT. We now consider a set of papers that demonstrate ***Andy's morphing*** into an IT guru.

3.2 From Productionland to MISland - The Morphing of Andy

We have argued that Andy's primary view of the world comes from production theory. Further, we have also argued that he has continuously dealt with the tension between the insights and power of the mathematical statement of the theory in economics and the difficulty of stating the problems and solving them in real world environments. In addition, we have observed that over time Andy has moved his focus from economics and operations management to information systems. To illustrate our points we move now to describe a collection of papers that represent Andy's work as a continual product and as a continual morphing or transition. These papers span the period from the early 1970's to the mid 1990's and include a diversity of topics. For each, we address four basic issues: 1) how the topic in the paper can be represented as a production problem – in particular, what is output, 2) the general technology of the paper, 3) where the topic fits into Andy's movement to IT, and 4) linkages to previous papers.

3.2.1 Water Resource Planning

First, consider a series of papers in water resource planning (Graves, Hatfield, and Whinston, 1969, 1972; and Pingry and Whinston, 1973). These papers each describe a classic cost minimization problem in economics, that is, minimize the cost of the inputs subject to the constraint that a target level of output, as described by a production function, is reached. The objective is to minimize the cost of the resources invested in treatment plants, bypass piping, in-stream aeration, low flow augmentation, or other treatment strategies subject to the constraint that the quality of the water at specific points in the river meet mandated goals. The relationship between the treatment strategies and the water quality is a production function.

The water quality problem as it is described in these three papers requires the use of various mathematical programming techniques for solution. In these three papers the complexity of solution is determined by the nonlinearity of the cost function and the production function. Of course, the introduction of the nonlinearities is what allows for the expansion of the applicability of the model. The specific evolutions of the models in these papers include: introducing economies (with respect to volume) and diseconomies (with respect to treatment rates) of scale in the cost functions, expansion of treatment alternatives that realistically require an nonlinear representation of the quality model, changing the dissolved oxygen quality model in the stream from linear transfer coefficient to a nonlinear model, and the addition of other measures of quality (temperature) that interact with the level of dissolved oxygen. Each of these changes increased the difficulty of solution and required compromises with respect to guarantees of optimal solutions.

These papers are excellent examples of Andy's early interests. They are attempts to mathematically capture the dimensions of a complex, real world, timely production function and to utilize techniques of operations research to solve the cost-minimizing problem. Further, the evolution of these water quality papers reflects the evolution of Andy's career. He pushes the envelope of solvability to gain a better representation of the motivating problem. His ability to accomplish this is based on his understanding of economics, operations management, and water quality modeling.

3.2.2 School Bus Scheduling

Angel, Caudle, Noonen, and Whinston, 1972, address a different production problem. In this case they are trying to "obtain a bus loading pattern such that:

(1) the number of routes is minimized,
(2) mileage is kept at a minimum,
(3) no bus is overloaded, and
(4) the time required to traverse any route does not exceed a maximum allowed by policy."

The objective here is not a single valued function, like cost. The authors attempt to generate better feasible solutions for evaluation by a bus scheduler that meet the various production constraints. In theory, enumeration or a modified traveling salesman algorithm could solve this problem. In practice, these approaches are uneconomical for realistic sized problems. A two-stage process is proposed that utilizes a clustering algorithm and a modified traveling salesman problem (Noonan and Whinston, 1969 and Graves and Whinston, 1970).

This paper illustrates several interesting aspects of the evolution of Andy's career. First, again it indicates his willingness to deal with complex solvability in order to get realistic solutions. Second, it illustrates his involvement in creating new solution techniques to further that goal. Third, it further illustrates his willingness to go to great lengths to acquire the detailed understanding of the application area. (One of the authors of this paper can directly attest to this, having gone to waste treatment school and to law school to acquire the detailed understanding necessary for a particular project.)

This paper also indicates a movement from the traditional view of operations research – where getting an optimal or satisficing solution is the responsibility of the algorithm in the computer -- toward a decision support environment, where the machine supports the decision-maker in a cooperative environment. The bus scheduler is an important part of the solution in this paper.

3.2.3 Document-Centered Information Systems

The problem addressed in Balakrishnan, Kalakota, Ow, and Whinston, 1995, is a multileveled production problem. The specific objective of the system presented in the paper is to improve reactive problem solving (in this case the problem of unanticipated materials shortages) in a manufacturing process. The outputs are solved materials shortage problems. These materials shortage problems are imbedded in the overall production problem, which is that of assembling and testing electronic cards.

Although, like the papers in water and bus scheduling, this paper addresses a production problem, the approach to solving the problem is quite different. In this case the pretense of optimization or sub-optimization, in the sense of operations research, is gone. The effort is aimed toward creating a decision support infrastructure that "best matches" the decision problem faced by the decision makers. In effect, the decision-makers in the process, and the information that they rely on, have become an integral part of the production process. In the case of water and bus scheduling the decision maker could ask what if questions to a model. In the case of electronic cards, there is no model producing a correct answer based on the assumed parameters.

What is produced is an ambitious information infrastructure for decision support based on the manufacturing problem (electronic cards), a framework for problem solving (based on those of Dewey, Simon,

Mintsberg, Rittel, March, and others), computing formalisms (hypermedia), models of collaborative problem solving (Issue Based Information Systems and Toulmin's schema of Argumentation), and a text and multimedia document database that includes structured documents based on Open Document Architecture and SGML.

Again, this paper represents Andy's willingness to push the envelope of realism. Rather than viewing the production process as a static, deterministic process, this paper treats it as a dynamic, uncertain process where the availability and structure of the information to the decision-maker matters. However, the goal is the same – model a production process.

This paper also represents Andy's further movement into information technology. The technical knowledge underlying the first two topics, water and buses, was the solution techniques of operation research. The technical knowledge for this paper includes computer formalisms, models cooperative problem solving, database, etc.

3.2.4 Resource Allocation

The topic addressed in Moore, Rao, and Whinston, 1996, at first glance, would appear to have little to do with production or information technology. However, in the larger context of Andy's career a case can be made that this paper is part of a natural evolution from production theory and information technology. In fact, this paper demonstrates the reflexive nature of Andy Whinston as a reference discipline. The evolution we have described so far has migrated from formal operations management models to frameworks and schemas – all aimed at solving production problems. This resource allocation paper reverses the direction. It looks back at generalized allocation mechanisms in the context of economics and attempts to deal with the role of information gathering for a "coordinator" that is attempting to allocate resources in a way that maximizes social welfare. Unlike the previous papers, the motivation is not to deal with a "realistic" instance of a production problem. To the contrary, the motivation is to deal with the role of information when the goal is to produce "social welfare maximizing allocations" in a general, theoretical context. The recognition of the role of information in the specific case has motivated an examination of the role of information in the general case.

Interestingly enough, even in this paper the search is for "real solutions." As the authors note, "Our goal has been to develop a process implementing what has seemed a very natural procedure; getting enough information about individual preferences to make an allocation which maximizes, or at least nearly maximizes, a social welfare function. This provides a fairly concrete and computable model of a system of obtaining and evaluating information which terminates in a finite number of steps." Later they add, "The goal of the three works cited (Hurwicz, 1977, Mount and Reiter, 1974, and Hurwicz and T. Marschak, 1985) was, of course considerably more ambitious than ours, and the models developed are considerable more general. However, in each case, it is the equilibrium of a process of message exchange which is being analyzed, as opposed to the choice of a stopping point of such a system and satisficing rule for a solution, which was our focal point here."

These last statements say it all. Even when returning to his economic roots and the rarified theoretical environment of resource allocation mechanisms, Andy is still focused, not on characterizing solutions, but on generating solutions. True to his production view of the world, he is looking for ways to produce "social welfare maximizing allocations" in a more efficient way. True to his migration to information systems, the more efficient way involves information systems.

4. CONCLUDING REMARKS ON ANDYISM OR PERHAPS A PRELUDE

Early in these musings, we suggested four characteristics of an ideal IT researcher. We also suggested that, for MIS to fully establish itself as a discipline, it must have reflexive RefD (reference discipline) relations with other disciplines. The goal should be mutual gain by leveraging across disciplines to yield mutual research gains and progress.

While certainly a bit tongue-in-cheek, our argument that Andy Whinston is a reference discipline for MIS has much merit. Using a production theory view, he has continues to push outward the MIS research boundaries in his economic analyses of e-commerce, network management, and intelligent agents. His work has impacted economists' research streams and methods. In our terms, Andy Whinston is a reflexive RefD! Andy is the ideal IT researcher.

Consider Banville and Landry's suggestion, noted earlier, that MIS researchers should not "refuse any help from other disciplines....There is room for the indispensable free enterprise will." We have argued that Andy epitomizes the "***free enterprise will***". Andy has contributed to MIS and an array of reference disciplines to such a degree that he himself has become a reflexive reference discipline. We argue that in reality, "Andy Whinston" is interchangeable with Robey's concept of "collaboration across methodologies." In our terms, the free-enterprise, methodological pluralism approach is, in fact, "Andyism."

Of course, as those who know Andy are certainly aware, he has contributed even more in the time span between the writing and publishing of this tome. Thus these concluding remarks might better be labeled, The Prelude.

Through his generosity and considerate nature, Andy has given much to all of us. He has help push us to go deep in our understanding of reference disciplines. He has helped position us to be able to leverage IT knowledge to successfully push out the boundaries of the reference disciplines. Most importantly, he has given us intellectual stimulation, nurtured our curiosity, and been our own personal reference discipline.

REFERENCES

Alavi, Maryan, Patricia Carlson, and Geoffrey Brooke, "The Ecology of MIS Research: A Twenty Year Status Review," Proceedings of the Tenth International Conference on Information Systems, Boston, MA, 363-375

Angel, R.D., W.L. Caudle, R. Noonan, and A Whinston, "Computer-Assisted School Bus Scheduling," Management Science, Volume 18, Number 6, February 1972.

Balakrishnan, Anant, Ravi Kalakota, Peng Si Ow and Andrew B. Whinston, "Document-Centered Information Systems to Support Reactive Problem-Solving in Manufacturing," Production Economics, Volume 38, 1995.

Banville, Claude and Maurice Landry, "Can the Field of MIS be Disciplined?" Communications of the ACM, Volume 32, Number 1, January 1989.

Baroudi, J.J., and W.J. Orlikowski, "Misinformation in MIS Research: The Problem of Statistical Power," working paper, CRIS 125, center for Research on Information Systems, Graduate School of Business Administration, New York University, June, 1986.

Benbasat, Izak and Ron Weber, "Research Commentary: Rethinking 'Diversity' in Information Systems Research," Information Systems Research, Volume 7, Number 4, December 1996.

Bever, R., J.R. Marsden, and A. Whinston, "Point Estimation and Process Models - The Spline Function Alternative," International Journal on Policy and Information, (1982)

Bever, R., J.R. Marsden, V. Salas-Fumas, and A. Whinston, "Process Model Specification and the Provision of Summary Information," Advances in Applied Microeconomics, 3: 43-69 (1982)

Cheon, Myun J., Choong, C. Lee and Varun Grover, "Research in MIS – Points of Work and Reference: A Replication and Extension of the Culnan and Swanson Study, Data Base, Spring 1991.

Cule, Paul E. and Varun Grover, "Into the Next Millennium: Some Thoughts on IS Practice and Research, Data Base, May 1994.

Graves, G.W., G.B. Hatfield and A. Whinston, "Water Pollution Control Using By-Pass Piping," Water Resources Research, Volume 3, Number 1, February 1969.

Graves, G.W., and A.B. Whinston, "An Algorithm for Quadratic Assignment Problem," Management Science, Volume 17, Number 7, March 1970.

Graves, G.W., G.B. Hatfield and A. Whinston, "Mathematical Programming for Regional Water Quality Management," Water Resources Research, Volume 8, Number 2, April 1972.

Hurwicz, L., "On the dimensional requirements of informationally decentralized Pareto-satisfactory processes," in Kenneth J. Arrow and L. Hurwicz (eds.), Studies in resource allocation processes, Cambridge University Press, 1977.

Hurwicz, L. and T. Marschak, Discrete allocation mechanisms: dimensional requirements for resource allocation mechanisms when desired out comes are unbounded," Journal of Complexity, Volume 1, 1985.

Keen, Peter G.W., "MIS Research: Reference Disciplines and a Cumulative Tradition, Proceedings of the First International Conference on Information Systems, Philadelphia, Pennsylvania, December 8-10, 1980.

Marsden, James R., David E. Pingry, and Andrew Whinston, "Production function theory and the optimal design of waste treatment facilities," Applied Economics, Volume 4, 1972.

Marsden, J.R., D.E. Pingry, and A. Whinston, "The Process Alternative to Statistical Cost Functions: Comment," The American Economic Review, September 1974.

Marsden, James, David Pingry and Andrew Whinston, "Engineering Foundations of Production Functions," Journal of Economic Theory, Volume 9, Number 2, October 1974.

Marsden, James R. and David E. Pingry, "Engineering Production Functions and the Testing of Quantitative Economic Hypotheses," Economica, Volume 53.

Moore, James C., H. Raghav Rao and Andrew B. Whinston, "Information processing for a finite resource allocation mechanism," Economic Theory, Volume 8, 1996.

Mount, K. and S. Reiter, "The informational size of message spaces," Journal of Economic Theory, Volume 8, 1974.

Noonan, R. and A. Whinston, "Ann Information System for Vehicle Scheduling," Software Age, December 1969.

Pingry, David E. and Andrew B. Whinston, "Multigoal Water Quality Planning Model," Journal of the Environmental Engineering Division, American Society of Civil Engineers, Volume 99, Number EE6, December 1973.

Robey, Daniel, "Research Commentary: Diversity in Information Systems Research: Threat, Promise, and Responsibility," Information Systems Research, Volume 7, Number 4, December 1996.

Swanson, E. Burton and Neil C. Ramiller, "Information Systems Research Thematics: Submissions to a New Journal, 1987-1992," Information Systems Research, Volume 4, Number 4, December 1993.

Teng, James T.C. and Dennis Galletta, "MIS Research Directions: A Survey of Researchers' Views," Data Base, Winter/Spring 1991.

Index

Index

MIX
Papier aus verantwortungsvollen Quellen
Paper from responsible sources
FSC® C105338

If you have any concerns about our products,
you can contact us on
ProductSafety@springernature.com

In case Publisher is established outside the EU,
the EU authorized representative is:
Springer Nature Customer Service Center GmbH
Europaplatz 3, 69115 Heidelberg, Germany

Printed by Libri Plureos GmbH
in Hamburg, Germany